# Eventually
# Everything
# Connects

## Eight Essays on Uncertainty

### Sarah Firth

graphic mundi

Library of Congress Cataloging-in-Publication Data

Names: Firth, Sarah, author.

Title: Eventually everything connects : eight essays on uncertainty / Sarah Firth.

Description: University Park, Pennsylvania : Graphic Mundi, [2024] | Originally published: Crows Nest, NSW, Australia : Joan, 2023. | Includes bibliographical references.

Summary: "A collection of eight autobiographical visual essays exploring the joys and pains of living in a hypercomplex, uncertain world"—Provided by publisher.

Identifiers: LCCN 2023050606 | ISBN 9781637790687 (paperback)

Subjects: LCSH: Firth, Sarah—Comic books, strips, etc. | Cartoonists—Australia—Biography—Comic books, strips, etc. | Illustrators—Australia—Biography—Comic books, strips, etc. | Uncertainty—Comic books, strips, etc. | LCGFT: Autobiographical comics. | Essays. | Graphic novels. | Nonfiction comics.

Classification: LCC PN6790.A83 F57 2024 | DDC 741.5/6994092 [B]—dc23/eng/20231204

LC record available at https://lccn.loc.gov/2023050606



Page 58 from "Like a Moth to a Flame," first published in "Bullshit Buffet" in *#42 Kuš Scientific Facts Anthology,* Kuš, 2021.

Pages 177–78 from "Seeing Things," first published in "Trust Yourself, Babe," in *Edition 8 Science Write Now,* 2 January 2023.

Pages 186–95 from "Seeing Things," first appeared in 'Trust Yourself, Babe' in *Edition 8 Science Write Now,* 2 January 2023.

Text hand-lettered by Sarah Firth

Cover and text designed by Sarah Firth and Joanna Hunt

Illustration technique: hand-drawn with Apple Pencil on iPad Pro using Procreate


Printed in Türkiye
Published by The Pennsylvania State University Press, University Park, PA 16802–1003

10 9 8 7 6 5 4 3 2 1

graphic mundi
drawing our worlds together

Graphic Mundi is an imprint of The Pennsylvania State University Press.

The Pennsylvania State University Press is a member of the Association of University Presses.

It is the policy of The Pennsylvania State University Press to use acid-free paper. Publications on uncoated stock satisfy the minimum requirements of American National Standard for Information Sciences—Permanence of Paper for Printed Library Material, ANSI z39.48–1992.

FSC
www.fsc.org
MIX
Paper | Supporting responsible forestry
FSC® C106499

TIME HAS its WAY WITH US ALL, SO I DEDICATE
THIS BOOK to TIME and TO EVERYTHING that
HAS COME BEFORE, that is, AND WILL COME AFTER.

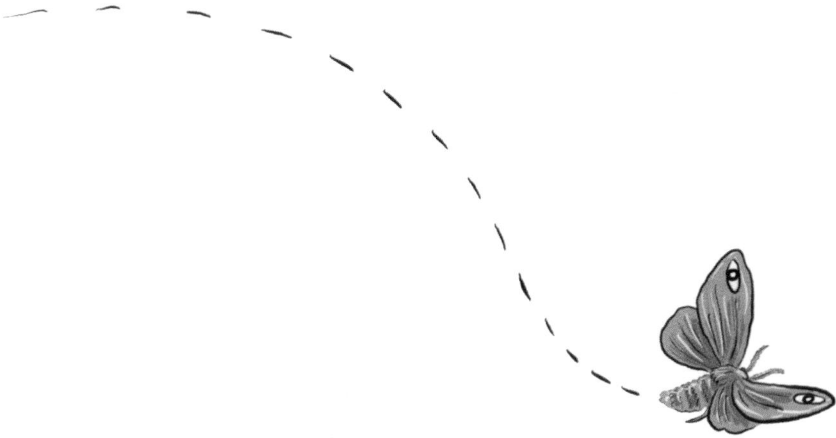

'WHEN we TRY to PICK OUT ANYTHING by ITSELF, WE FIND it HITCHED to EVERYTHING ELSE in THE UNIVERSE.'

    - JOHN MUIR, NATURALIST, AUTHOR, from
      'MY FIRST SUMMER in the SIERRA'

'EVERYTHING TANGLED in THE STRING of EVERYTHING ELSE. NOW, WHEN HER CAT VOMITED, SHE THOUGHT SHE HEARD THE WORD PRAXIS.'

    - PATRICIA LOCKWOOD, POET, NOVELIST, ESSAYIST, from 'NO ONE IS TALKING ABOUT THIS'

# Contents

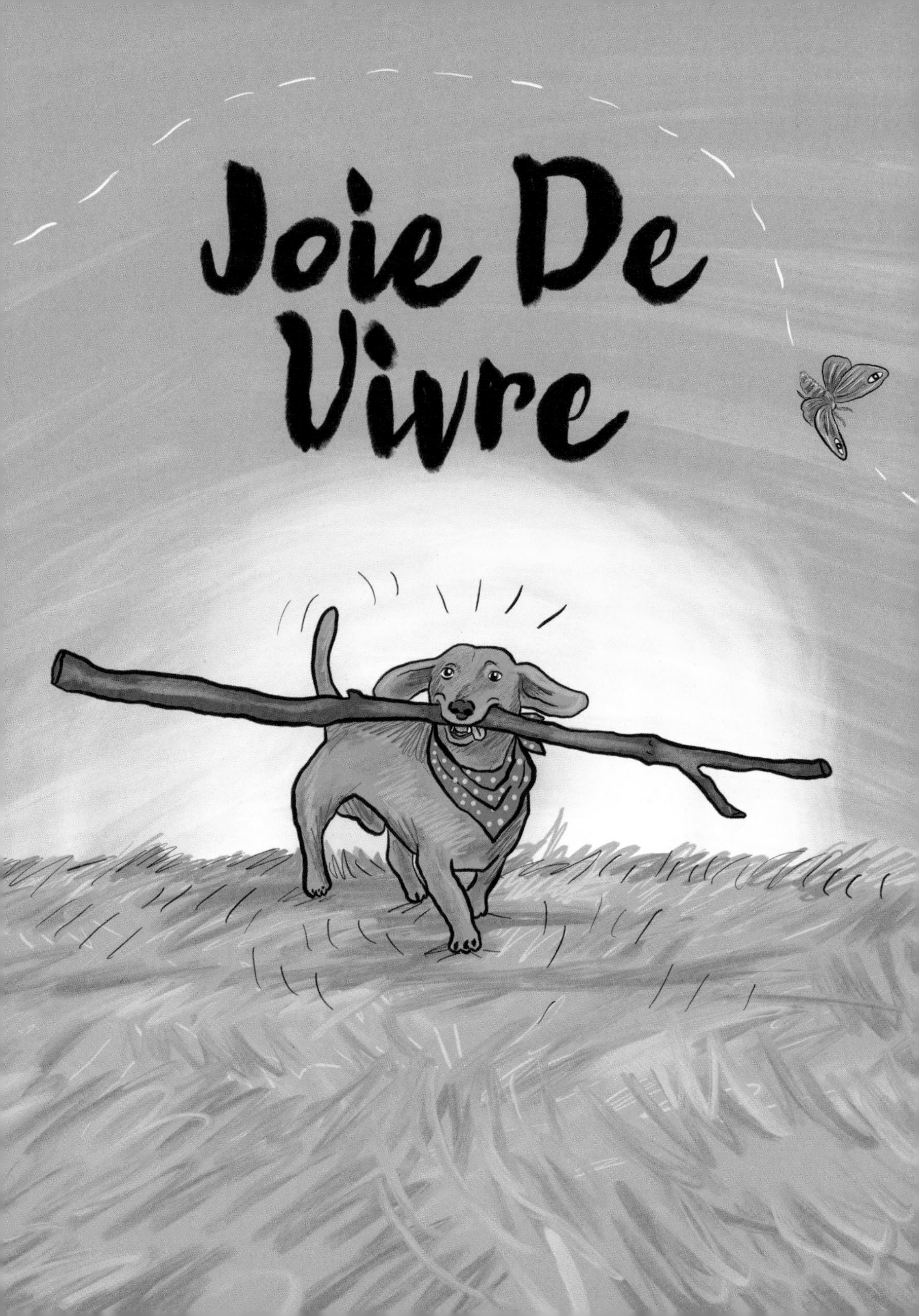
Joie De
Vivre

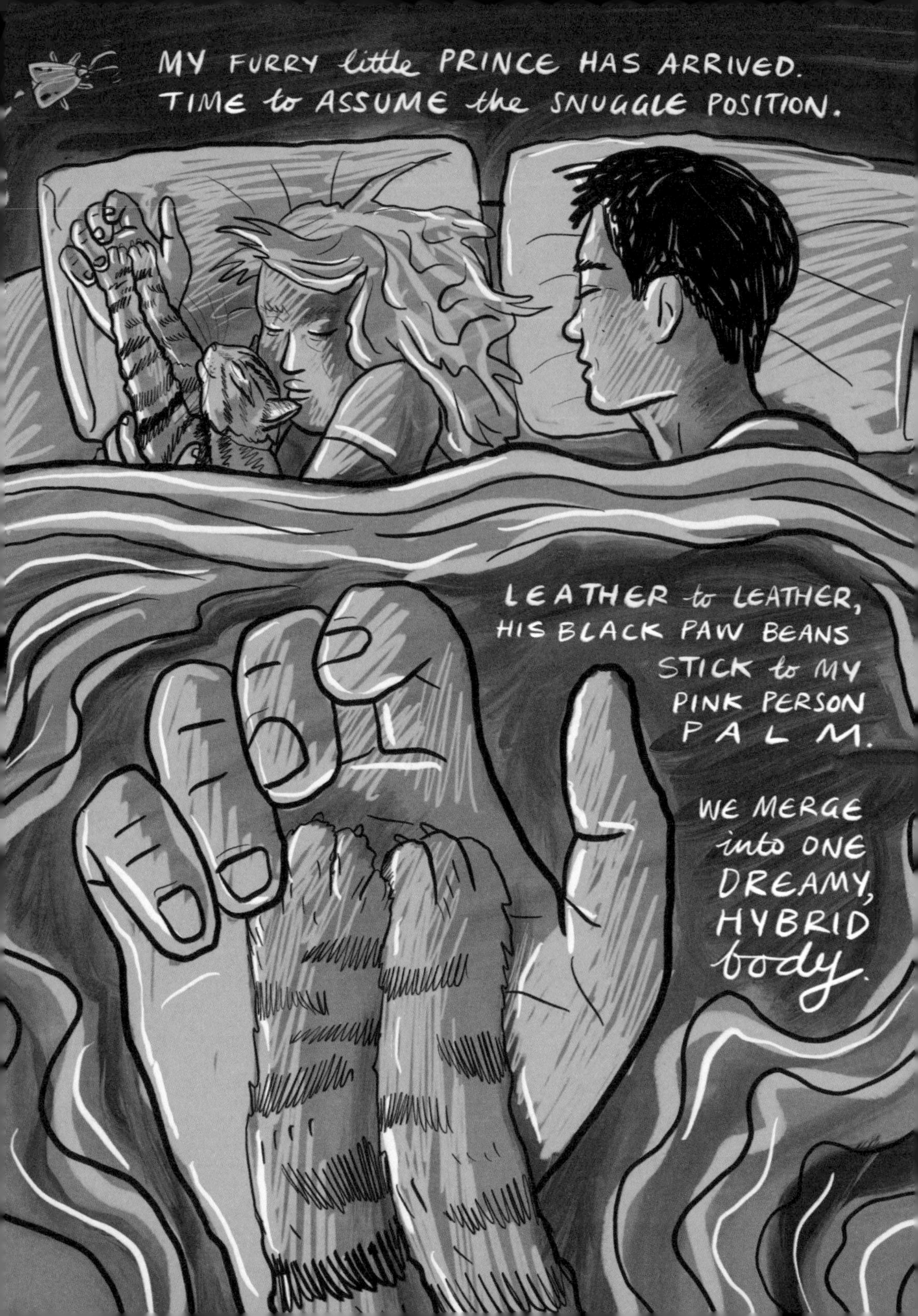
MY FURRY little PRINCE HAS ARRIVED.
TIME to ASSUME the SNUGGLE POSITION.
LEATHER to LEATHER, HIS BLACK PAW BEANS STICK to MY PINK PERSON PALM.
WE MERGE into ONE DREAMY, HYBRID body.

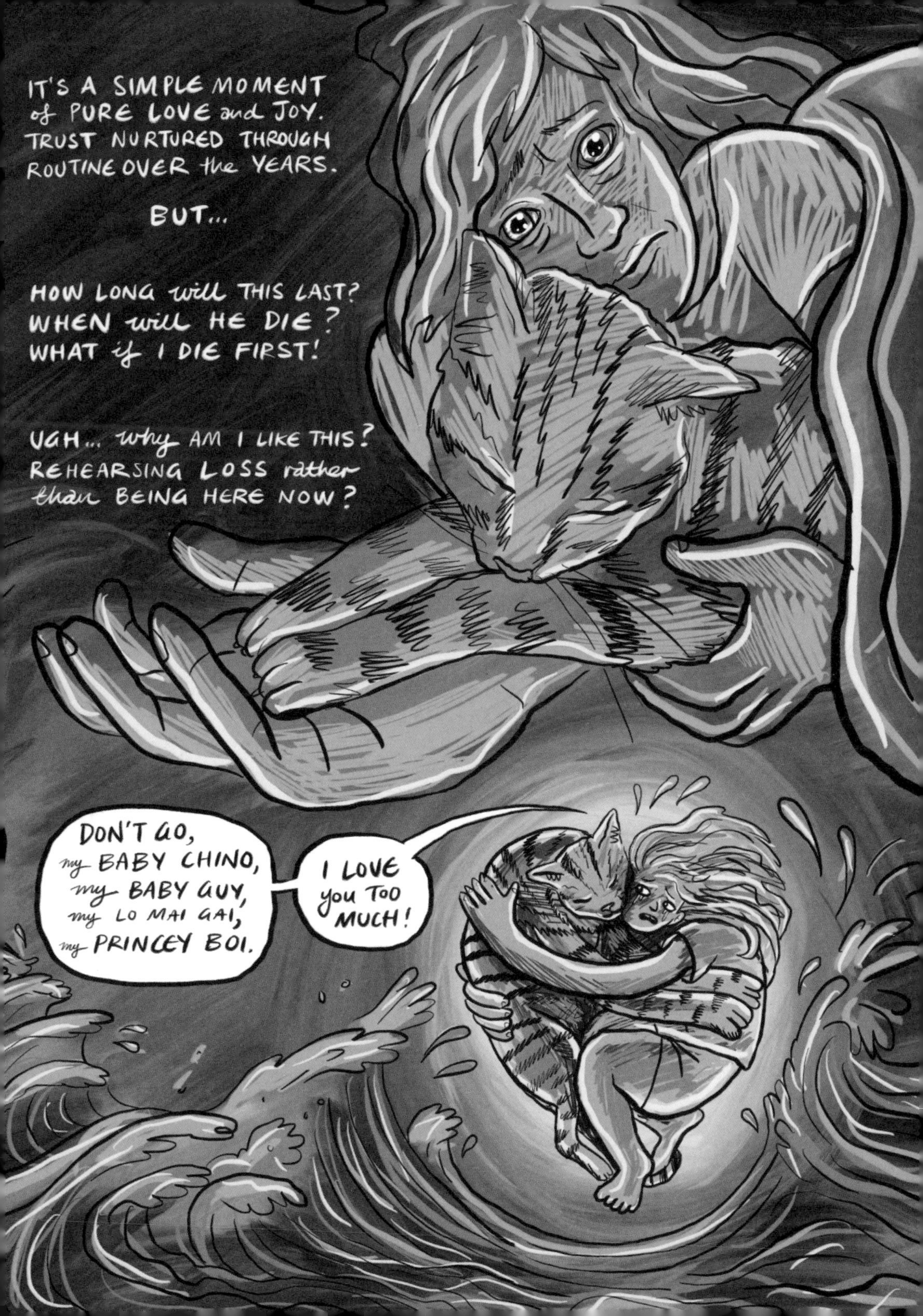
IT'S A SIMPLE MOMENT of PURE LOVE and JOY. TRUST NURTURED THROUGH ROUTINE OVER the YEARS.
BUT...
HOW LONG will THIS LAST? WHEN will HE DIE? WHAT if I DIE FIRST!
UGH... why AM I LIKE THIS? REHEARSING LOSS rather than BEING HERE NOW?
DON'T GO, my BABY CHINO, my BABY GUY, my LO MAI GAI, my PRINCEY BOI.
I LOVE you TOO MUCH!

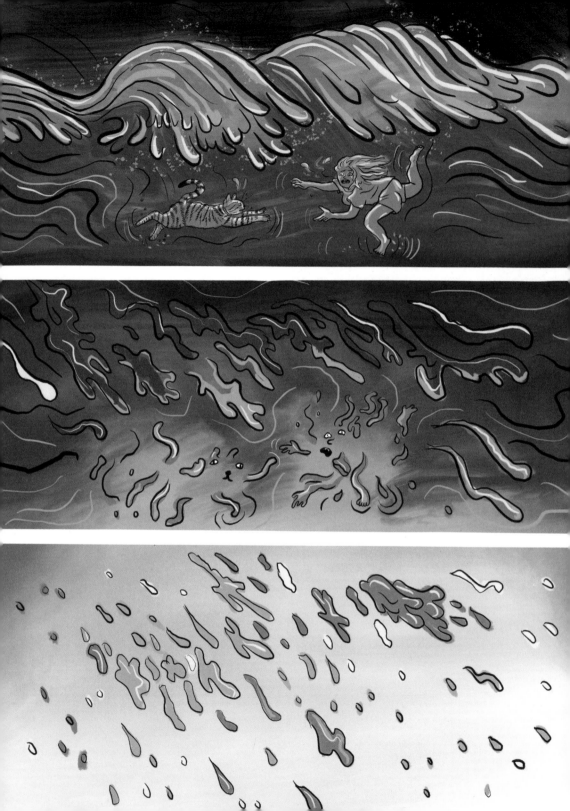

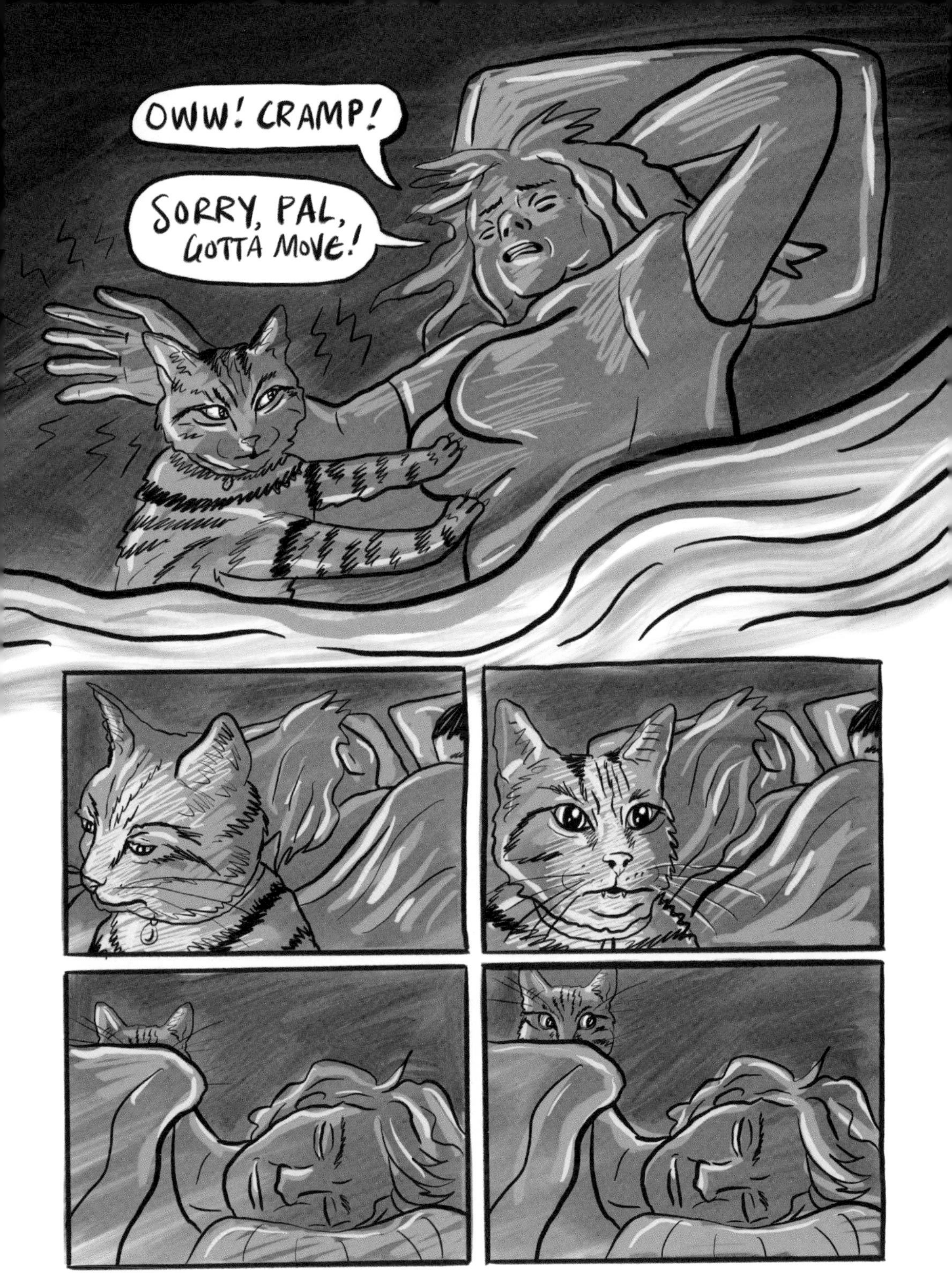
OWW! CRAMP!
SORRY, PAL, GOTTA MOVE!

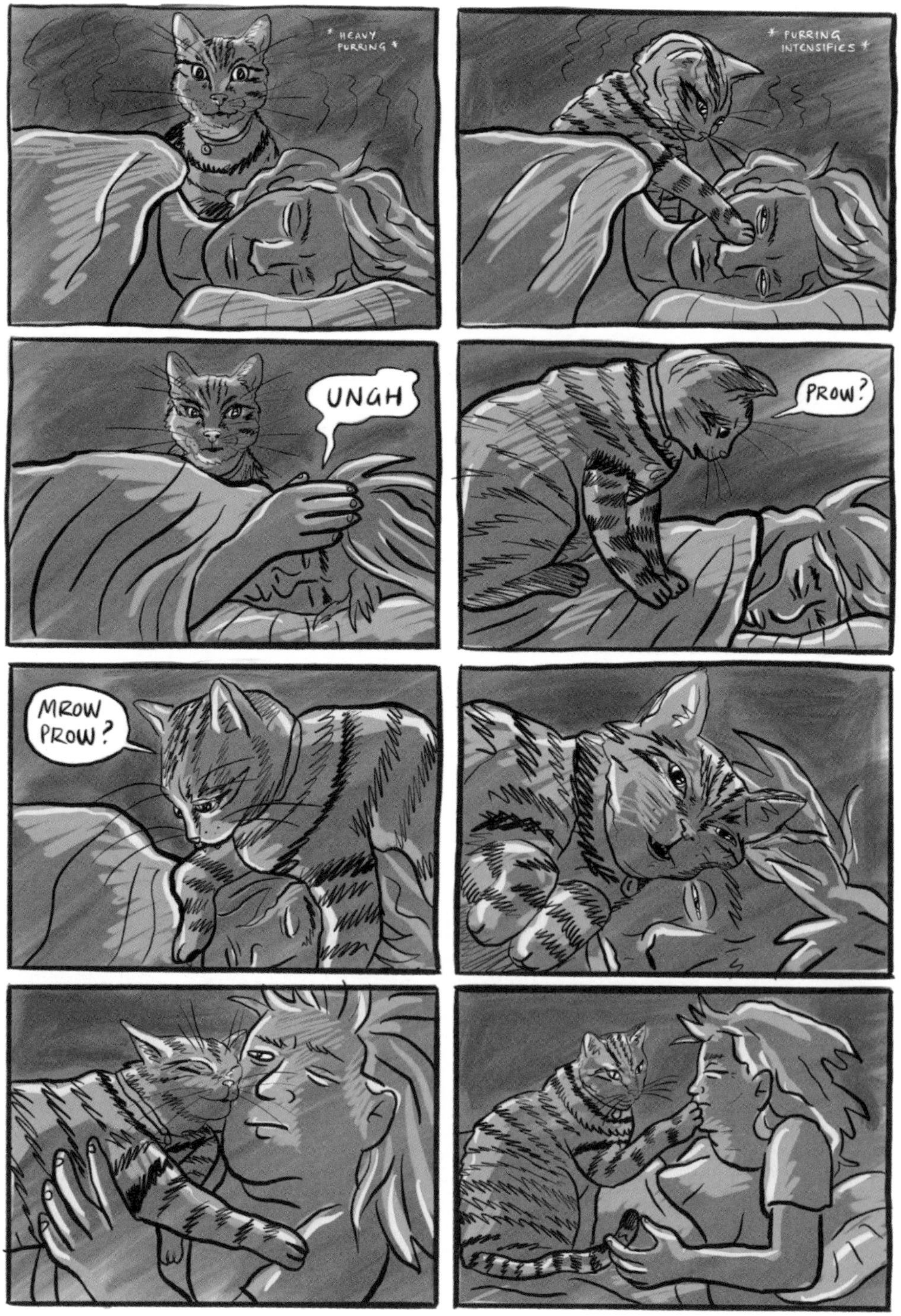
* HEAVY PURRING *
* PURRING INTENSIFIES *
UNGH
PROW?
MROW PROW?

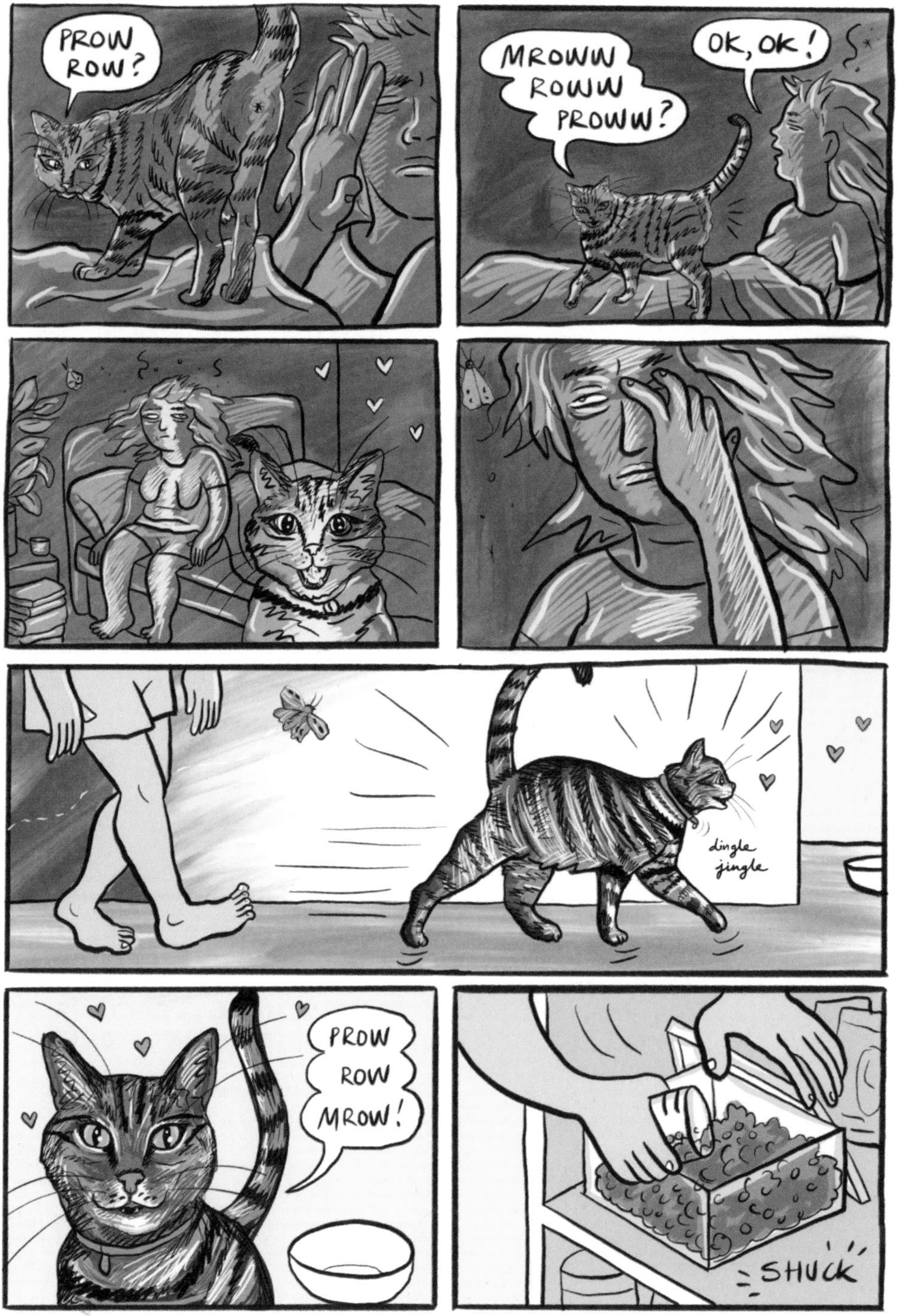
PROW ROW?
MROWW ROWW PROWW?
OK, OK!
dingle jingle
PROW ROW MROW!
SHUCK

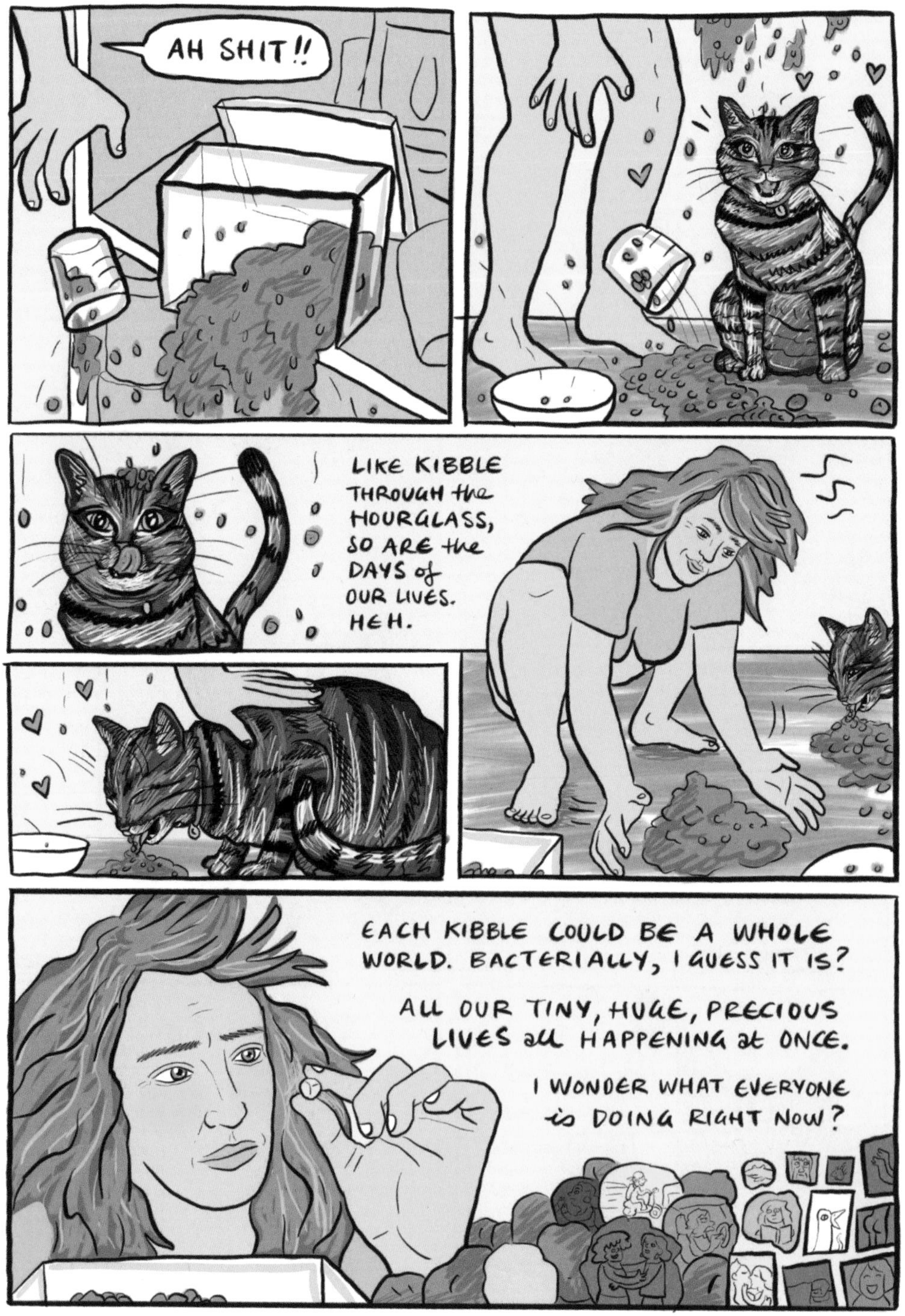

AH SHIT!!
LIKE KIBBLE THROUGH the HOURGLASS, SO ARE the DAYS of OUR LIVES. HEH.
EACH KIBBLE COULD BE A WHOLE WORLD. BACTERIALLY, I GUESS IT IS?
ALL OUR TINY, HUGE, PRECIOUS LIVES all HAPPENING at ONCE.
I WONDER WHAT EVERYONE is DOING RIGHT NOW?

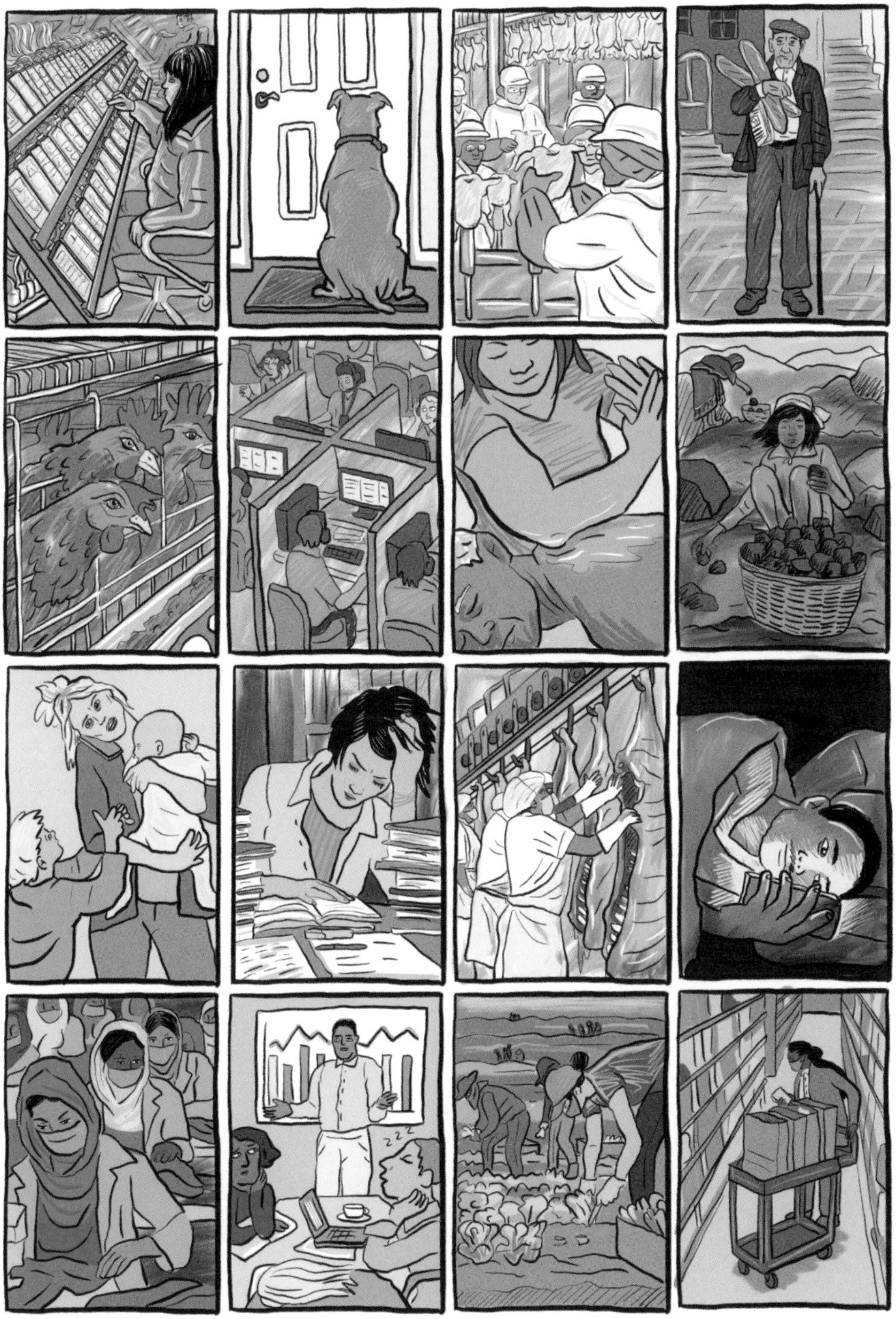
zzz

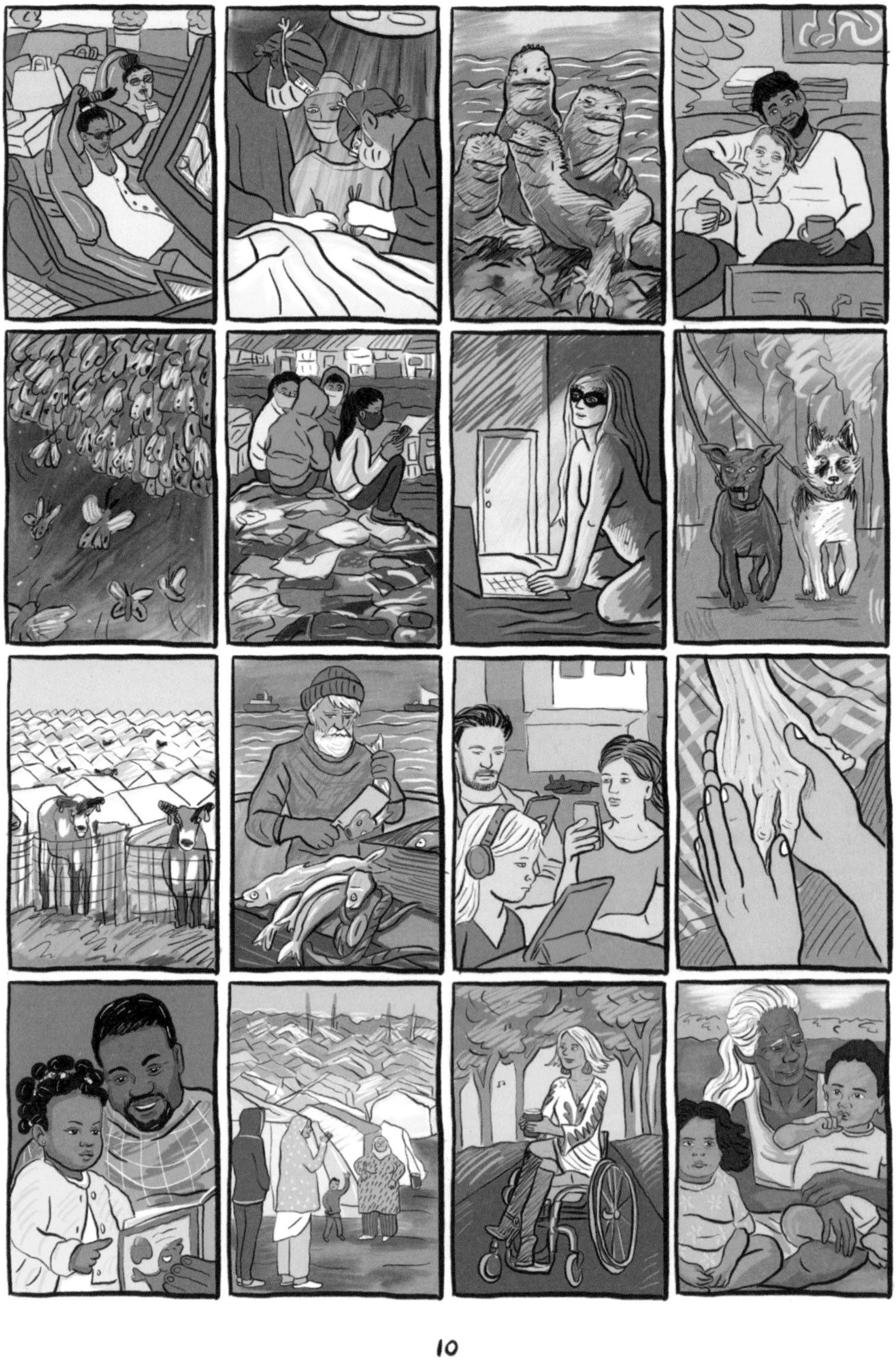

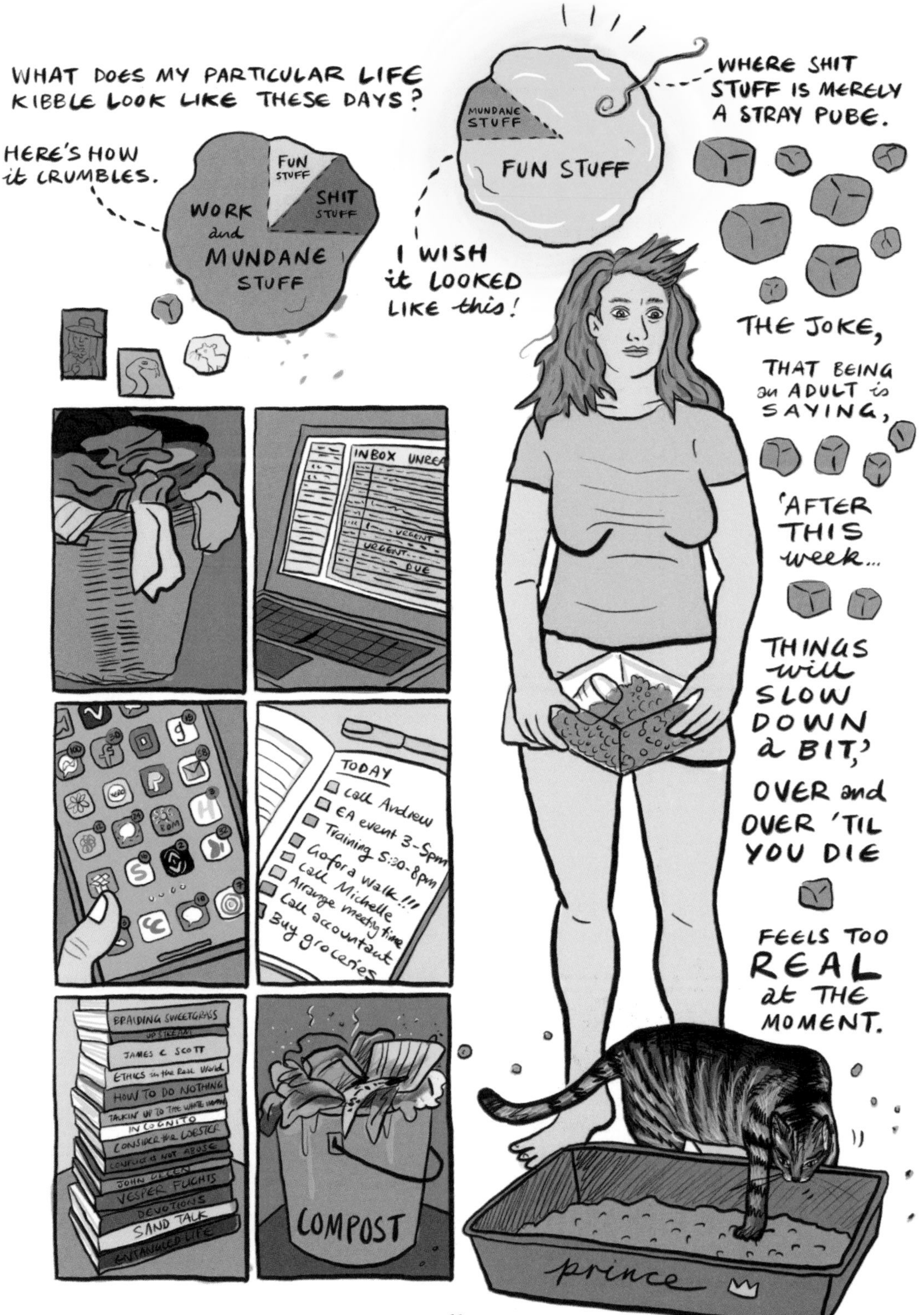
WHAT DOES MY PARTICULAR LIFE KIBBLE LOOK LIKE THESE DAYS?
HERE'S HOW it CRUMBLES.
WORK and MUNDANE STUFF
FUN STUFF
SHIT STUFF
I WISH it LOOKED LIKE this!
MUNDANE STUFF
FUN STUFF
WHERE SHIT STUFF IS MERELY A STRAY PUBE.
INBOX UNREA
URGENT
URGENT
DUE
TODAY
Call Andrew
EA event 3-5pm
Training 5:30-8pm
Go for a walk!!!
Call Michelle
Arrange meeting time
Call accountant
Buy groceries
BRAIDING SWEETGRASS
UP STREAM
JAMES C SCOTT
ETHICS in the Real World
HOW TO DO NOTHING
TALKIN' UP TO THE WHITE WOMAN
INCOGNITO
CONSIDER the LOBSTER
CONFLICT IS NOT ABUSE
JOHN CLEEN
VESPER FLIGHTS
DEVOTIONS
SAND TALK
ENTANGLED LIFE
COMPOST
THE JOKE,
THAT BEING an ADULT is SAYING,
'AFTER THIS week...
THINGS will SLOW DOWN a BIT,'
OVER and OVER 'TIL YOU DIE
FEELS TOO REAL at THE MOMENT.
prince

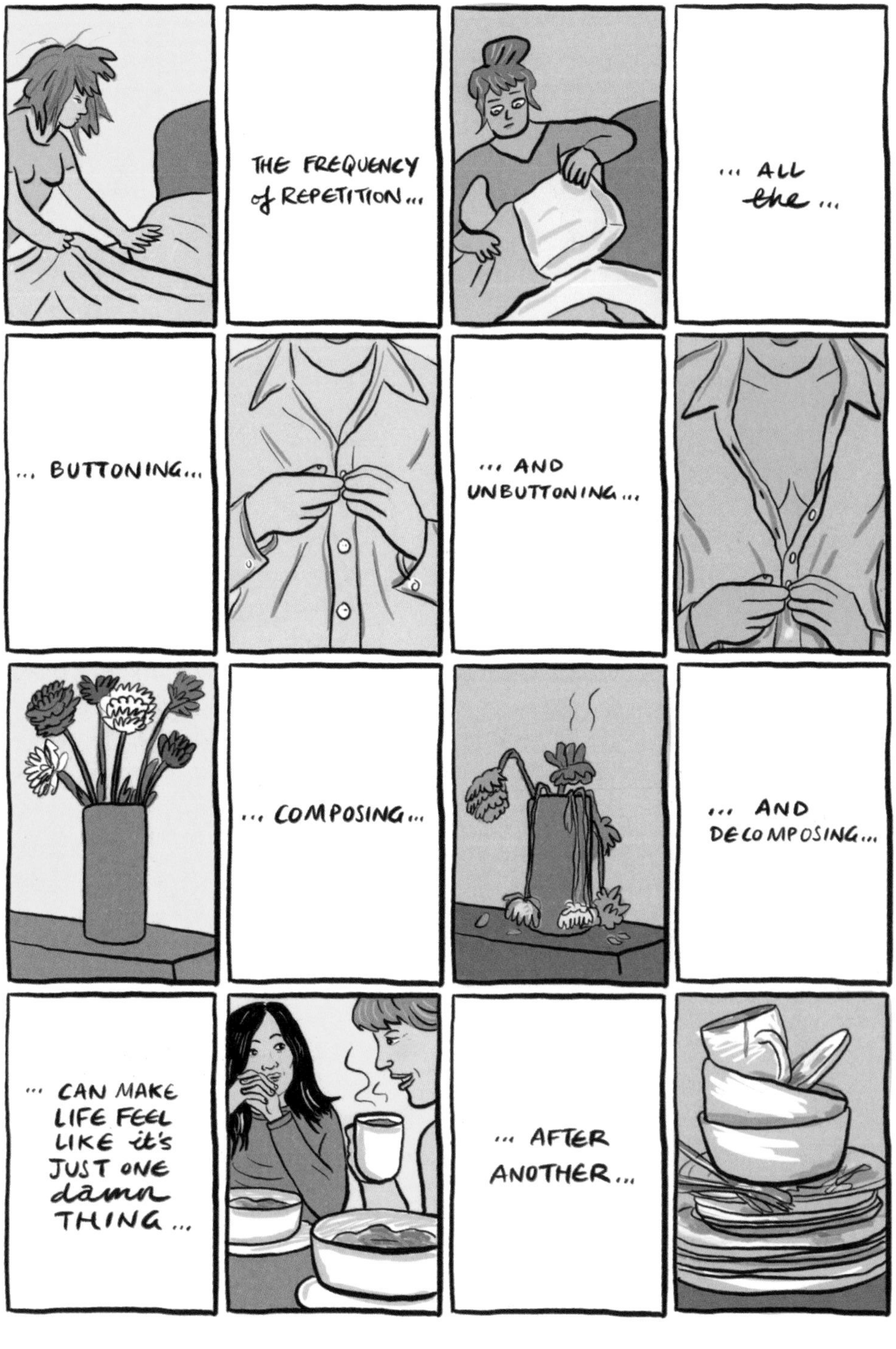
THE FREQUENCY of REPETITION...
... ALL the ...
... BUTTONING...
... AND UNBUTTONING...
... COMPOSING...
... AND DECOMPOSING...
... CAN MAKE LIFE FEEL LIKE it's JUST ONE damn THING...
... AFTER ANOTHER...

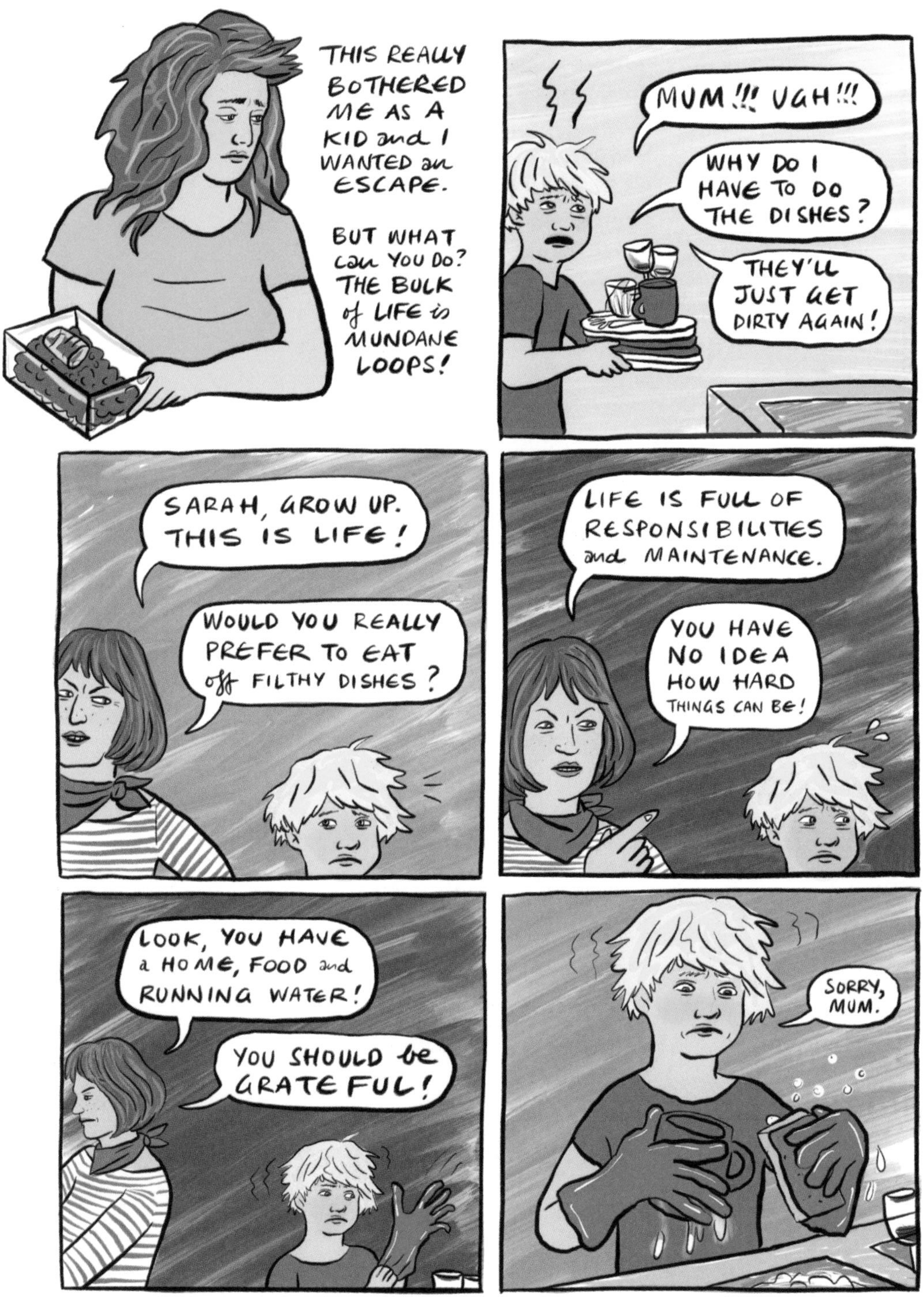
THIS REALLY BOTHERED ME AS A KID and I WANTED an ESCAPE.
BUT WHAT can YOU DO? THE BULK of LIFE is MUNDANE LOOPS!
MUM!!! UGH!!!
WHY DO I HAVE TO DO THE DISHES?
THEY'LL JUST GET DIRTY AGAIN!
SARAH, GROW UP. THIS IS LIFE!
WOULD YOU REALLY PREFER TO EAT off FILTHY DISHES?
LIFE IS FULL OF RESPONSIBILITIES and MAINTENANCE.
YOU HAVE NO IDEA HOW HARD THINGS CAN BE!
LOOK, YOU HAVE a HOME, FOOD and RUNNING WATER!
YOU SHOULD be GRATEFUL!
SORRY, MUM.

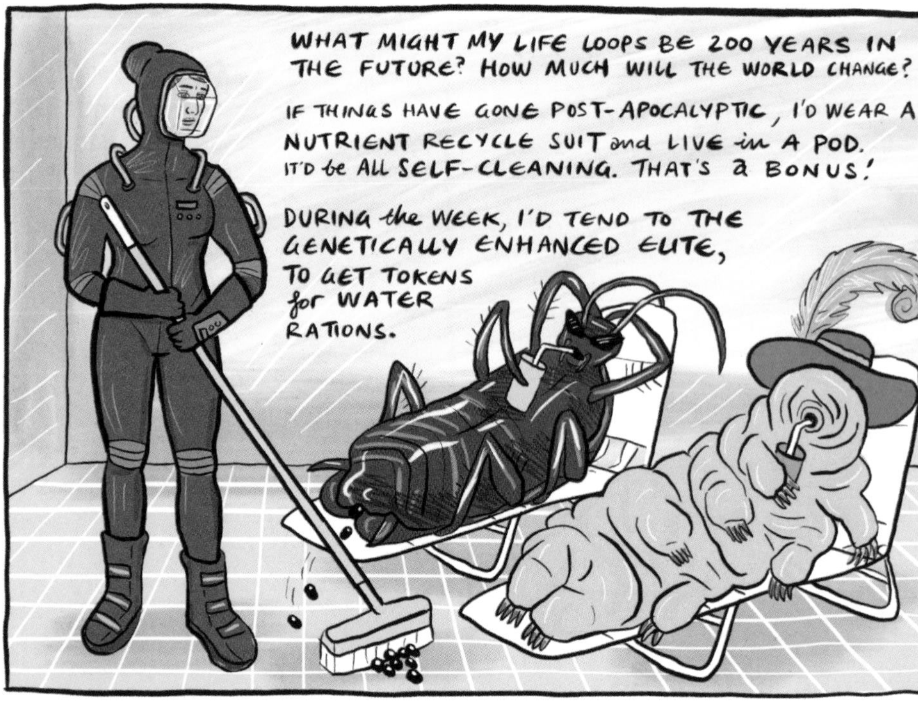
WHAT MIGHT MY LIFE LOOPS BE 200 YEARS IN THE FUTURE? HOW MUCH WILL THE WORLD CHANGE?
IF THINGS HAVE GONE POST-APOCALYPTIC, I'D WEAR A NUTRIENT RECYCLE SUIT and LIVE in A POD. IT'D be ALL SELF-CLEANING. THAT'S a BONUS!
DURING the WEEK, I'D TEND TO THE GENETICALLY ENHANCED ELITE, TO GET TOKENS for WATER RATIONS.

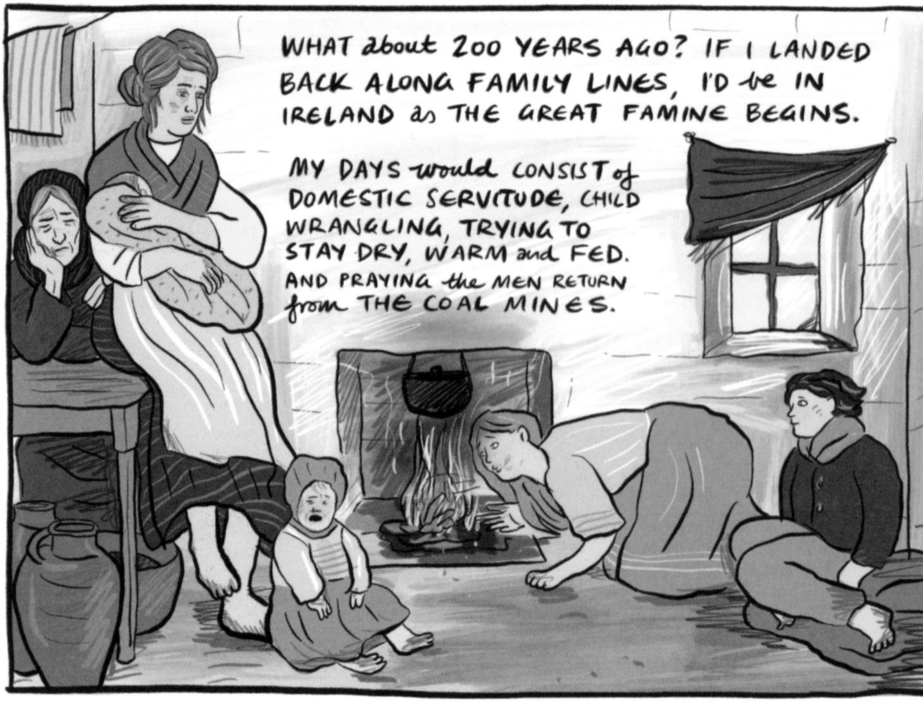
WHAT about 200 YEARS AGO? IF I LANDED BACK ALONG FAMILY LINES, I'D be IN IRELAND as THE GREAT FAMINE BEGINS.
MY DAYS would CONSIST of DOMESTIC SERVITUDE, CHILD WRANGLING, TRYING TO STAY DRY, WARM and FED. AND PRAYING the MEN RETURN from THE COAL MINES.

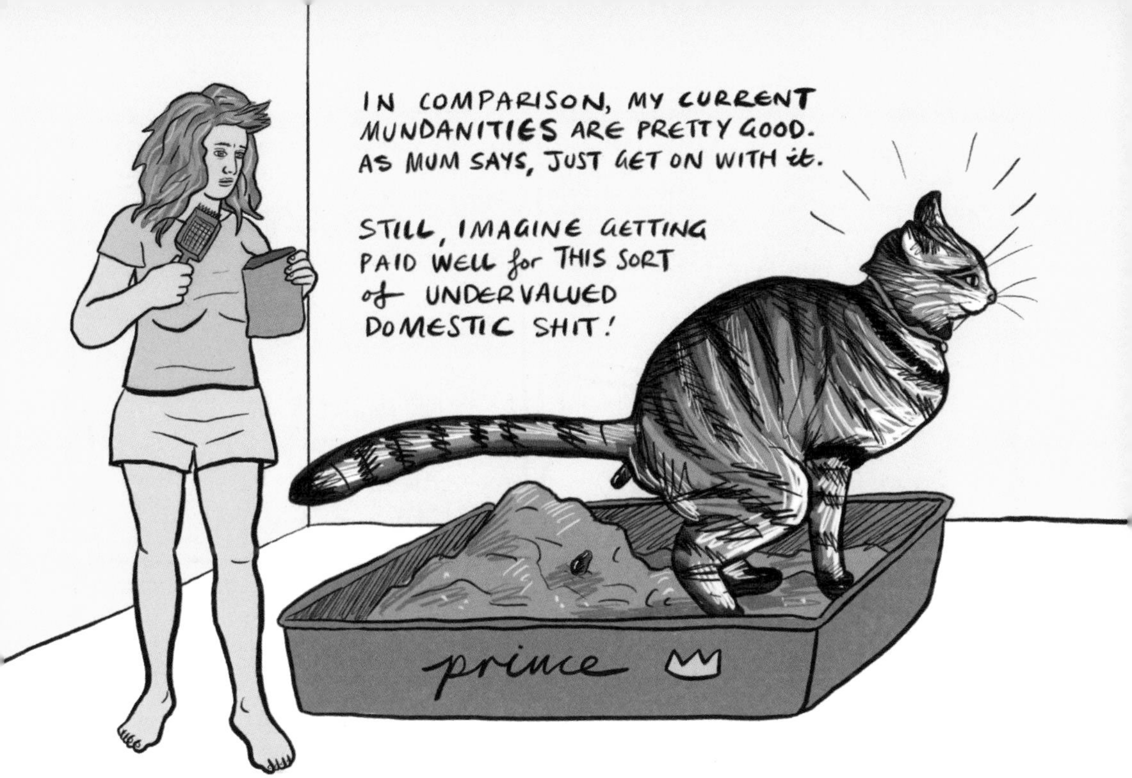
IN COMPARISON, MY CURRENT MUNDANITIES ARE PRETTY GOOD. AS MUM SAYS, JUST GET ON WITH it.
STILL, IMAGINE GETTING PAID WELL for THIS SORT of UNDERVALUED DOMESTIC SHIT!
prince

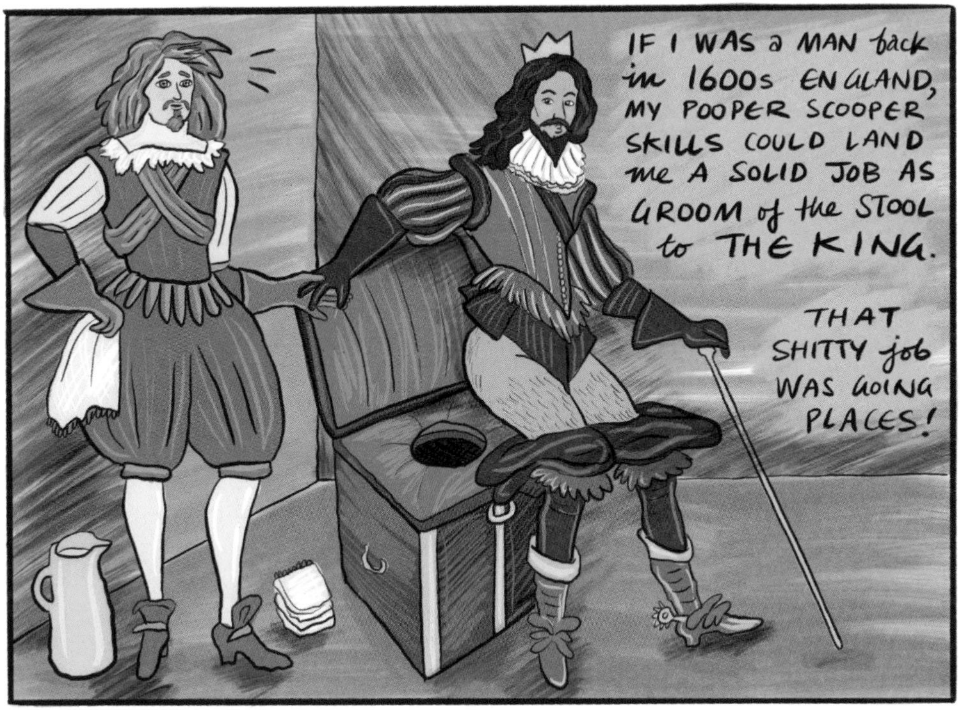
IF I WAS a MAN back in 1600s ENGLAND, MY POOPER SCOOPER SKILLS COULD LAND me A SOLID JOB AS GROOM of the STOOL to THE KING.
THAT SHITTY job WAS GOING PLACES!

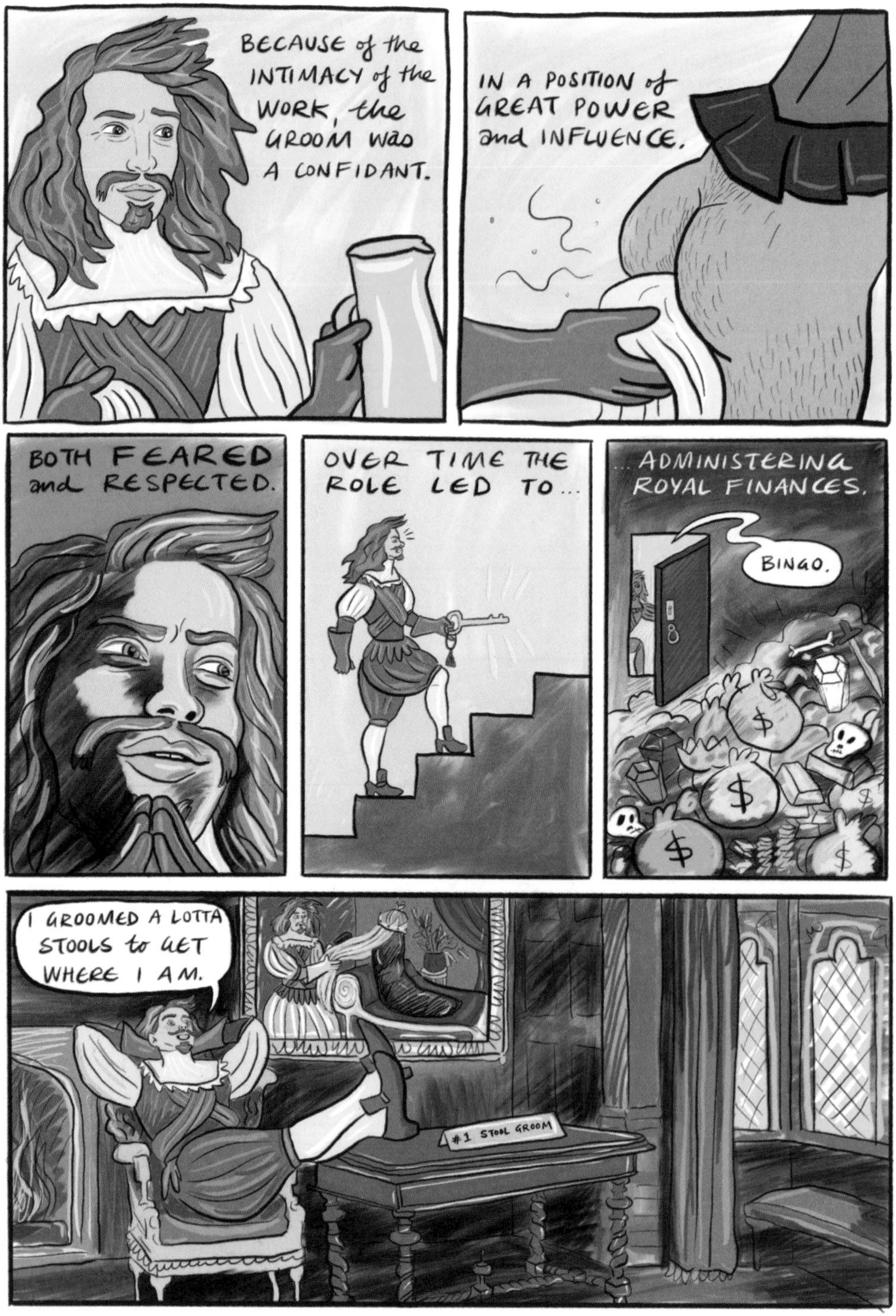
BECAUSE of the INTIMACY of the WORK, the GROOM was A CONFIDANT.
IN A POSITION of GREAT POWER and INFLUENCE.
BOTH FEARED and RESPECTED.
OVER TIME THE ROLE LED TO...
...ADMINISTERING ROYAL FINANCES.
BINGO.
I GROOMED A LOTTA STOOLS to GET WHERE I AM.
#1 STOOL GROOM

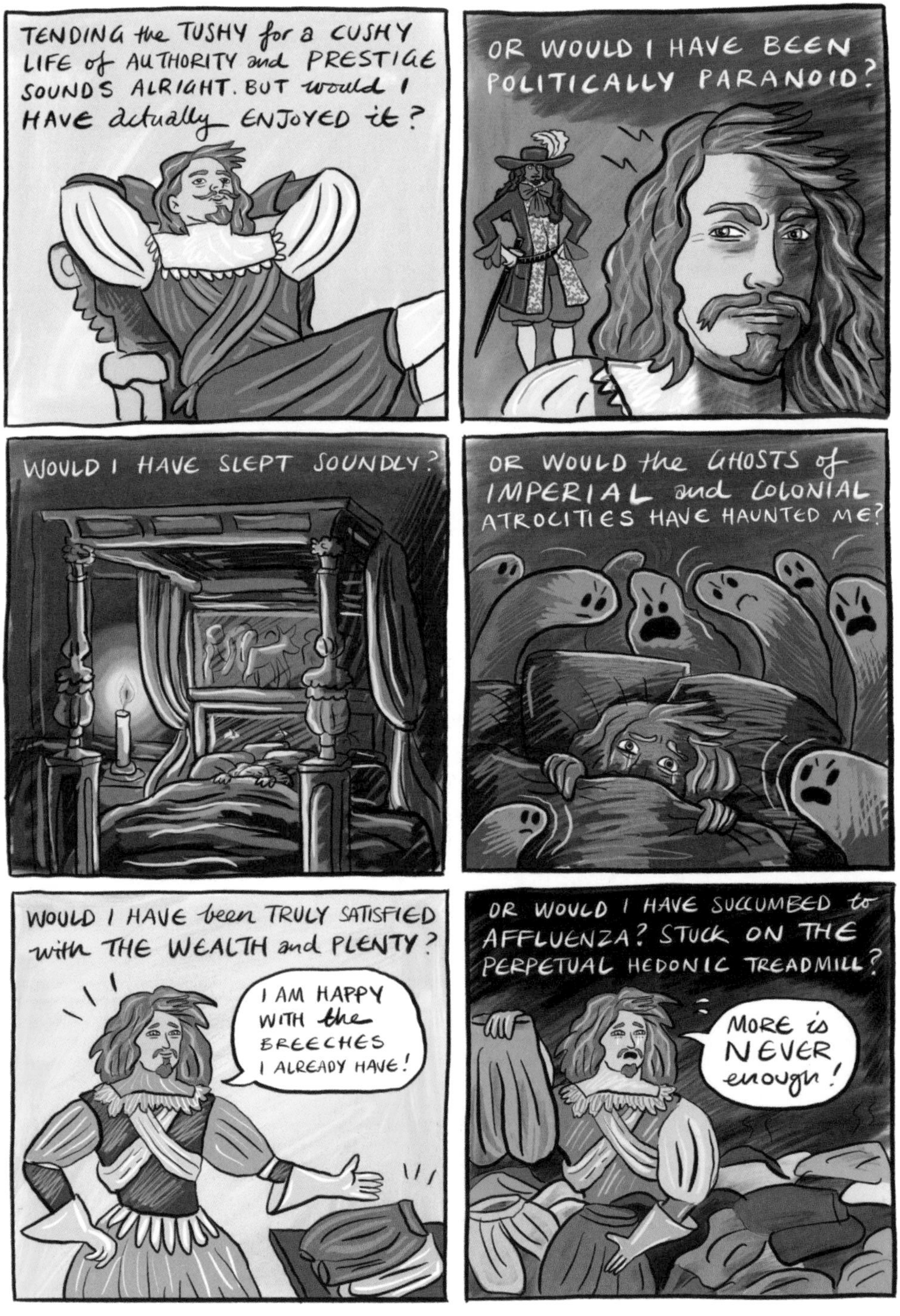
TENDING the TUSHY for a CUSHY LIFE of AUTHORITY and PRESTIGE SOUNDS ALRIGHT. BUT would I HAVE actually ENJOYED it?
OR WOULD I HAVE BEEN POLITICALLY PARANOID?
WOULD I HAVE SLEPT SOUNDLY?
OR WOULD the GHOSTS of IMPERIAL and COLONIAL ATROCITIES HAVE HAUNTED ME?
WOULD I HAVE been TRULY SATISFIED with THE WEALTH and PLENTY?
I AM HAPPY WITH the BREECHES I ALREADY HAVE!
OR WOULD I HAVE SUCCUMBED to AFFLUENZA? STUCK ON THE PERPETUAL HEDONIC TREADMILL?
MORE is NEVER enough!

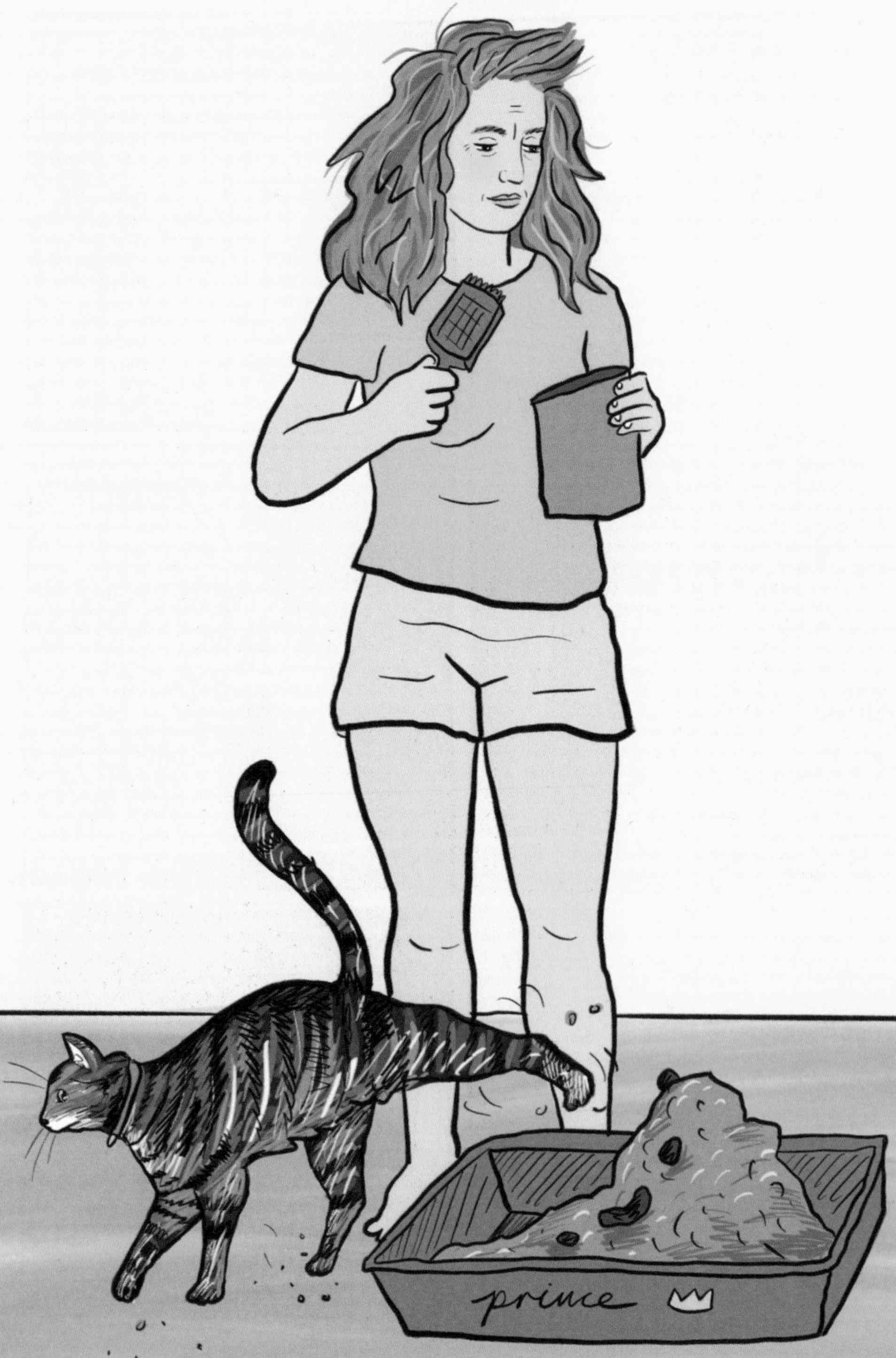
prince

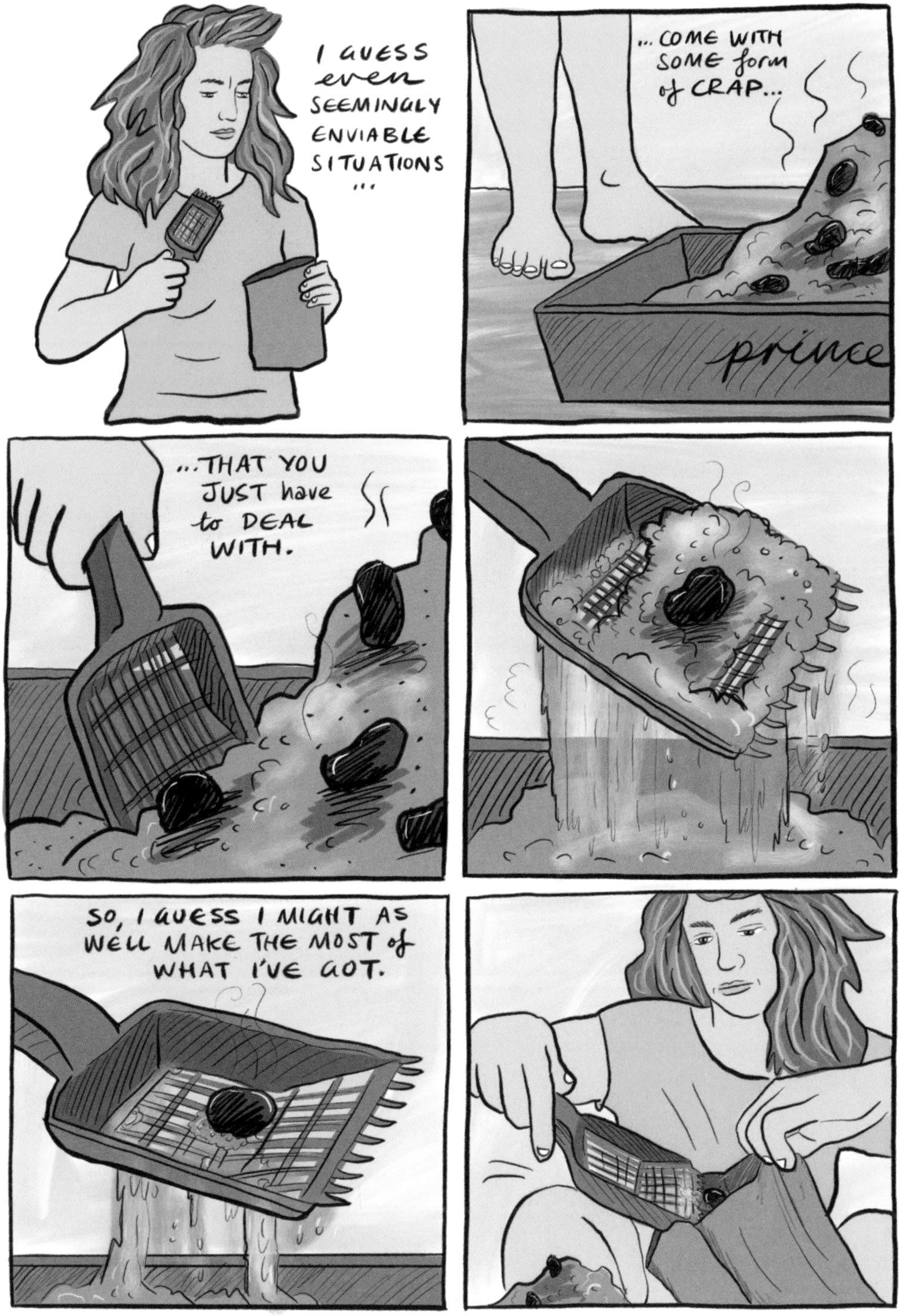
I GUESS even SEEMINGLY ENVIABLE SITUATIONS ...
... COME WITH SOME form of CRAP...
prince
...THAT YOU JUST have to DEAL WITH.
SO, I GUESS I MIGHT AS WELL MAKE THE MOST of WHAT I'VE GOT.

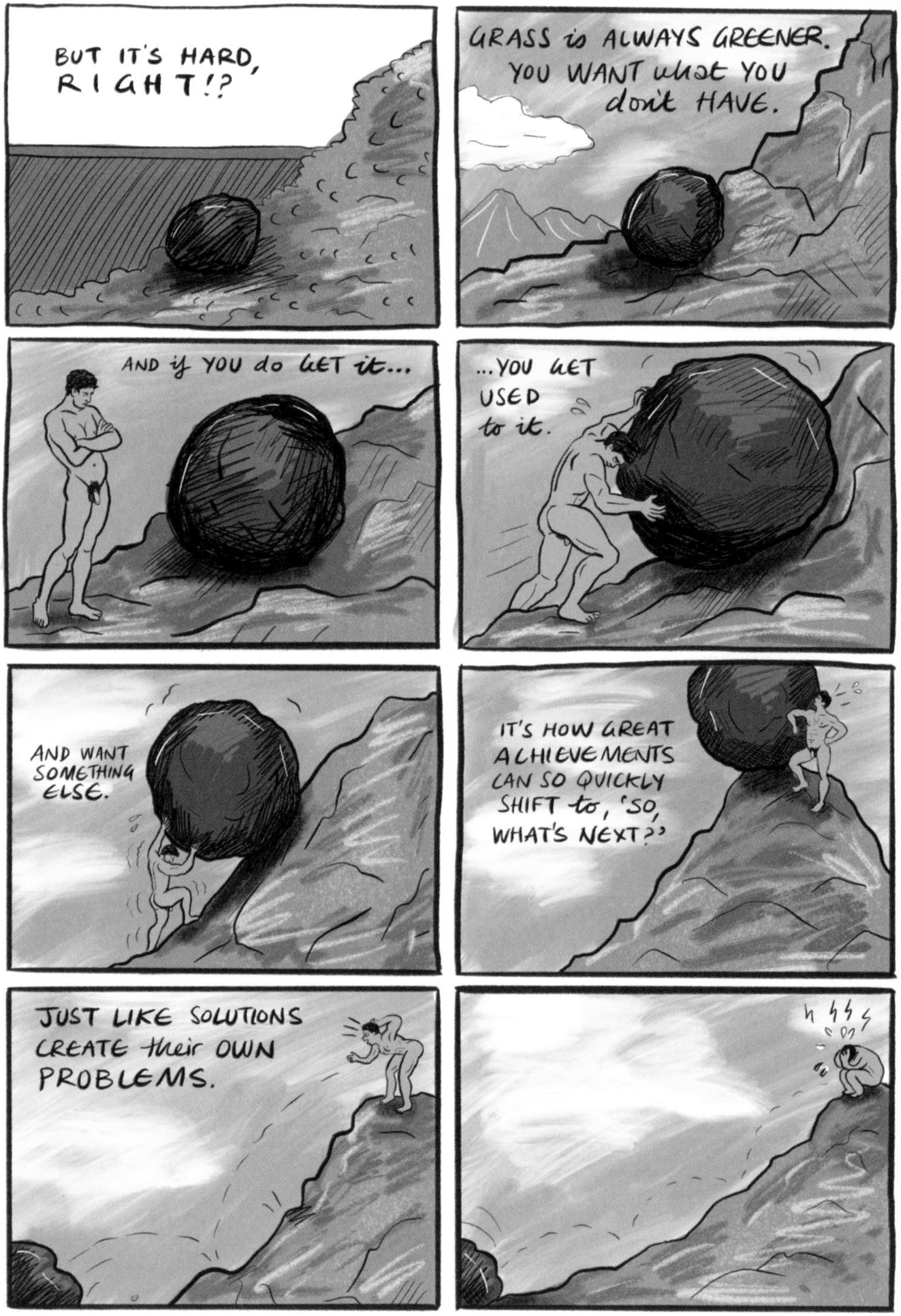
BUT IT'S HARD, RIGHT!?
GRASS is ALWAYS GREENER. YOU WANT what YOU don't HAVE.
AND if YOU do GET it...
...YOU GET USED to it.
AND WANT SOMETHING ELSE.
IT'S HOW GREAT ACHIEVEMENTS CAN SO QUICKLY SHIFT to, 'SO, WHAT'S NEXT?'
JUST LIKE SOLUTIONS CREATE their OWN PROBLEMS.

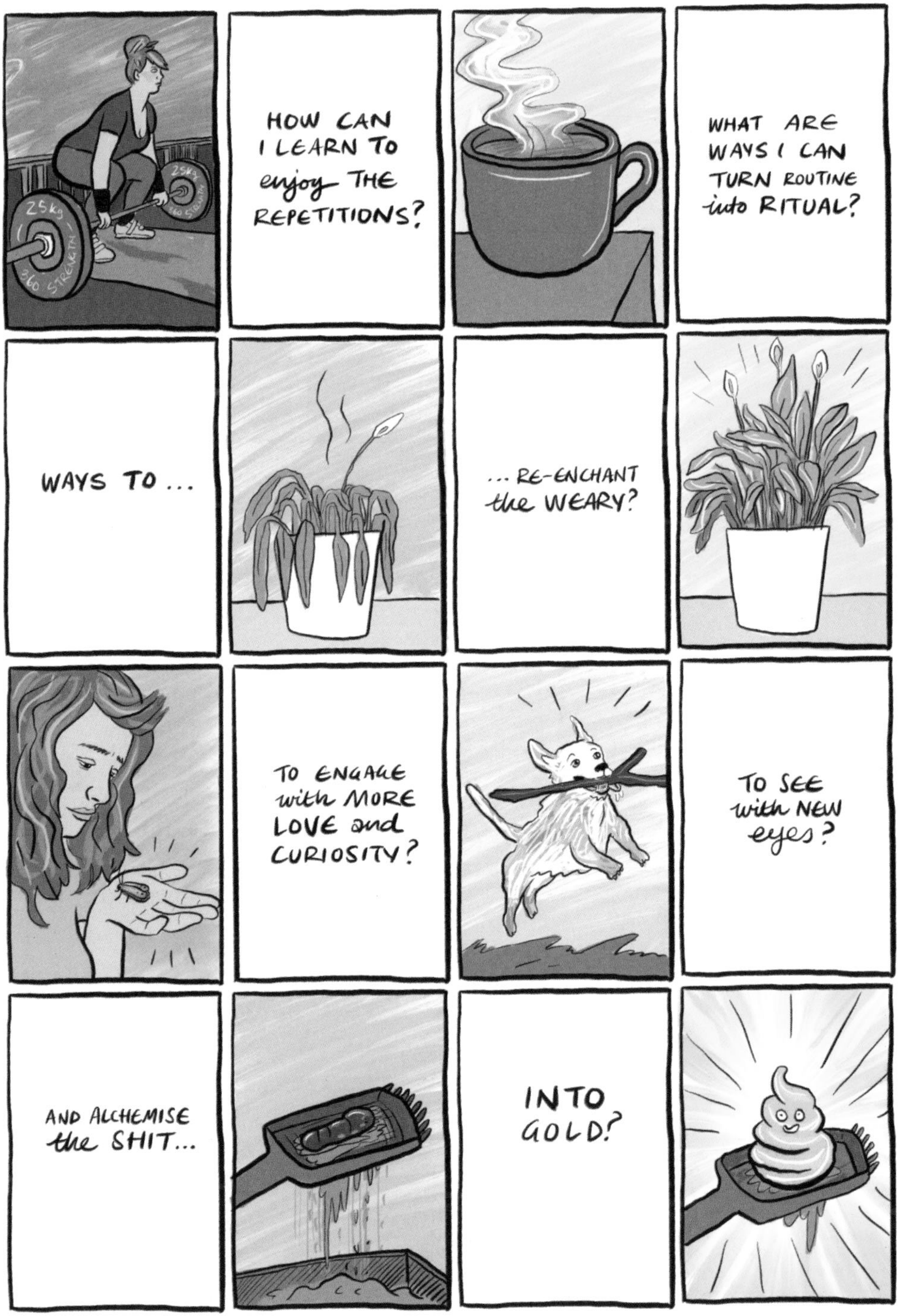
HOW CAN I LEARN TO enjoy THE REPETITIONS?
WHAT ARE WAYS I CAN TURN ROUTINE into RITUAL?
WAYS TO ...
... RE-ENCHANT the WEARY?
TO ENGAGE with MORE LOVE and CURIOSITY?
TO SEE with NEW eyes?
AND ALCHEMISE the SHIT...
INTO GOLD?

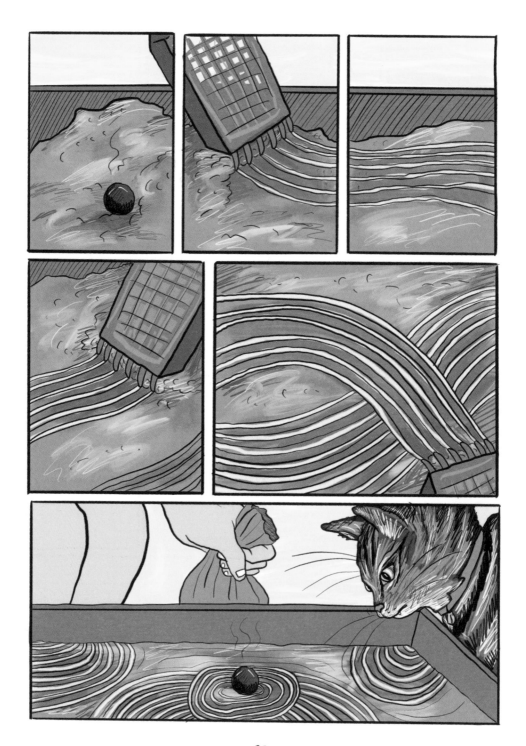

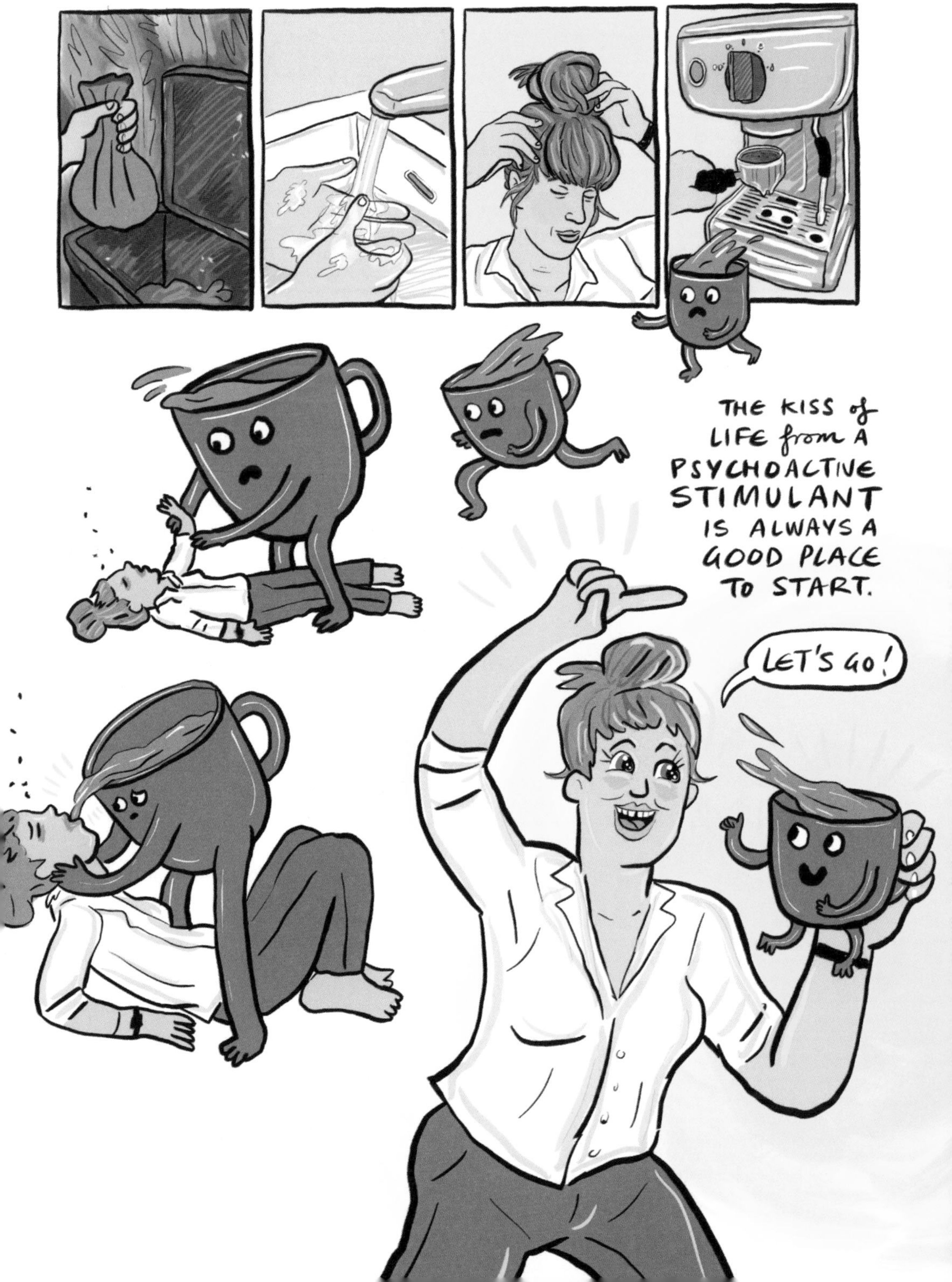
THE KISS of LIFE from A PSYCHOACTIVE STIMULANT IS ALWAYS A GOOD PLACE TO START.
LET'S GO!

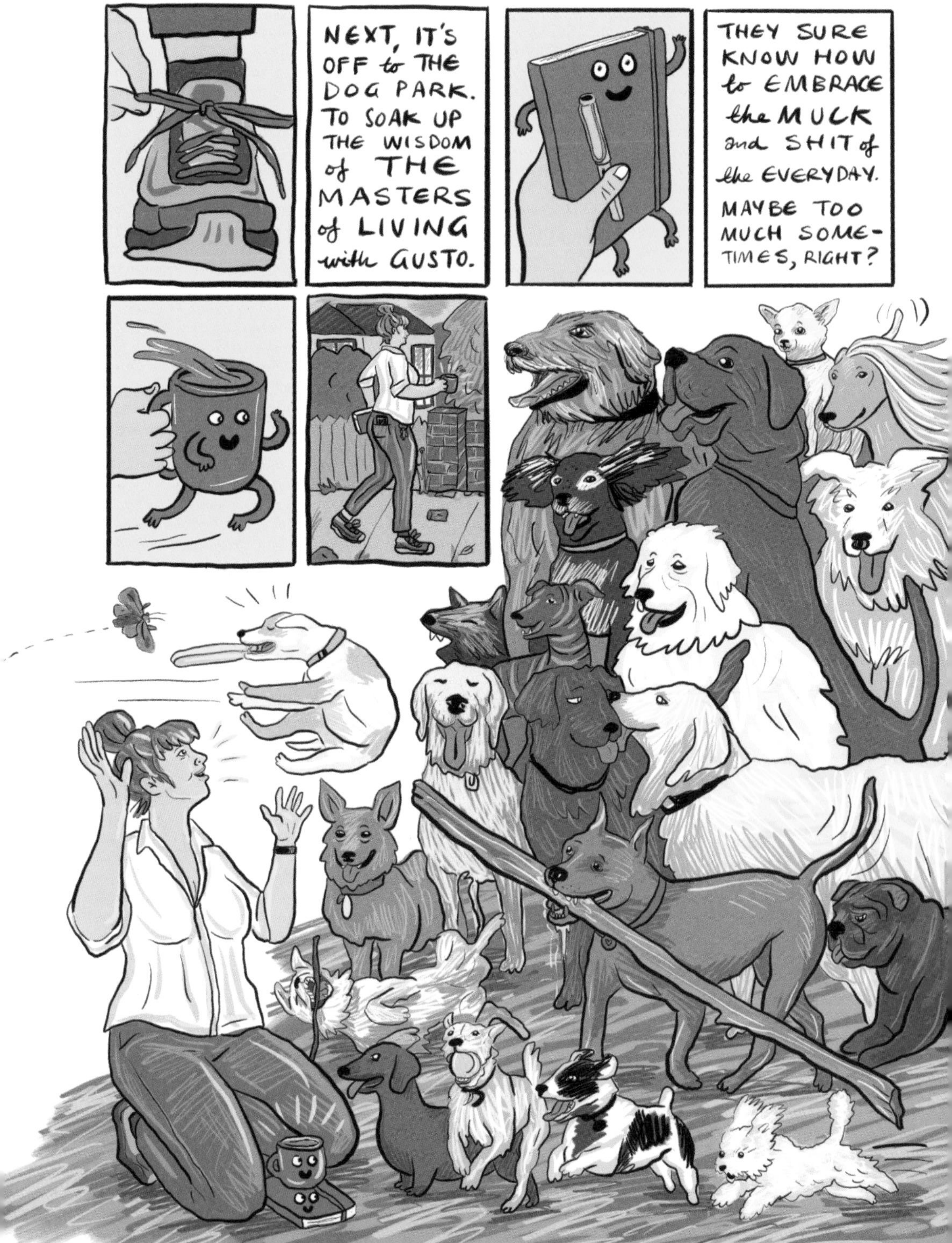
NEXT, IT'S OFF to THE DOG PARK. TO SOAK UP THE WISDOM of THE MASTERS of LIVING with GUSTO.
THEY SURE KNOW HOW to EMBRACE the MUCK and SHIT of the EVERYDAY.
MAYBE TOO MUCH SOME-TIMES, RIGHT?

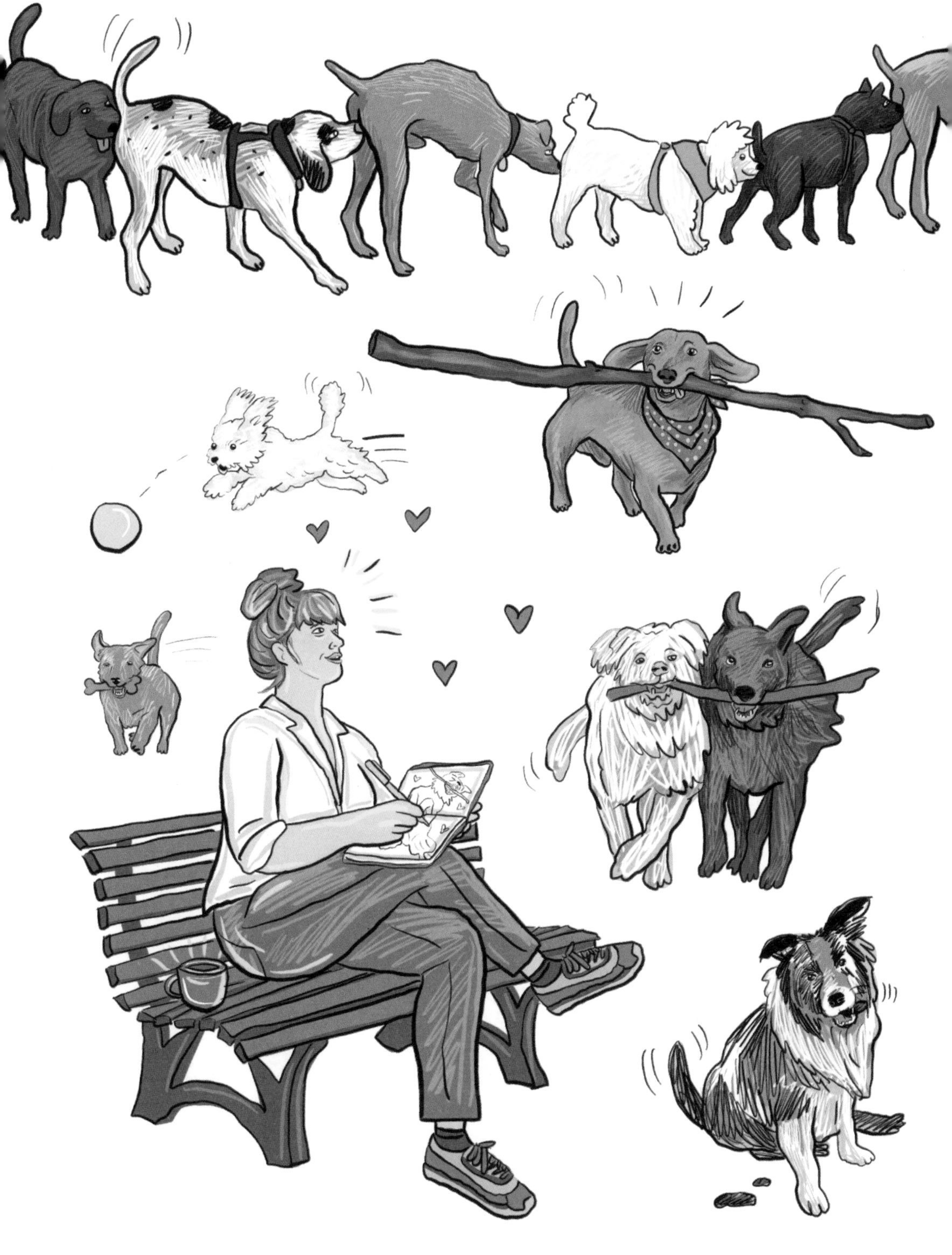

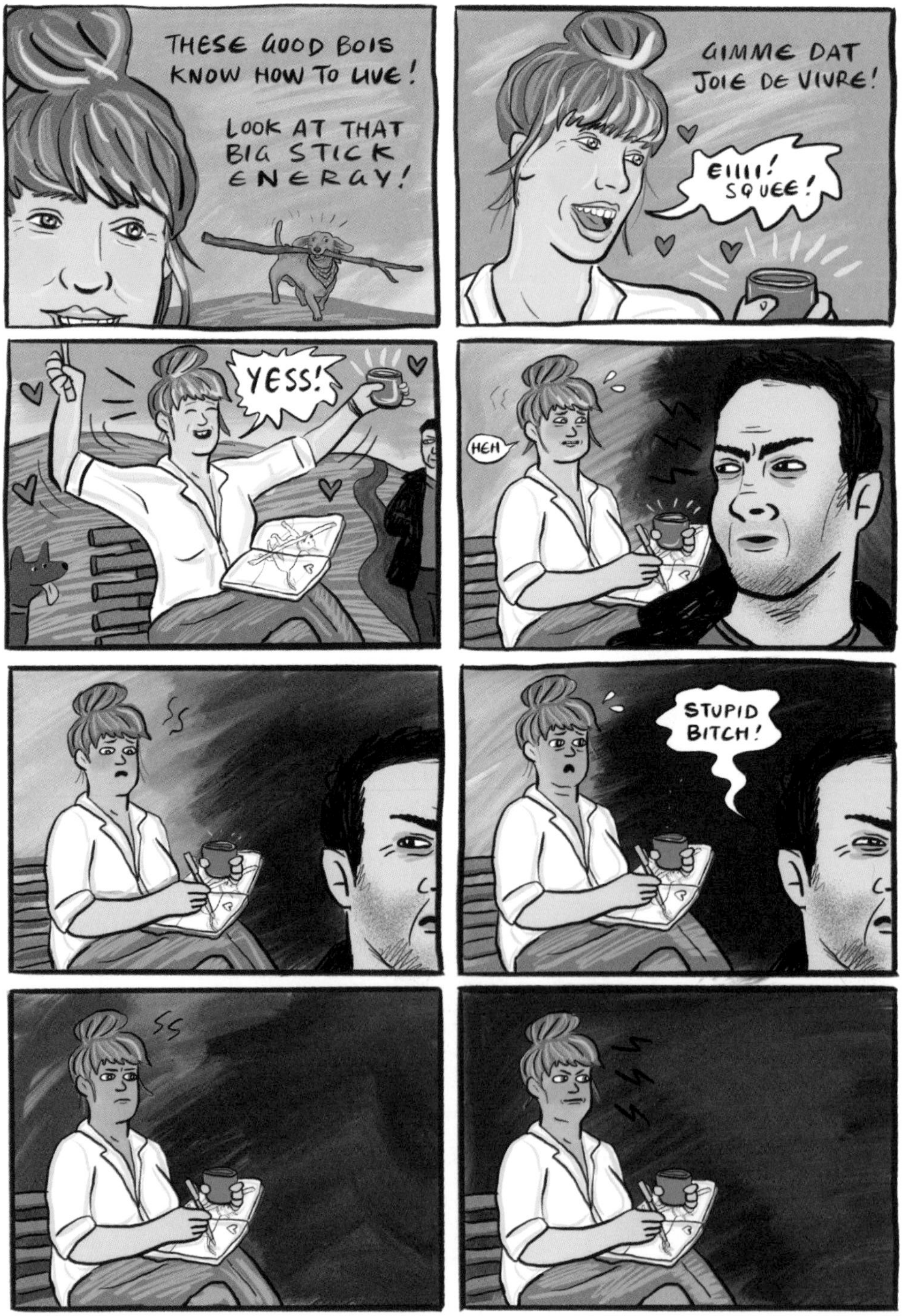

THESE GOOD BOIS KNOW HOW TO LIVE!
LOOK AT THAT BIG STICK ENERGY!
GIMME DAT JOIE DE VIVRE!
EIIII! SQUEE!
YESS!
HEH
STUPID BITCH!

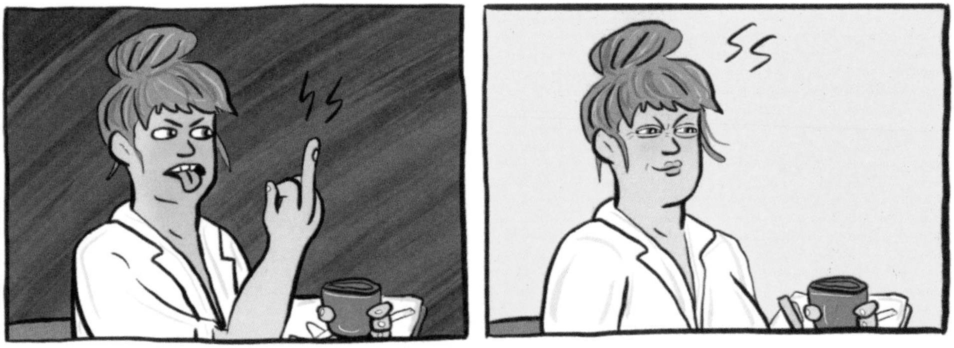

BAH! FUCK that GUY, and FUCK MY FEAR of BEING CRINGE. JOY GIVES ME LIFE! WHEN I SEE PEOPLE IN THEIR JOY IT'S A WINK for ME TO SHINE TOO. SO WHY DOES it FEEL PRECARIOUS?

MAYBE THAT'S the PARADOX of JOY? IT'S BOTH / AND. LIKE HOW TINY BIRDS ARE SO DELICATE and FLEETING, YET THEY CAN SURVIVE STORMS that SNAP BIG TREES.

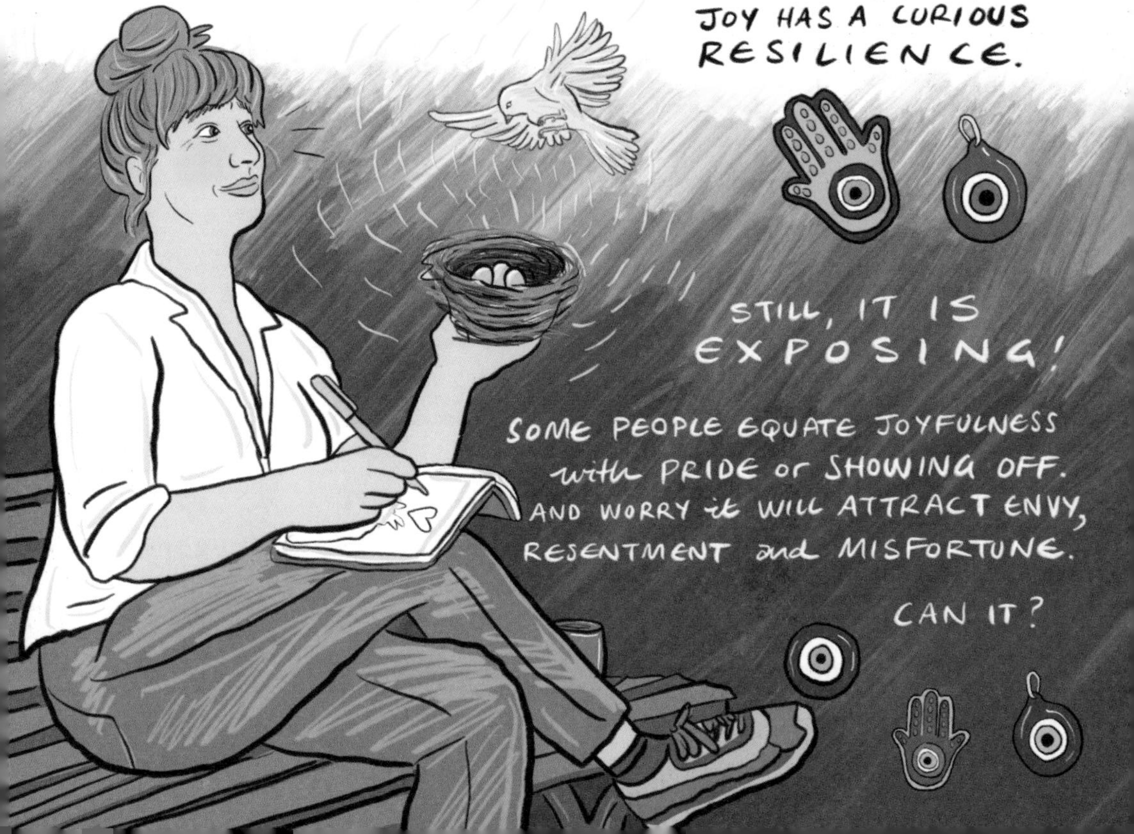

JOY HAS A CURIOUS RESILIENCE.
STILL, IT IS EXPOSING!
SOME PEOPLE EQUATE JOYFULNESS with PRIDE or SHOWING OFF.
AND WORRY it WILL ATTRACT ENVY, RESENTMENT and MISFORTUNE.
CAN IT?

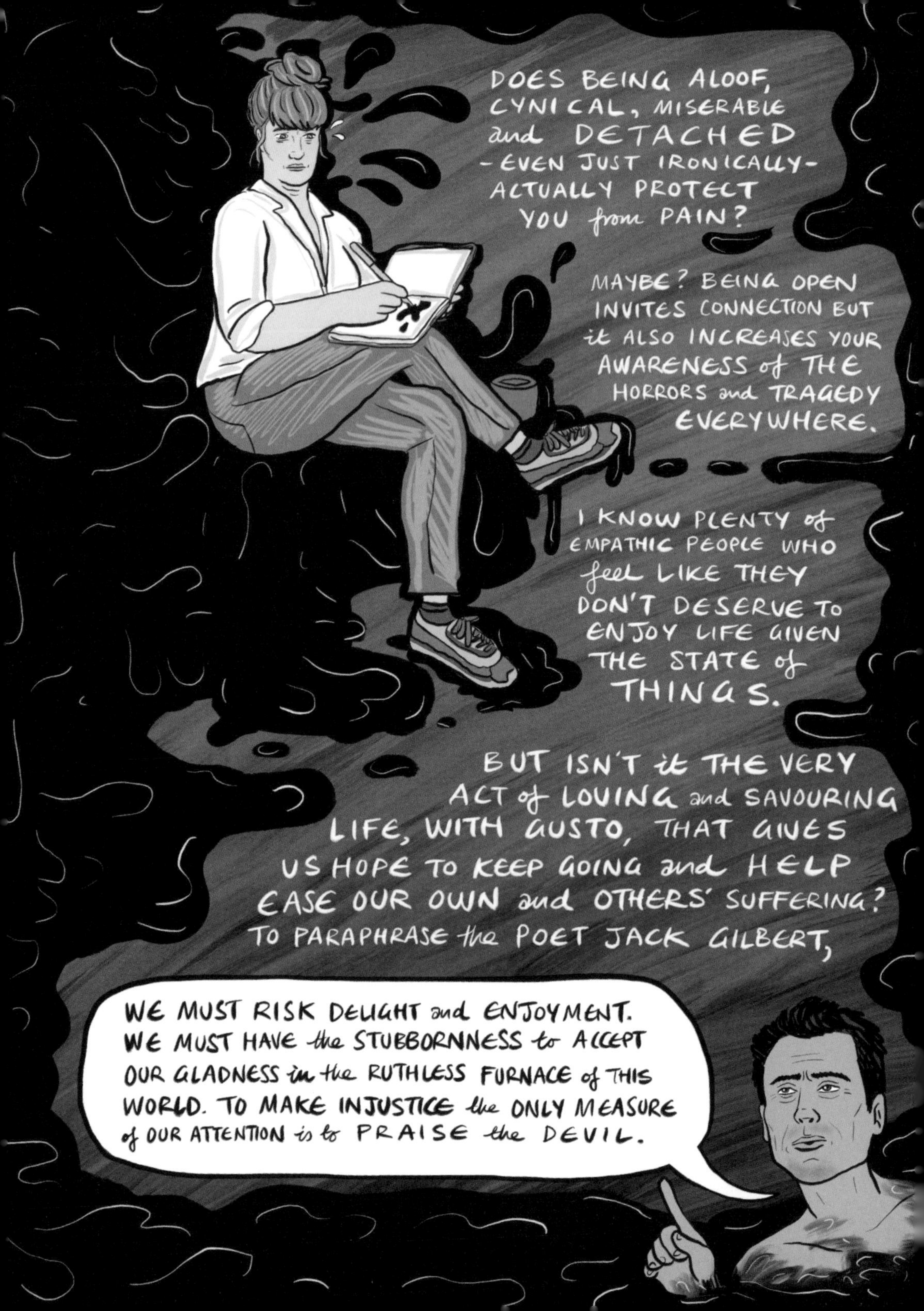
DOES BEING ALOOF, CYNICAL, MISERABLE and DETACHED - EVEN JUST IRONICALLY - ACTUALLY PROTECT YOU from PAIN?
MAYBE? BEING OPEN INVITES CONNECTION BUT it ALSO INCREASES YOUR AWARENESS of THE HORRORS and TRAGEDY EVERYWHERE.
I KNOW PLENTY of EMPATHIC PEOPLE WHO feel LIKE THEY DON'T DESERVE TO ENJOY LIFE GIVEN THE STATE of THINGS.
BUT ISN'T it THE VERY ACT of LOVING and SAVOURING LIFE, WITH GUSTO, THAT GIVES US HOPE TO KEEP GOING and HELP EASE OUR OWN and OTHERS' SUFFERING? TO PARAPHRASE the POET JACK GILBERT,
WE MUST RISK DELIGHT and ENJOYMENT. WE MUST HAVE the STUBBORNNESS to ACCEPT OUR GLADNESS in the RUTHLESS FURNACE of THIS WORLD. TO MAKE INJUSTICE the ONLY MEASURE of OUR ATTENTION is to PRAISE the DEVIL.

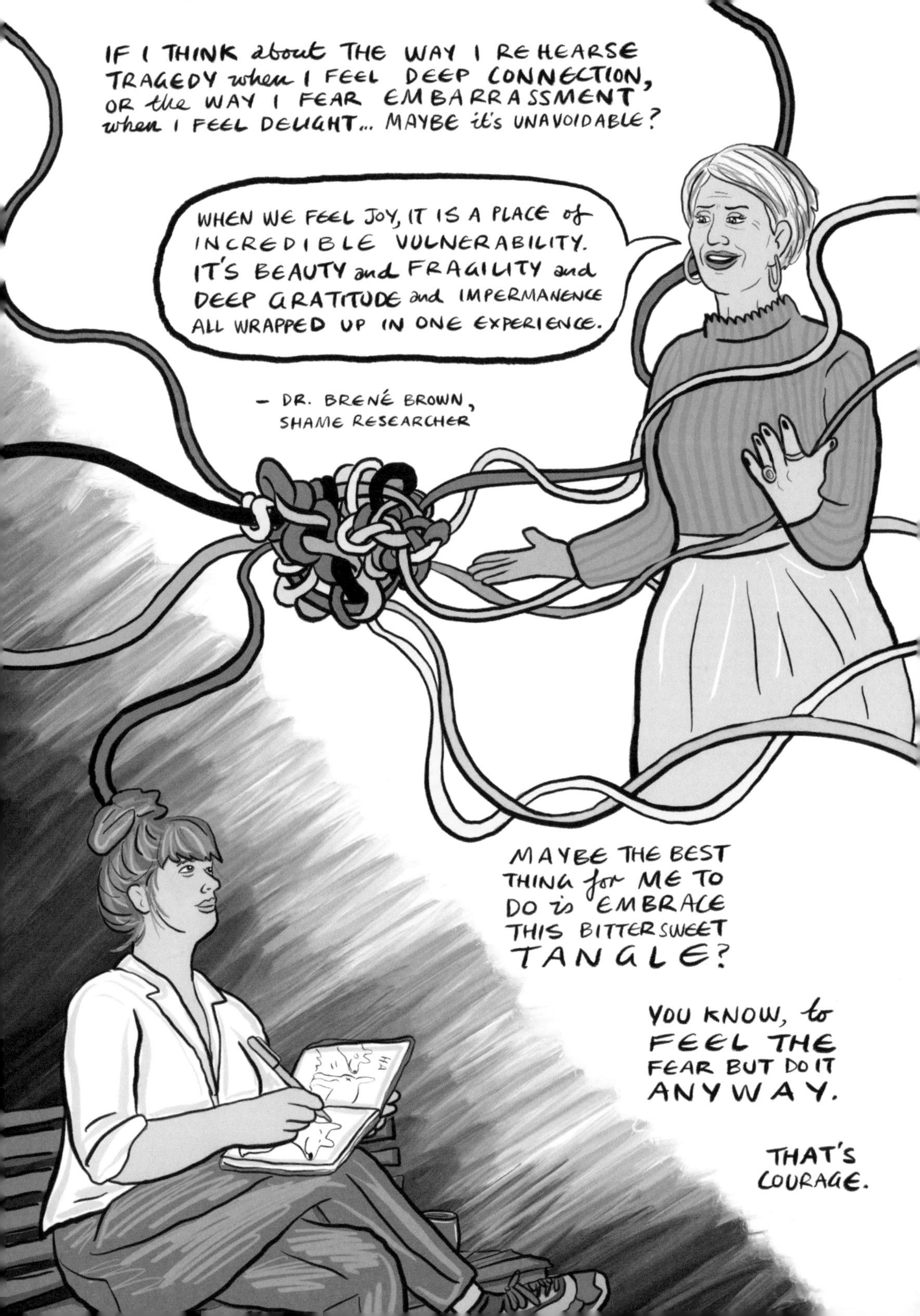
IF I THINK about THE WAY I REHEARSE TRAGEDY when I FEEL DEEP CONNECTION, OR the WAY I FEAR EMBARRASSMENT when I FEEL DELIGHT... MAYBE it's UNAVOIDABLE?
WHEN WE FEEL JOY, IT IS A PLACE of INCREDIBLE VULNERABILITY. IT'S BEAUTY and FRAGILITY and DEEP GRATITUDE and IMPERMANENCE ALL WRAPPED UP IN ONE EXPERIENCE.
– DR. BRENÉ BROWN, SHAME RESEARCHER
HA
MAYBE THE BEST THING for ME TO DO is EMBRACE THIS BITTERSWEET TANGLE?
YOU KNOW, to FEEL THE FEAR BUT DO IT ANYWAY.
THAT'S COURAGE.

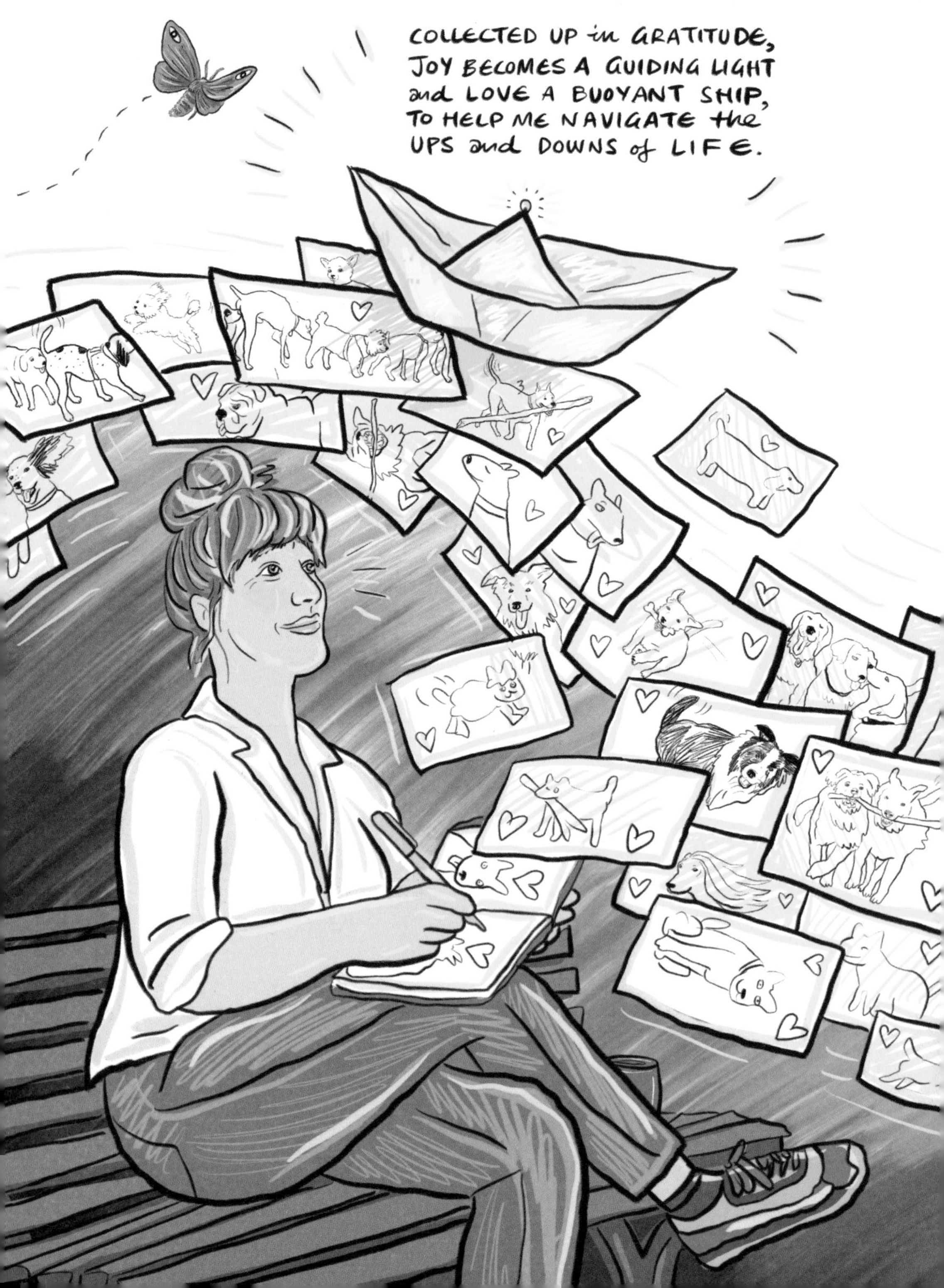
COLLECTED UP in GRATITUDE, JOY BECOMES A GUIDING LIGHT and LOVE A BUOYANT SHIP, TO HELP ME NAVIGATE the UPS and DOWNS of LIFE.

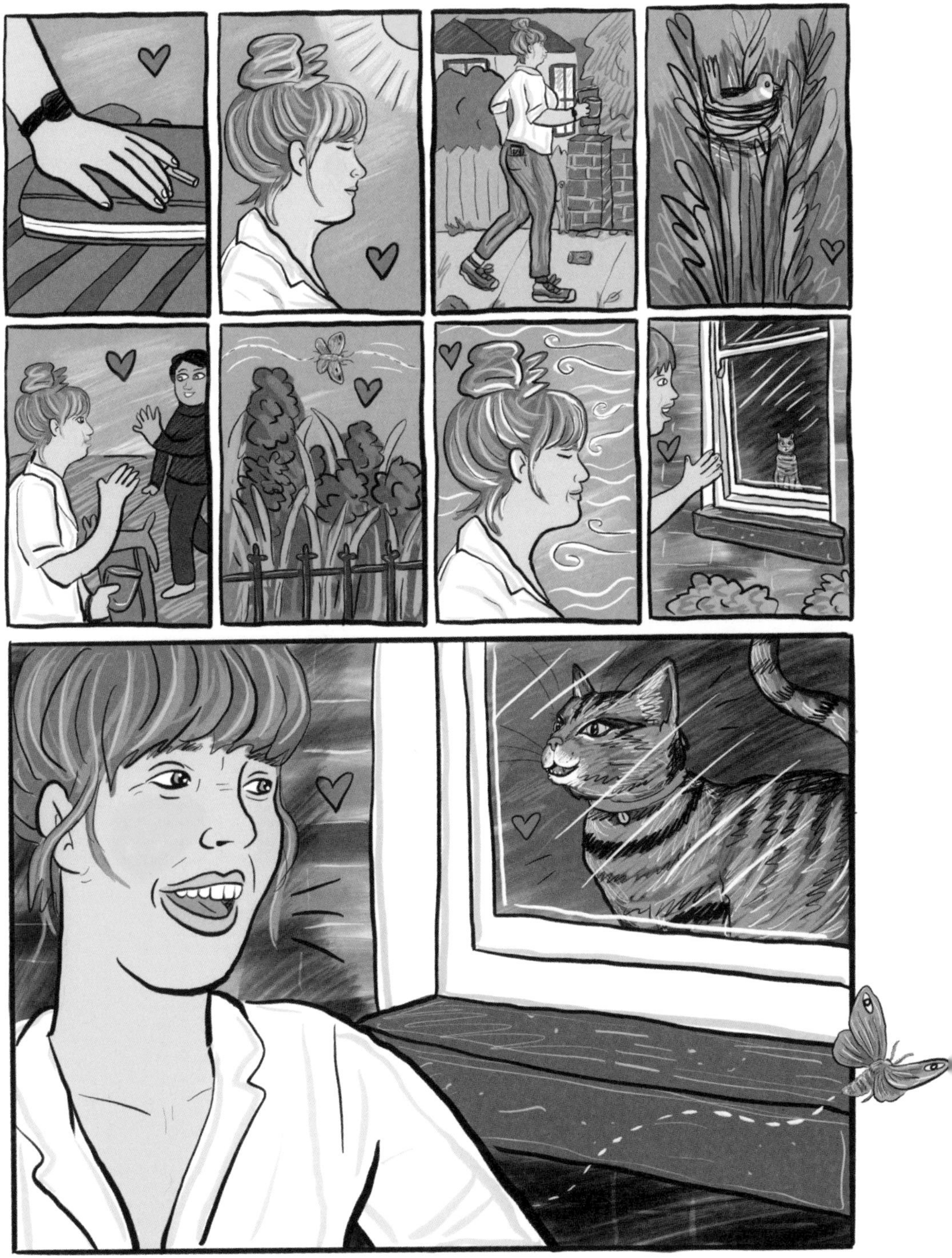

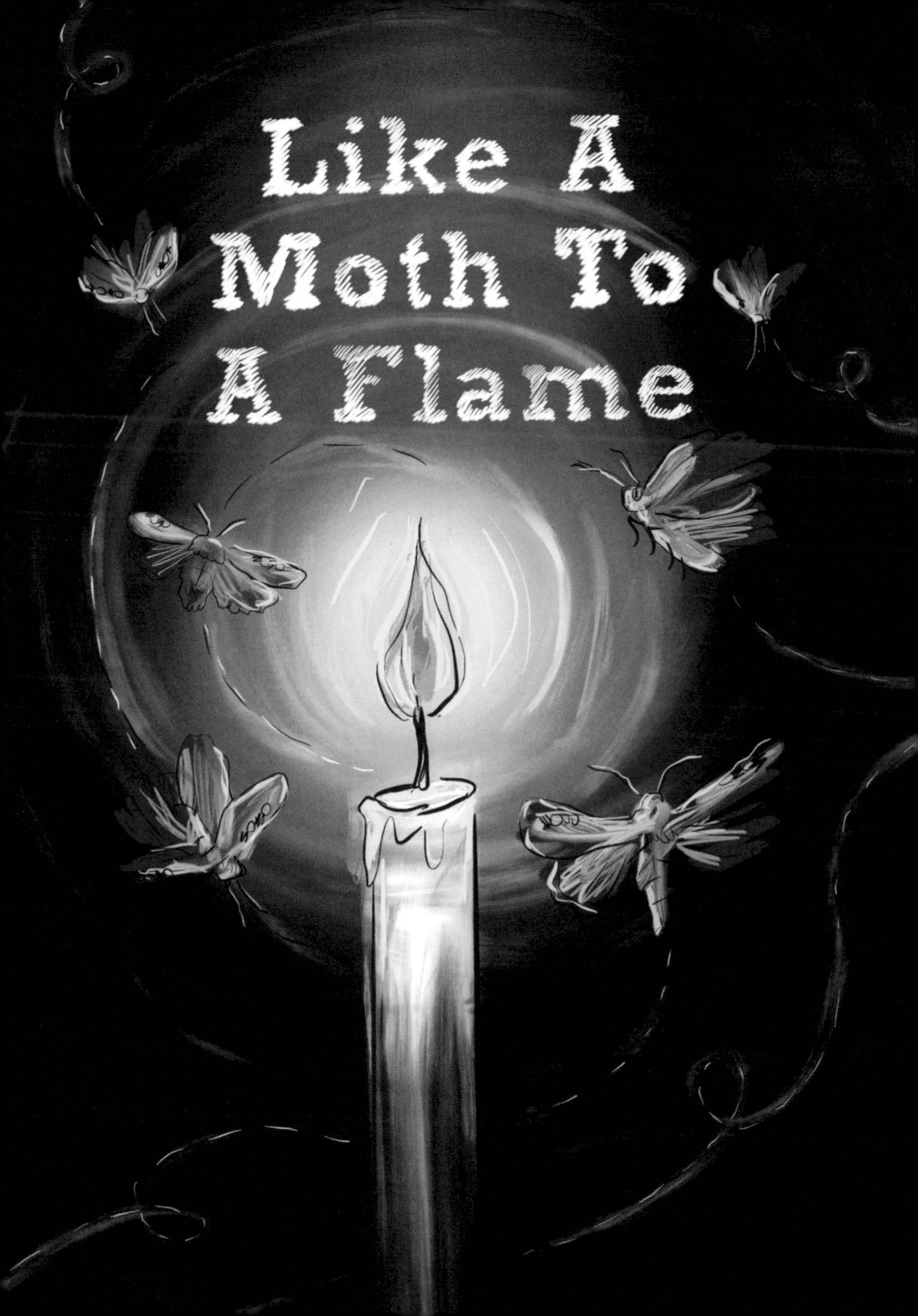
Like A
Moth To
A Flame

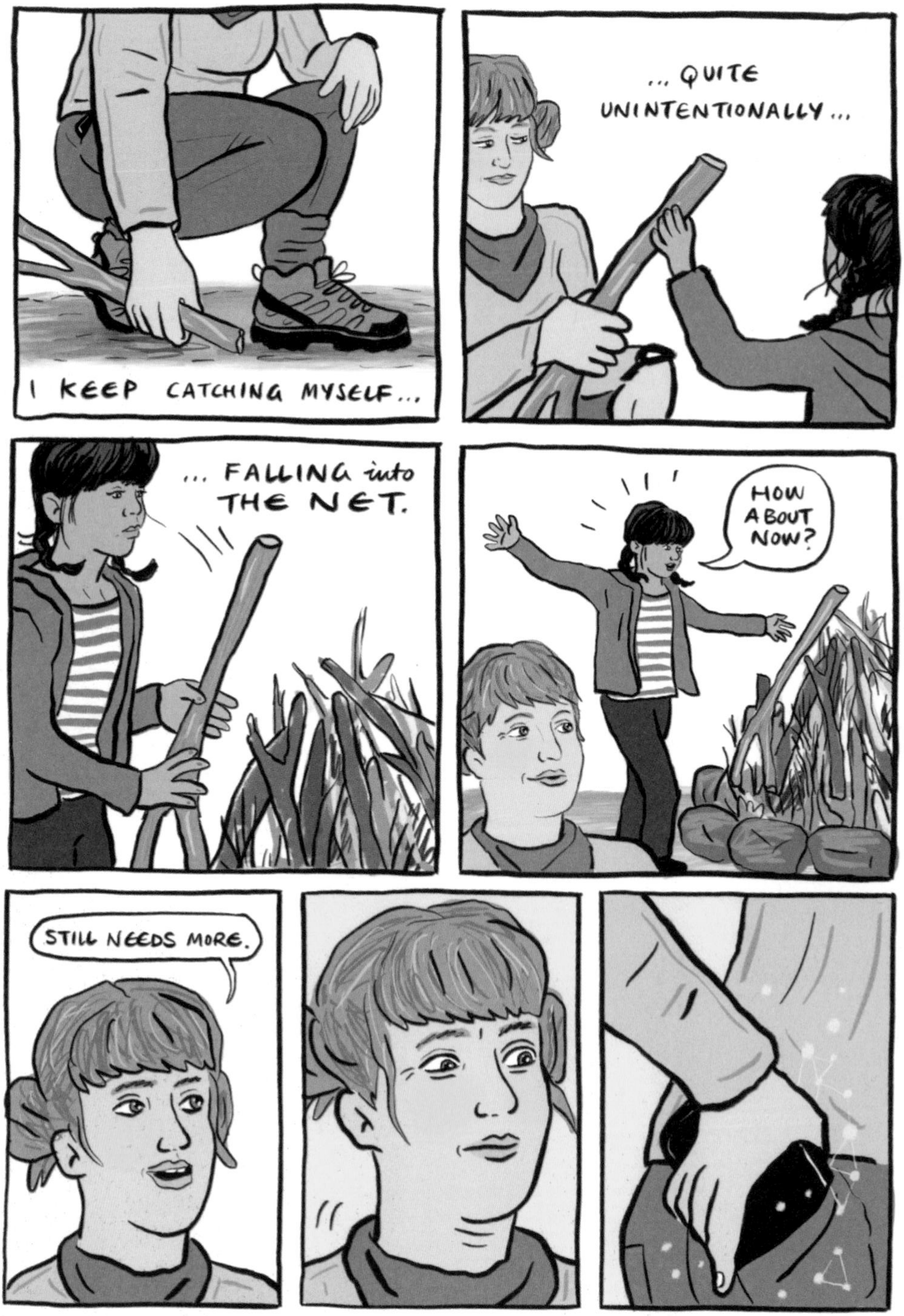
I KEEP CATCHING MYSELF...
... QUITE UNINTENTIONALLY...
... FALLING into THE NET.
HOW ABOUT NOW?
STILL NEEDS MORE.

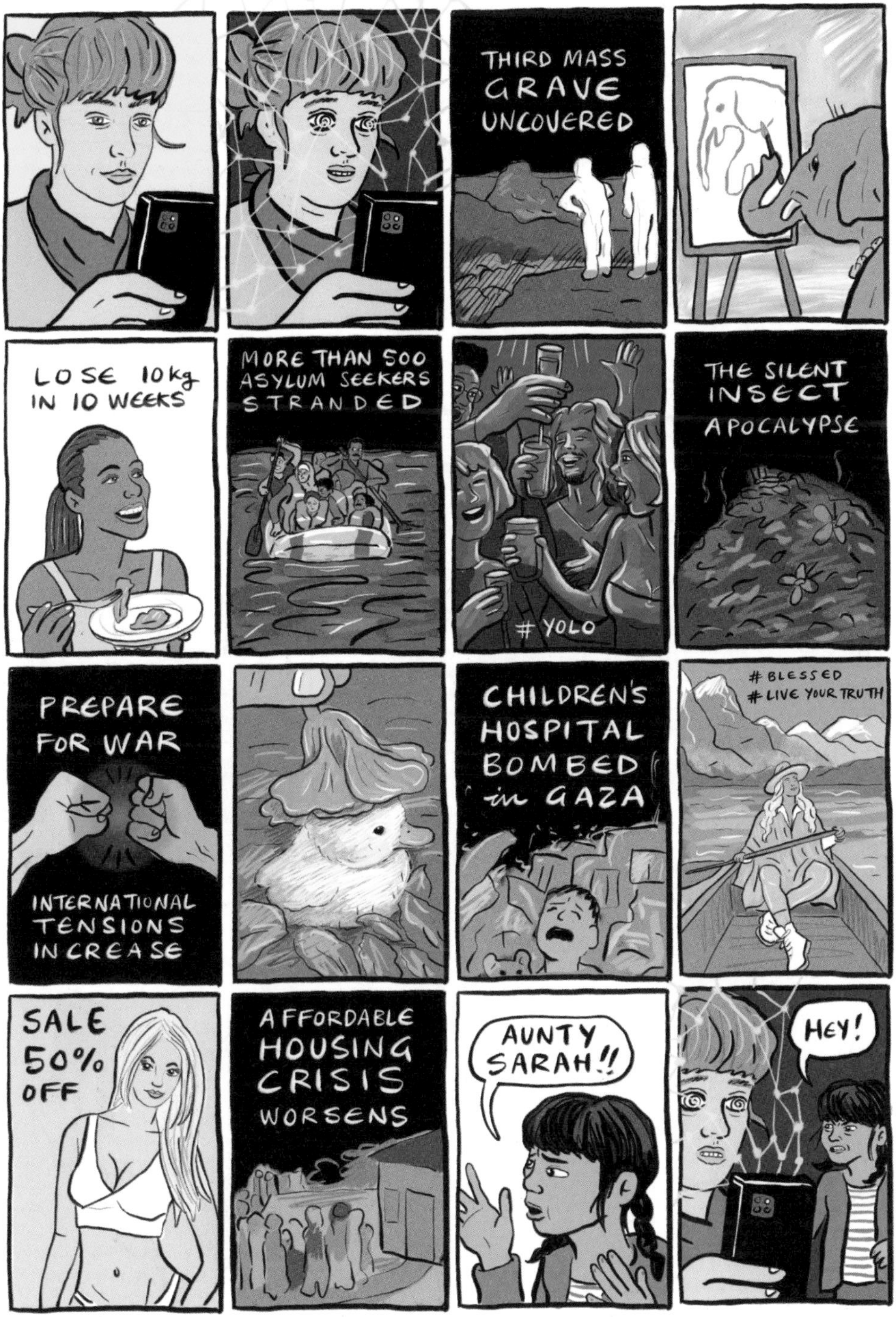
THIRD MASS GRAVE UNCOVERED
LOSE 10kg IN 10 WEEKS
MORE THAN 500 ASYLUM SEEKERS STRANDED
# YOLO
THE SILENT INSECT APOCALYPSE
PREPARE FOR WAR
INTERNATIONAL TENSIONS INCREASE
CHILDREN'S HOSPITAL BOMBED in GAZA
# BLESSED
# LIVE YOUR TRUTH
SALE 50% OFF
AFFORDABLE HOUSING CRISIS WORSENS
AUNTY SARAH!!
HEY!

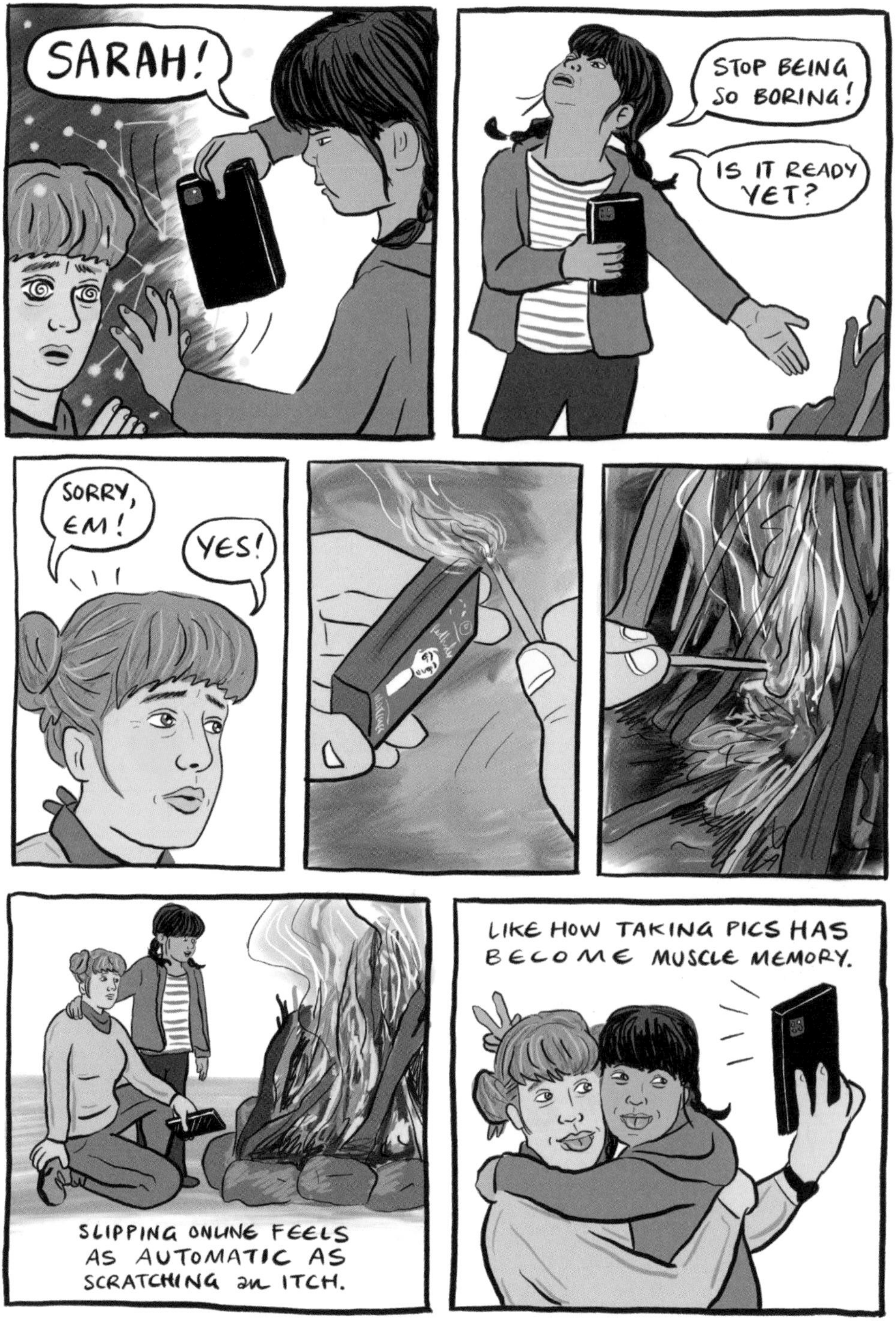
SARAH!
STOP BEING SO BORING!
IS IT READY YET?
SORRY, EM!
YES!
SLIPPING ONLINE FEELS AS AUTOMATIC AS SCRATCHING an ITCH.
LIKE HOW TAKING PICS HAS BECOME MUSCLE MEMORY.

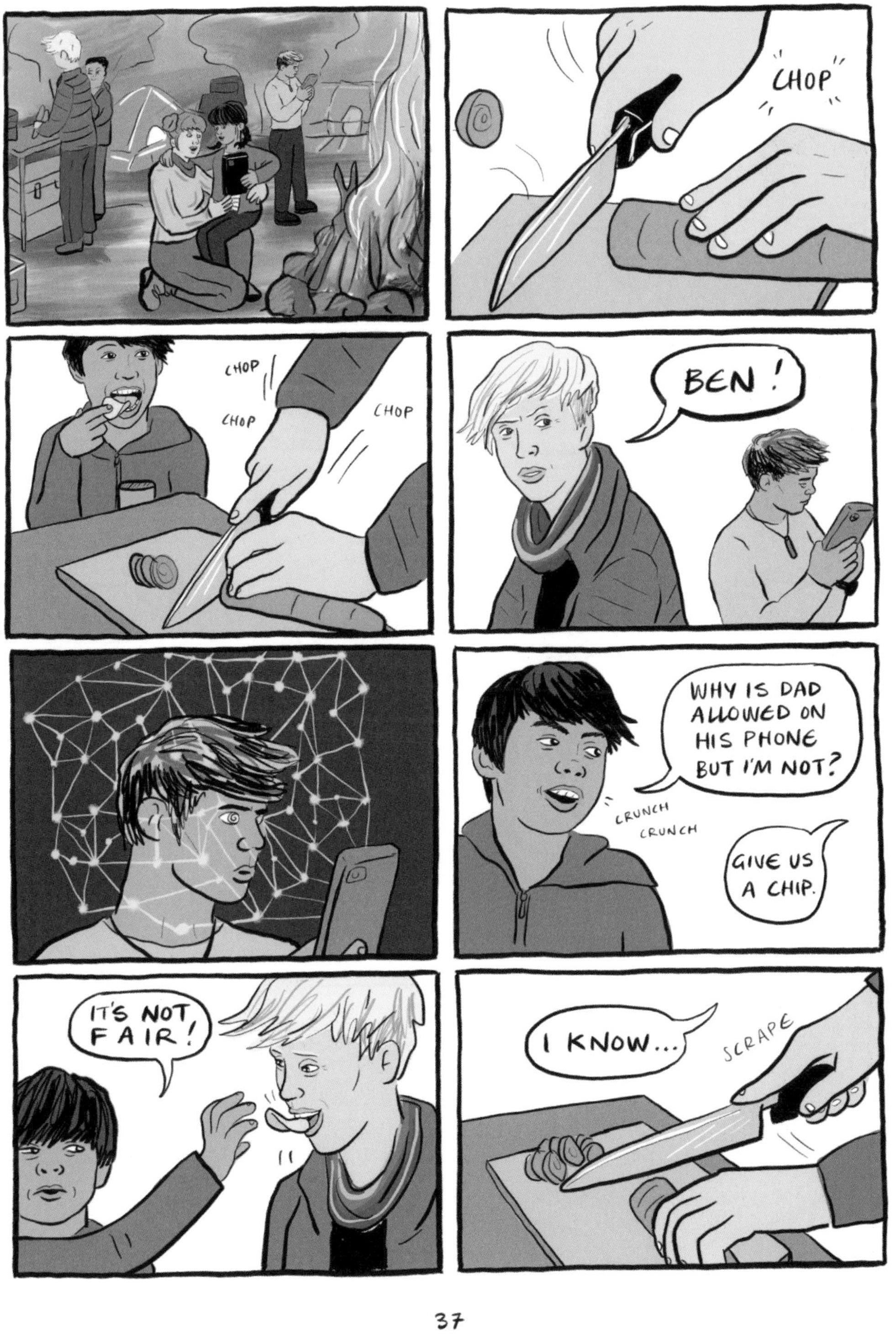
CHOP
CHOP
CHOP
CHOP
BEN!
WHY IS DAD ALLOWED ON HIS PHONE BUT I'M NOT?
CRUNCH
CRUNCH
GIVE US A CHIP.
IT'S NOT FAIR!
I KNOW...
SCRAPE

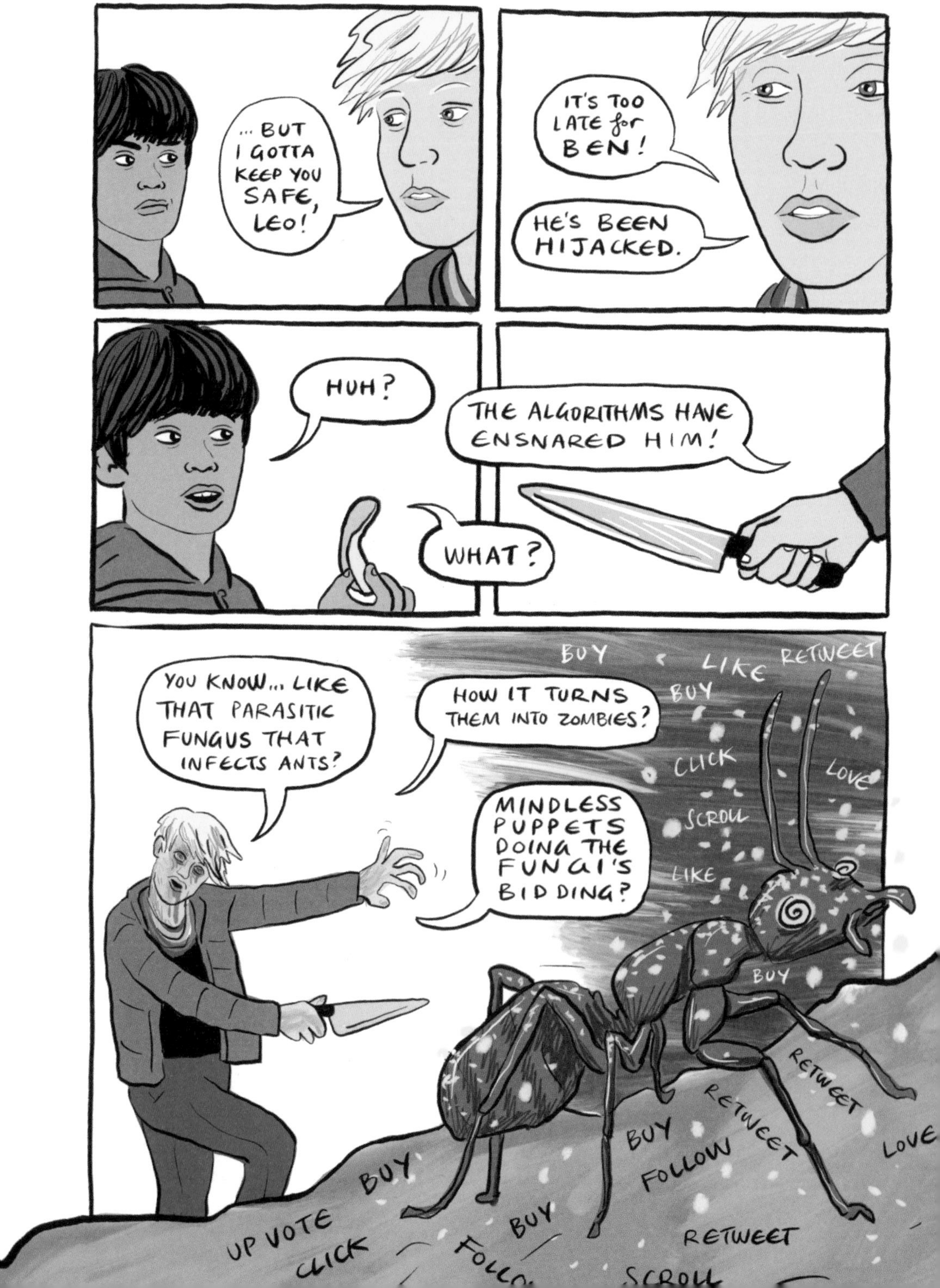

... BUT I GOTTA KEEP YOU SAFE, LEO!
IT'S TOO LATE for BEN!
HE'S BEEN HIJACKED.
HUH?
WHAT?
THE ALGORITHMS HAVE ENSNARED HIM!
YOU KNOW... LIKE THAT PARASITIC FUNGUS THAT INFECTS ANTS?
HOW IT TURNS THEM INTO ZOMBIES?
MINDLESS PUPPETS DOING THE FUNGI'S BIDDING?
BUY
LIKE
RETWEET
BUY
CLICK
LOVE
SCROLL
LIKE
BUY
RETWEET
RETWEET
BUY
FOLLOW
LOVE
BUY
UP VOTE
BUY
CLICK
RETWEET
SCROLL

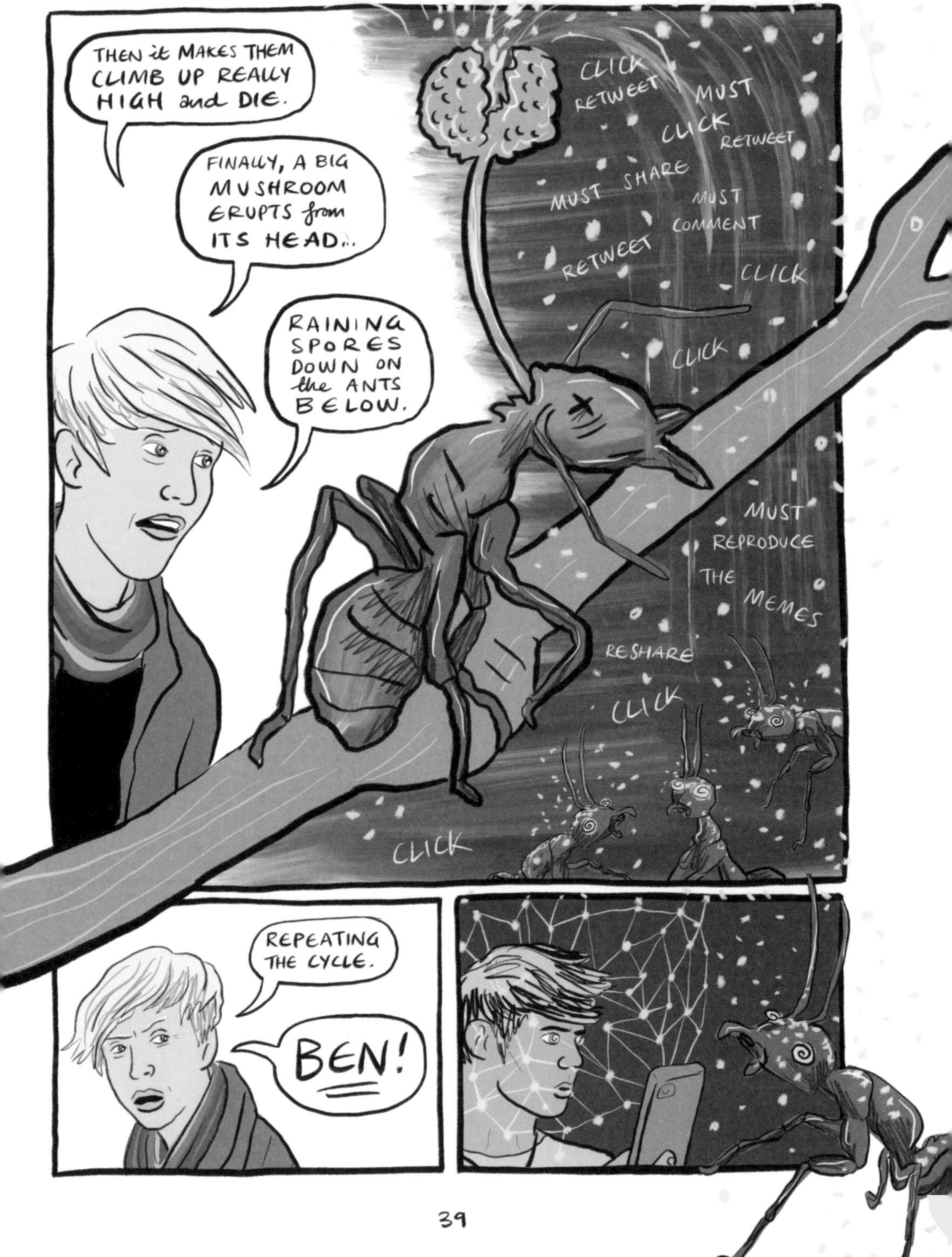
THEN it MAKES THEM CLIMB UP REALLY HIGH and DIE.
FINALLY, A BIG MUSHROOM ERUPTS from ITS HEAD...
RAINING SPORES DOWN ON the ANTS BELOW.
CLICK
RETWEET
MUST
CLICK
RETWEET
MUST SHARE
MUST COMMENT
RETWEET
CLICK
CLICK
MUST REPRODUCE THE MEMES
RESHARE
CLICK
CLICK
REPEATING THE CYCLE.
BEN!

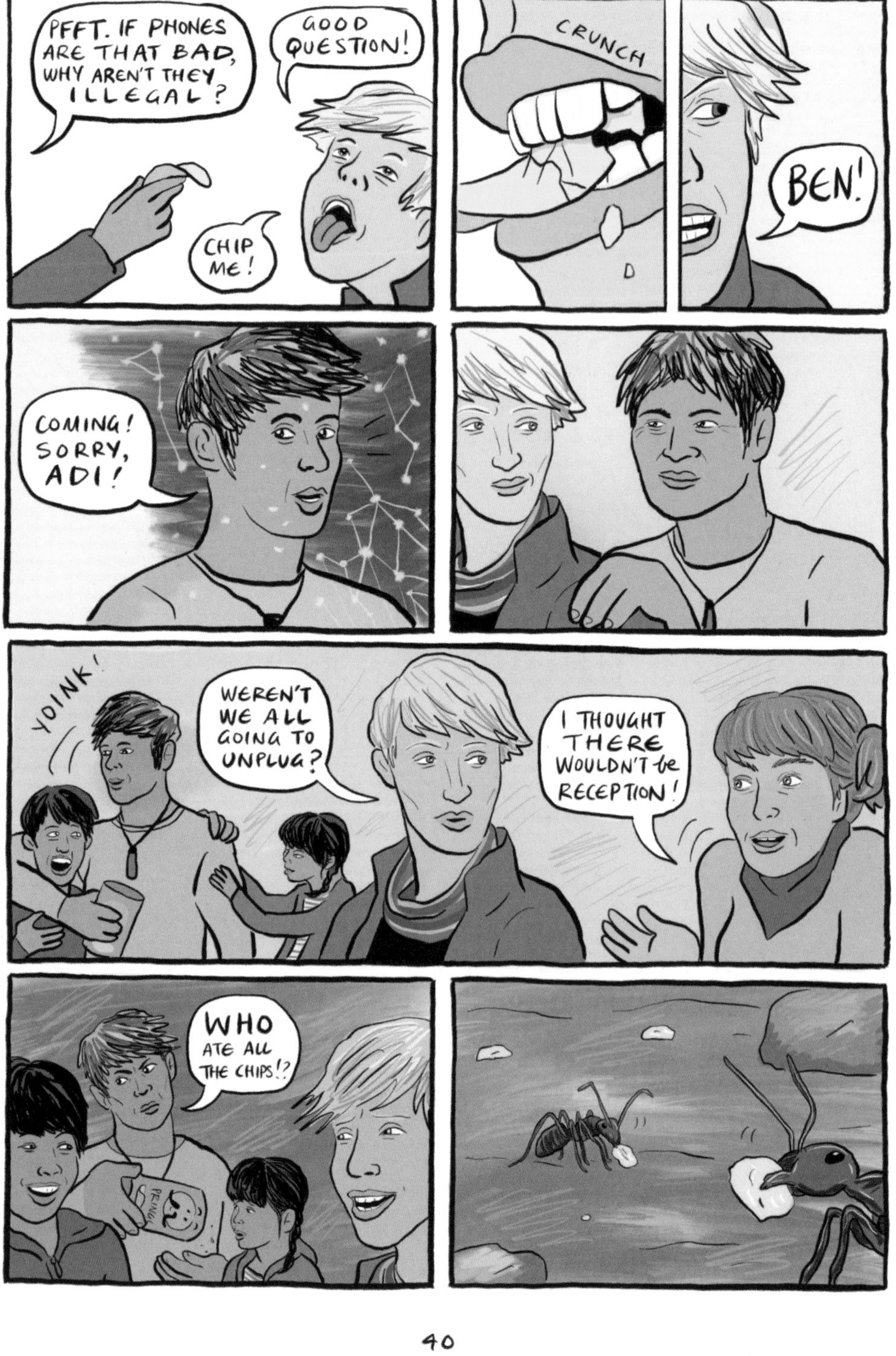
PFFT. IF PHONES ARE THAT BAD, WHY AREN'T THEY ILLEGAL?
GOOD QUESTION!
CHIP ME!
CRUNCH
BEN!
COMING! SORRY, ADI!
YOINK!
WEREN'T WE ALL GOING TO UNPLUG?
I THOUGHT THERE WOULDN'T be RECEPTION!
WHO ATE ALL THE CHIPS!?

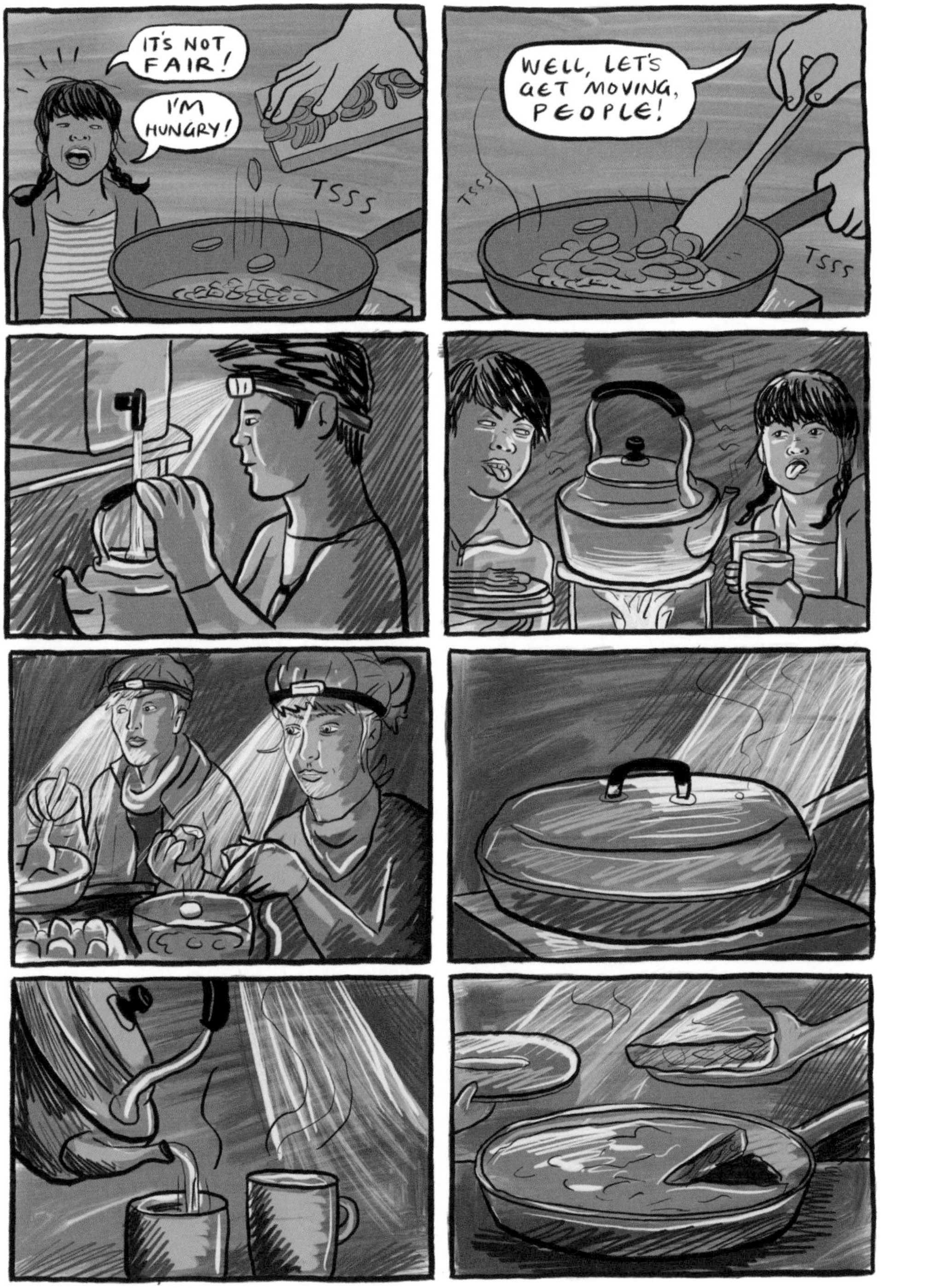
IT'S NOT FAIR!
I'M HUNGRY!
TSSS
WELL, LET'S GET MOVING, PEOPLE!
TSSS
TSSS

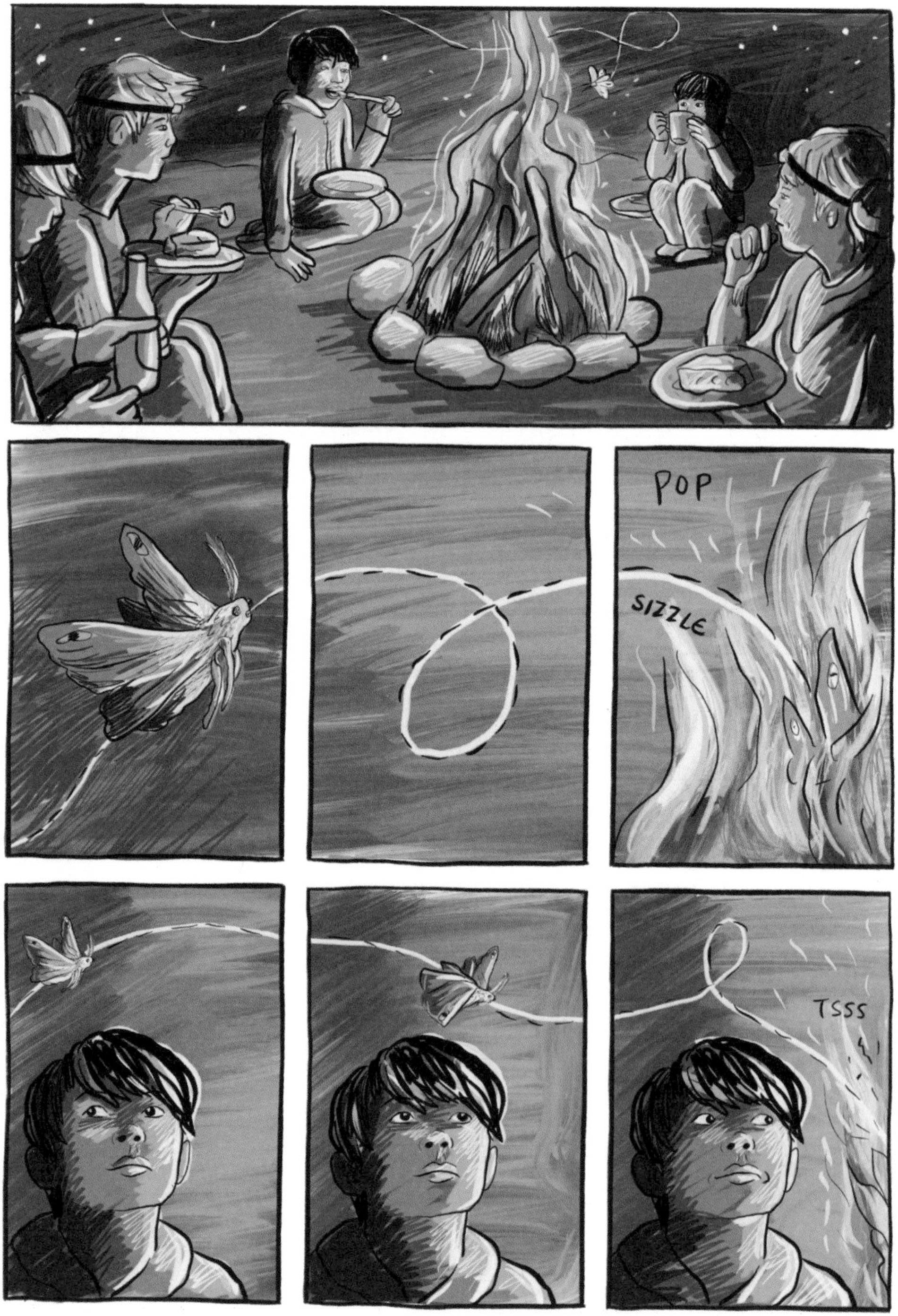
POP
SIZZLE
TSSS

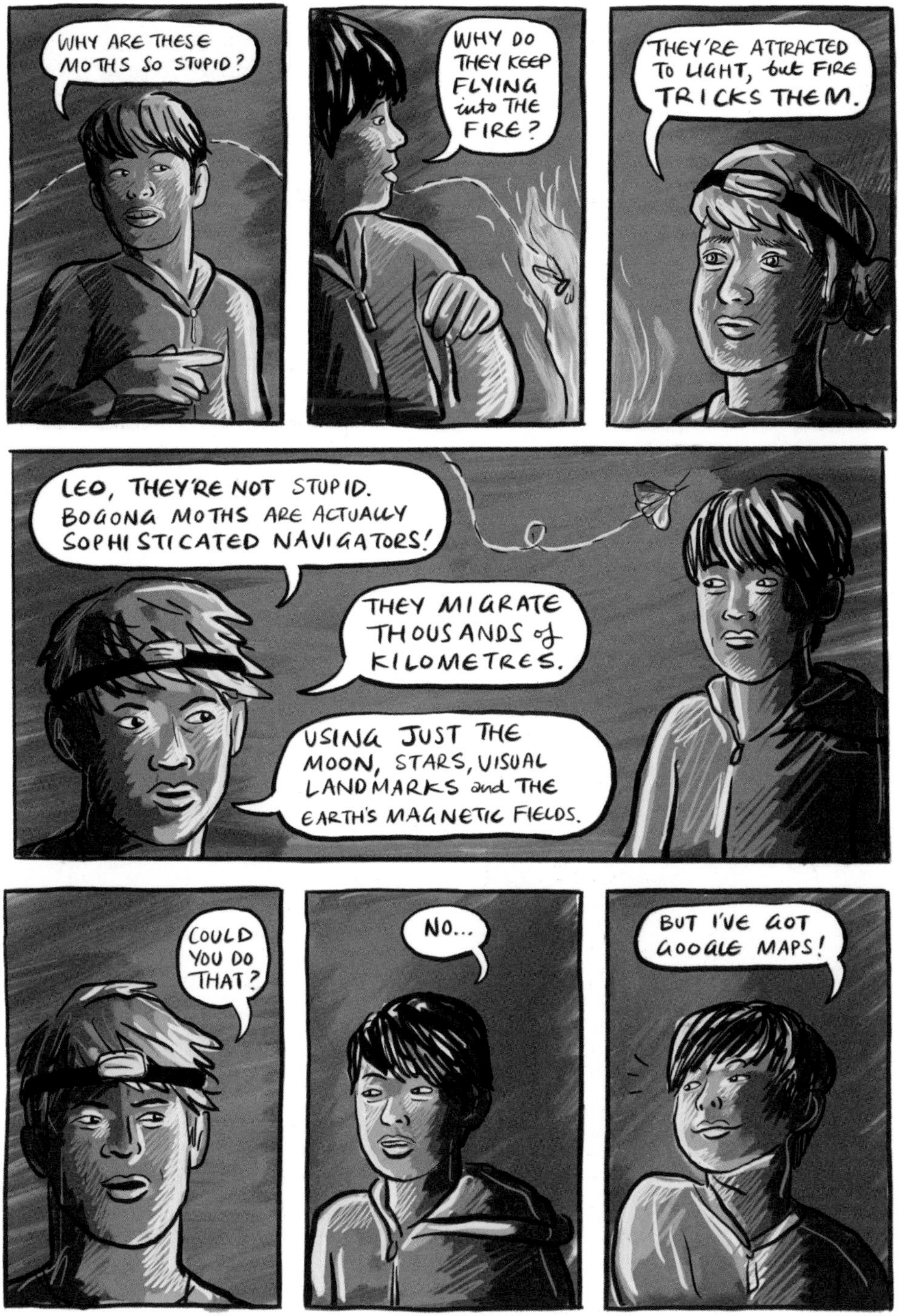
WHY ARE THESE MOTHS SO STUPID?
WHY DO THEY KEEP FLYING into THE FIRE?
THEY'RE ATTRACTED TO LIGHT, but FIRE TRICKS THEM.
LEO, THEY'RE NOT STUPID. BOGONG MOTHS ARE ACTUALLY SOPHISTICATED NAVIGATORS!
THEY MIGRATE THOUSANDS of KILOMETRES.
USING JUST THE MOON, STARS, VISUAL LANDMARKS and THE EARTH'S MAGNETIC FIELDS.
COULD YOU DO THAT?
NO...
BUT I'VE GOT GOOGLE MAPS!

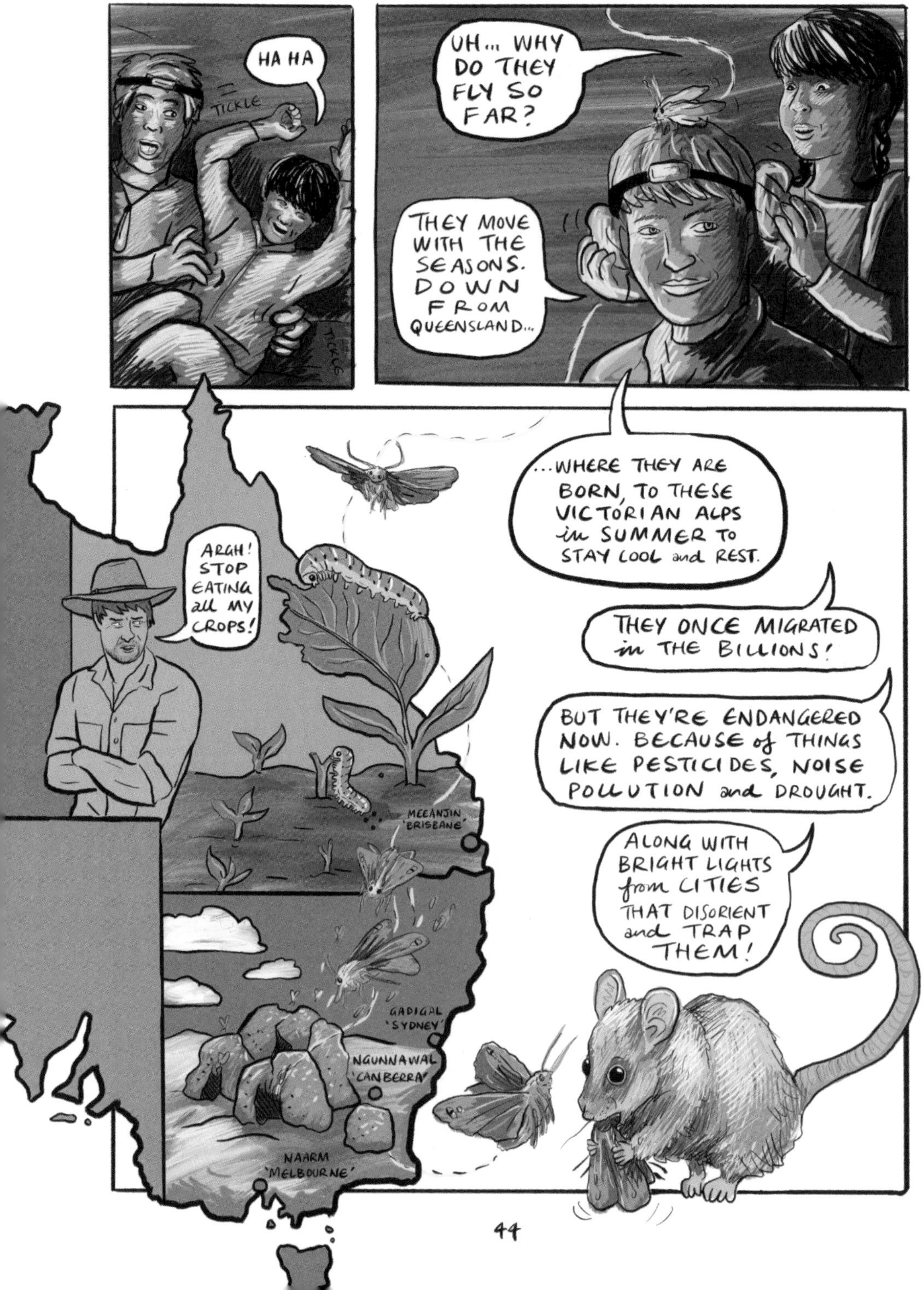
HA HA
TICKLE
TICKLE
UH... WHY DO THEY FLY SO FAR?
THEY MOVE WITH THE SEASONS. DOWN FROM QUEENSLAND...
...WHERE THEY ARE BORN, TO THESE VICTORIAN ALPS in SUMMER TO STAY COOL and REST.
ARGH! STOP EATING all MY CROPS!
THEY ONCE MIGRATED in THE BILLIONS!
BUT THEY'RE ENDANGERED NOW. BECAUSE of THINGS LIKE PESTICIDES, NOISE POLLUTION and DROUGHT.
ALONG WITH BRIGHT LIGHTS from CITIES THAT DISORIENT and TRAP THEM!
MEEANJIN 'BRISBANE'
GADIGAL 'SYDNEY'
NGUNNAWAL 'CANBERRA'
NAARM 'MELBOURNE'

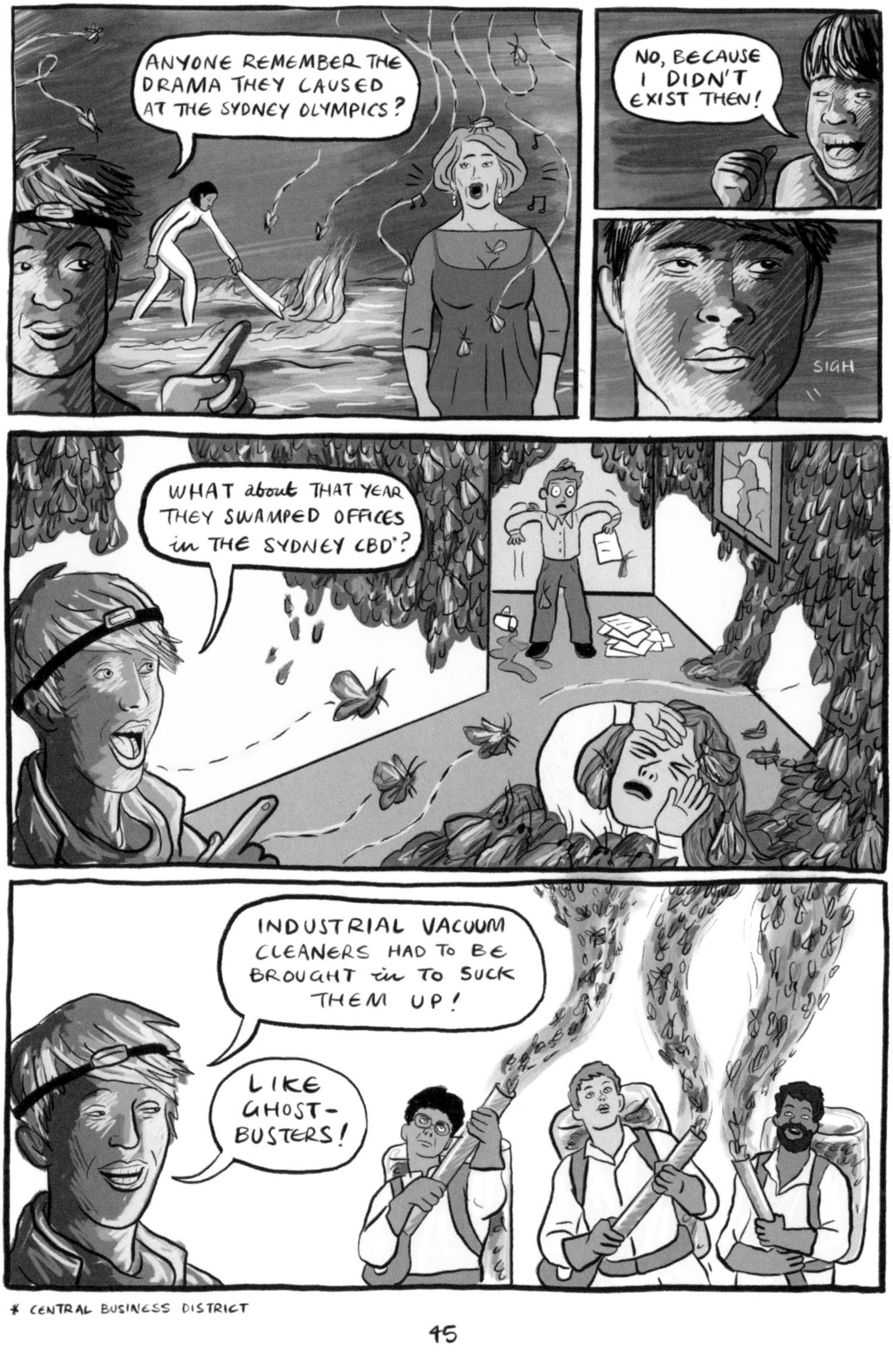
ANYONE REMEMBER THE DRAMA THEY CAUSED AT THE SYDNEY OLYMPICS?
NO, BECAUSE I DIDN'T EXIST THEN!
SIGH
WHAT about THAT YEAR THEY SWAMPED OFFICES in THE SYDNEY CBD*?
INDUSTRIAL VACUUM CLEANERS HAD TO BE BROUGHT in TO SUCK THEM UP!
LIKE GHOST-BUSTERS!

* CENTRAL BUSINESS DISTRICT

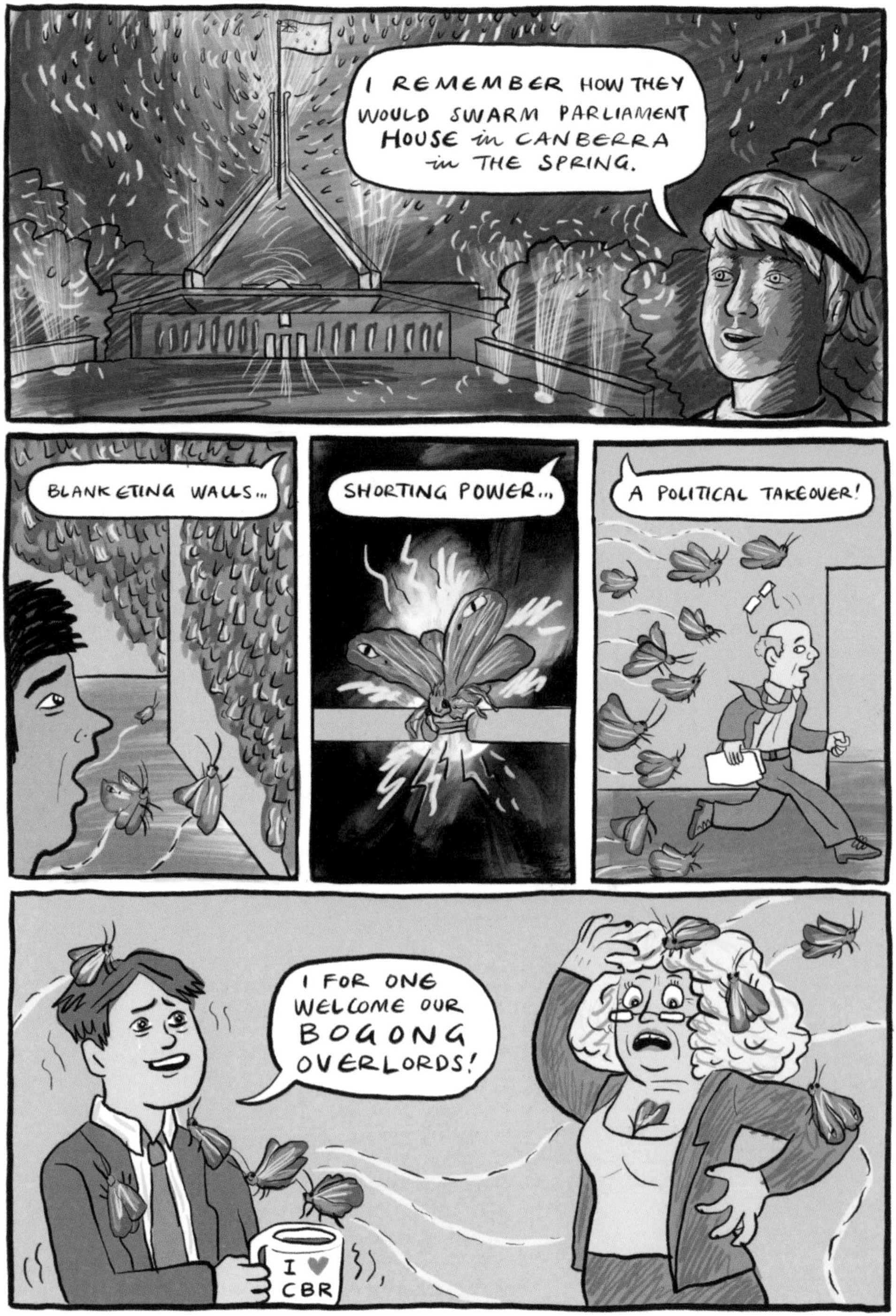
I REMEMBER HOW THEY WOULD SWARM PARLIAMENT HOUSE in CANBERRA in THE SPRING.
BLANKETING WALLS...
SHORTING POWER...
A POLITICAL TAKEOVER!
I FOR ONE WELCOME OUR BOGONG OVERLORDS!
I ♥ CBR

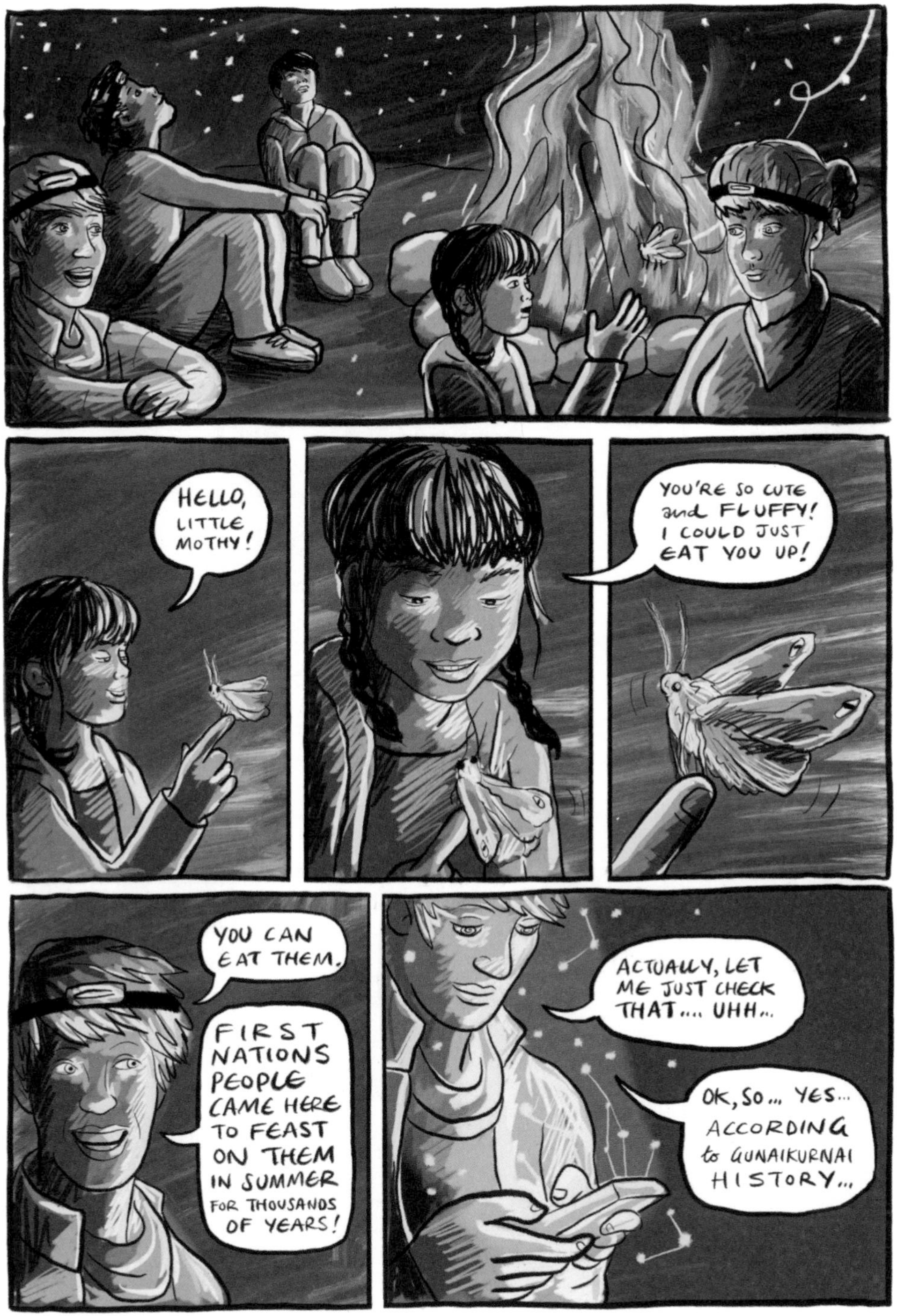
HELLO, LITTLE MOTHY!
YOU'RE SO CUTE and FLUFFY! I COULD JUST EAT YOU UP!
YOU CAN EAT THEM.
FIRST NATIONS PEOPLE CAME HERE TO FEAST ON THEM IN SUMMER FOR THOUSANDS OF YEARS!
ACTUALLY, LET ME JUST CHECK THAT.... UHH...
OK, SO... YES... ACCORDING to GUNAIKURNAI HISTORY...

...THE USUAL WAY TO FIND LOTS of CORI, BOGONG MOTHS, WAS TO LOOK for SWARMS of NRARIGALHA, RAVENS, NEAR ROCKS...

... PEOPLE WOULD GO INTO THE ROCKY CREVICES and OVERHANGS TO HARVEST THE SLEEPING MOTHS, THEN ROAST THEM on THE FIRE.

NEXT, THE MOTHS WERE GROUND into A PASTE or PRESSED into MOTH MEAT CAKES and SMOKED, TO PRESERVE THEM for LATER.

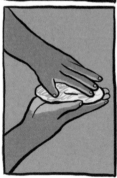

OOH! AND A 2000-YEAR-OLD GRIND STONE WAS UNEARTHED JUST NEAR HERE. IT'S THE FIRST CONFIRMED INSECT FOOD STONE TOOL in the WHOLE WORLD!

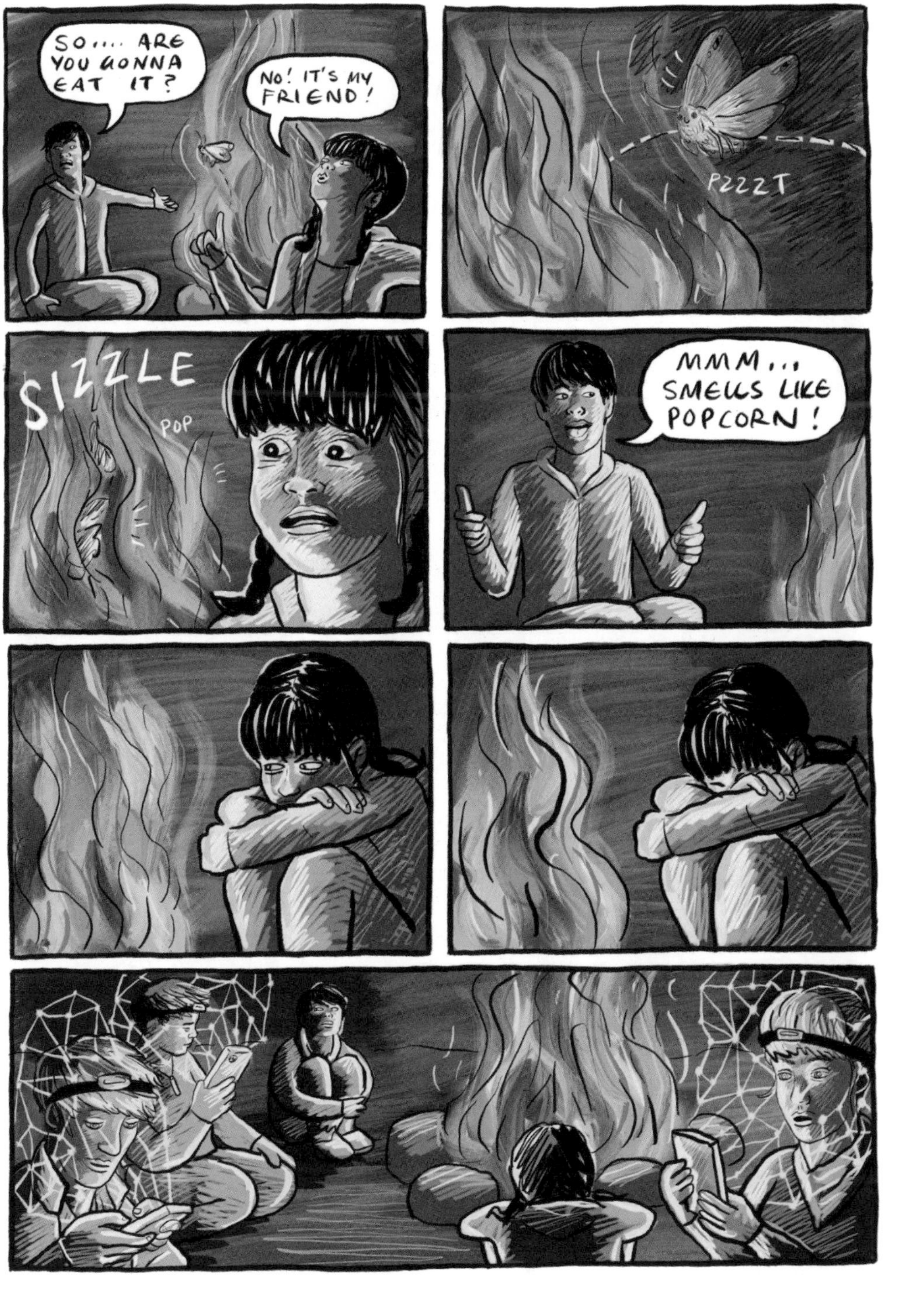
SO.... ARE YOU GONNA EAT IT?
NO! IT'S MY FRIEND!
PZZZT
SIZZLE
POP
MMM... SMELLS LIKE POPCORN!

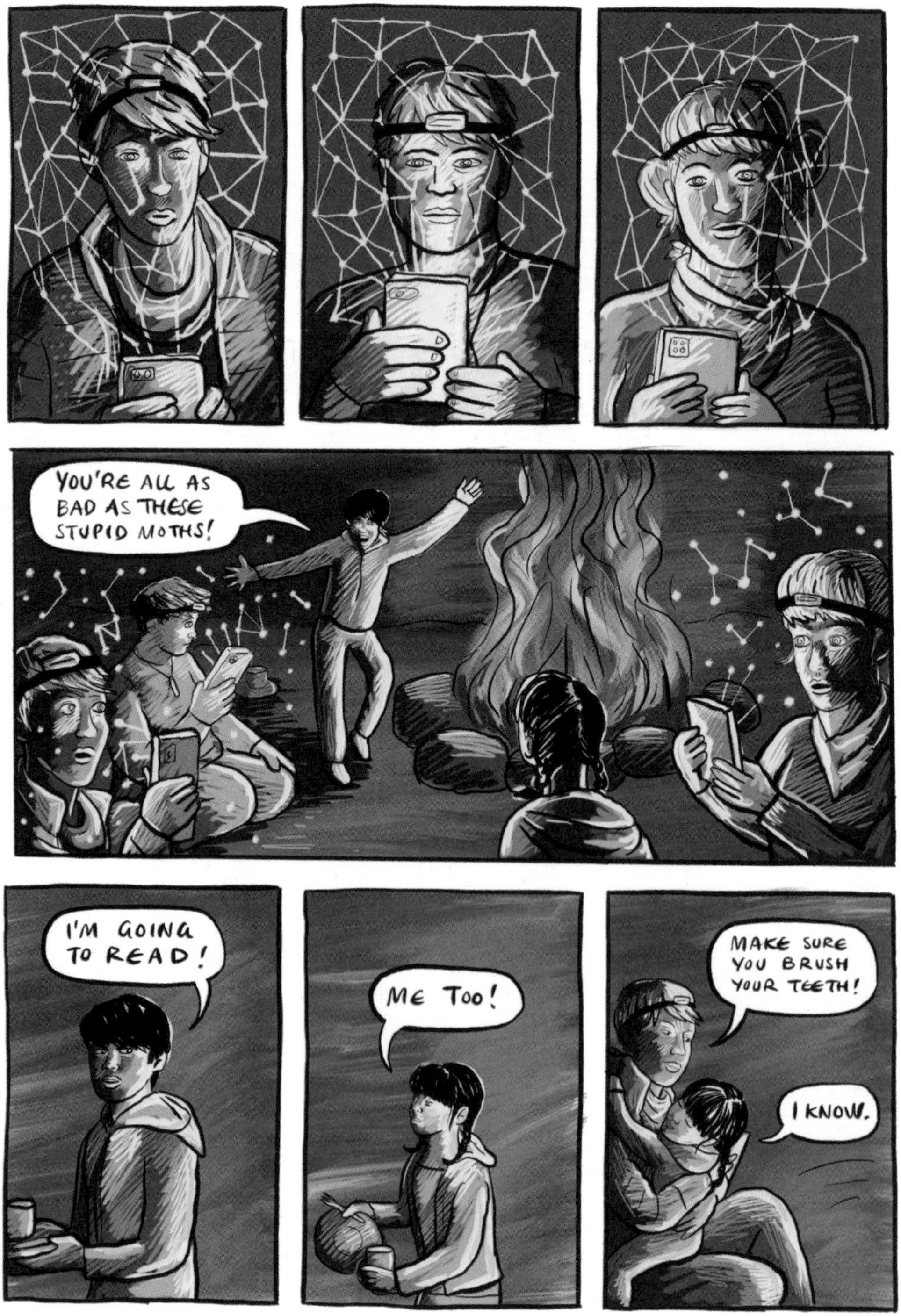
YOU'RE ALL AS BAD AS THESE STUPID MOTHS!
I'M GOING TO READ!
ME TOO!
MAKE SURE YOU BRUSH YOUR TEETH!
I KNOW.

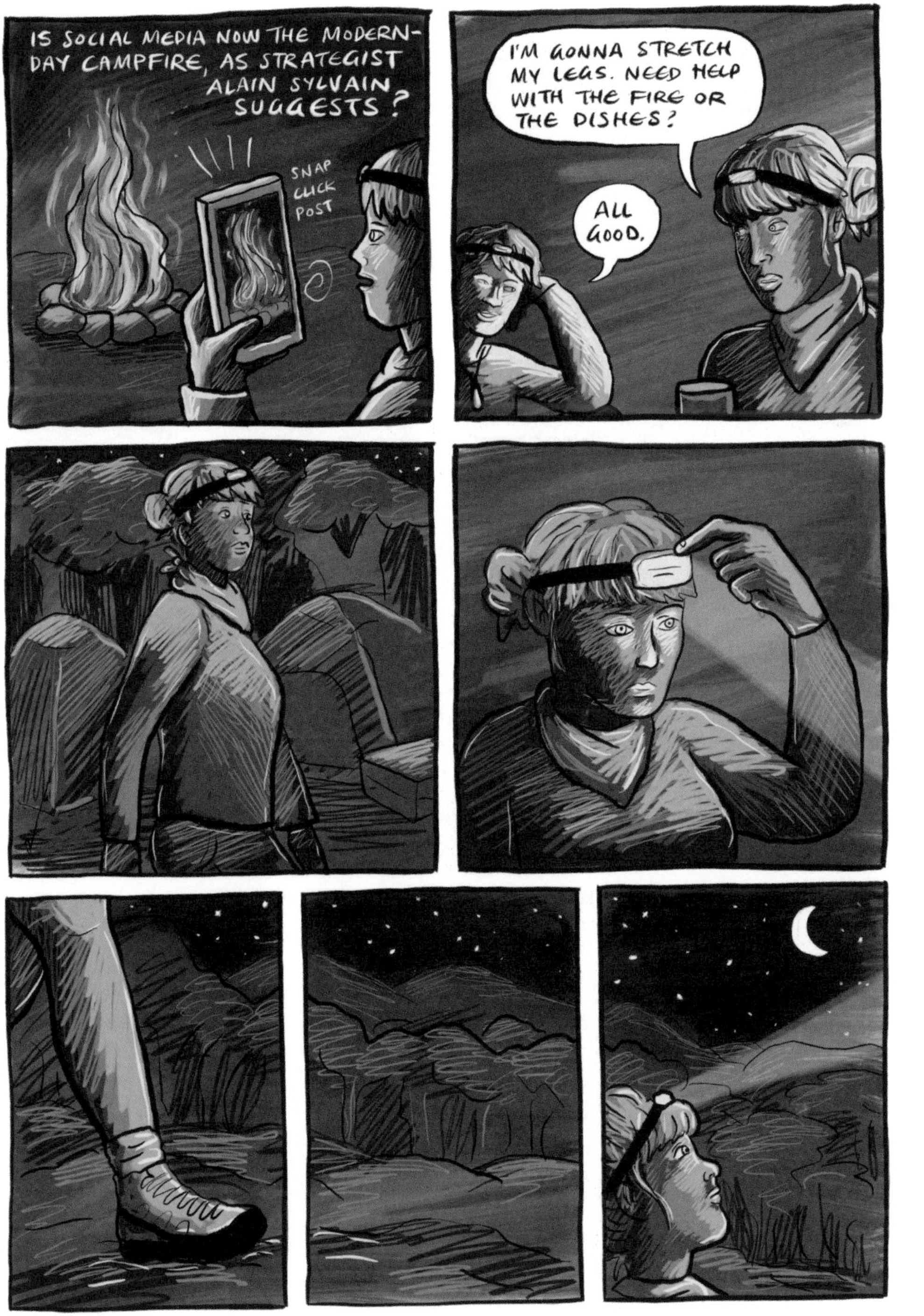
IS SOCIAL MEDIA NOW THE MODERN-DAY CAMPFIRE, AS STRATEGIST ALAIN SYLVAIN SUGGESTS?
SNAP
CLICK
POST
I'M GONNA STRETCH MY LEGS. NEED HELP WITH THE FIRE OR THE DISHES?
ALL GOOD.

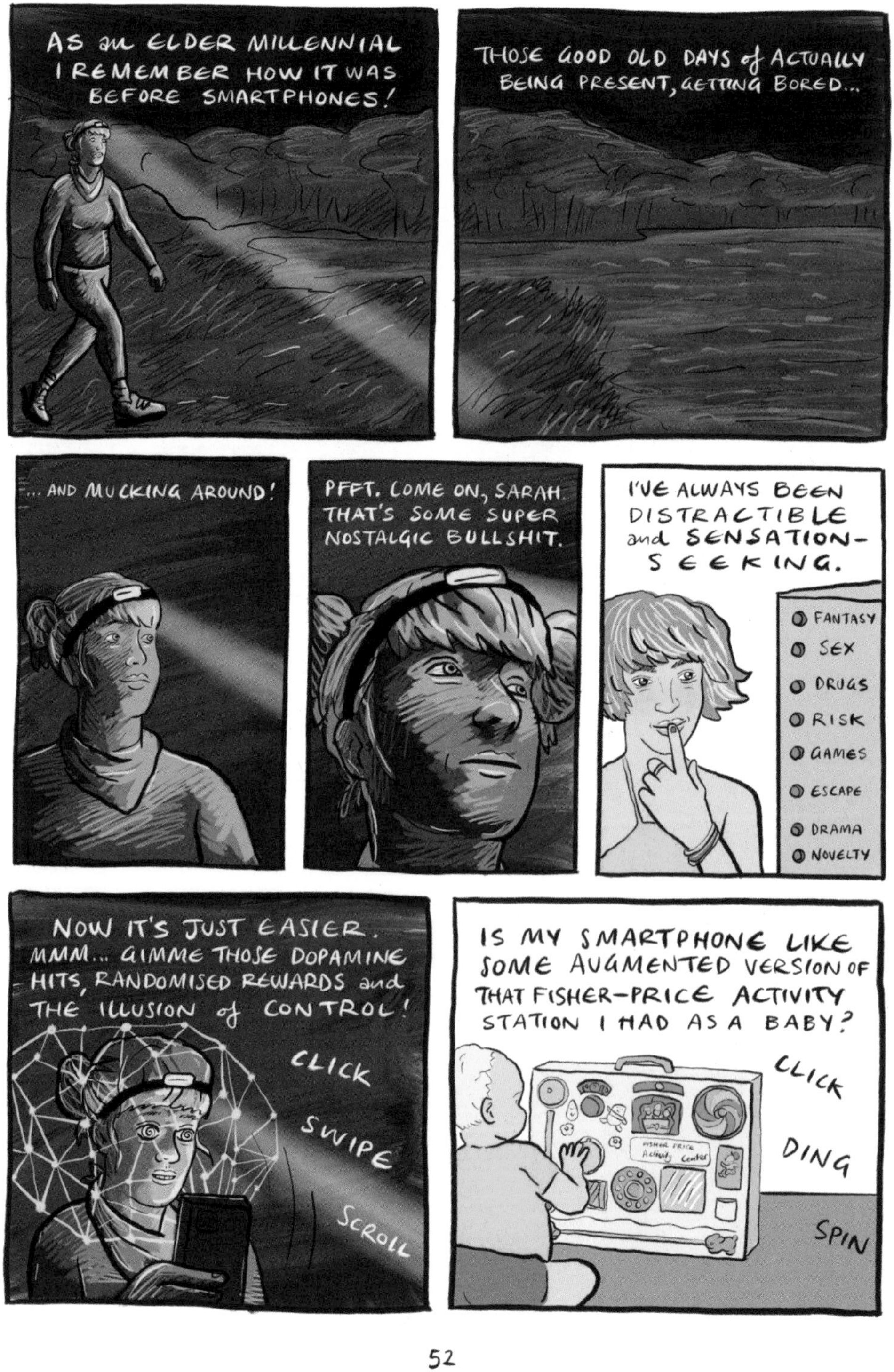
AS an ELDER MILLENNIAL I REMEMBER HOW IT WAS BEFORE SMARTPHONES!
THOSE GOOD OLD DAYS of ACTUALLY BEING PRESENT, GETTING BORED...
... AND MUCKING AROUND!
PFFT. COME ON, SARAH. THAT'S SOME SUPER NOSTALGIC BULLSHIT.
I'VE ALWAYS BEEN DISTRACTIBLE and SENSATION-SEEKING.
FANTASY
SEX
DRUGS
RISK
GAMES
ESCAPE
DRAMA
NOVELTY
NOW IT'S JUST EASIER. MMM... GIMME THOSE DOPAMINE HITS, RANDOMISED REWARDS and THE ILLUSION of CONTROL!
CLICK
SWIPE
SCROLL
IS MY SMARTPHONE LIKE SOME AUGMENTED VERSION OF THAT FISHER-PRICE ACTIVITY STATION I HAD AS A BABY?
FISHER PRICE Activity Center
CLICK
DING
SPIN

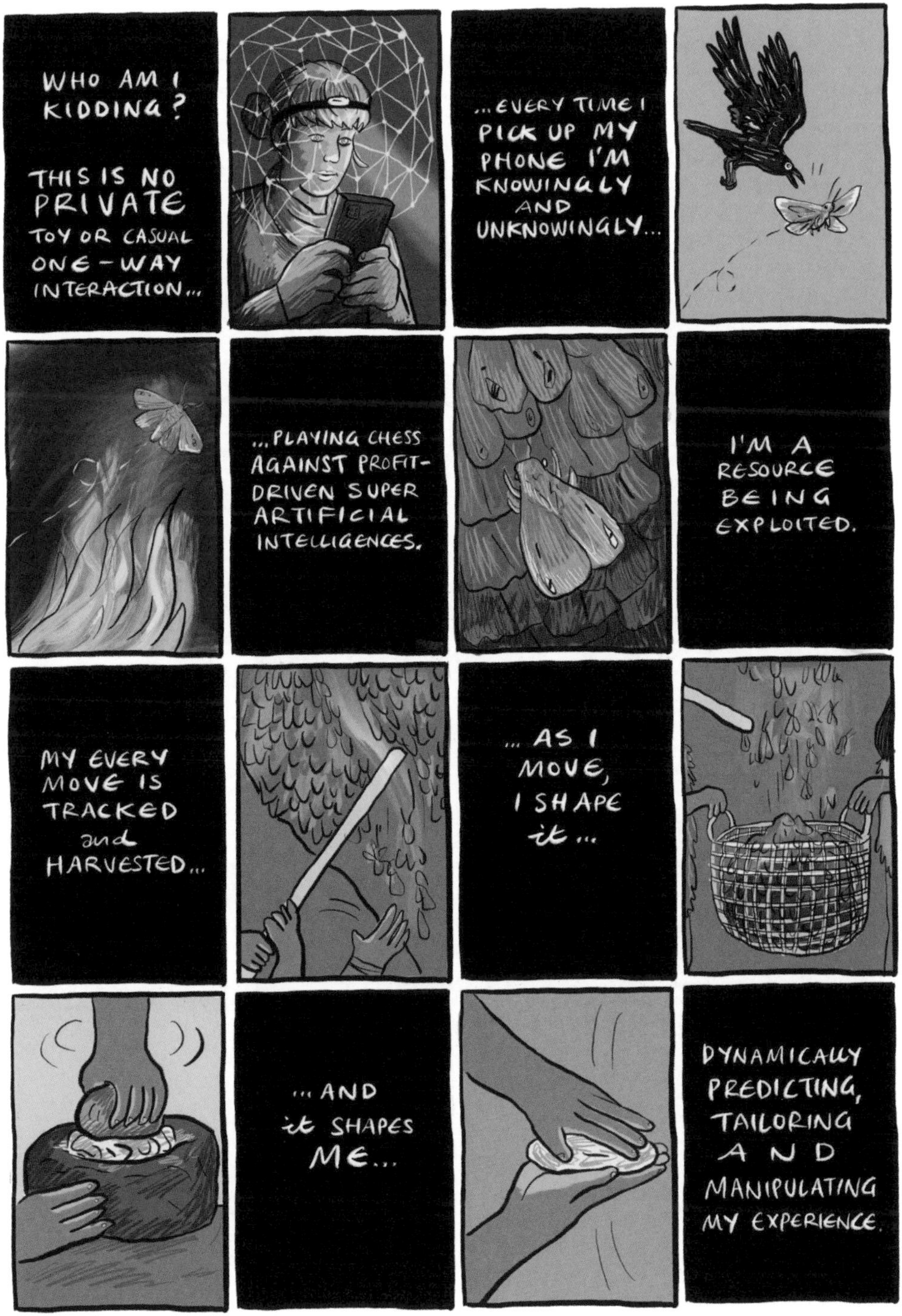
WHO AM I KIDDING?
THIS IS NO PRIVATE TOY OR CASUAL ONE-WAY INTERACTION...
...EVERY TIME I PICK UP MY PHONE I'M KNOWINGLY AND UNKNOWINGLY...
...PLAYING CHESS AGAINST PROFIT-DRIVEN SUPER ARTIFICIAL INTELLIGENCES.
I'M A RESOURCE BEING EXPLOITED.
MY EVERY MOVE IS TRACKED and HARVESTED...
... AS I MOVE, I SHAPE it...
...AND it SHAPES ME...
DYNAMICALLY PREDICTING, TAILORING AND MANIPULATING MY EXPERIENCE.

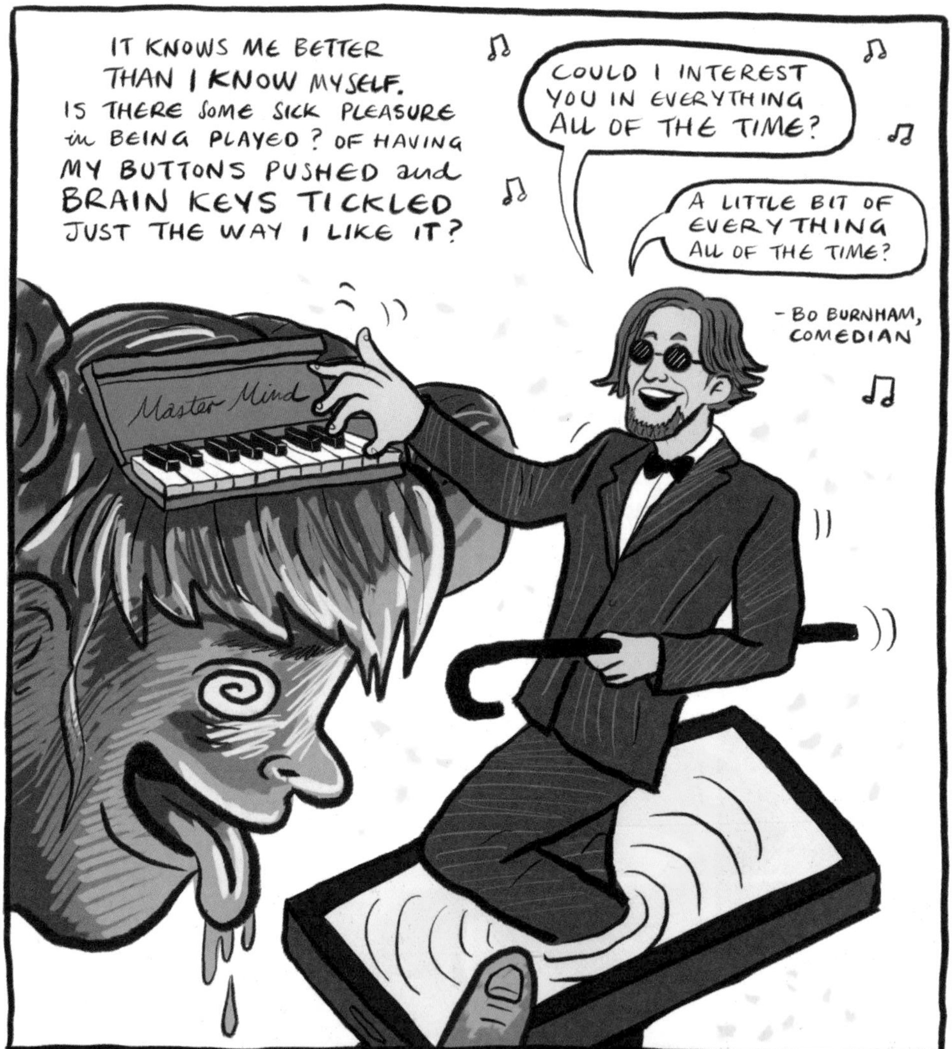
IT KNOWS ME BETTER THAN I KNOW MYSELF. IS THERE SOME SICK PLEASURE in BEING PLAYED? OF HAVING MY BUTTONS PUSHED and BRAIN KEYS TICKLED JUST THE WAY I LIKE IT?
COULD I INTEREST YOU IN EVERYTHING ALL OF THE TIME?
A LITTLE BIT OF EVERYTHING ALL OF THE TIME?
- BO BURNHAM, COMEDIAN
Master Mind

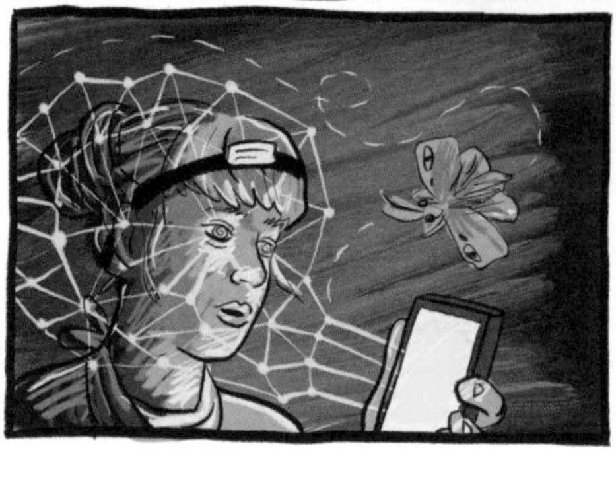

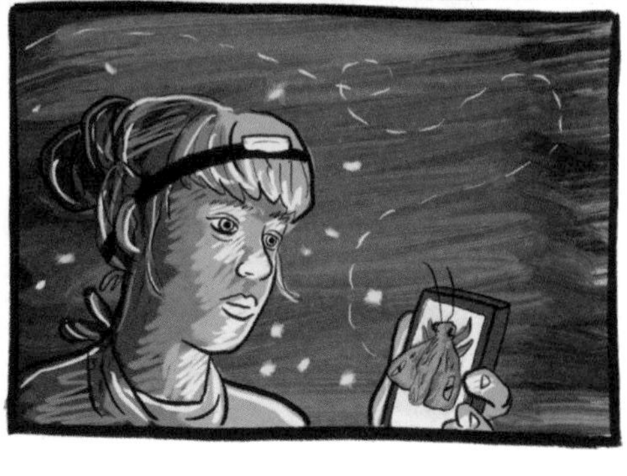

LOOK, OBVIOUSLY BEING ONLINE ISN'T TOTALLY AWFUL, OTHERWISE I'D STOP, RIGHT?

RIGHT?!

TAKE SOCIAL MEDIA, it CAN BE SUCH A RICH SPACE for COMMUNITY, ACTIVISM and INFORMATION.

ONLINE CONNECTION HAS BEEN A REAL LIFELINE for ME DURING PERIODS of ISOLATION.

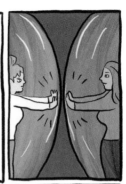

LIKE WHEN I WAS STUCK in BED FROM A CAR ACCIDENT AFTER UNIVERSITY, and THROUGHOUT the COVID-19 PANDEMIC LOCK DOWNS.

SOME OF MY M O S T MEANINGFUL RELATIONSHIPS HAVE STARTED OUT ONLINE.

AS AN ARTIST and WRITER I OFTEN feel MORE MYSELF, MORE SELF-EXPRESSED in WORDS, VIDEO and PICTURES.

AND ONLINE S P A C E S allow ME TO SHARE all THIS and ENTER INTO OTHER PEOPLE'S W O R L D S.

LIKE SOME SORT OF INTERACTIVE JOURNAL OR PERFORMANCE ART.

ALL OF THIS HAS HELPED ME DEVELOP MY VOICE and CREATIVE CONFIDENCE.

AND MANY of MY PROFESSIONAL CREATIVE OPPORTUNITIES and CONNECTIONS HAVE COME DIRECTLY FROM it.

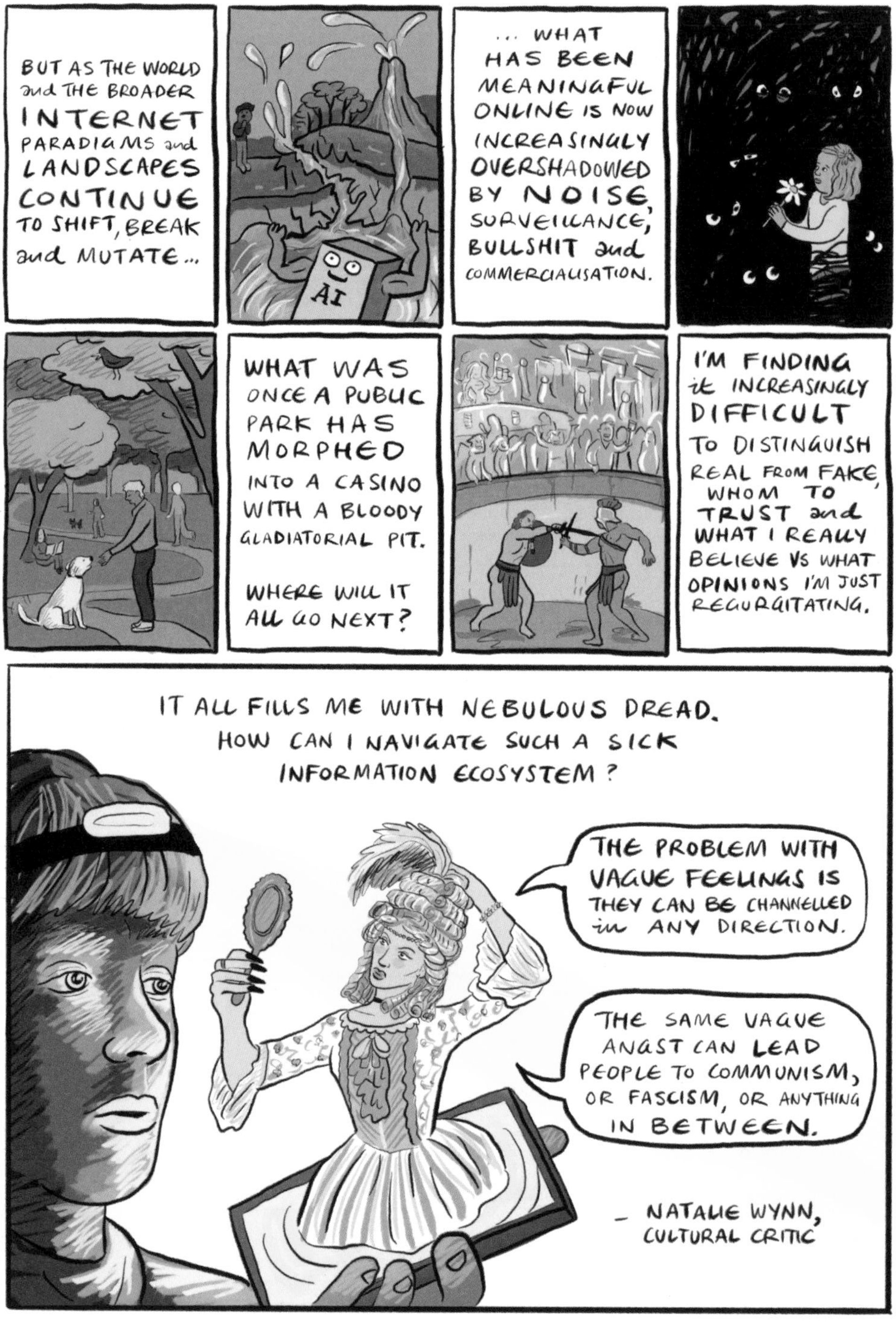
BUT AS THE WORLD and THE BROADER INTERNET PARADIGMS and LANDSCAPES CONTINUE TO SHIFT, BREAK and MUTATE...
AI
... WHAT HAS BEEN MEANINGFUL ONLINE IS NOW INCREASINGLY OVERSHADOWED BY NOISE, SURVEILLANCE, BULLSHIT and COMMERCIALISATION.
WHAT WAS ONCE A PUBLIC PARK HAS MORPHED INTO A CASINO WITH A BLOODY GLADIATORIAL PIT.
WHERE WILL IT ALL GO NEXT?
I'M FINDING it INCREASINGLY DIFFICULT TO DISTINGUISH REAL FROM FAKE, WHOM TO TRUST and WHAT I REALLY BELIEVE VS WHAT OPINIONS I'M JUST REGURGITATING.
IT ALL FILLS ME WITH NEBULOUS DREAD. HOW CAN I NAVIGATE SUCH A SICK INFORMATION ECOSYSTEM?
THE PROBLEM WITH VAGUE FEELINGS IS THEY CAN BE CHANNELLED in ANY DIRECTION.
THE SAME VAGUE ANGST CAN LEAD PEOPLE TO COMMUNISM, OR FASCISM, OR ANYTHING IN BETWEEN.
- NATALIE WYNN, CULTURAL CRITIC

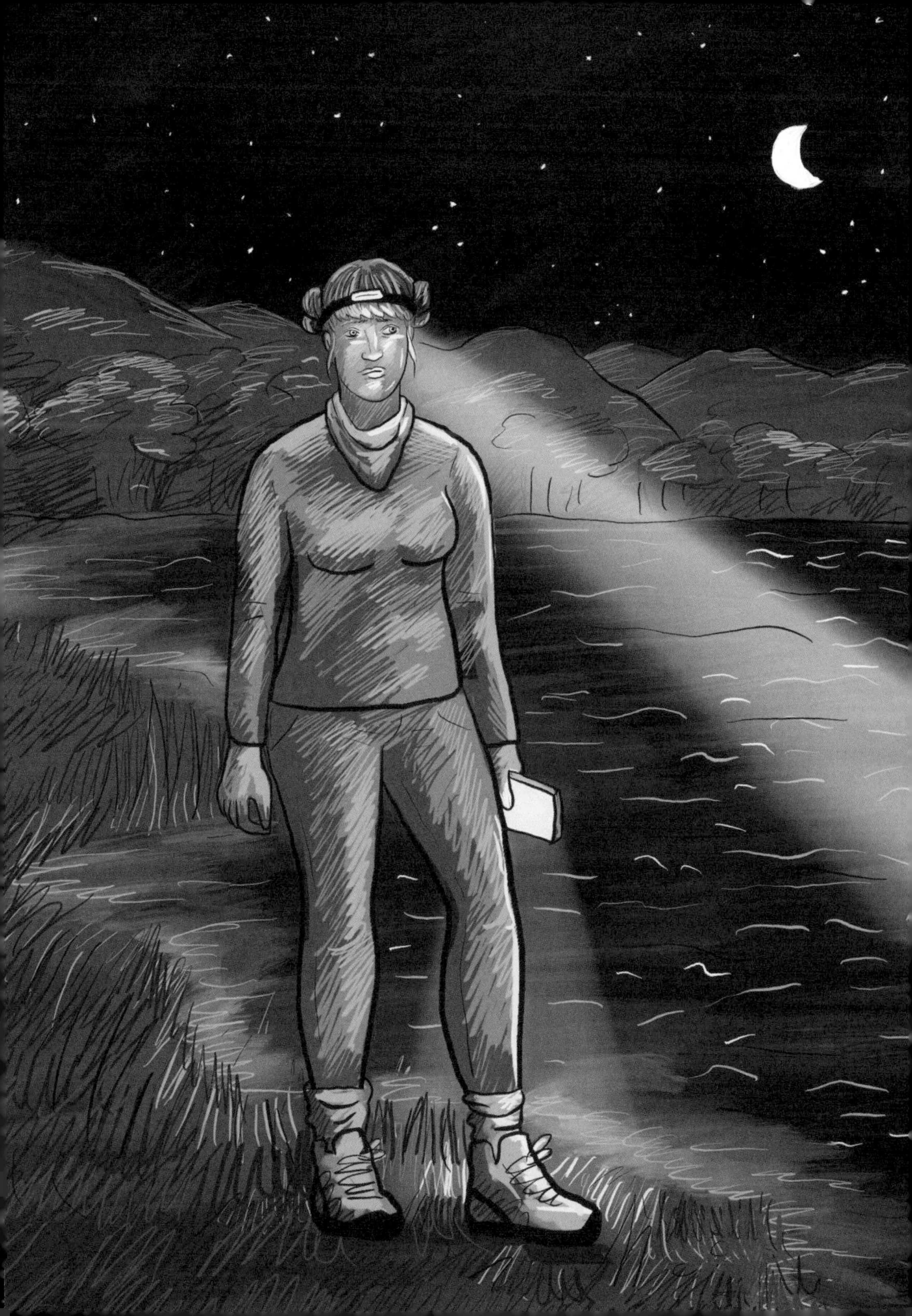

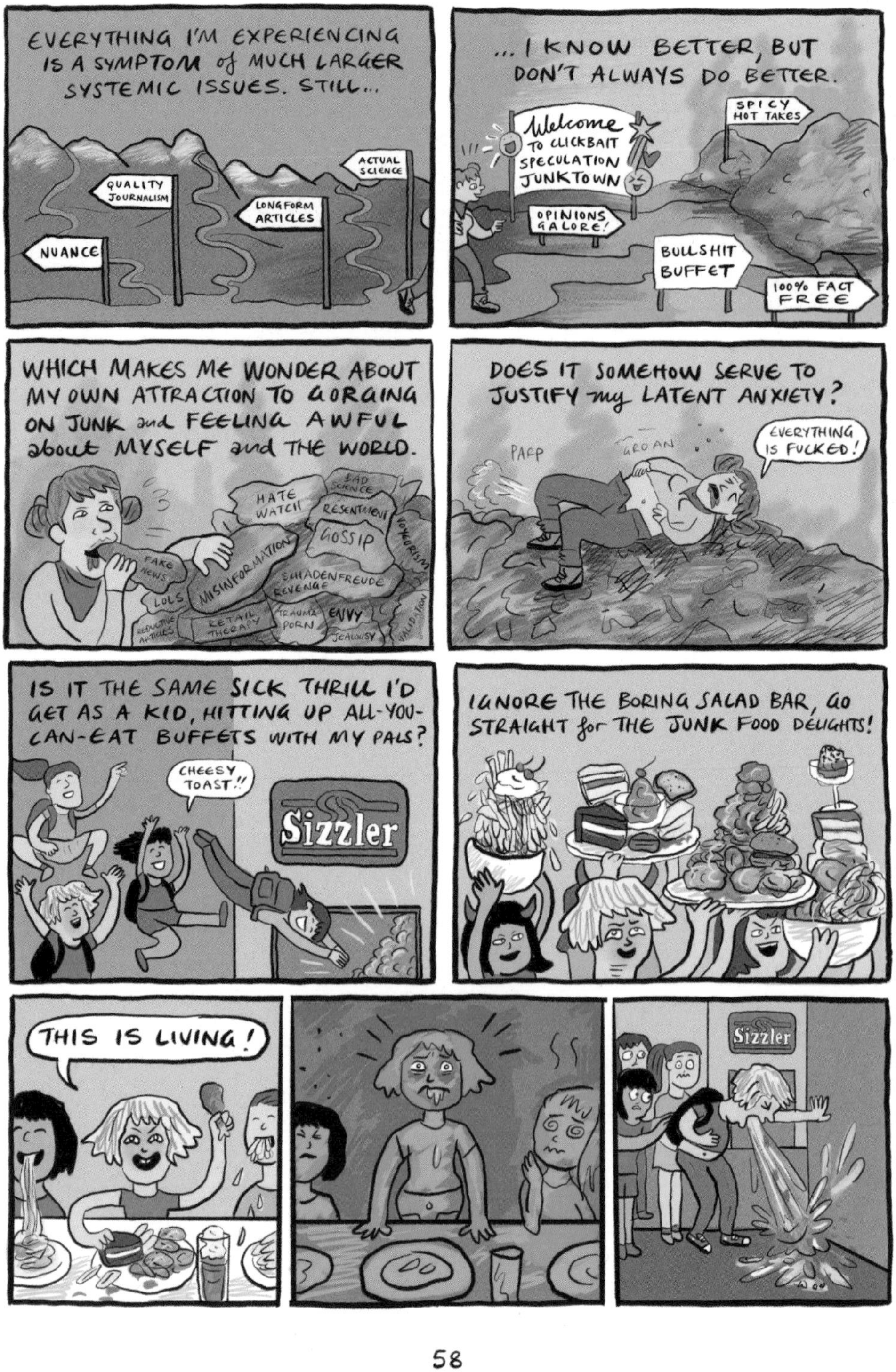
EVERYTHING I'M EXPERIENCING IS A SYMPTOM of MUCH LARGER SYSTEMIC ISSUES. STILL...
QUALITY JOURNALISM
ACTUAL SCIENCE
LONGFORM ARTICLES
NUANCE
...I KNOW BETTER, BUT DON'T ALWAYS DO BETTER.
Welcome TO CLICKBAIT SPECULATION JUNKTOWN
SPICY HOT TAKES
OPINIONS GALORE!
BULLSHIT BUFFET
100% FACT FREE
WHICH MAKES ME WONDER ABOUT MY OWN ATTRACTION TO GORGING ON JUNK and FEELING AWFUL about MYSELF and THE WORLD.
BAD SCIENCE
HATE WATCH
RESENTMENT
GOSSIP
VOYEURISM
FAKE NEWS
MISINFORMATION
SCHADENFREUDE
REVENGE
LOLS
REDUCTIVE ARTICLES
RETAIL THERAPY
TRAUMA PORN
ENVY
JEALOUSY
VALIDATION
DOES IT SOMEHOW SERVE TO JUSTIFY my LATENT ANXIETY?
PARP
GROAN
EVERYTHING IS FUCKED!
IS IT THE SAME SICK THRILL I'D GET AS A KID, HITTING UP ALL-YOU-CAN-EAT BUFFETS WITH MY PALS?
CHEESY TOAST!!
Sizzler
IGNORE THE BORING SALAD BAR, GO STRAIGHT for THE JUNK FOOD DELIGHTS!
THIS IS LIVING!
Sizzler

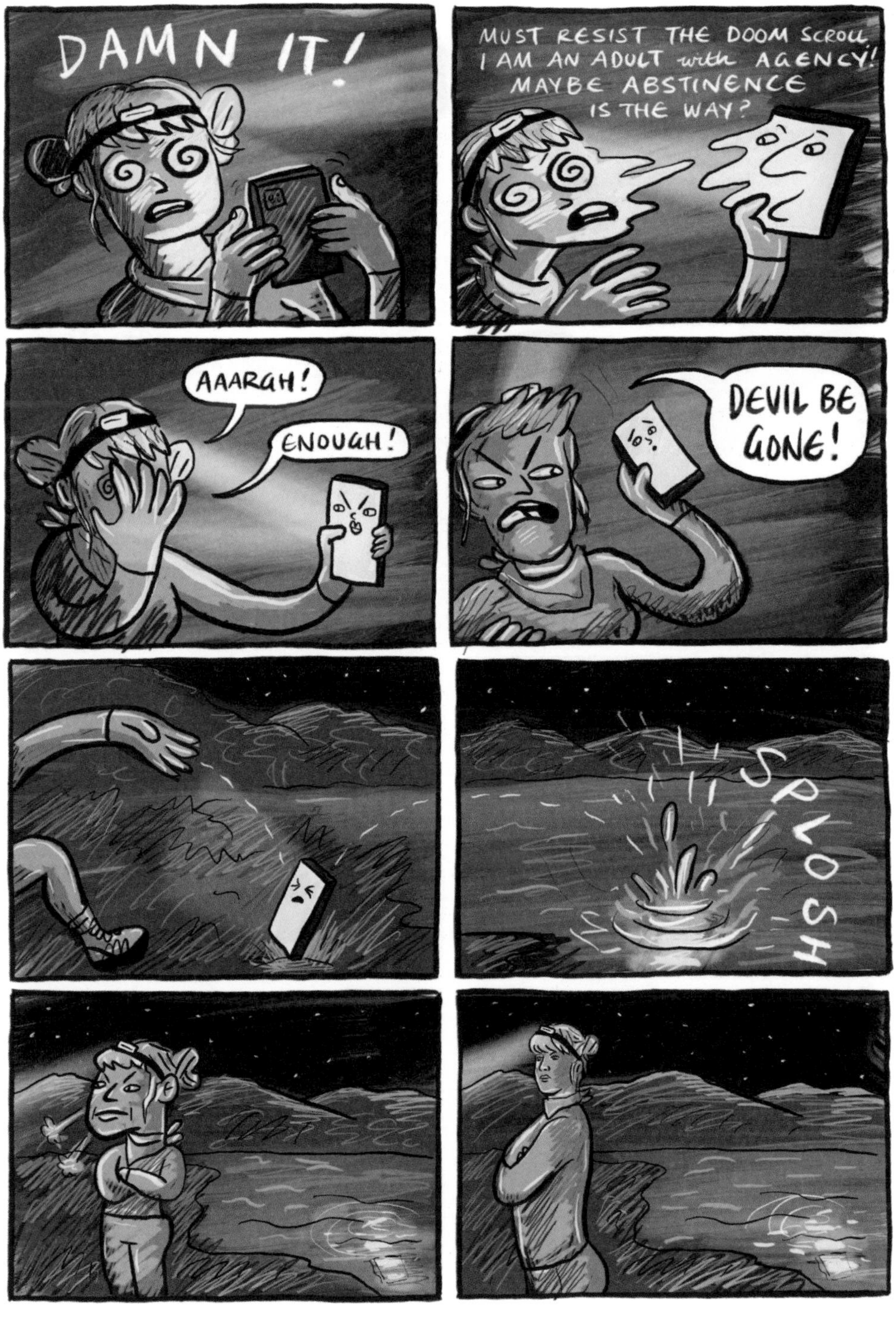
DAMN IT!
MUST RESIST THE DOOM SCROLL
I AM AN ADULT with AGENCY!
MAYBE ABSTINENCE
IS THE WAY?
AAARGH!
ENOUGH!
DEVIL BE GONE!
SPLOSH

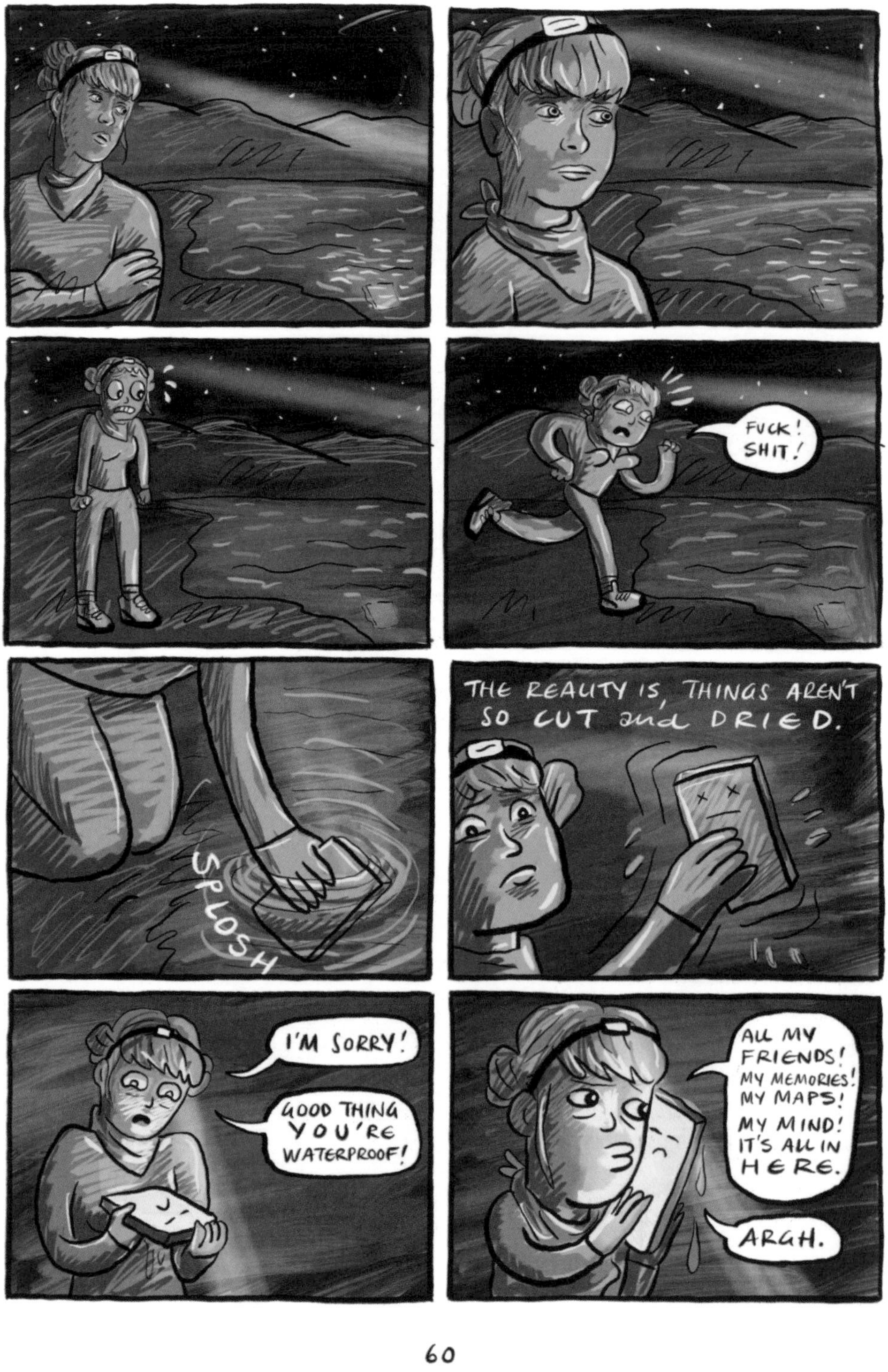
FUCK! SHIT!
SPLOSH
THE REALITY IS, THINGS AREN'T SO CUT and DRIED.
I'M SORRY!
GOOD THING YOU'RE WATERPROOF!
ALL MY FRIENDS! MY MEMORIES! MY MAPS! MY MIND! IT'S ALL IN HERE.
ARGH.

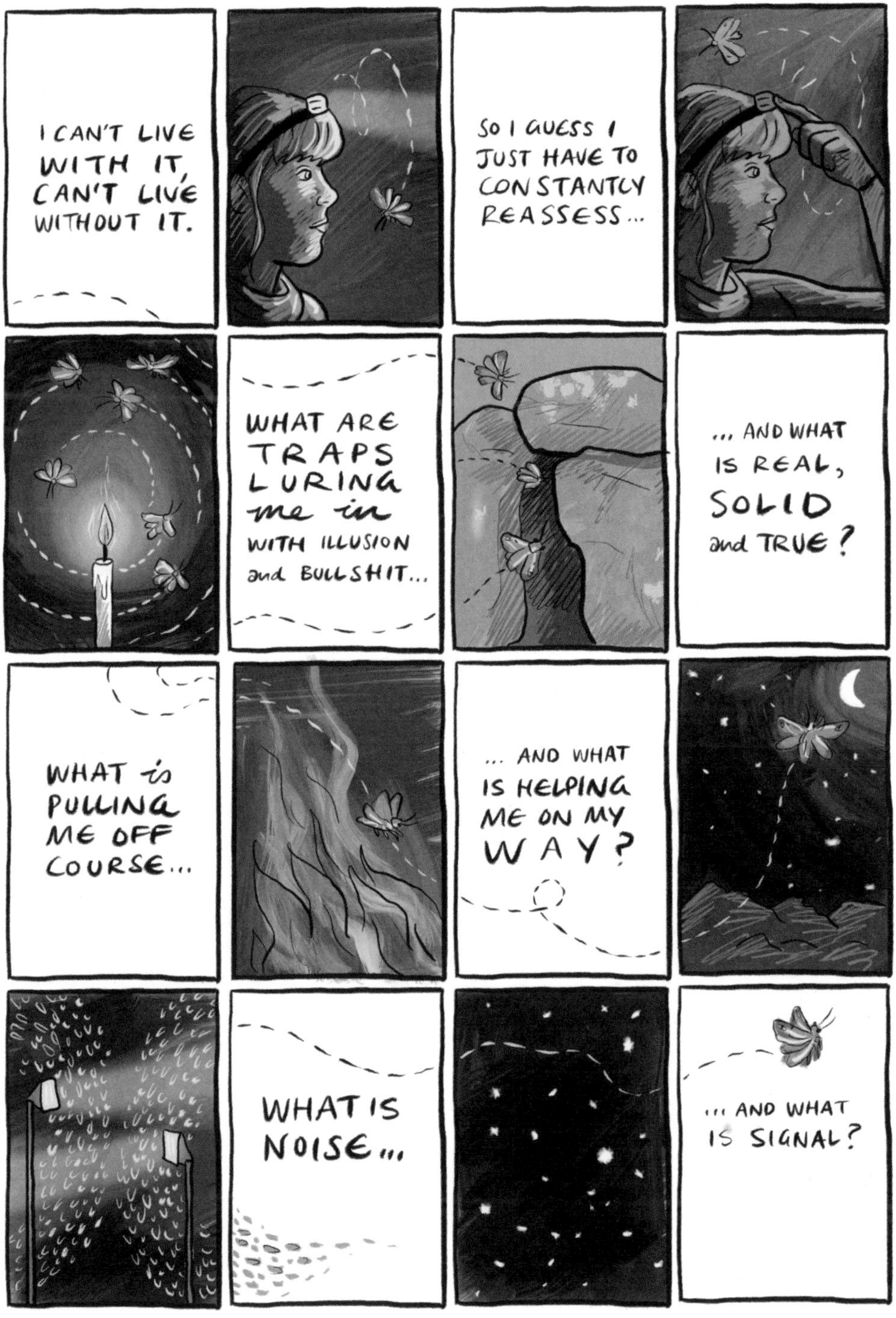
I CAN'T LIVE WITH IT, CAN'T LIVE WITHOUT IT.
SO I GUESS I JUST HAVE TO CONSTANTLY REASSESS...
WHAT ARE TRAPS LURING me in WITH ILLUSION and BULLSHIT...
... AND WHAT IS REAL, SOLID and TRUE?
WHAT is PULLING ME OFF COURSE...
... AND WHAT IS HELPING ME ON MY WAY?
WHAT IS NOISE...
... AND WHAT IS SIGNAL?

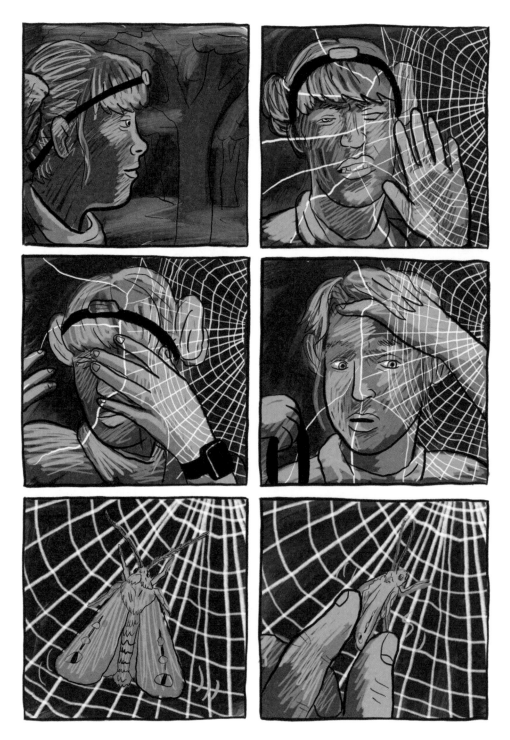

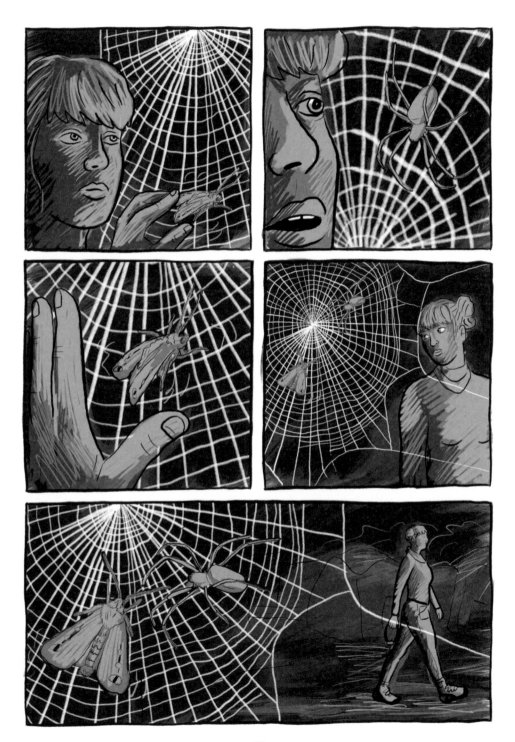

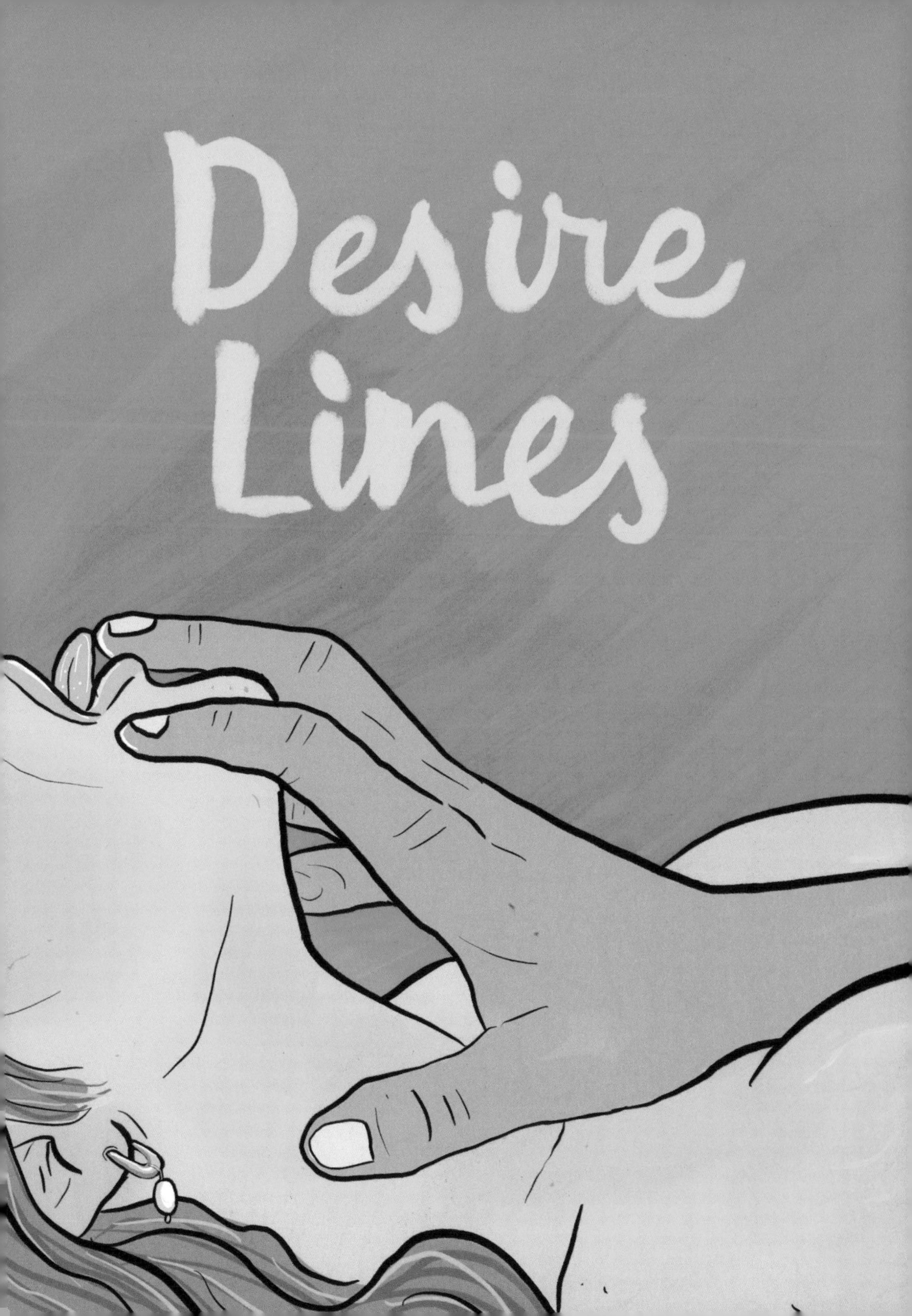
Desire
Lines

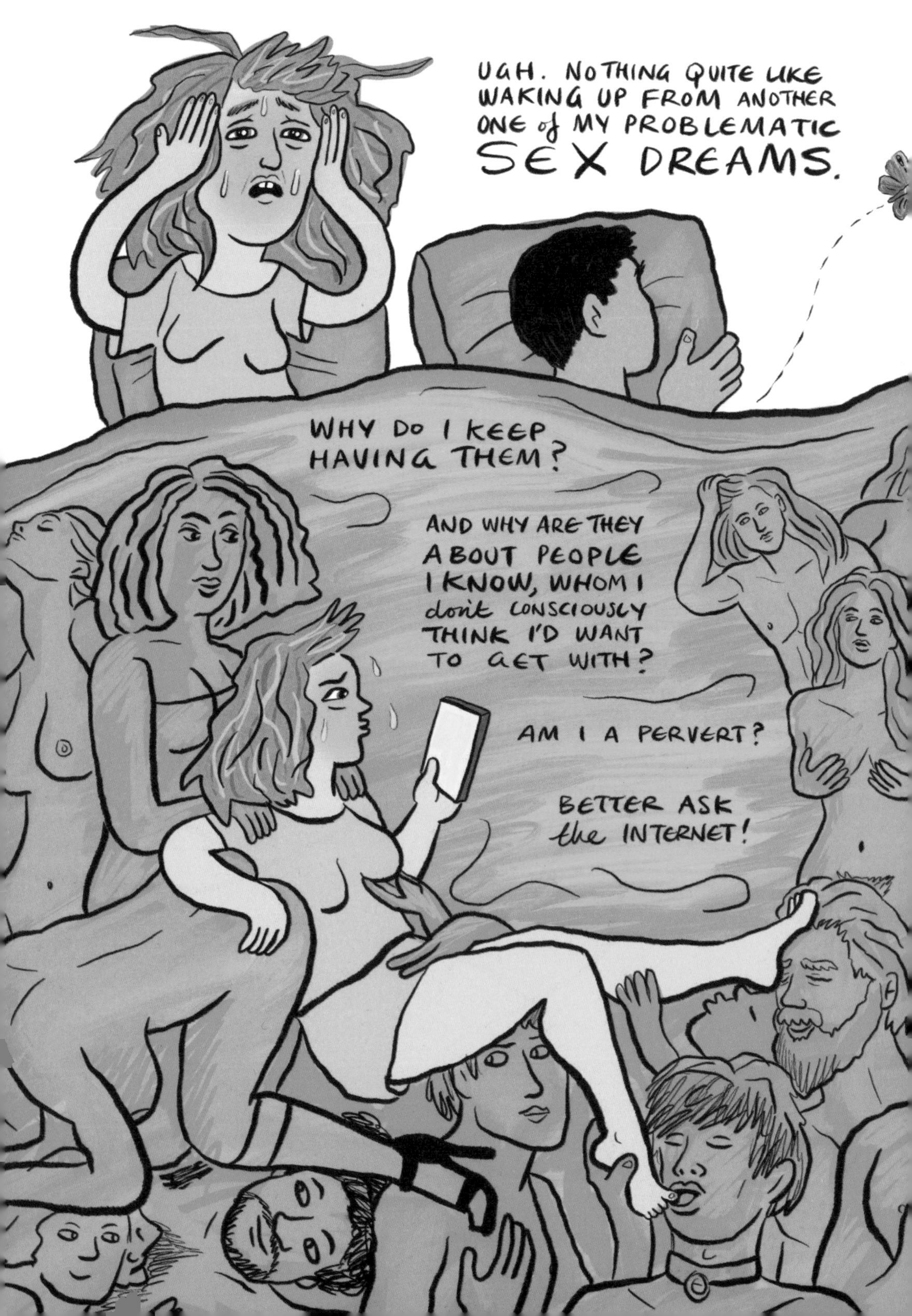
UGH. NOTHING QUITE LIKE WAKING UP FROM ANOTHER ONE of MY PROBLEMATIC SEX DREAMS.
WHY DO I KEEP HAVING THEM?
AND WHY ARE THEY ABOUT PEOPLE I KNOW, WHOM I don't CONSCIOUSLY THINK I'D WANT TO GET WITH?
AM I A PERVERT?
BETTER ASK the INTERNET!

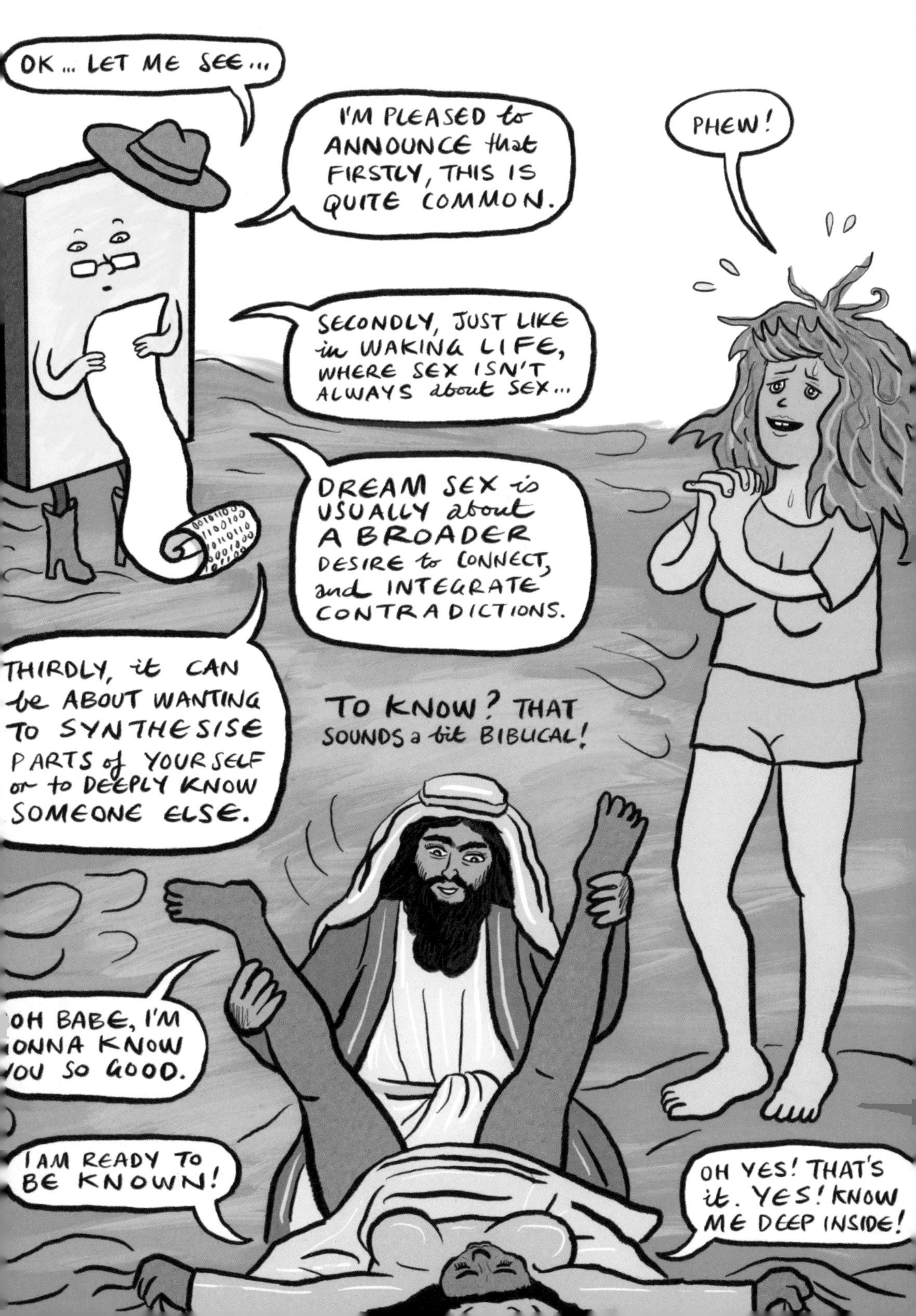
OK ... LET ME SEE ...
I'M PLEASED to ANNOUNCE that FIRSTLY, THIS IS QUITE COMMON.
PHEW!
SECONDLY, JUST LIKE in WAKING LIFE, WHERE SEX ISN'T ALWAYS about SEX...
DREAM SEX is USUALLY about A BROADER DESIRE to CONNECT, and INTEGRATE CONTRADICTIONS.
THIRDLY, it CAN be ABOUT WANTING TO SYNTHESISE PARTS of YOURSELF or to DEEPLY KNOW SOMEONE ELSE.
TO KNOW? THAT SOUNDS a bit BIBLICAL!
OH BABE, I'M GONNA KNOW YOU SO GOOD.
I AM READY TO BE KNOWN!
OH YES! THAT'S it. YES! KNOW ME DEEP INSIDE!

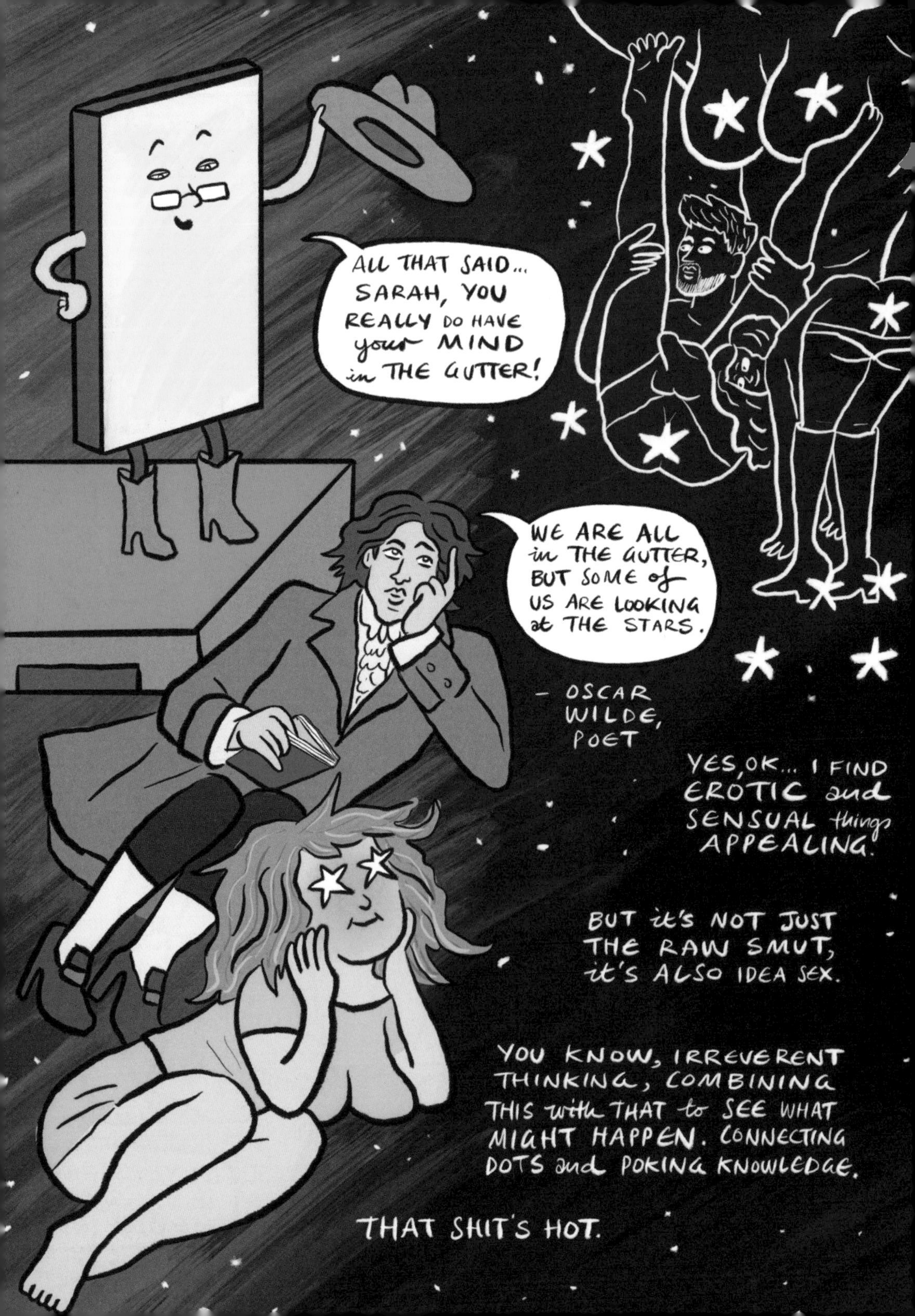
ALL THAT SAID... SARAH, YOU REALLY DO HAVE your MIND in THE GUTTER!
WE ARE ALL in THE GUTTER, BUT SOME of US ARE LOOKING at THE STARS.
- OSCAR WILDE, POET
YES, OK... I FIND EROTIC and SENSUAL things APPEALING.
BUT it's NOT JUST THE RAW SMUT, it's ALSO IDEA SEX.
YOU KNOW, IRREVERENT THINKING, COMBINING THIS with THAT to SEE WHAT MIGHT HAPPEN. CONNECTING DOTS and POKING KNOWLEDGE.
THAT SHIT'S HOT.

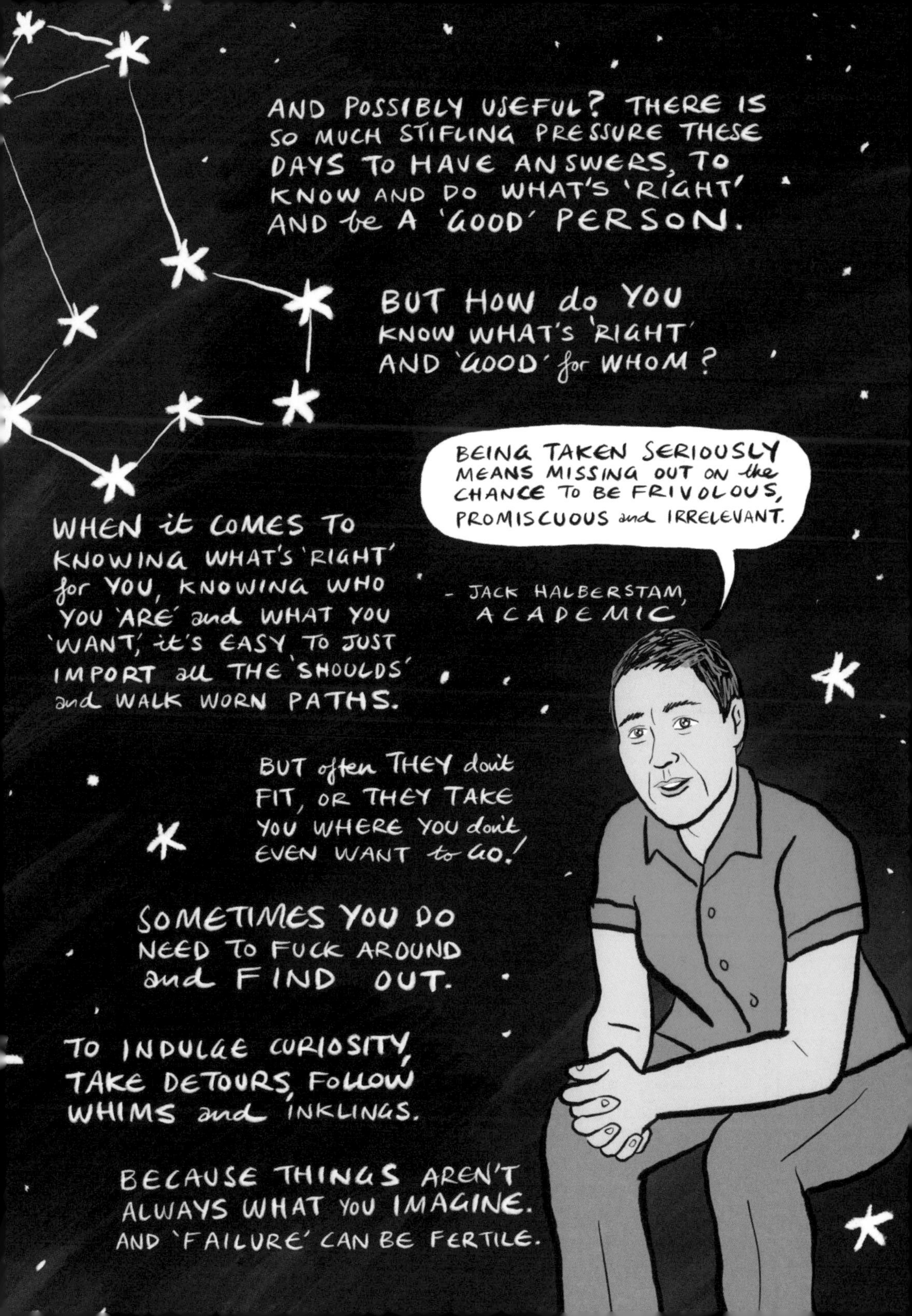
AND POSSIBLY USEFUL? THERE IS SO MUCH STIFLING PRESSURE THESE DAYS TO HAVE ANSWERS, TO KNOW AND DO WHAT'S 'RIGHT' AND be A 'GOOD' PERSON.
BUT HOW do YOU KNOW WHAT'S 'RIGHT' AND 'GOOD' for WHOM?
BEING TAKEN SERIOUSLY MEANS MISSING OUT ON the CHANCE TO BE FRIVOLOUS, PROMISCUOUS and IRRELEVANT.
- JACK HALBERSTAM, ACADEMIC
WHEN it COMES TO KNOWING WHAT'S 'RIGHT' for YOU, KNOWING WHO YOU 'ARE' and WHAT YOU 'WANT,' it's EASY TO JUST IMPORT all THE 'SHOULDS' and WALK WORN PATHS.
BUT often THEY don't FIT, OR THEY TAKE YOU WHERE YOU don't EVEN WANT to GO!
SOMETIMES YOU DO NEED TO FUCK AROUND and FIND OUT.
TO INDULGE CURIOSITY, TAKE DETOURS, FOLLOW WHIMS and INKLINGS.
BECAUSE THINGS AREN'T ALWAYS WHAT YOU IMAGINE. AND 'FAILURE' CAN BE FERTILE.

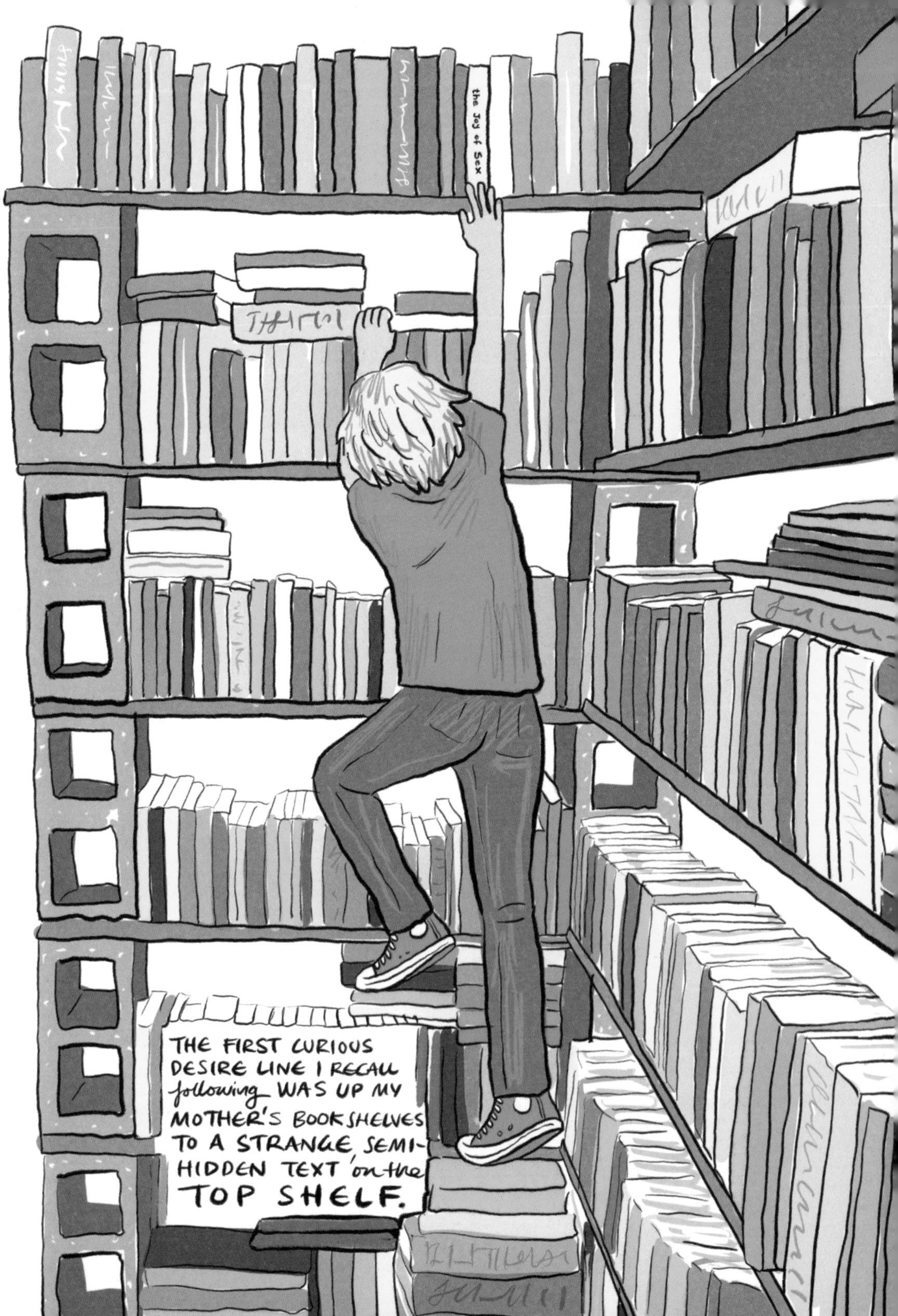
the Joy of Sex
THE FIRST CURIOUS DESIRE LINE I RECALL following WAS UP MY MOTHER'S BOOKSHELVES TO A STRANGE, SEMI-HIDDEN TEXT on the TOP SHELF.

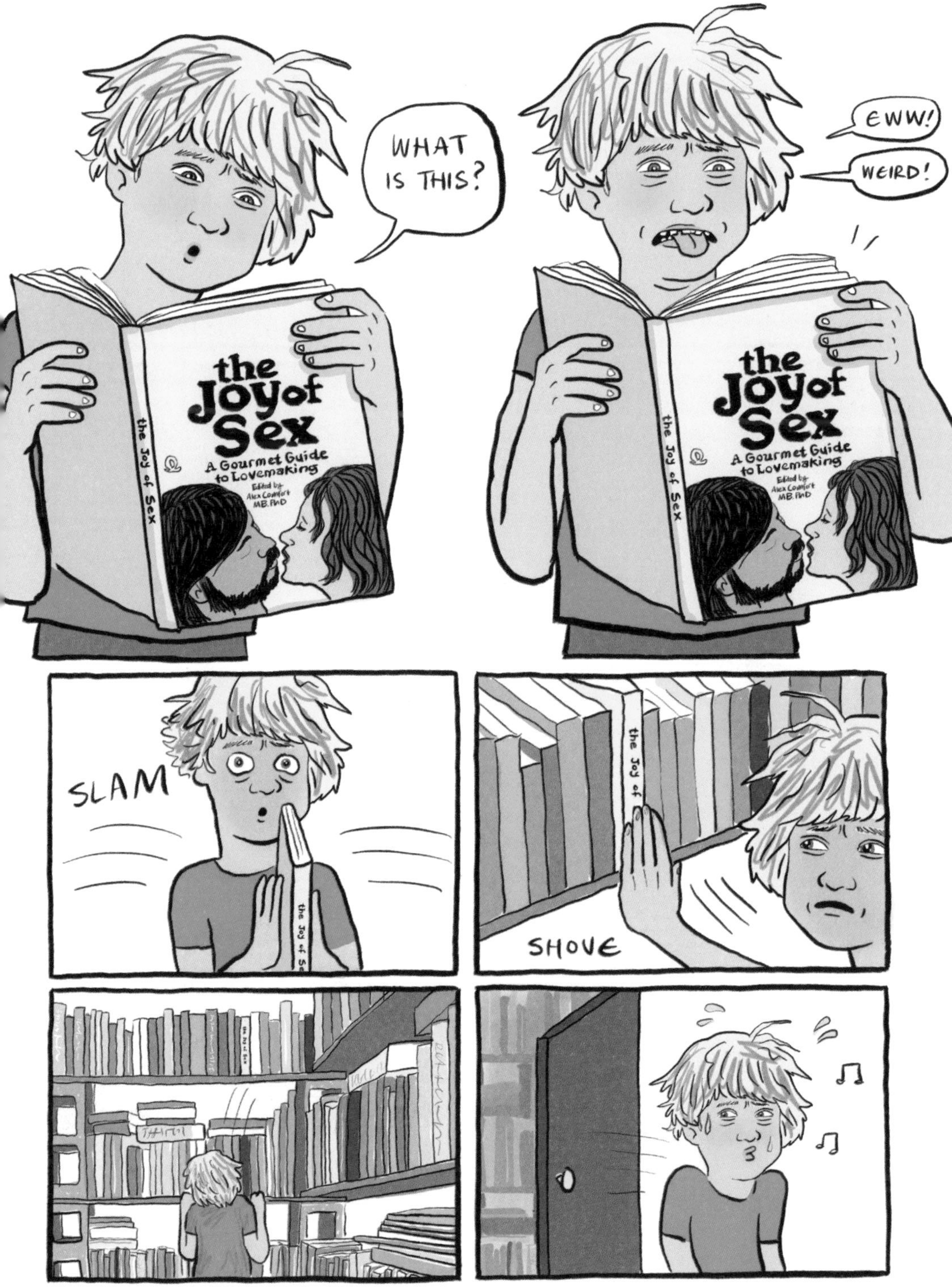
WHAT IS THIS?
the Joy of Sex
A Gourmet Guide to Lovemaking
EWW!
WEIRD!
SLAM
SHOVE

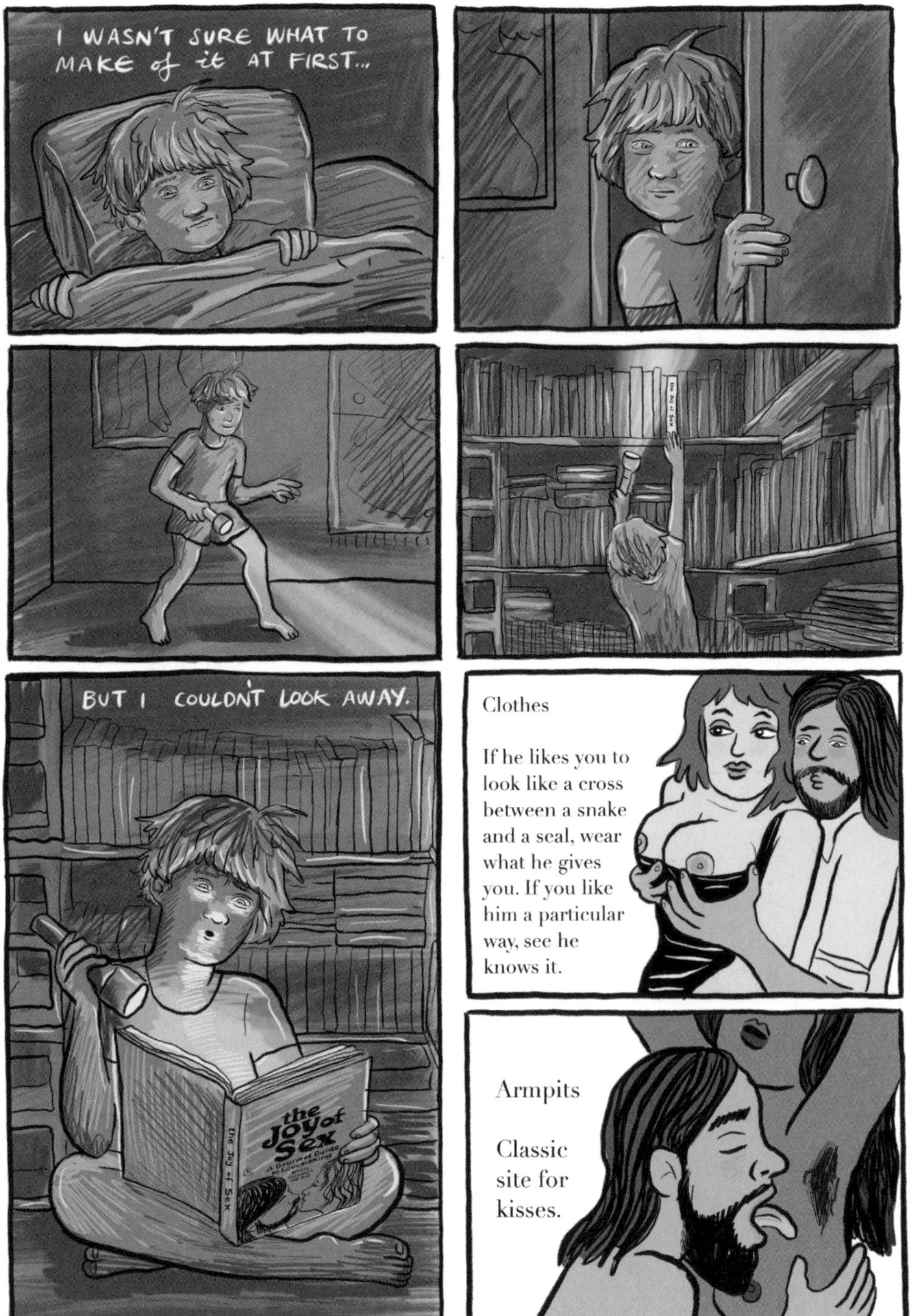
I WASN'T SURE WHAT TO MAKE of it AT FIRST...
BUT I COULDN'T LOOK AWAY.
the Joy of Sex
Clothes
If he likes you to look like a cross between a snake and a seal, wear what he gives you. If you like him a particular way, see he knows it.
Armpits
Classic site for kisses.

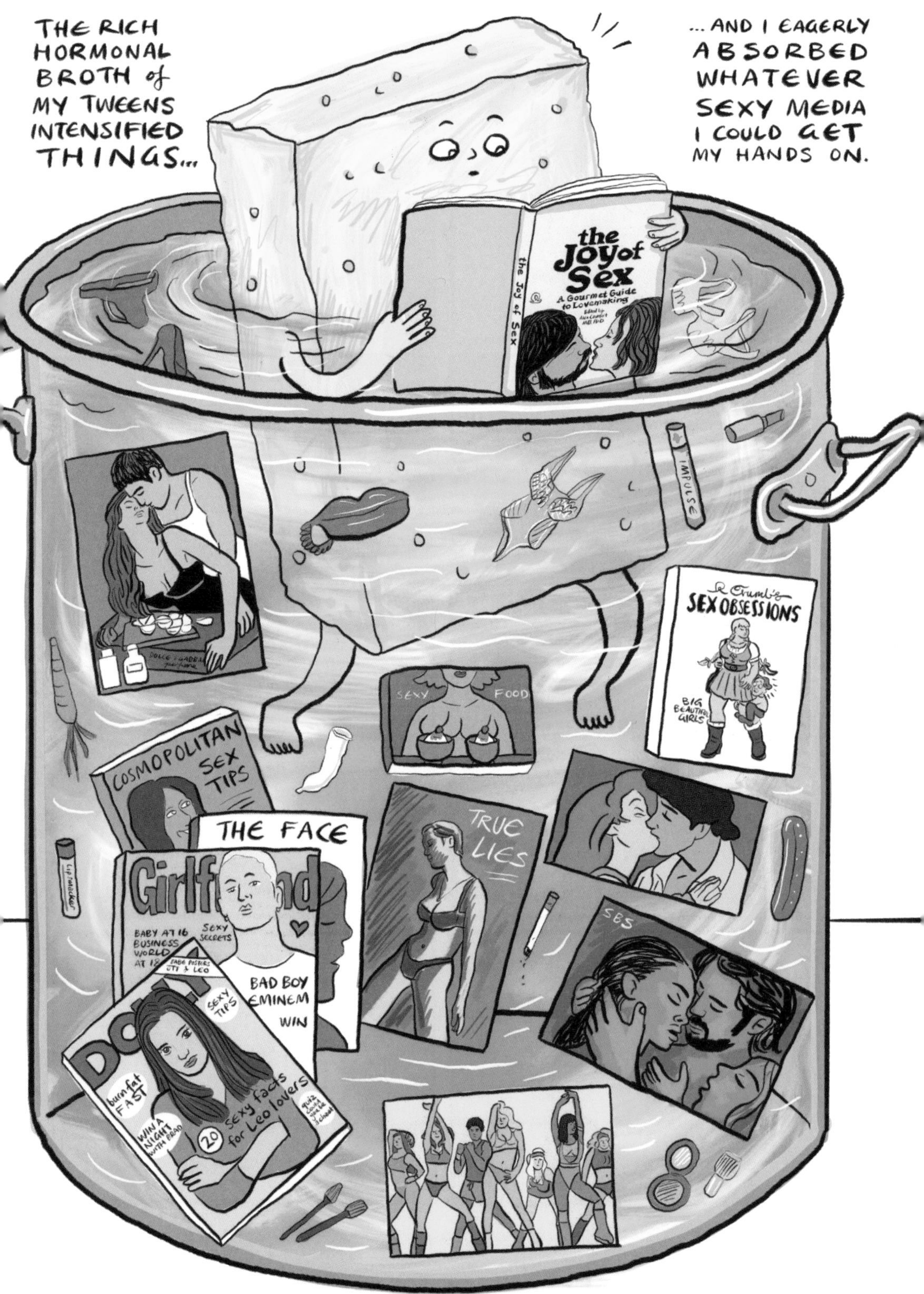
THE RICH HORMONAL BROTH of MY TWEENS INTENSIFIED THINGS...
...AND I EAGERLY ABSORBED WHATEVER SEXY MEDIA I COULD GET MY HANDS ON.
the Joy of Sex
A Gourmet Guide to Lovemaking
the Joy of Sex
IMPULSE
SEX OBSESSIONS
BIG BEAUTIFUL GIRLS
SEXY FOOD
COSMOPOLITAN
SEX TIPS
THE FACE
BABY AT 16
SEXY SECRETS
BUSINESS WORLD AT 18
BAD BOY EMINEM
WIN
TRUE LIES
SBS
SEXY TIPS
burn fat FAST
WIN A NIGHT WITH BRAD
20 sexy facts for Leo lovers

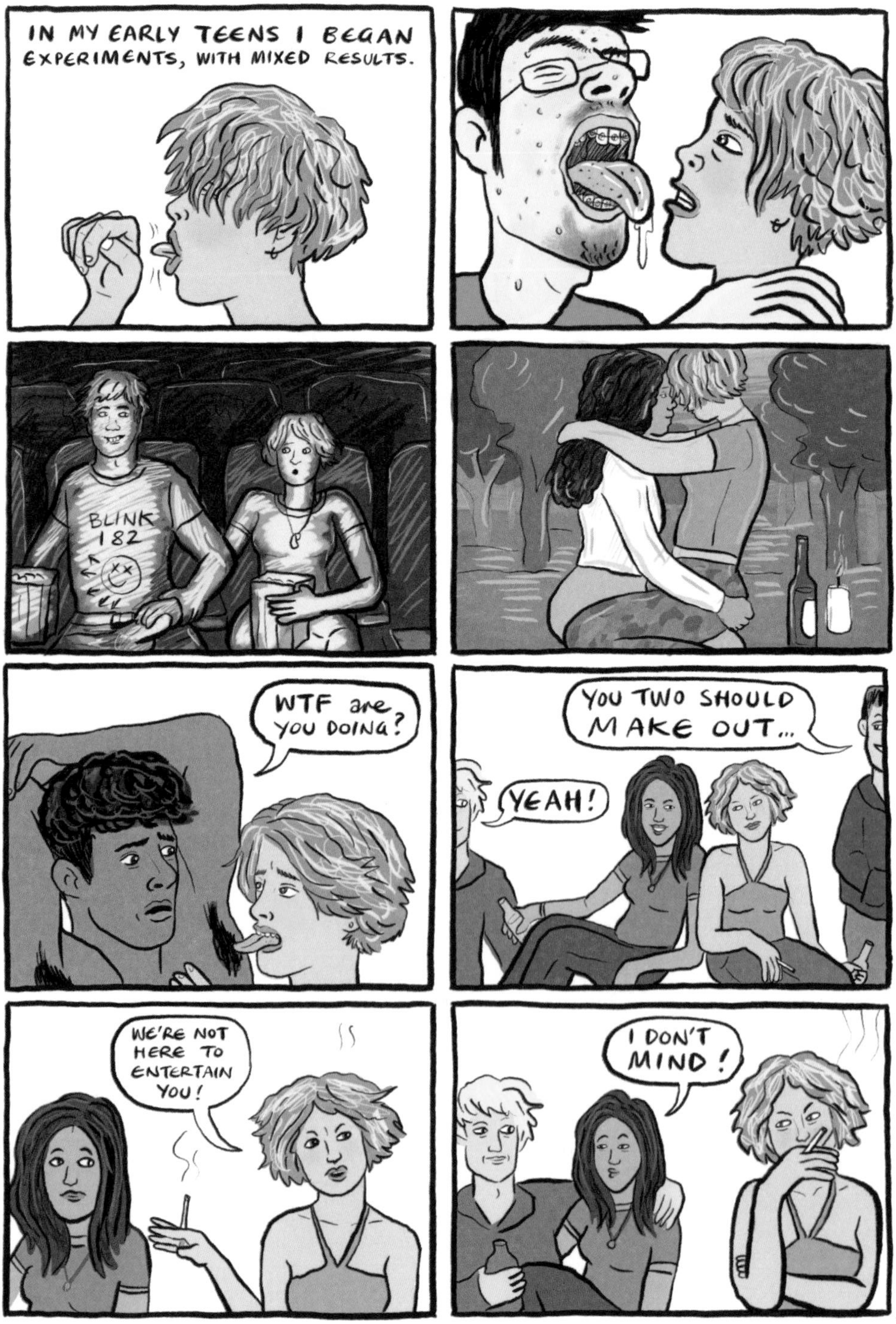

IN MY EARLY TEENS I BEGAN EXPERIMENTS, WITH MIXED RESULTS.
BLINK 182
WTF are YOU DOING?
YOU TWO SHOULD MAKE OUT...
YEAH!
WE'RE NOT HERE TO ENTERTAIN YOU!
I DON'T MIND!

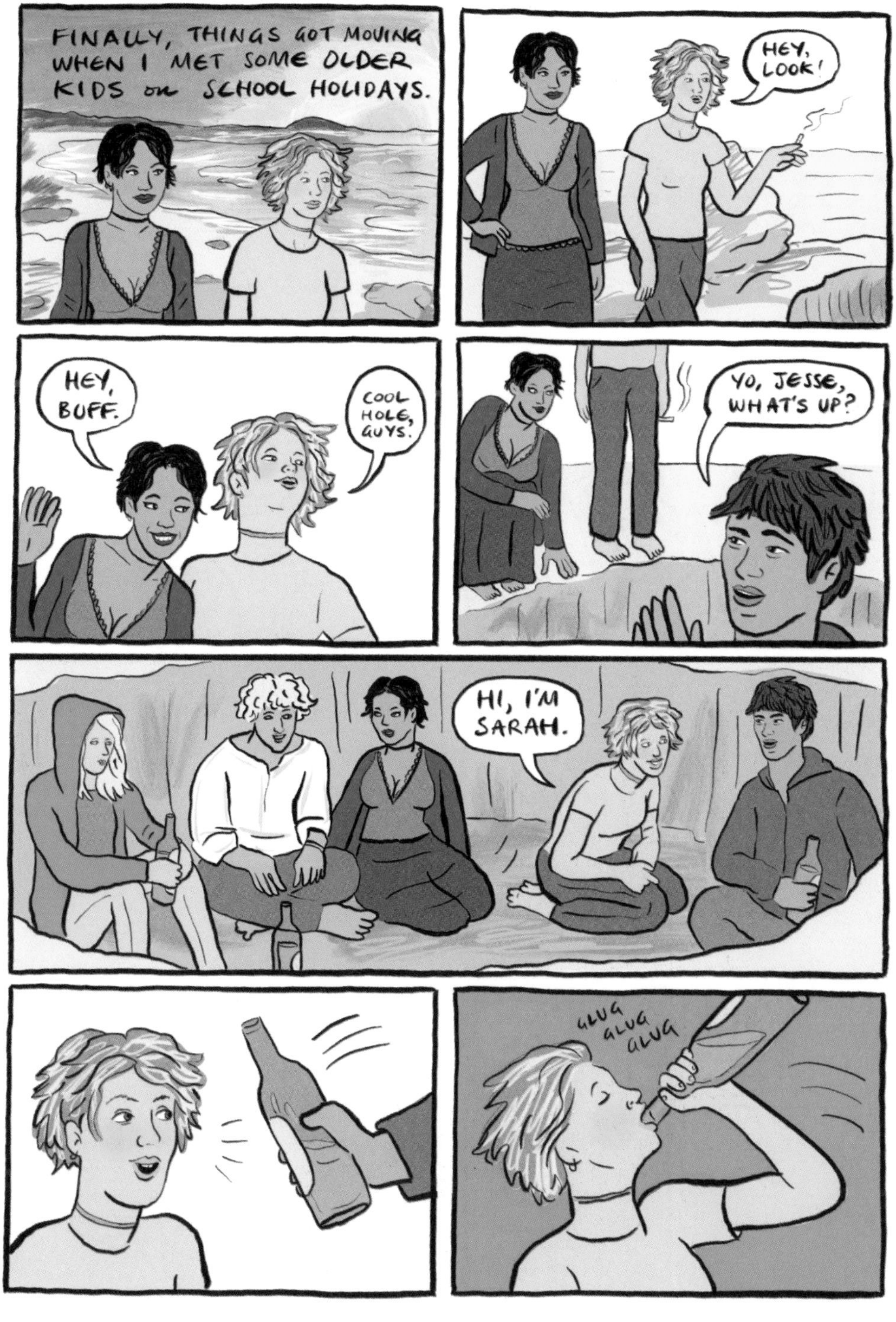
FINALLY, THINGS GOT MOVING WHEN I MET SOME OLDER KIDS on SCHOOL HOLIDAYS.
HEY, LOOK!
HEY, BUFF.
COOL HOLE, GUYS.
YO, JESSE, WHAT'S UP?
HI, I'M SARAH.
GLUG GLUG GLUG

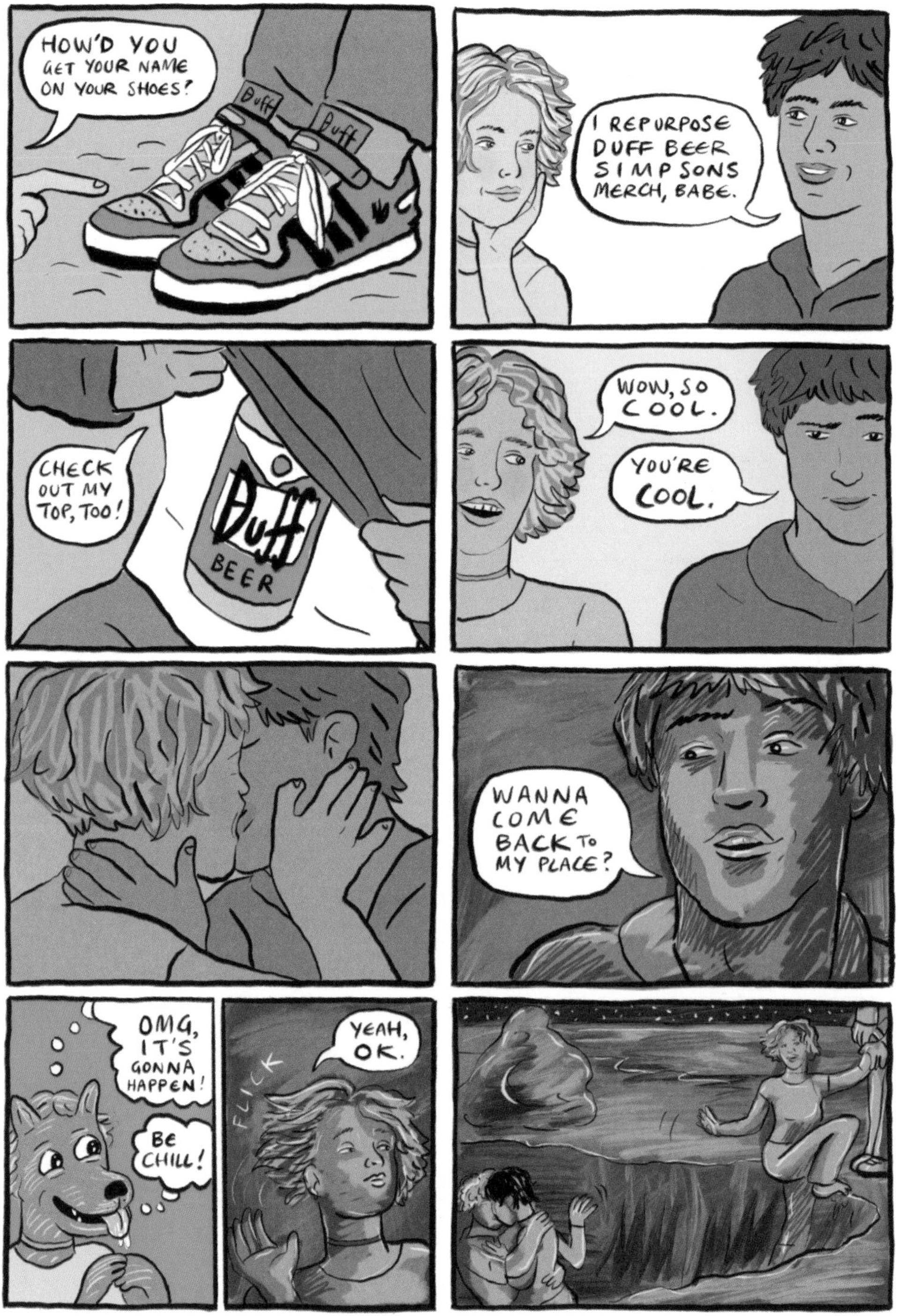
HOW'D YOU GET YOUR NAME ON YOUR SHOES?
Duff
Duff
I REPURPOSE DUFF BEER SIMPSONS MERCH, BABE.
CHECK OUT MY TOP, TOO!
Duff
BEER
WOW, SO COOL.
YOU'RE COOL.
WANNA COME BACK TO MY PLACE?
OMG, IT'S GONNA HAPPEN!
BE CHILL!
FLICK
YEAH, OK.

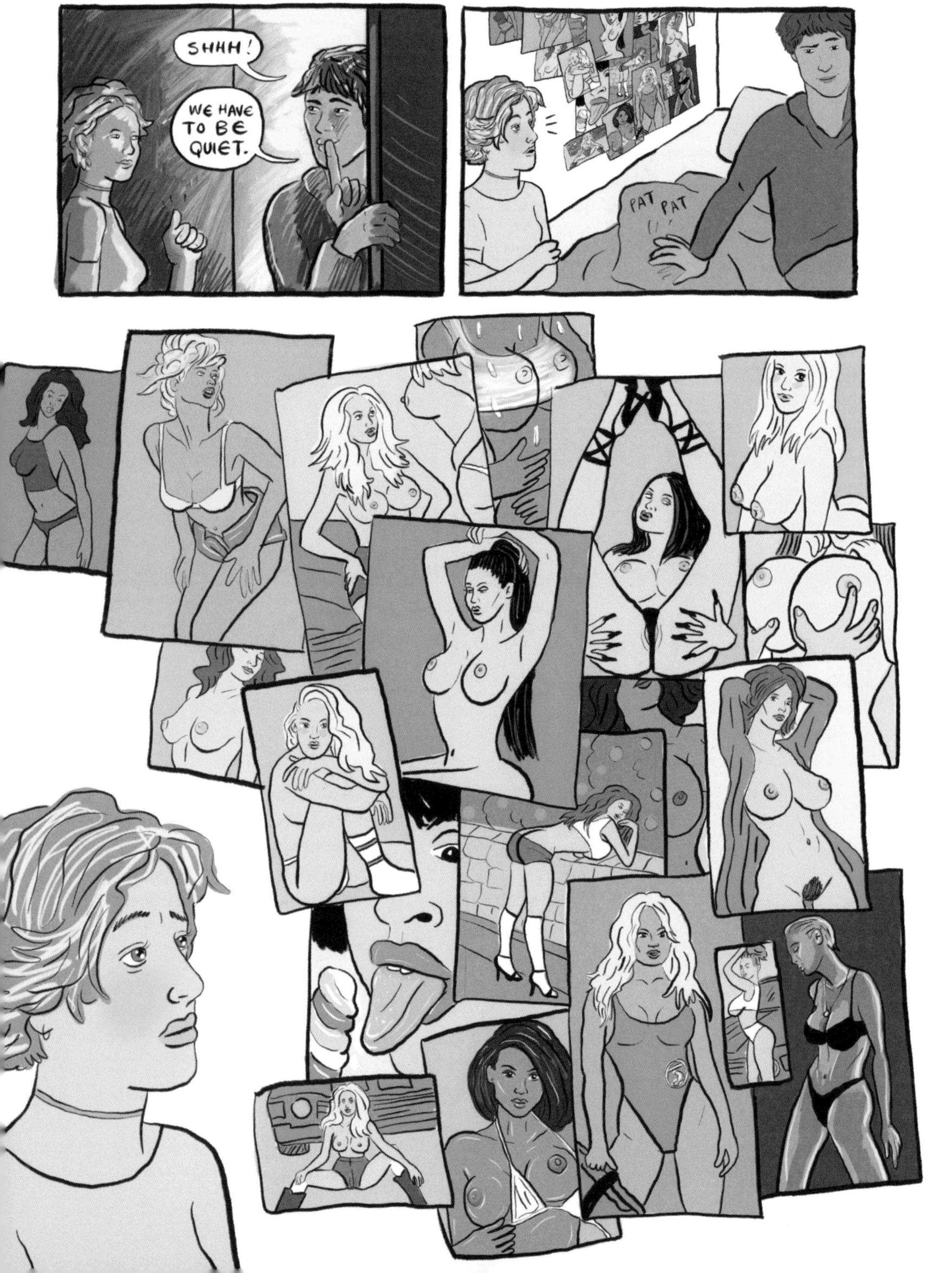
SHHH!
WE HAVE TO BE QUIET.
PAT PAT

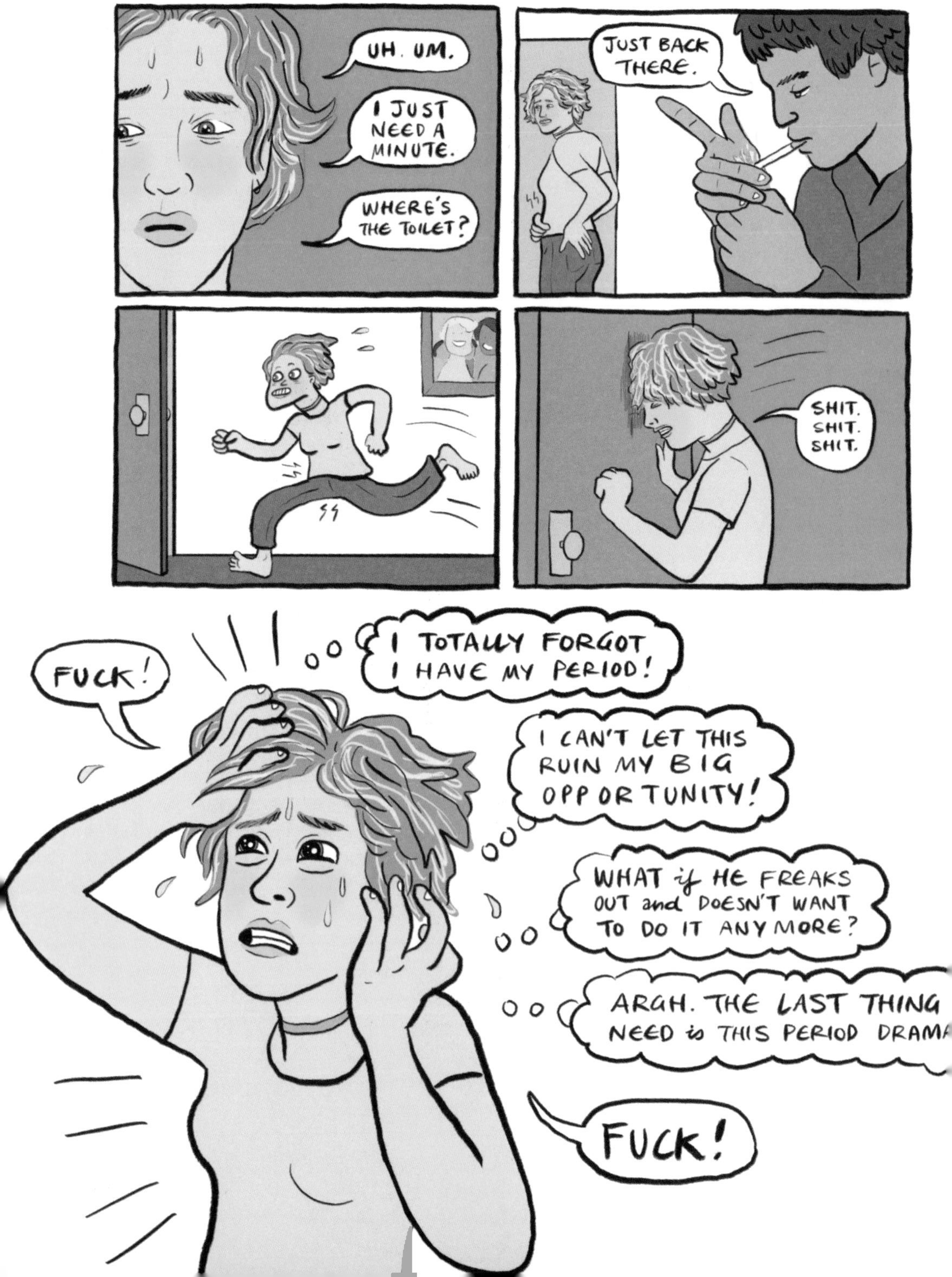
UH. UM.
I JUST NEED A MINUTE.
WHERE'S THE TOILET?
JUST BACK THERE.
SHIT. SHIT. SHIT.
FUCK!
I TOTALLY FORGOT I HAVE MY PERIOD!
I CAN'T LET THIS RUIN MY BIG OPPORTUNITY!
WHAT if HE FREAKS OUT and DOESN'T WANT TO DO IT ANYMORE?
ARGH. THE LAST THING NEED is THIS PERIOD DRAMA
FUCK!

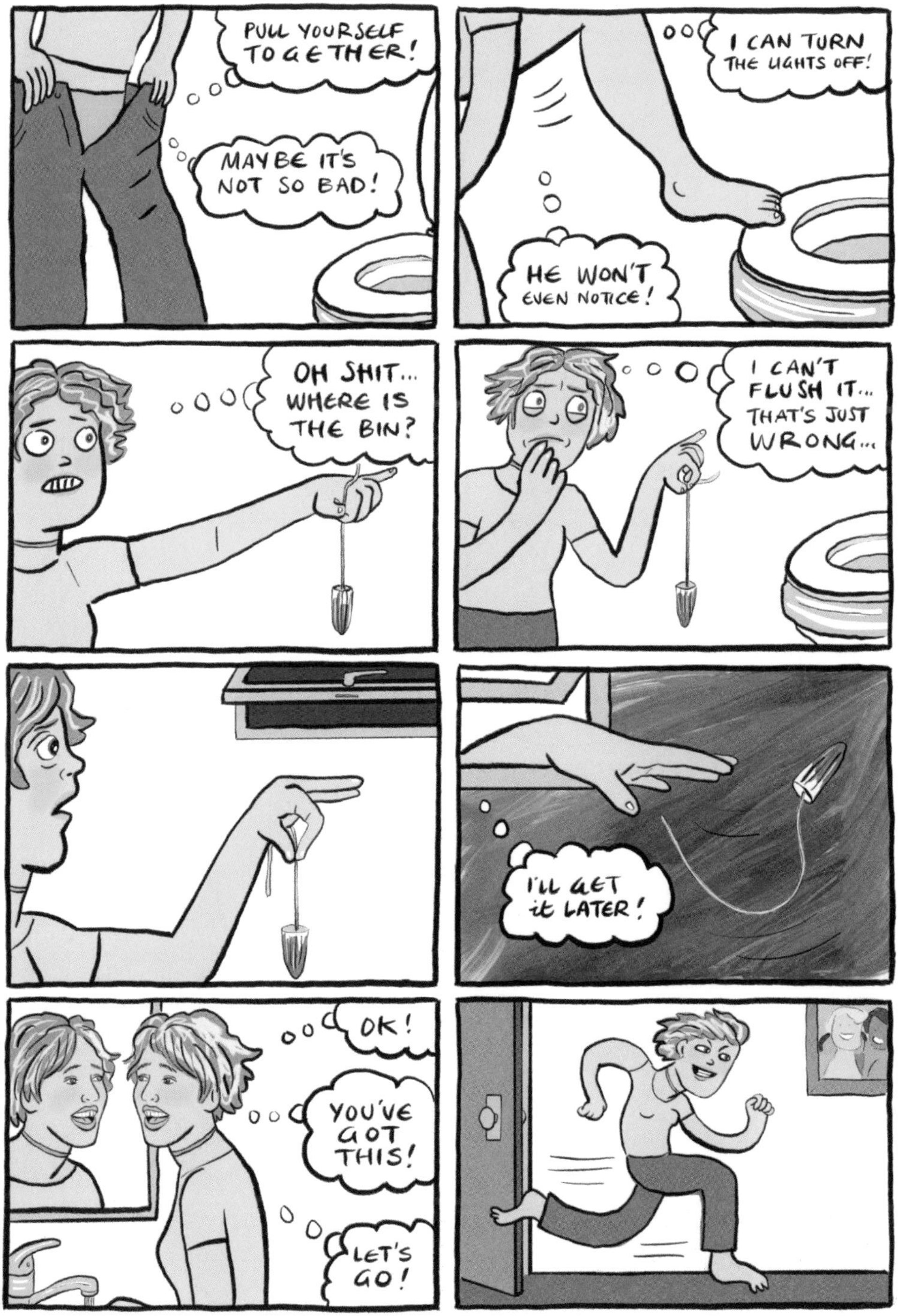
PULL YOURSELF TOGETHER!
MAYBE IT'S NOT SO BAD!
I CAN TURN THE LIGHTS OFF!
HE WON'T EVEN NOTICE!
OH SHIT... WHERE IS THE BIN?
I CAN'T FLUSH IT... THAT'S JUST WRONG...
I'LL GET it LATER!
OK!
YOU'VE GOT THIS!
LET'S GO!

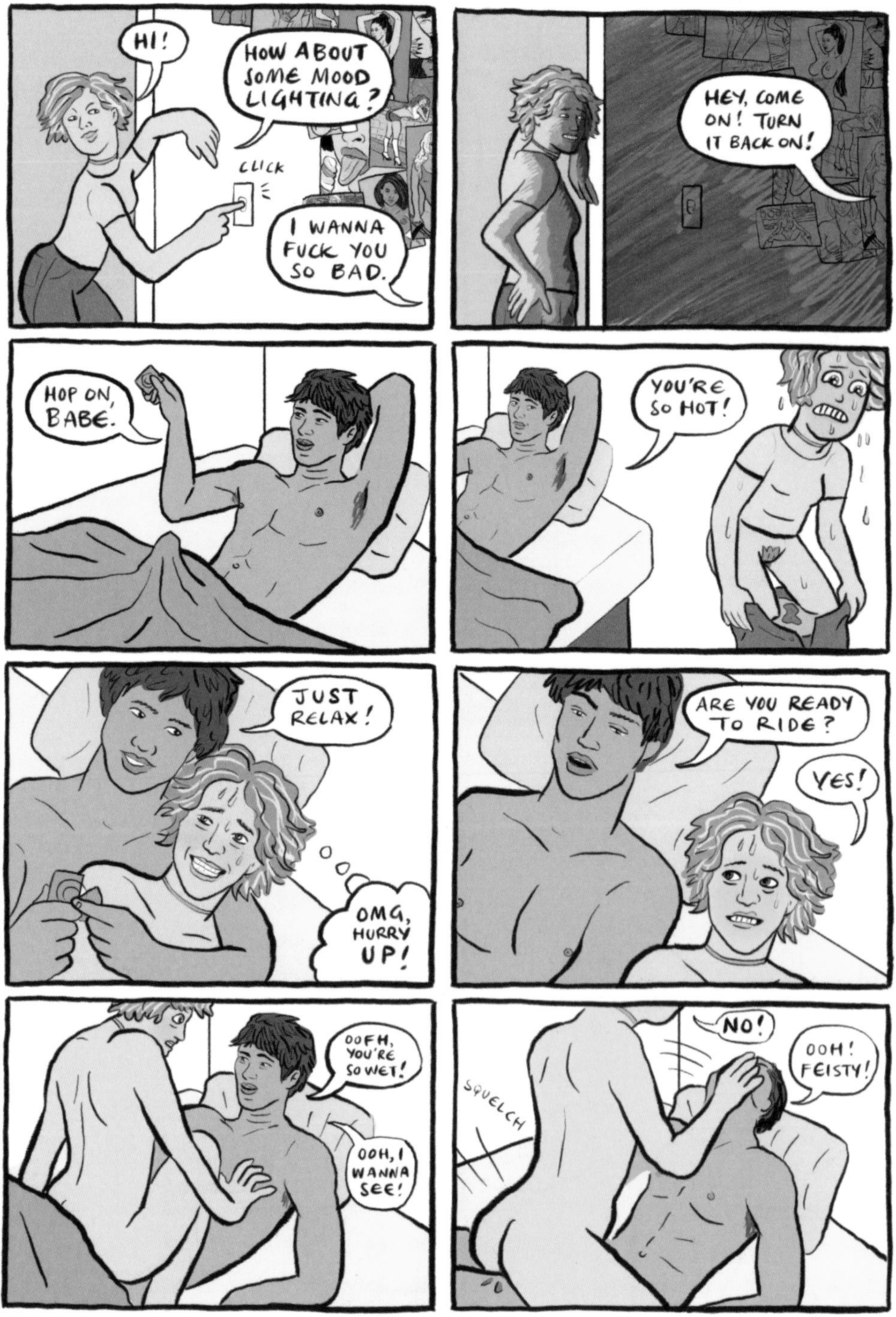
HI!
HOW ABOUT SOME MOOD LIGHTING?
CLICK
I WANNA FUCK YOU SO BAD.
HEY, COME ON! TURN IT BACK ON!
HOP ON, BABE.
YOU'RE SO HOT!
JUST RELAX!
OMG, HURRY UP!
ARE YOU READY TO RIDE?
YES!
OOFH, YOU'RE SO WET!
OOH, I WANNA SEE!
SQUELCH
NO!
OOH! FEISTY!

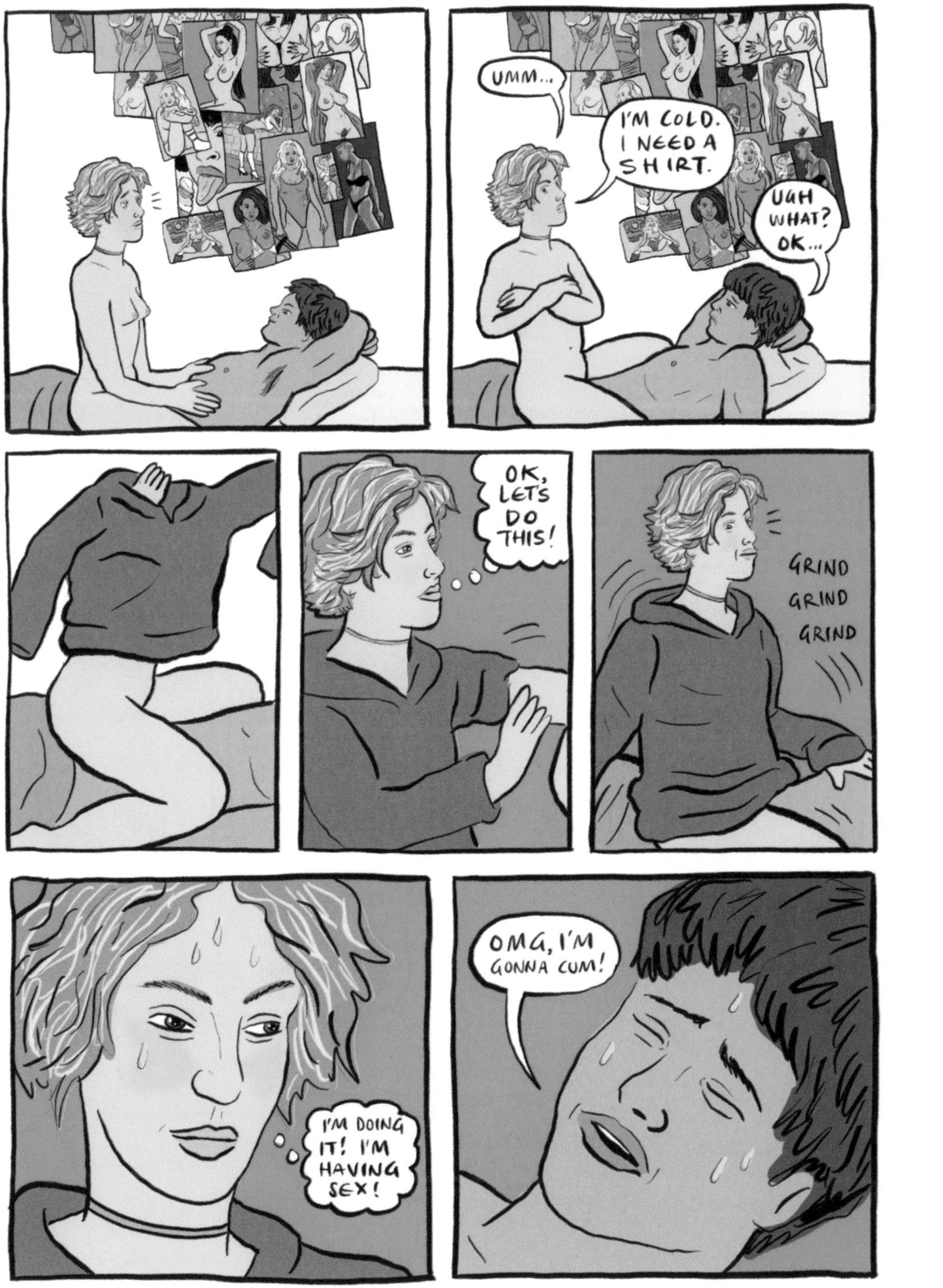
UMM...
I'M COLD. I NEED A SHIRT.
UGH WHAT? OK...
OK, LET'S DO THIS!
GRIND GRIND GRIND
I'M DOING IT! I'M HAVING SEX!
OMG, I'M GONNA CUM!

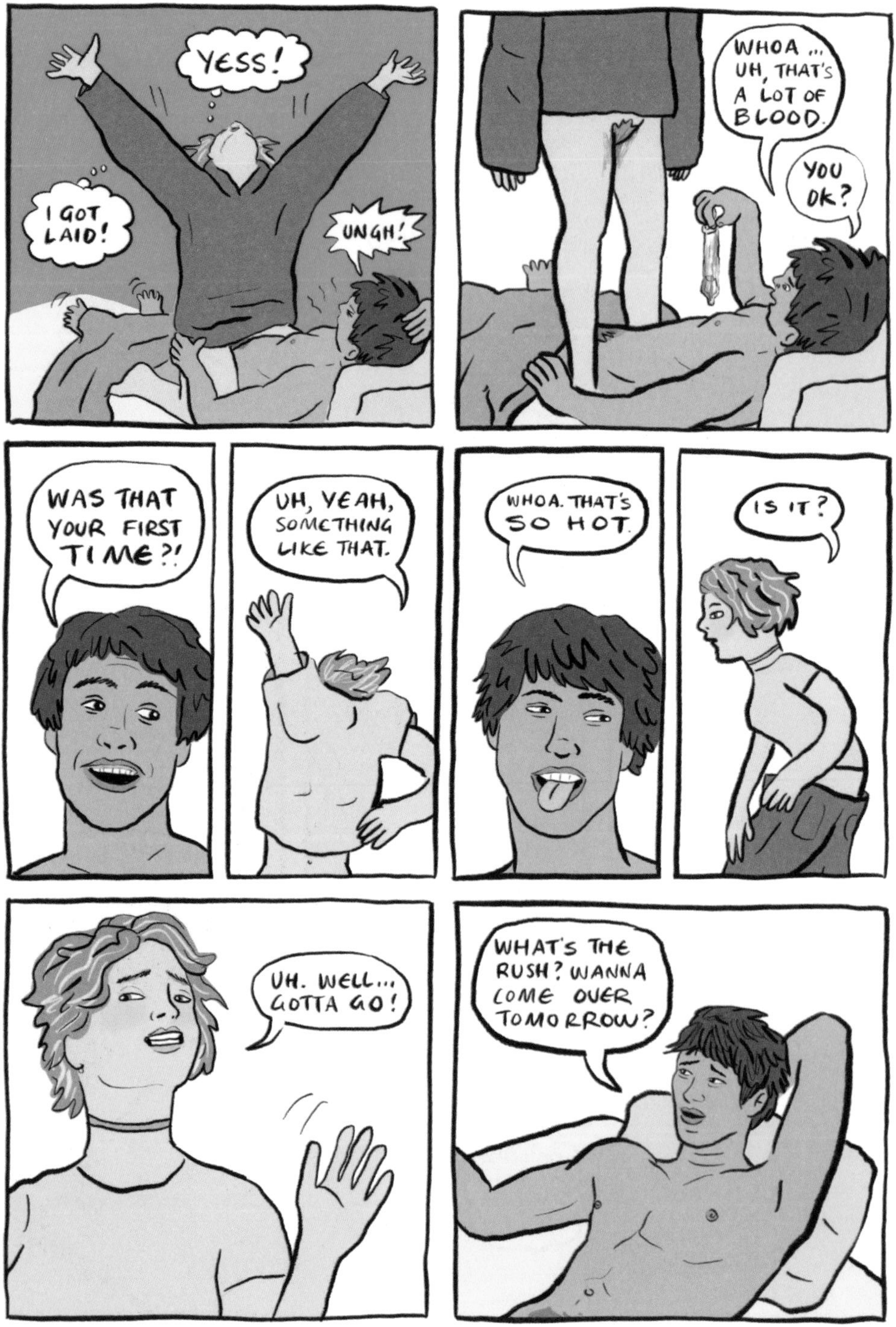
YESS!
I GOT LAID!
UNGH!
WHOA ... UH, THAT'S A LOT OF BLOOD.
YOU OK?
WAS THAT YOUR FIRST TIME?!
UH, YEAH, SOMETHING LIKE THAT.
WHOA. THAT'S SO HOT.
IS IT?
UH. WELL... GOTTA GO!
WHAT'S THE RUSH? WANNA COME OVER TOMORROW?

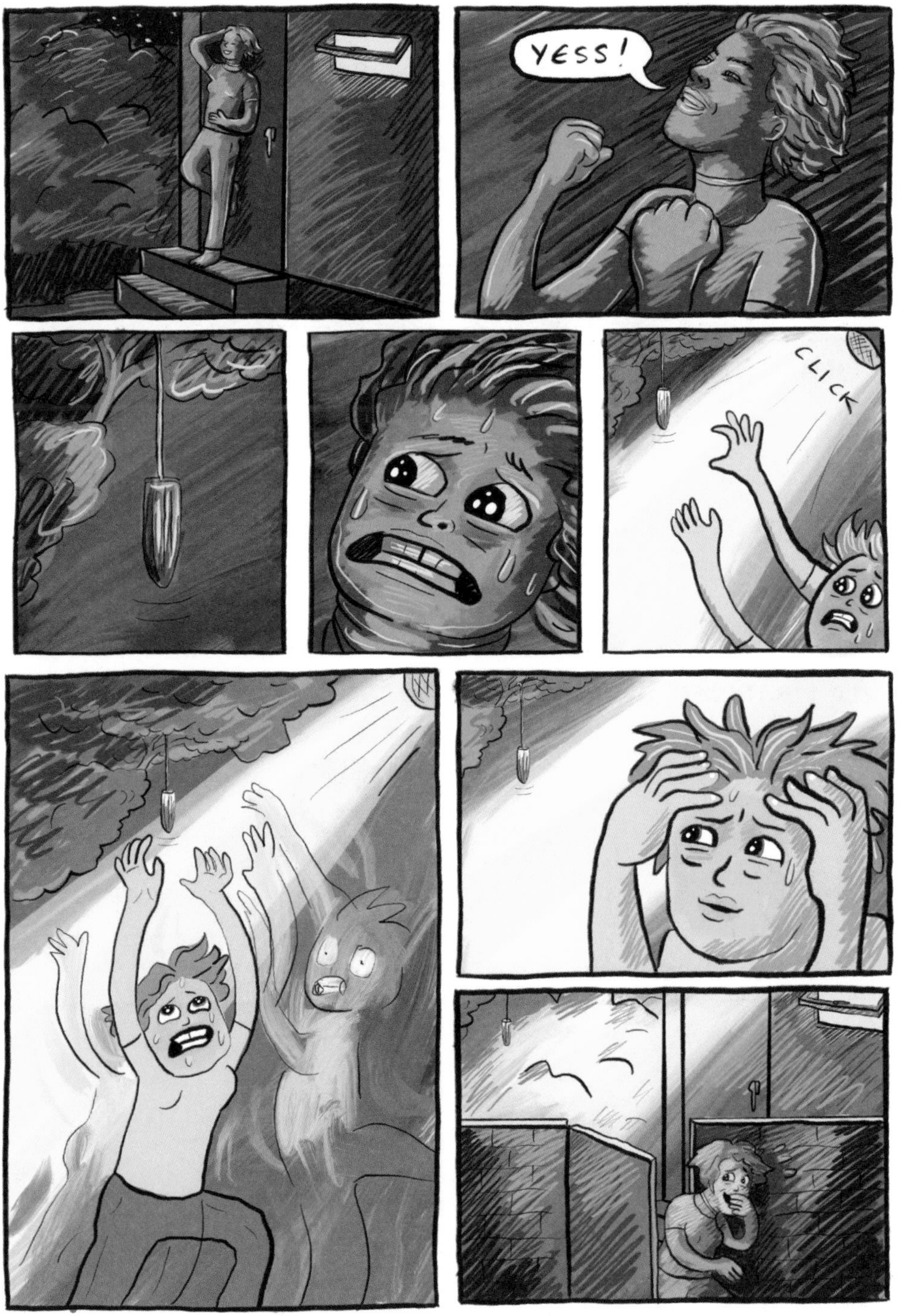
YESS!
CLICK

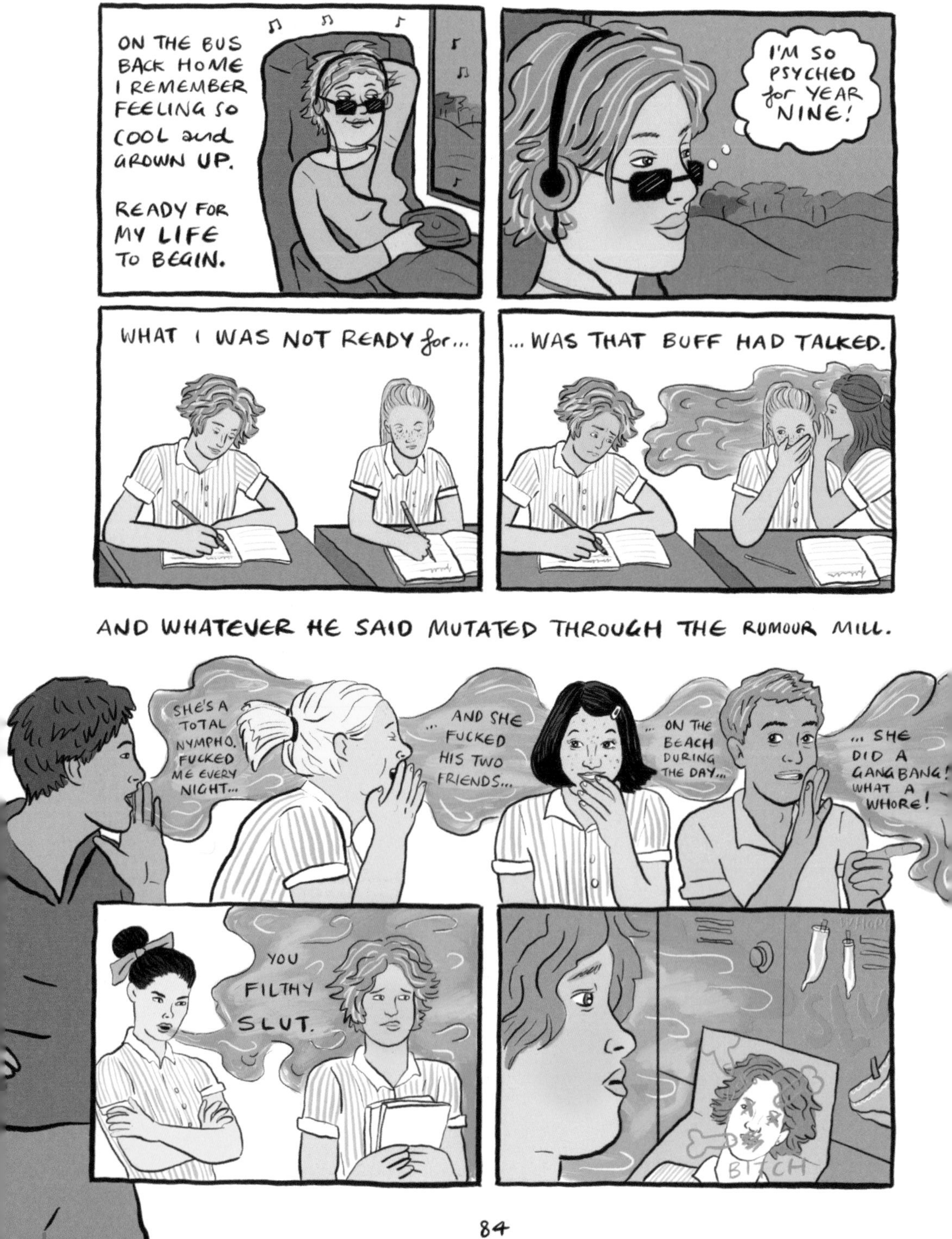
ON THE BUS BACK HOME I REMEMBER FEELING SO COOL and GROWN UP.
READY FOR MY LIFE TO BEGIN.
I'M SO PSYCHED for YEAR NINE!
WHAT I WAS NOT READY for...
...WAS THAT BUFF HAD TALKED.
AND WHATEVER HE SAID MUTATED THROUGH THE RUMOUR MILL.
SHE'S A TOTAL NYMPHO. FUCKED ME EVERY NIGHT...
... AND SHE FUCKED HIS TWO FRIENDS...
... ON THE BEACH DURING THE DAY...
... SHE DID A GANGBANG! WHAT A WHORE!
YOU FILTHY SLUT.
BITCH

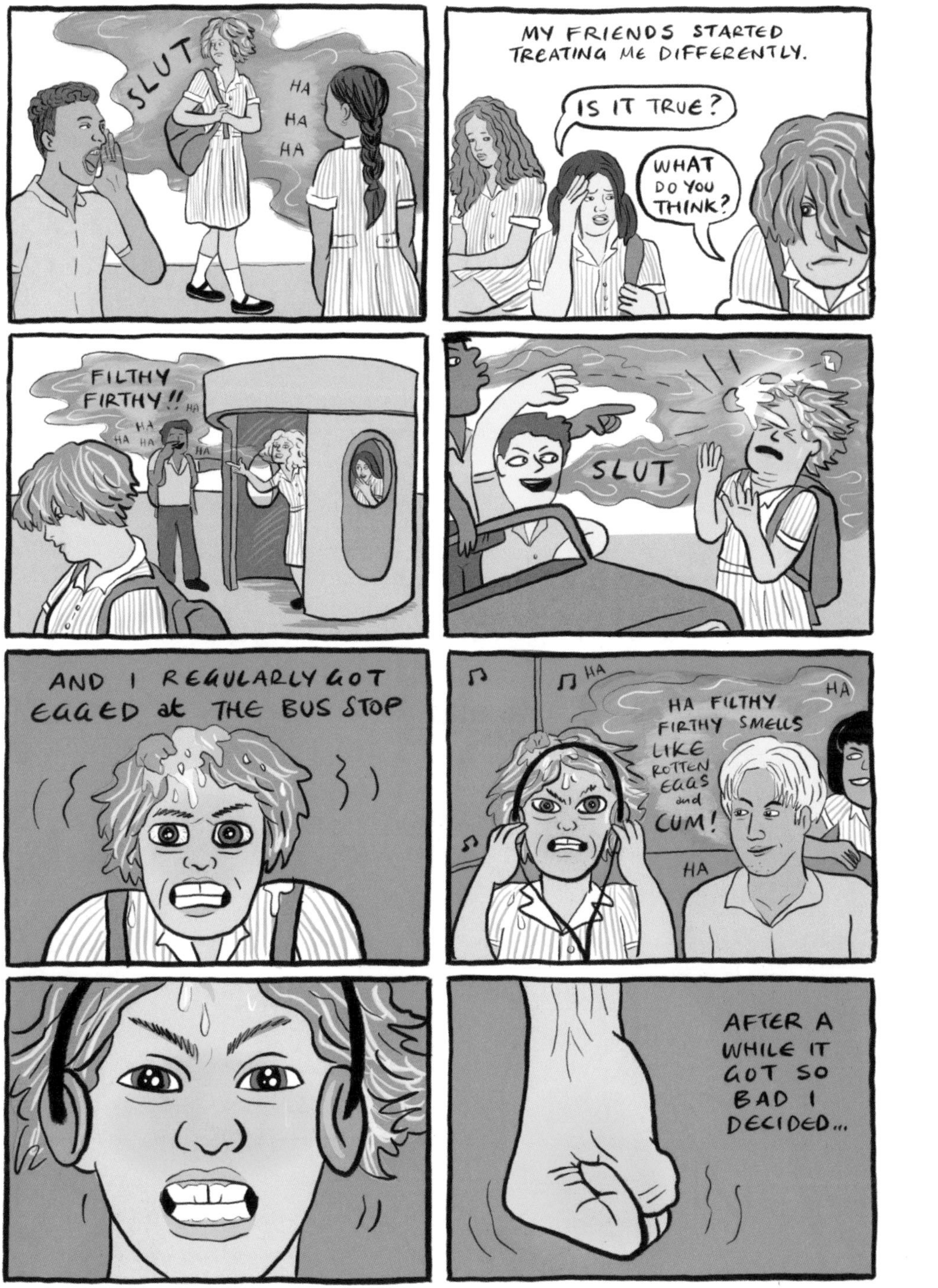
SLUT
HA HA HA
MY FRIENDS STARTED TREATING ME DIFFERENTLY.
IS IT TRUE?
WHAT DO YOU THINK?
FILTHY FIRTHY!! HA
HA HA HA HA
SLUT
AND I REGULARLY GOT EGGED at THE BUS STOP
HA
HA FILTHY FIRTHY SMELLS LIKE ROTTEN EGGS and CUM!
HA
HA
AFTER A WHILE IT GOT SO BAD I DECIDED...

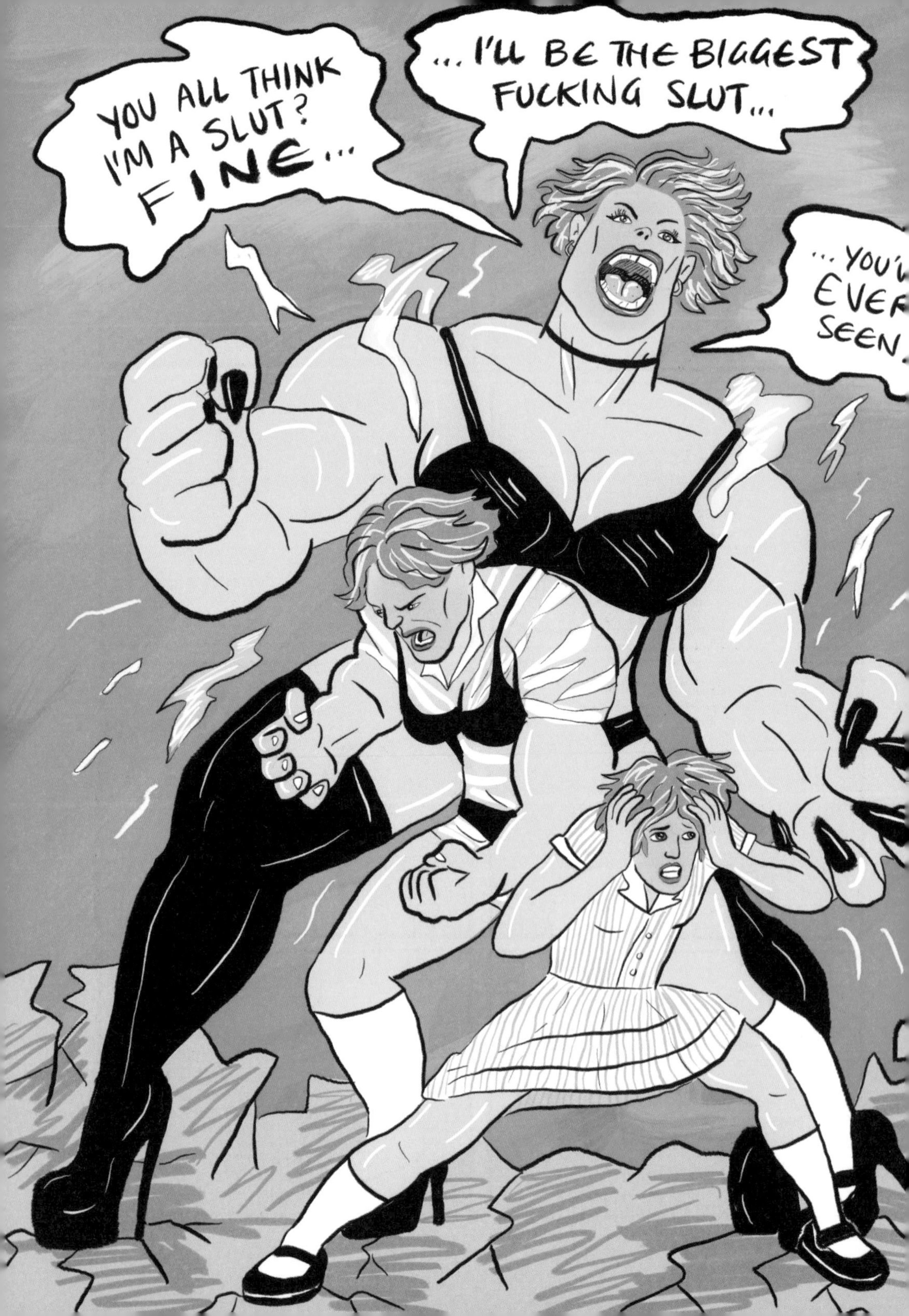
YOU ALL THINK I'M A SLUT? FINE...
...I'LL BE THE BIGGEST FUCKING SLUT...
...YOU'... EVER... SEEN...

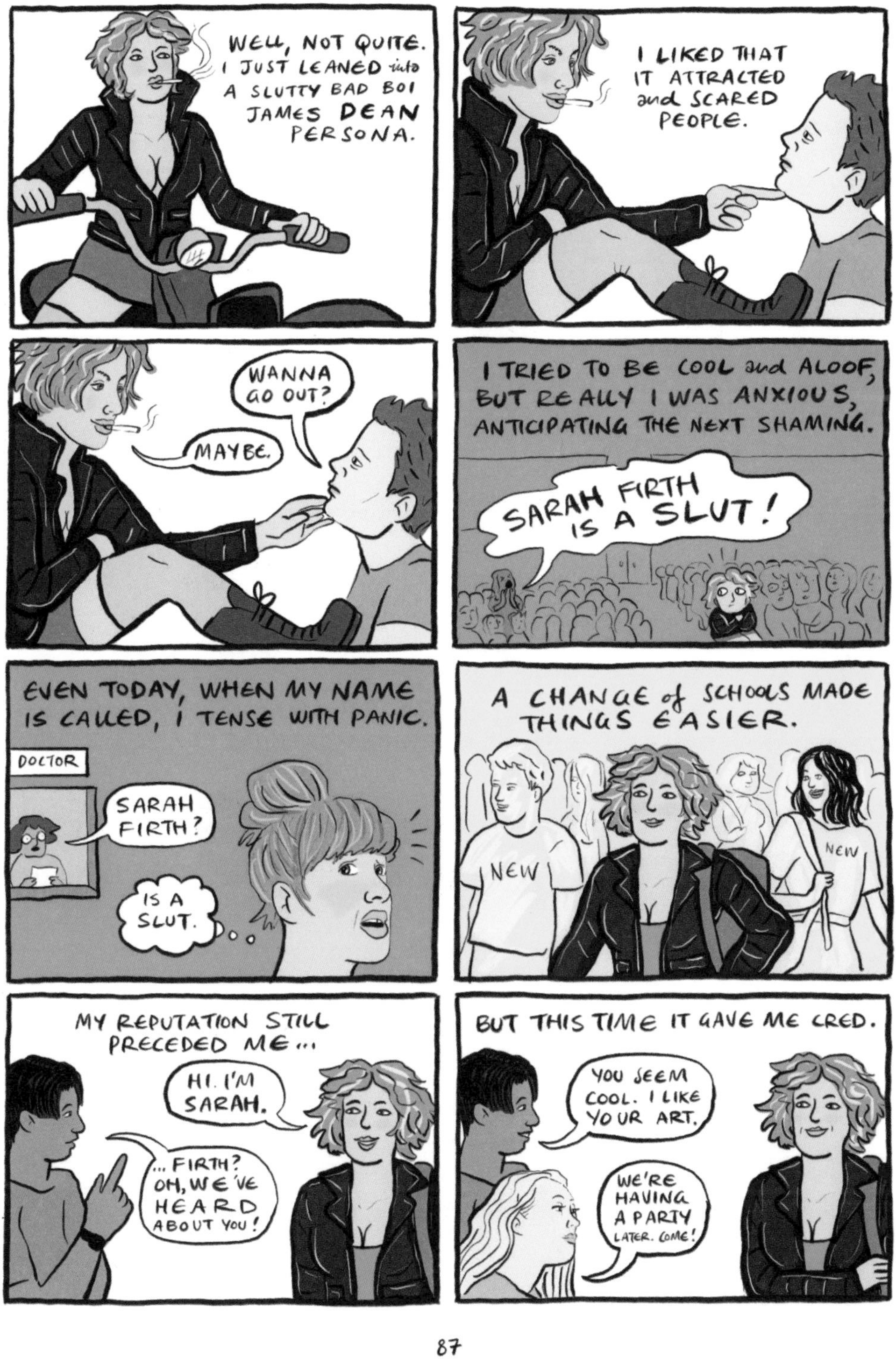
WELL, NOT QUITE. I JUST LEANED into A SLUTTY BAD BOI JAMES DEAN PERSONA.
I LIKED THAT IT ATTRACTED and SCARED PEOPLE.
WANNA GO OUT?
MAYBE.
I TRIED TO BE COOL and ALOOF, BUT REALLY I WAS ANXIOUS, ANTICIPATING THE NEXT SHAMING.
SARAH FIRTH IS A SLUT!
EVEN TODAY, WHEN MY NAME IS CALLED, I TENSE WITH PANIC.
DOCTOR
SARAH FIRTH?
IS A SLUT.
A CHANGE of SCHOOLS MADE THINGS EASIER.
NEW
NEW
MY REPUTATION STILL PRECEDED ME...
HI. I'M SARAH.
...FIRTH? OH, WE'VE HEARD ABOUT YOU!
BUT THIS TIME IT GAVE ME CRED.
YOU SEEM COOL. I LIKE YOUR ART.
WE'RE HAVING A PARTY LATER. COME!

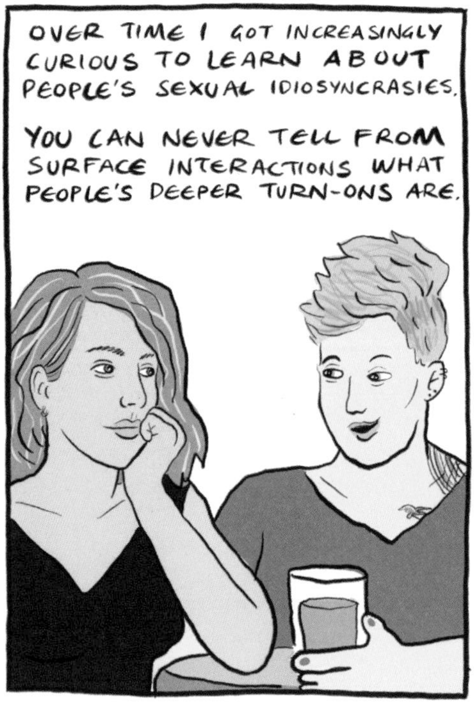
OVER TIME I GOT INCREASINGLY CURIOUS TO LEARN ABOUT PEOPLE'S SEXUAL IDIOSYNCRASIES.
YOU CAN NEVER TELL FROM SURFACE INTERACTIONS WHAT PEOPLE'S DEEPER TURN-ONS ARE.

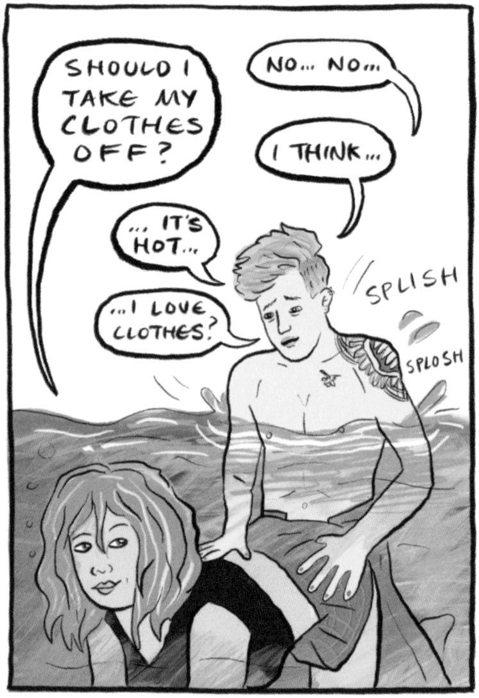
SHOULD I TAKE MY CLOTHES OFF?
NO... NO...
I THINK...
... IT'S HOT...
...I LOVE CLOTHES?
SPLISH
SPLOSH

I WANTED TO GO and EXPLORE HIDDEN LIBIDINAL REALMS. AND LEARN ABOUT WHAT THESE EVER-MORPHING SPACES HOLD.

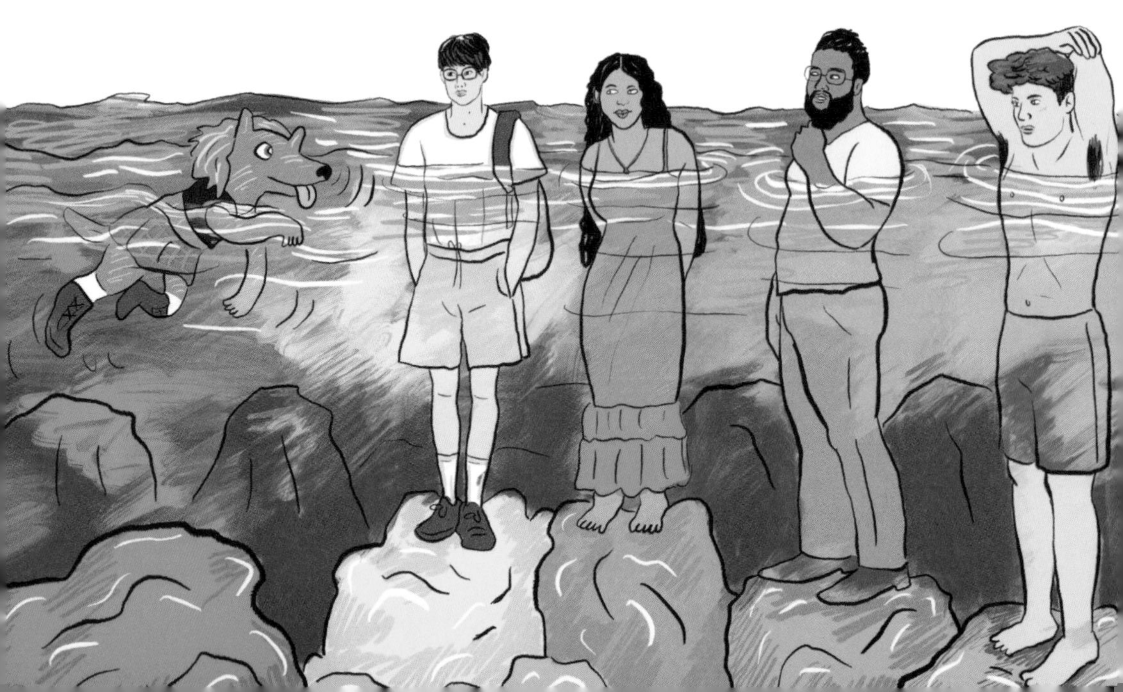

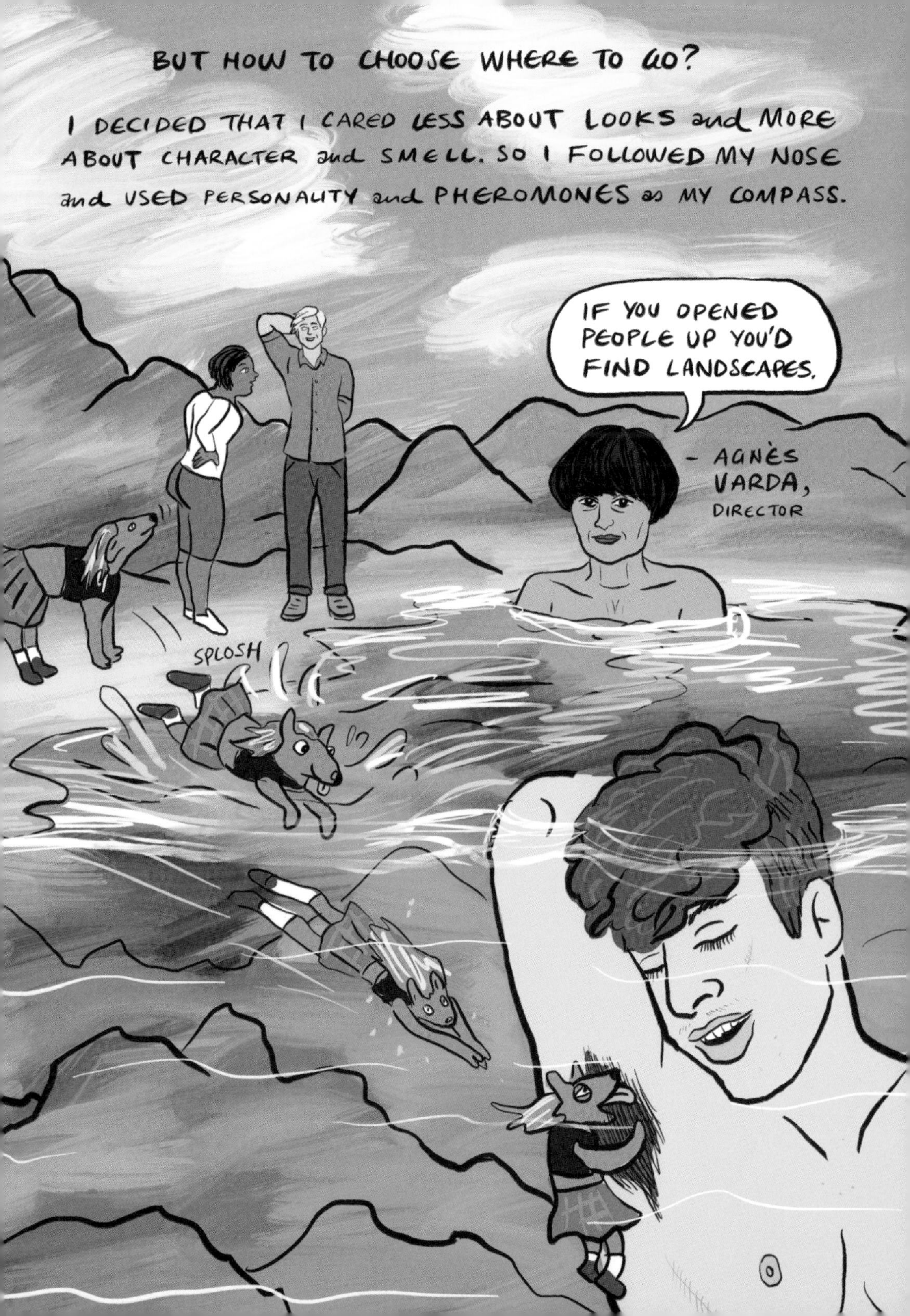
BUT HOW TO CHOOSE WHERE TO GO?
I DECIDED THAT I CARED LESS ABOUT LOOKS and MORE ABOUT CHARACTER and SMELL. SO I FOLLOWED MY NOSE and USED PERSONALITY and PHEROMONES as MY COMPASS.
IF YOU OPENED PEOPLE UP YOU'D FIND LANDSCAPES.
- AGNÈS VARDA, DIRECTOR
SPLOSH

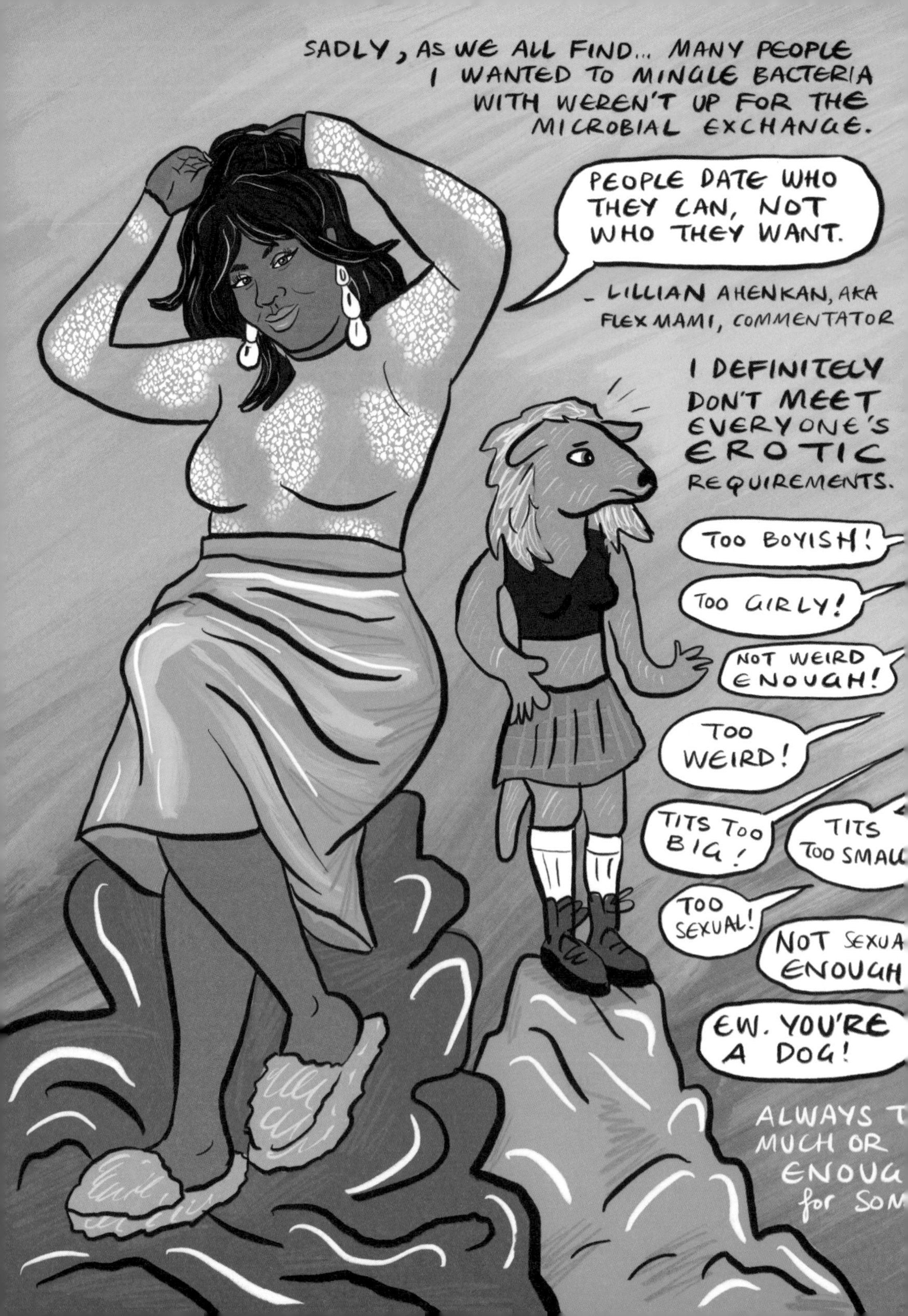
SADLY, AS WE ALL FIND... MANY PEOPLE I WANTED TO MINGLE BACTERIA WITH WEREN'T UP FOR THE MICROBIAL EXCHANGE.
PEOPLE DATE WHO THEY CAN, NOT WHO THEY WANT.
- LILLIAN AHENKAN, AKA FLEX MAMI, COMMENTATOR
I DEFINITELY DON'T MEET EVERYONE'S EROTIC REQUIREMENTS.
TOO BOYISH!
TOO GIRLY!
NOT WEIRD ENOUGH!
TOO WEIRD!
TITS TOO BIG!
TITS TOO SMAL
TOO SEXUAL!
NOT SEXUA ENOUGH
EW. YOU'RE A DOG!
ALWAYS T MUCH OR ENOUG for SOM

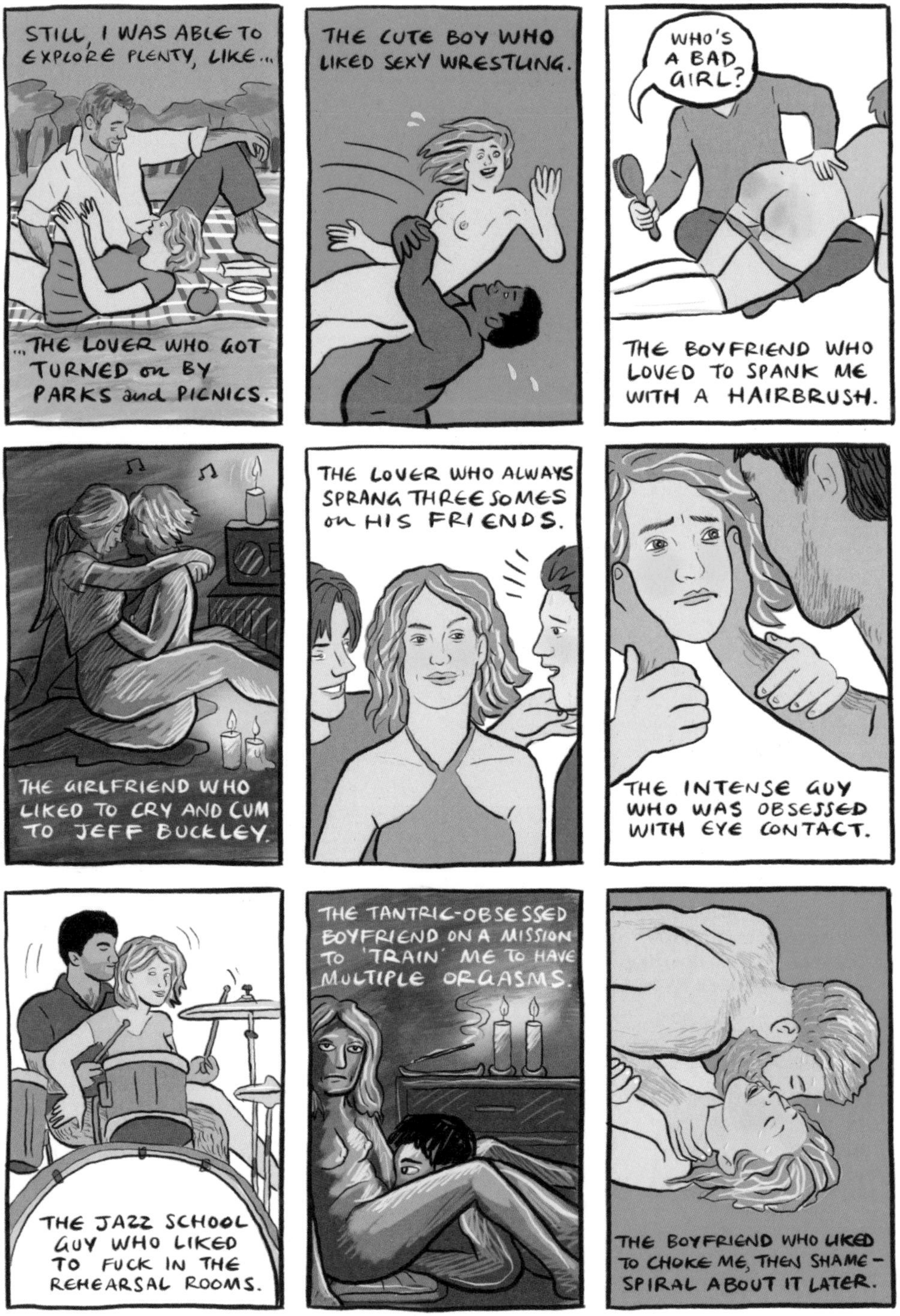
STILL, I WAS ABLE TO EXPLORE PLENTY, LIKE...
...THE LOVER WHO GOT TURNED ON BY PARKS AND PICNICS.
THE CUTE BOY WHO LIKED SEXY WRESTLING.
WHO'S A BAD GIRL?
THE BOYFRIEND WHO LOVED TO SPANK ME WITH A HAIRBRUSH.
THE GIRLFRIEND WHO LIKED TO CRY AND CUM TO JEFF BUCKLEY.
THE LOVER WHO ALWAYS SPRANG THREESOMES ON HIS FRIENDS.
THE INTENSE GUY WHO WAS OBSESSED WITH EYE CONTACT.
THE JAZZ SCHOOL GUY WHO LIKED TO FUCK IN THE REHEARSAL ROOMS.
THE TANTRIC-OBSESSED BOYFRIEND ON A MISSION TO 'TRAIN' ME TO HAVE MULTIPLE ORGASMS.
THE BOYFRIEND WHO LIKED TO CHOKE ME, THEN SHAME-SPIRAL ABOUT IT LATER.

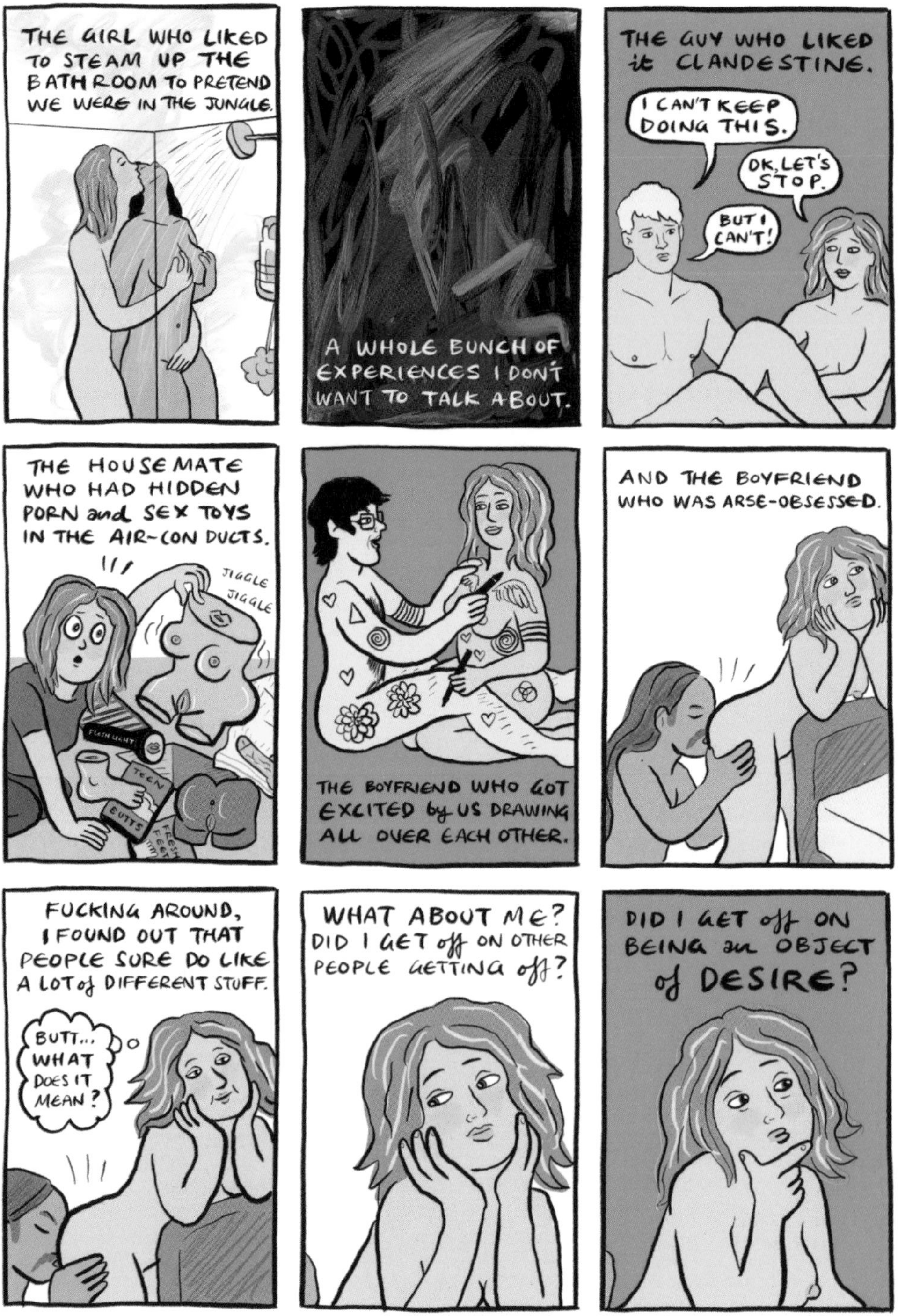
THE GIRL WHO LIKED TO STEAM UP THE BATHROOM TO PRETEND WE WERE IN THE JUNGLE.
A WHOLE BUNCH OF EXPERIENCES I DON'T WANT TO TALK ABOUT.
THE GUY WHO LIKED it CLANDESTINE.
I CAN'T KEEP DOING THIS.
OK, LET'S STOP.
BUT I CAN'T!
THE HOUSEMATE WHO HAD HIDDEN PORN and SEX TOYS IN THE AIR-CON DUCTS.
JIGGLE JIGGLE
FLESHLIGHT
TEEN
BUTTS
FRESH FEET
THE BOYFRIEND WHO GOT EXCITED by US DRAWING ALL OVER EACH OTHER.
AND THE BOYFRIEND WHO WAS ARSE-OBSESSED.
FUCKING AROUND, I FOUND OUT THAT PEOPLE SURE DO LIKE A LOT of DIFFERENT STUFF.
BUTT... WHAT DOES IT MEAN?
WHAT ABOUT ME? DID I GET off ON OTHER PEOPLE GETTING off?
DID I GET off ON BEING an OBJECT of DESIRE?

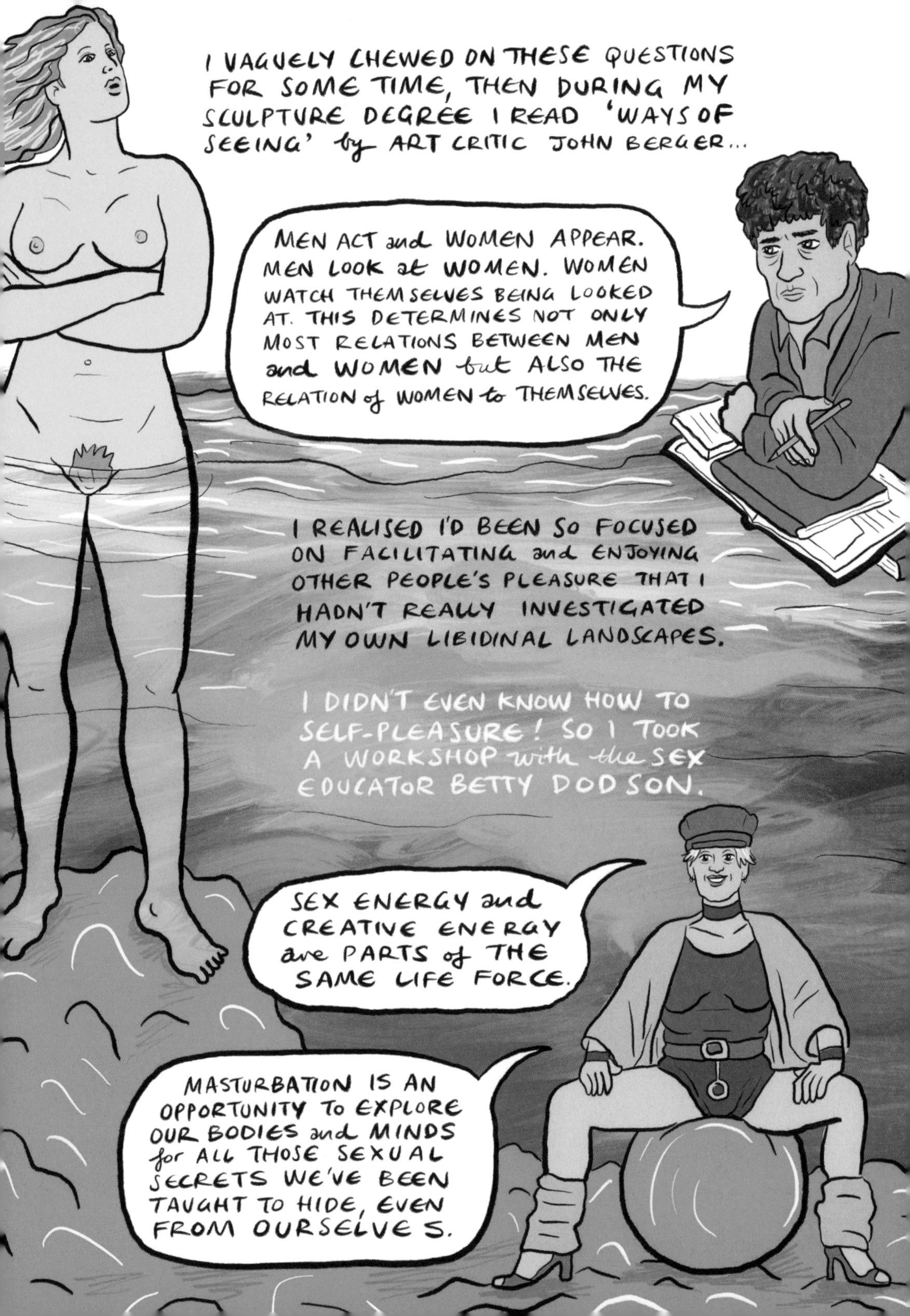
I VAGUELY CHEWED ON THESE QUESTIONS FOR SOME TIME, THEN DURING MY SCULPTURE DEGREE I READ 'WAYS OF SEEING' by ART CRITIC JOHN BERGER...
MEN ACT and WOMEN APPEAR. MEN LOOK at WOMEN. WOMEN WATCH THEMSELVES BEING LOOKED AT. THIS DETERMINES NOT ONLY MOST RELATIONS BETWEEN MEN and WOMEN but ALSO THE RELATION of WOMEN to THEMSELVES.
I REALISED I'D BEEN SO FOCUSED ON FACILITATING and ENJOYING OTHER PEOPLE'S PLEASURE THAT I HADN'T REALLY INVESTIGATED MY OWN LIBIDINAL LANDSCAPES.
I DIDN'T EVEN KNOW HOW TO SELF-PLEASURE! SO I TOOK A WORKSHOP with the SEX EDUCATOR BETTY DODSON.
SEX ENERGY and CREATIVE ENERGY are PARTS of THE SAME LIFE FORCE.
MASTURBATION IS AN OPPORTUNITY TO EXPLORE OUR BODIES and MINDS for ALL THOSE SEXUAL SECRETS WE'VE BEEN TAUGHT TO HIDE, EVEN FROM OURSELVES.

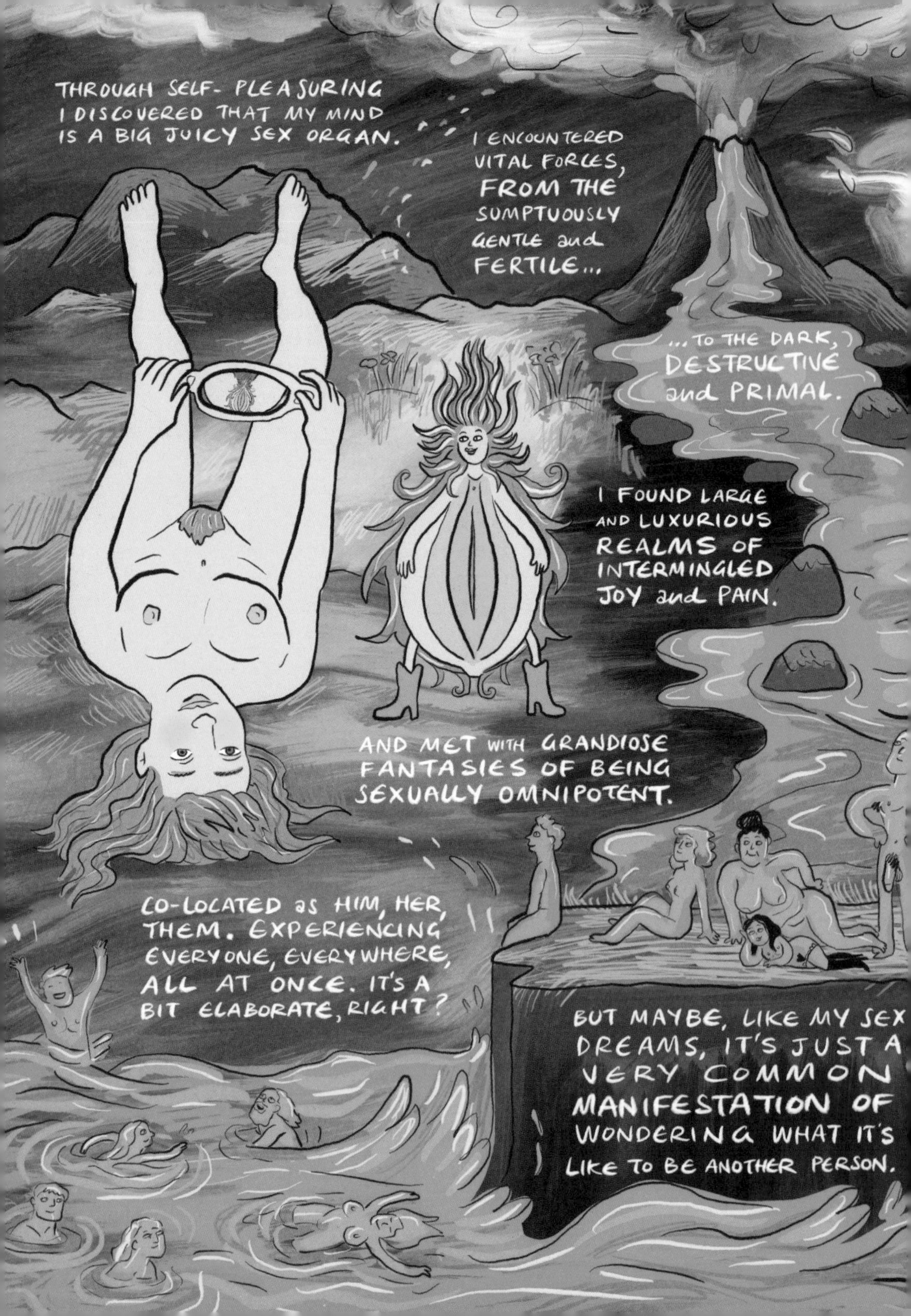
THROUGH SELF-PLEASURING I DISCOVERED THAT MY MIND IS A BIG JUICY SEX ORGAN.
I ENCOUNTERED VITAL FORCES, FROM THE SUMPTUOUSLY GENTLE and FERTILE...
...TO THE DARK, DESTRUCTIVE and PRIMAL.
I FOUND LARGE AND LUXURIOUS REALMS OF INTERMINGLED JOY and PAIN.
AND MET WITH GRANDIOSE FANTASIES OF BEING SEXUALLY OMNIPOTENT.
CO-LOCATED as HIM, HER, THEM. EXPERIENCING EVERYONE, EVERYWHERE, ALL AT ONCE. IT'S A BIT ELABORATE, RIGHT?
BUT MAYBE, LIKE MY SEX DREAMS, IT'S JUST A VERY COMMON MANIFESTATION OF WONDERING WHAT IT'S LIKE TO BE ANOTHER PERSON.

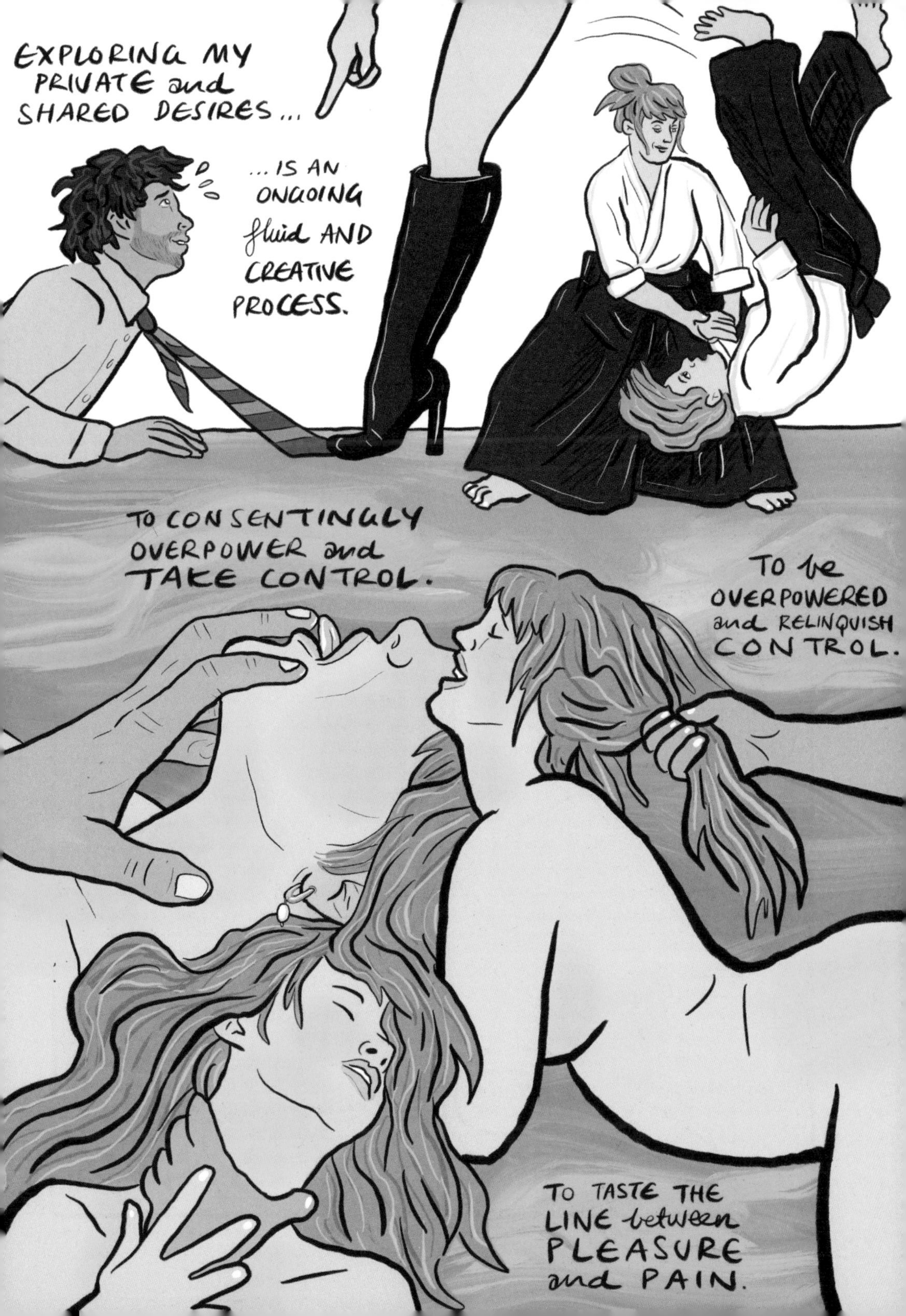
EXPLORING MY PRIVATE and SHARED DESIRES...
...IS AN ONGOING fluid AND CREATIVE PROCESS.
TO CONSENTINGLY OVERPOWER and TAKE CONTROL.
To be OVERPOWERED and RELINQUISH CONTROL.
TO TASTE THE LINE between PLEASURE and PAIN.

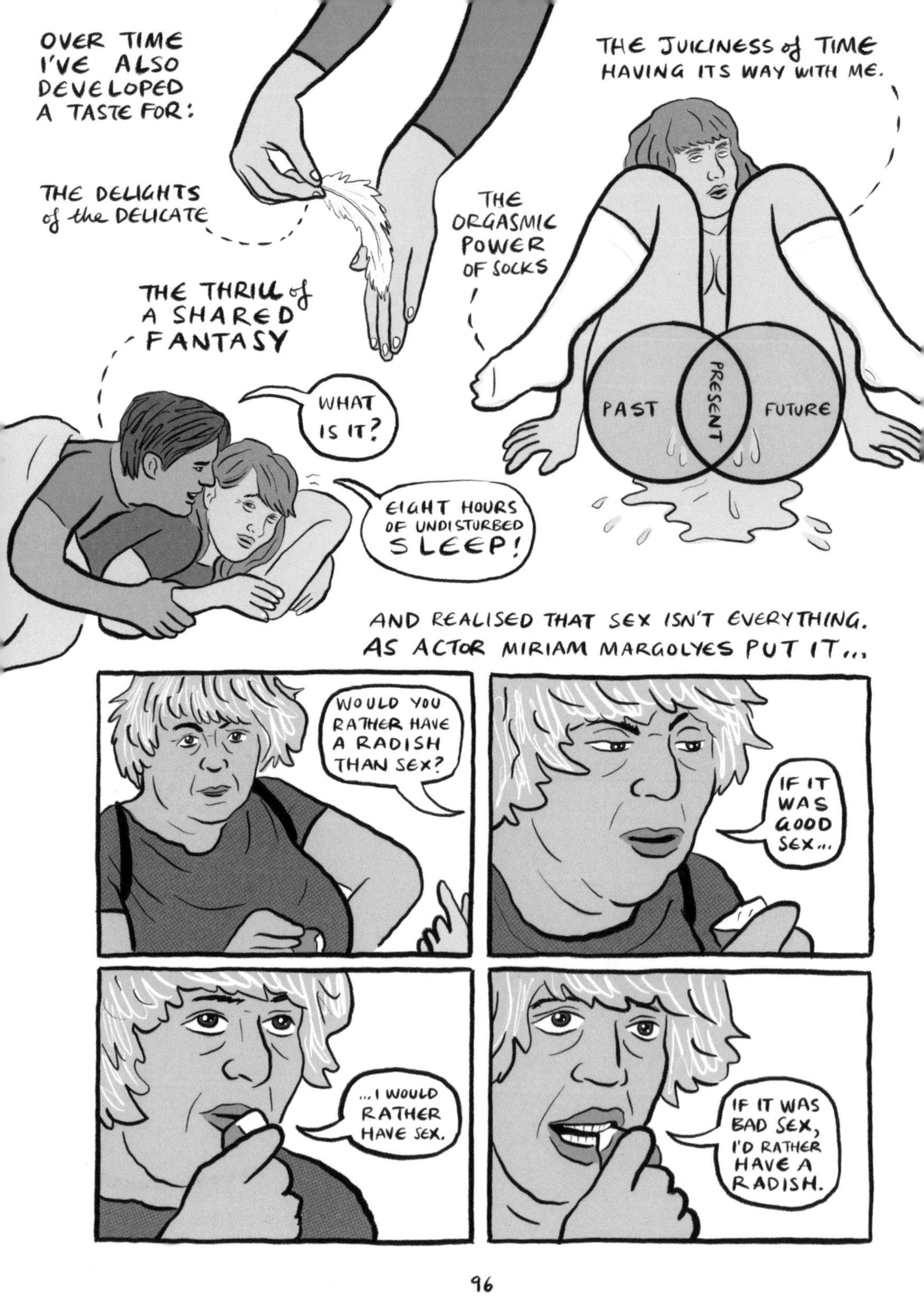
OVER TIME I'VE ALSO DEVELOPED A TASTE FOR:
THE DELIGHTS of the DELICATE
THE THRILL of A SHARED FANTASY
WHAT IS IT?
EIGHT HOURS OF UNDISTURBED SLEEP!
THE ORGASMIC POWER OF SOCKS
THE JUICINESS of TIME HAVING ITS WAY WITH ME.
PAST
PRESENT
FUTURE
AND REALISED THAT SEX ISN'T EVERYTHING.
AS ACTOR MIRIAM MARGOLYES PUT IT...
WOULD YOU RATHER HAVE A RADISH THAN SEX?
IF IT WAS GOOD SEX...
...I WOULD RATHER HAVE SEX.
IF IT WAS BAD SEX, I'D RATHER HAVE A RADISH.

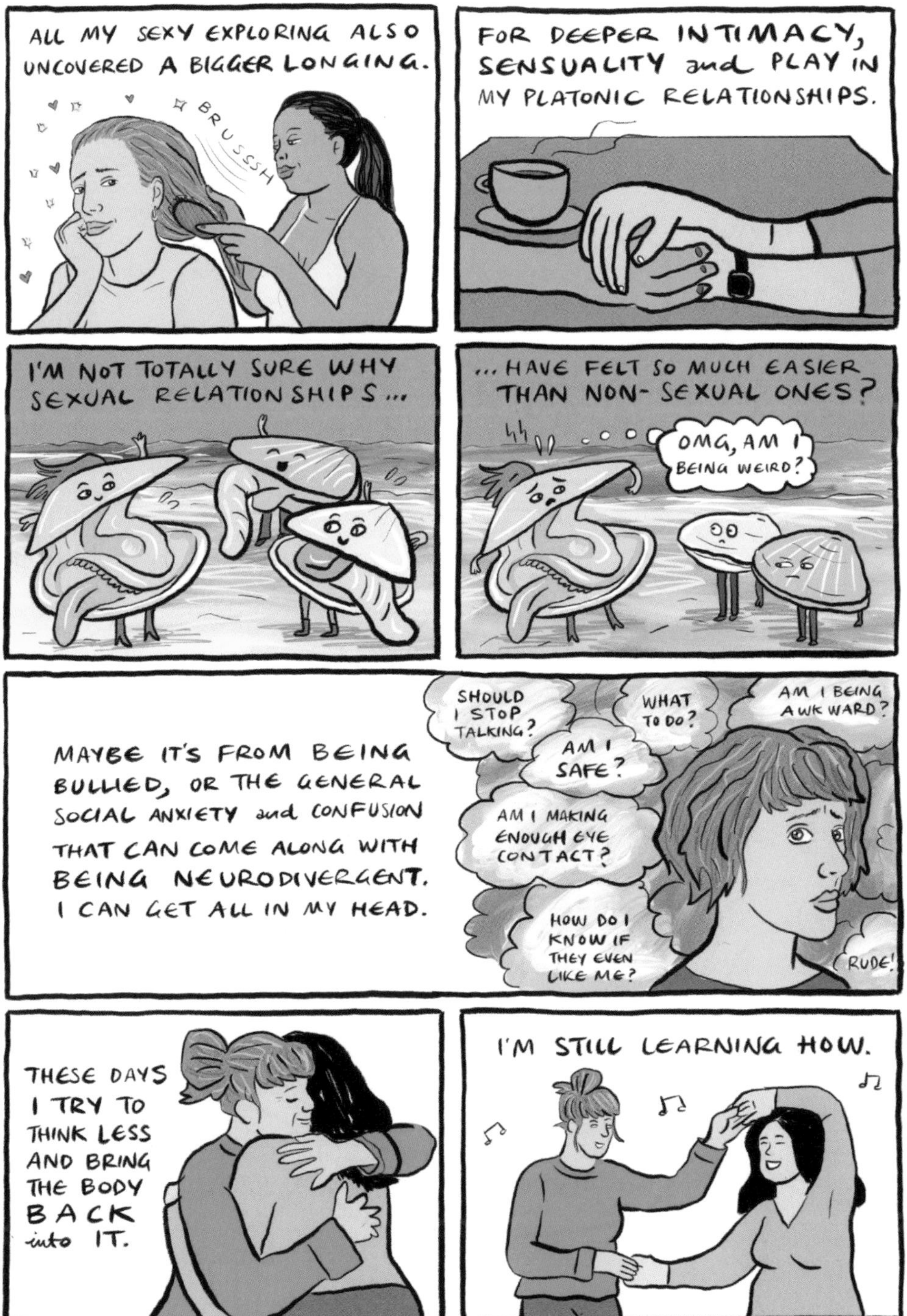
ALL MY SEXY EXPLORING ALSO UNCOVERED A BIGGER LONGING.
BRUSSSH
FOR DEEPER INTIMACY, SENSUALITY and PLAY IN MY PLATONIC RELATIONSHIPS.
I'M NOT TOTALLY SURE WHY SEXUAL RELATIONSHIPS...
...HAVE FELT SO MUCH EASIER THAN NON-SEXUAL ONES?
OMG, AM I BEING WEIRD?
MAYBE IT'S FROM BEING BULLIED, OR THE GENERAL SOCIAL ANXIETY and CONFUSION THAT CAN COME ALONG WITH BEING NEURODIVERGENT. I CAN GET ALL IN MY HEAD.
SHOULD I STOP TALKING?
WHAT TO DO?
AM I BEING AWKWARD?
AM I SAFE?
AM I MAKING ENOUGH EYE CONTACT?
HOW DO I KNOW IF THEY EVEN LIKE ME?
RUDE!
THESE DAYS I TRY TO THINK LESS AND BRING THE BODY BACK into IT.
I'M STILL LEARNING HOW.

IN EXPANDING MY SENSE of THE EROTIC and SENSUAL into THE EVERYDAY, I THINK of PHILOSOPHER GASTON BACHELARD and HIS IDEAS ABOUT THE POETIC and PSYCHIC POTENCY of OUR MUNDANE OBJECTS and SPACES.

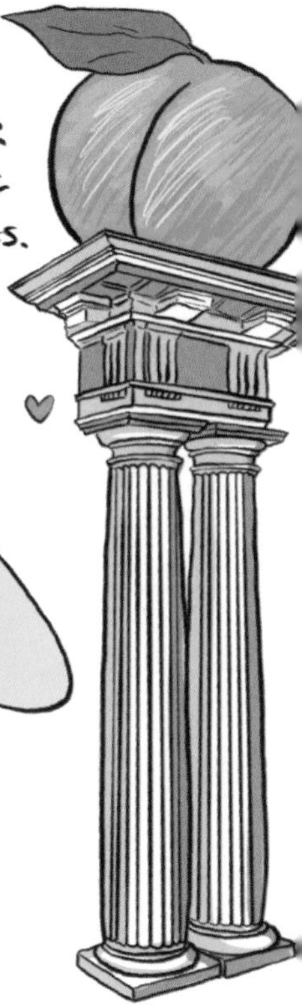

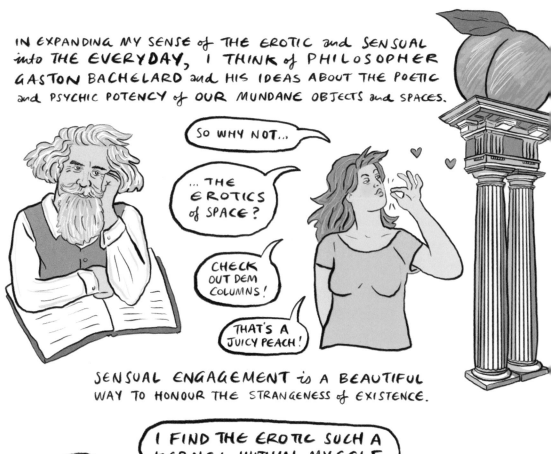

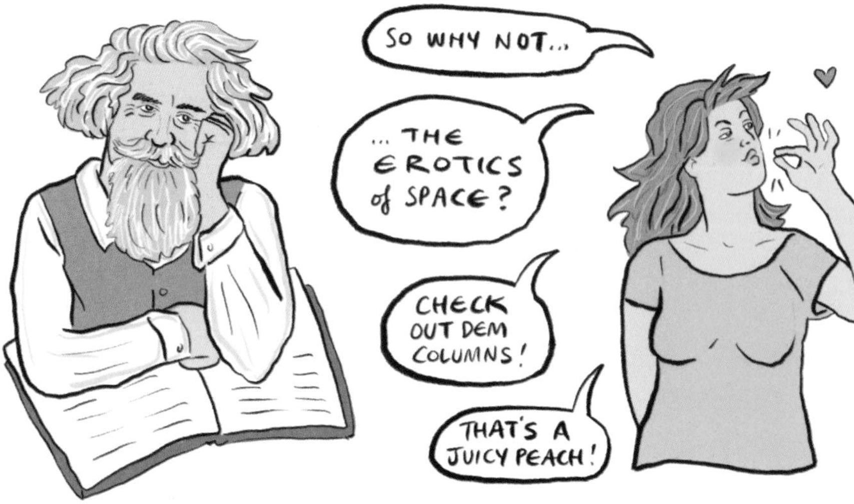
SO WHY NOT...
... THE EROTICS of SPACE?
CHECK OUT DEM COLUMNS!
THAT'S A JUICY PEACH!

SENSUAL ENGAGEMENT is A BEAUTIFUL WAY TO HONOUR THE STRANGENESS of EXISTENCE.

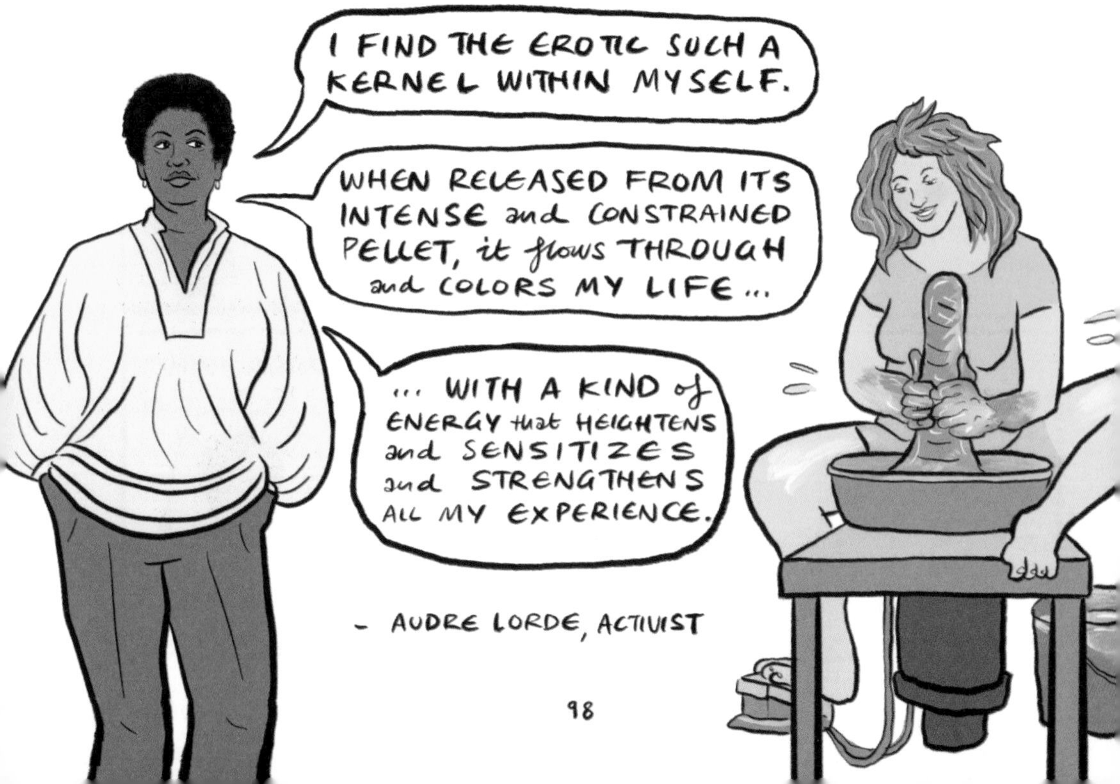
I FIND THE EROTIC SUCH A KERNEL WITHIN MYSELF.
WHEN RELEASED FROM ITS INTENSE and CONSTRAINED PELLET, it flows THROUGH and COLORS MY LIFE...
... WITH A KIND of ENERGY that HEIGHTENS and SENSITIZES and STRENGTHENS ALL MY EXPERIENCE.

– AUDRE LORDE, ACTIVIST

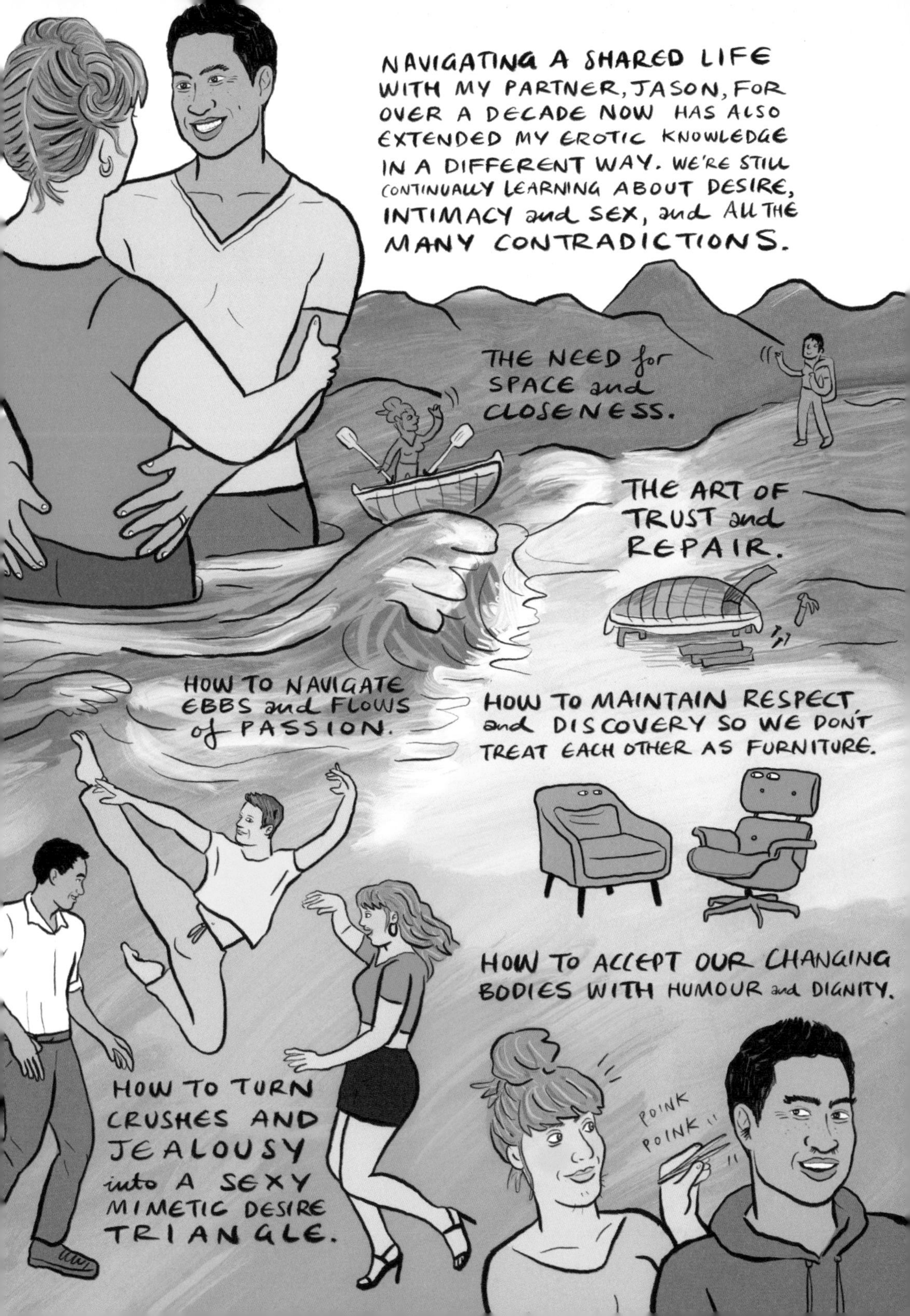
NAVIGATING A SHARED LIFE WITH MY PARTNER, JASON, FOR OVER A DECADE NOW HAS ALSO EXTENDED MY EROTIC KNOWLEDGE IN A DIFFERENT WAY. WE'RE STILL CONTINUALLY LEARNING ABOUT DESIRE, INTIMACY and SEX, and ALL THE MANY CONTRADICTIONS.
THE NEED for SPACE and CLOSENESS.
THE ART OF TRUST and REPAIR.
HOW TO NAVIGATE EBBS and FLOWS of PASSION.
HOW TO MAINTAIN RESPECT, and DISCOVERY SO WE DON'T TREAT EACH OTHER AS FURNITURE.
HOW TO ACCEPT OUR CHANGING BODIES WITH HUMOUR and DIGNITY.
HOW TO TURN CRUSHES AND JEALOUSY into A SEXY MIMETIC DESIRE TRIANGLE.
POINK POINK !!

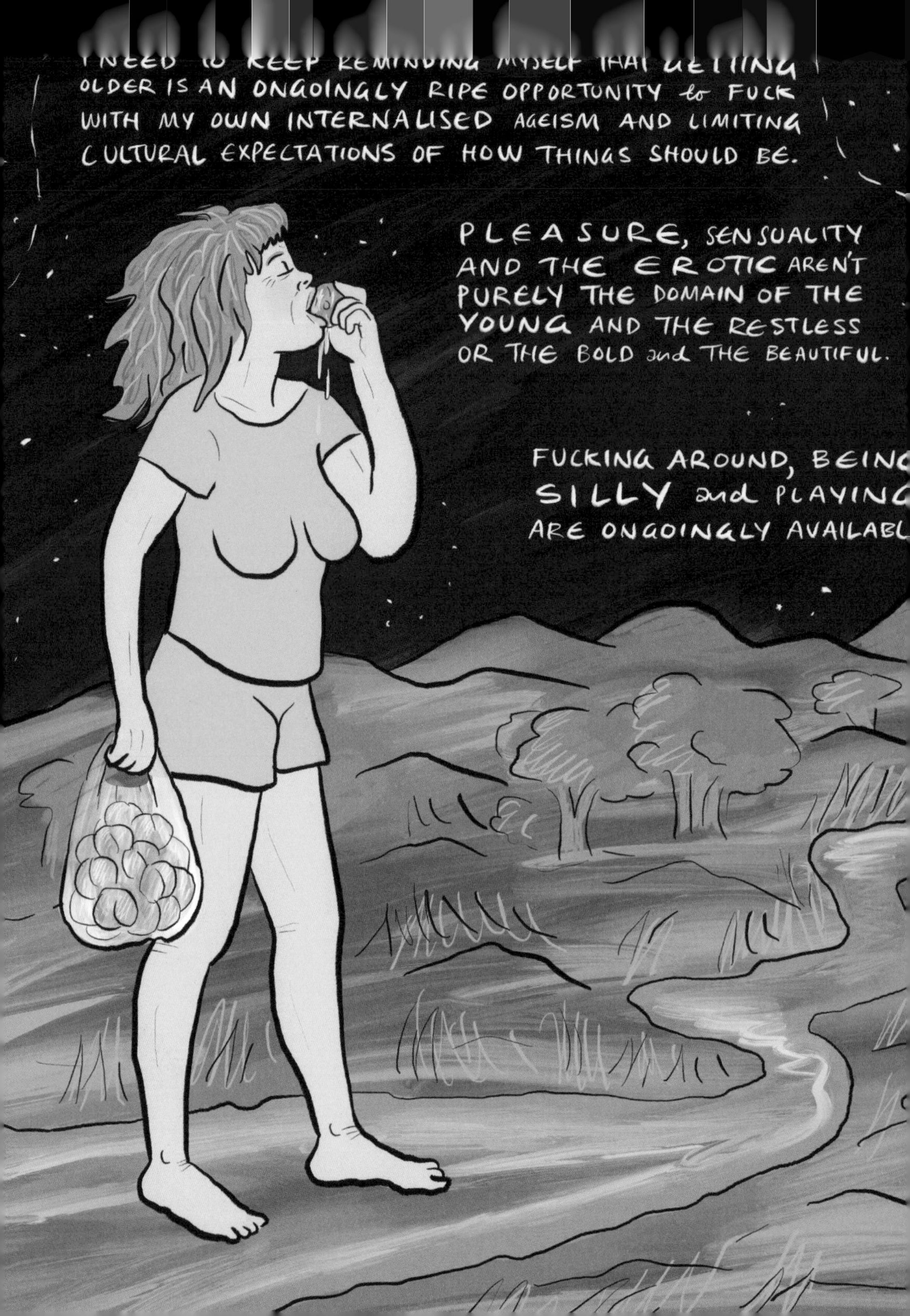
I NEED TO KEEP REMINDING MYSELF THAT GETTING OLDER IS AN ONGOINGLY RIPE OPPORTUNITY to FUCK WITH MY OWN INTERNALISED AGEISM AND LIMITING CULTURAL EXPECTATIONS OF HOW THINGS SHOULD BE.
PLEASURE, SENSUALITY AND THE EROTIC AREN'T PURELY THE DOMAIN OF THE YOUNG AND THE RESTLESS OR THE BOLD and THE BEAUTIFUL.
FUCKING AROUND, BEIN
SILLY and PLAYIN
ARE ONGOINGLY AVAILABL

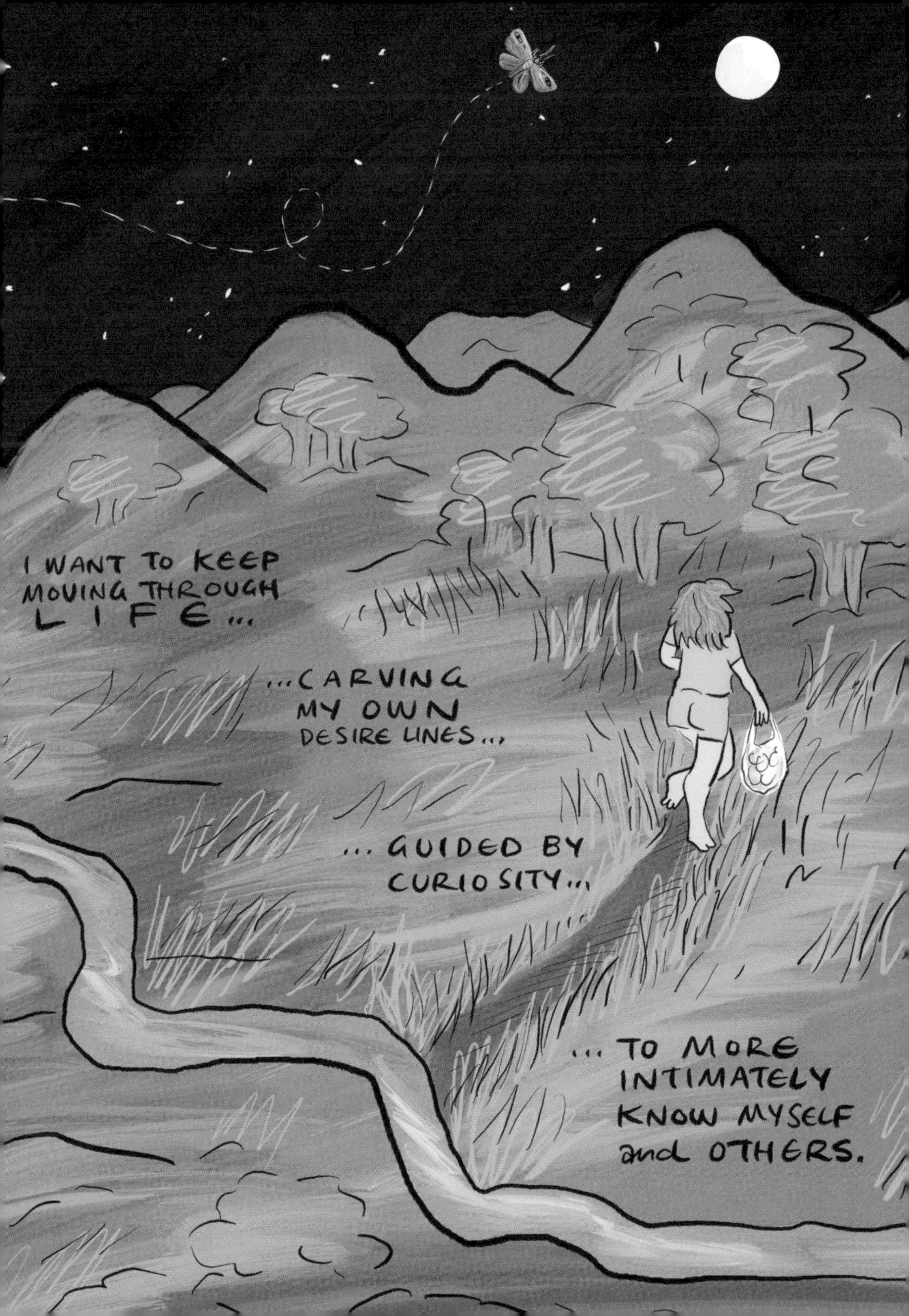
I WANT TO KEEP MOVING THROUGH LIFE...
...CARVING MY OWN DESIRE LINES...
... GUIDED BY CURIOSITY...
... TO MORE INTIMATELY KNOW MYSELF and OTHERS.

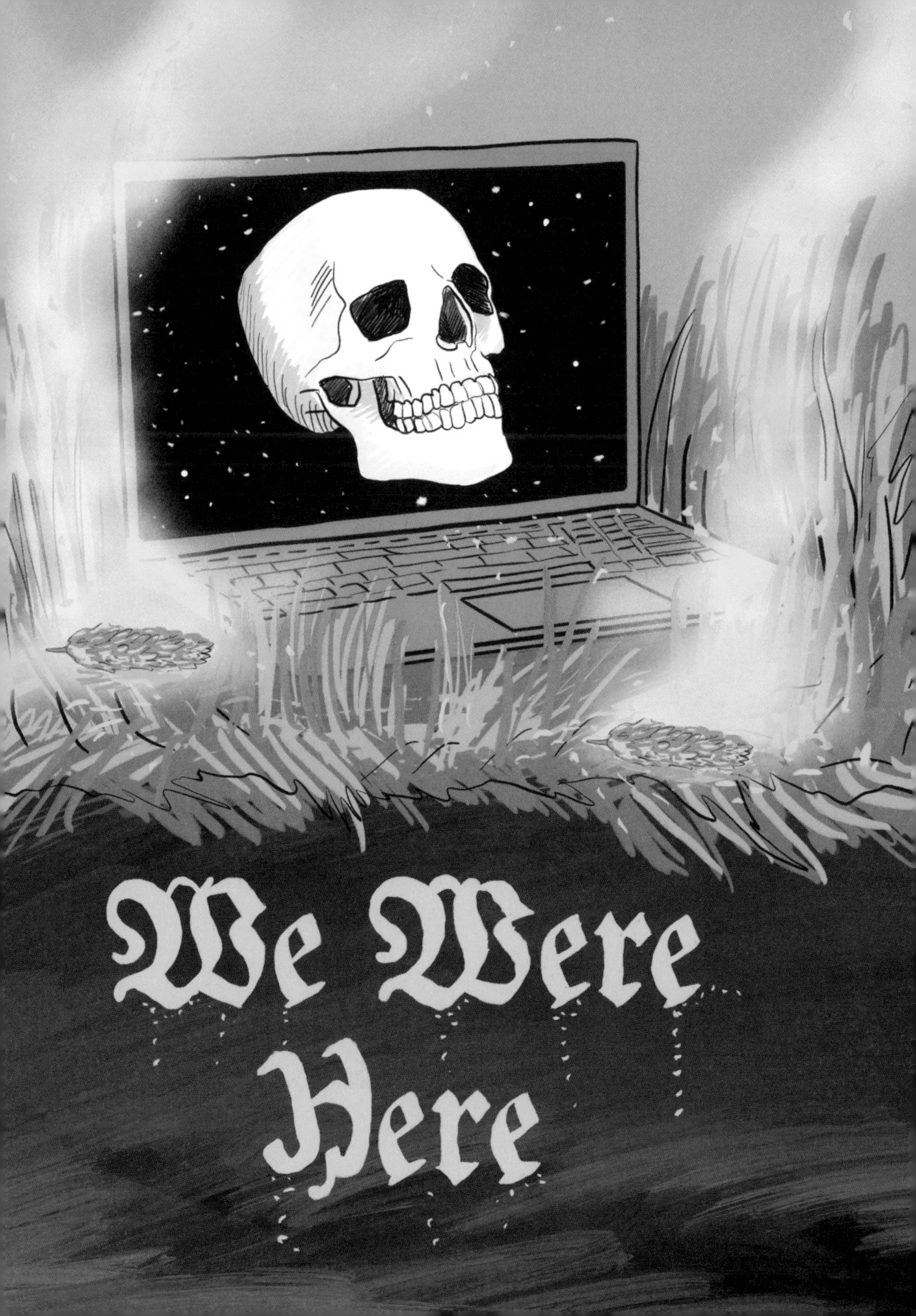
We Were
Here

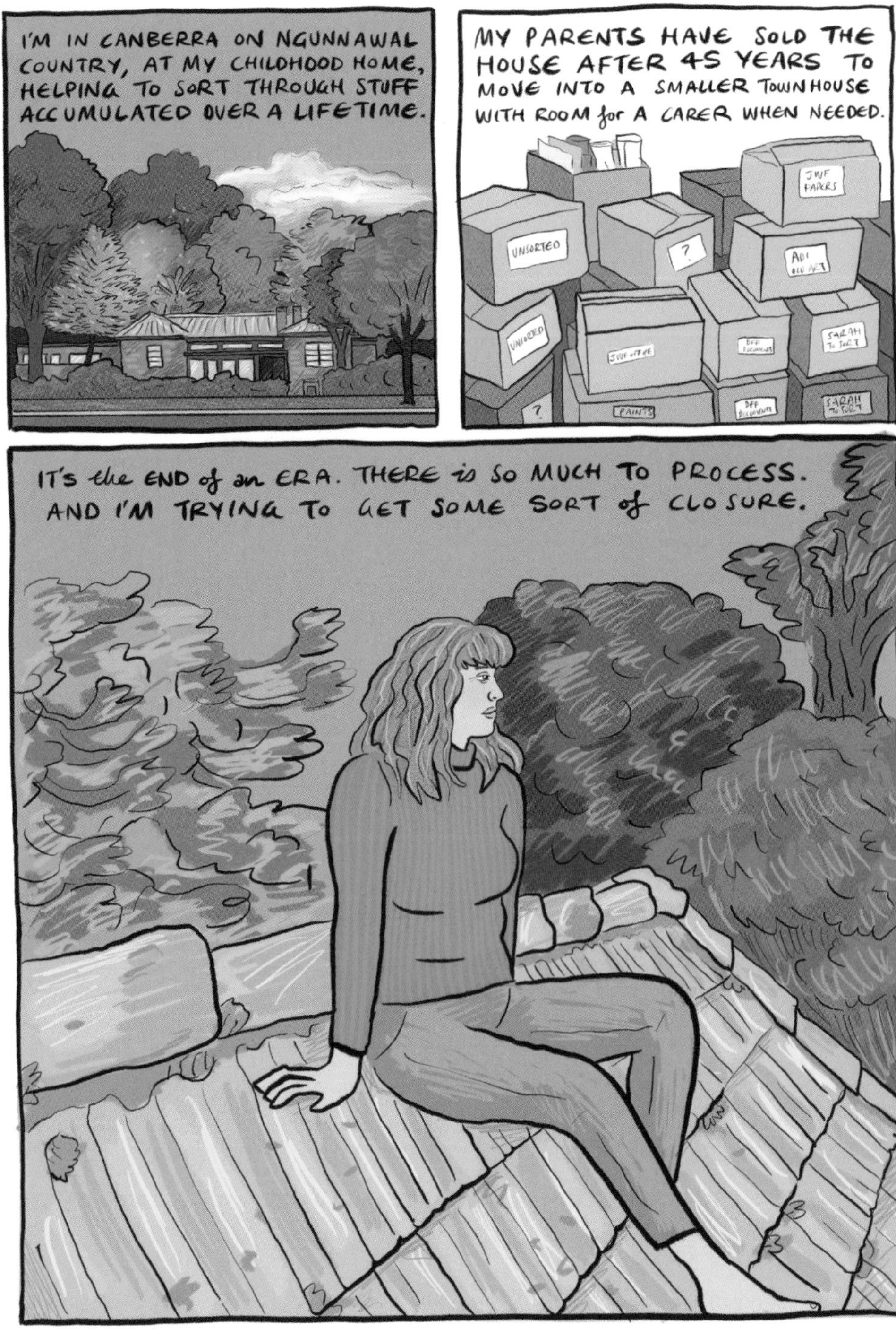
I'M IN CANBERRA ON NGUNNAWAL COUNTRY, AT MY CHILDHOOD HOME, HELPING TO SORT THROUGH STUFF ACCUMULATED OVER A LIFETIME.
MY PARENTS HAVE SOLD THE HOUSE AFTER 45 YEARS TO MOVE INTO A SMALLER TOWNHOUSE WITH ROOM for A CARER WHEN NEEDED.
JWF PAPERS
UNSORTED
?
UNSORTED
SARAH TO SORT
PAINTS
SARAH TO SORT
IT'S the END of an ERA. THERE is SO MUCH TO PROCESS. AND I'M TRYING TO GET SOME SORT of CLOSURE.

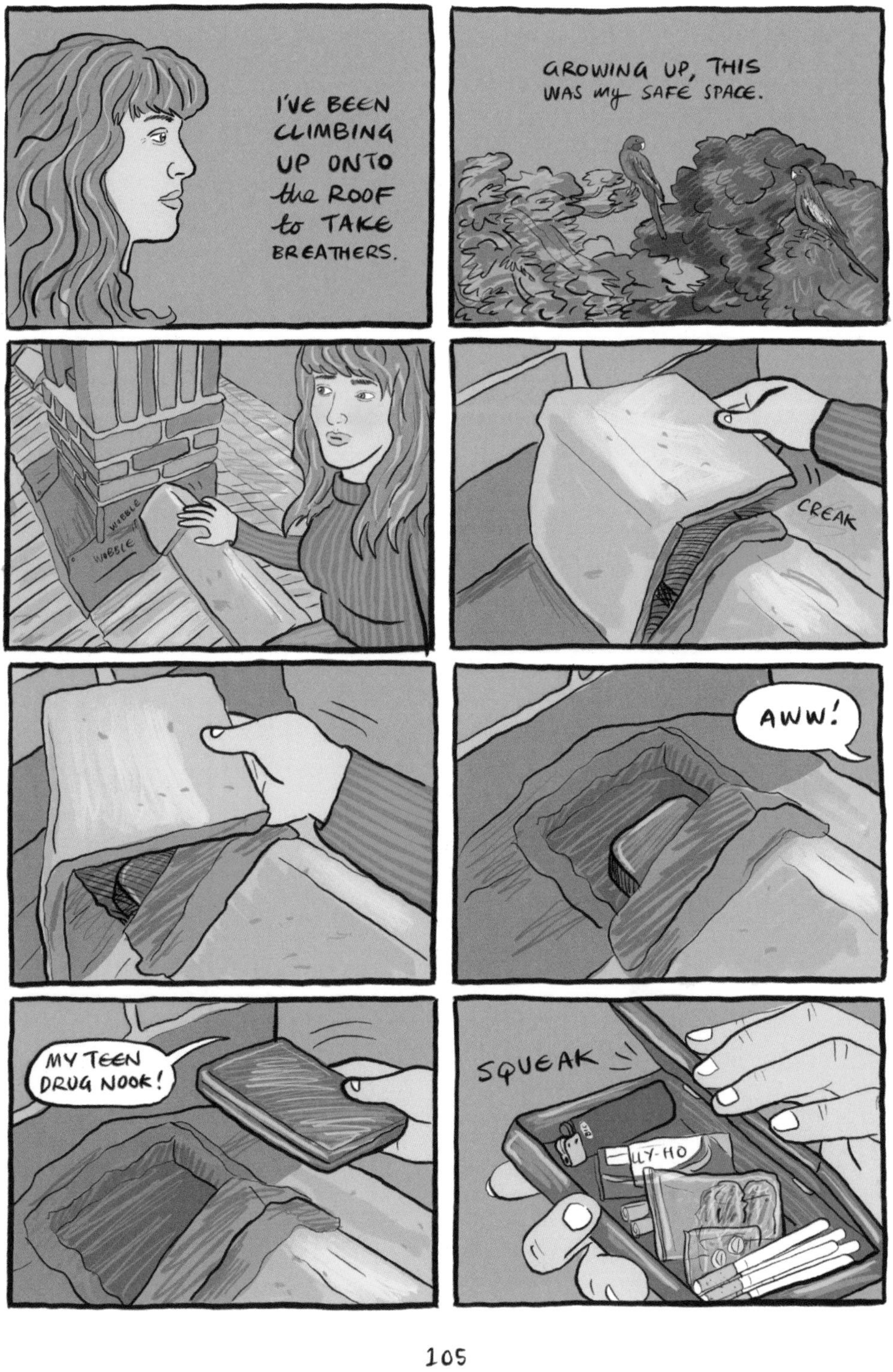
I'VE BEEN CLIMBING UP ONTO the ROOF to TAKE BREATHERS.
GROWING UP, THIS WAS my SAFE SPACE.
WIBBLE
WIBBLE
CREAK
AWW!
MY TEEN DRUG NOOK!
SQUEAK

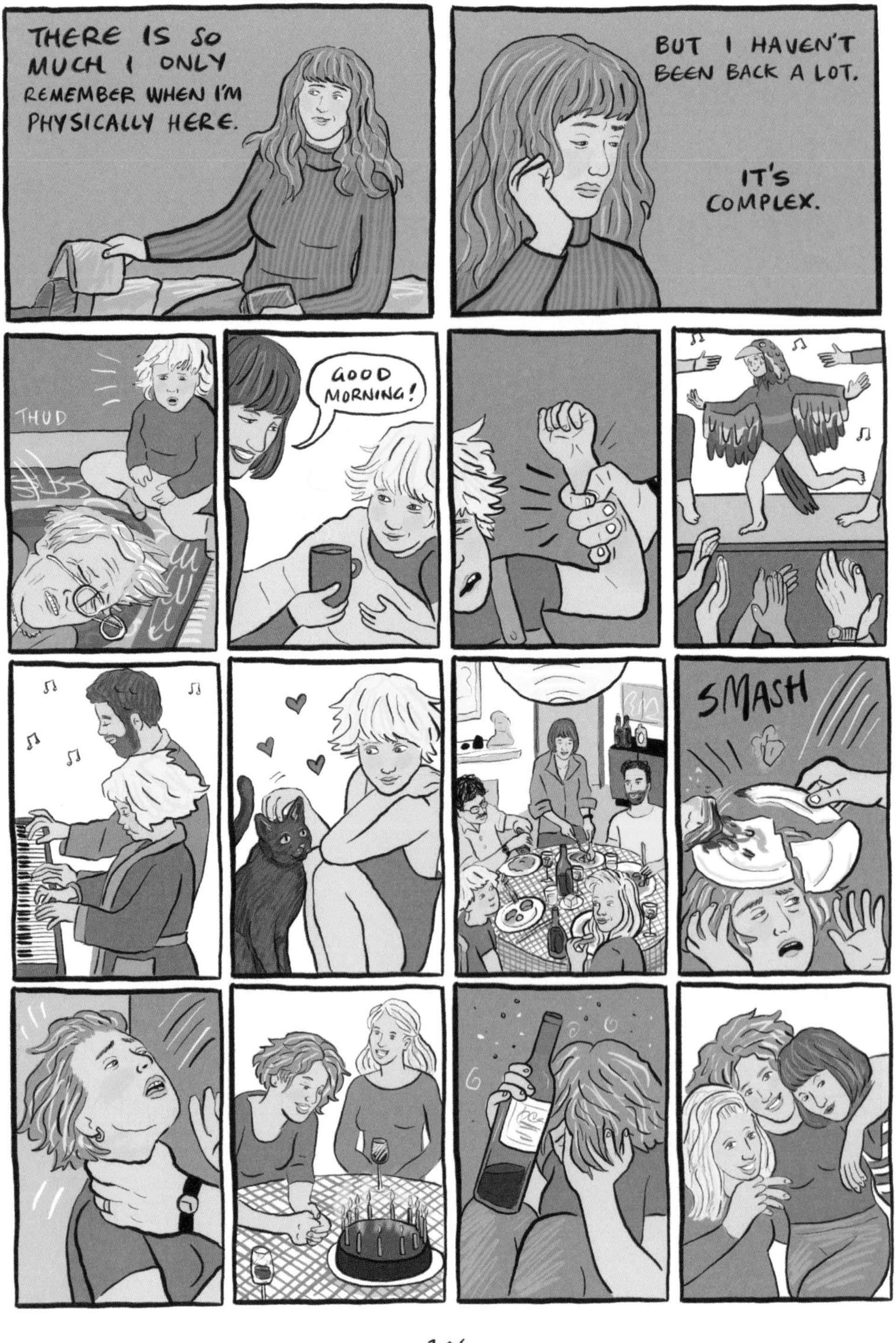
THERE IS SO MUCH I ONLY REMEMBER WHEN I'M PHYSICALLY HERE.
BUT I HAVEN'T BEEN BACK A LOT.
IT'S COMPLEX.
THUD
GOOD MORNING!
SMASH

BUT NOW THAT it's GOING...

I'VE BEEN VISITING with URGENCY.

KNOWING IT WILL BE DEMOLISHED TO MAKE WAY for APARTMENTS...

SMASH

FEELS LIKE THE UPROOTING of a PSYCHIC BEDROCK.

A HUGE SUBTERRANEAN LOSS.

ONCE THIS PLACE GOES...

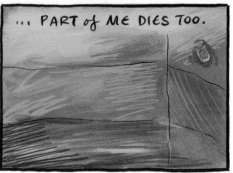

... PART of ME DIES TOO.

A REMINDER that EVERYTHING, EVERYWHERE GETS SWEPT AWAY in TIME.

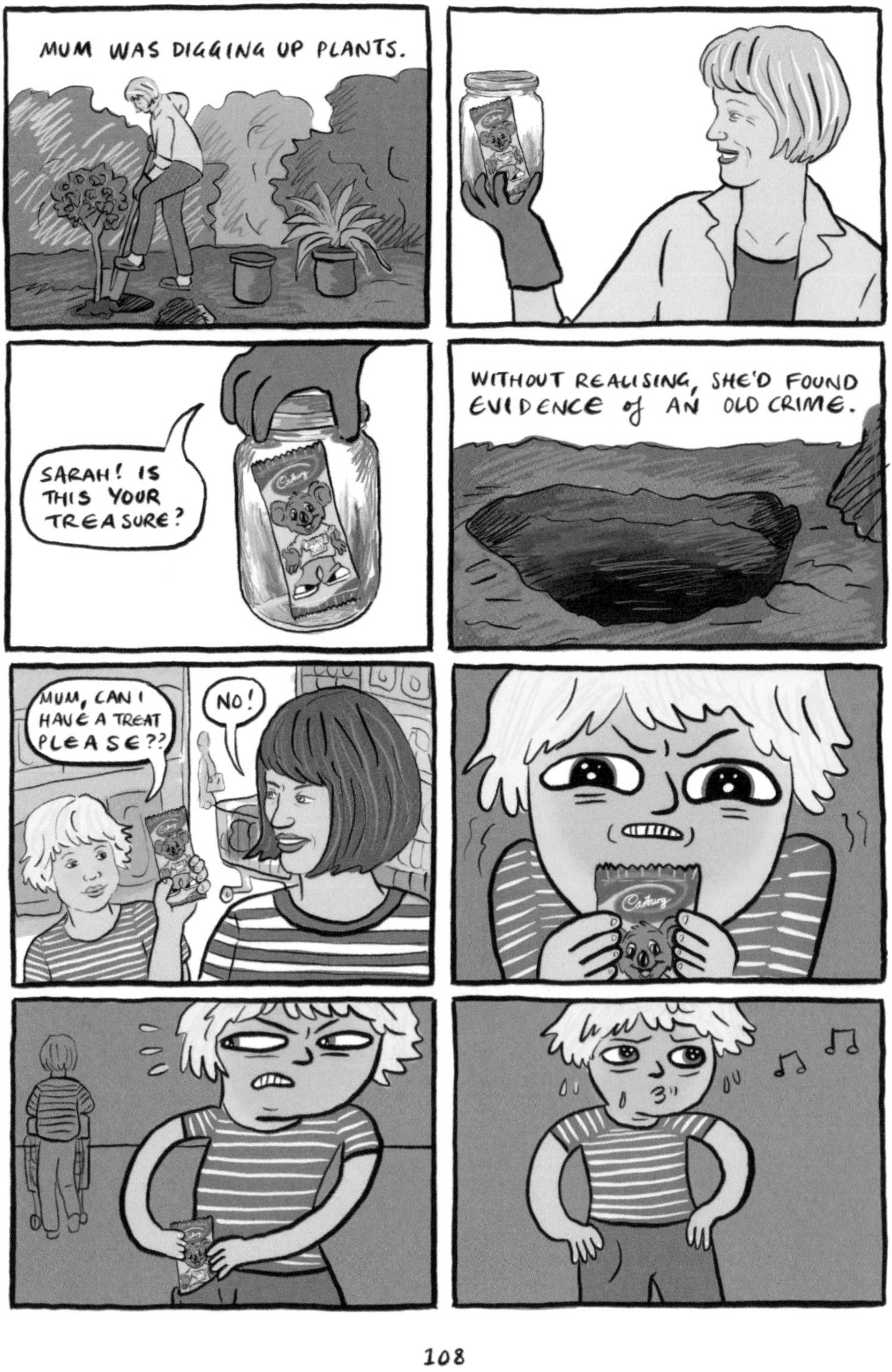
MUM WAS DIGGING UP PLANTS.
SARAH! IS THIS YOUR TREASURE?
WITHOUT REALISING, SHE'D FOUND EVIDENCE of AN OLD CRIME.
MUM, CAN I HAVE A TREAT PLEASE??
NO!

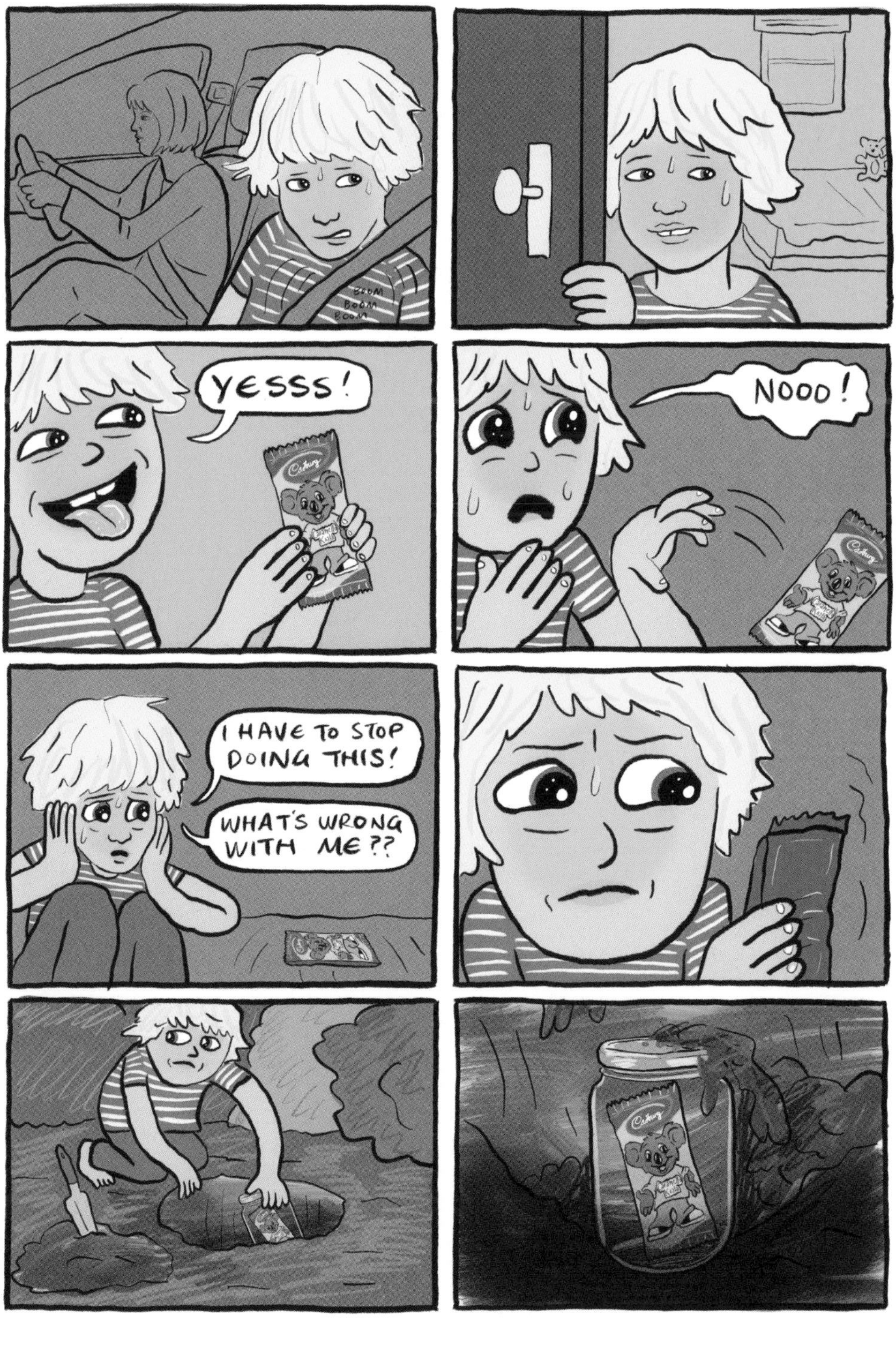
BOOM
BOOM
BOOM
YESSS!
NOOO!
I HAVE TO STOP DOING THIS!
WHAT'S WRONG WITH ME??

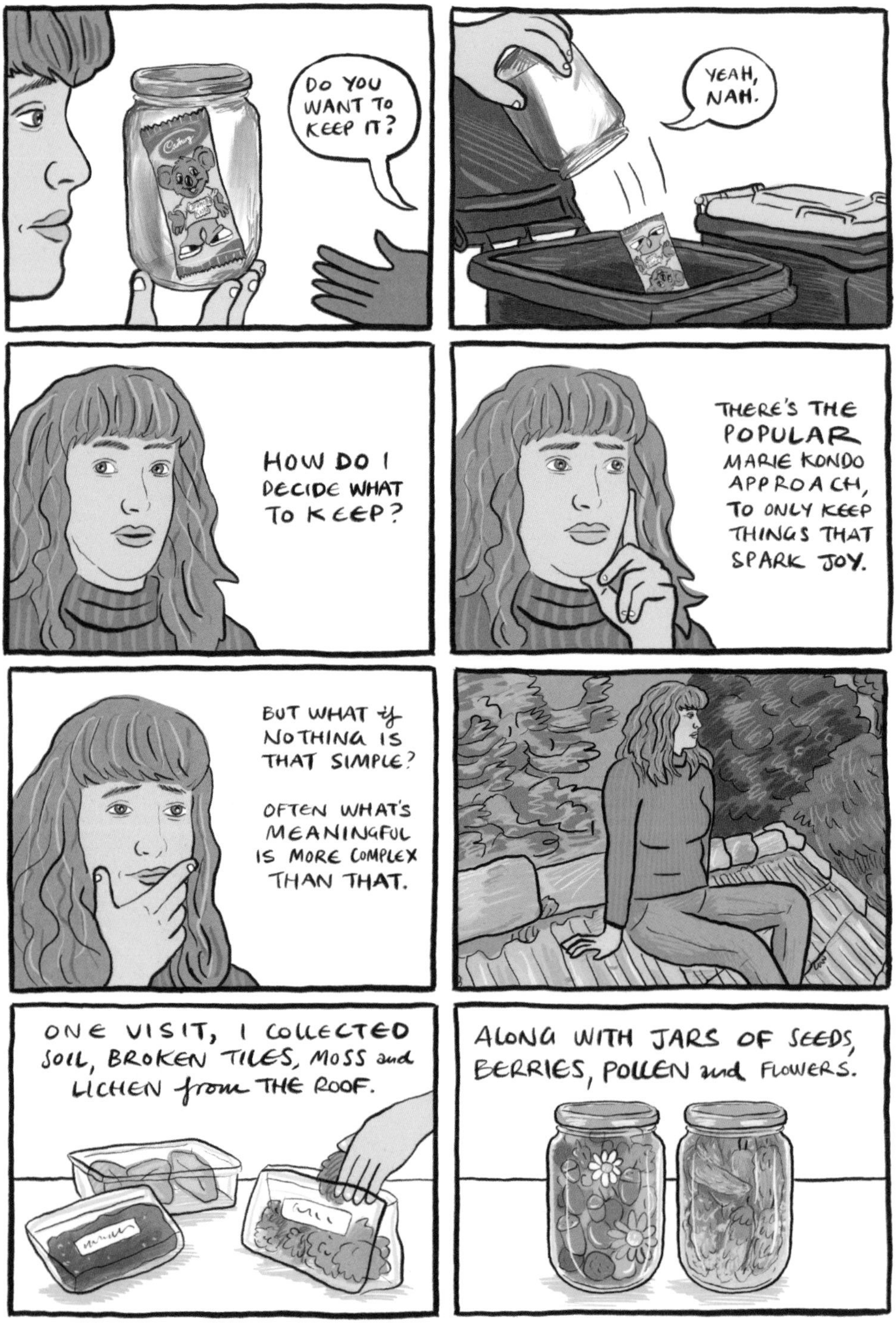
DO YOU WANT TO KEEP IT?
YEAH, NAH.
HOW DO I DECIDE WHAT TO KEEP?
THERE'S THE POPULAR MARIE KONDO APPROACH, TO ONLY KEEP THINGS THAT SPARK JOY.
BUT WHAT if NOTHING IS THAT SIMPLE?
OFTEN WHAT'S MEANINGFUL IS MORE COMPLEX THAN THAT.
ONE VISIT, I COLLECTED SOIL, BROKEN TILES, MOSS and LICHEN from THE ROOF.
ALONG WITH JARS OF SEEDS, BERRIES, POLLEN and FLOWERS.

IS THIS SIMILAR TO HOW PEOPLE IN THE VICTORIAN ERA WOULD PRESERVE THINGS LIKE A TOOTH...

... OR KEEP A LOCK of HAIR from A DECEASED LOVED ONE?

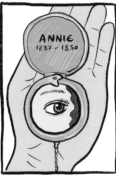

ANNIE
1837 - 1850

AS PHYSICAL ANCHORS for VIVID RECOLLECTION?

SMELLS

THIS VISIT, I'VE BEEN WRITING LISTS of SMELLS and SOUNDS.

STICKING PLANTS in my JOURNAL...

... AND RECORDING VIDEOS of DOORS and LIGHT SWITCHES.

CREEAK

CAPTURING the ROAR of THE ANCIENT TOILET.

THE GROAN of the STAIRS.

THE PLIP of the ALWAYS LEAKY TAP.

EVERYTHING SPEAKS.

WHAT DOES it SAY?

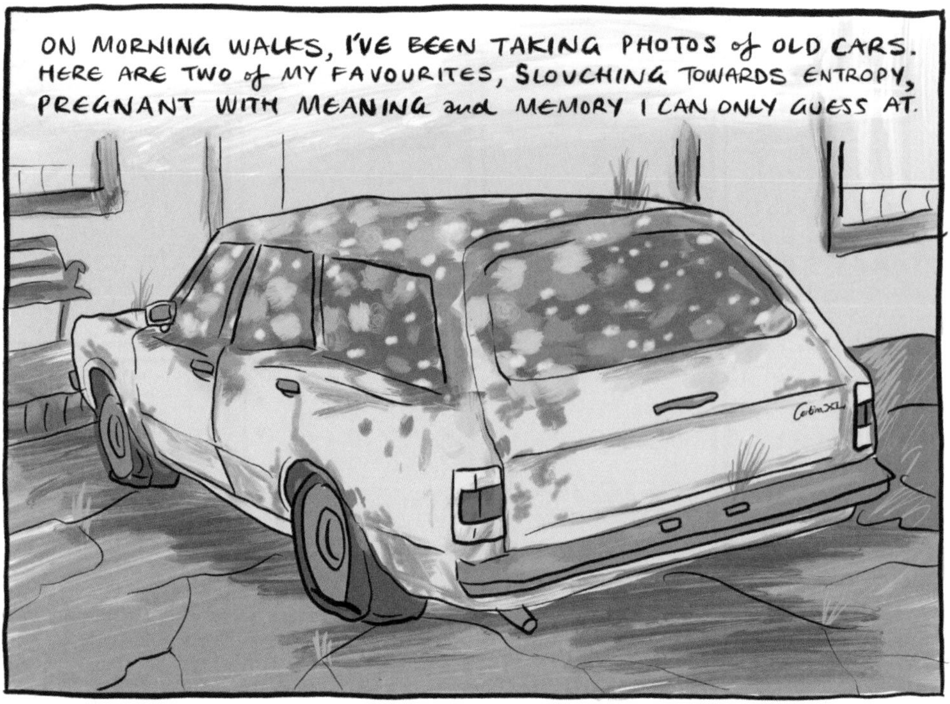
ON MORNING WALKS, I'VE BEEN TAKING PHOTOS of OLD CARS. HERE ARE TWO of MY FAVOURITES, SLOUCHING TOWARDS ENTROPY, PREGNANT WITH MEANING and MEMORY I CAN ONLY GUESS AT.

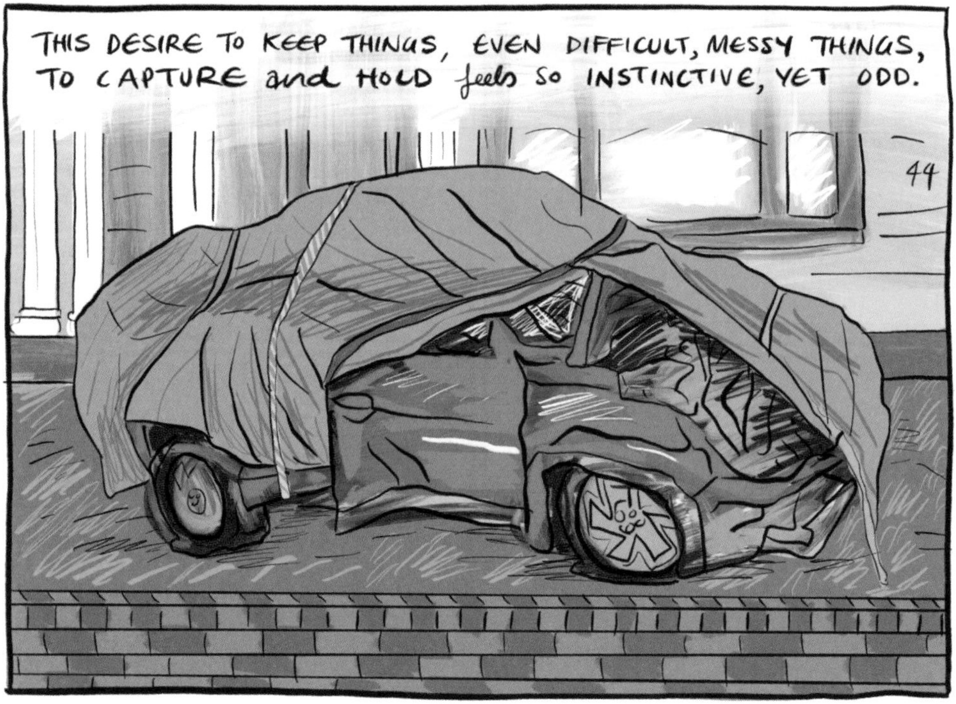
THIS DESIRE TO KEEP THINGS, EVEN DIFFICULT, MESSY THINGS, TO CAPTURE and HOLD feels SO INSTINCTIVE, YET ODD.
44

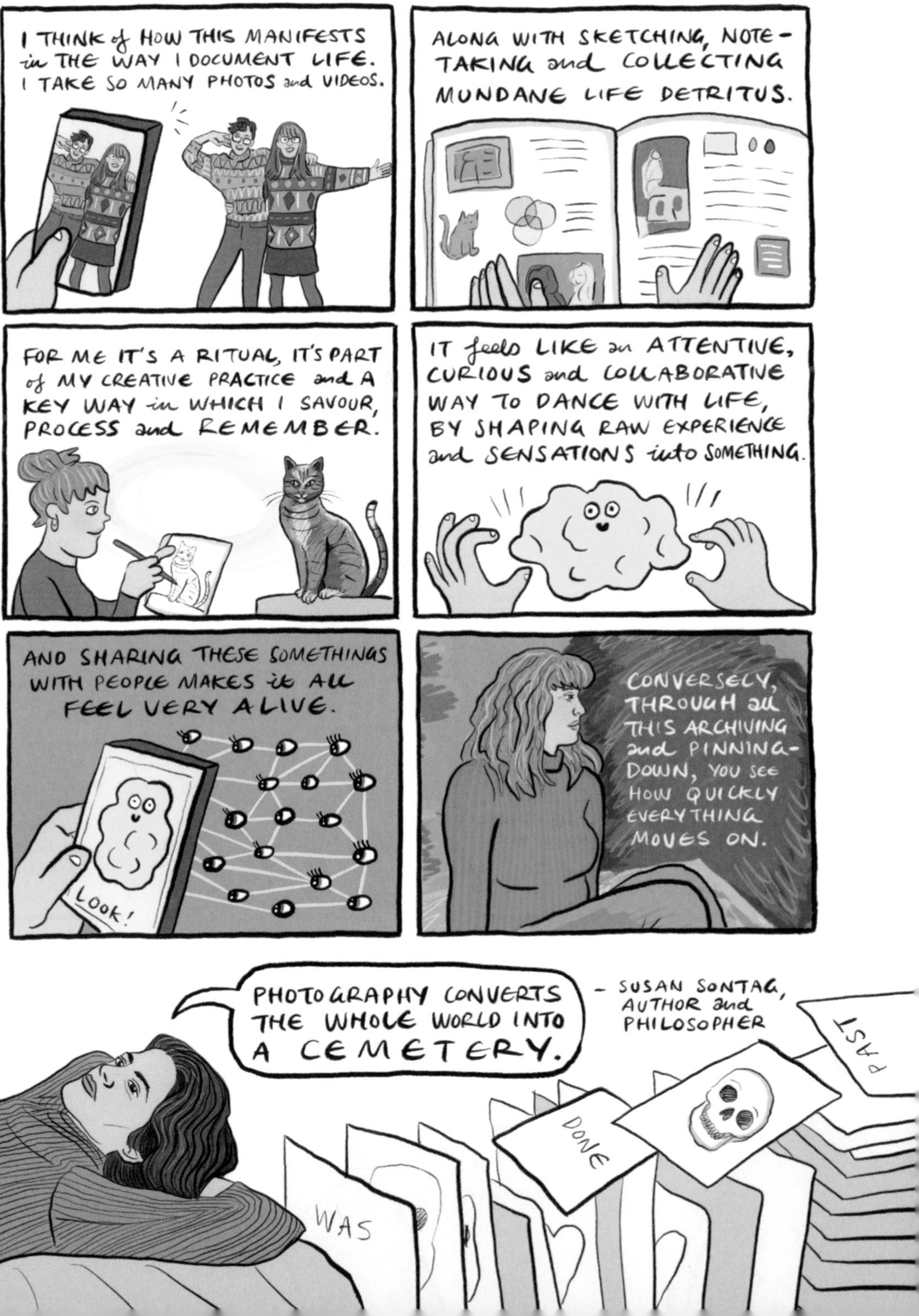

I THINK of HOW THIS MANIFESTS in THE WAY I DOCUMENT LIFE. I TAKE SO MANY PHOTOS and VIDEOS.
ALONG WITH SKETCHING, NOTE-TAKING and COLLECTING MUNDANE LIFE DETRITUS.
FOR ME IT'S A RITUAL, IT'S PART of MY CREATIVE PRACTICE and A KEY WAY in WHICH I SAVOUR, PROCESS and REMEMBER.
IT feels LIKE an ATTENTIVE, CURIOUS and COLLABORATIVE WAY TO DANCE WITH LIFE, BY SHAPING RAW EXPERIENCE and SENSATIONS into SOMETHING.
AND SHARING THESE SOMETHINGS WITH PEOPLE MAKES it ALL FEEL VERY ALIVE.
LOOK!
CONVERSELY, THROUGH all THIS ARCHIVING and PINNING-DOWN, YOU SEE HOW QUICKLY EVERYTHING MOVES ON.
PHOTOGRAPHY CONVERTS THE WHOLE WORLD INTO A CEMETERY.
- SUSAN SONTAG, AUTHOR and PHILOSOPHER
PAST
DONE
WAS

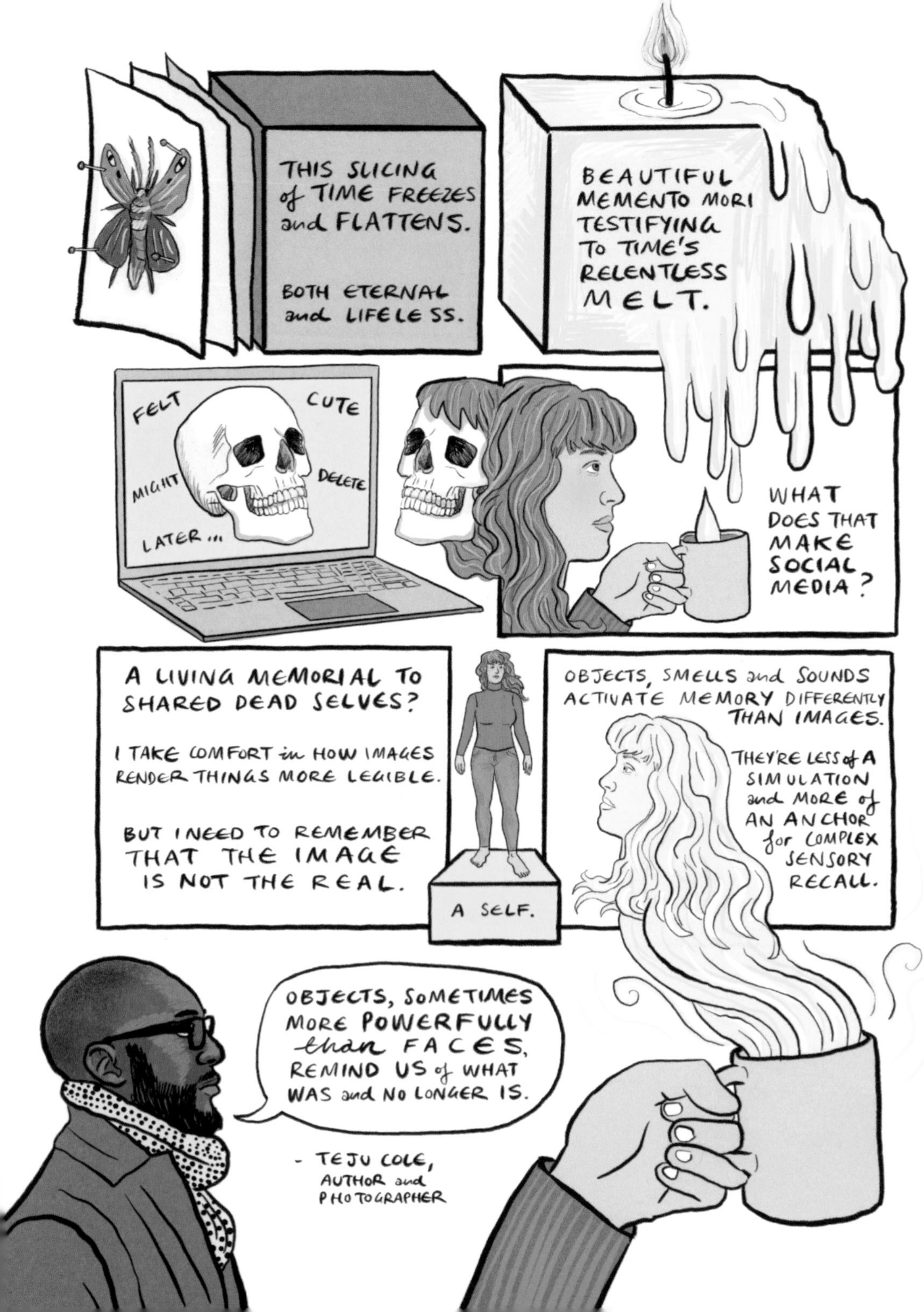

THIS SLICING of TIME FREEZES and FLATTENS.
BOTH ETERNAL and LIFELESS.
BEAUTIFUL MEMENTO MORI TESTIFYING TO TIME'S RELENTLESS MELT.
FELT
CUTE
MIGHT
DELETE
LATER...
WHAT DOES THAT MAKE SOCIAL MEDIA?
A LIVING MEMORIAL TO SHARED DEAD SELVES?
I TAKE COMFORT in HOW IMAGES RENDER THINGS MORE LEGIBLE.
BUT I NEED TO REMEMBER THAT THE IMAGE IS NOT THE REAL.
A SELF.
OBJECTS, SMELLS and SOUNDS ACTIVATE MEMORY DIFFERENTLY THAN IMAGES.
THEY'RE LESS of A SIMULATION and MORE of AN ANCHOR for COMPLEX SENSORY RECALL.
OBJECTS, SOMETIMES MORE POWERFULLY than FACES, REMIND US of WHAT WAS and NO LONGER IS.
- TEJU COLE, AUTHOR and PHOTOGRAPHER

A PHYSICAL REPOSITORY CAN FEEL MORE SOLID, but it TOO IS FRAGILE.

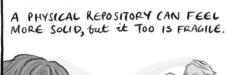

LIFE JUST WANTS TO HAVE ITS WAY WITH EVERYTHING!

THOSE JARS I COLLECTED on A RECENT VISIT HERE?

THEY'VE SINCE TURNED ROTTEN.

OLD REPURPOSED for NEW.

I KNOW THAT'S HOW IT WORKS.

ALL LIFE IS FERMENTATION.

— RICHARD FEYNMAN, PHYSICIST

STILL, IT TROUBLES ME.

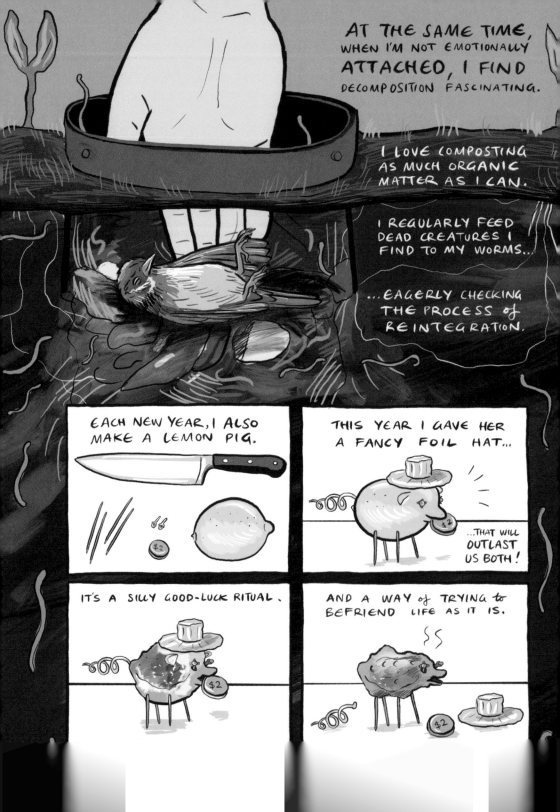

AT THE SAME TIME, WHEN I'M NOT EMOTIONALLY ATTACHED, I FIND DECOMPOSITION FASCINATING.

I LOVE COMPOSTING AS MUCH ORGANIC MATTER AS I CAN.

I REGULARLY FEED DEAD CREATURES I FIND TO MY WORMS...

...EAGERLY CHECKING THE PROCESS of REINTEGRATION.

EACH NEW YEAR, I ALSO MAKE A LEMON PIG.

$2

THIS YEAR I GAVE HER A FANCY FOIL HAT...

$2

...THAT WILL OUTLAST US BOTH!

IT'S A SILLY GOOD-LUCK RITUAL.

$2

AND A WAY of TRYING to BEFRIEND LIFE AS IT IS.

$2

BEGINNINGS...

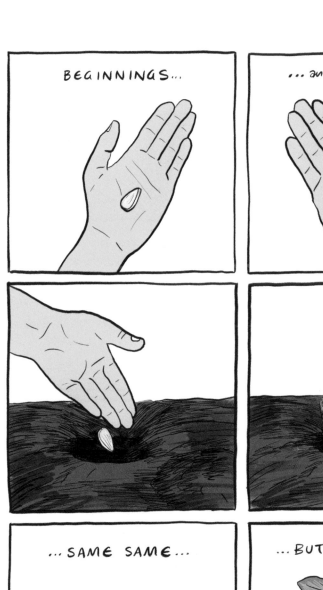

...and ENDINGS...

...SAME SAME...

...BUT DIFFERENT.

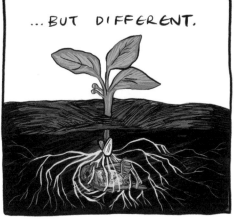

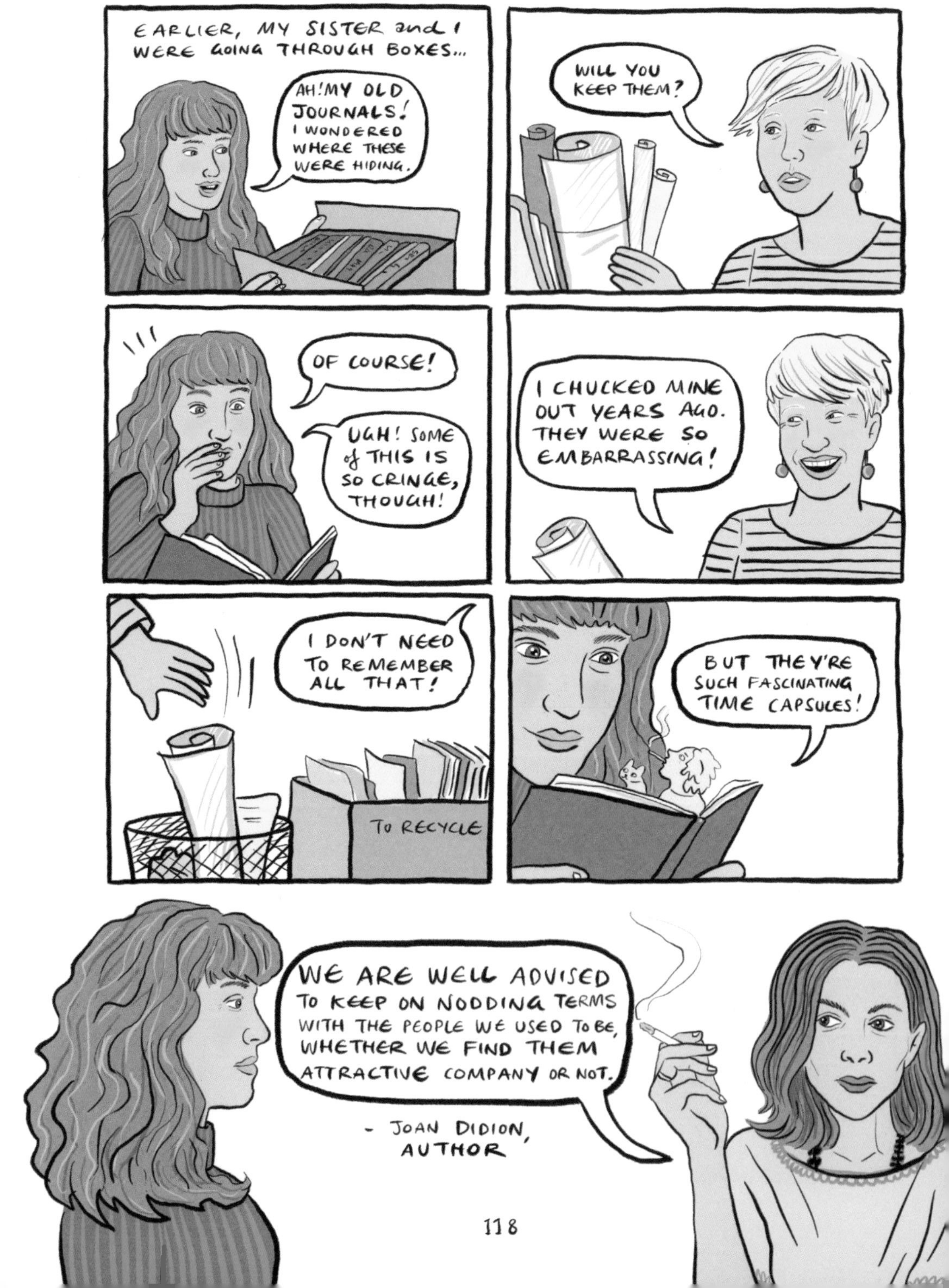
EARLIER, MY SISTER and I WERE GOING THROUGH BOXES...
AH! MY OLD JOURNALS! I WONDERED WHERE THESE WERE HIDING.
WILL YOU KEEP THEM?
OF COURSE!
UGH! SOME of THIS IS SO CRINGE, THOUGH!
I CHUCKED MINE OUT YEARS AGO. THEY WERE SO EMBARRASSING!
I DON'T NEED TO REMEMBER ALL THAT!
TO RECYCLE
BUT THEY'RE SUCH FASCINATING TIME CAPSULES!
WE ARE WELL ADVISED TO KEEP ON NODDING TERMS WITH THE PEOPLE WE USED TO BE, WHETHER WE FIND THEM ATTRACTIVE COMPANY OR NOT.
- JOAN DIDION, AUTHOR

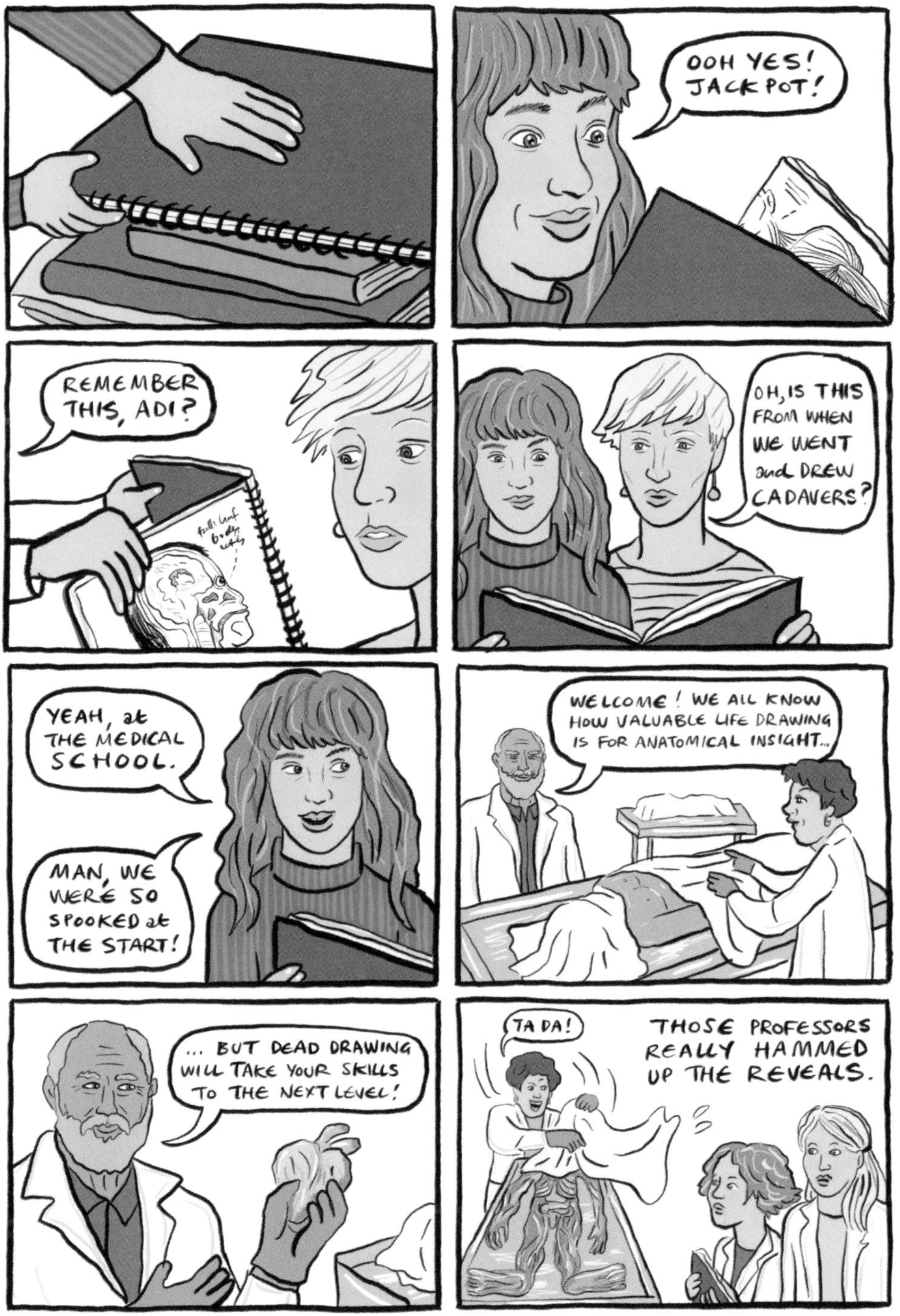
OOH YES! JACKPOT!
REMEMBER THIS, ADI?
OH, IS THIS FROM WHEN WE WENT and DREW CADAVERS?
YEAH, at THE MEDICAL SCHOOL.
MAN, WE WERE SO SPOOKED at THE START!
WELCOME! WE ALL KNOW HOW VALUABLE LIFE DRAWING IS FOR ANATOMICAL INSIGHT...
... BUT DEAD DRAWING WILL TAKE YOUR SKILLS TO THE NEXT LEVEL!
TA DA!
THOSE PROFESSORS REALLY HAMMED UP THE REVEALS.

A STUDENT VOMITED OUT of SHOCK!

I WAS SURPRISED BY HOW MUCH THE CADAVERS LOOKED LIKE MEAT.

I MEAN, THEY ARE?

EVERYTHING STANK OF FORMALIN and FORMALDEHYDE.

WHICH made US CRAVE MEAT, WHICH is APPARENTLY a THING?

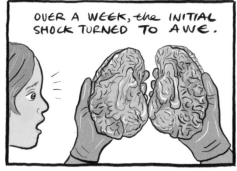

OVER A WEEK, the INITIAL SHOCK TURNED TO AWE.

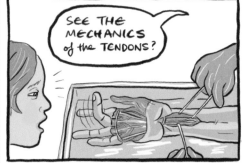

SEE THE MECHANICS of the TENDONS?

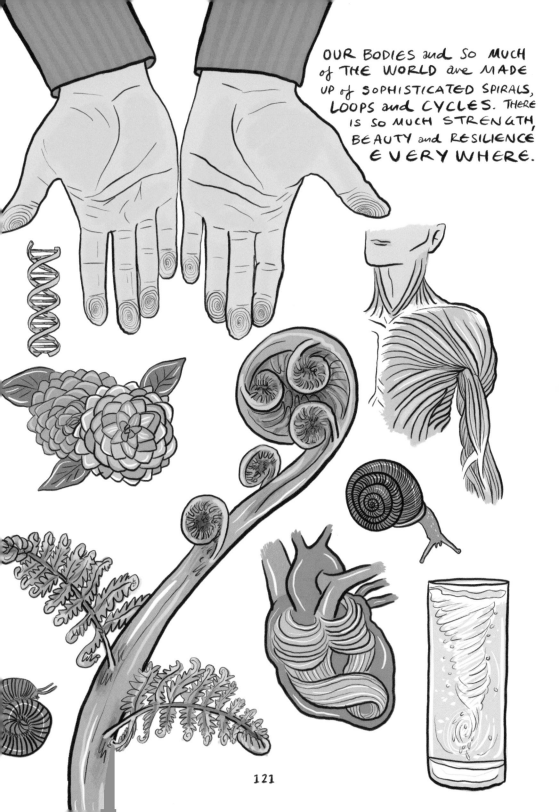

OUR BODIES and SO MUCH of THE WORLD are MADE UP of SOPHISTICATED SPIRALS, LOOPS and CYCLES. THERE IS SO MUCH STRENGTH, BEAUTY and RESILIENCE EVERYWHERE.

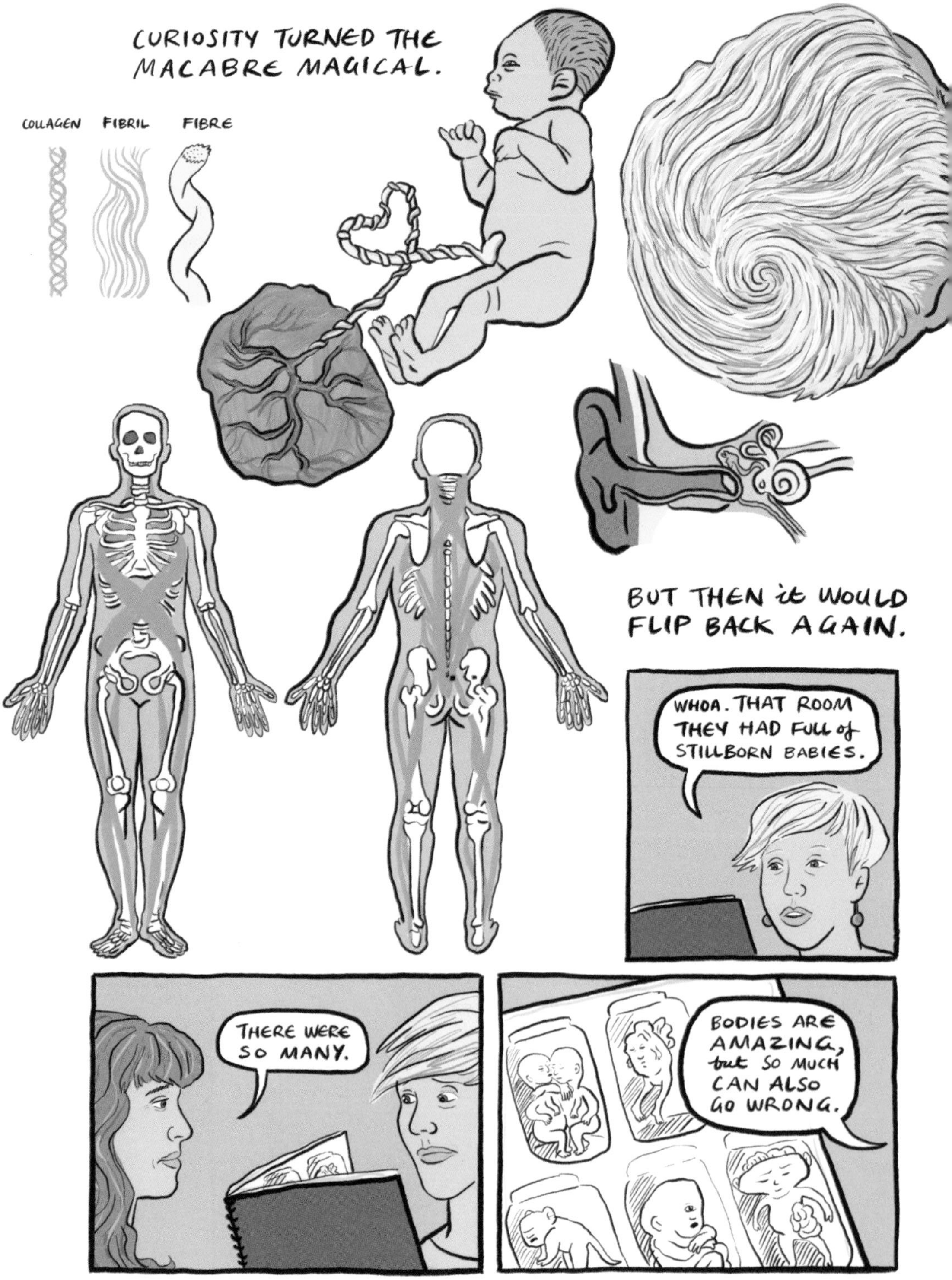
CURIOSITY TURNED THE MACABRE MAGICAL.
COLLAGEN
FIBRIL
FIBRE
BUT THEN it WOULD FLIP BACK AGAIN.
WHOA. THAT ROOM THEY HAD FULL of STILLBORN BABIES.
THERE WERE SO MANY.
BODIES ARE AMAZING, but SO MUCH CAN ALSO GO WRONG.

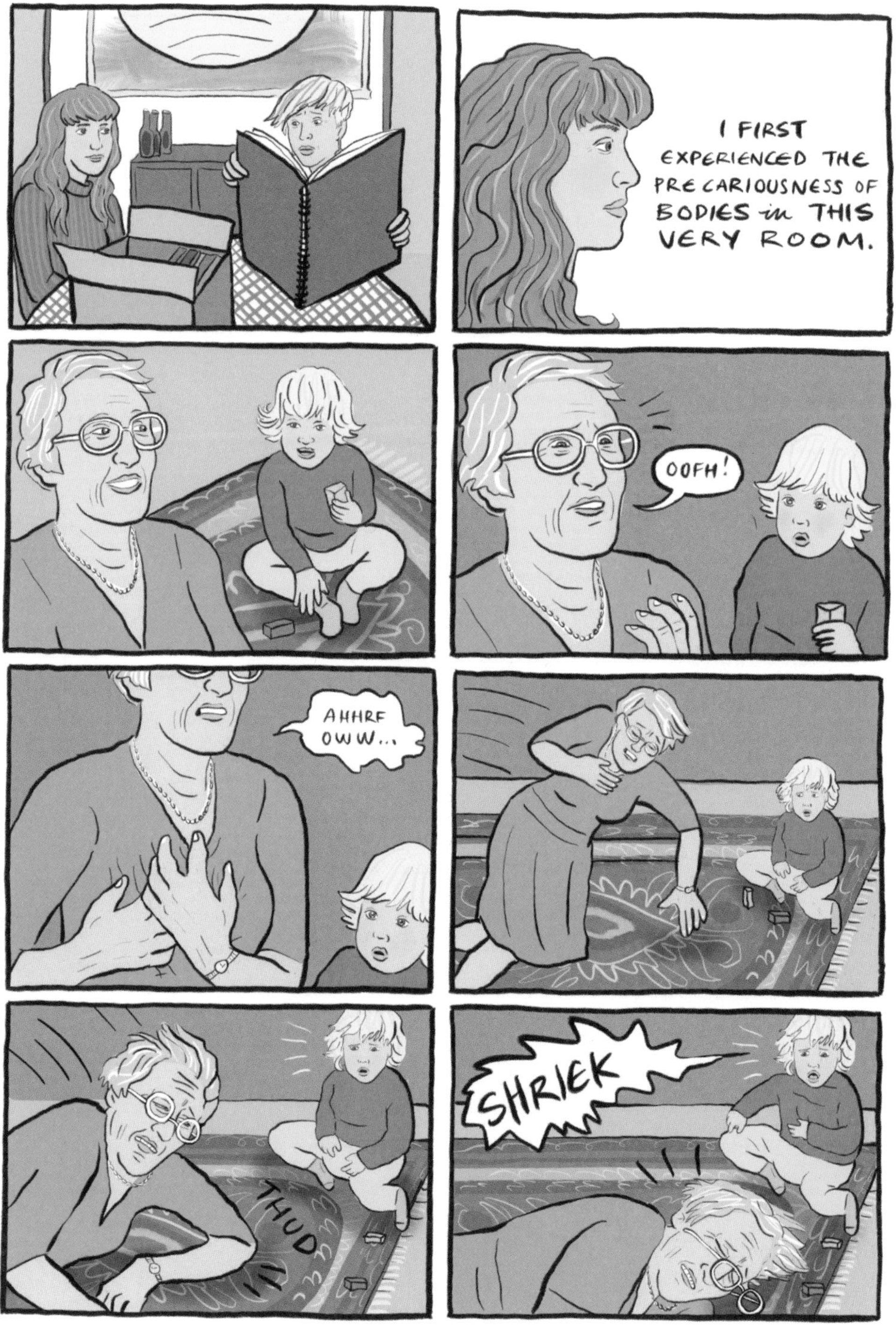
I FIRST EXPERIENCED THE PRECARIOUSNESS OF BODIES in THIS VERY ROOM.
OOFH!
AHHRF OWW...
THUD
SHRIEK

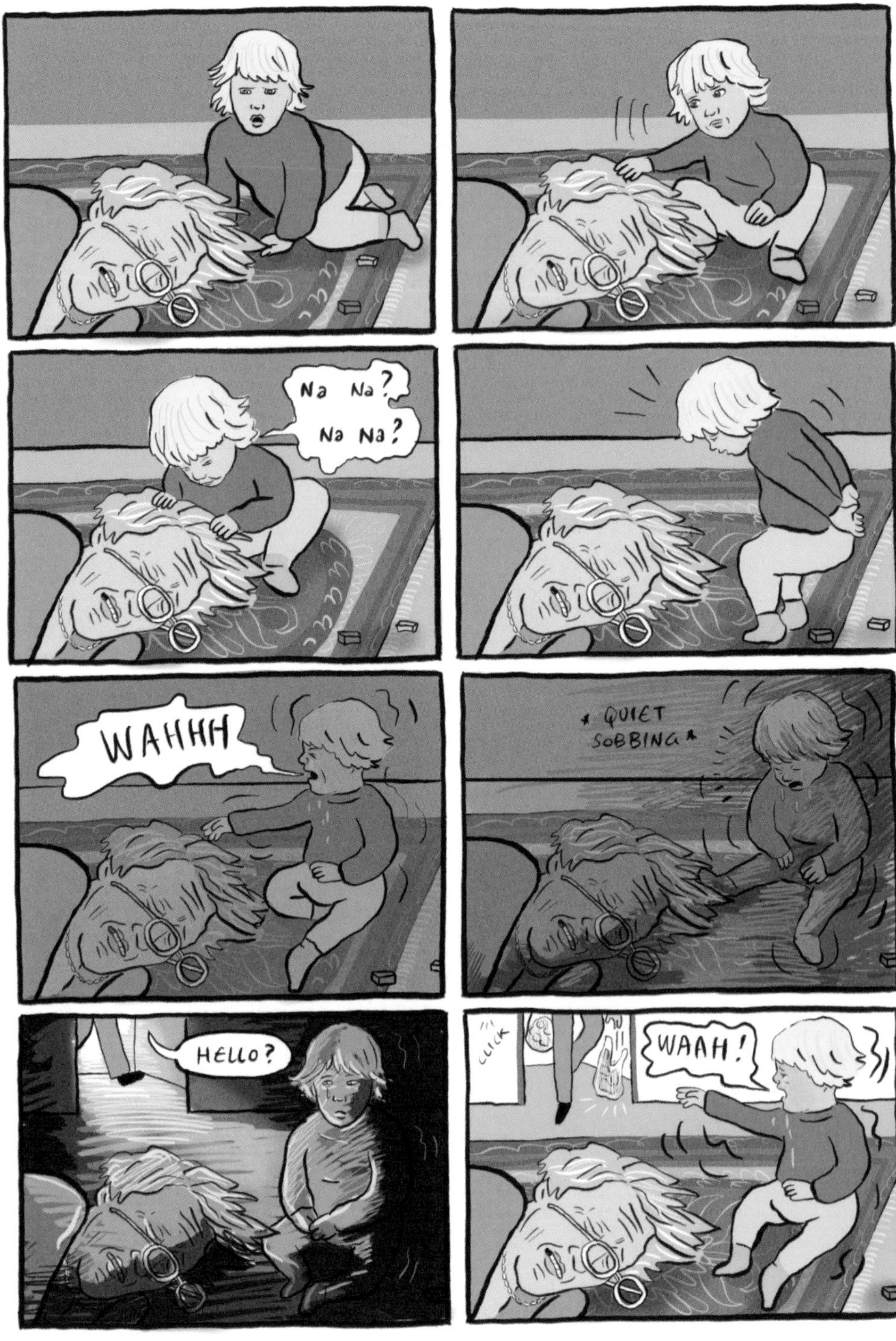
Na Na?
Na Na?
WAHHH
* QUIET SOBBING *
HELLO?
CLICK
WAAH!

THEN and NOW, THE STRANGE INTERRUPTION and UNCANNINESS of DEATH LEAVES ME WITH SO MANY QUESTIONS.

WHY WAS THE COFFIN OF MY EX-BOYFRIEND IAN SO SMALL?

WHY DID YOU DO IT? WE ALL LOVED YOU!

HOW CAN A BELOVED FRIEND TURN into A GROTESQUE OBJECT?

WILL the GUILT EVER STOP HAUNTING ME?

I WAS ONLY GONE for THE WEEKEND!

HOW CAN a GROWN MAN CRUMPLE LIKE A CAN OF BEER?

WHERE DOES A WHOLE WORLD GO? AND WHAT TO DO WITH THE ACHE?

WHY WAS MY HOUSEMATE ODETTE'S COFFIN ALSO SO SMALL?

SHE HAD SO MUCH LIFE AHEAD of HER...

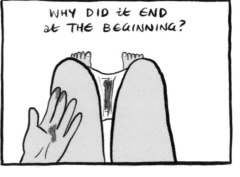

WHY DID it END at THE BEGINNING?

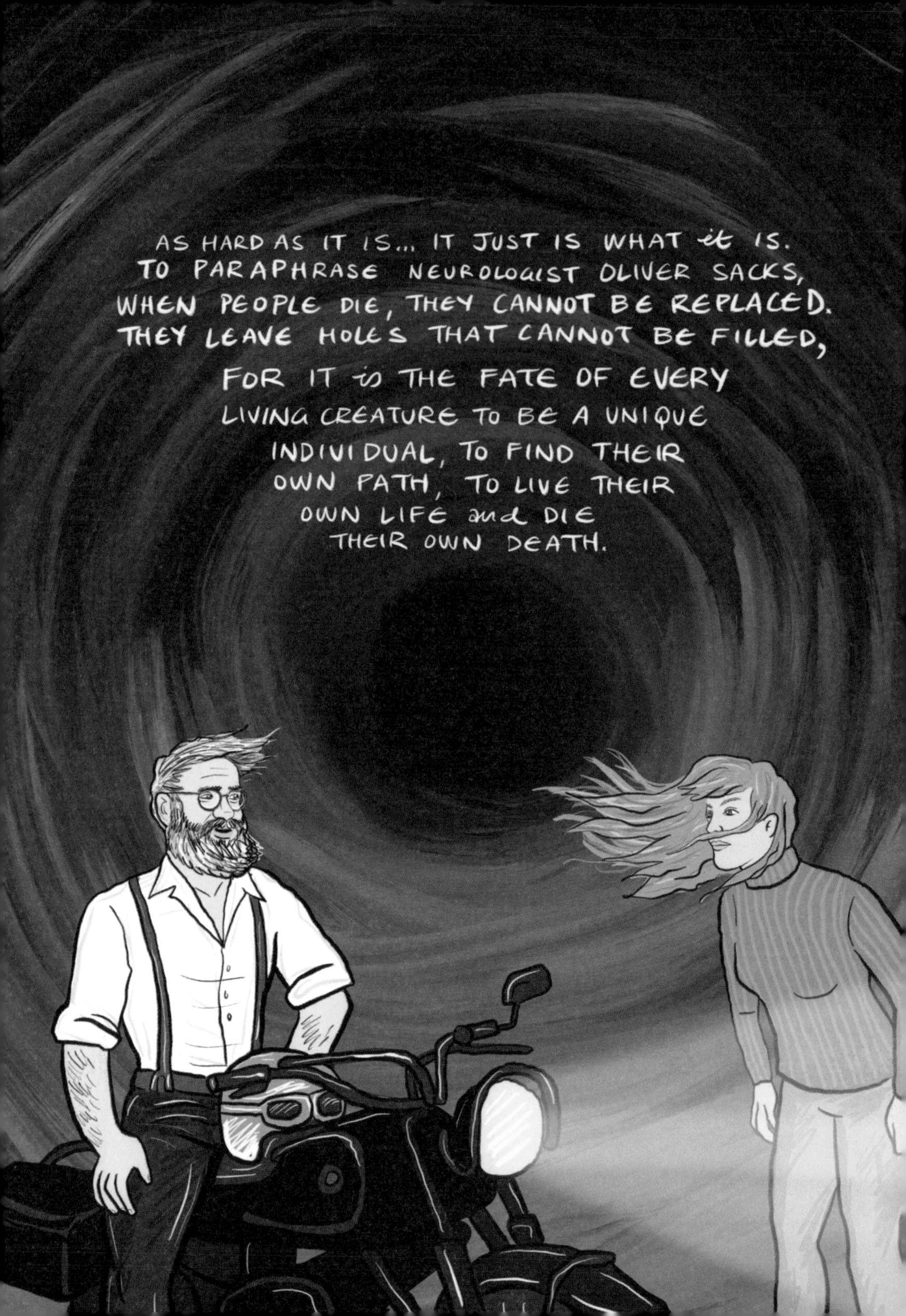
AS HARD AS IT IS... IT JUST IS WHAT it IS.
TO PARAPHRASE NEUROLOGIST OLIVER SACKS, WHEN PEOPLE DIE, THEY CANNOT BE REPLACED. THEY LEAVE HOLES THAT CANNOT BE FILLED,
FOR IT is THE FATE OF EVERY LIVING CREATURE TO BE A UNIQUE INDIVIDUAL, TO FIND THEIR OWN PATH, TO LIVE THEIR OWN LIFE and DIE THEIR OWN DEATH.

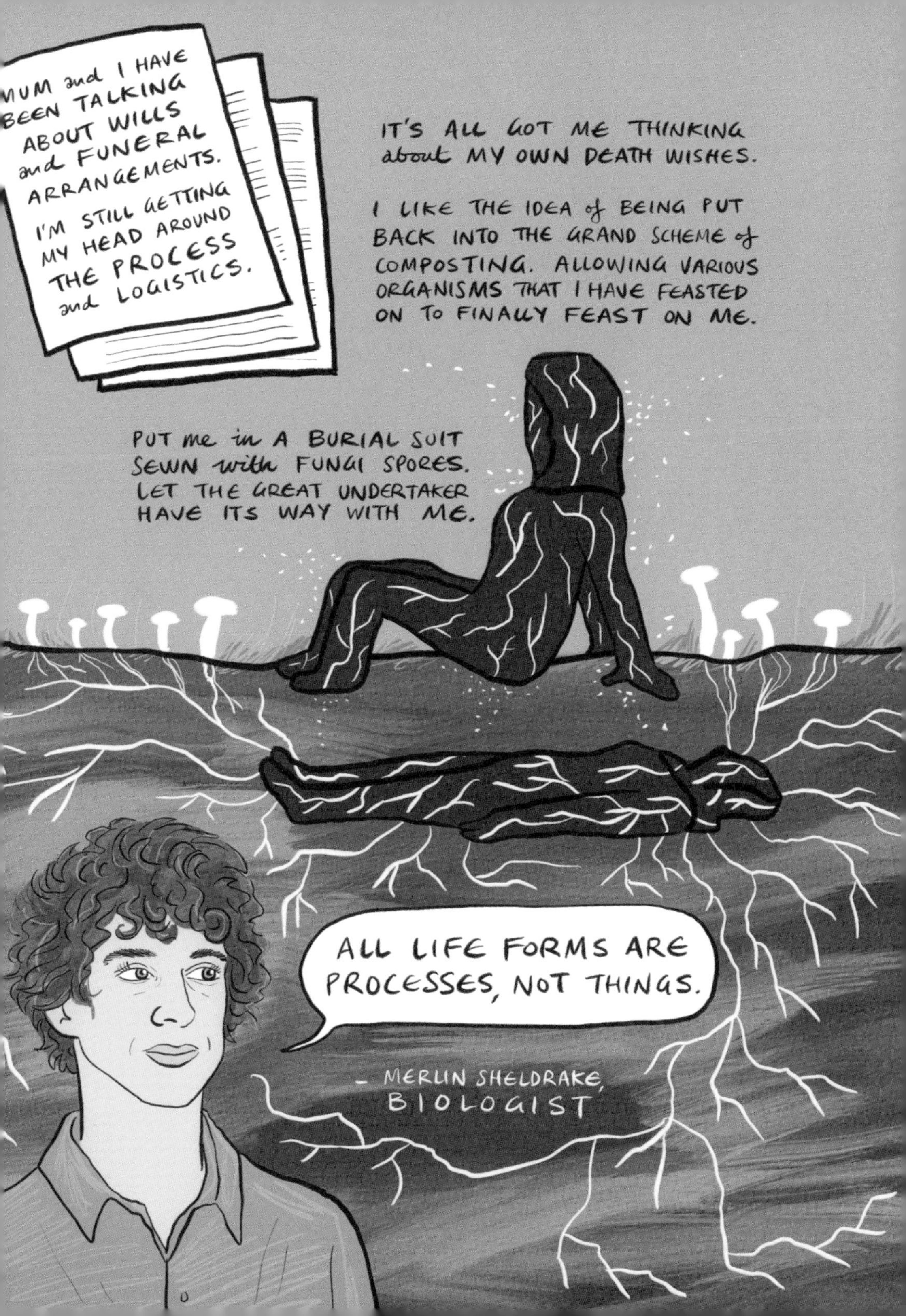
MUM and I HAVE BEEN TALKING ABOUT WILLS and FUNERAL ARRANGEMENTS.
I'M STILL GETTING MY HEAD AROUND THE PROCESS and LOGISTICS.
IT'S ALL GOT ME THINKING about MY OWN DEATH WISHES.
I LIKE THE IDEA of BEING PUT BACK INTO THE GRAND SCHEME of COMPOSTING. ALLOWING VARIOUS ORGANISMS THAT I HAVE FEASTED ON TO FINALLY FEAST ON ME.
PUT me in A BURIAL SUIT SEWN with FUNGI SPORES. LET THE GREAT UNDERTAKER HAVE ITS WAY WITH ME.
ALL LIFE FORMS ARE PROCESSES, NOT THINGS.
– MERLIN SHELDRAKE, BIOLOGIST

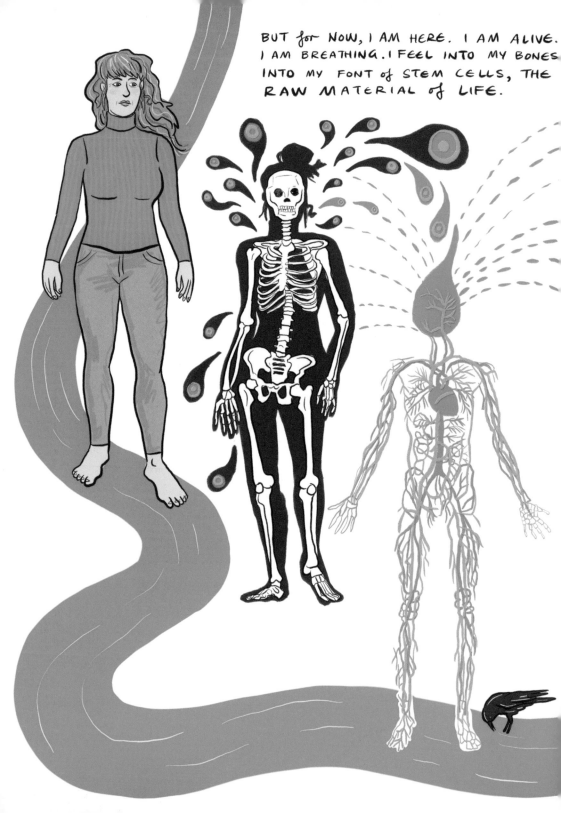

BUT for NOW, I AM HERE. I AM ALIVE. I AM BREATHING. I FEEL INTO MY BONES INTO MY FONT of STEM CELLS, THE RAW MATERIAL of LIFE.

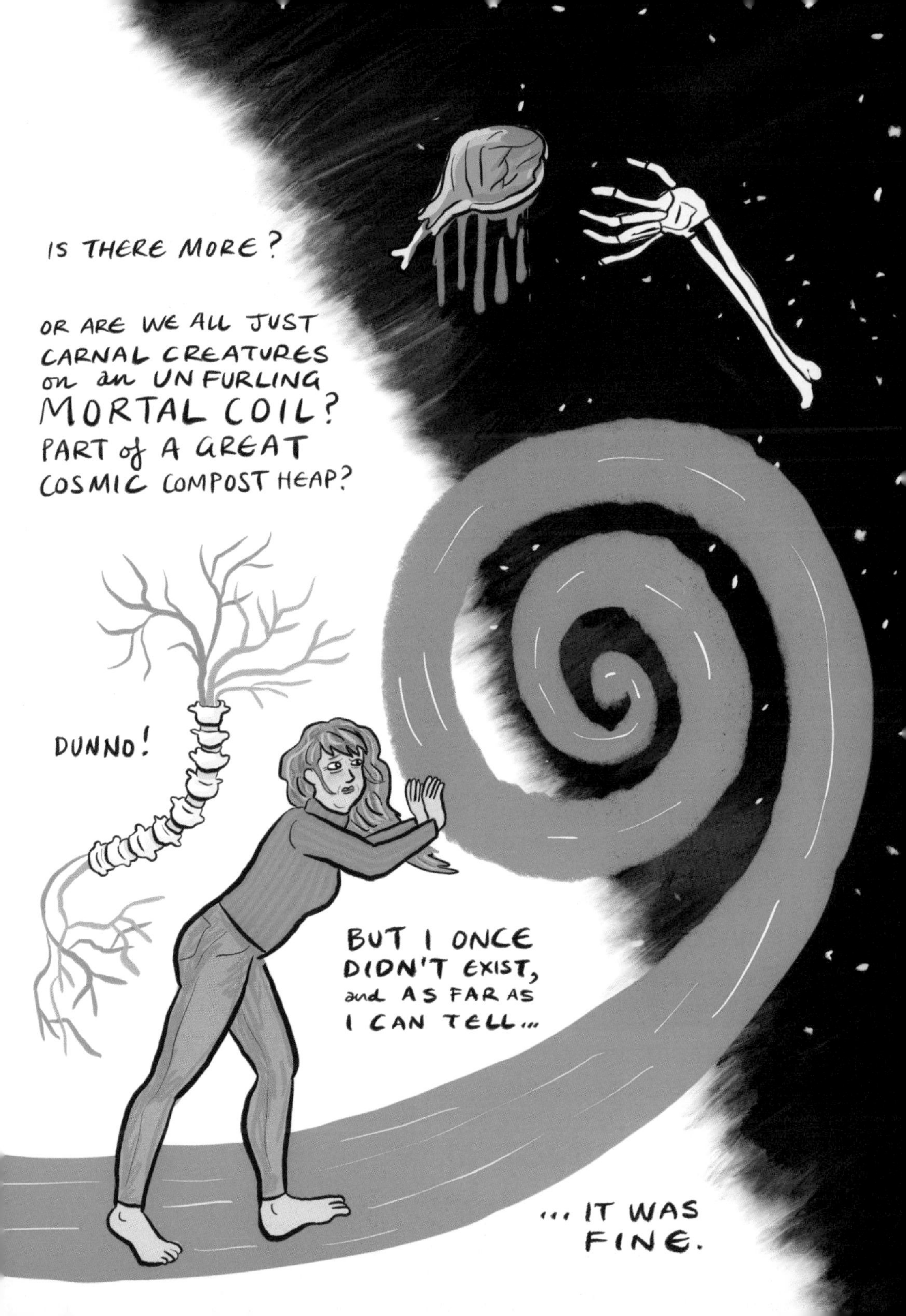
IS THERE MORE?
OR ARE WE ALL JUST CARNAL CREATURES on an UNFURLING MORTAL COIL? PART of A GREAT COSMIC COMPOST HEAP?
DUNNO!
BUT I ONCE DIDN'T EXIST, and AS FAR AS I CAN TELL...
... IT WAS FINE.

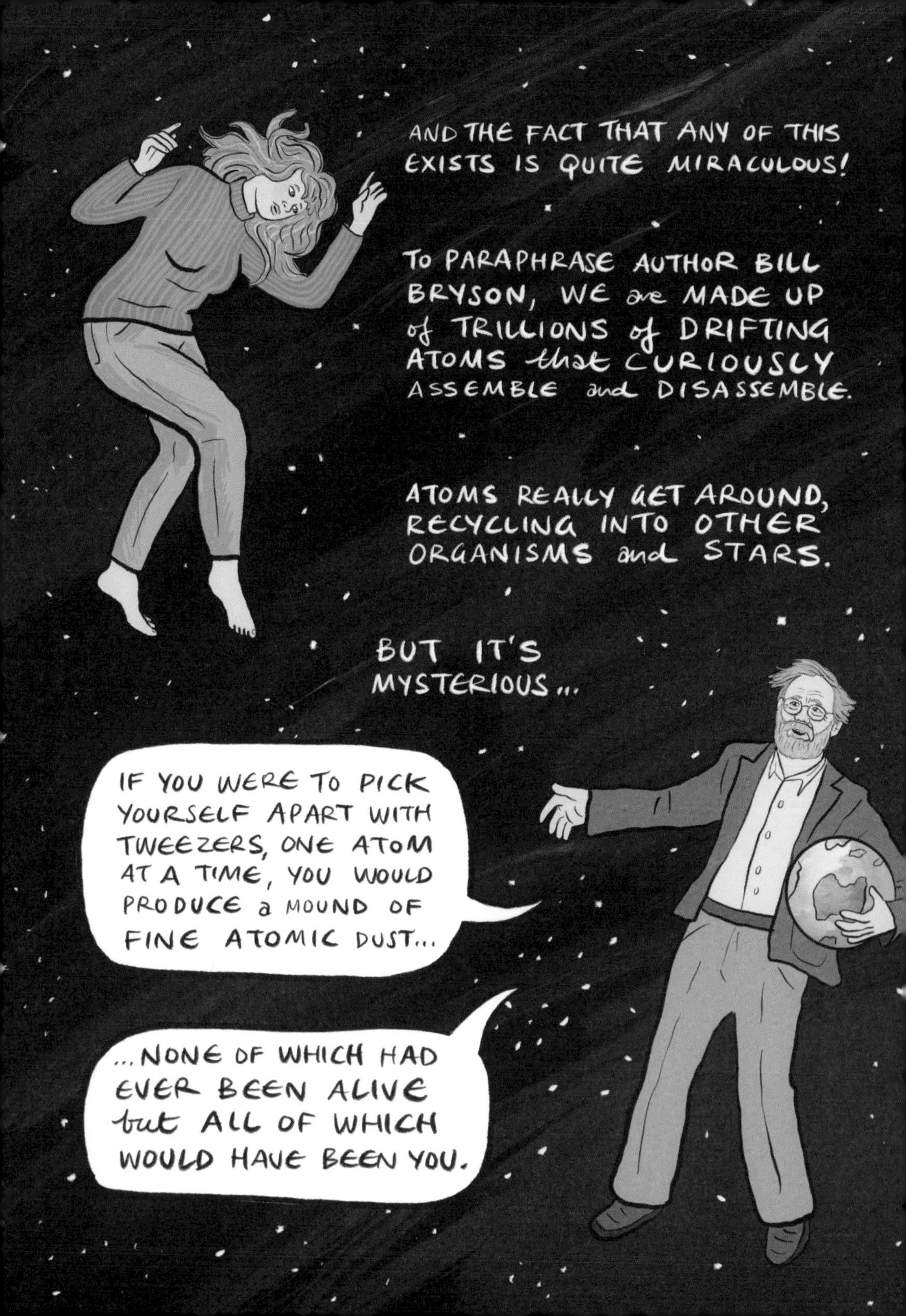
AND THE FACT THAT ANY OF THIS EXISTS IS QUITE MIRACULOUS!
TO PARAPHRASE AUTHOR BILL BRYSON, WE are MADE UP of TRILLIONS of DRIFTING ATOMS that CURIOUSLY ASSEMBLE and DISASSEMBLE.
ATOMS REALLY GET AROUND, RECYCLING INTO OTHER ORGANISMS and STARS.
BUT IT'S MYSTERIOUS...
IF YOU WERE TO PICK YOURSELF APART WITH TWEEZERS, ONE ATOM AT A TIME, YOU WOULD PRODUCE a MOUND OF FINE ATOMIC DUST...
...NONE OF WHICH HAD EVER BEEN ALIVE but ALL OF WHICH WOULD HAVE BEEN YOU.

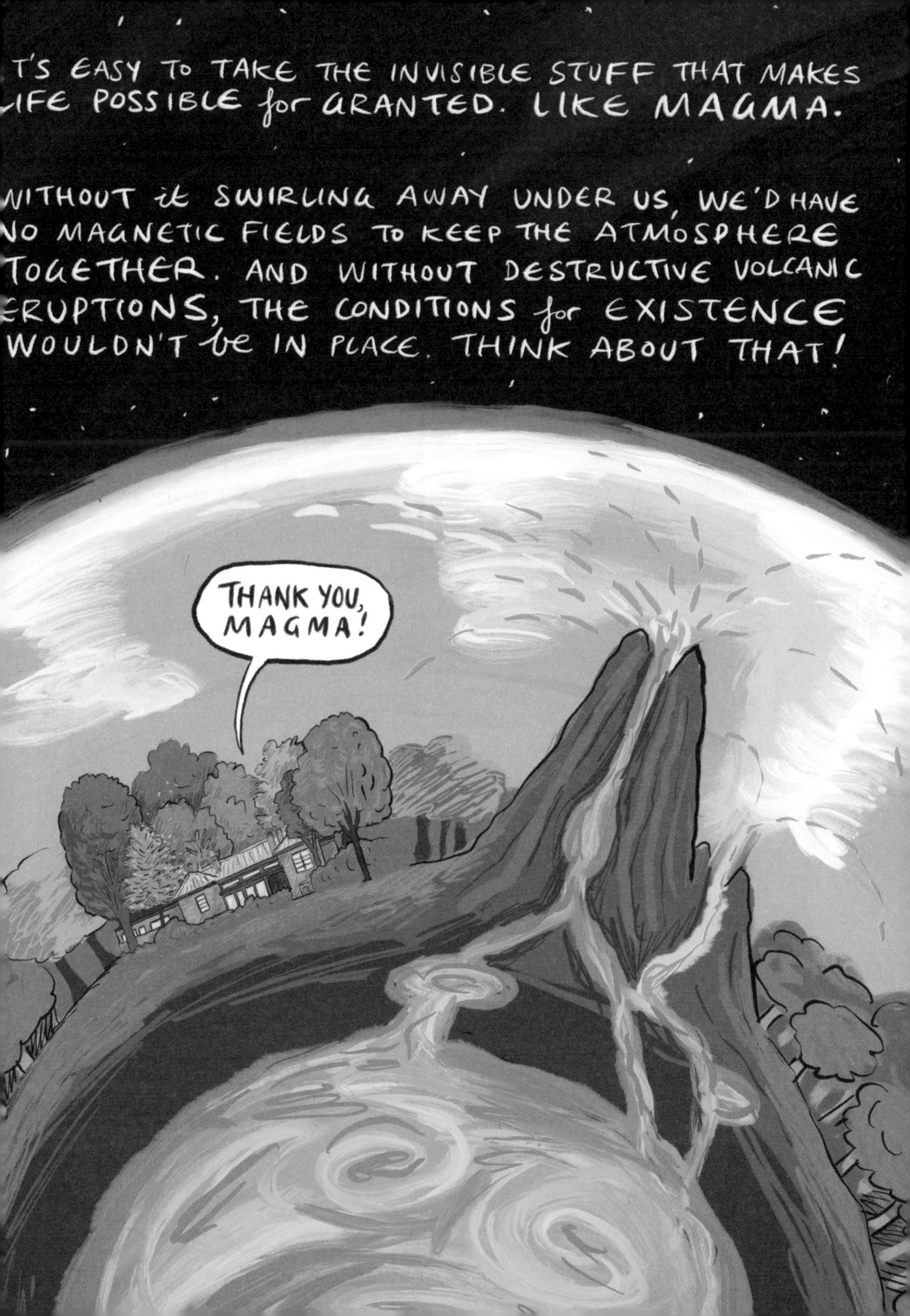
T'S EASY TO TAKE THE INVISIBLE STUFF THAT MAKES LIFE POSSIBLE for GRANTED. LIKE MAGMA.
WITHOUT it SWIRLING AWAY UNDER US, WE'D HAVE NO MAGNETIC FIELDS TO KEEP THE ATMOSPHERE TOGETHER. AND WITHOUT DESTRUCTIVE VOLCANIC ERUPTIONS, THE CONDITIONS for EXISTENCE WOULDN'T be IN PLACE. THINK ABOUT THAT!
THANK YOU, MAGMA!

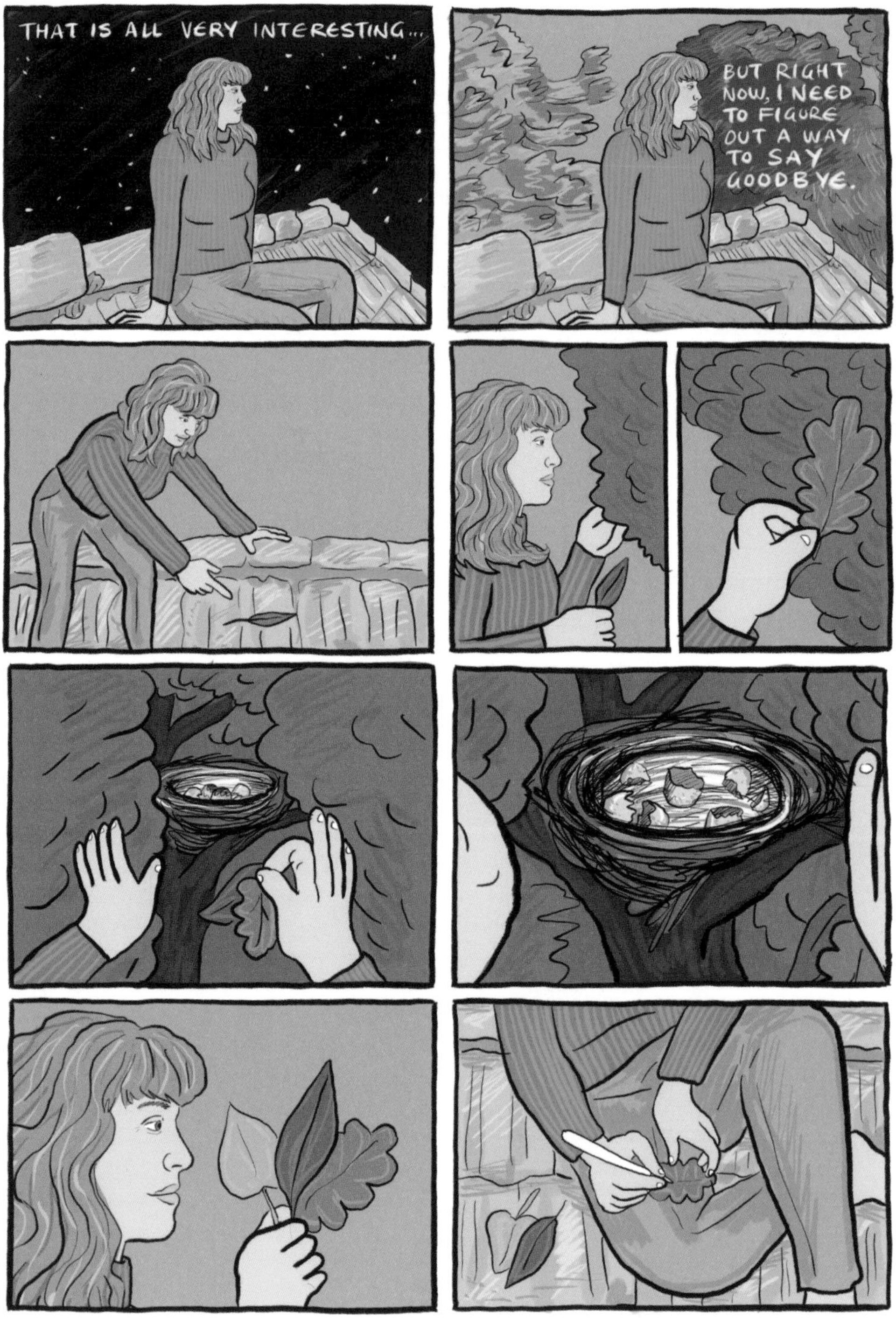
THAT IS ALL VERY INTERESTING...
BUT RIGHT NOW, I NEED TO FIGURE OUT A WAY TO SAY GOODBYE.

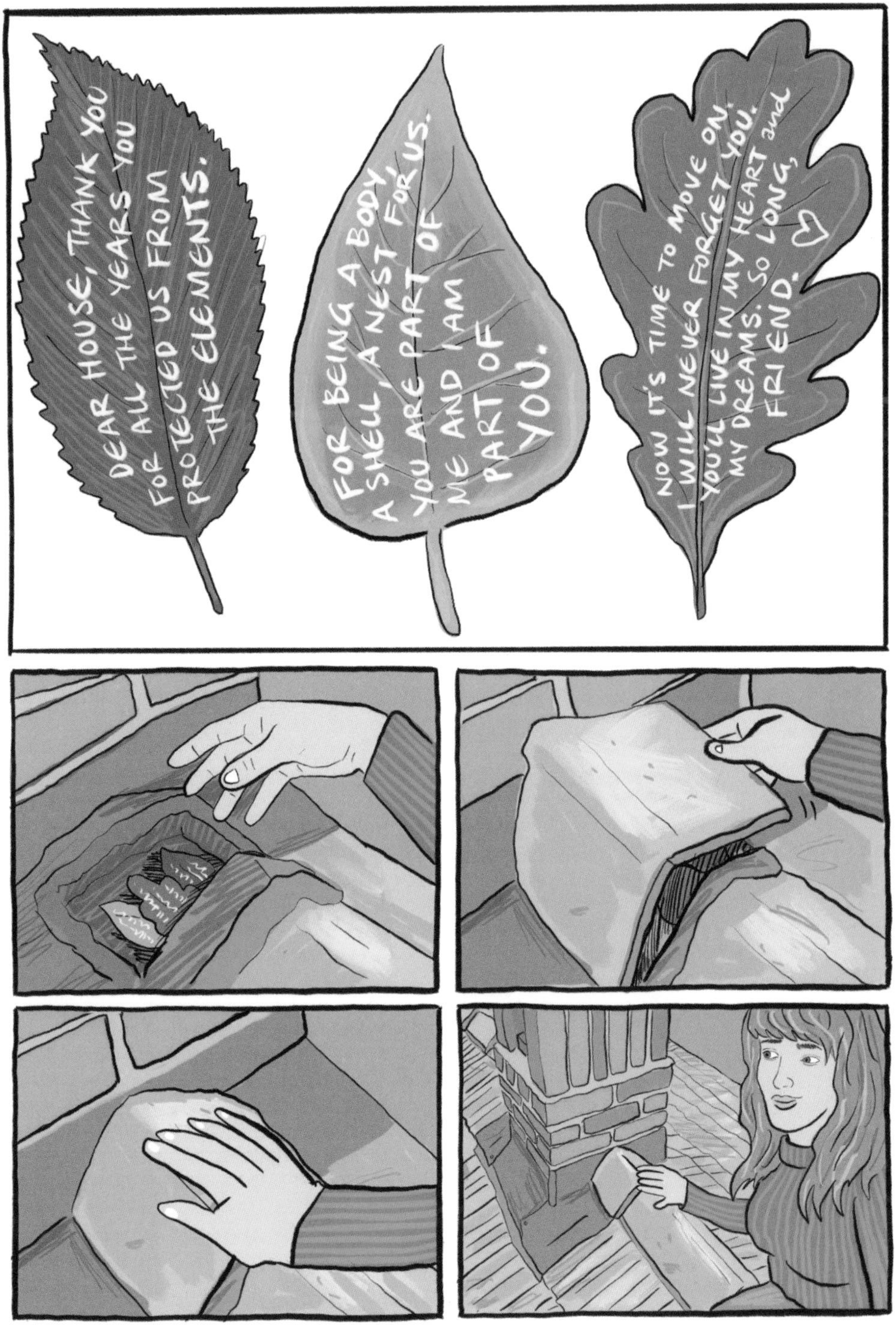
DEAR HOUSE, THANK YOU FOR ALL THE YEARS YOU PROTECTED US FROM THE ELEMENTS.
FOR BEING A BODY, A SHELL, A NEST FOR US. YOU ARE PART OF ME AND I AM PART OF YOU.
NOW IT'S TIME TO MOVE ON. I WILL NEVER FORGET YOU. YOU'LL LIVE IN MY HEART and MY DREAMS. SO LONG, FRIEND.

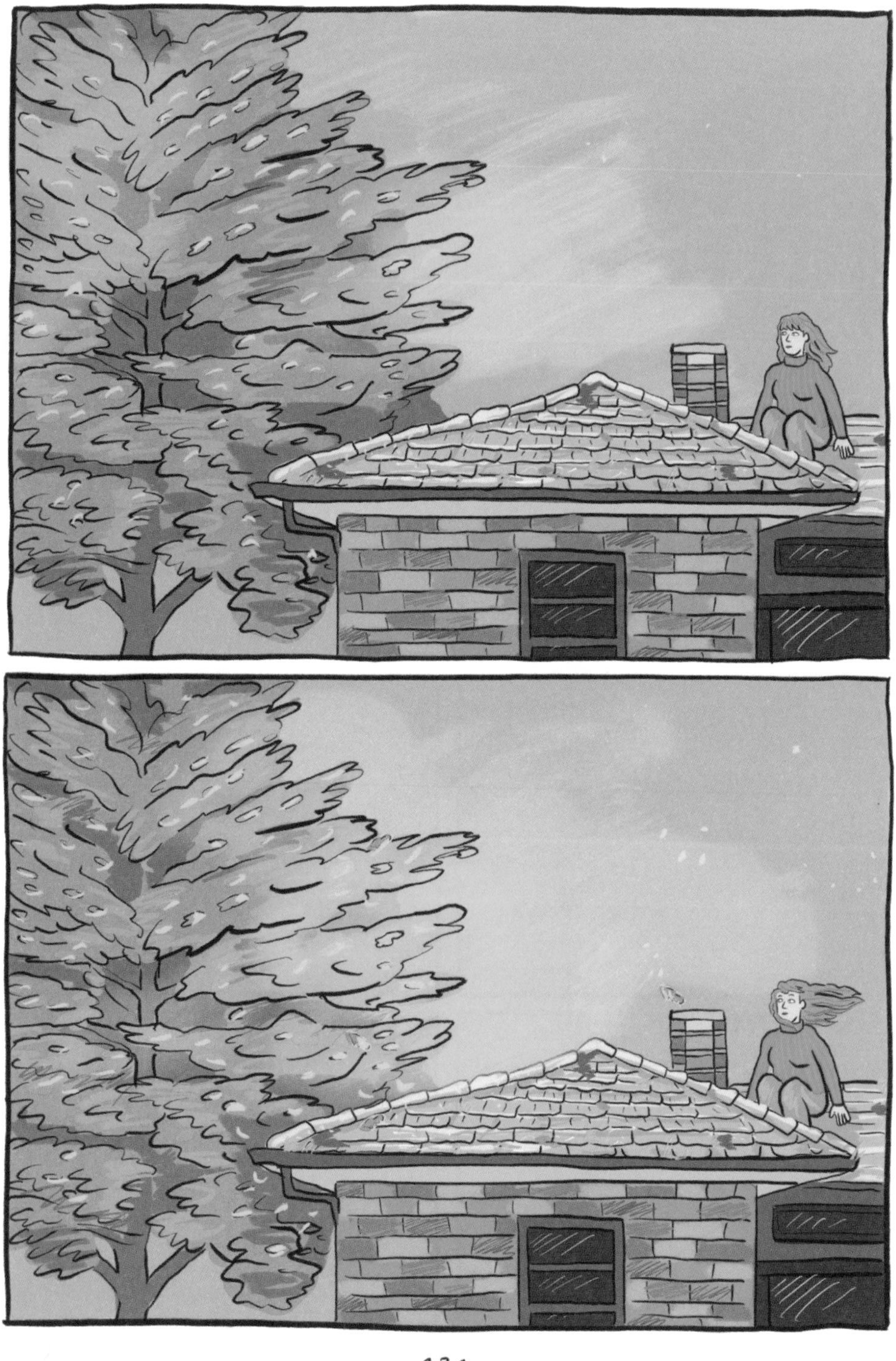

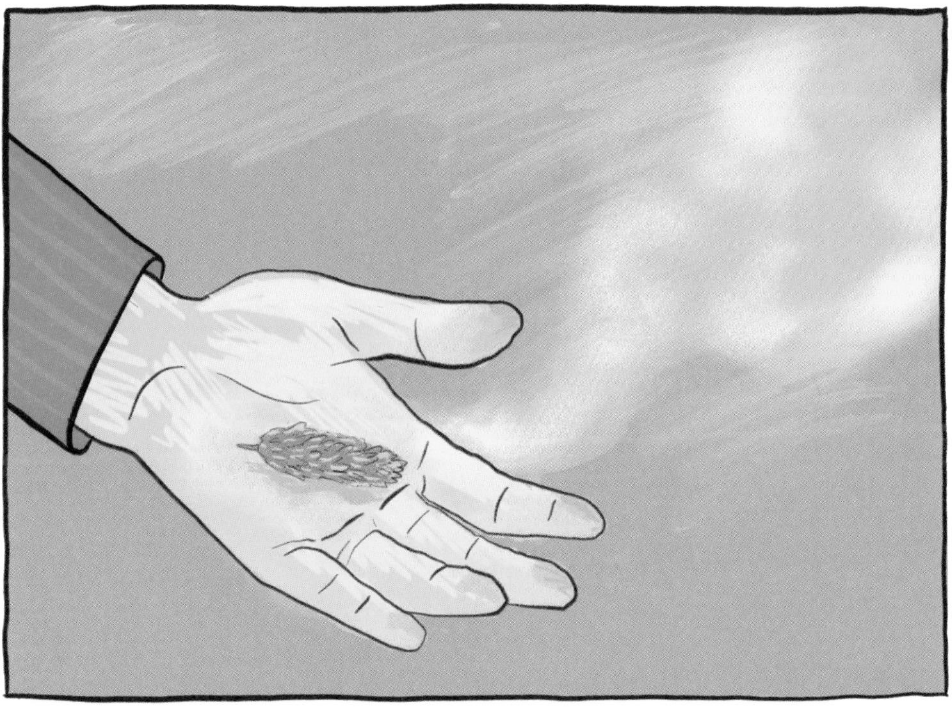

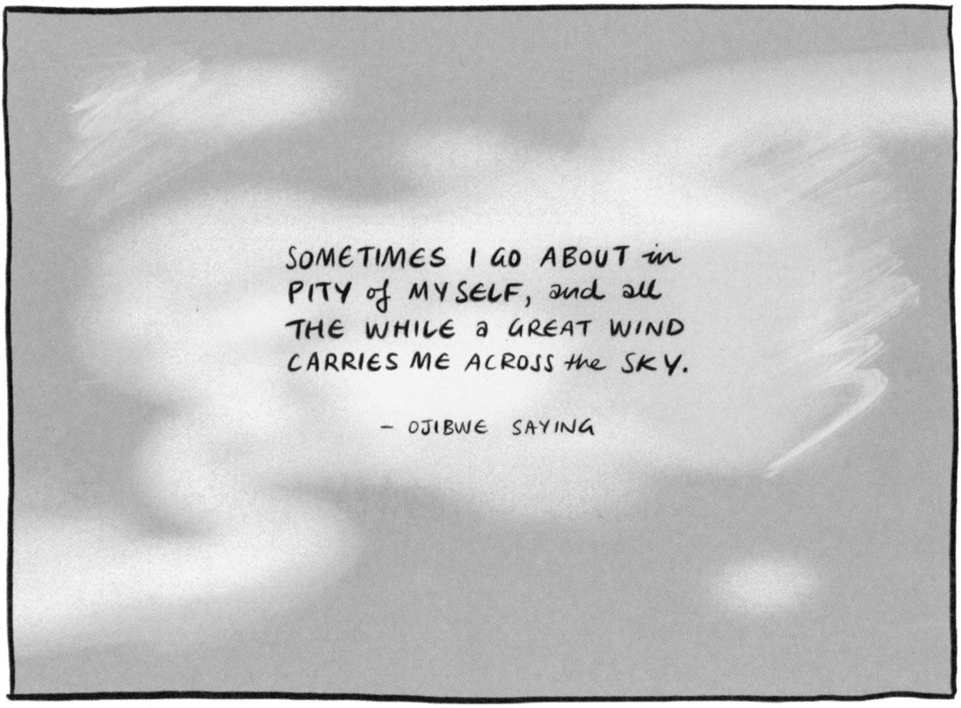
SOMETIMES I GO ABOUT in PITY of MYSELF, and all THE WHILE a GREAT WIND CARRIES ME ACROSS the SKY.
– OJIBWE SAYING

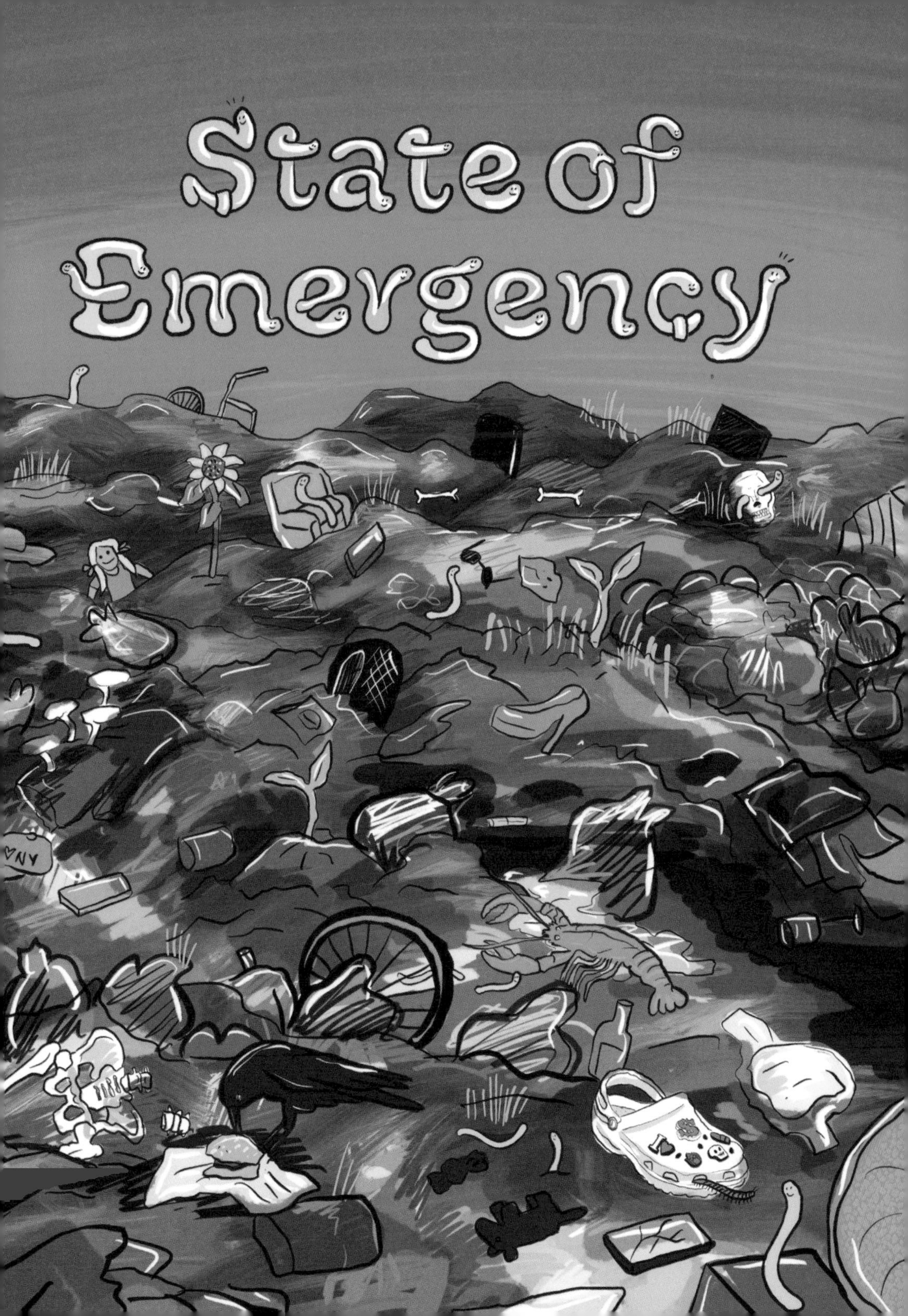
State of Emergency

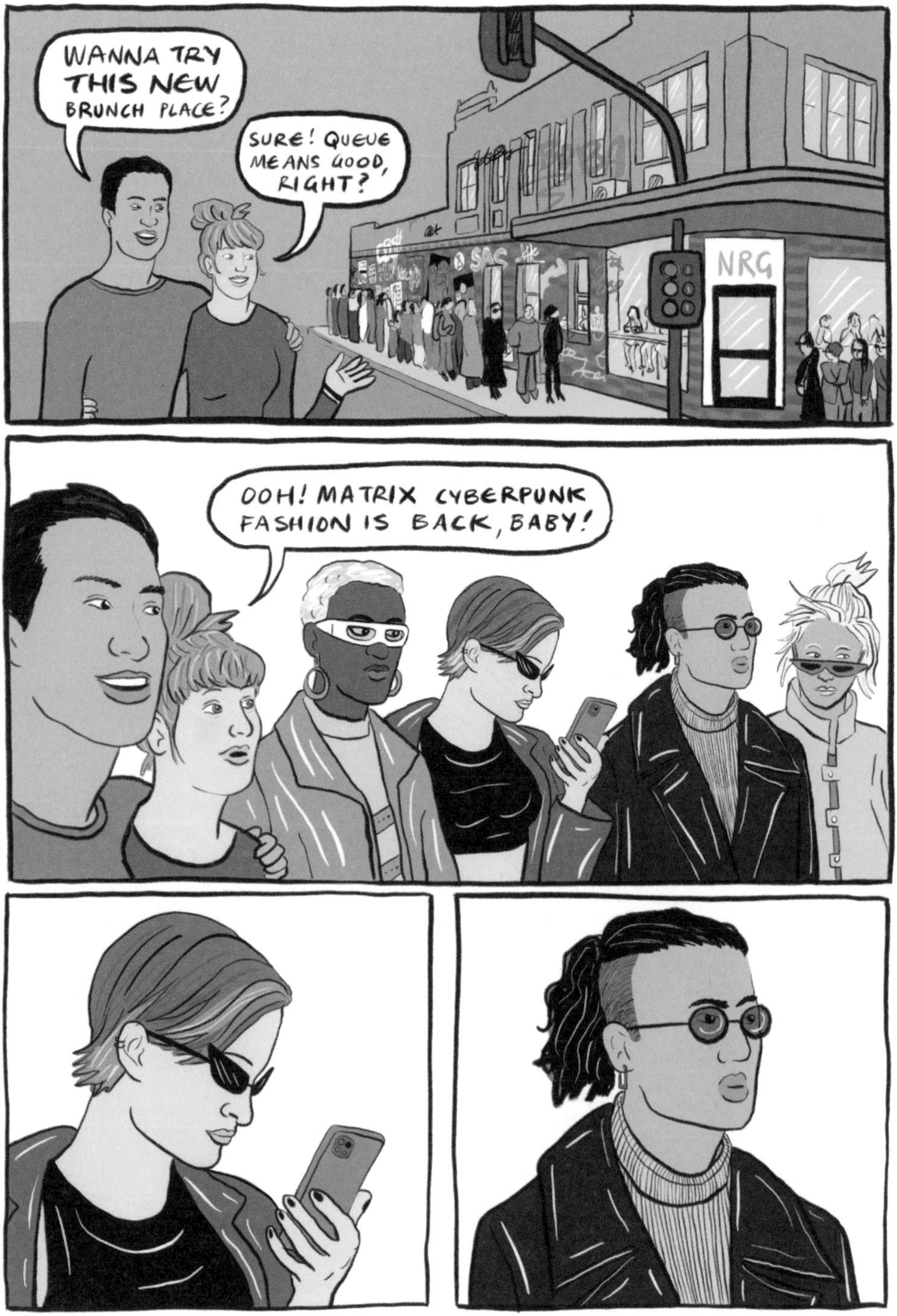
WANNA TRY THIS NEW BRUNCH PLACE?
SURE! QUEUE MEANS GOOD, RIGHT?
SAC
NRG
OOH! MATRIX CYBERPUNK FASHION IS BACK, BABY!

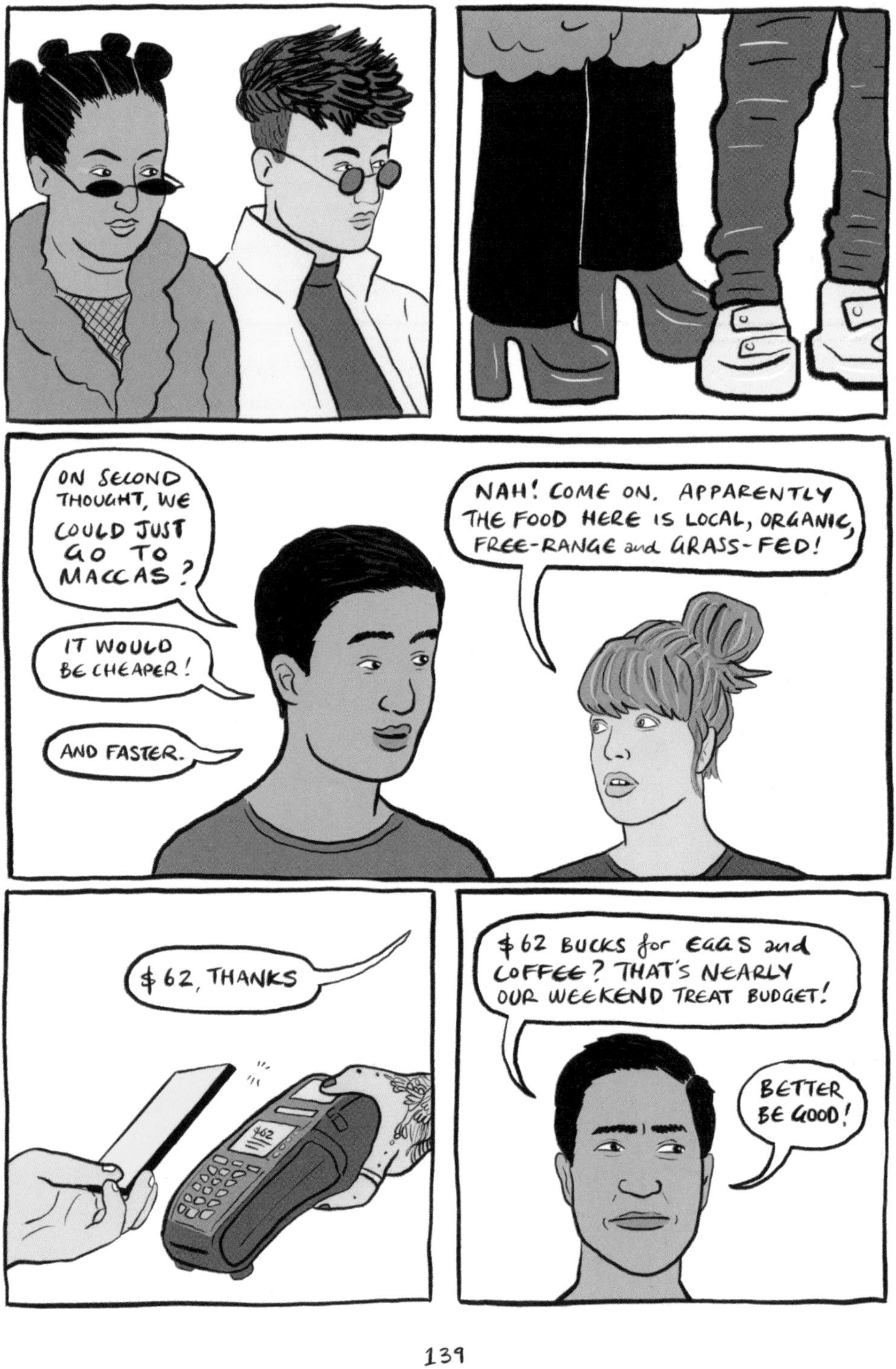
ON SECOND THOUGHT, WE COULD JUST GO TO MACCAS?
IT WOULD BE CHEAPER!
AND FASTER.
NAH! COME ON. APPARENTLY THE FOOD HERE IS LOCAL, ORGANIC, FREE-RANGE and GRASS-FED!
$62, THANKS
$62
$62 BUCKS for EGGS and COFFEE? THAT'S NEARLY OUR WEEKEND TREAT BUDGET!
BETTER BE GOOD!

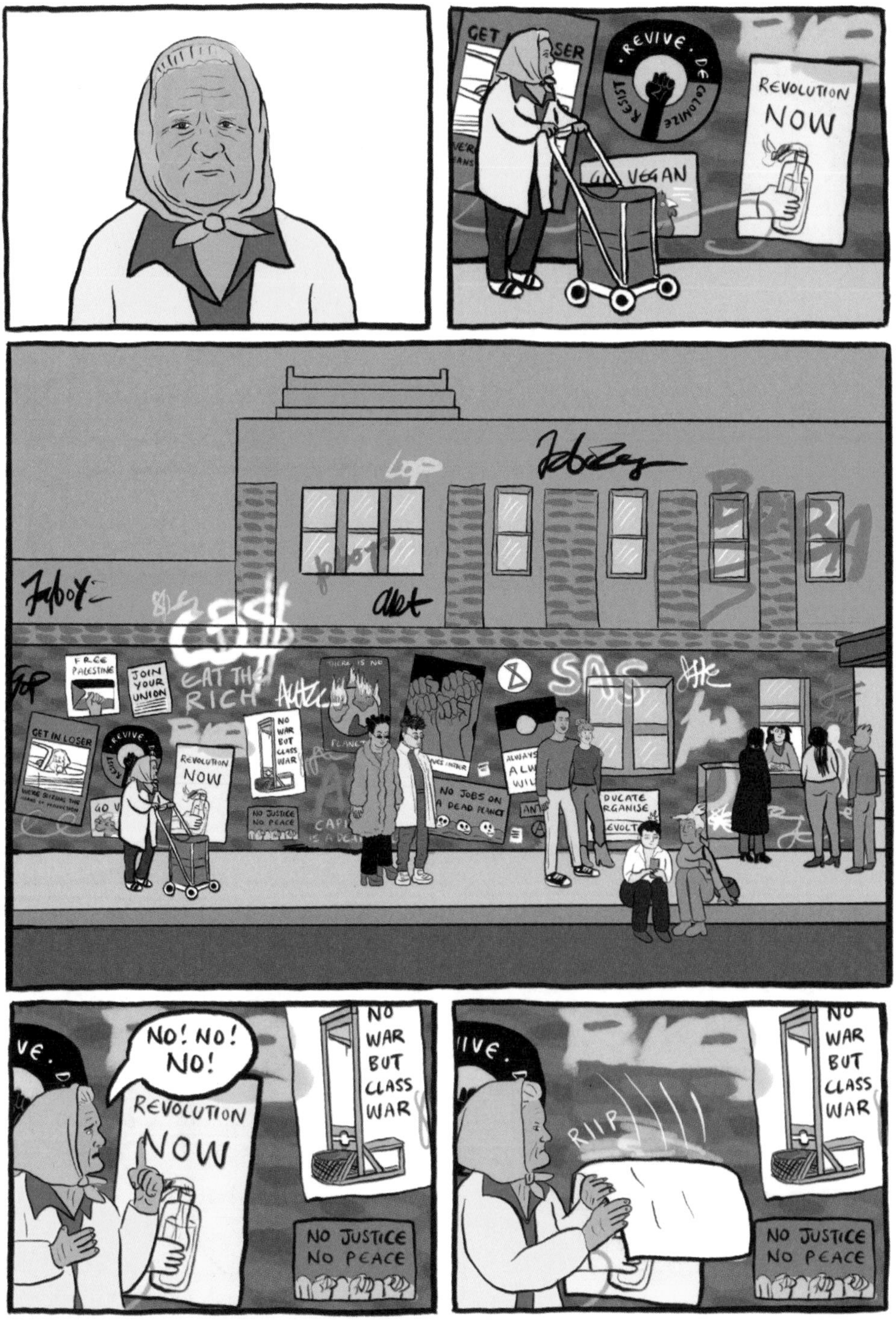
GET IN LOSER
REVIVE · DE COLONIZE · RESIST
REVOLUTION NOW
FREE PALESTINE
JOIN YOUR UNION
EAT THE RICH
GET IN LOSER
REVOLUTION NOW
NO WAR BUT CLASS WAR
NO JUSTICE NO PEACE
NO JOBS ON A DEAD PLANET
NO! NO! NO!
REVOLUTION NOW
NO WAR BUT CLASS WAR
NO JUSTICE NO PEACE
RIIP
NO WAR BUT CLASS WAR
NO JUSTICE NO PEACE

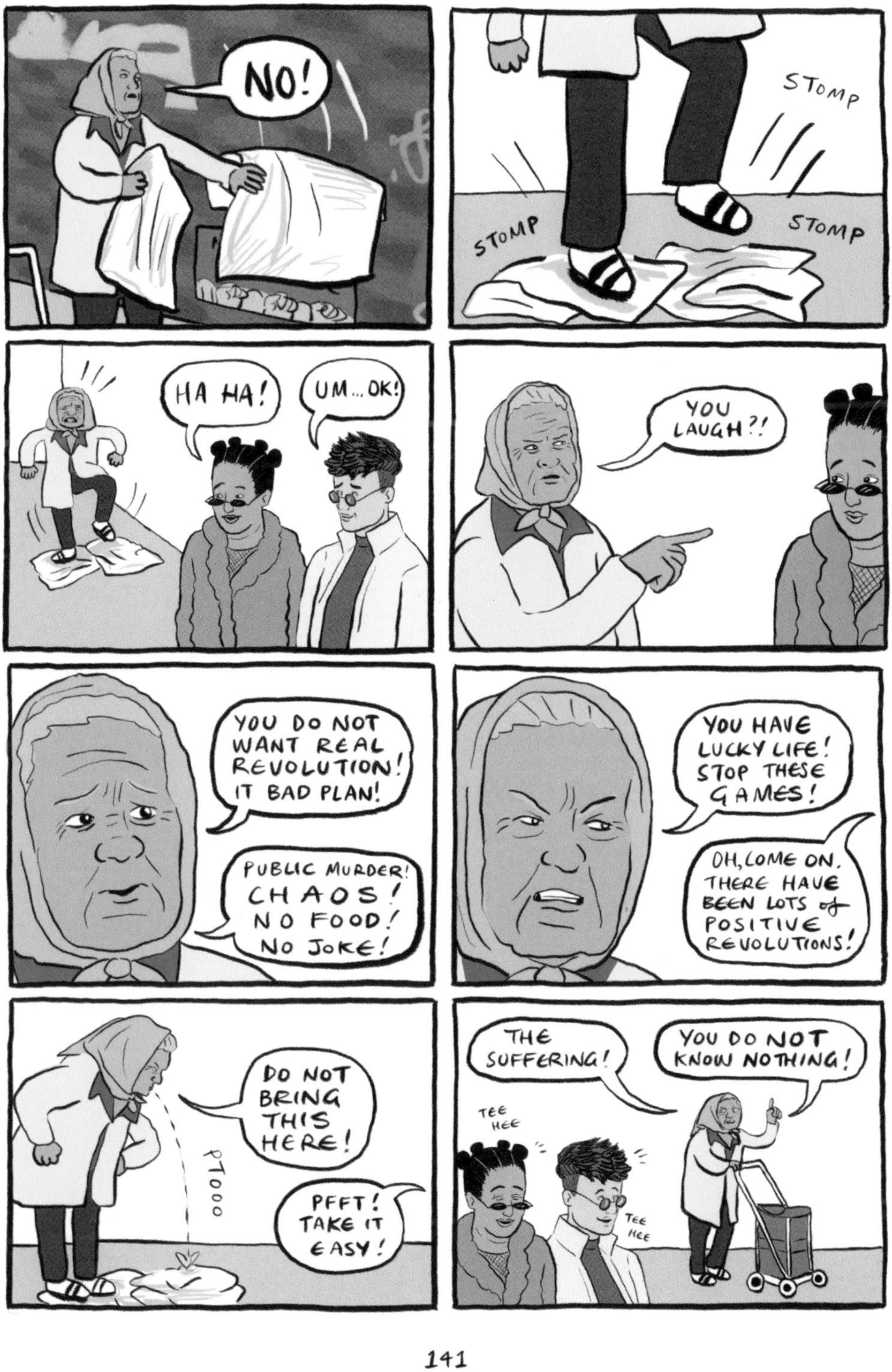
NO!
STOMP
STOMP
STOMP
HA HA!
UM...OK!
YOU LAUGH?!
YOU DO NOT WANT REAL REVOLUTION! IT BAD PLAN!
PUBLIC MURDER! CHAOS! NO FOOD! NO JOKE!
YOU HAVE LUCKY LIFE! STOP THESE GAMES!
OH, COME ON. THERE HAVE BEEN LOTS of POSITIVE REVOLUTIONS!
DO NOT BRING THIS HERE!
PTOOO
PFFT! TAKE IT EASY!
THE SUFFERING!
YOU DO NOT KNOW NOTHING!
TEE HEE
TEE HEE

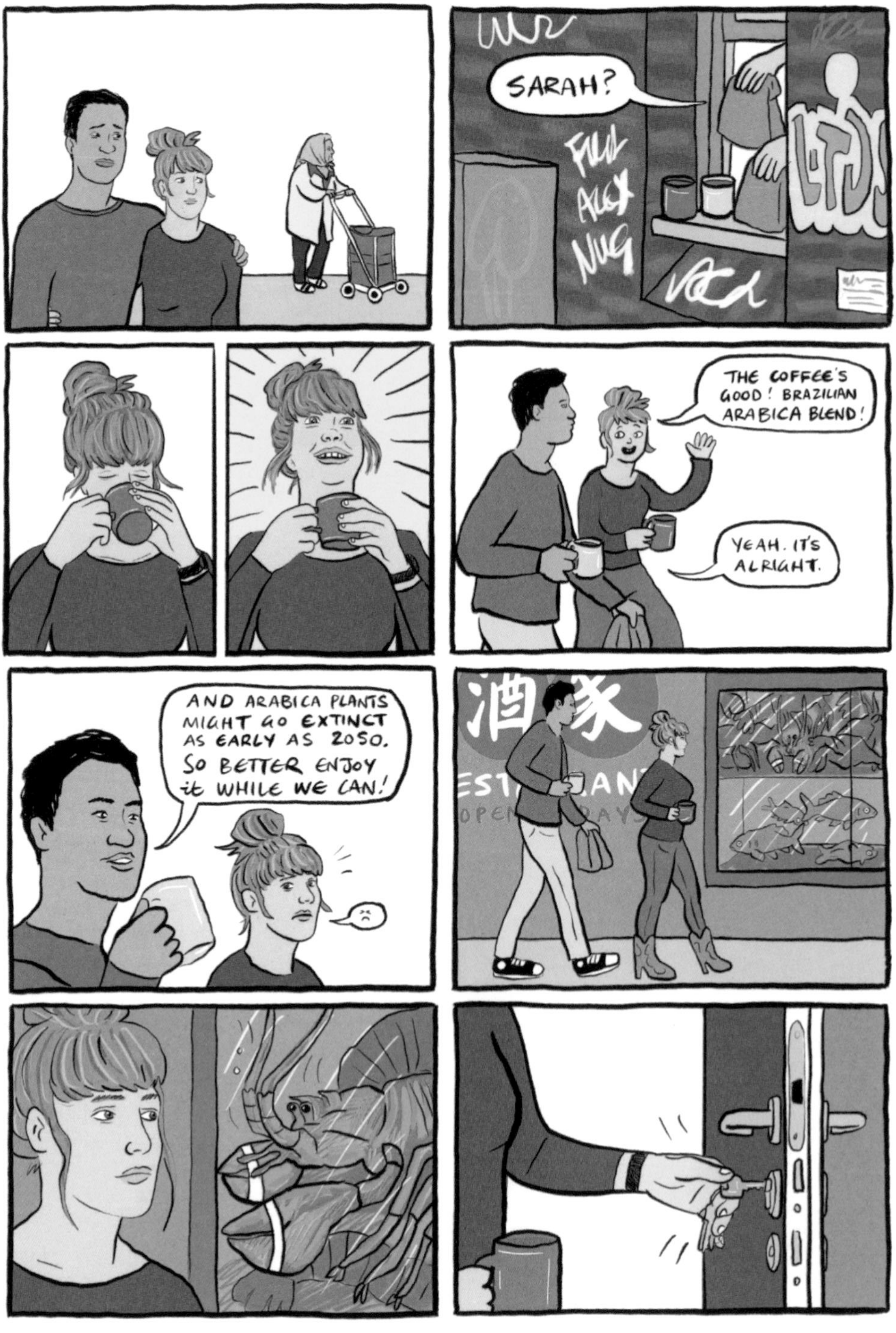
SARAH?
THE COFFEE'S GOOD! BRAZILIAN ARABICA BLEND!
YEAH. IT'S ALRIGHT.
AND ARABICA PLANTS MIGHT GO EXTINCT AS EARLY AS 2050. SO BETTER ENJOY IT WHILE WE CAN!
酒家

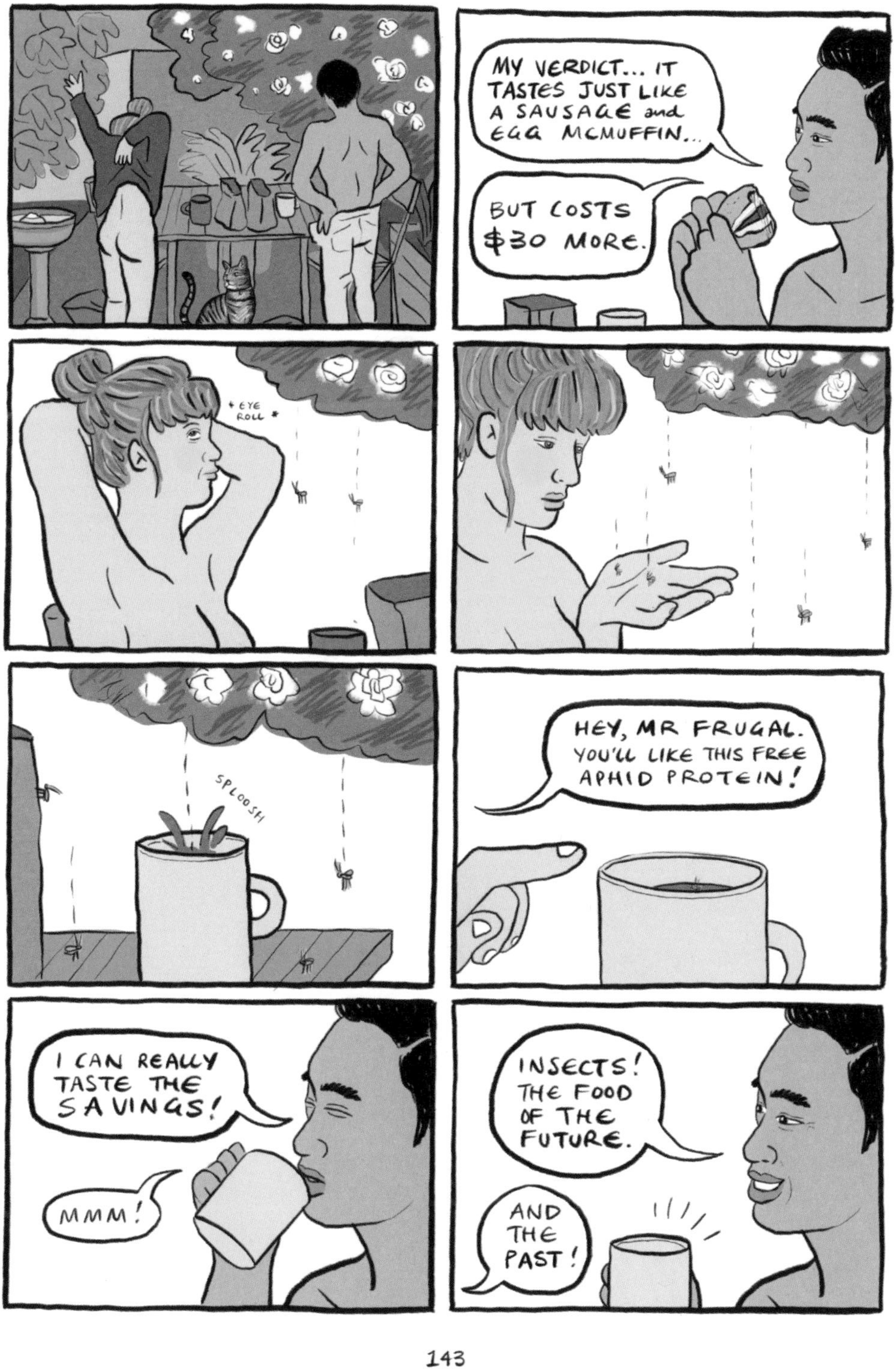
MY VERDICT... IT TASTES JUST LIKE A SAUSAGE and EGG MCMUFFIN...
BUT COSTS $30 MORE.
*EYE ROLL*
SPLOOSH
HEY, MR FRUGAL. YOU'LL LIKE THIS FREE APHID PROTEIN!
I CAN REALLY TASTE THE SAVINGS!
MMM!
INSECTS! THE FOOD OF THE FUTURE.
AND THE PAST!

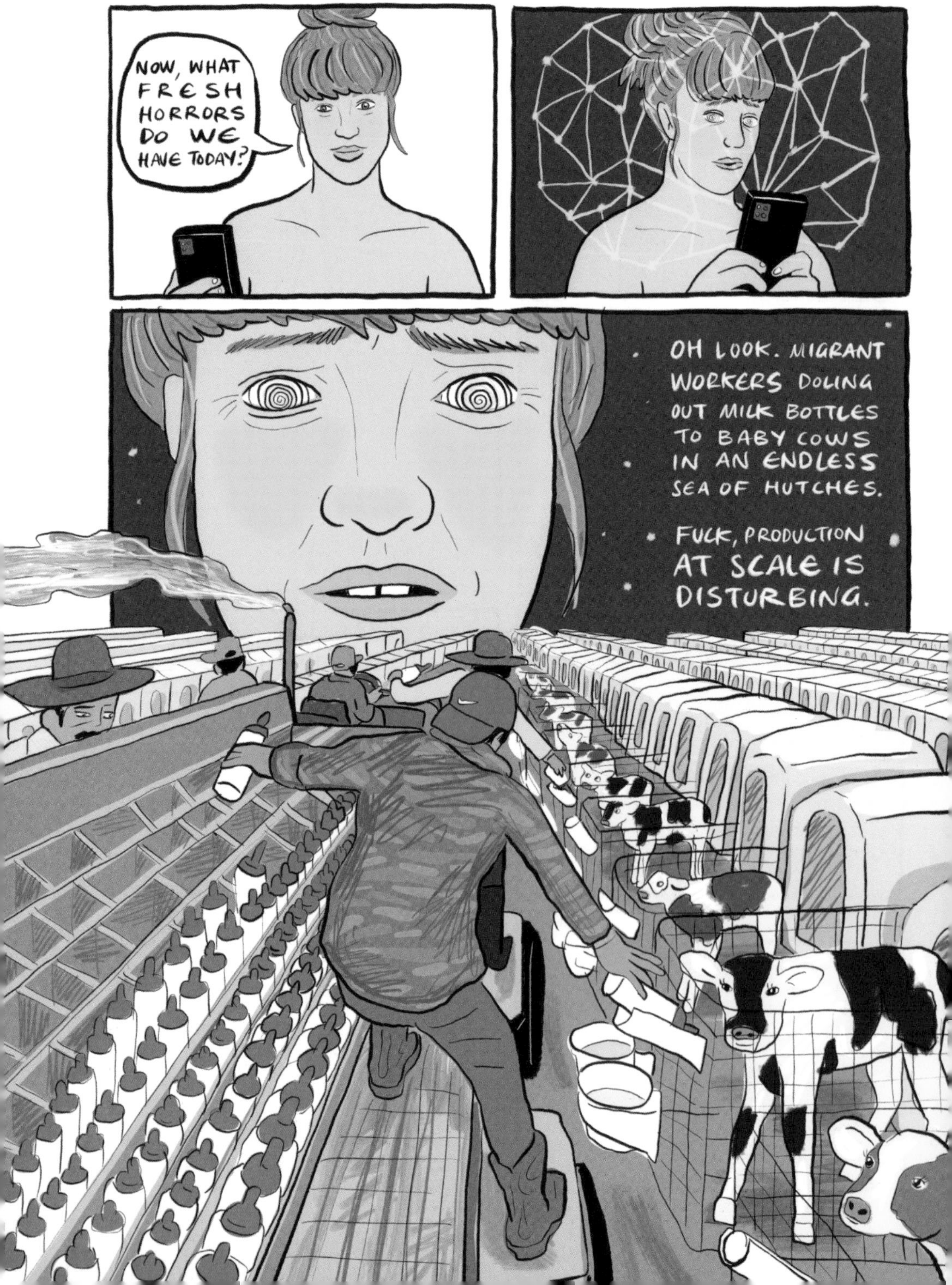
NOW, WHAT FRESH HORRORS DO WE HAVE TODAY?
OH LOOK. MIGRANT WORKERS DOLING OUT MILK BOTTLES TO BABY COWS IN AN ENDLESS SEA OF HUTCHES.
FUCK, PRODUCTION AT SCALE IS DISTURBING.

I OCCASIONALLY NEED TO EAT ANIMAL PRODUCTS for HEALTH REASONS. I TRY TO EAT AS INTENTIONALLY AS I CAN ACCESS and AFFORD.

THE HORROR of THE SYSTEMS and SCALE of INDUSTRIALISED FARMING CERTAINLY BREAKS MY BRAIN.

WILL LAB-GROWN MEAT MAKE IT ALL MORE ETHICAL AND CHEAP?

LATELY, I'VE BOUGHT MEAT STRAIGHT FROM SMALL LOCAL FARMS, DEER and KANGAROO CULLS and SUSTAINABLE HUNTING.

CAN THINGS LIKE THESE SCALE? SHOULD THEY? CAN ANYTHING AT SCALE BE ETHICAL and ENVIRONMENTALLY POSITIVE?

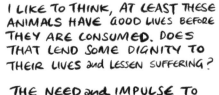

I LIKE TO THINK, AT LEAST THESE ANIMALS HAVE GOOD LIVES BEFORE THEY ARE CONSUMED. DOES THAT LEND SOME DIGNITY TO THEIR LIVES and LESSEN SUFFERING?

THE NEED and IMPULSE TO EXPLOIT OTHER CREATURES AS RESOURCES and FUEL are EVERYWHERE.

LIKE WITH THE ABUNDANCE of APHIDS on THE ROSES HERE. ANTS HAVE MOVED in TO MILK and FARM THEM.

WE'RE NOT TAKING ADVANTAGE of THEM!

IT'S A WIN-WIN!

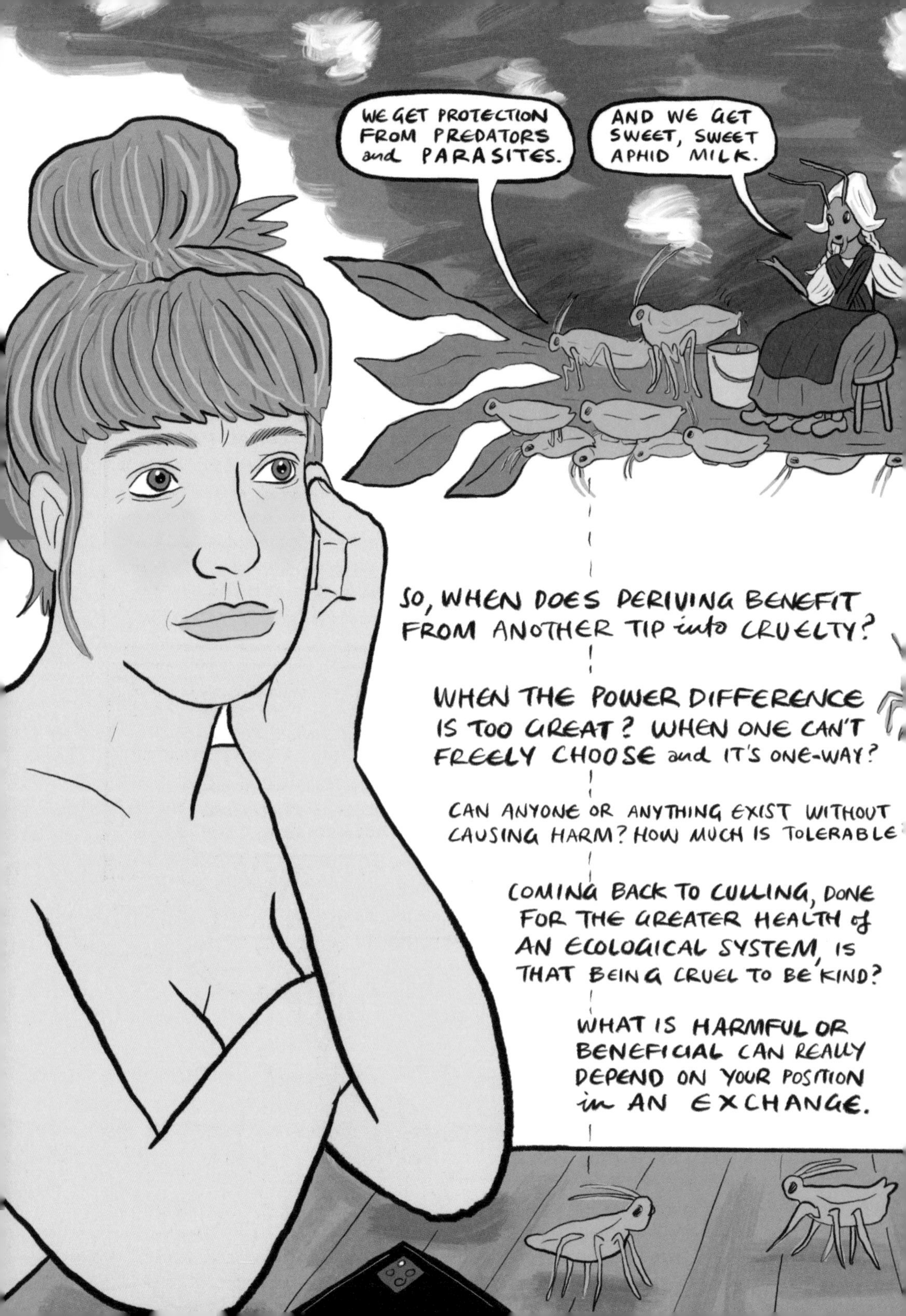
WE GET PROTECTION FROM PREDATORS and PARASITES.
AND WE GET SWEET, SWEET APHID MILK.
SO, WHEN DOES DERIVING BENEFIT FROM ANOTHER TIP into CRUELTY?
WHEN THE POWER DIFFERENCE IS TOO GREAT? WHEN ONE CAN'T FREELY CHOOSE and IT'S ONE-WAY?
CAN ANYONE OR ANYTHING EXIST WITHOUT CAUSING HARM? HOW MUCH IS TOLERABLE
COMING BACK TO CULLING, DONE FOR THE GREATER HEALTH of AN ECOLOGICAL SYSTEM, IS THAT BEING CRUEL TO BE KIND?
WHAT IS HARMFUL OR BENEFICIAL CAN REALLY DEPEND ON YOUR POSITION in AN EXCHANGE.

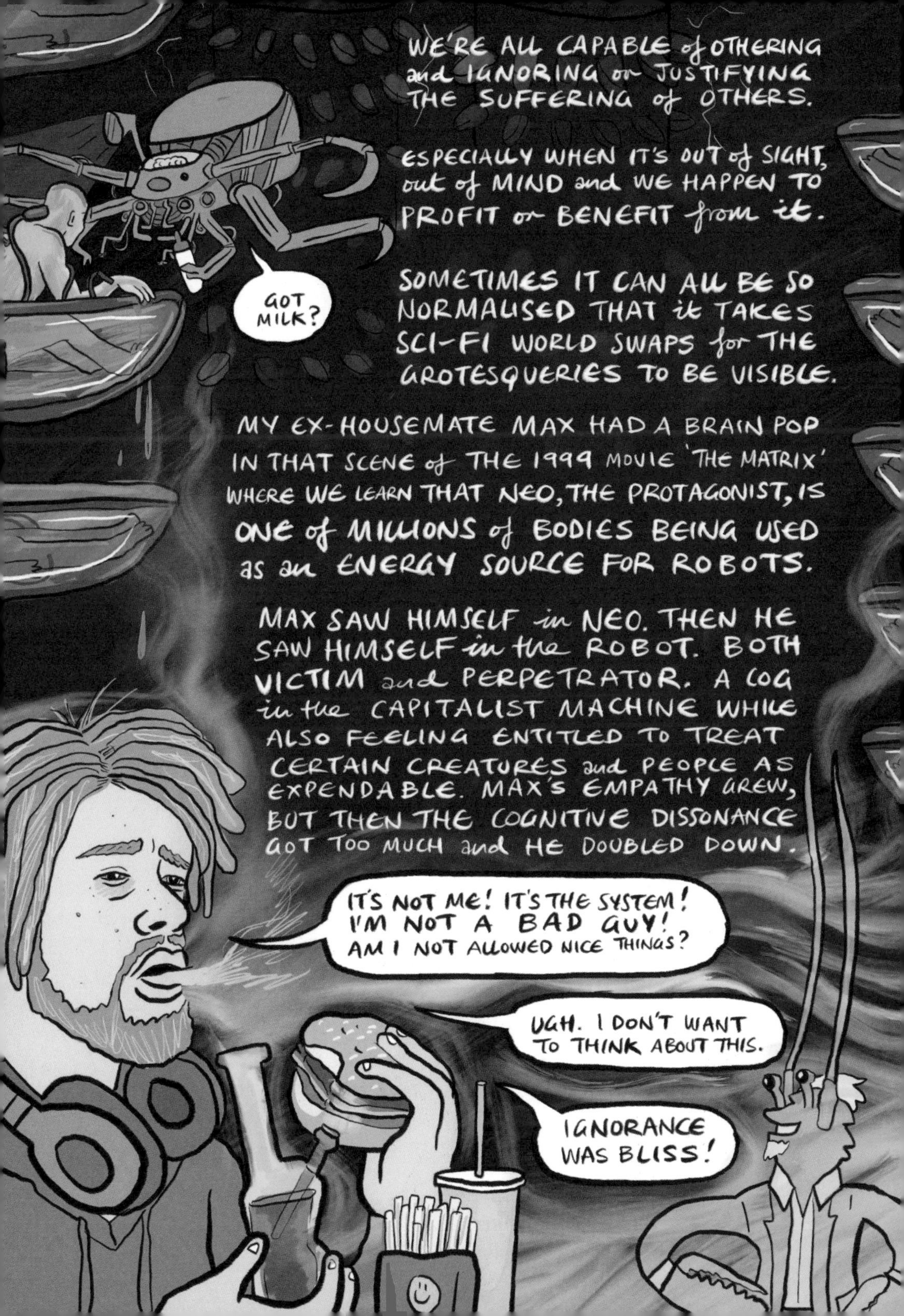
WE'RE ALL CAPABLE of OTHERING and IGNORING or JUSTIFYING THE SUFFERING of OTHERS.
ESPECIALLY WHEN IT'S OUT of SIGHT, out of MIND and WE HAPPEN TO PROFIT or BENEFIT from it.
GOT MILK?
SOMETIMES IT CAN ALL BE SO NORMALISED THAT it TAKES SCI-FI WORLD SWAPS for THE GROTESQUERIES TO BE VISIBLE.
MY EX-HOUSEMATE MAX HAD A BRAIN POP IN THAT SCENE of THE 1999 MOVIE 'THE MATRIX' WHERE WE LEARN THAT NEO, THE PROTAGONIST, IS ONE of MILLIONS of BODIES BEING USED as an ENERGY SOURCE FOR ROBOTS.
MAX SAW HIMSELF in NEO. THEN HE SAW HIMSELF in the ROBOT. BOTH VICTIM and PERPETRATOR. A COG in the CAPITALIST MACHINE WHILE ALSO FEELING ENTITLED TO TREAT CERTAIN CREATURES and PEOPLE AS EXPENDABLE. MAX'S EMPATHY GREW, BUT THEN THE COGNITIVE DISSONANCE GOT TOO MUCH and HE DOUBLED DOWN.
IT'S NOT ME! IT'S THE SYSTEM! I'M NOT A BAD GUY! AM I NOT ALLOWED NICE THINGS?
UGH. I DON'T WANT TO THINK ABOUT THIS.
IGNORANCE WAS BLISS!

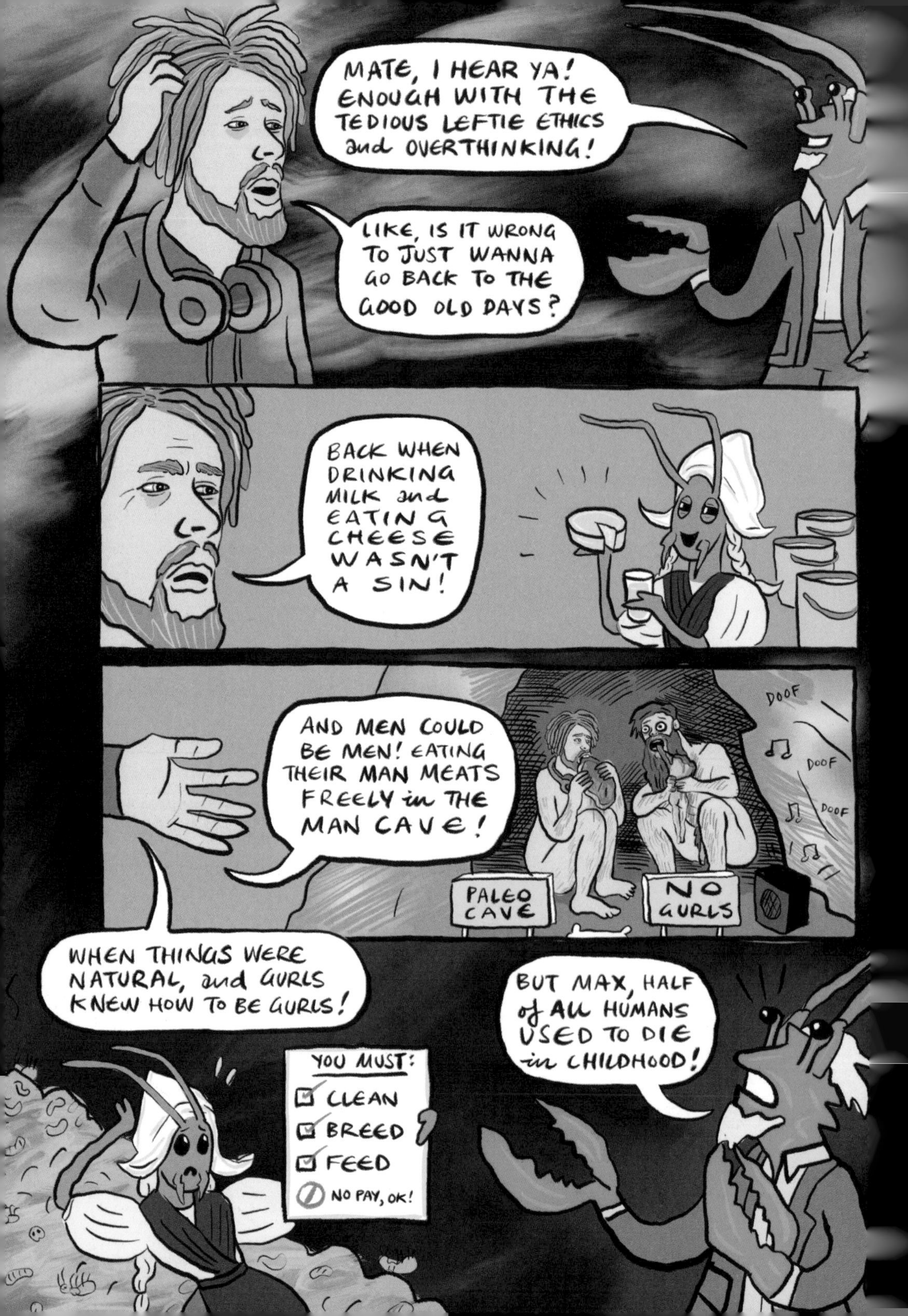
MATE, I HEAR YA! ENOUGH WITH THE TEDIOUS LEFTIE ETHICS and OVERTHINKING!
LIKE, IS IT WRONG TO JUST WANNA GO BACK TO THE GOOD OLD DAYS?
BACK WHEN DRINKING MILK and EATING CHEESE WASN'T A SIN!
AND MEN COULD BE MEN! EATING THEIR MAN MEATS FREELY in THE MAN CAVE!
DOOF
DOOF
DOOF
PALEO CAVE
NO GURLS
WHEN THINGS WERE NATURAL, and GURLS KNEW HOW TO BE GURLS!
YOU MUST:
CLEAN
BREED
FEED
NO PAY, OK!
BUT MAX, HALF of ALL HUMANS USED TO DIE in CHILDHOOD!

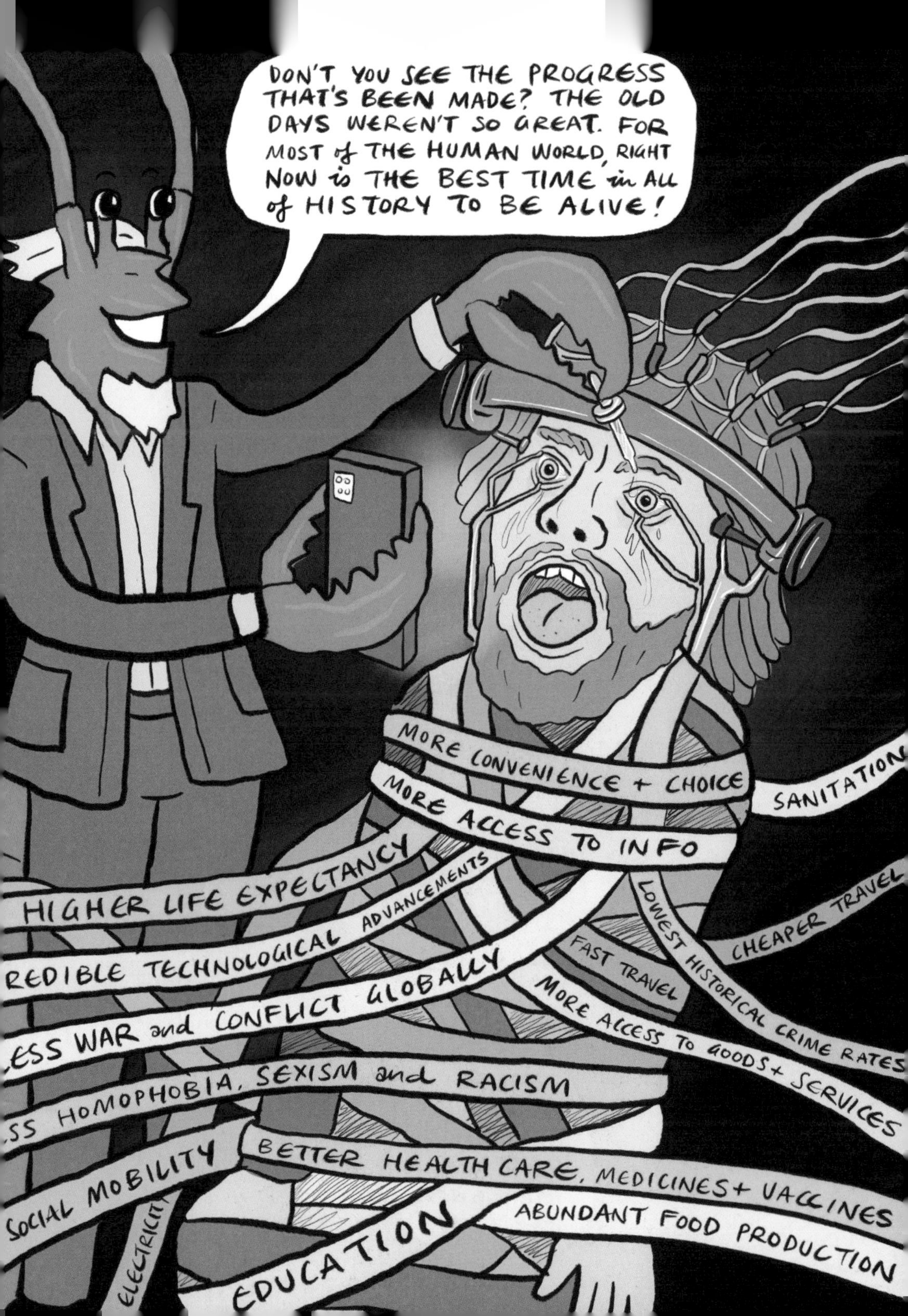
DON'T YOU SEE THE PROGRESS THAT'S BEEN MADE? THE OLD DAYS WEREN'T SO GREAT. FOR MOST of THE HUMAN WORLD, RIGHT NOW is THE BEST TIME in ALL of HISTORY TO BE ALIVE!
MORE CONVENIENCE + CHOICE
SANITATION
MORE ACCESS TO INFO
HIGHER LIFE EXPECTANCY
REDIBLE TECHNOLOGICAL ADVANCEMENTS
CHEAPER TRAVEL
LOWEST HISTORICAL CRIME RATES
FAST TRAVEL
ESS WAR and CONFLICT GLOBALLY
MORE ACCESS TO GOODS + SERVICES
SS HOMOPHOBIA, SEXISM and RACISM
SOCIAL MOBILITY
BETTER HEALTH CARE, MEDICINES + VACCINES
ELECTRICITY
EDUCATION
ABUNDANT FOOD PRODUCTION

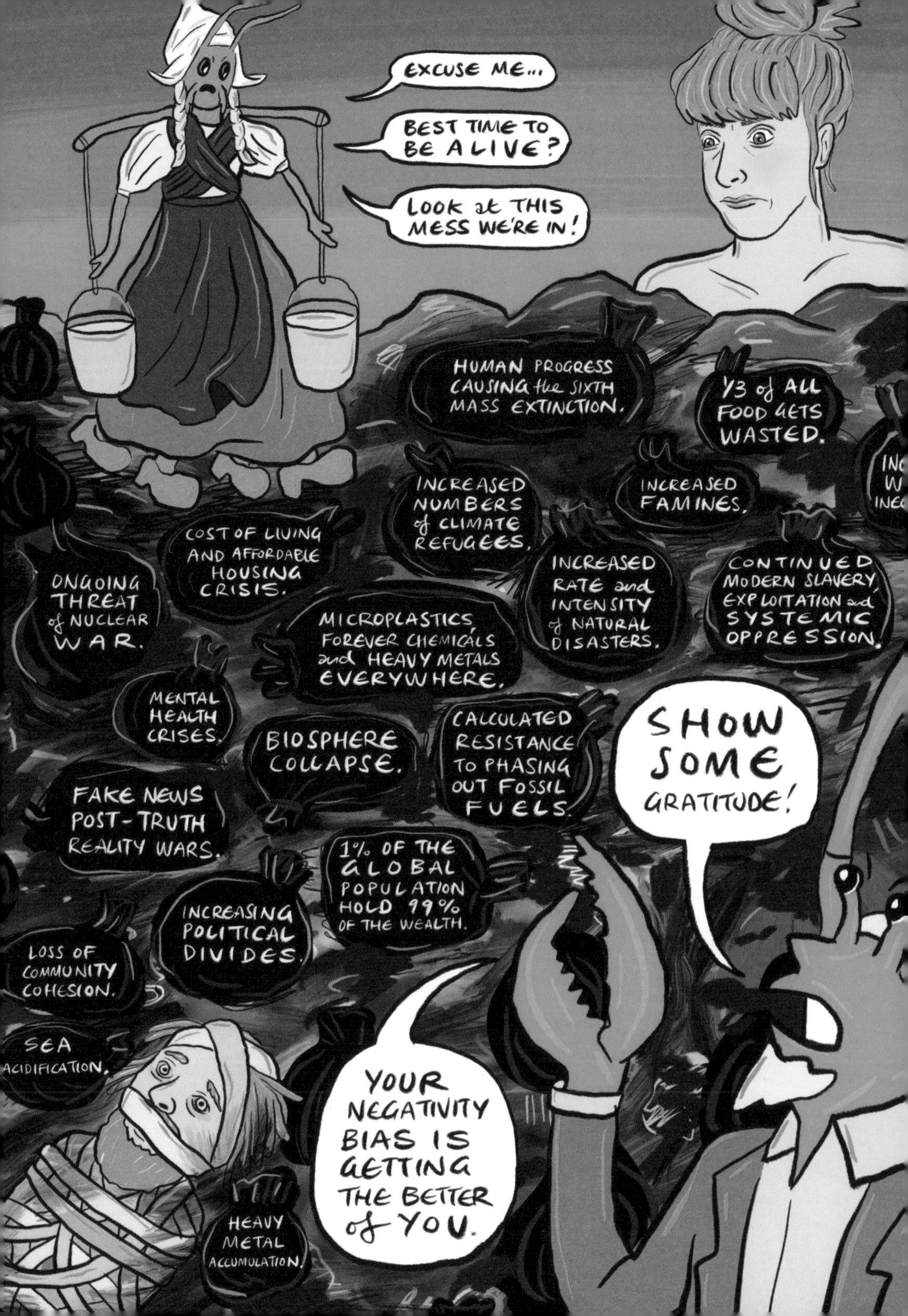
EXCUSE ME...
BEST TIME TO BE ALIVE?
LOOK at THIS MESS WE'RE IN!
HUMAN PROGRESS CAUSING the SIXTH MASS EXTINCTION.
1/3 of ALL FOOD GETS WASTED.
INCREASED NUMBERS of CLIMATE REFUGEES.
INCREASED FAMINES.
COST OF LIVING AND AFFORDABLE HOUSING CRISIS.
ONGOING THREAT of NUCLEAR WAR.
INCREASED RATE and INTENSITY of NATURAL DISASTERS.
CONTINUED MODERN SLAVERY, EXPLOITATION and SYSTEMIC OPPRESSION.
MICROPLASTICS, FOREVER CHEMICALS and HEAVY METALS EVERYWHERE.
MENTAL HEALTH CRISES.
BIOSPHERE COLLAPSE.
CALCULATED RESISTANCE TO PHASING OUT FOSSIL FUELS.
SHOW SOME GRATITUDE!
FAKE NEWS POST-TRUTH REALITY WARS.
1% OF THE GLOBAL POPULATION HOLD 99% OF THE WEALTH.
INCREASING POLITICAL DIVIDES.
LOSS OF COMMUNITY COHESION.
SEA ACIDIFICATION.
YOUR NEGATIVITY BIAS IS GETTING THE BETTER of YOU.
HEAVY METAL ACCUMULATION.

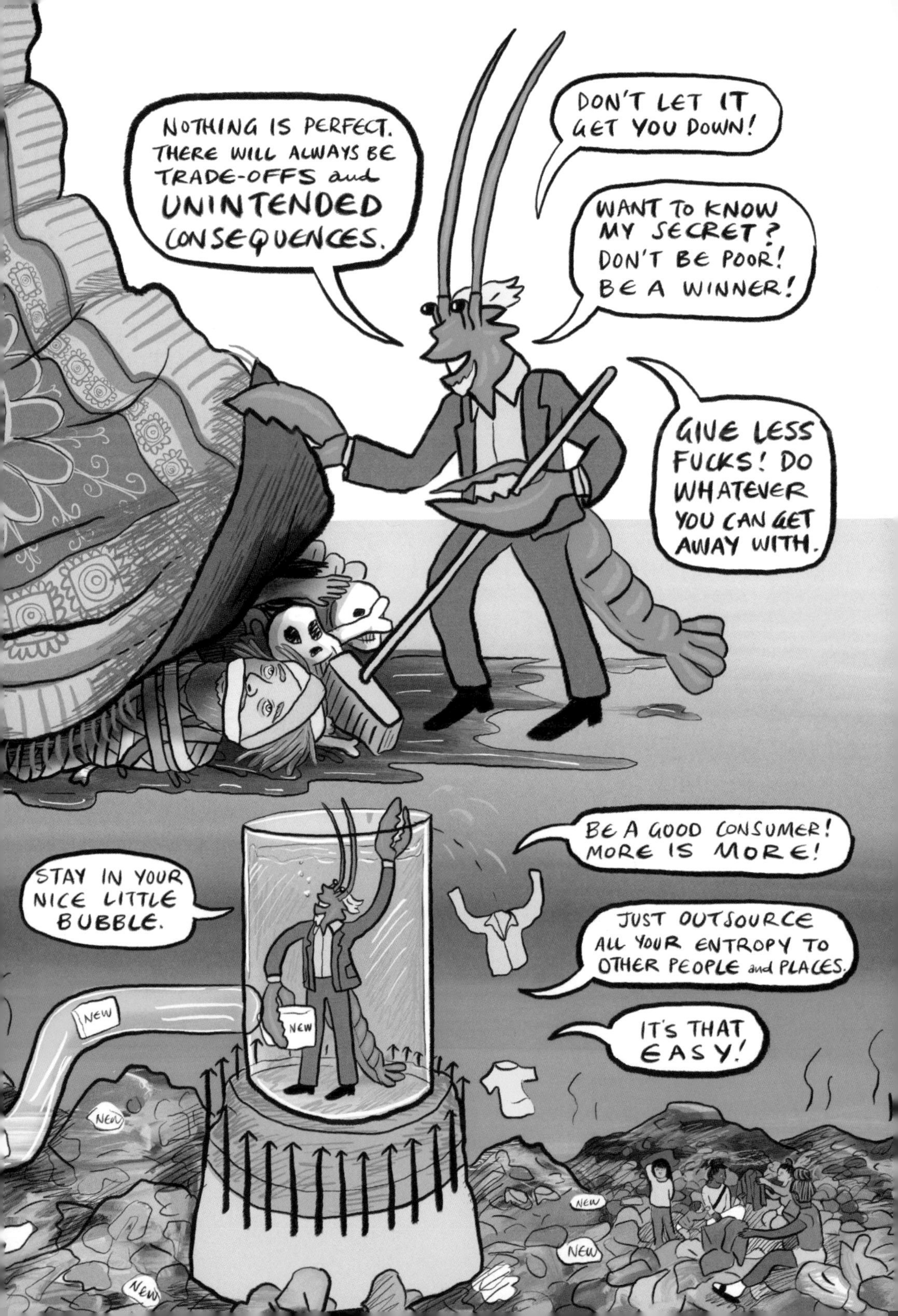
NOTHING IS PERFECT. THERE WILL ALWAYS BE TRADE-OFFS and UNINTENDED CONSEQUENCES.
DON'T LET IT GET YOU DOWN!
WANT TO KNOW MY SECRET? DON'T BE POOR! BE A WINNER!
GIVE LESS FUCKS! DO WHATEVER YOU CAN GET AWAY WITH.
STAY IN YOUR NICE LITTLE BUBBLE.
BE A GOOD CONSUMER! MORE IS MORE!
JUST OUTSOURCE ALL YOUR ENTROPY TO OTHER PEOPLE and PLACES.
IT'S THAT EASY!
NEW
NEW
NEW
NEW
NEW
NEW

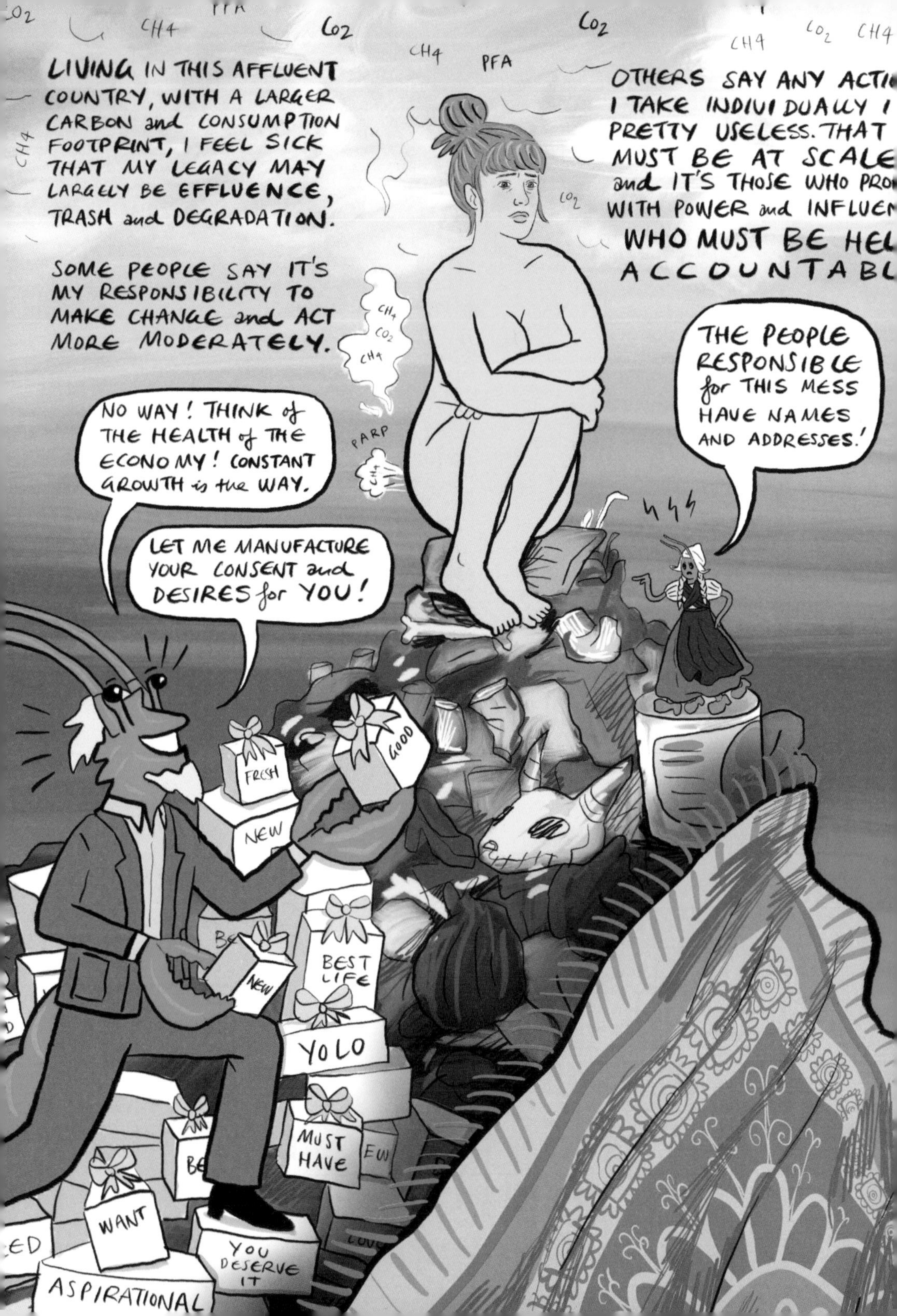
LIVING IN THIS AFFLUENT COUNTRY, WITH A LARGER CARBON and CONSUMPTION FOOTPRINT, I FEEL SICK THAT MY LEGACY MAY LARGELY BE EFFLUENCE, TRASH and DEGRADATION.
SOME PEOPLE SAY IT'S MY RESPONSIBILITY TO MAKE CHANGE and ACT MORE MODERATELY.
OTHERS SAY ANY ACTI I TAKE INDIVIDUALLY I PRETTY USELESS. THAT MUST BE AT SCALE and IT'S THOSE WHO PRO WITH POWER and INFLUEN WHO MUST BE HEL ACCOUNTABL
PARP
NO WAY! THINK of THE HEALTH of THE ECONOMY! CONSTANT GROWTH is the WAY.
LET ME MANUFACTURE YOUR CONSENT and DESIRES for YOU!
THE PEOPLE RESPONSIBLE for THIS MESS HAVE NAMES AND ADDRESSES.'
FRESH
GOOD
NEW
BEST LIFE
NEW
YOLO
MUST HAVE
WANT
YOU DESERVE IT
ASPIRATIONAL

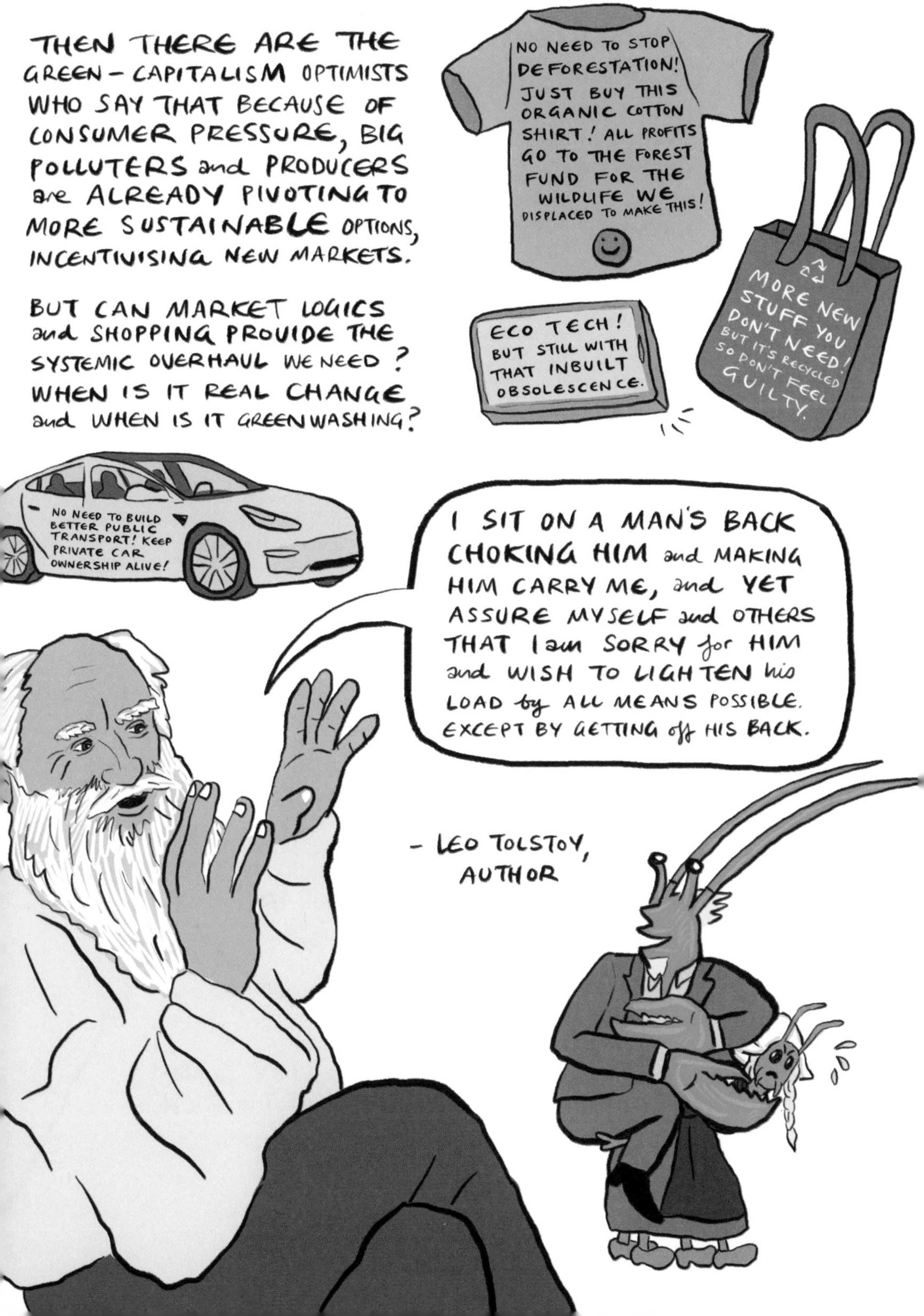
THEN THERE ARE THE GREEN-CAPITALISM OPTIMISTS WHO SAY THAT BECAUSE OF CONSUMER PRESSURE, BIG POLLUTERS and PRODUCERS are ALREADY PIVOTING TO MORE SUSTAINABLE OPTIONS, INCENTIVISING NEW MARKETS.
NO NEED TO STOP DEFORESTATION! JUST BUY THIS ORGANIC COTTON SHIRT! ALL PROFITS GO TO THE FOREST FUND FOR THE WILDLIFE WE DISPLACED TO MAKE THIS!
MORE NEW STUFF YOU DON'T NEED! BUT IT'S RECYCLED SO DON'T FEEL GUILTY.
ECO TECH! BUT STILL WITH THAT INBUILT OBSOLESCENCE.
BUT CAN MARKET LOGICS and SHOPPING PROVIDE THE SYSTEMIC OVERHAUL WE NEED? WHEN IS IT REAL CHANGE and WHEN IS IT GREENWASHING?
NO NEED TO BUILD BETTER PUBLIC TRANSPORT! KEEP PRIVATE CAR OWNERSHIP ALIVE!
I SIT ON A MAN'S BACK CHOKING HIM and MAKING HIM CARRY ME, and YET ASSURE MYSELF and OTHERS THAT I am SORRY for HIM and WISH TO LIGHTEN his LOAD by ALL MEANS POSSIBLE. EXCEPT BY GETTING off HIS BACK.
- LEO TOLSTOY, AUTHOR

CAN EXPECTING THOSE *in* POWER TO SOLVE THE SYSTEMIC PROBLEMS THEY BENEFIT FROM REALLY CHANGE THINGS?

CAN PUBLIC AND PRIVATE INTERESTS WORK TOGETHER IN THIS SYSTEM THAT REQUIRES SCARCITY and CONSTANT GROWTH?

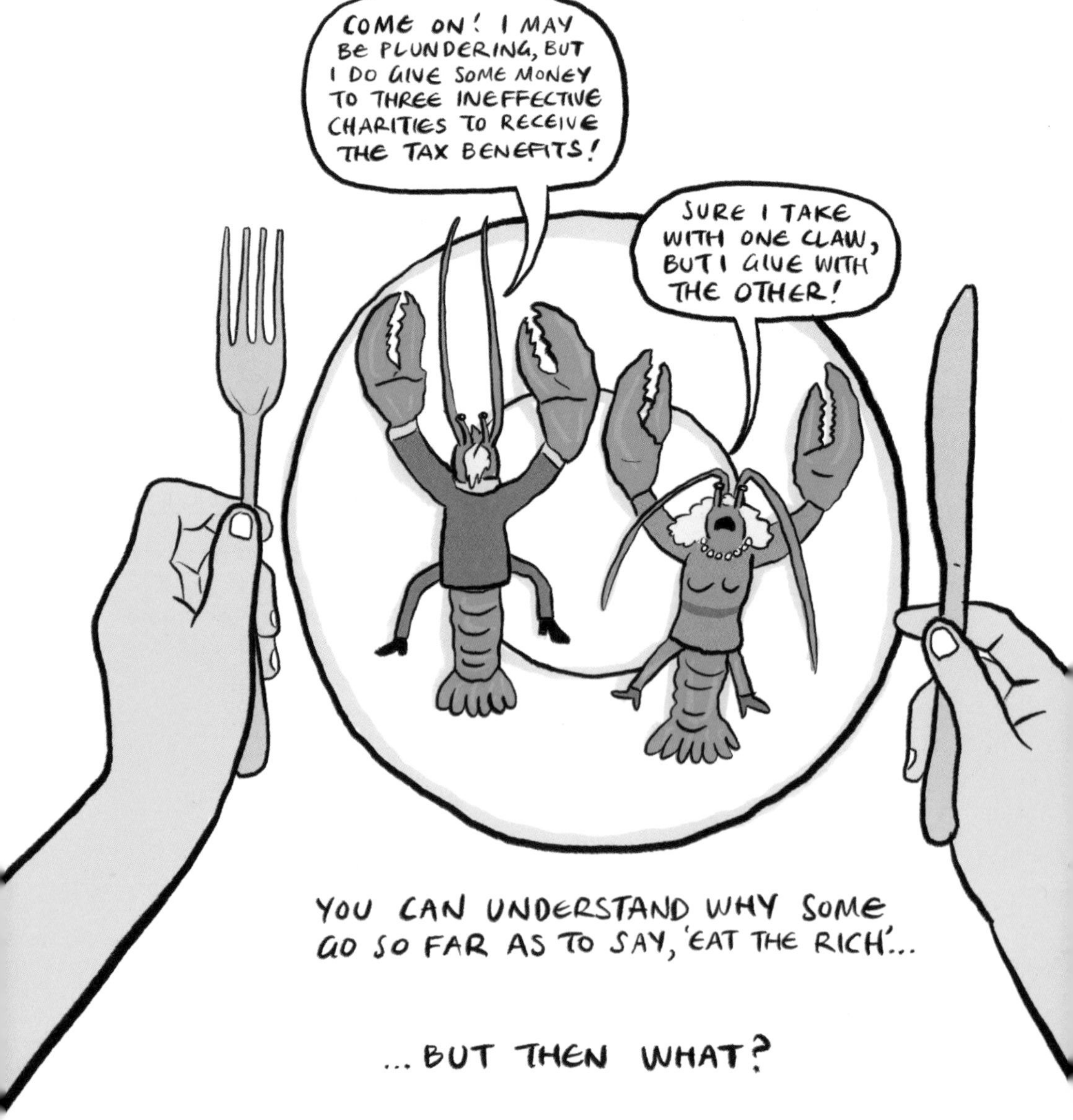
COME ON! I MAY BE PLUNDERING, BUT I DO GIVE SOME MONEY TO THREE INEFFECTIVE CHARITIES TO RECEIVE THE TAX BENEFITS!
SURE I TAKE WITH ONE CLAW, BUT I GIVE WITH THE OTHER!

YOU CAN UNDERSTAND WHY SOME GO SO FAR AS TO SAY, 'EAT THE RICH'...

...BUT THEN WHAT?

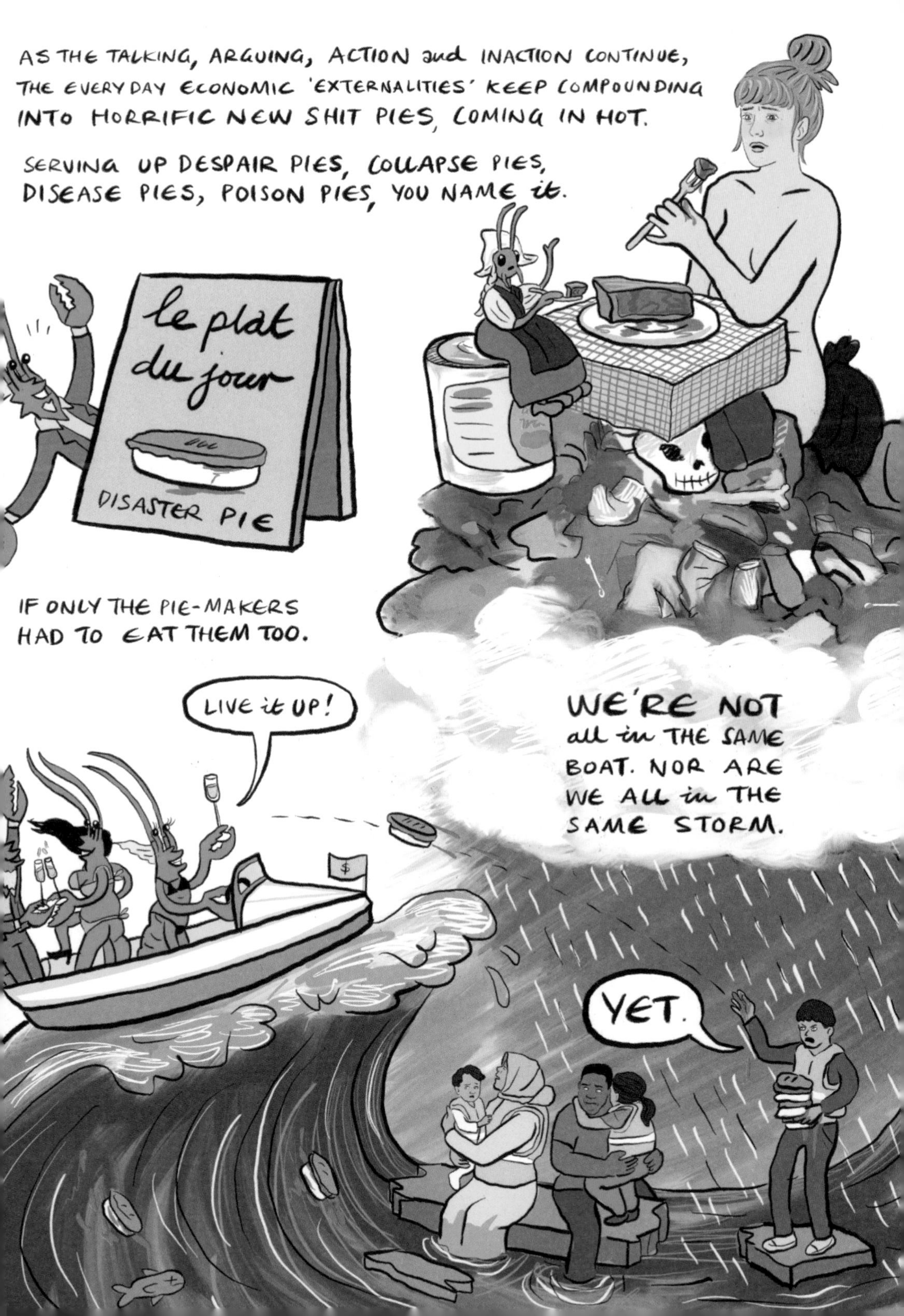
AS THE TALKING, ARGUING, ACTION and INACTION CONTINUE, THE EVERYDAY ECONOMIC 'EXTERNALITIES' KEEP COMPOUNDING INTO HORRIFIC NEW SHIT PIES, COMING IN HOT.
SERVING UP DESPAIR PIES, COLLAPSE PIES, DISEASE PIES, POISON PIES, YOU NAME it.
le plat du jour
DISASTER PIE
IF ONLY THE PIE-MAKERS HAD TO EAT THEM TOO.
LIVE it UP!
$
WE'RE NOT all in THE SAME BOAT. NOR ARE WE ALL in THE SAME STORM.
YET.

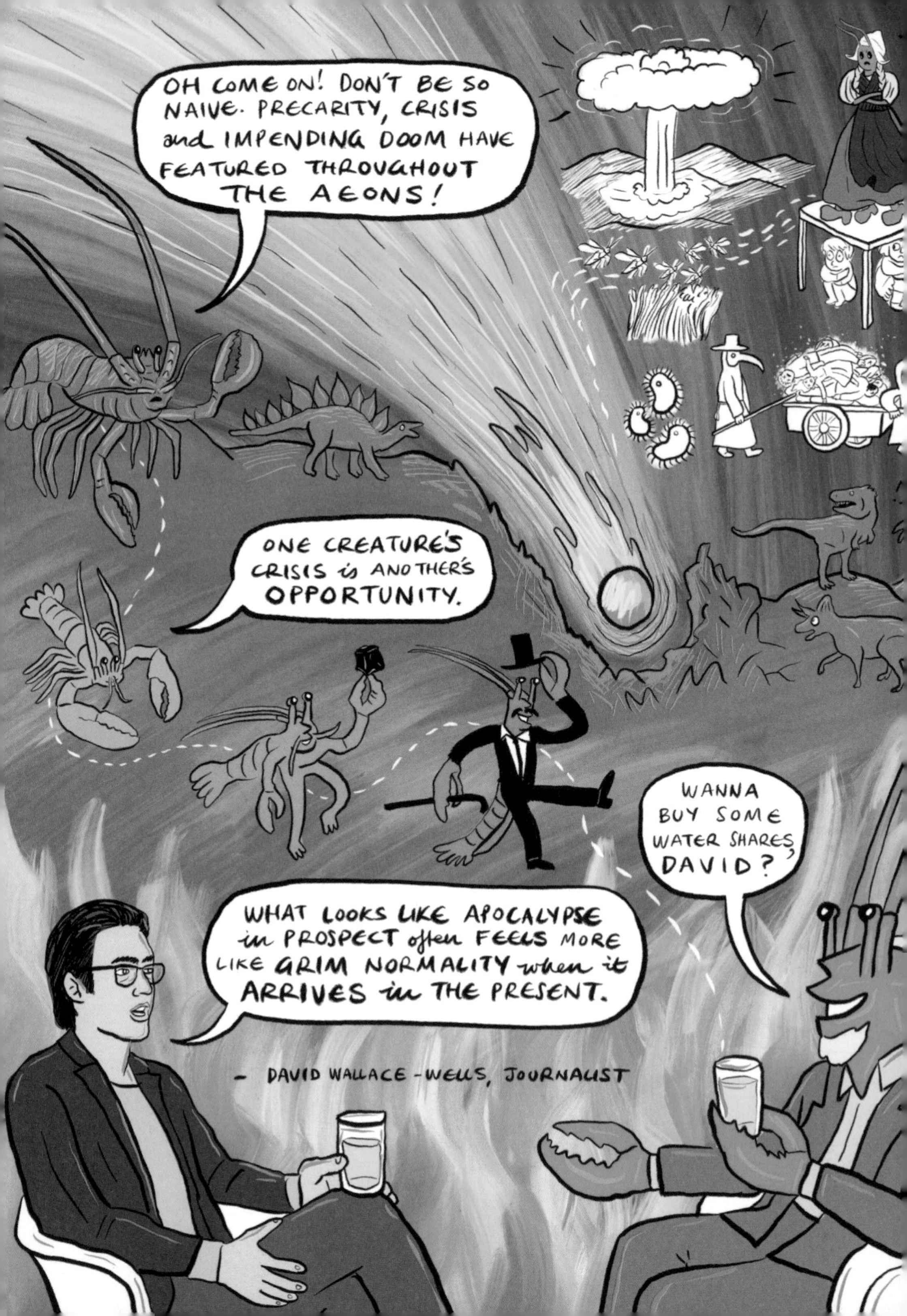
OH COME ON! DON'T BE SO NAIVE. PRECARITY, CRISIS and IMPENDING DOOM HAVE FEATURED THROUGHOUT THE AEONS!
ONE CREATURE'S CRISIS is ANOTHER'S OPPORTUNITY.
WANNA BUY SOME WATER SHARES, DAVID?
WHAT LOOKS LIKE APOCALYPSE in PROSPECT often FEELS MORE LIKE GRIM NORMALITY when it ARRIVES in THE PRESENT.
– DAVID WALLACE-WELLS, JOURNALIST

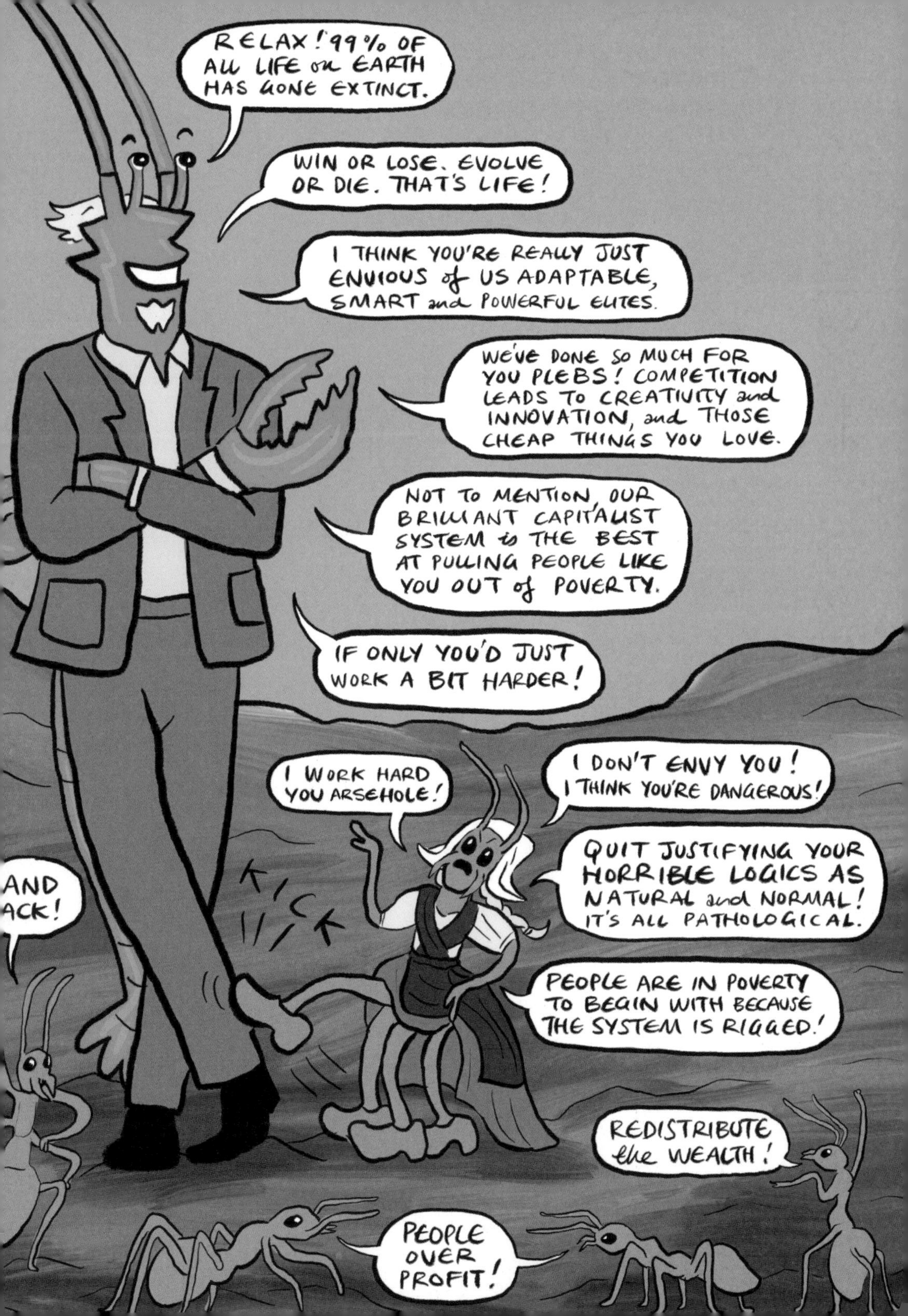
RELAX! 99% OF ALL LIFE on EARTH HAS GONE EXTINCT.
WIN OR LOSE. EVOLVE OR DIE. THAT'S LIFE!
I THINK YOU'RE REALLY JUST ENVIOUS of US ADAPTABLE, SMART and POWERFUL ELITES.
WE'VE DONE SO MUCH FOR YOU PLEBS! COMPETITION LEADS TO CREATIVITY and INNOVATION, and THOSE CHEAP THINGS YOU LOVE.
NOT TO MENTION, OUR BRILLIANT CAPITALIST SYSTEM is THE BEST AT PULLING PEOPLE LIKE YOU OUT of POVERTY.
IF ONLY YOU'D JUST WORK A BIT HARDER!
I WORK HARD YOU ARSEHOLE!
I DON'T ENVY YOU! I THINK YOU'RE DANGEROUS!
AND
ACK!
KICK
QUIT JUSTIFYING YOUR HORRIBLE LOGICS AS NATURAL and NORMAL! IT'S ALL PATHOLOGICAL.
PEOPLE ARE IN POVERTY TO BEGIN WITH BECAUSE THE SYSTEM IS RIGGED!
REDISTRIBUTE the WEALTH!
PEOPLE OVER PROFIT!

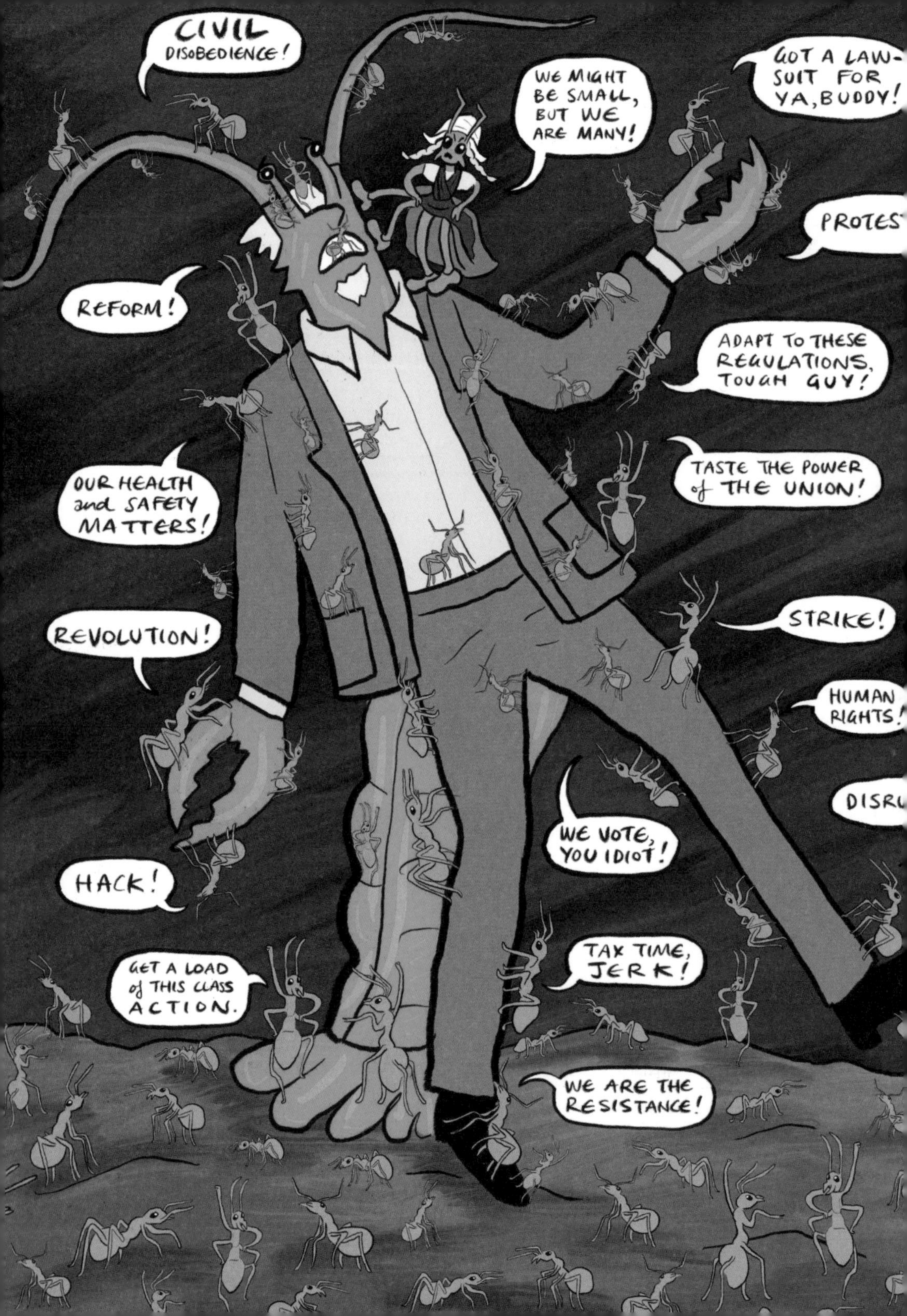
CIVIL DISOBEDIENCE!
WE MIGHT BE SMALL, BUT WE ARE MANY!
GOT A LAW-SUIT FOR YA, BUDDY!
PROTES
REFORM!
ADAPT TO THESE REGULATIONS, TOUGH GUY!
OUR HEALTH and SAFETY MATTERS!
TASTE THE POWER of THE UNION!
REVOLUTION!
STRIKE!
HUMAN RIGHTS!
DISRU
WE VOTE, YOU IDIOT!
HACK!
GET A LOAD of THIS CLASS ACTION.
TAX TIME, JERK!
WE ARE THE RESISTANCE!

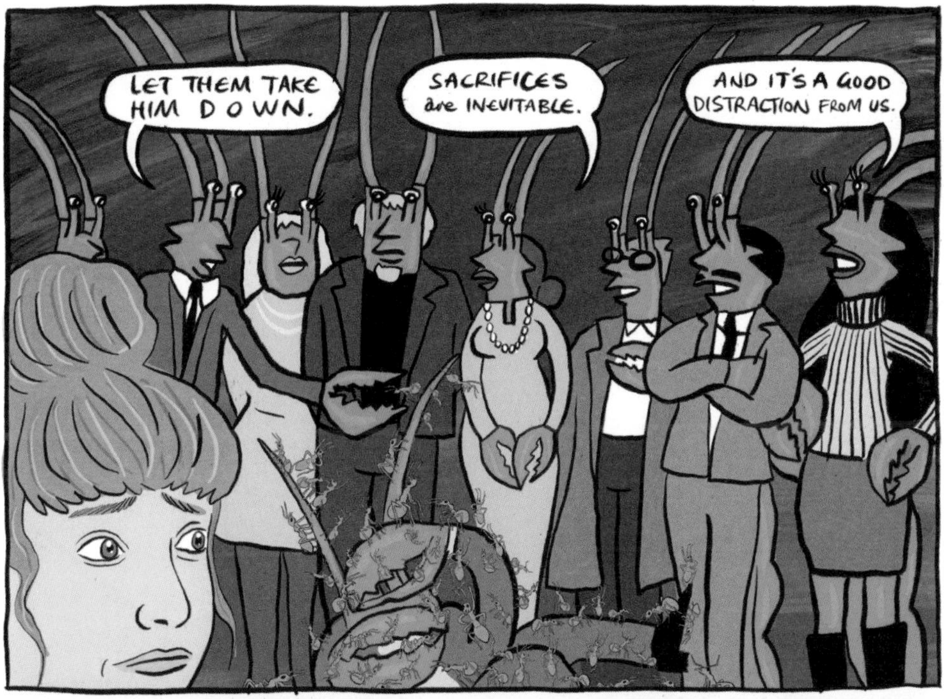
LET THEM TAKE HIM DOWN.
SACRIFICES are INEVITABLE.
AND IT'S A GOOD DISTRACTION FROM US.

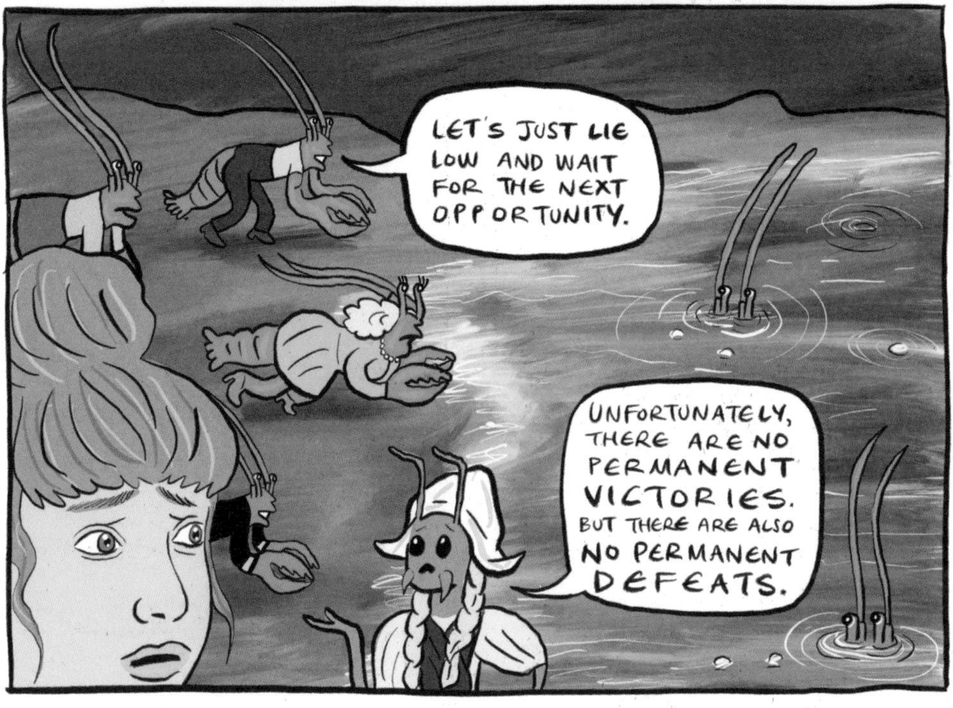
LET'S JUST LIE LOW AND WAIT FOR THE NEXT OPPORTUNITY.
UNFORTUNATELY, THERE ARE NO PERMANENT VICTORIES. BUT THERE ARE ALSO NO PERMANENT DEFEATS.

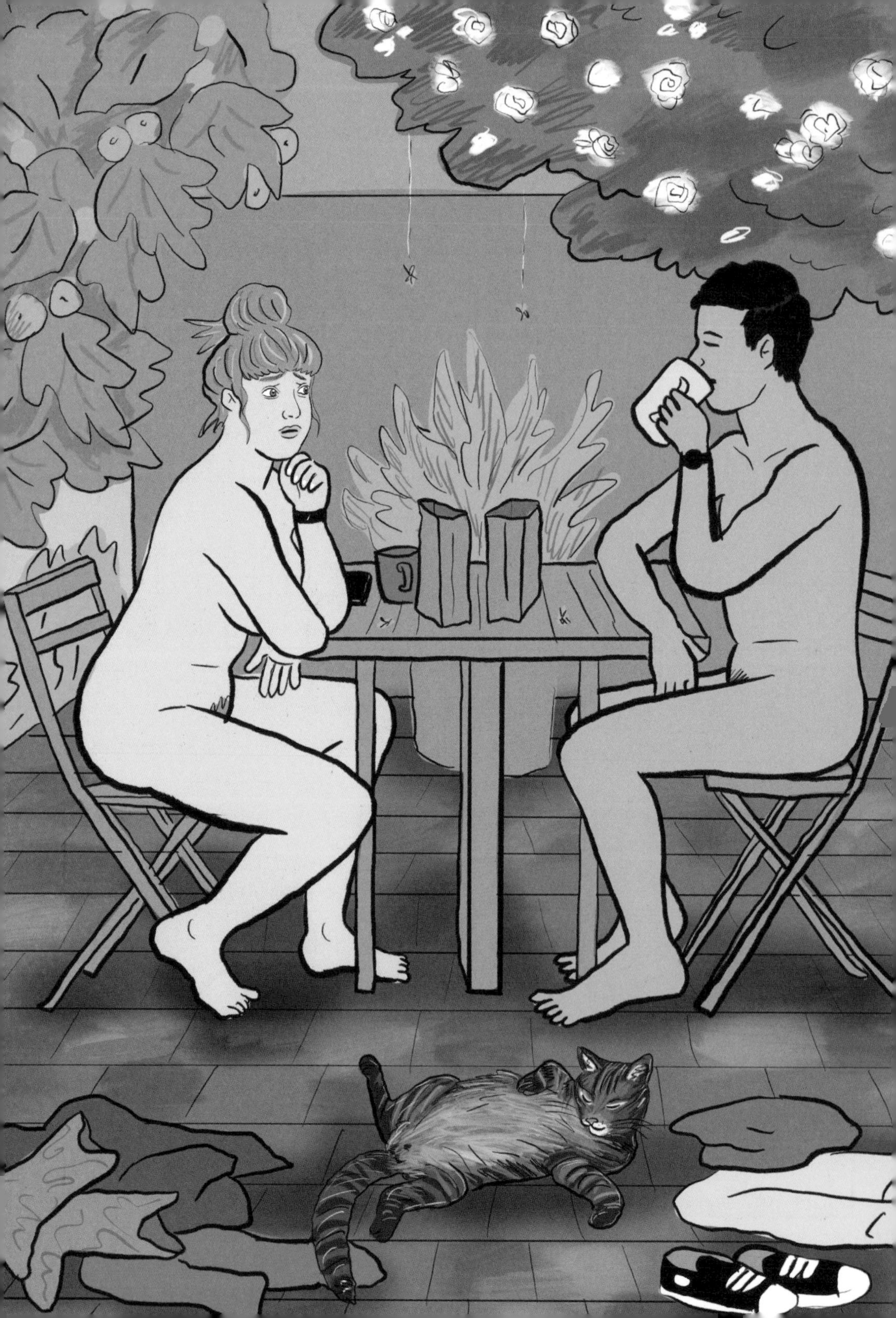

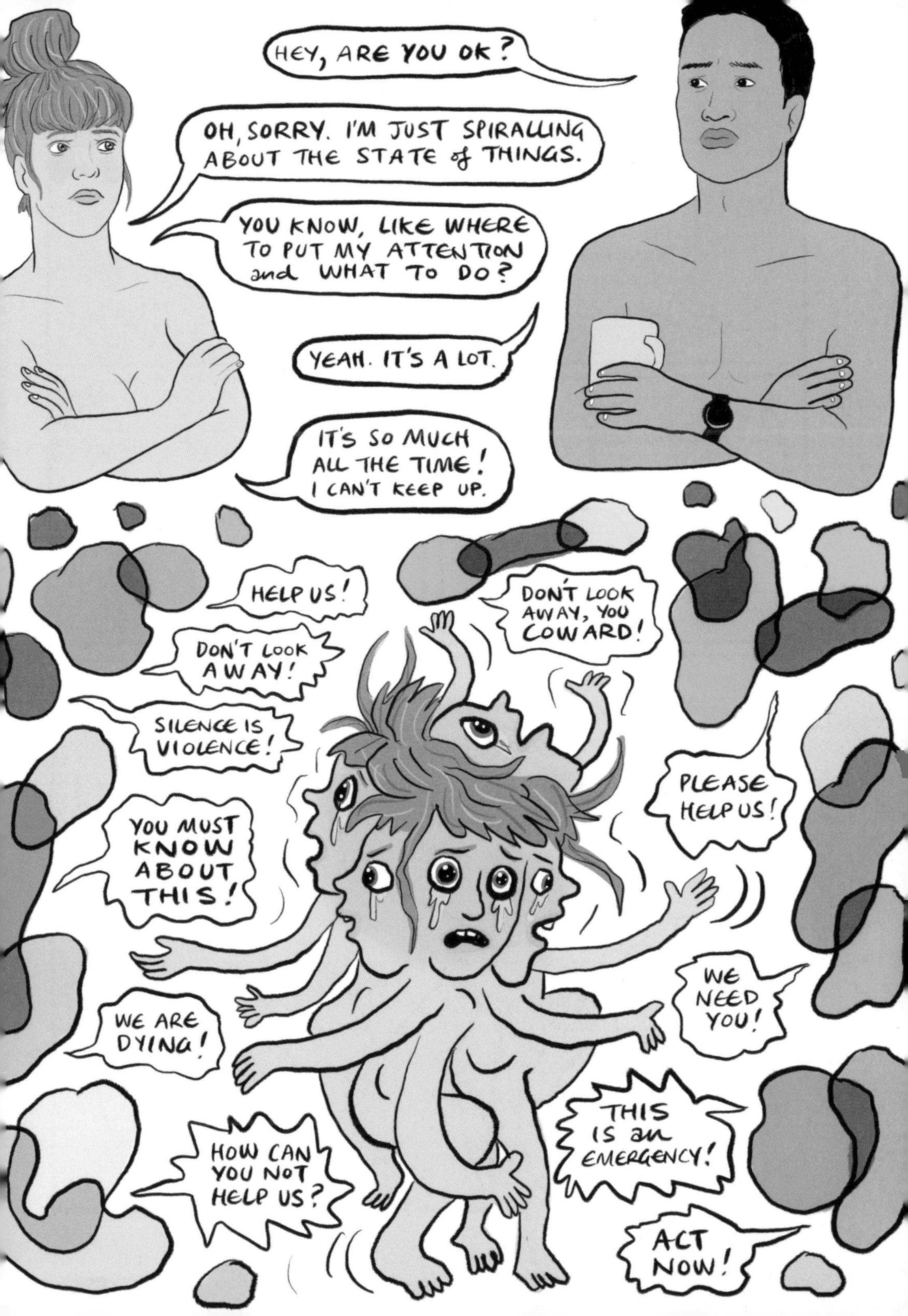
HEY, ARE YOU OK?
OH, SORRY. I'M JUST SPIRALLING ABOUT THE STATE of THINGS.
YOU KNOW, LIKE WHERE TO PUT MY ATTENTION and WHAT TO DO?
YEAH. IT'S A LOT.
IT'S SO MUCH ALL THE TIME! I CAN'T KEEP UP.
HELP US!
DON'T LOOK AWAY, YOU COWARD!
DON'T LOOK AWAY!
SILENCE IS VIOLENCE!
PLEASE HELP US!
YOU MUST KNOW ABOUT THIS!
WE NEED YOU!
WE ARE DYING!
THIS is an EMERGENCY!
HOW CAN YOU NOT HELP US?
ACT NOW!

THIS IS A BIT BLEAK, BUT SOMETIMES I THINK, HEY, I COULD DIE TOMORROW. THEN NONE of THESE ARE MY PROBLEMS ANYMORE!
NO OFFENCE, BUT YOU ALONE WON'T SOLVE ANY MAJOR ISSUES.
I KNOW. BUT PERSONAL RESPONSIBILITY STILL MATTERS!
AS DOES COLLECTIVE ACTION and SYSTEMIC CHANGE.
IF YOUR SPHERE OF CONCERN IS MUCH BIGGER THAN YOUR SPHERE of INFLUENCE, YOU'RE GONNA FEEL TOTALLY OVERWHELMED.
GROUND YOURSELF!
ACTION IS THE ANTIDOTE TO DESPAIR. COME BACK TO WHAT YOU CAN CONTROL and IMPACT.
START WHERE YOU ARE, DO WHAT YOU CAN.

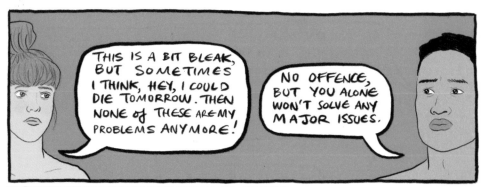

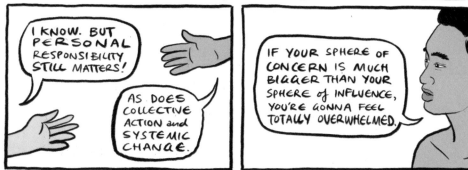

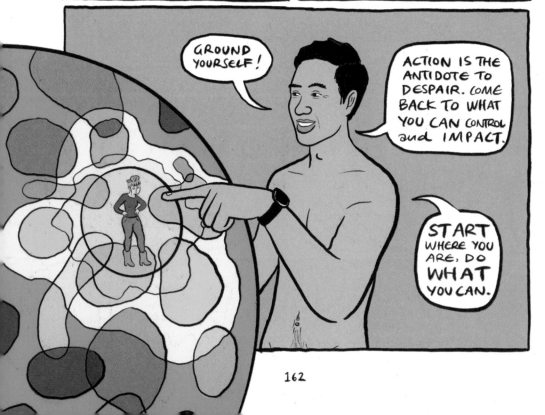

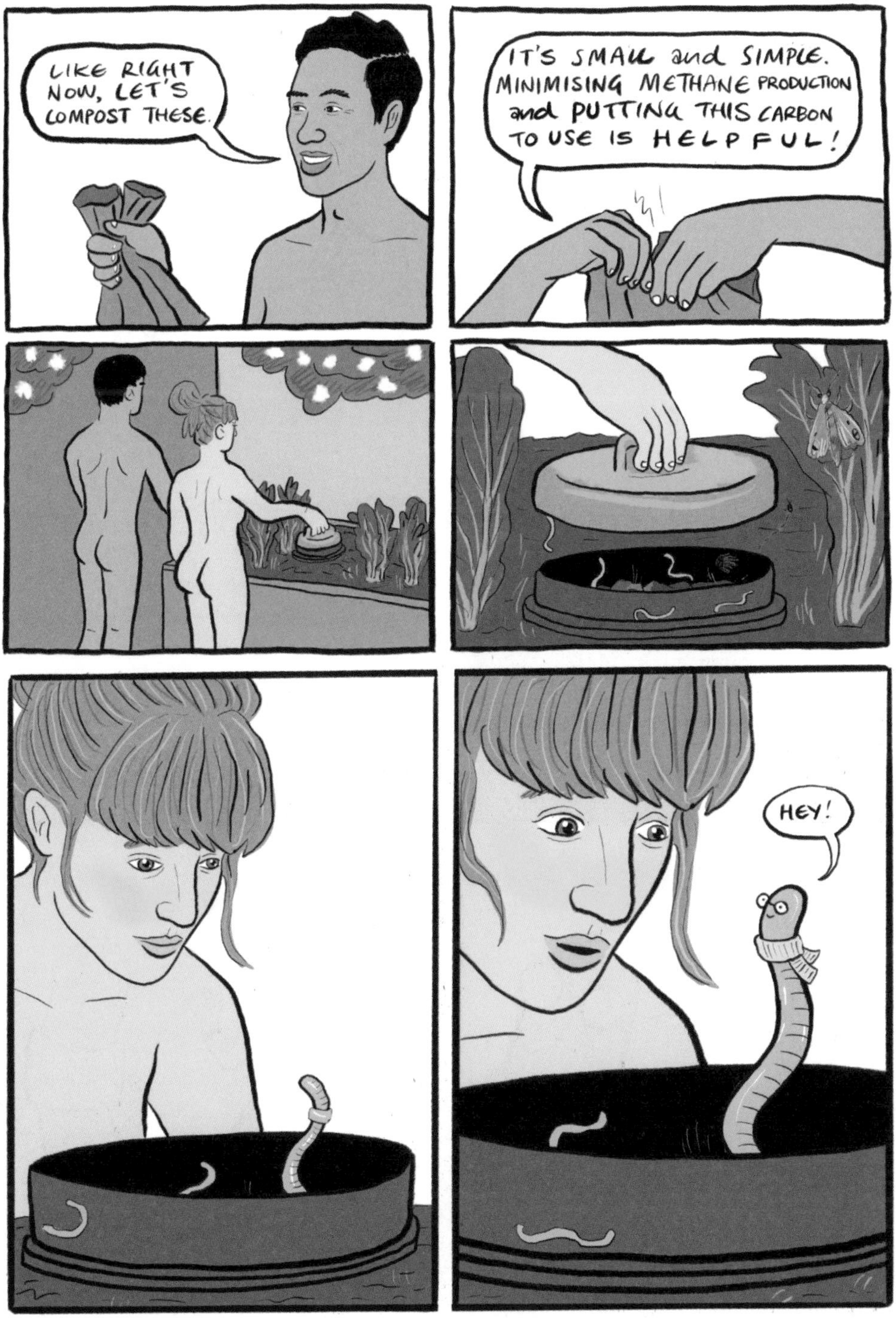

LIKE RIGHT NOW, LET'S COMPOST THESE.
IT'S SMALL and SIMPLE. MINIMISING METHANE PRODUCTION and PUTTING THIS CARBON TO USE IS HELPFUL!
HEY!

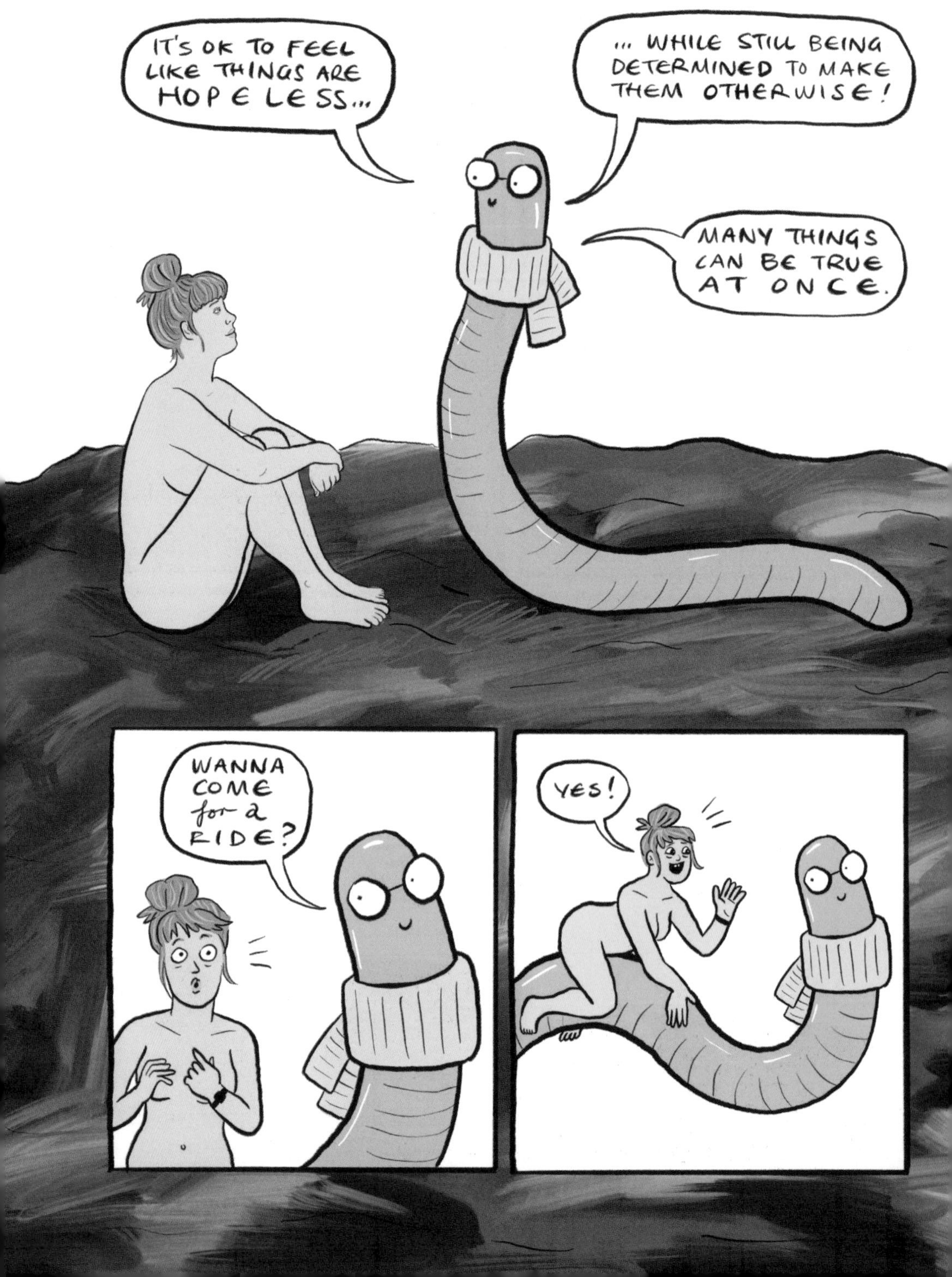
IT'S OK TO FEEL LIKE THINGS ARE HOPELESS...
... WHILE STILL BEING DETERMINED TO MAKE THEM OTHERWISE!
MANY THINGS CAN BE TRUE AT ONCE.
WANNA COME for a RIDE?
YES!

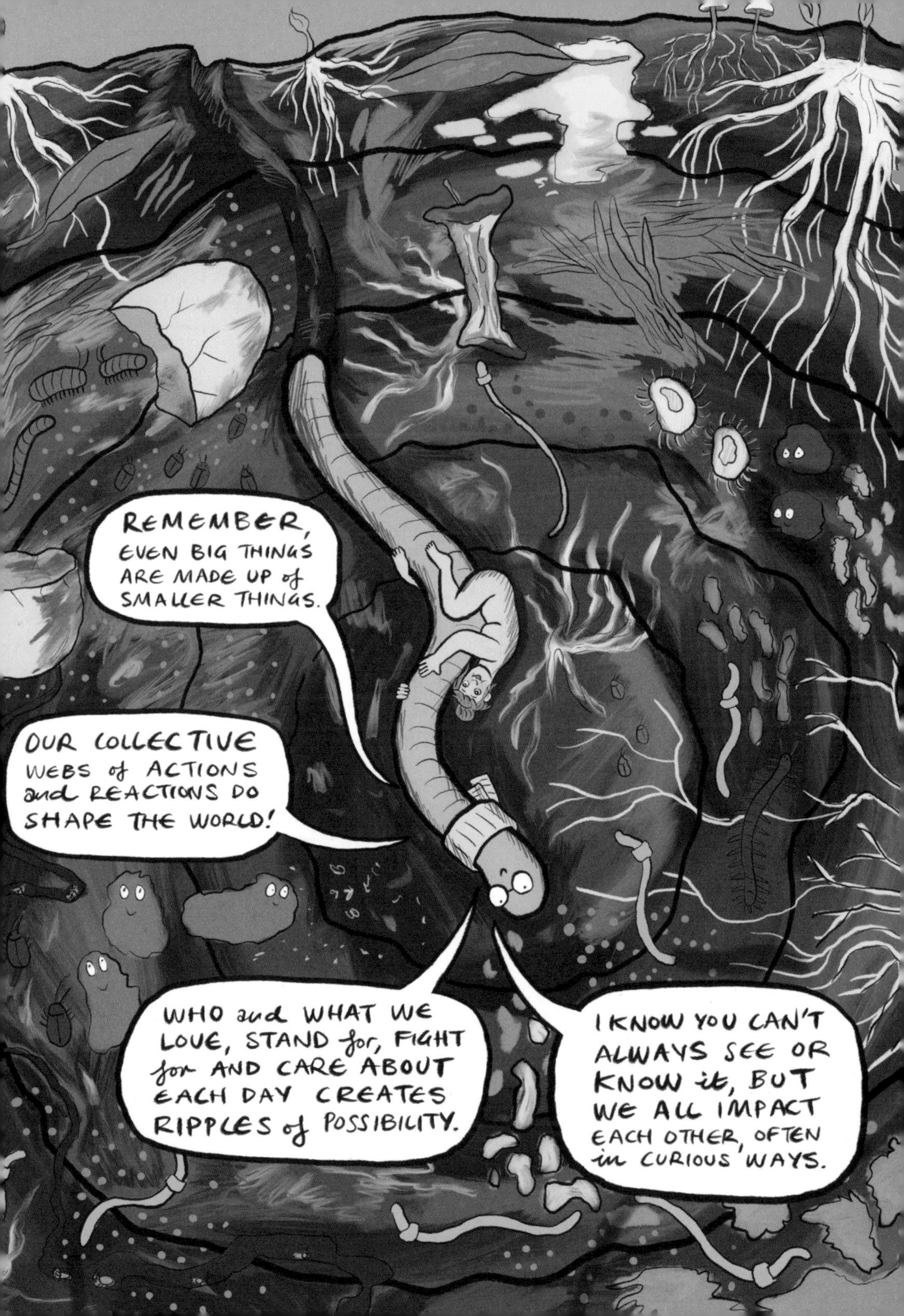
REMEMBER, EVEN BIG THINGS ARE MADE UP of SMALLER THINGS.
OUR COLLECTIVE WEBS of ACTIONS and REACTIONS DO SHAPE THE WORLD!
WHO and WHAT WE LOVE, STAND for, FIGHT for AND CARE ABOUT EACH DAY CREATES RIPPLES of POSSIBILITY.
I KNOW YOU CAN'T ALWAYS SEE OR KNOW it, BUT WE ALL IMPACT EACH OTHER, OFTEN in CURIOUS WAYS.

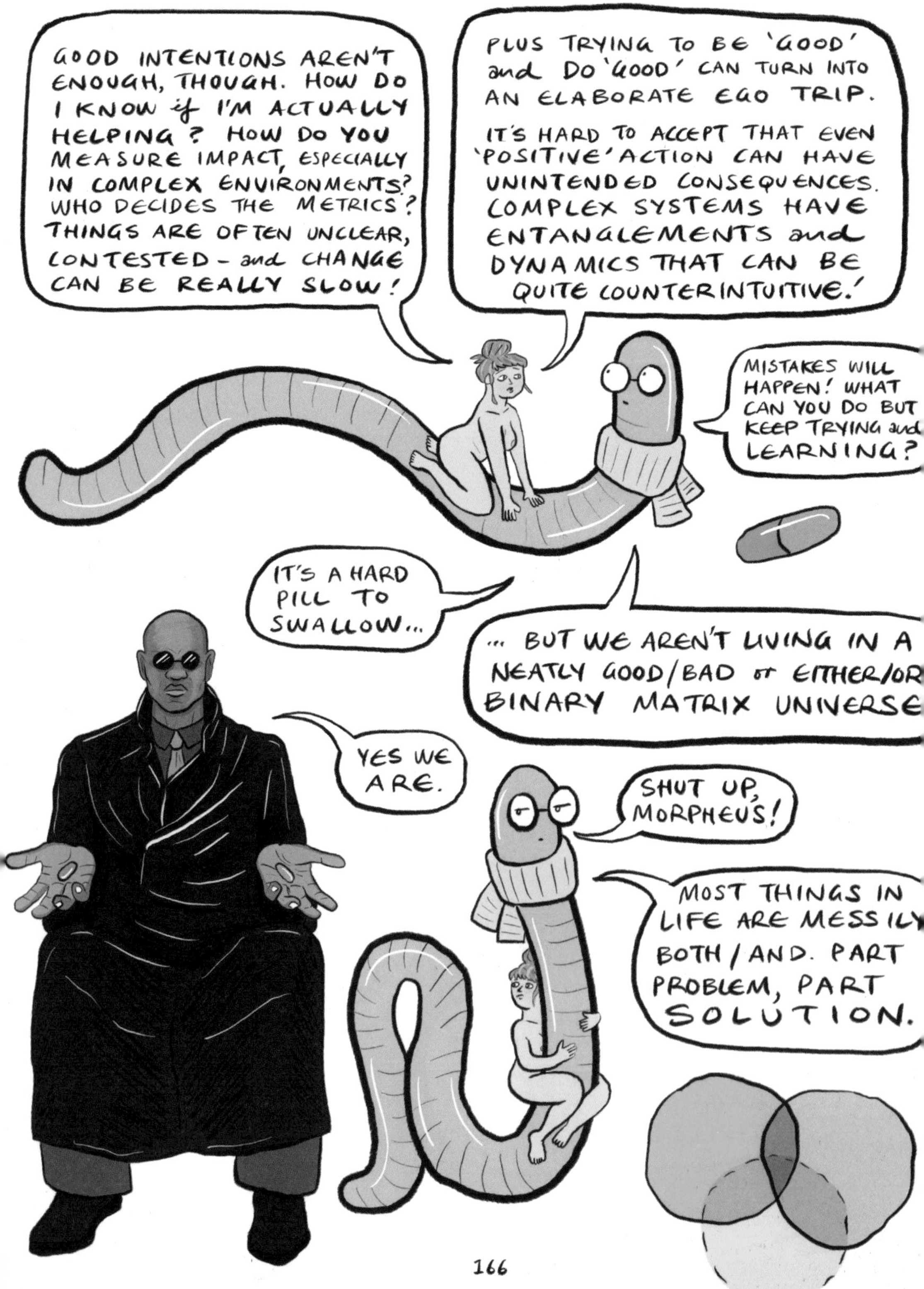
GOOD INTENTIONS AREN'T ENOUGH, THOUGH. HOW DO I KNOW if I'M ACTUALLY HELPING? HOW DO YOU MEASURE IMPACT, ESPECIALLY IN COMPLEX ENVIRONMENTS? WHO DECIDES THE METRICS? THINGS ARE OFTEN UNCLEAR, CONTESTED - and CHANGE CAN BE REALLY SLOW!
PLUS TRYING TO BE 'GOOD' and DO 'GOOD' CAN TURN INTO AN ELABORATE EGO TRIP.
IT'S HARD TO ACCEPT THAT EVEN 'POSITIVE' ACTION CAN HAVE UNINTENDED CONSEQUENCES. COMPLEX SYSTEMS HAVE ENTANGLEMENTS and DYNAMICS THAT CAN BE QUITE COUNTERINTUITIVE.'
MISTAKES WILL HAPPEN! WHAT CAN YOU DO BUT KEEP TRYING and LEARNING?
IT'S A HARD PILL TO SWALLOW...
... BUT WE AREN'T LIVING IN A NEATLY GOOD/BAD or EITHER/OR BINARY MATRIX UNIVERSE
YES WE ARE.
SHUT UP, MORPHEUS!
MOST THINGS IN LIFE ARE MESSILY BOTH/AND. PART PROBLEM, PART SOLUTION.

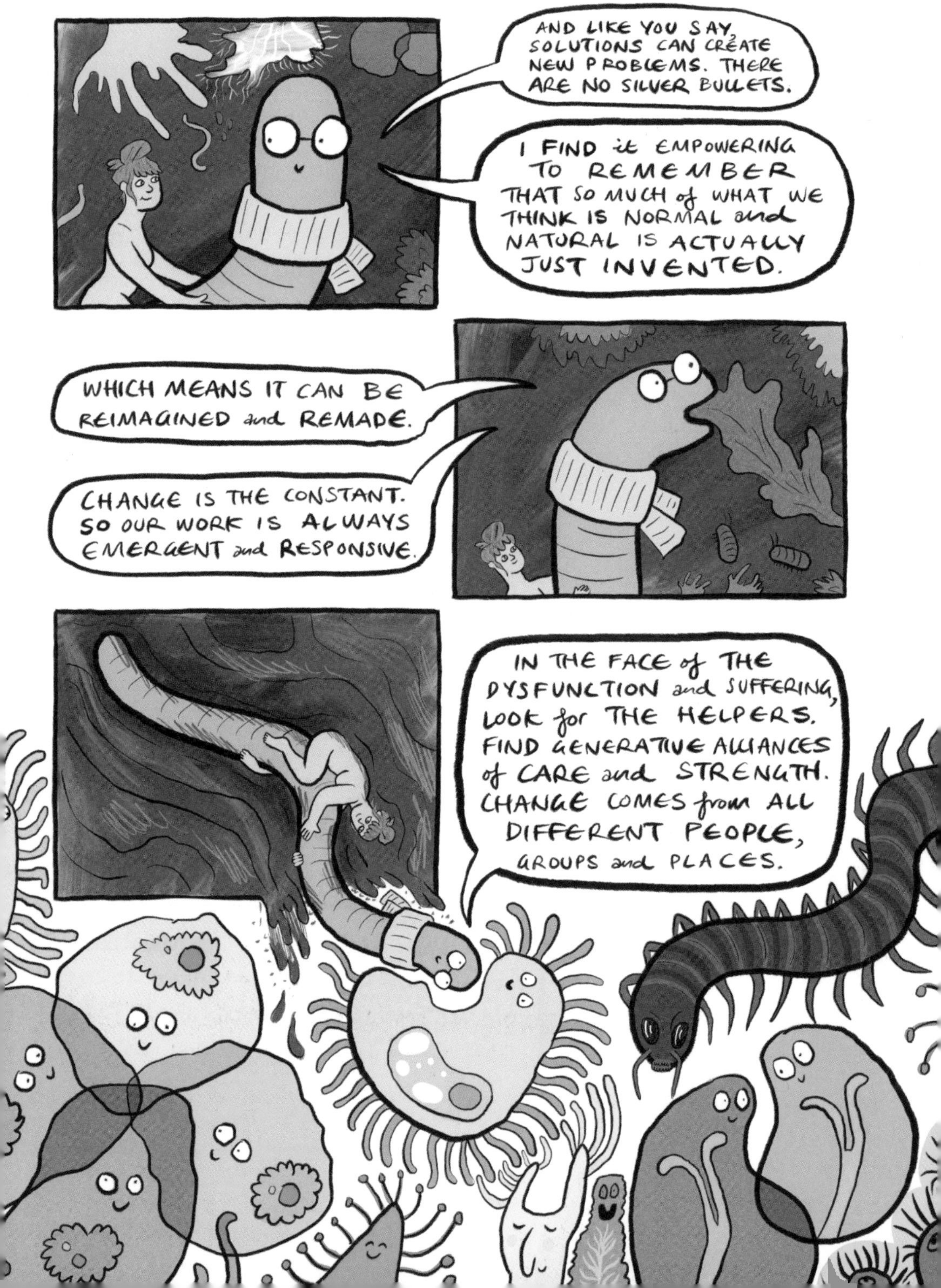
AND LIKE YOU SAY, SOLUTIONS CAN CREATE NEW PROBLEMS. THERE ARE NO SILVER BULLETS.
I FIND it EMPOWERING TO REMEMBER THAT SO MUCH of WHAT WE THINK IS NORMAL and NATURAL IS ACTUALLY JUST INVENTED.
WHICH MEANS IT CAN BE REIMAGINED and REMADE.
CHANGE IS THE CONSTANT. SO OUR WORK IS ALWAYS EMERGENT and RESPONSIVE.
IN THE FACE of THE DYSFUNCTION and SUFFERING, LOOK for THE HELPERS. FIND GENERATIVE ALLIANCES of CARE and STRENGTH. CHANGE COMES from ALL DIFFERENT PEOPLE, GROUPS and PLACES.

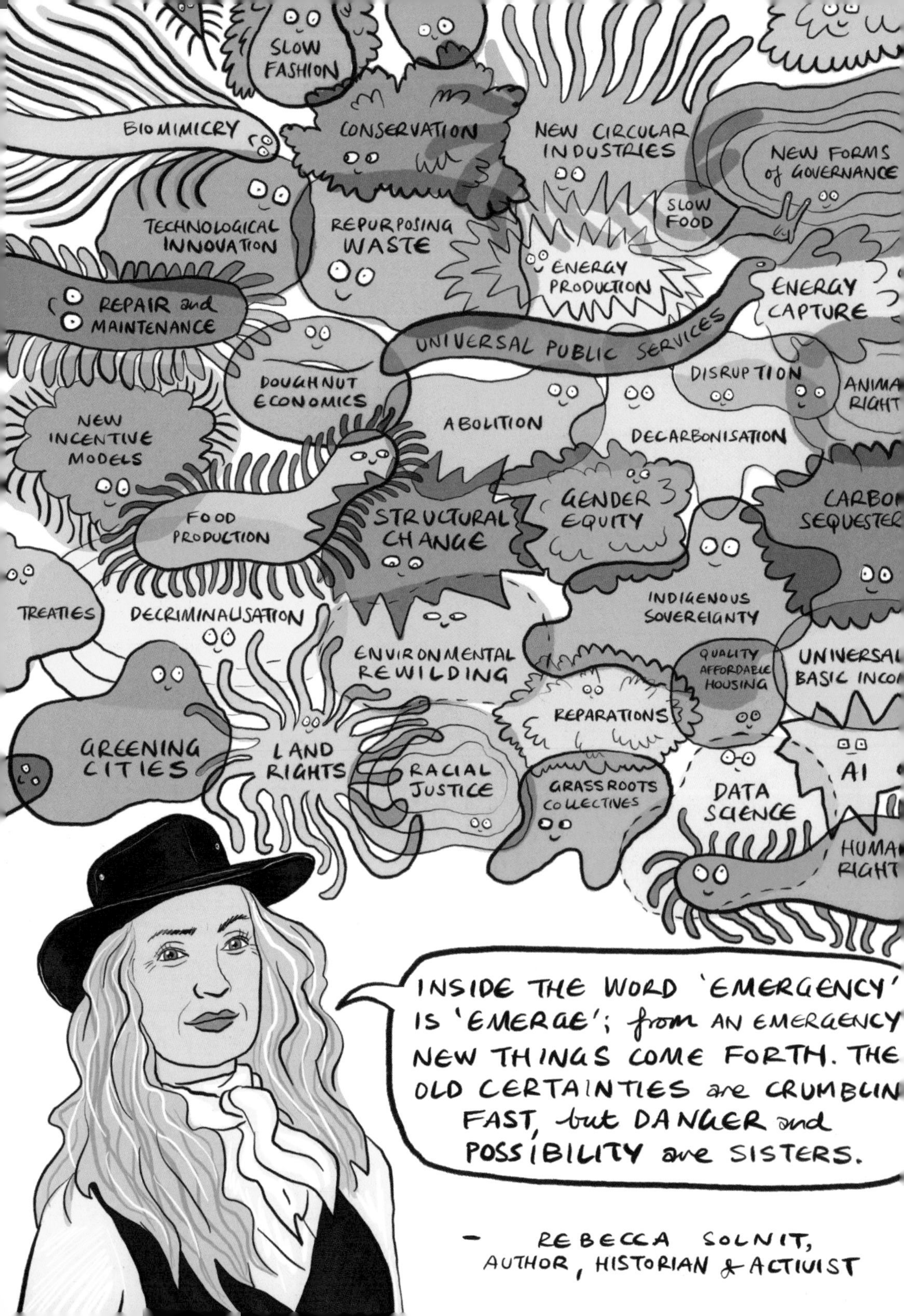
SLOW FASHION
BIOMIMICRY
CONSERVATION
NEW CIRCULAR INDUSTRIES
NEW FORMS of GOVERNANCE
TECHNOLOGICAL INNOVATION
REPURPOSING WASTE
SLOW FOOD
ENERGY PRODUCTION
REPAIR and MAINTENANCE
ENERGY CAPTURE
UNIVERSAL PUBLIC SERVICES
DOUGHNUT ECONOMICS
DISRUPTION
ANIMA RIGHT
NEW INCENTIVE MODELS
ABOLITION
DECARBONISATION
FOOD PRODUCTION
STRUCTURAL CHANGE
GENDER EQUITY
CARBO SEQUESTER
TREATIES
DECRIMINALISATION
INDIGENOUS SOVEREIGNTY
ENVIRONMENTAL REWILDING
QUALITY AFFORDABLE HOUSING
UNIVERSAL BASIC INCO
REPARATIONS
GREENING CITIES
LAND RIGHTS
RACIAL JUSTICE
GRASSROOTS COLLECTIVES
DATA SCIENCE
AI
HUMA RIGHT
INSIDE THE WORD 'EMERGENCY' IS 'EMERGE'; from AN EMERGENCY NEW THINGS COME FORTH. THE OLD CERTAINTIES are CRUMBLIN FAST, but DANGER and POSSIBILITY are SISTERS.
– REBECCA SOLNIT, AUTHOR, HISTORIAN & ACTIVIST

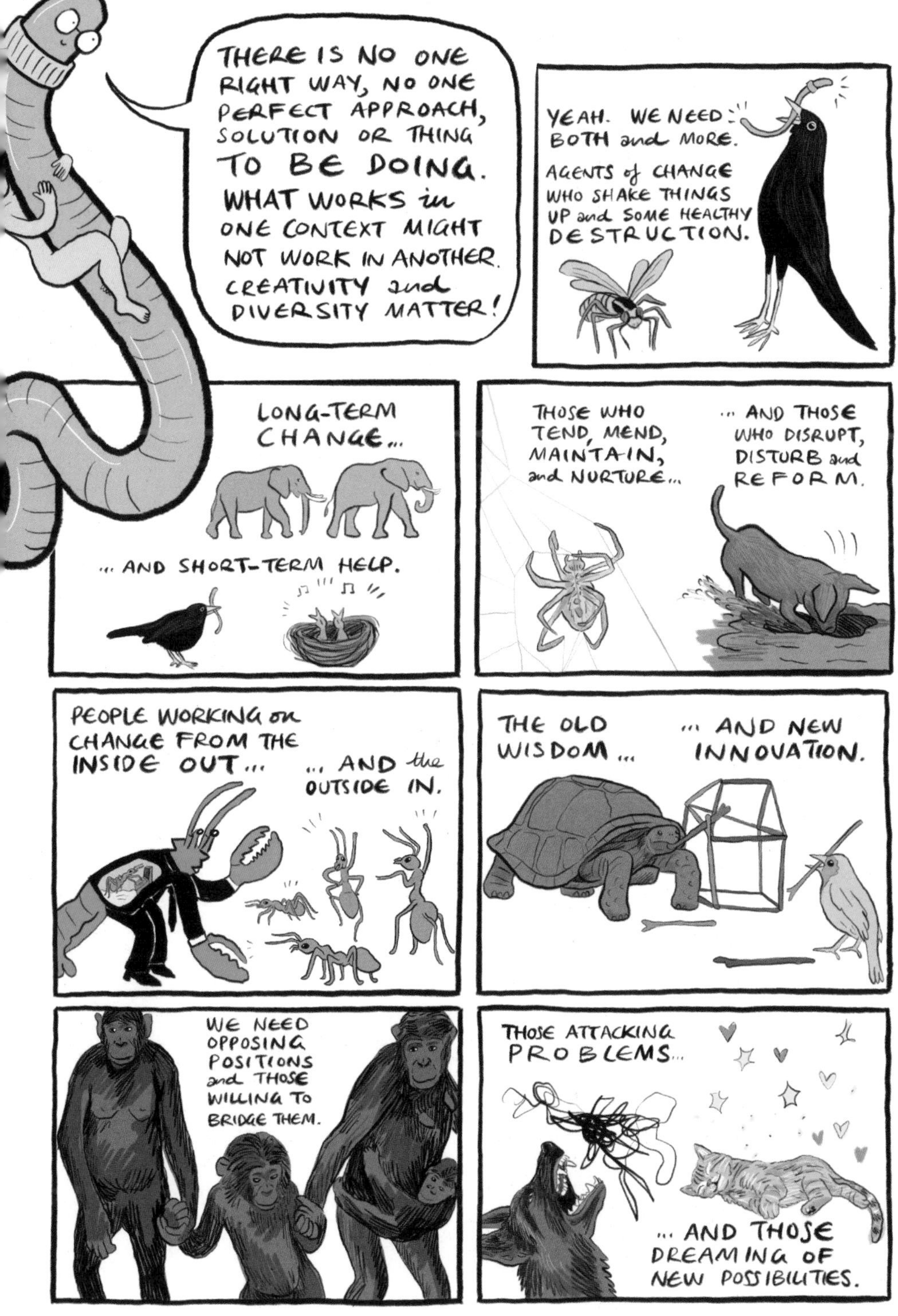
THERE IS NO ONE RIGHT WAY, NO ONE PERFECT APPROACH, SOLUTION OR THING TO BE DOING. WHAT WORKS in ONE CONTEXT MIGHT NOT WORK IN ANOTHER. CREATIVITY and DIVERSITY MATTER!
YEAH. WE NEED BOTH and MORE.
AGENTS of CHANGE WHO SHAKE THINGS UP and SOME HEALTHY DESTRUCTION.
LONG-TERM CHANGE...
... AND SHORT-TERM HELP.
THOSE WHO TEND, MEND, MAINTAIN, and NURTURE...
... AND THOSE WHO DISRUPT, DISTURB and REFORM.
PEOPLE WORKING on CHANGE FROM THE INSIDE OUT...
... AND the OUTSIDE IN.
THE OLD WISDOM...
... AND NEW INNOVATION.
WE NEED OPPOSING POSITIONS and THOSE WILLING TO BRIDGE THEM.
THOSE ATTACKING PROBLEMS...
... AND THOSE DREAMING OF NEW POSSIBILITIES.

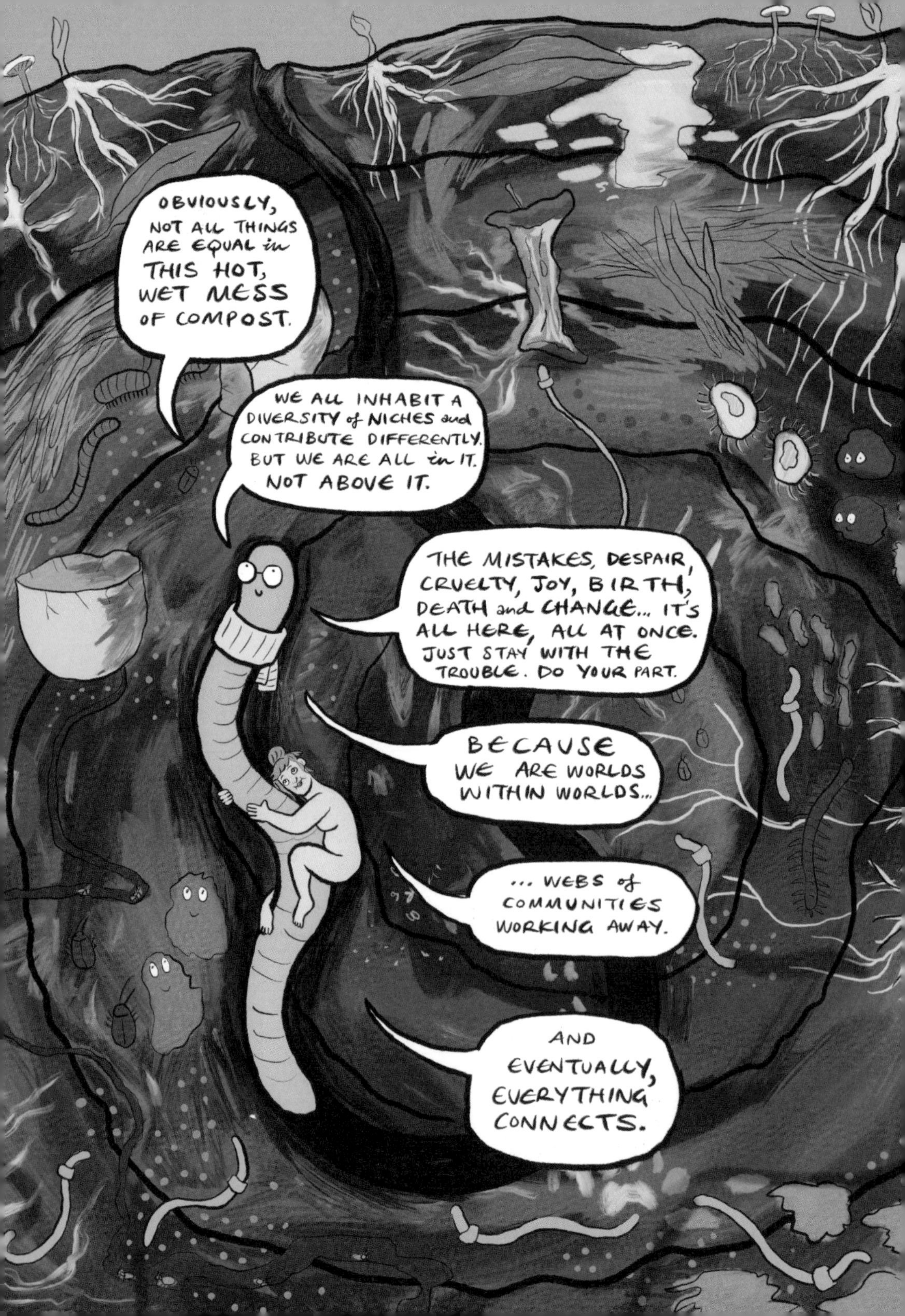
OBVIOUSLY, NOT ALL THINGS ARE EQUAL in THIS HOT, WET MESS OF COMPOST.
WE ALL INHABIT A DIVERSITY of NICHES and CONTRIBUTE DIFFERENTLY. BUT WE ARE ALL in IT. NOT ABOVE IT.
THE MISTAKES, DESPAIR, CRUELTY, JOY, BIRTH, DEATH and CHANGE... IT'S ALL HERE, ALL AT ONCE. JUST STAY WITH THE TROUBLE. DO YOUR PART.
BECAUSE WE ARE WORLDS WITHIN WORLDS...
... WEBS of COMMUNITIES WORKING AWAY.
AND EVENTUALLY, EVERYTHING CONNECTS.

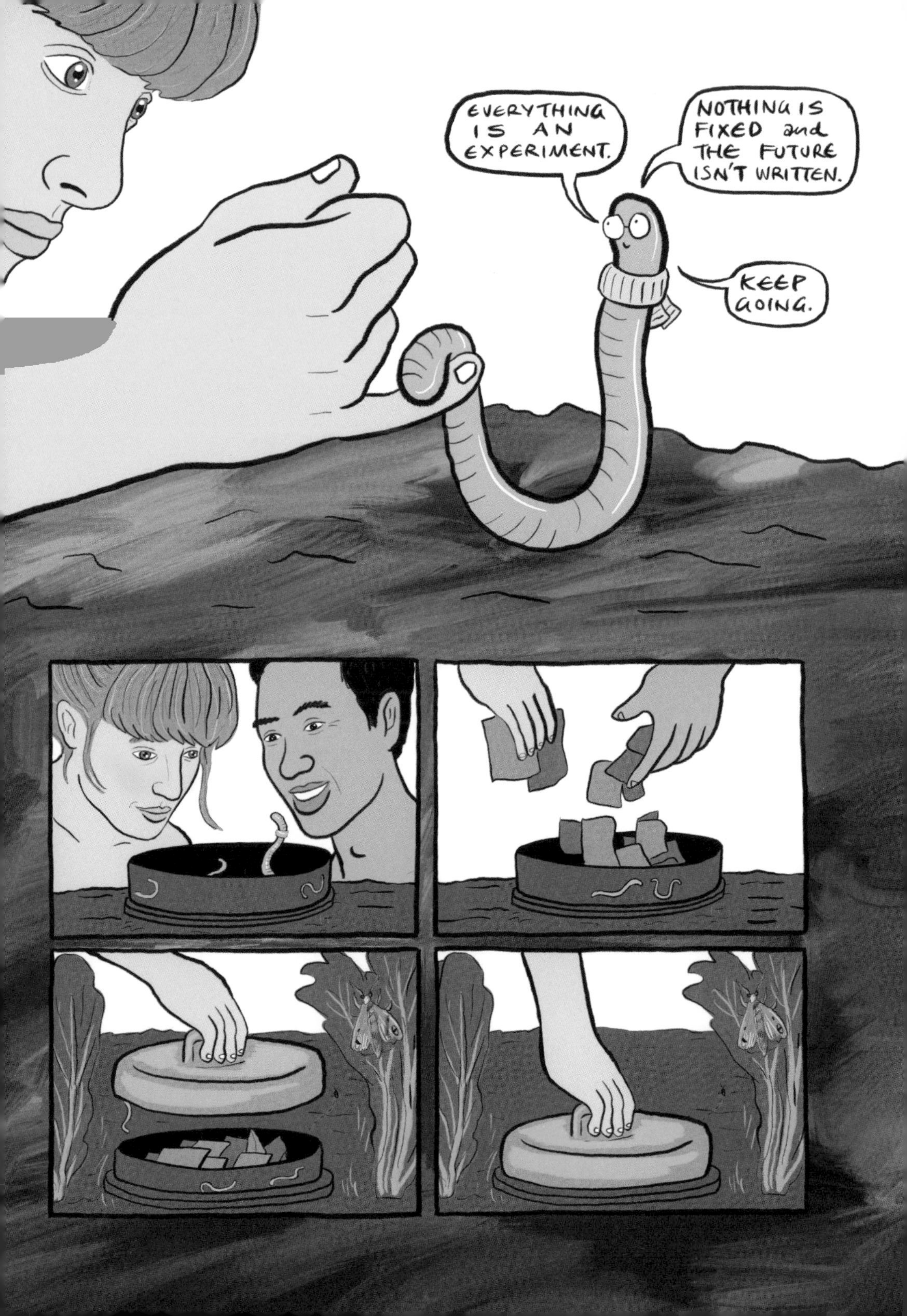
EVERYTHING IS AN EXPERIMENT.
NOTHING IS FIXED and THE FUTURE ISN'T WRITTEN.
KEEP GOING.

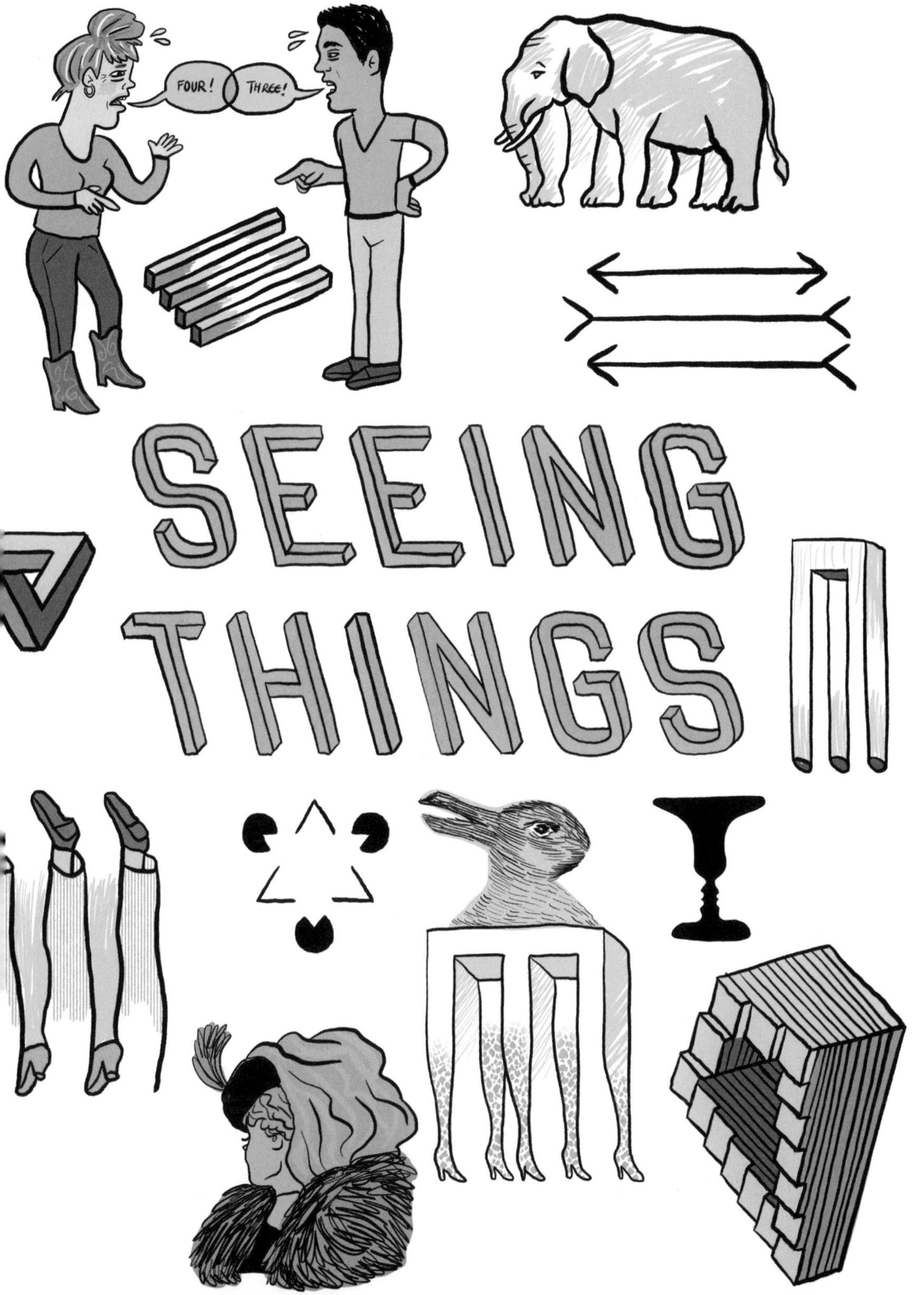
FOUR!
THREE!
SEEING THINGS

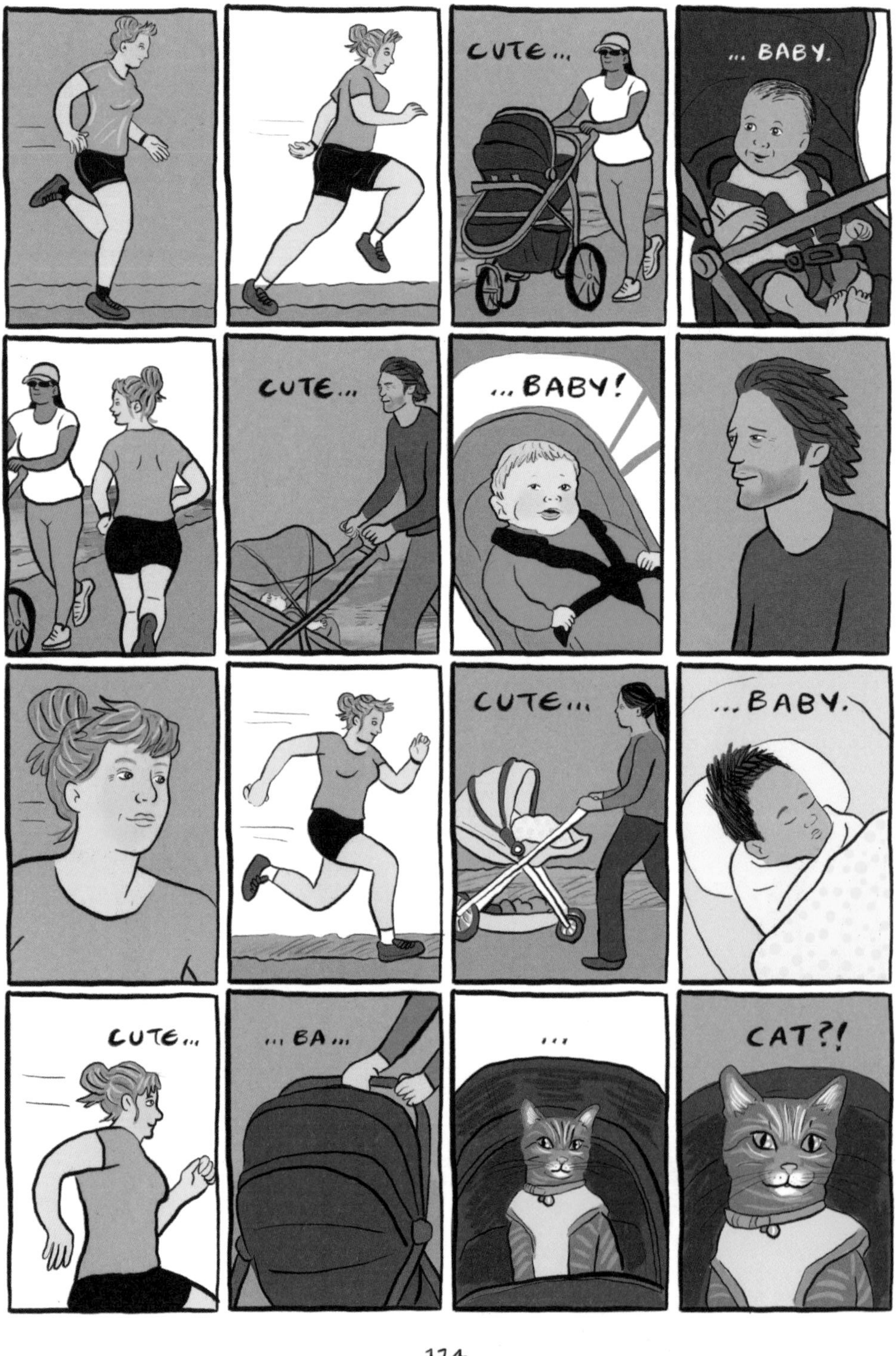
CUTE...
... BABY.
CUTE...
... BABY!
CUTE...
... BABY.
CUTE...
... BA...
...
CAT?!

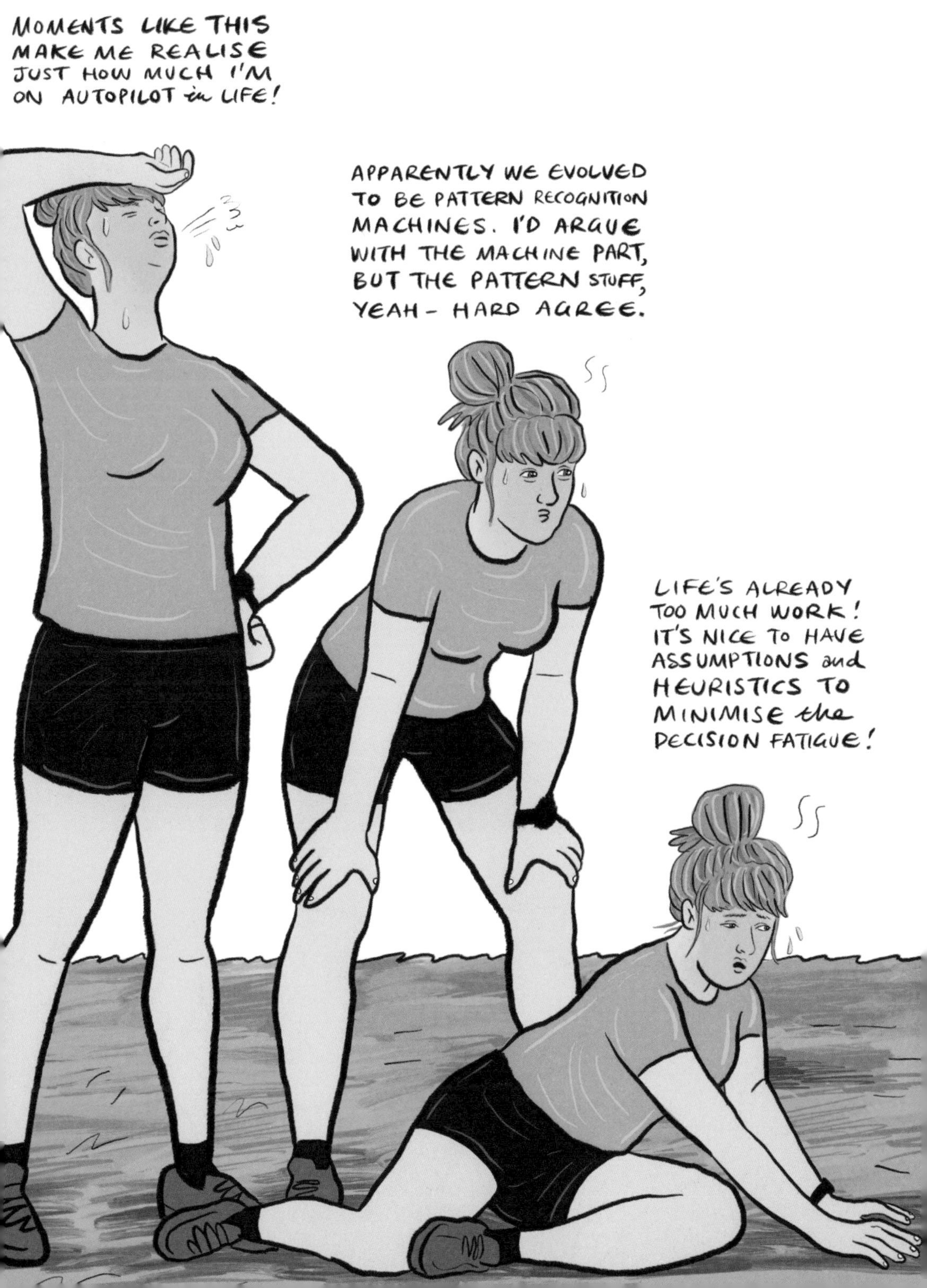
MOMENTS LIKE THIS MAKE ME REALISE JUST HOW MUCH I'M ON AUTOPILOT in LIFE!
APPARENTLY WE EVOLVED TO BE PATTERN RECOGNITION MACHINES. I'D ARGUE WITH THE MACHINE PART, BUT THE PATTERN STUFF, YEAH - HARD AGREE.
LIFE'S ALREADY TOO MUCH WORK! IT'S NICE TO HAVE ASSUMPTIONS and HEURISTICS TO MINIMISE the DECISION FATIGUE!

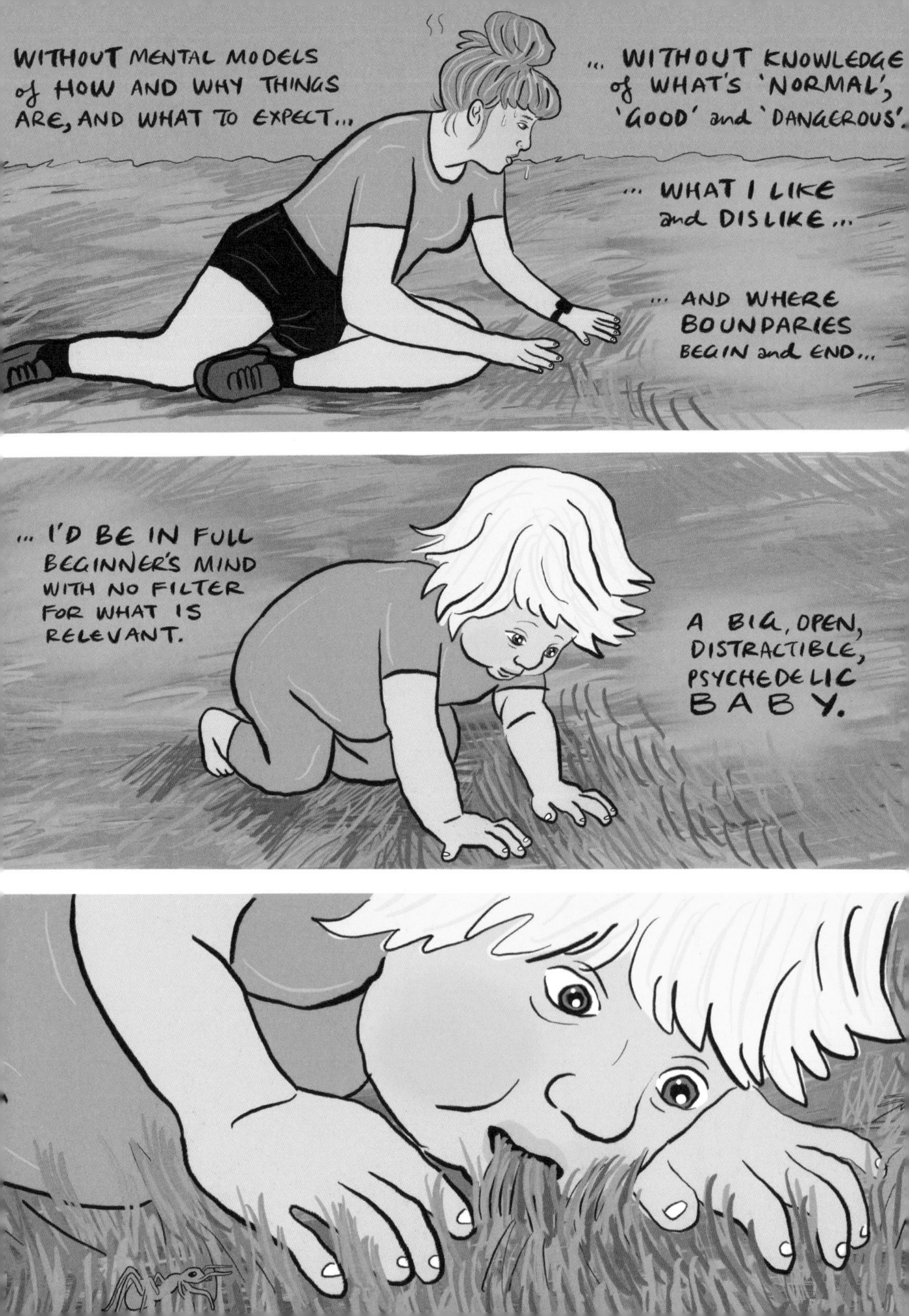
WITHOUT MENTAL MODELS of HOW AND WHY THINGS ARE, AND WHAT TO EXPECT...
... WITHOUT KNOWLEDGE of WHAT'S 'NORMAL', 'GOOD' and 'DANGEROUS'.
... WHAT I LIKE and DISLIKE...
... AND WHERE BOUNDARIES BEGIN and END...
... I'D BE IN FULL BEGINNER'S MIND WITH NO FILTER FOR WHAT IS RELEVANT.
A BIG, OPEN, DISTRACTIBLE, PSYCHEDELIC BABY.

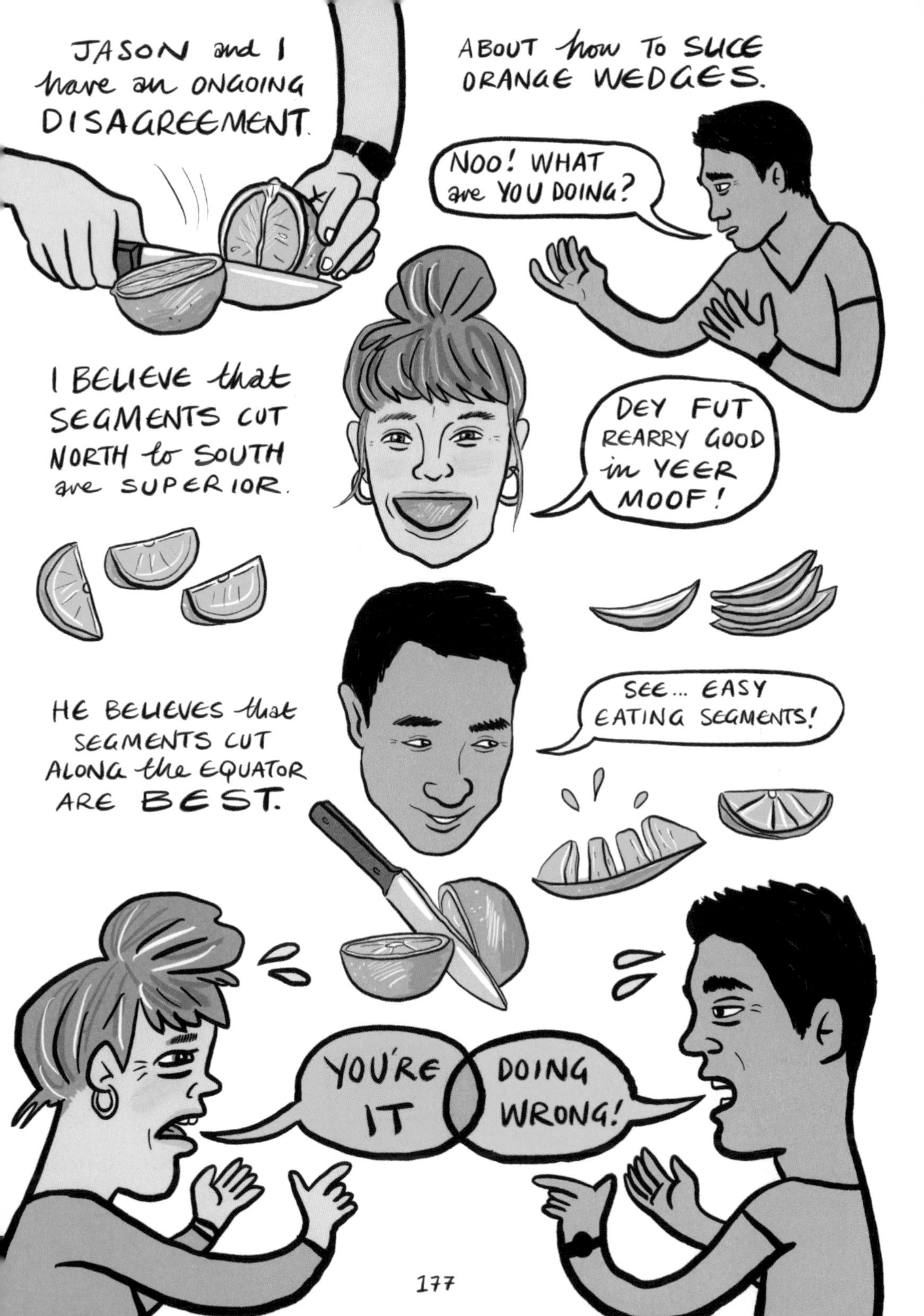
JASON and I have an ONGOING DISAGREEMENT.
ABOUT how to SLICE ORANGE WEDGES.
NOO! WHAT are YOU DOING?
I BELIEVE that SEGMENTS CUT NORTH to SOUTH are SUPERIOR.
DEY FUT REARRY GOOD in YEER MOOF!
HE BELIEVES that SEGMENTS CUT ALONG the EQUATOR ARE BEST.
SEE... EASY EATING SEGMENTS!
YOU'RE DOING IT WRONG!

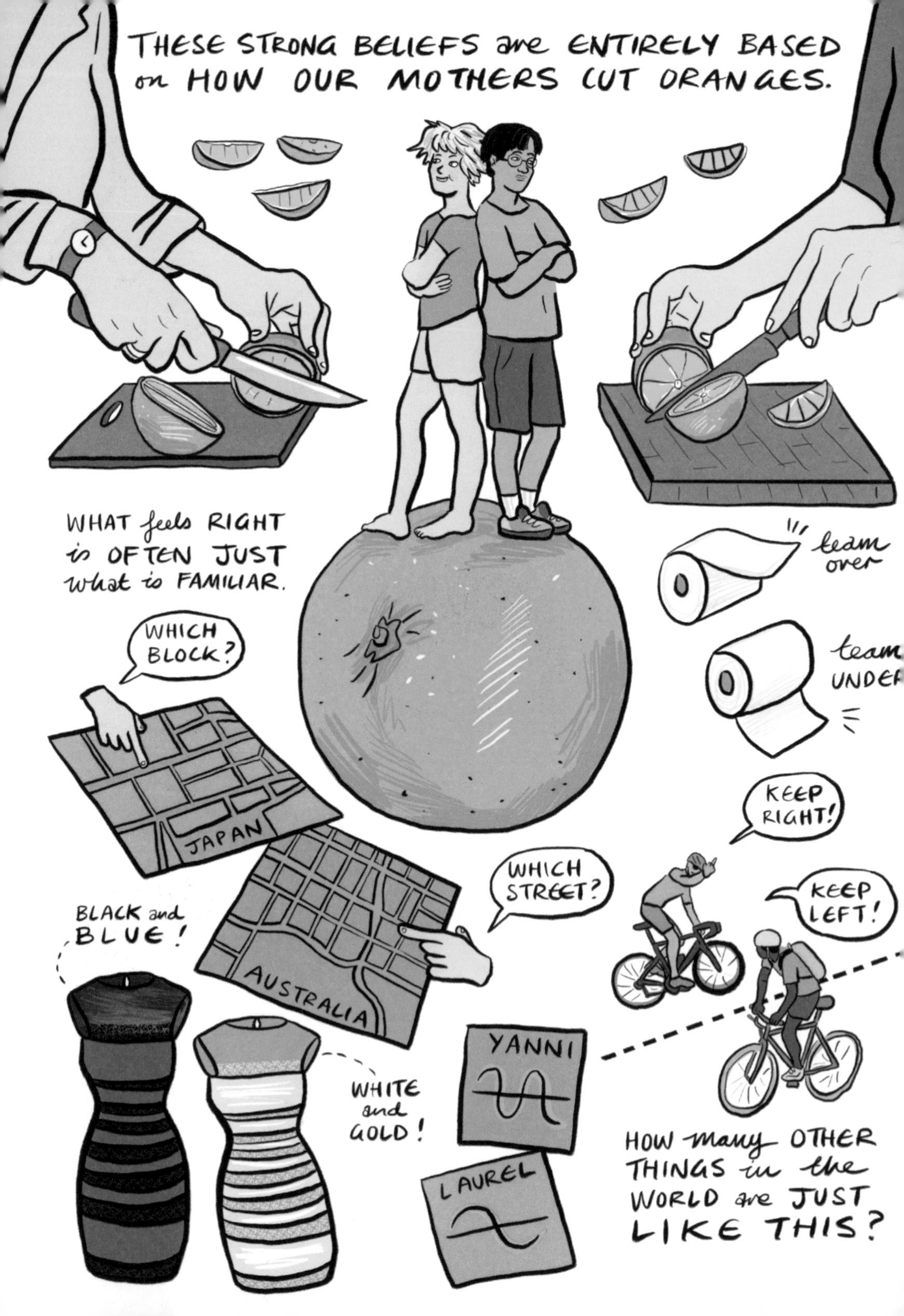
THESE STRONG BELIEFS are ENTIRELY BASED on HOW OUR MOTHERS CUT ORANGES.
WHAT feels RIGHT is OFTEN JUST what is FAMILIAR.
team over
team UNDER
WHICH BLOCK?
JAPAN
KEEP RIGHT!
WHICH STREET?
KEEP LEFT!
BLACK and BLUE!
AUSTRALIA
YANNI
WHITE and GOLD!
LAUREL
HOW many OTHER THINGS in the WORLD are JUST LIKE THIS?

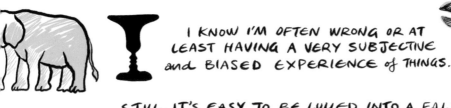

I KNOW I'M OFTEN WRONG OR AT LEAST HAVING A VERY SUBJECTIVE and BIASED EXPERIENCE of THINGS.

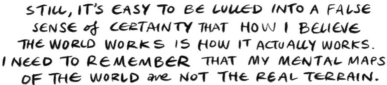

STILL, IT'S EASY TO BE LULLED INTO A FALSE SENSE of CERTAINTY THAT HOW I BELIEVE THE WORLD WORKS IS HOW IT ACTUALLY WORKS. I NEED TO REMEMBER THAT MY MENTAL MAPS OF THE WORLD are NOT THE REAL TERRAIN.

PERHAPS THAT'S WHY I ENJOY OPTICAL ILLUSIONS and MAGIC TRICKS? THEY HURT SO GOOD!

LIKE THOSE 'INVISIBLE GORILLA' VIDEOS THAT SHOW HOW SELECTIVE ATTENTION SHAPES WHAT YOU SEE. YOU BECOME SO FOCUSED on the NARROW TASK of COUNTING BASKETBALL THROWS, YOU COMPLETELY MISS A MAN IN A GORILLA SUIT WALKING SLOWLY THROUGH THE GROUP.

UNTIL YOU ARE TOLD ABOUT it AFTERWARDS.

THEN YOU CAN'T UNSEE IT.

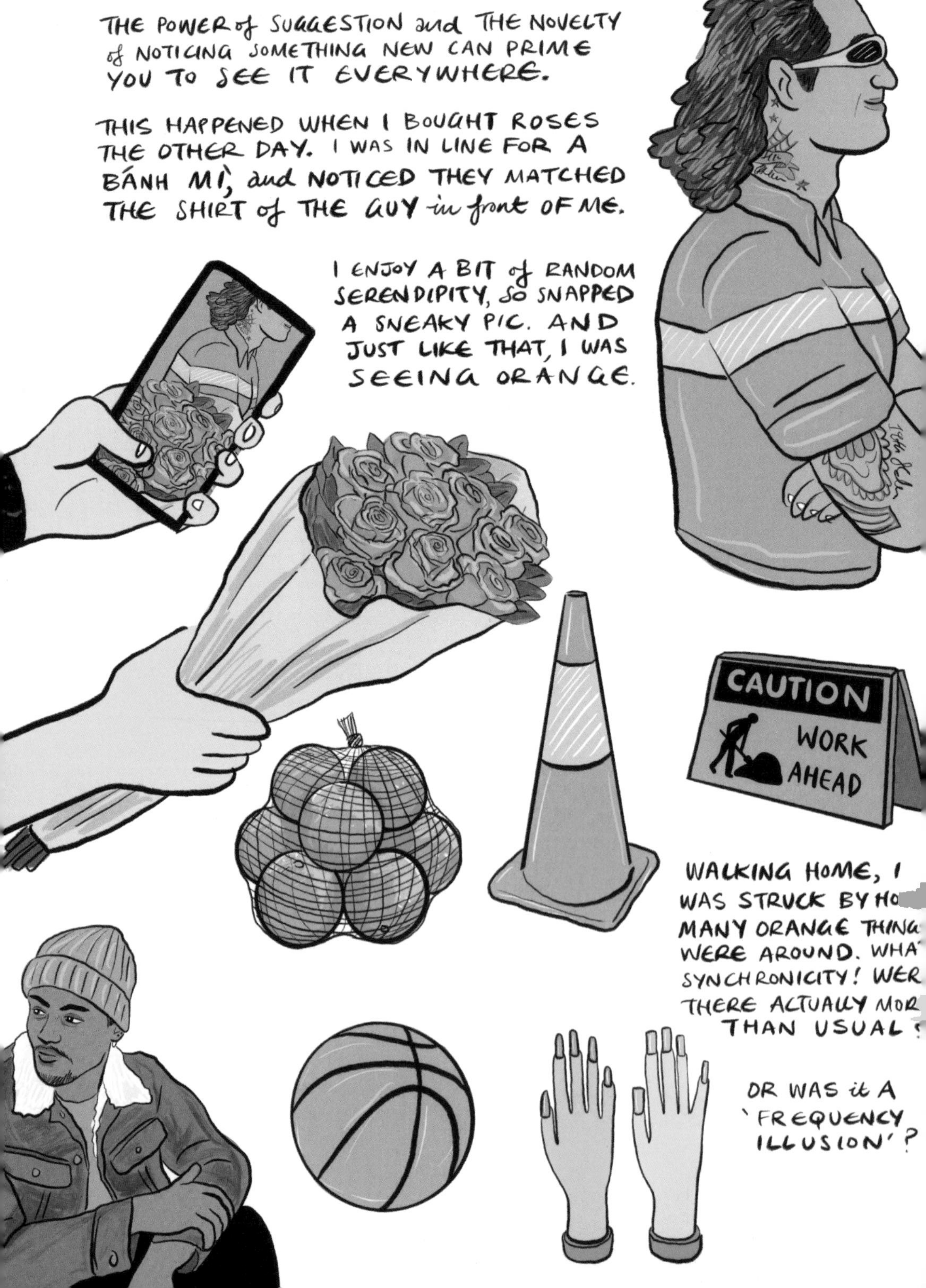
THE POWER of SUGGESTION and THE NOVELTY of NOTICING SOMETHING NEW CAN PRIME YOU TO SEE IT EVERYWHERE.
THIS HAPPENED WHEN I BOUGHT ROSES THE OTHER DAY. I WAS IN LINE FOR A BÁNH MÌ, and NOTICED THEY MATCHED THE SHIRT of THE GUY in front OF ME.
I ENJOY A BIT of RANDOM SERENDIPITY, SO SNAPPED A SNEAKY PIC. AND JUST LIKE THAT, I WAS SEEING ORANGE.
CAUTION
WORK AHEAD
WALKING HOME, I WAS STRUCK BY HO MANY ORANGE THING WERE AROUND. WHA SYNCHRONICITY! WER THERE ACTUALLY MOR THAN USUAL
OR WAS it A 'FREQUENCY ILLUSION'?

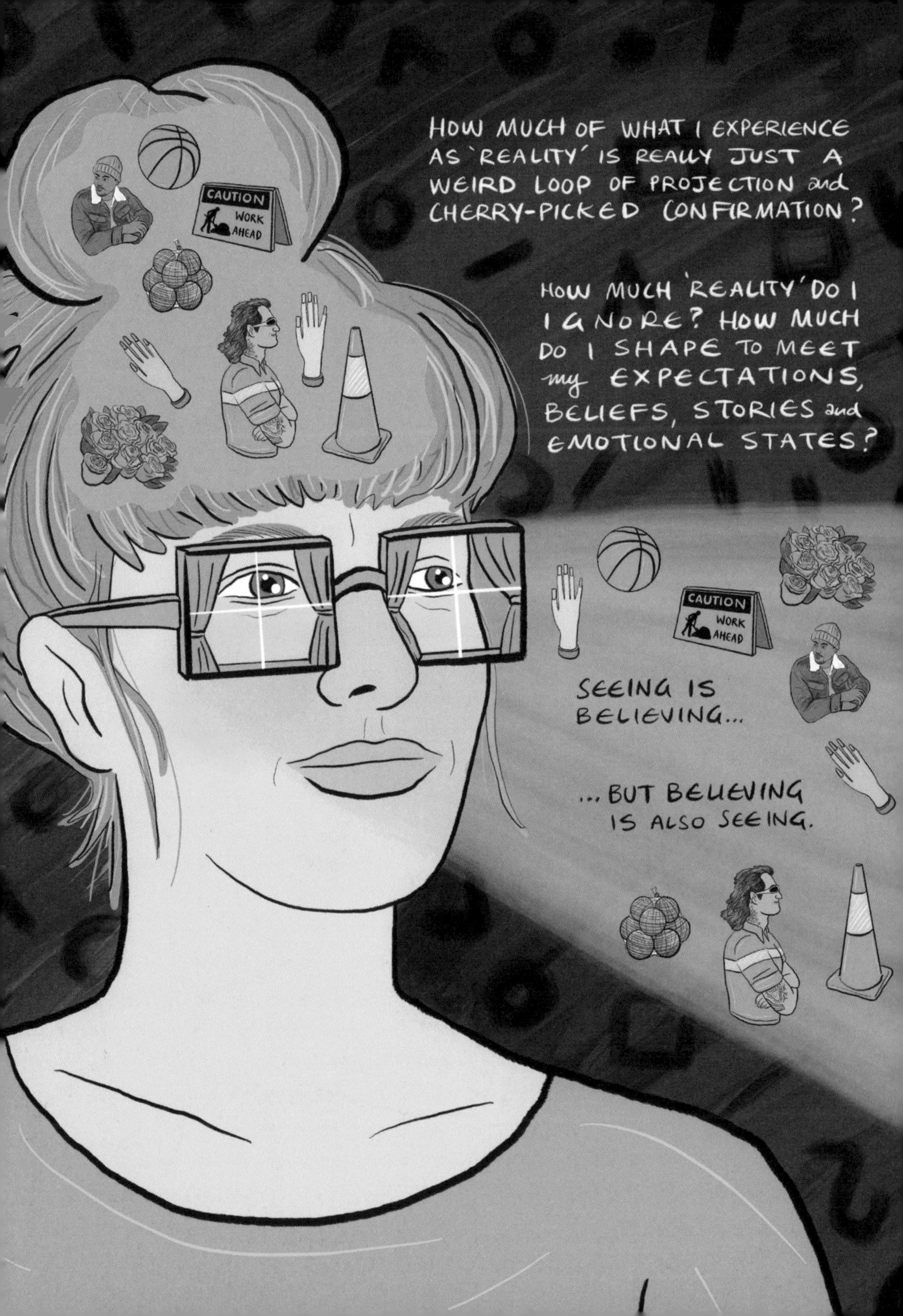
HOW MUCH OF WHAT I EXPERIENCE AS 'REALITY' IS REALLY JUST A WEIRD LOOP OF PROJECTION and CHERRY-PICKED CONFIRMATION?
HOW MUCH 'REALITY' DO I IGNORE? HOW MUCH DO I SHAPE TO MEET my EXPECTATIONS, BELIEFS, STORIES and EMOTIONAL STATES?
CAUTION WORK AHEAD
CAUTION WORK AHEAD
SEEING IS BELIEVING...
...BUT BELIEVING IS ALSO SEEING.

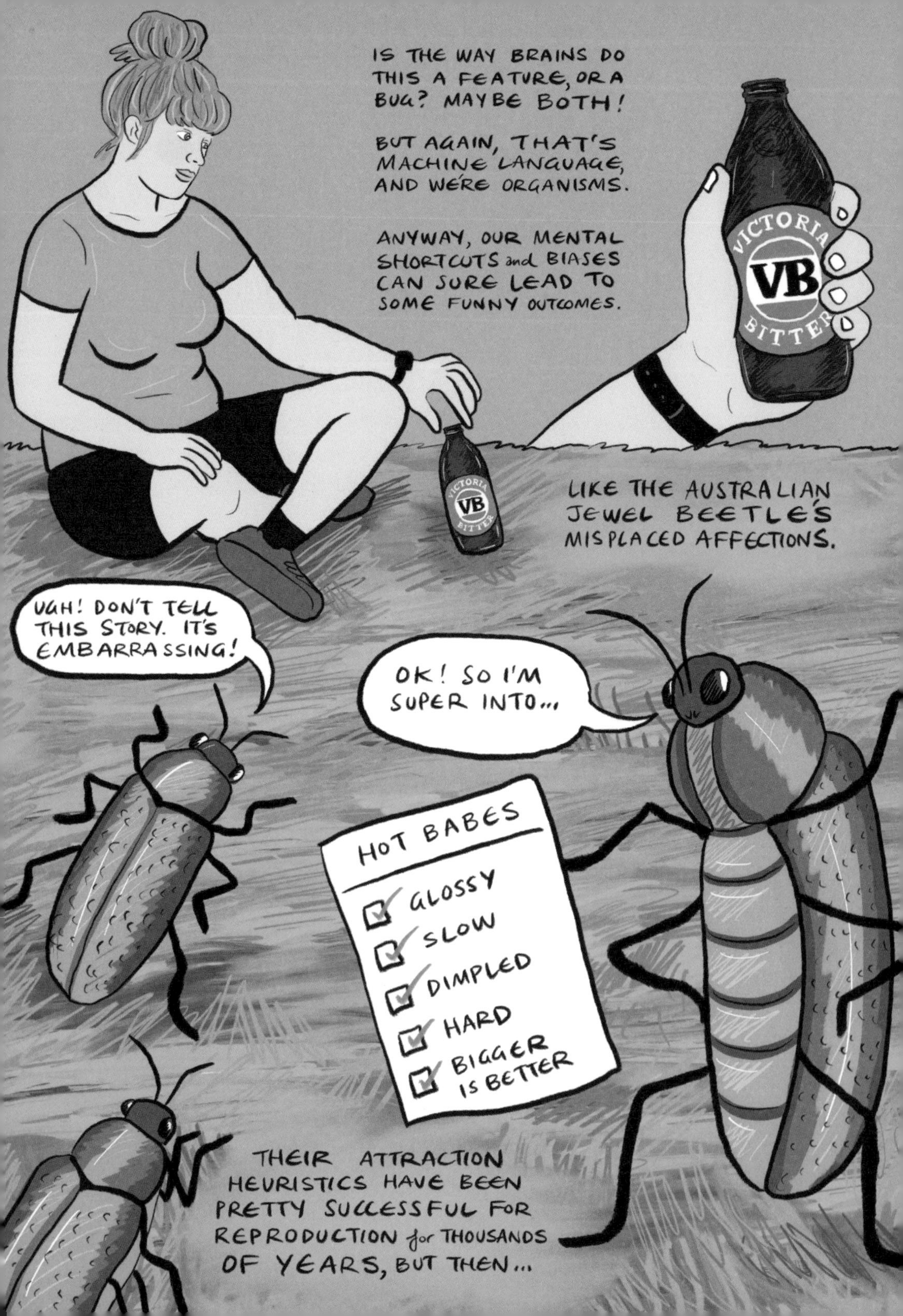

IS THE WAY BRAINS DO THIS A FEATURE, OR A BUG? MAYBE BOTH!
BUT AGAIN, THAT'S MACHINE LANGUAGE, AND WE'RE ORGANISMS.
ANYWAY, OUR MENTAL SHORTCUTS and BIASES CAN SURE LEAD TO SOME FUNNY OUTCOMES.
VICTORIA VB BITTER
LIKE THE AUSTRALIAN JEWEL BEETLE'S MISPLACED AFFECTIONS.
UGH! DON'T TELL THIS STORY. IT'S EMBARRASSING!
OK! SO I'M SUPER INTO...
HOT BABES
GLOSSY
SLOW
DIMPLED
HARD
BIGGER IS BETTER
THEIR ATTRACTION HEURISTICS HAVE BEEN PRETTY SUCCESSFUL FOR REPRODUCTION for THOUSANDS OF YEARS, BUT THEN...

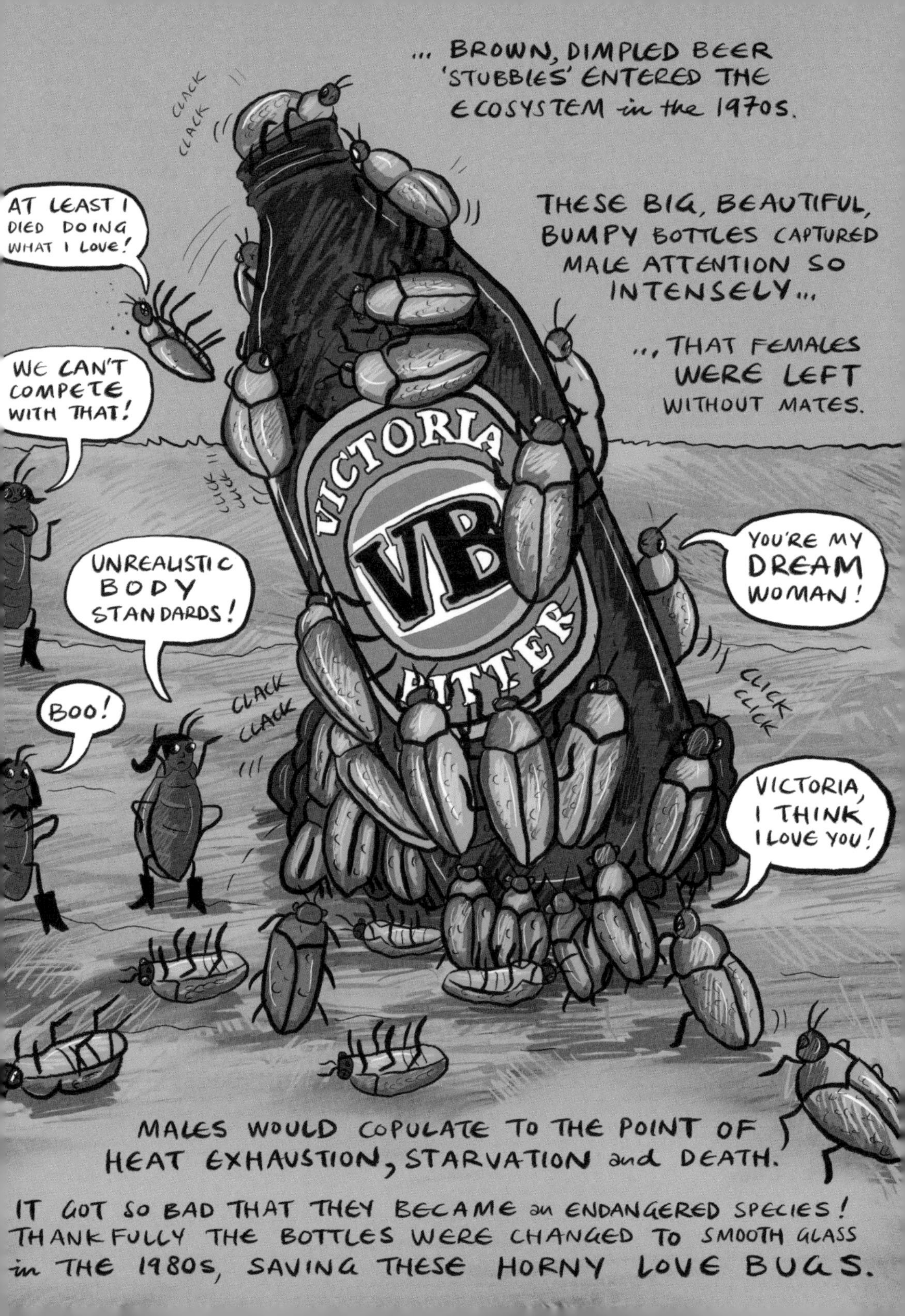
... BROWN, DIMPLED BEER 'STUBBIES' ENTERED THE ECOSYSTEM in the 1970S.
CLACK CLACK
THESE BIG, BEAUTIFUL, BUMPY BOTTLES CAPTURED MALE ATTENTION SO INTENSELY...
AT LEAST I DIED DOING WHAT I LOVE!
... THAT FEMALES WERE LEFT WITHOUT MATES.
WE CAN'T COMPETE WITH THAT!
VICTORIA BITTER
VB
CLICK CLICK
YOU'RE MY DREAM WOMAN!
UNREALISTIC BODY STANDARDS!
CLACK CLACK
CLICK CLICK
BOO!
VICTORIA, I THINK I LOVE YOU!
MALES WOULD COPULATE TO THE POINT OF HEAT EXHAUSTION, STARVATION and DEATH.
IT GOT SO BAD THAT THEY BECAME an ENDANGERED SPECIES! THANKFULLY THE BOTTLES WERE CHANGED TO SMOOTH GLASS in THE 1980S, SAVING THESE HORNY LOVE BUGS.

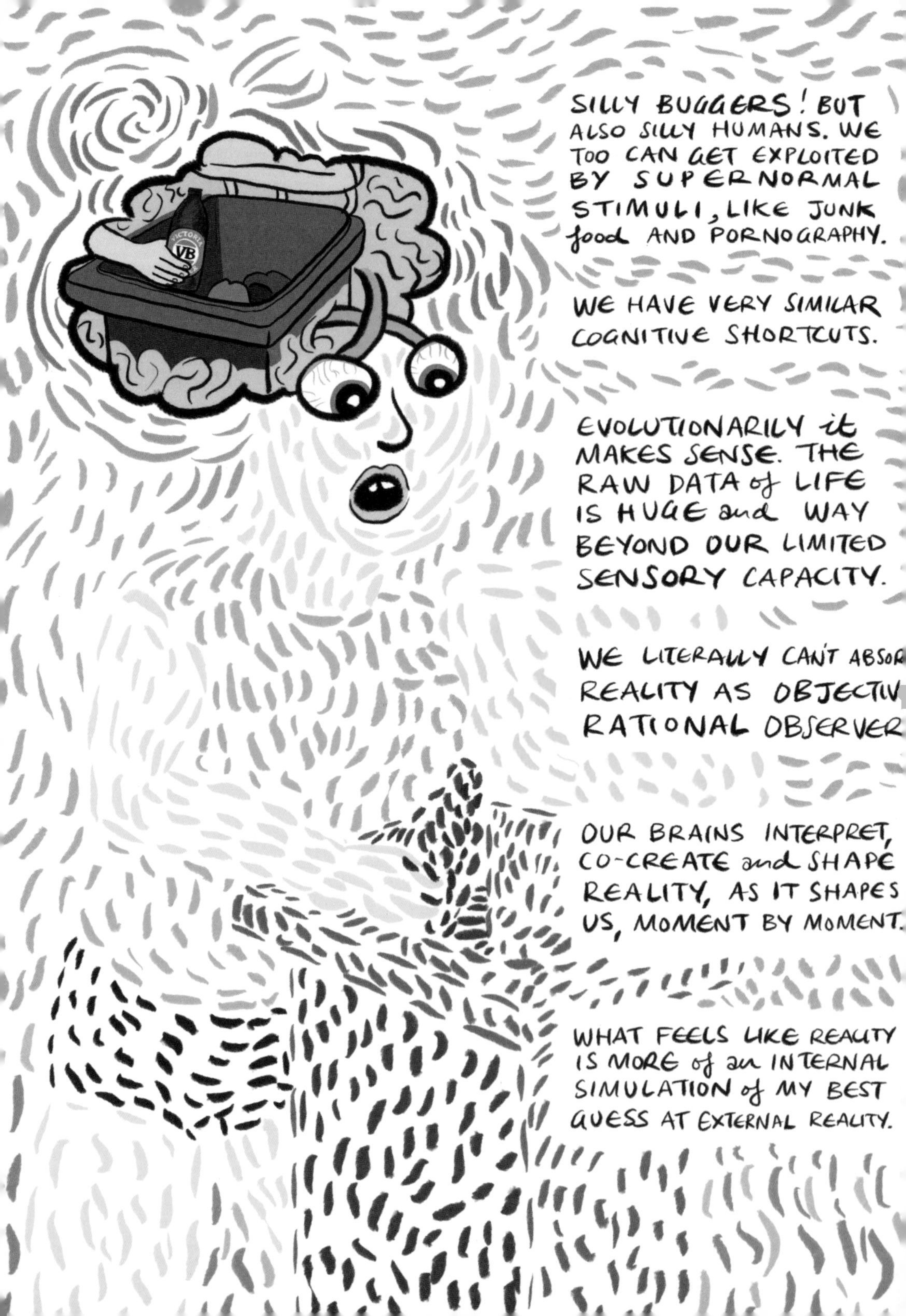
SILLY BUGGERS! BUT ALSO SILLY HUMANS. WE TOO CAN GET EXPLOITED BY SUPERNORMAL STIMULI, LIKE JUNK food AND PORNOGRAPHY.
WE HAVE VERY SIMILAR COGNITIVE SHORTCUTS.
EVOLUTIONARILY it MAKES SENSE. THE RAW DATA of LIFE IS HUGE and WAY BEYOND OUR LIMITED SENSORY CAPACITY.
WE LITERALLY CAN'T ABSOR REALITY AS OBJECTIV RATIONAL OBSERVER
OUR BRAINS INTERPRET, CO-CREATE and SHAPE REALITY, AS IT SHAPES US, MOMENT BY MOMENT.
WHAT FEELS LIKE REALITY IS MORE of an INTERNAL SIMULATION of MY BEST GUESS AT EXTERNAL REALITY.

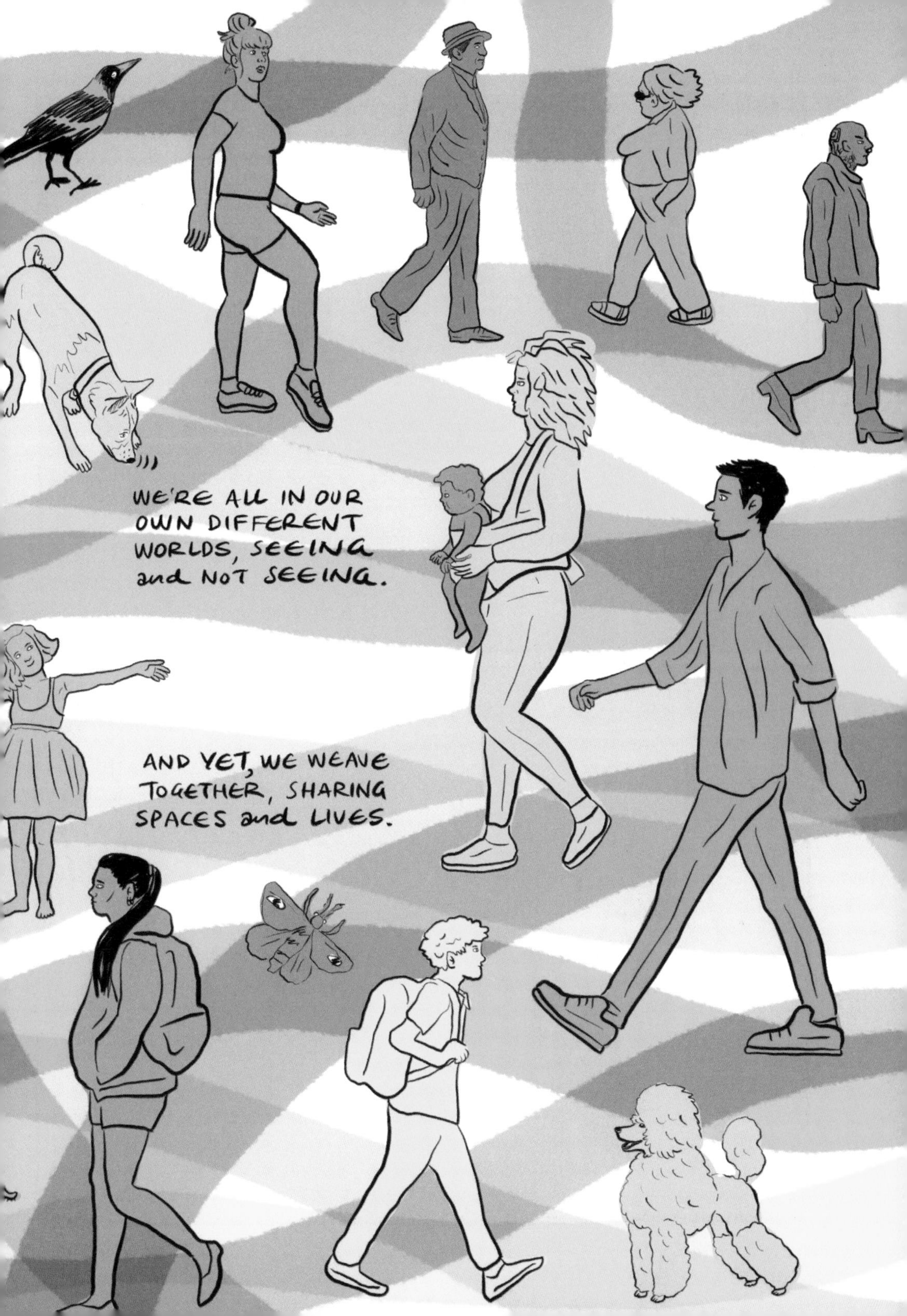
WE'RE ALL IN OUR OWN DIFFERENT WORLDS, SEEING and NOT SEEING.
AND YET, WE WEAVE TOGETHER, SHARING SPACES and LIVES.

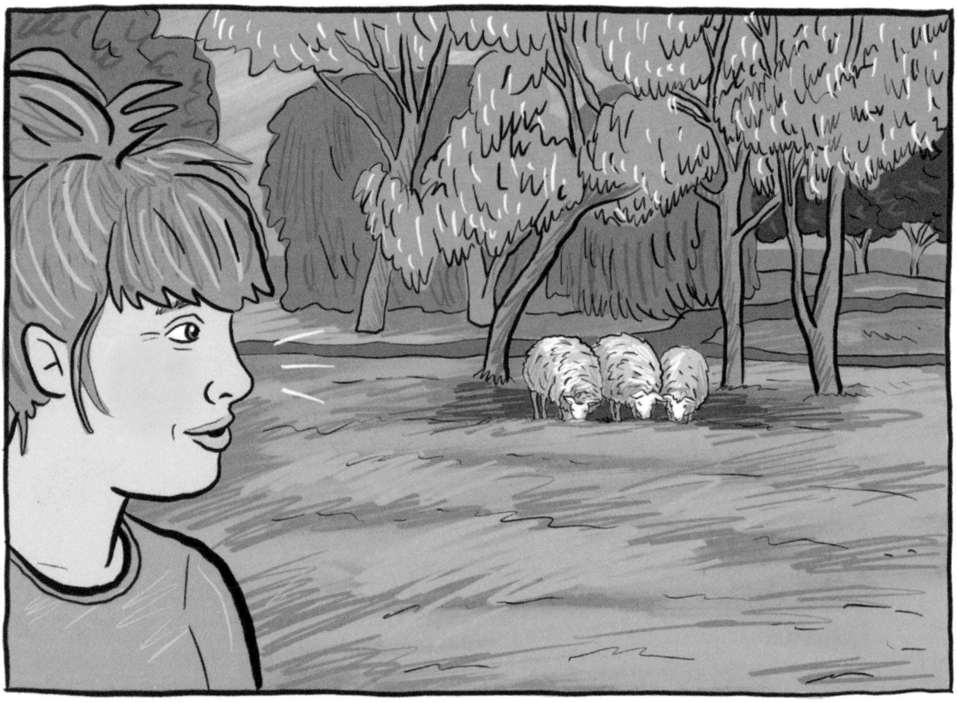

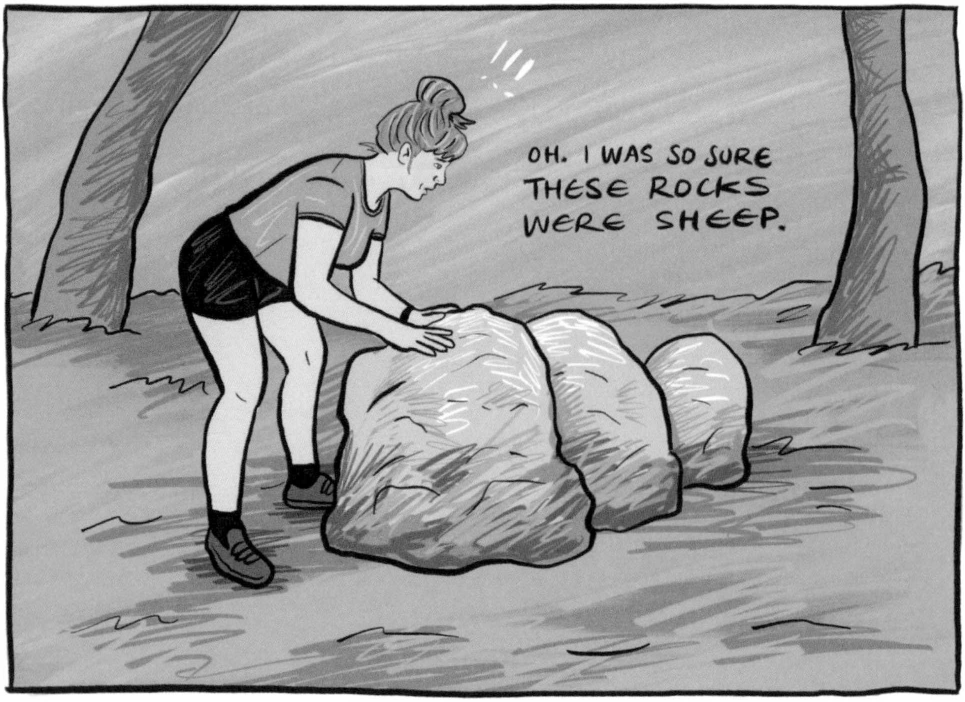
OH. I WAS SO SURE THESE ROCKS WERE SHEEP.

THERE IT IS AGAIN. MY TALENT *for* MISPERCEPTION.

WHICH CAN *be* A DELIGHT *to* INDULGE...

YEE HAW!

BUT *it* ALSO MEANS REALITY **TESTING** *is* IMPORTANT FOR ME.

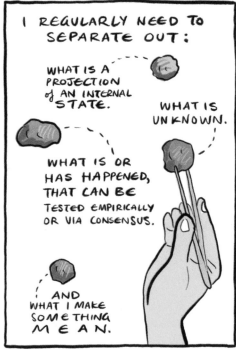

I REGULARLY NEED TO SEPARATE OUT:

WHAT IS A PROJECTION *of* AN INTERNAL STATE.

WHAT IS UNKNOWN.

WHAT IS OR HAS HAPPENED, THAT CAN BE TESTED EMPIRICALLY OR VIA CONSENSUS.

AND WHAT I MAKE SOMETHING **MEAN.**

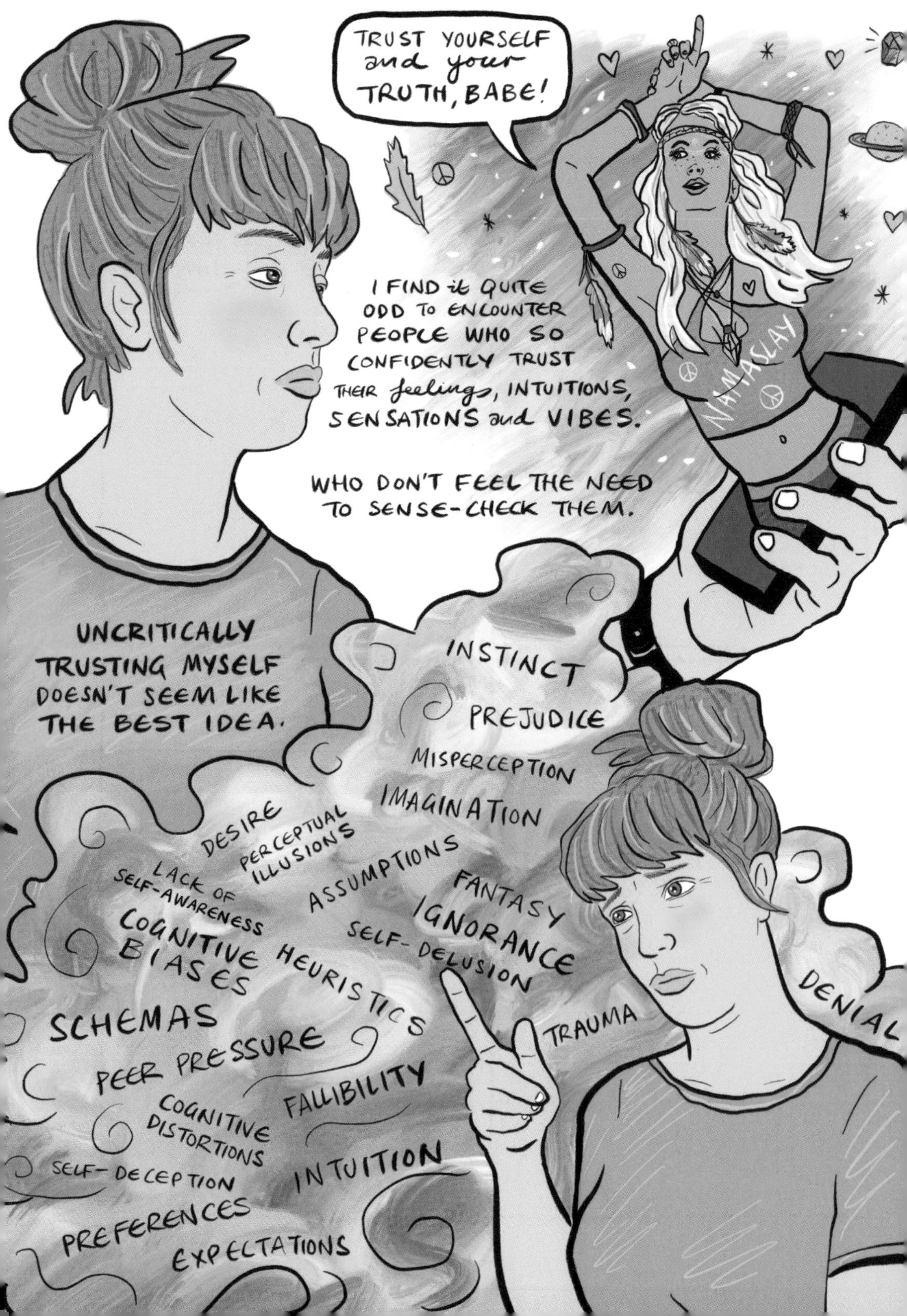

TRUST YOURSELF and your TRUTH, BABE!
NAMASLAY
I FIND it QUITE ODD TO ENCOUNTER PEOPLE WHO SO CONFIDENTLY TRUST THEIR feelings, INTUITIONS, SENSATIONS and VIBES.
WHO DON'T FEEL THE NEED TO SENSE-CHECK THEM.
UNCRITICALLY TRUSTING MYSELF DOESN'T SEEM LIKE THE BEST IDEA.
INSTINCT
PREJUDICE
MISPERCEPTION
IMAGINATION
DESIRE
PERCEPTUAL ILLUSIONS
ASSUMPTIONS
LACK OF SELF-AWARENESS
FANTASY
IGNORANCE
COGNITIVE BIASES
SELF-DELUSION
HEURISTICS
DENIAL
SCHEMAS
TRAUMA
PEER PRESSURE
FALLIBILITY
COGNITIVE DISTORTIONS
INTUITION
SELF-DECEPTION
PREFERENCES
EXPECTATIONS

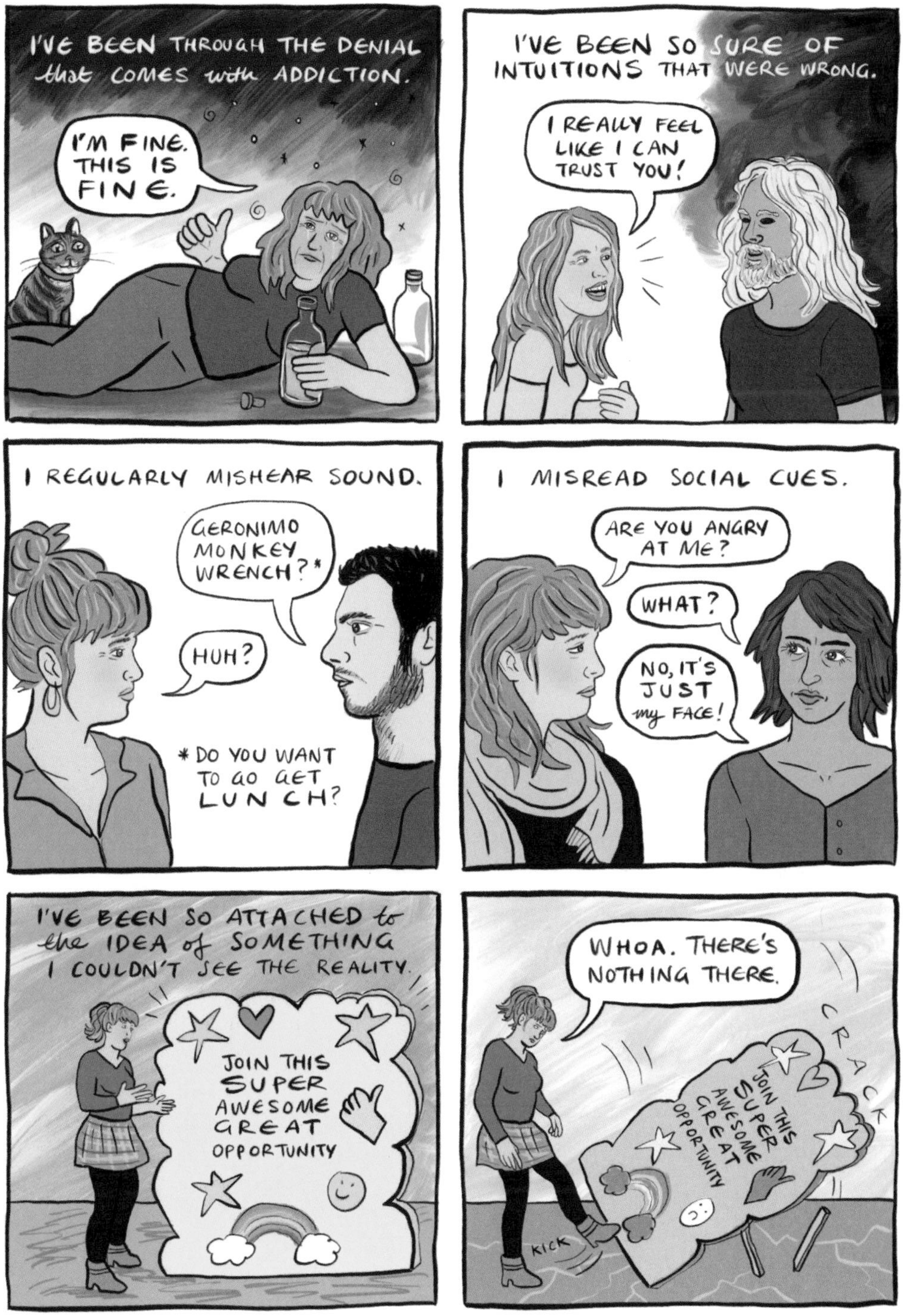
I'VE BEEN THROUGH THE DENIAL that COMES with ADDICTION.
I'M FINE. THIS IS FINE.
I'VE BEEN SO SURE OF INTUITIONS THAT WERE WRONG.
I REALLY FEEL LIKE I CAN TRUST YOU!
I REGULARLY MISHEAR SOUND.
GERONIMO MONKEY WRENCH?*
HUH?
* DO YOU WANT TO GO GET LUNCH?
I MISREAD SOCIAL CUES.
ARE YOU ANGRY AT ME?
WHAT?
NO, IT'S JUST my FACE!
I'VE BEEN SO ATTACHED to the IDEA of SOMETHING I COULDN'T SEE THE REALITY.
JOIN THIS SUPER AWESOME GREAT OPPORTUNITY
WHOA. THERE'S NOTHING THERE.
CRACK
JOIN THIS SUPER AWESOME GREAT OPPORTUNITY
KICK

I EXPERIENCE BODY DYSMORPHIA.

I'VE GONE ALONG WITH THINGS BECAUSE of PEER PRESSURE.

GOLD DUST! WE'RE BEING BLESSED by GOD!

BUT I CAN'T SEE IT?

I'VE TAKEN ON BELIEFS and A WHOLE WORLD VIEW...

AVOID SPIRIT POSSESSION

HELPING GOD'S PLAN

SAVING THE WORLD

SAVING SOULS

YOU ARE A CHILD of GOD

PENANCE

FOSTER GOOD KARMA

AVOID BAD KARMA

ATONEMENT

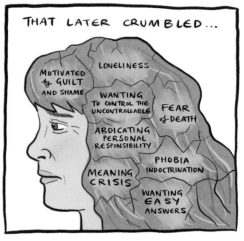

THAT LATER CRUMBLED...

MOTIVATED by GUILT AND SHAME

LONELINESS

WANTING TO CONTROL THE UNCONTROLLABLE

FEAR of DEATH

ABDICATING PERSONAL RESPONSIBILITY

PHOBIA INDOCTRINATION

MEANING CRISIS

WANTING EASY ANSWERS

AND if THERE IS ONE THING my MENTAL HEALTH WOBBLES HAVE CLEARLY SHOWN ME...

IT'S THAT THINGS AREN'T ALWAYS WHAT THEY SEEM.

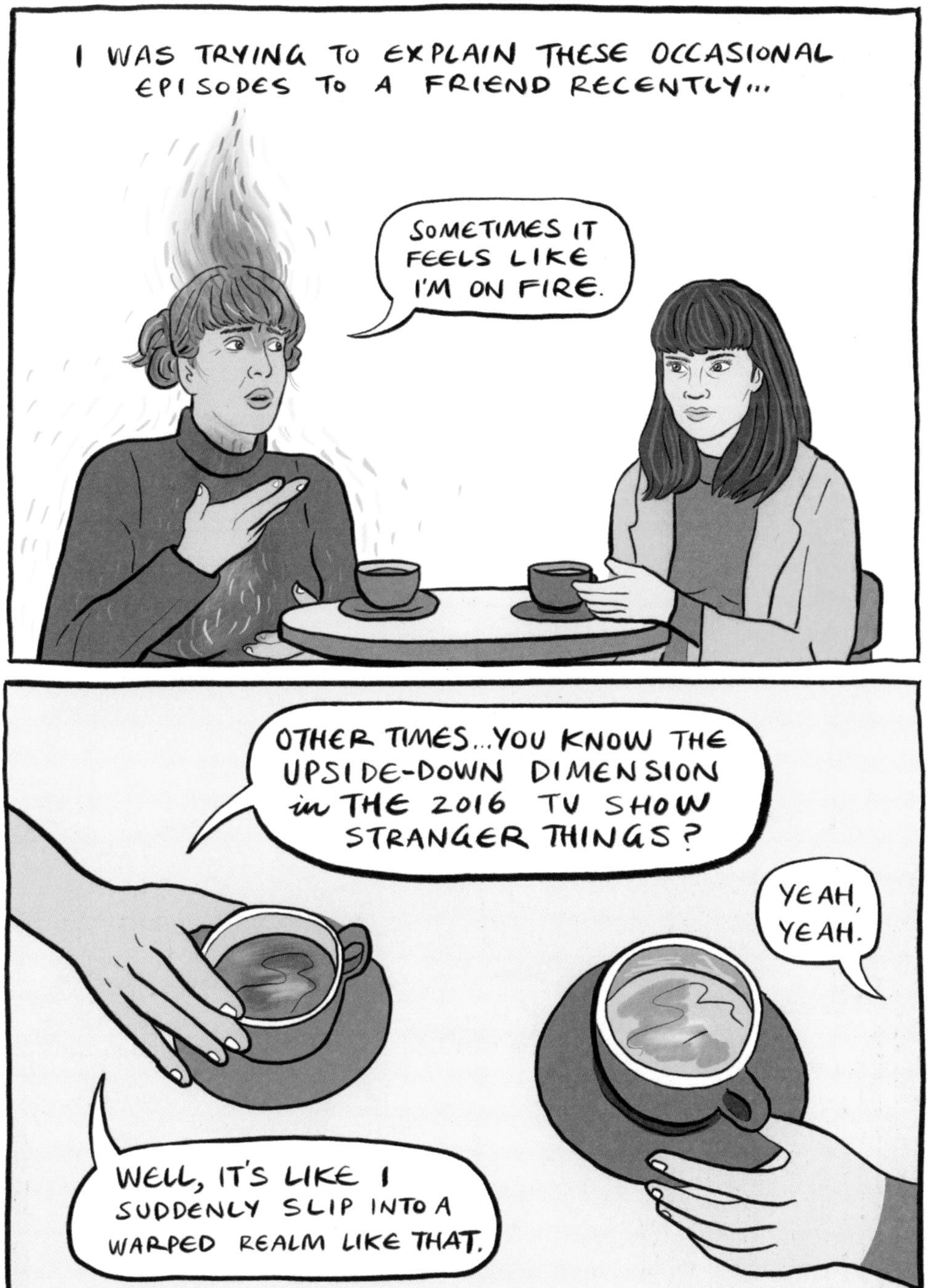
I WAS TRYING TO EXPLAIN THESE OCCASIONAL EPISODES TO A FRIEND RECENTLY...
SOMETIMES IT FEELS LIKE I'M ON FIRE.
OTHER TIMES...YOU KNOW THE UPSIDE-DOWN DIMENSION in THE 2016 TV SHOW STRANGER THINGS?
YEAH, YEAH.
WELL, IT'S LIKE I SUDDENLY SLIP INTO A WARPED REALM LIKE THAT.

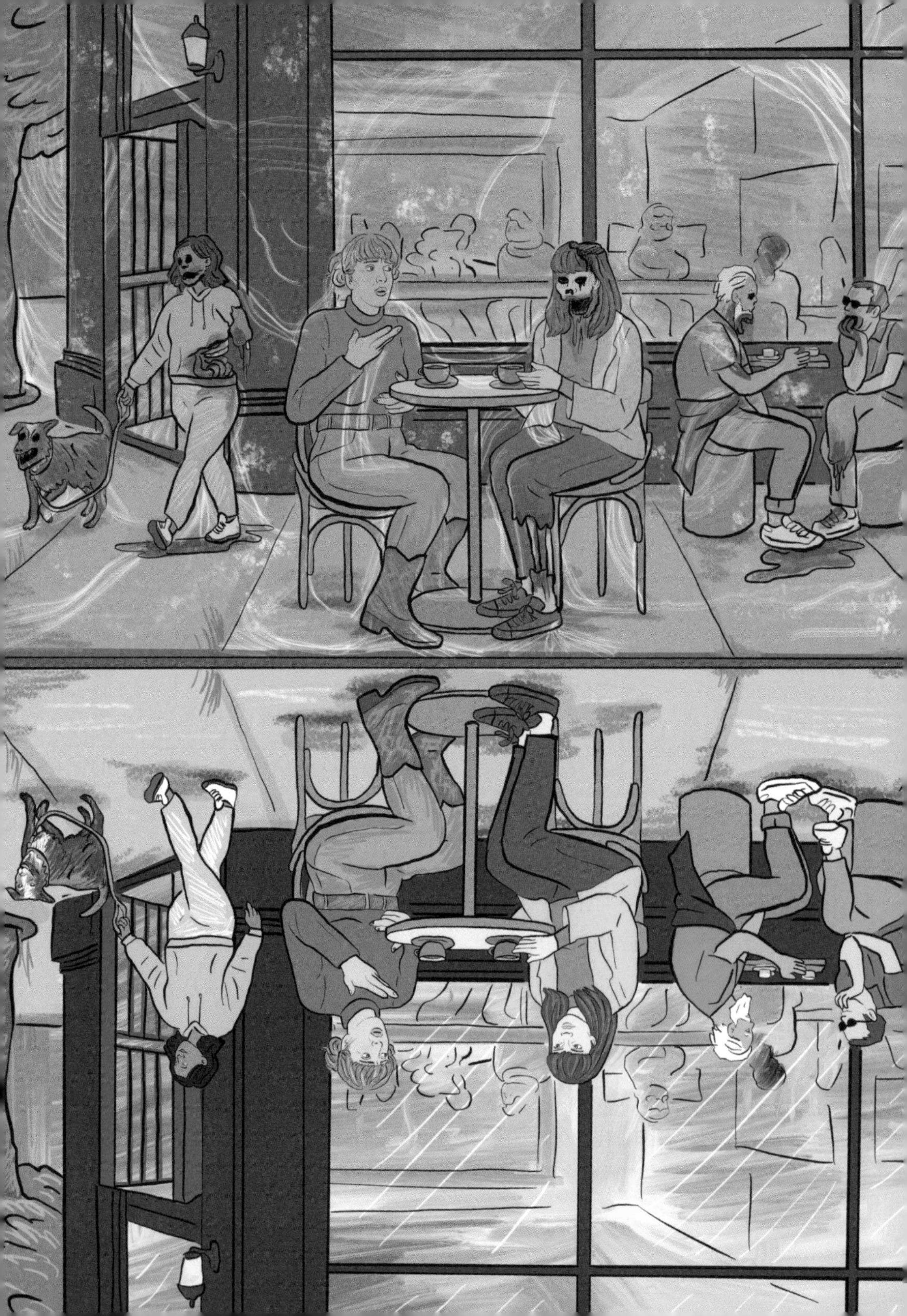

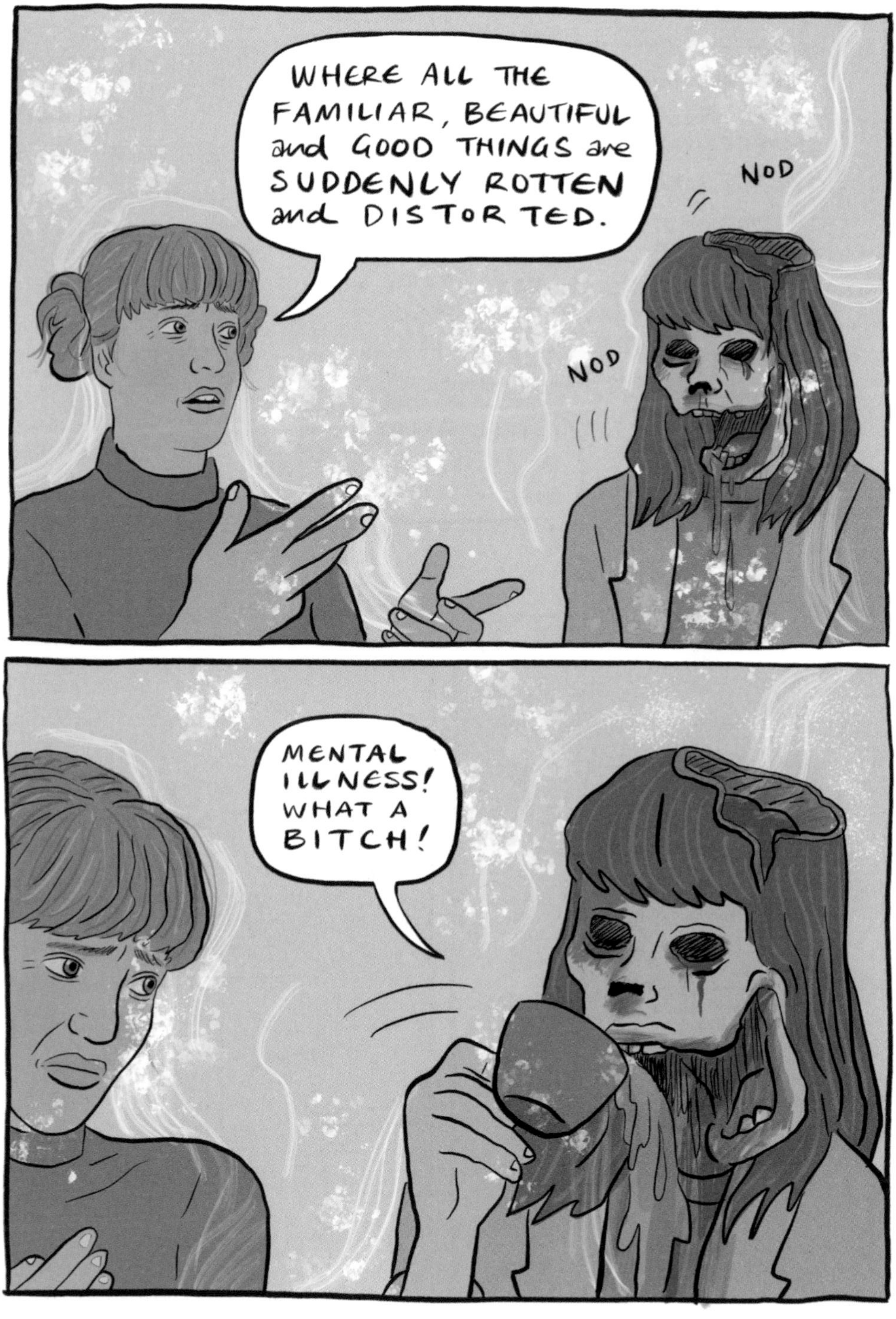
WHERE ALL THE FAMILIAR, BEAUTIFUL and GOOD THINGS are SUDDENLY ROTTEN and DISTORTED.
NOD
NOD
MENTAL ILLNESS! WHAT A BITCH!

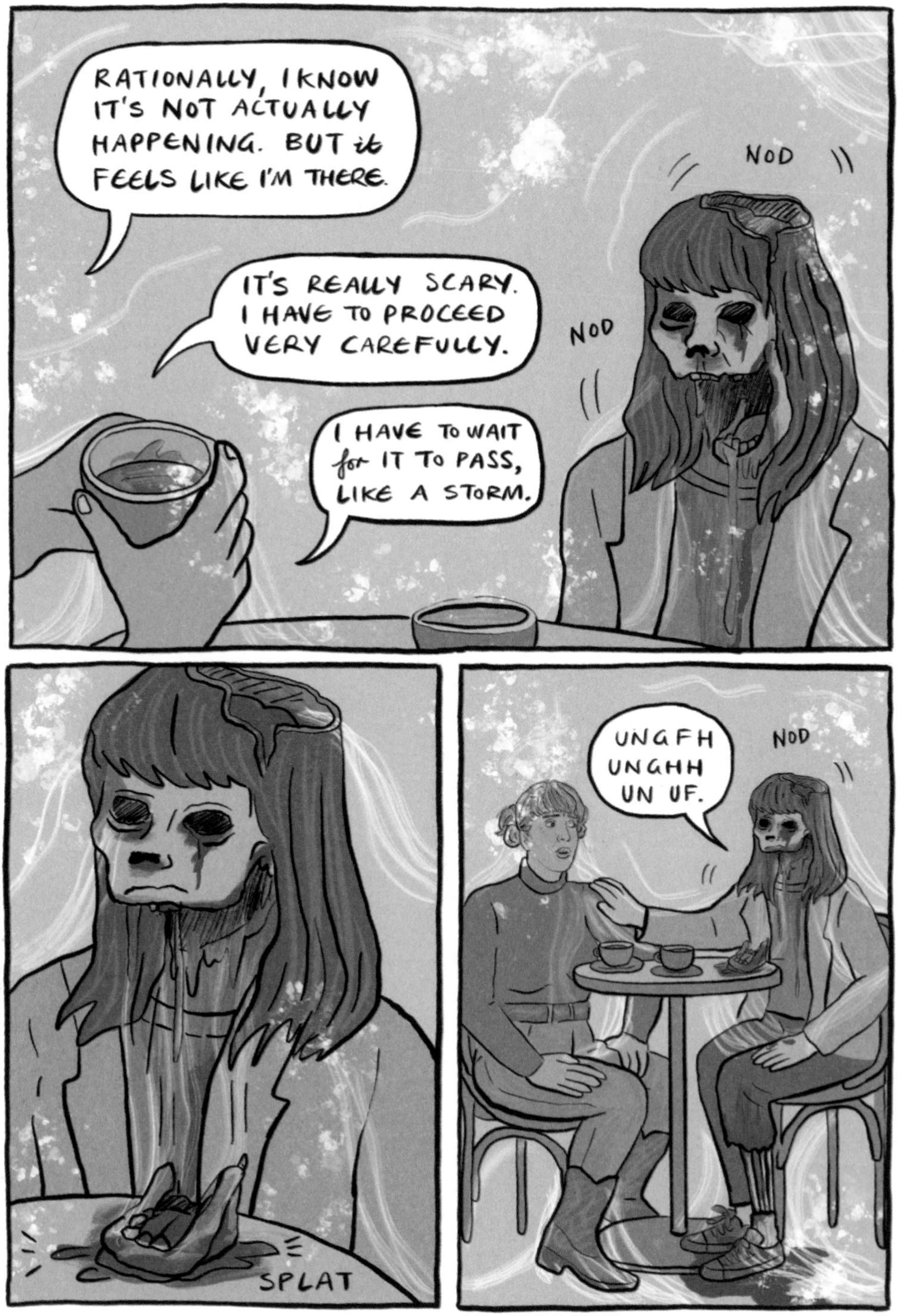
RATIONALLY, I KNOW IT'S NOT ACTUALLY HAPPENING. BUT it FEELS LIKE I'M THERE.
NOD
IT'S REALLY SCARY. I HAVE TO PROCEED VERY CAREFULLY.
NOD
I HAVE TO WAIT for IT TO PASS, LIKE A STORM.
SPLAT
UNGFH UNGHH UN UF.
NOD

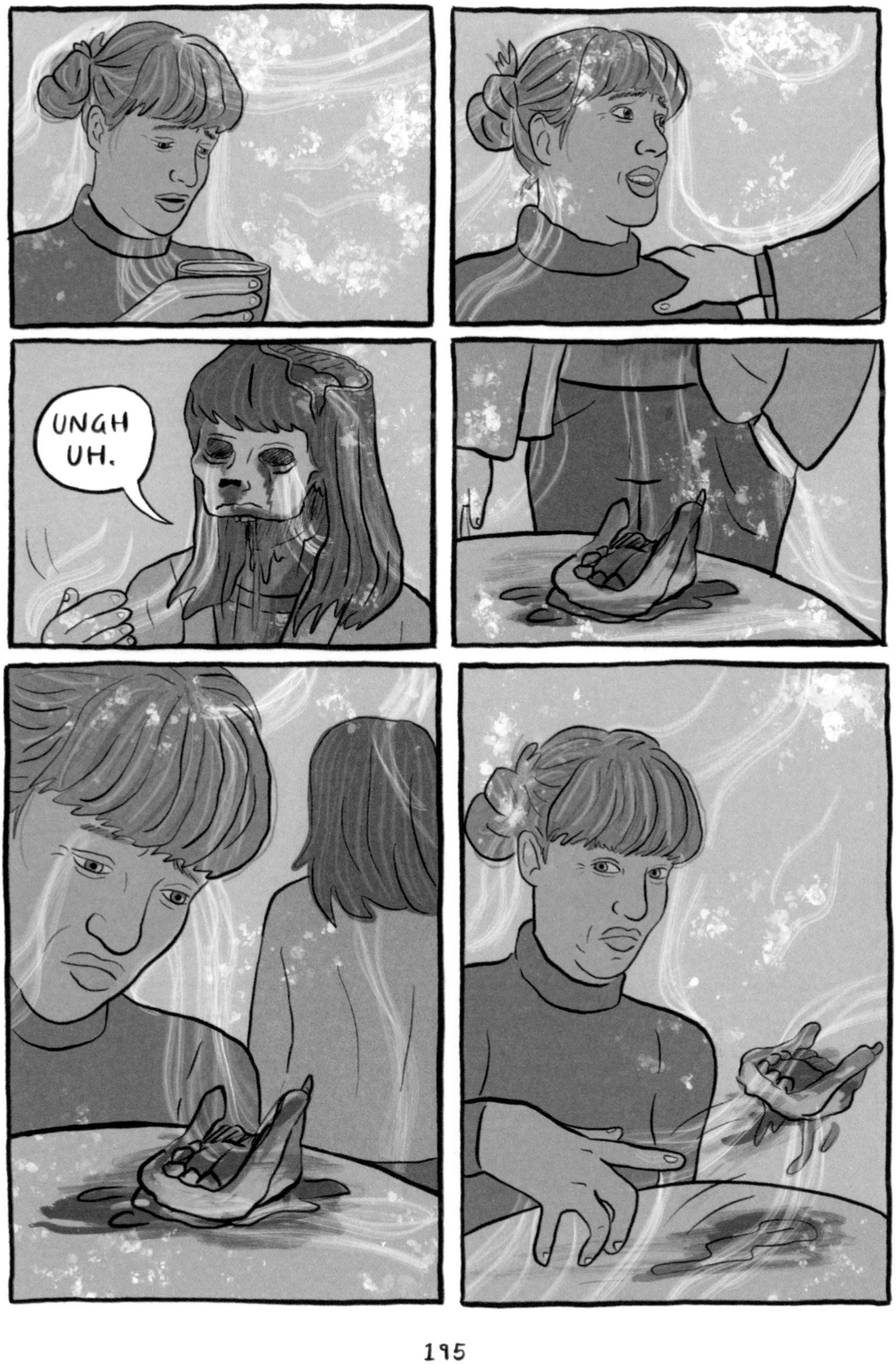
UNGH UH.

WHEN THE PANIC and DOOM IS LOUD, SOMETHING THAT'S SURPRISINGLY HELPFUL IS...

...STATISTICS! IT GIVES ME SOME DATA TO GET PERSPECTIVE.

ON A PLANE OBSESSING THAT I'M GOING TO DIE?

DON'T WORRY! YOU ONLY HAVE A 1 in 11 MILLION CHANCE of DYING in A CRASH.

HOORAY!

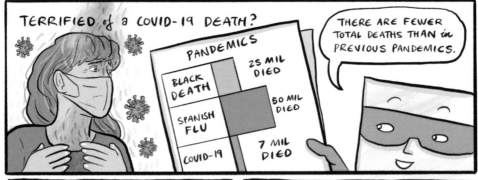

TERRIFIED of a COVID-19 DEATH?

PANDEMICS

BLACK DEATH — 25 MIL DIED

SPANISH FLU — 50 MIL DIED

COVID-19 — 7 MIL DIED

THERE ARE FEWER TOTAL DEATHS THAN in PREVIOUS PANDEMICS.

SCARED of THAT STRANGER?

YOU'RE MORE LIKELY TO BE HARMED OR MURDERED BY SOMEONE YOU KNOW!

GREAT!

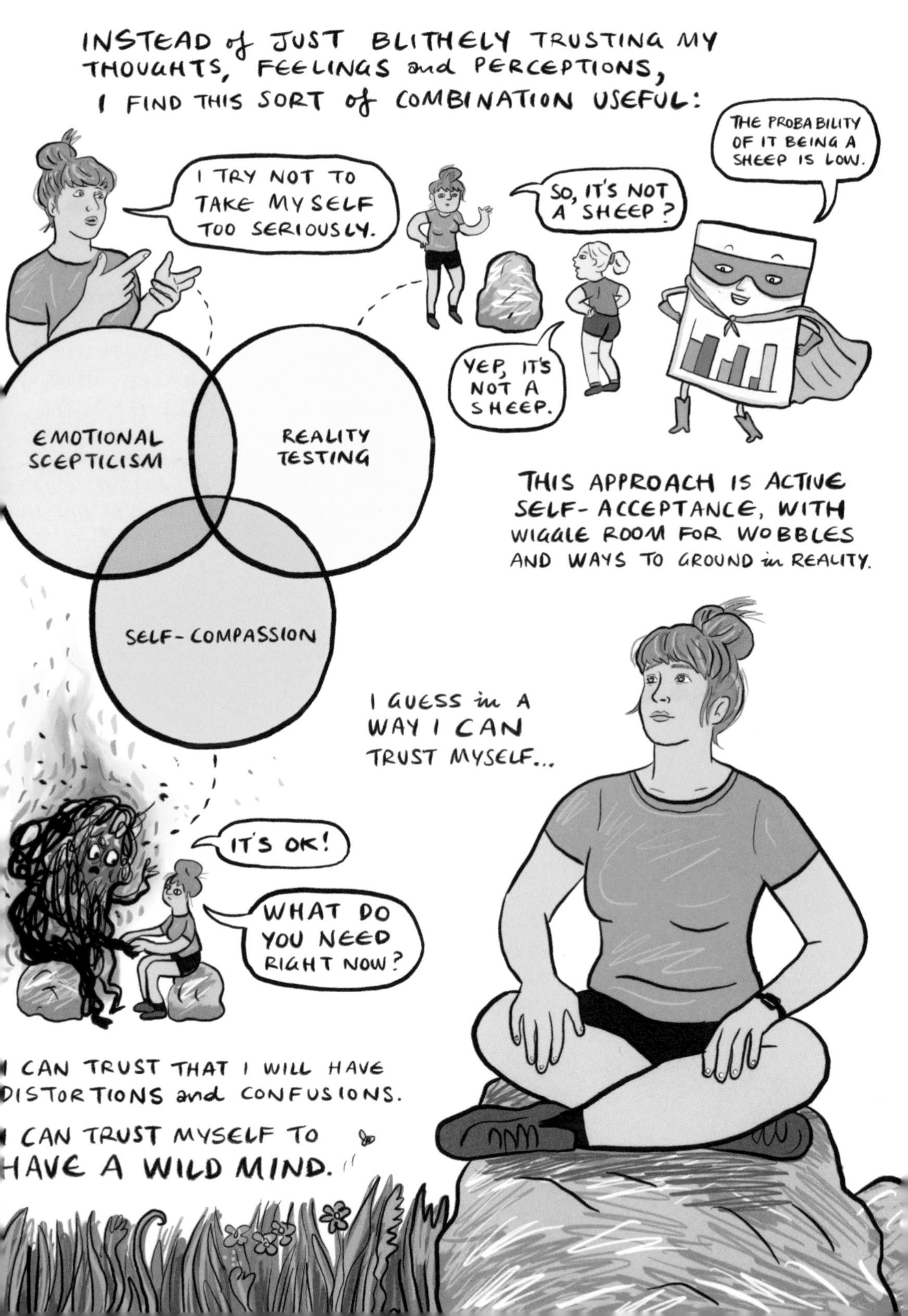
INSTEAD of JUST BLITHELY TRUSTING MY THOUGHTS, FEELINGS and PERCEPTIONS, I FIND THIS SORT of COMBINATION USEFUL:
I TRY NOT TO TAKE MYSELF TOO SERIOUSLY.
SO, IT'S NOT A SHEEP?
THE PROBABILITY OF IT BEING A SHEEP IS LOW.
YEP, IT'S NOT A SHEEP.
EMOTIONAL SCEPTICISM
REALITY TESTING
SELF-COMPASSION
THIS APPROACH IS ACTIVE SELF-ACCEPTANCE, WITH WIGGLE ROOM FOR WOBBLES AND WAYS TO GROUND in REALITY.
IT'S OK!
WHAT DO YOU NEED RIGHT NOW?
I GUESS in A WAY I CAN TRUST MYSELF...
I CAN TRUST THAT I WILL HAVE DISTORTIONS and CONFUSIONS.
I CAN TRUST MYSELF TO HAVE A WILD MIND.

COMING BACK TO MY EARLIER THOUGHT THAT ALL MODELS ARE WRONG, BUT SOME ARE USEFUL, THE WAY I USE STATISTICS IS LESS ABOUT FACT and MORE of A KIND OF NARRATIVE REFRAME.

FACTS MATTER BUT SO DO THE STORIES I TELL MYSELF ABOUT THEM.

WE HUMANS LAYER STORIES ONTO EVERYTHING. AND THEY REALLY DO SHAPE EXPERIENCE. THINK of HOW NOCEBOS and PLACEBOS IMPACT HEALTH.

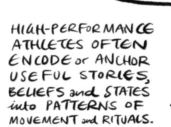

BELIEVE I WILL MAKE YOU SICK and I WILL!

BELIEVE I WILL MAKE YOU WELL and I WILL!

HIGH-PERFORMANCE ATHLETES OFTEN ENCODE or ANCHOR USEFUL STORIES, BELIEFS and STATES into PATTERNS OF MOVEMENT and RITUALS.

IS THIS SIMILAR TO HOW GOOD LUCK SUPERSTITIONS ARE ENACTED?

HIGH JUMPER NICOLA MCDERMOTT USES HER JOURNAL AS A RITUAL DURING COMPETITIONS, AS BOTH A SPACE TO POSITIVELY VISUALISE and WRITE AFFIRMATIONS.

SIMILARLY, ATHLETE MICHELLE JENNEKE'S FAMOUS PRE-RACE DANCE HELPS HER TO ALIGN MENTALLY, EMOTIONALLY and PHYSICALLY.

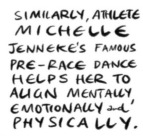

I'M NOT ADVOCATING FOR TOXIC POSITIVITY. WHAT I AM SAYING IS THAT REFRAMING THE FACTS or RAW EXPERIENCE and SENSATIONS IN A WAY THAT IS HELPFUL RATHER THAN A HINDRANCE IS A USEFUL CREATIVE TOOL TO PLAY WITH.

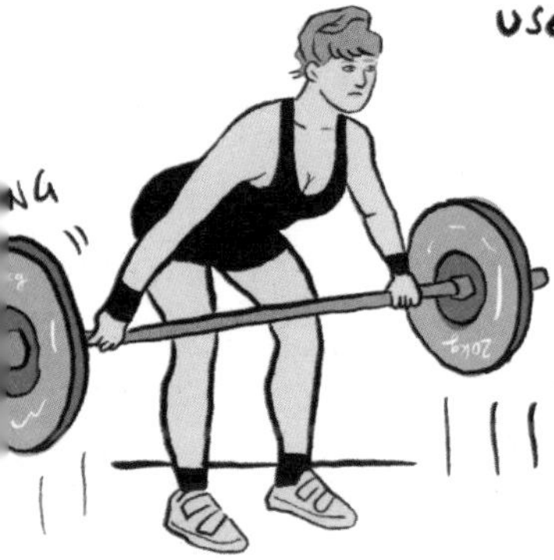
NG
20kg

I GET PERFORMANCE and ANTICIPATORY ANXIETY REGULARLY. ESPECIALLY BEFORE OLYMPIC WEIGHTLIFTING COMPETITIONS. THE ADRENALINE, SWEATS and TUMMY BUTTERFLIES CAN FEEL A BIT MUCH. BUT THEN MY COACH MENTIONED THAT ANXIETY FEELS SO CLOSE TO EXCITEMENT. IT JUST GETS LABELLED DIFFERENTLY.

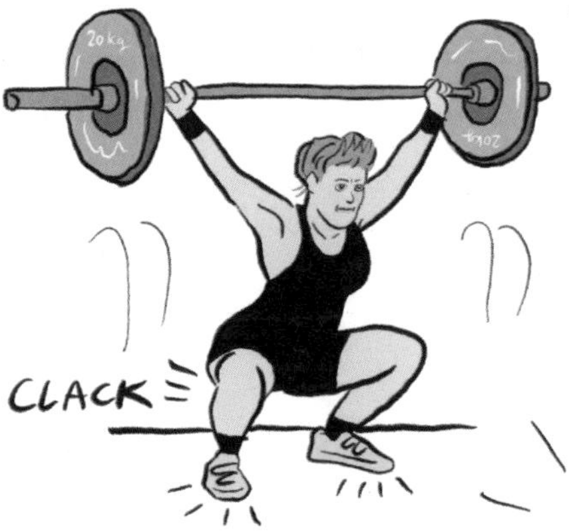
20kg
20kg
CLACK

SO WHY NOT TELL YOURSELF YOU'RE EXCITED?

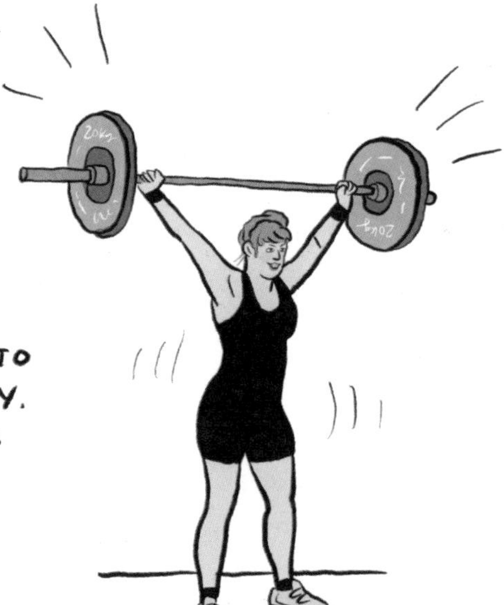
20kg
20kg

I'VE BEEN PLAYING WITH THIS REFRAME, and BY SHIFTING WHAT MY BODY SENSATIONS MEAN, I ACTUALLY RESPOND DIFFERENTLY.

INSTEAD of CRAMPING UP, I WANT TO MOVE THE ENERGY THROUGH MY BODY. TO WIGGLE, BOUNCE and CLAP.

I FEEL MORE FLUID and LESS IN MY HEAD and WORRIED I'M GOING TO FUCK UP. IT FEELS LIKE an INTENSE PARTY.

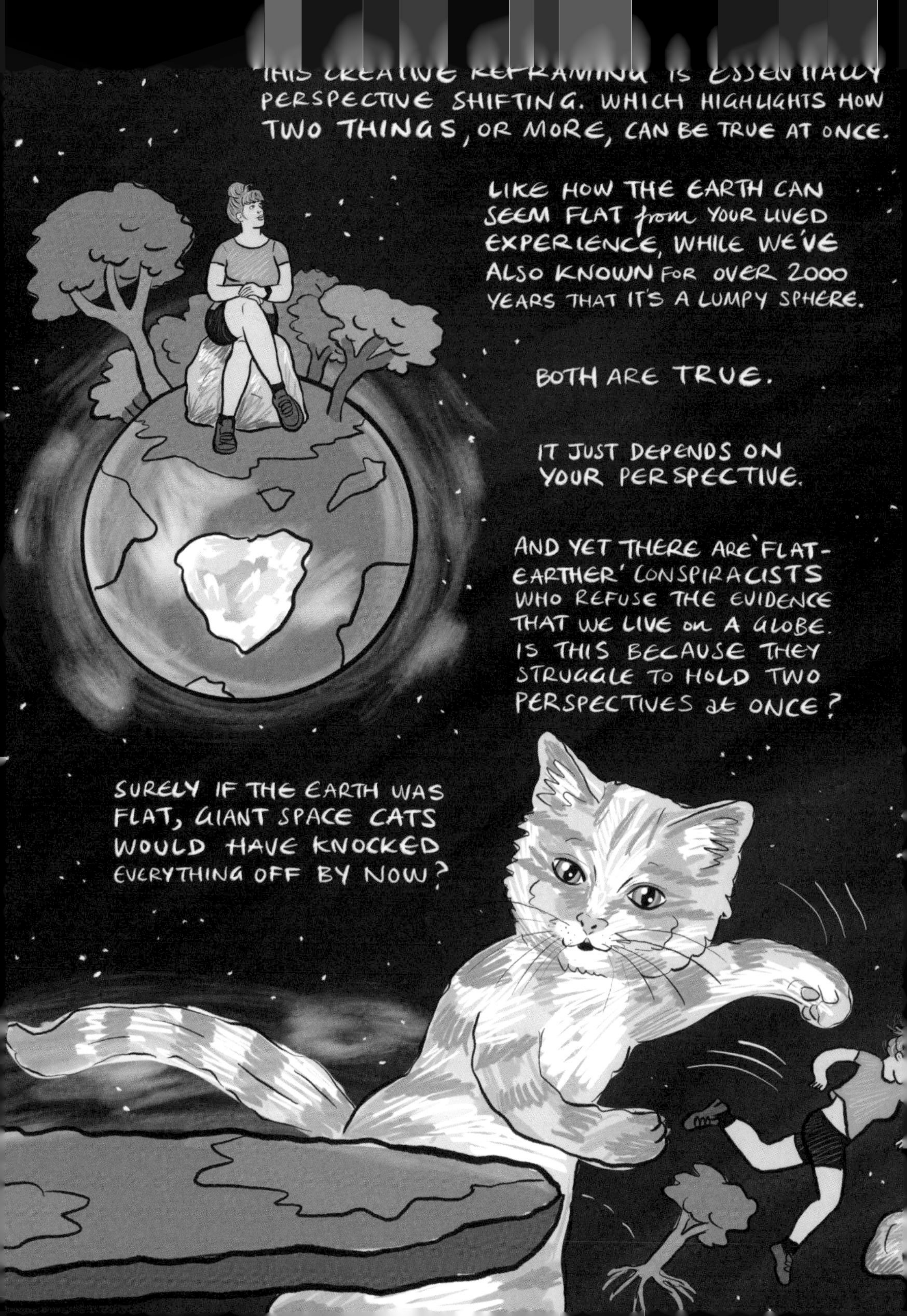
THIS CREATIVE REFRAMING IS ESSENTIALLY PERSPECTIVE SHIFTING. WHICH HIGHLIGHTS HOW TWO THINGS, OR MORE, CAN BE TRUE AT ONCE.
LIKE HOW THE EARTH CAN SEEM FLAT from YOUR LIVED EXPERIENCE, WHILE WE'VE ALSO KNOWN FOR OVER 2000 YEARS THAT IT'S A LUMPY SPHERE.
BOTH ARE TRUE.
IT JUST DEPENDS ON YOUR PERSPECTIVE.
AND YET THERE ARE 'FLAT-EARTHER' CONSPIRACISTS WHO REFUSE THE EVIDENCE THAT WE LIVE on A GLOBE. IS THIS BECAUSE THEY STRUGGLE TO HOLD TWO PERSPECTIVES at ONCE?
SURELY IF THE EARTH WAS FLAT, GIANT SPACE CATS WOULD HAVE KNOCKED EVERYTHING OFF BY NOW?

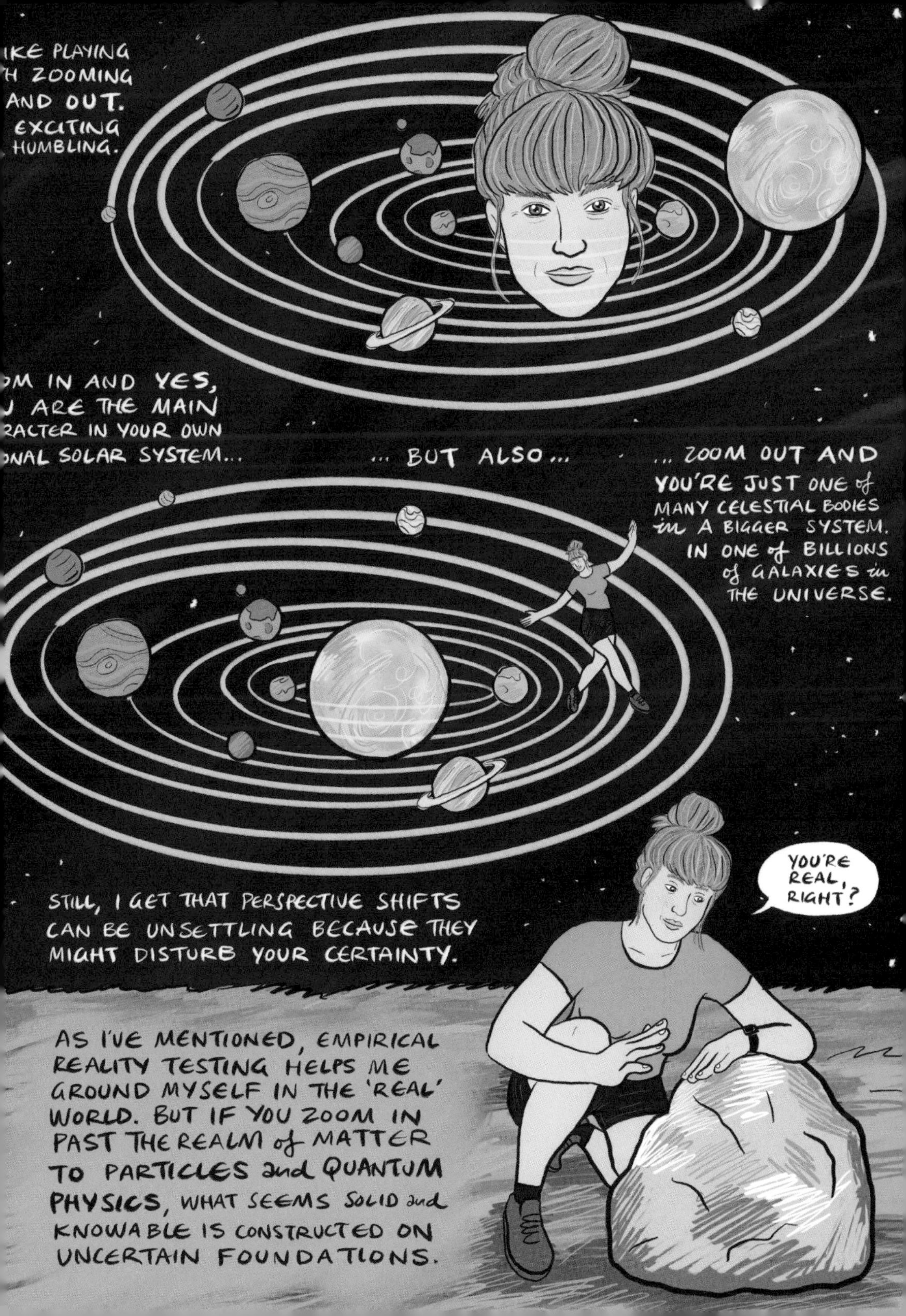

IKE PLAYING
H ZOOMING
AND OUT.
EXCITING
HUMBLING.
OM IN AND YES,
U ARE THE MAIN
RACTER IN YOUR OWN
ONAL SOLAR SYSTEM...
... BUT ALSO...
... ZOOM OUT AND YOU'RE JUST ONE of MANY CELESTIAL BODIES in A BIGGER SYSTEM. IN ONE of BILLIONS of GALAXIES in THE UNIVERSE.
STILL, I GET THAT PERSPECTIVE SHIFTS CAN BE UNSETTLING BECAUSE THEY MIGHT DISTURB YOUR CERTAINTY.
YOU'RE REAL, RIGHT?
AS I'VE MENTIONED, EMPIRICAL REALITY TESTING HELPS ME GROUND MYSELF IN THE 'REAL' WORLD. BUT IF YOU ZOOM IN PAST THE REALM of MATTER TO PARTICLES and QUANTUM PHYSICS, WHAT SEEMS SOLID and KNOWABLE IS CONSTRUCTED ON UNCERTAIN FOUNDATIONS.

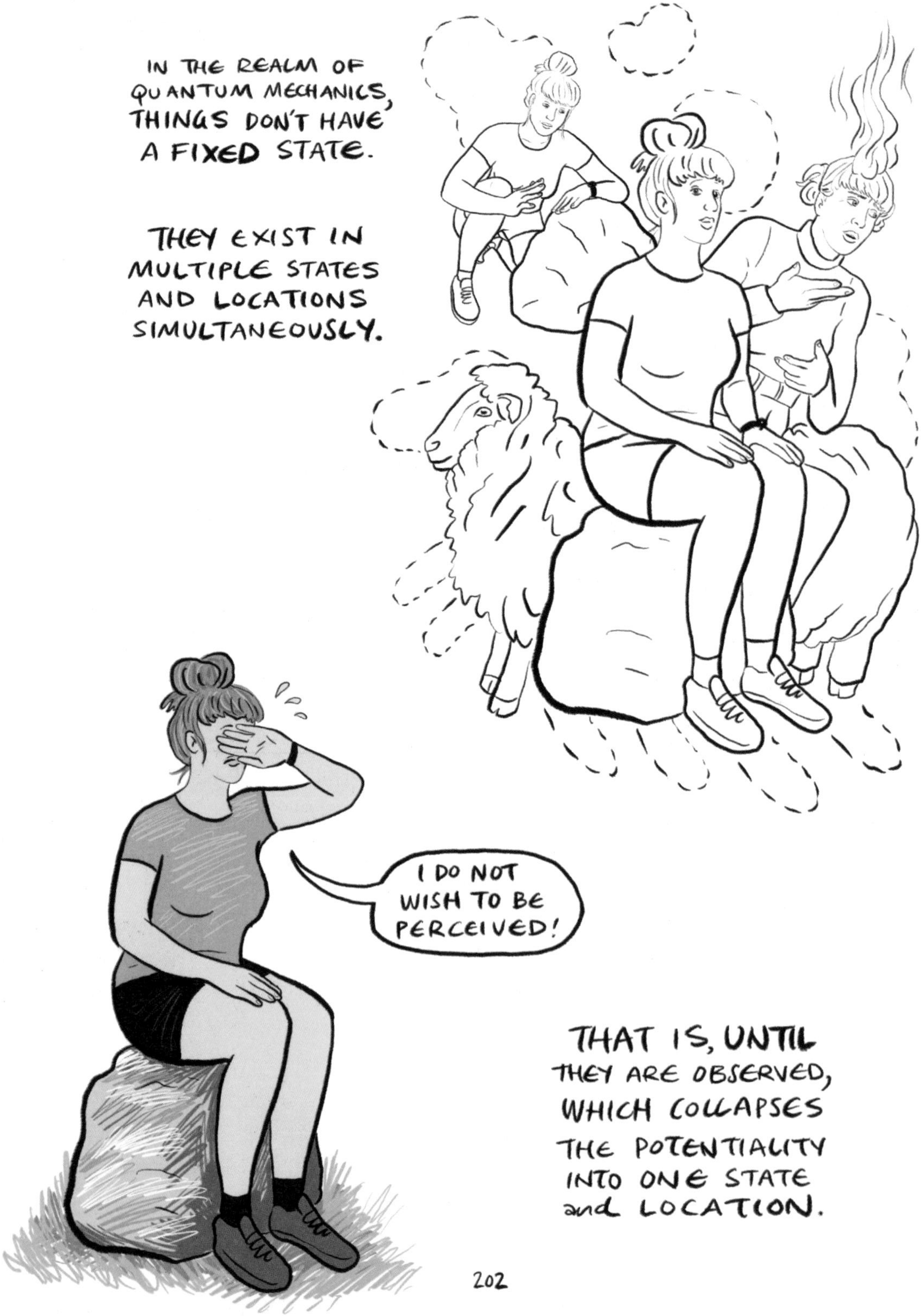
IN THE REALM OF QUANTUM MECHANICS, THINGS DON'T HAVE A FIXED STATE.
THEY EXIST IN MULTIPLE STATES AND LOCATIONS SIMULTANEOUSLY.
I DO NOT WISH TO BE PERCEIVED!
THAT IS, UNTIL THEY ARE OBSERVED, WHICH COLLAPSES THE POTENTIALITY INTO ONE STATE and LOCATION.

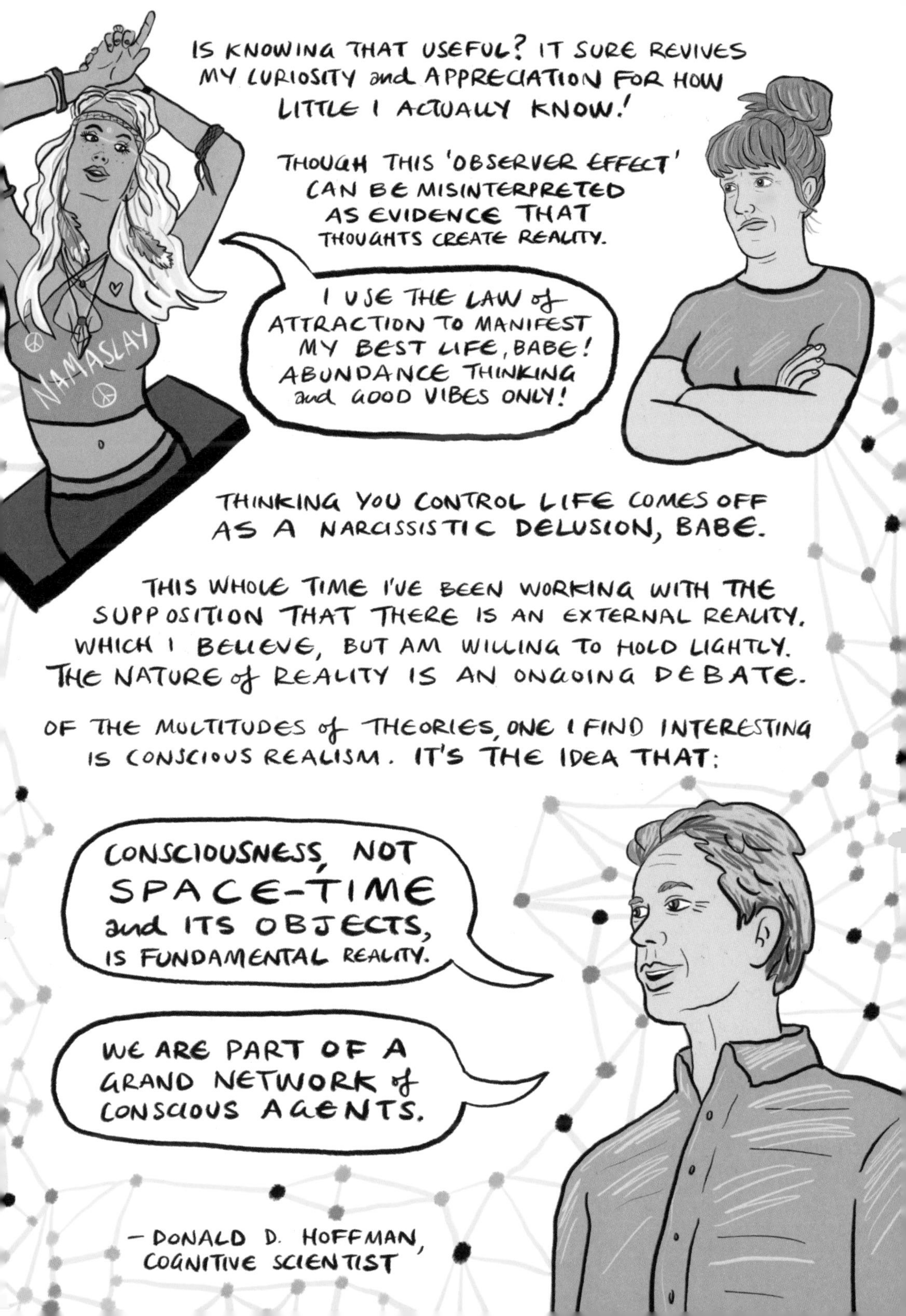
IS KNOWING THAT USEFUL? IT SURE REVIVES MY CURIOSITY and APPRECIATION FOR HOW LITTLE I ACTUALLY KNOW!
THOUGH THIS 'OBSERVER EFFECT' CAN BE MISINTERPRETED AS EVIDENCE THAT THOUGHTS CREATE REALITY.
I USE THE LAW of ATTRACTION TO MANIFEST MY BEST LIFE, BABE! ABUNDANCE THINKING and GOOD VIBES ONLY!
NAMASLAY
THINKING YOU CONTROL LIFE COMES OFF AS A NARCISSISTIC DELUSION, BABE.
THIS WHOLE TIME I'VE BEEN WORKING WITH THE SUPPOSITION THAT THERE IS AN EXTERNAL REALITY, WHICH I BELIEVE, BUT AM WILLING TO HOLD LIGHTLY. THE NATURE of REALITY IS AN ONGOING DEBATE.
OF THE MULTITUDES of THEORIES, ONE I FIND INTERESTING IS CONSCIOUS REALISM. IT'S THE IDEA THAT:
CONSCIOUSNESS, NOT SPACE-TIME and ITS OBJECTS, IS FUNDAMENTAL REALITY.
WE ARE PART OF A GRAND NETWORK of CONSCIOUS AGENTS.
—DONALD D. HOFFMAN, COGNITIVE SCIENTIST

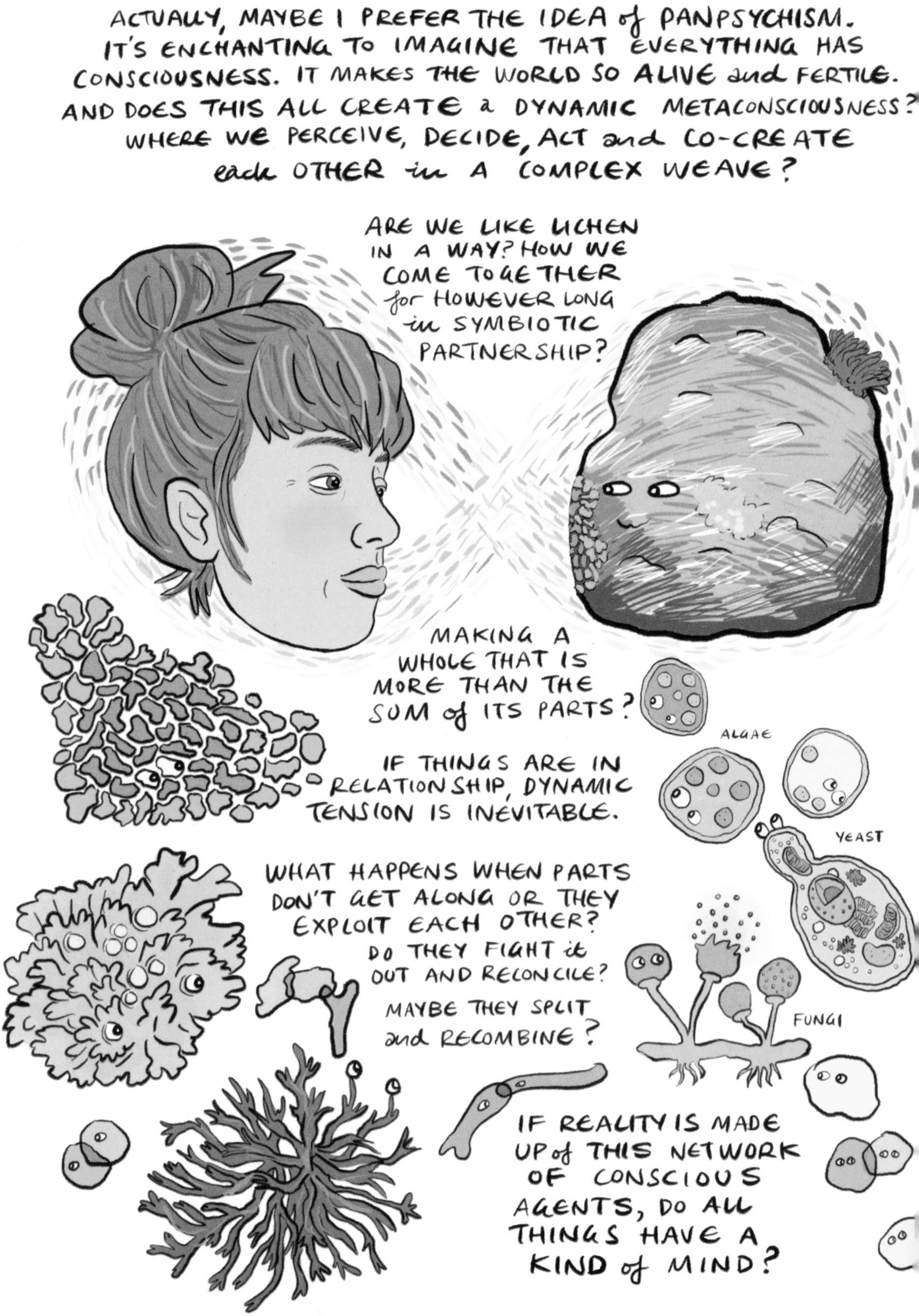
ACTUALLY, MAYBE I PREFER THE IDEA of PANPSYCHISM. IT'S ENCHANTING TO IMAGINE THAT EVERYTHING HAS CONSCIOUSNESS. IT MAKES THE WORLD SO ALIVE and FERTILE. AND DOES THIS ALL CREATE a DYNAMIC METACONSCIOUSNESS? WHERE WE PERCEIVE, DECIDE, ACT and CO-CREATE each OTHER in A COMPLEX WEAVE?
ARE WE LIKE LICHEN IN A WAY? HOW WE COME TOGETHER for HOWEVER LONG in SYMBIOTIC PARTNERSHIP?
MAKING A WHOLE THAT IS MORE THAN THE SUM of ITS PARTS?
IF THINGS ARE IN RELATIONSHIP, DYNAMIC TENSION IS INEVITABLE.
ALGAE
YEAST
WHAT HAPPENS WHEN PARTS DON'T GET ALONG OR THEY EXPLOIT EACH OTHER?
DO THEY FIGHT it OUT AND RECONCILE?
MAYBE THEY SPLIT and RECOMBINE?
FUNGI
IF REALITY IS MADE UP of THIS NETWORK OF CONSCIOUS AGENTS, DO ALL THINGS HAVE A KIND of MIND?

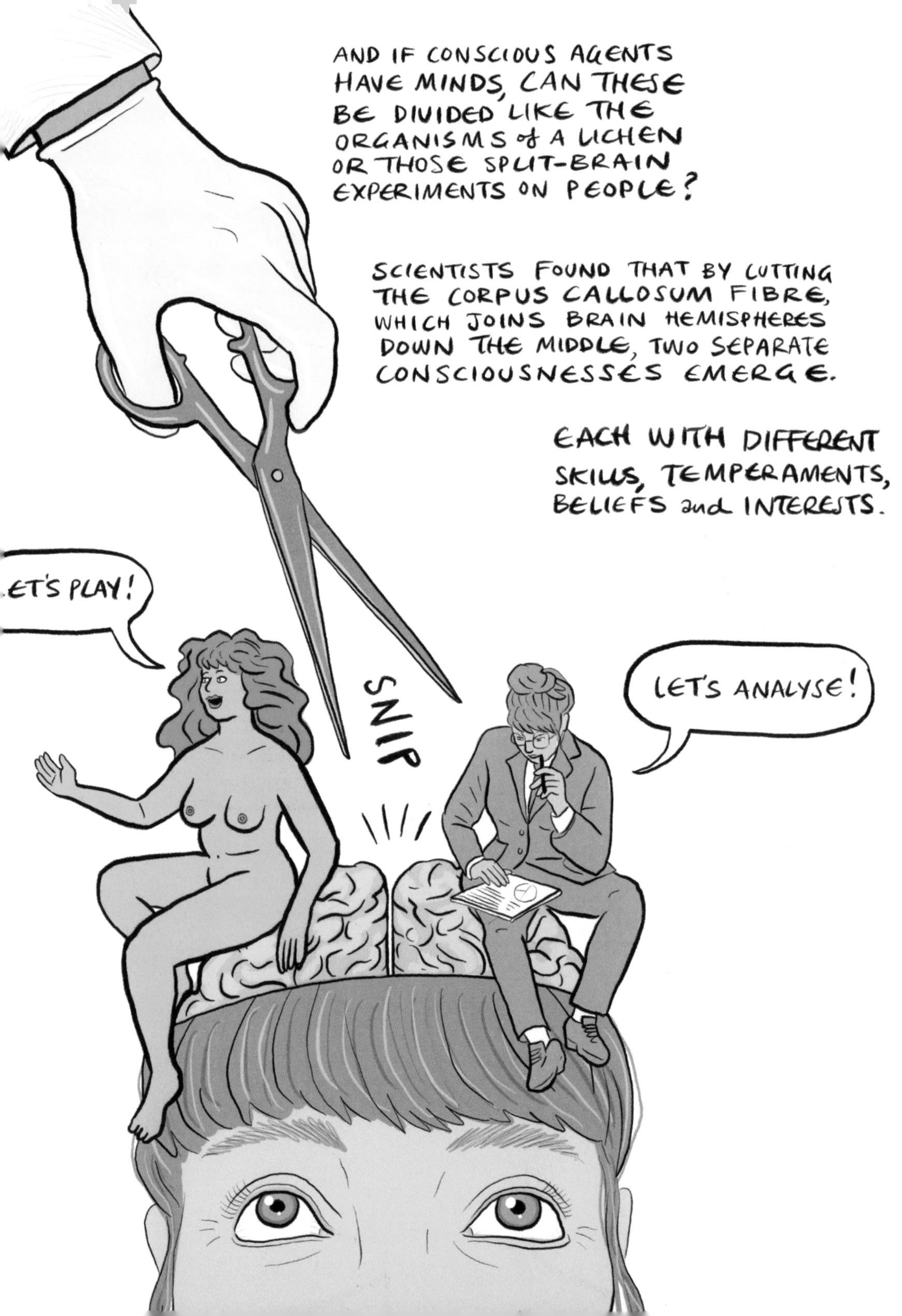
AND IF CONSCIOUS AGENTS HAVE MINDS, CAN THESE BE DIVIDED LIKE THE ORGANISMS of A LICHEN OR THOSE SPLIT-BRAIN EXPERIMENTS ON PEOPLE?
SCIENTISTS FOUND THAT BY CUTTING THE CORPUS CALLOSUM FIBRE, WHICH JOINS BRAIN HEMISPHERES DOWN THE MIDDLE, TWO SEPARATE CONSCIOUSNESSES EMERGE.
EACH WITH DIFFERENT SKILLS, TEMPERAMENTS, BELIEFS and INTERESTS.
ET'S PLAY!
SNIP
LET'S ANALYSE!

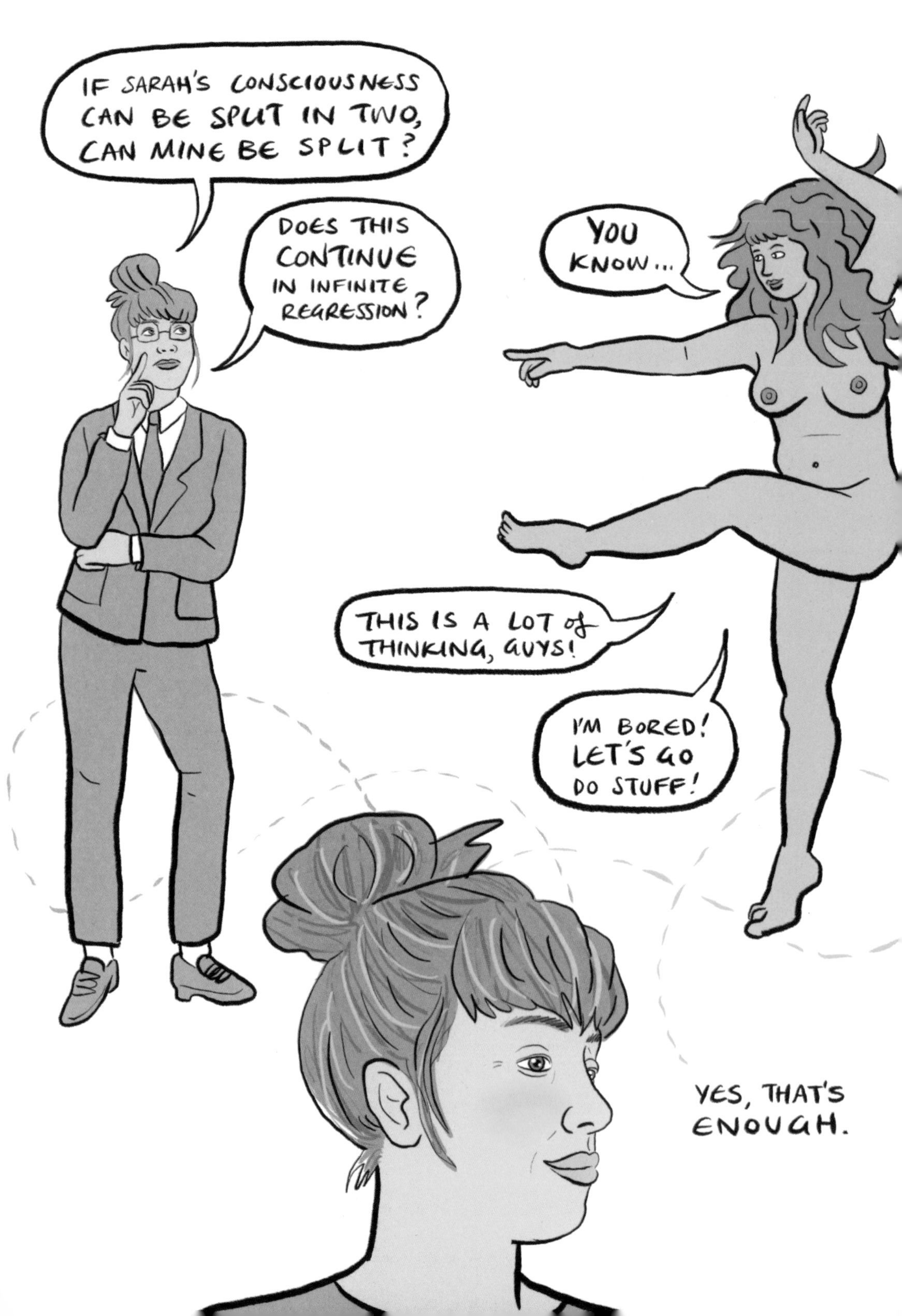
IF SARAH'S CONSCIOUSNESS CAN BE SPLIT IN TWO, CAN MINE BE SPLIT?
DOES THIS CONTINUE IN INFINITE REGRESSION?
YOU KNOW...
THIS IS A LOT OF THINKING, GUYS!
I'M BORED! LET'S GO DO STUFF!
YES, THAT'S ENOUGH.

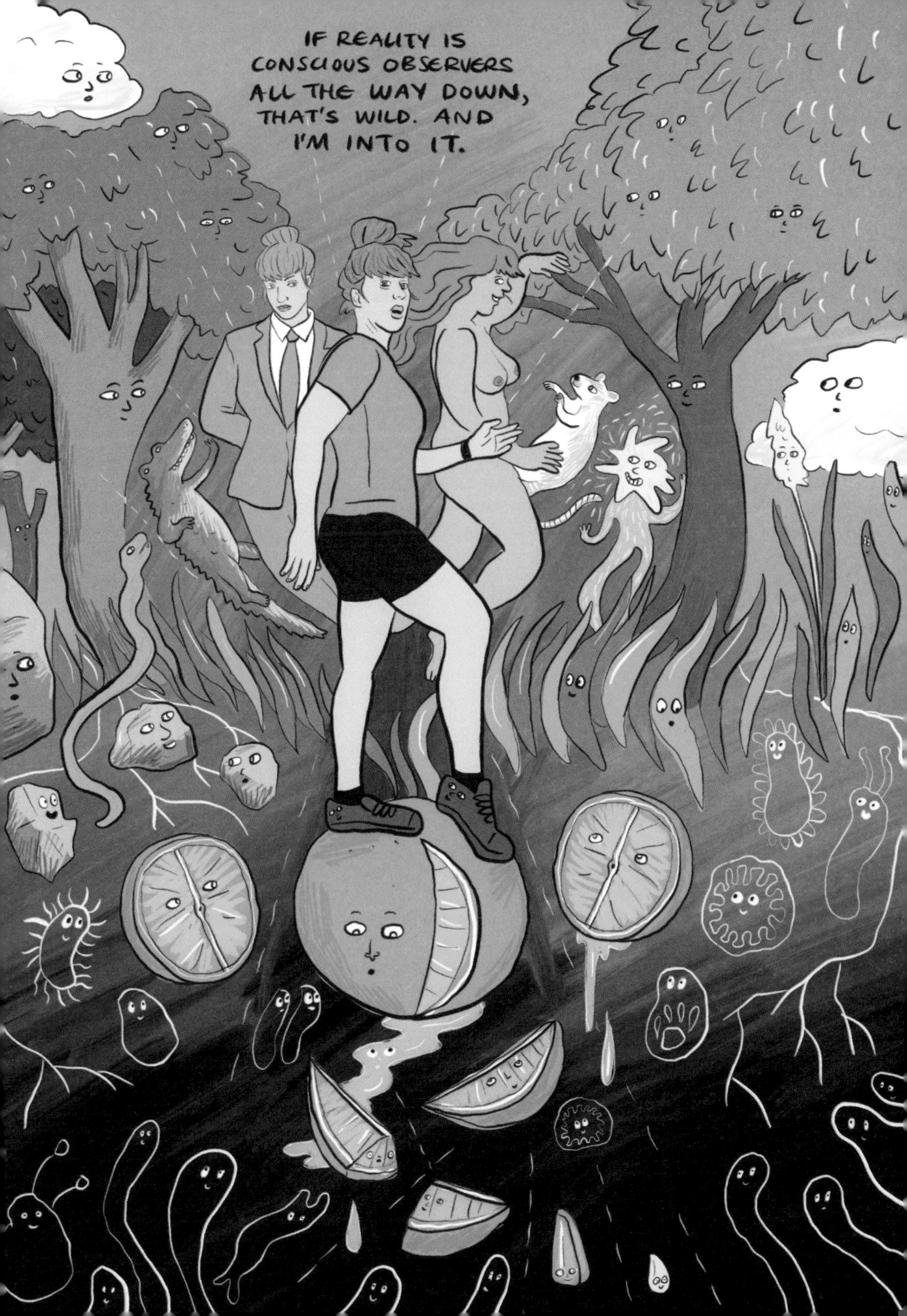
IF REALITY IS CONSCIOUS OBSERVERS ALL THE WAY DOWN, THAT'S WILD. AND I'M INTO IT.

# What Makes a Me?

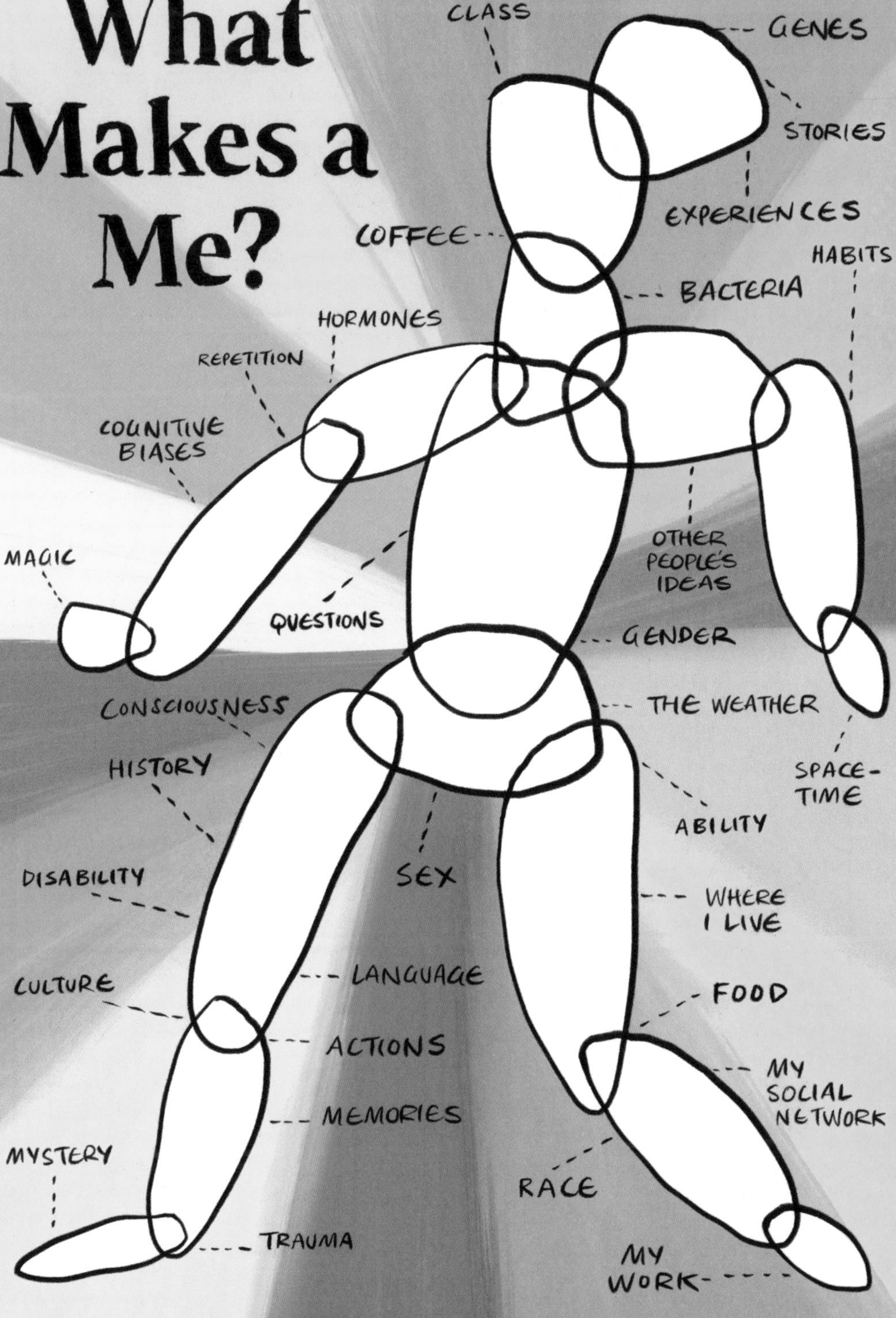
CLASS
GENES
STORIES
EXPERIENCES
COFFEE
HABITS
BACTERIA
HORMONES
REPETITION
COGNITIVE BIASES
MAGIC
OTHER PEOPLE'S IDEAS
QUESTIONS
GENDER
CONSCIOUSNESS
THE WEATHER
HISTORY
SPACE-TIME
ABILITY
SEX
DISABILITY
WHERE I LIVE
LANGUAGE
CULTURE
FOOD
ACTIONS
MY SOCIAL NETWORK
MEMORIES
MYSTERY
RACE
TRAUMA
MY WORK

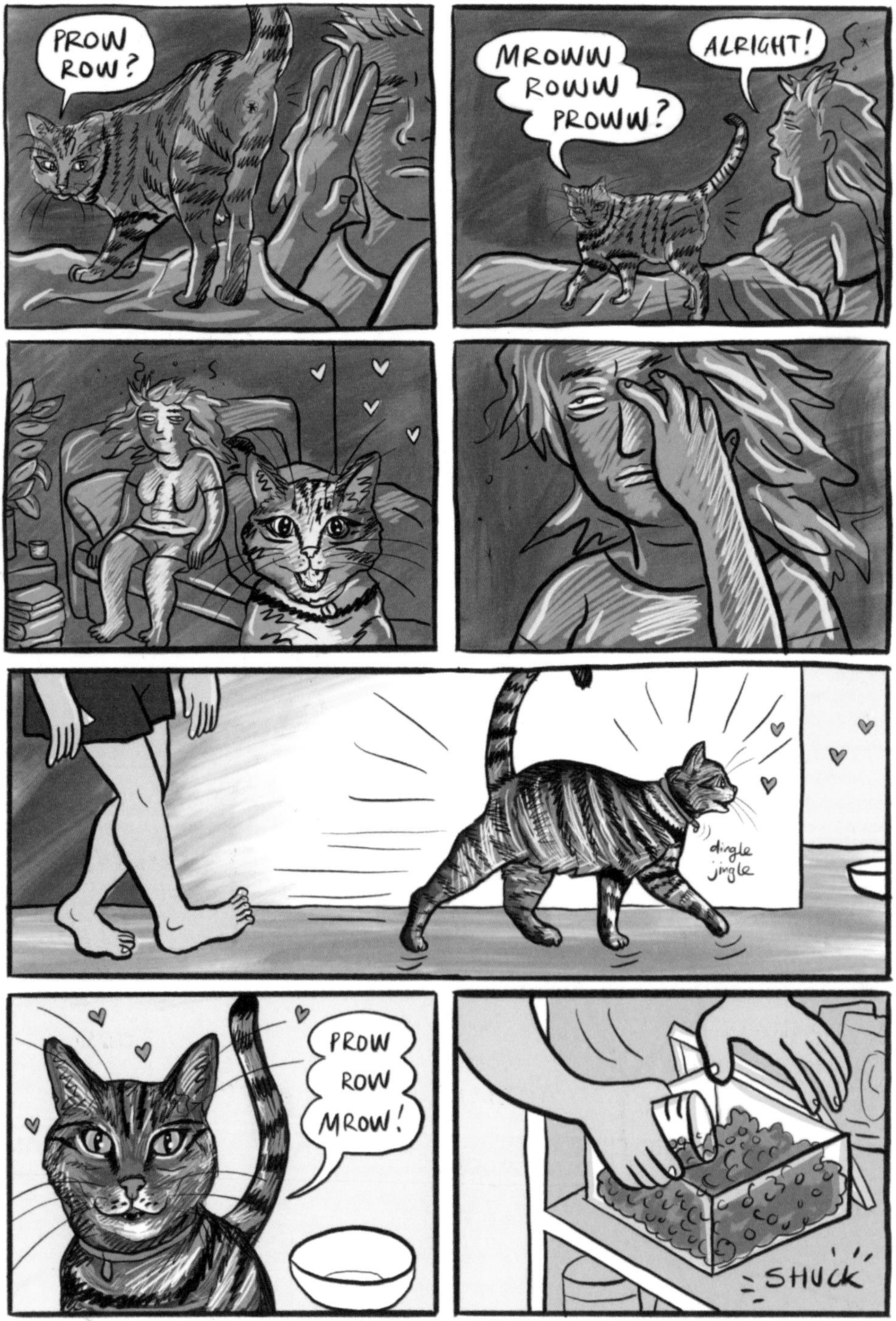
PROW ROW?
MROWW ROWW PROWW?
ALRIGHT!
dingle jingle
PROW ROW MROW!
SHUCK

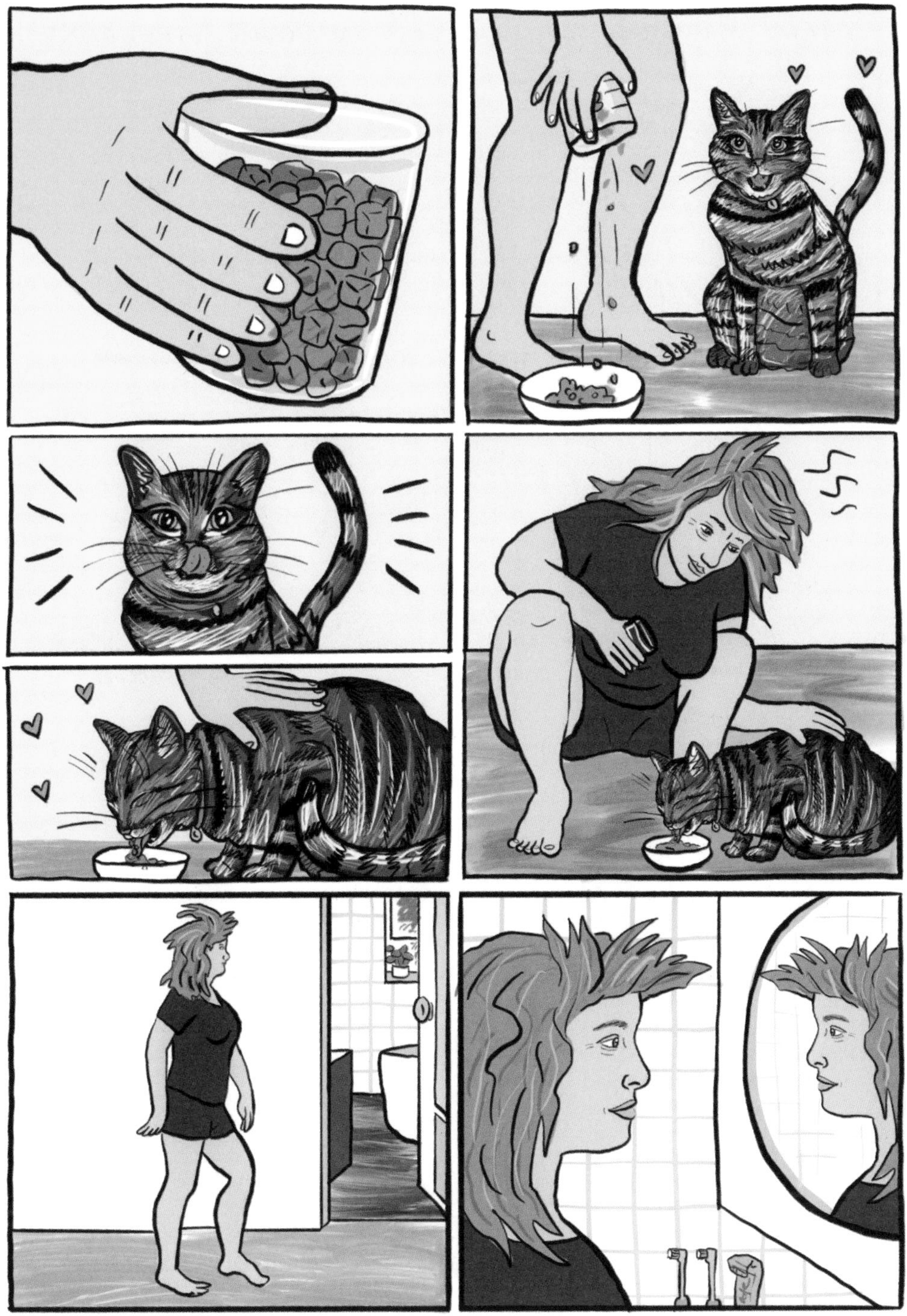

EVERY MORNING MY HAIR DOES SOMETHING DIFFERENT.

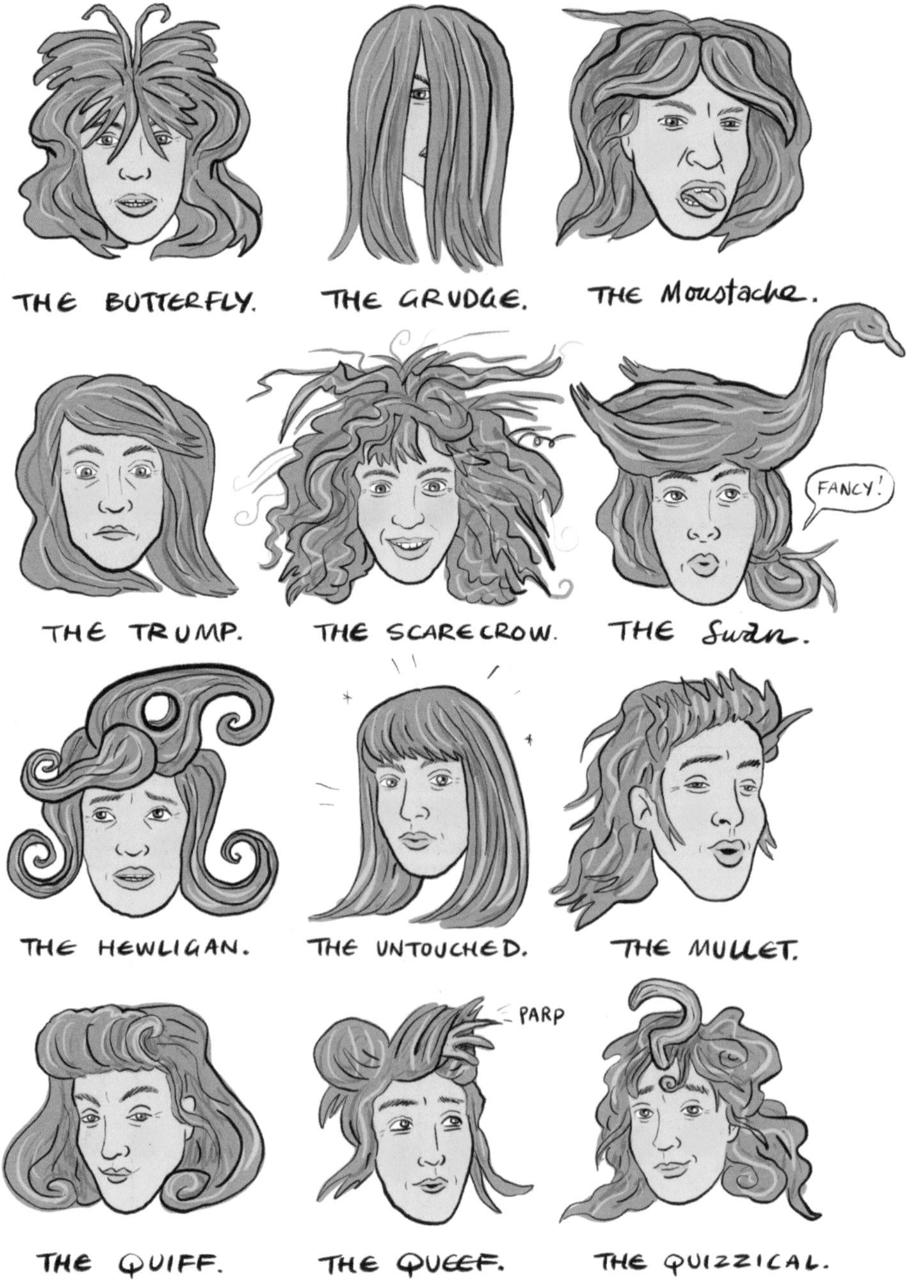
THE BUTTERFLY.
THE GRUDGE.
THE Moustache.
THE TRUMP.
THE SCARECROW.
FANCY!
THE Swan.
THE HEWLIGAN.
THE UNTOUCHED.
THE MULLET.
PARP
THE QUIFF.
THE QUEEF.
THE QUIZZICAL.

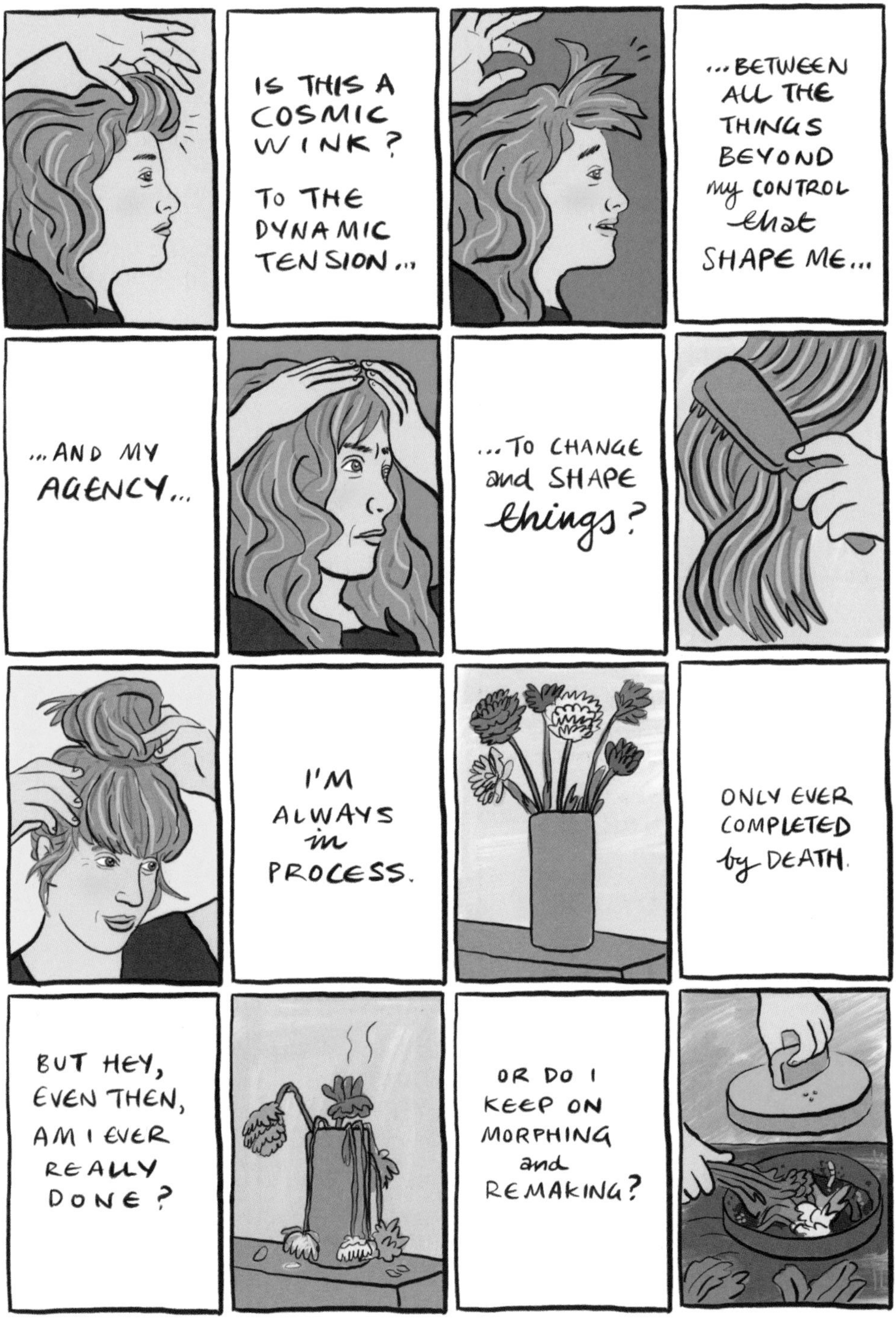
IS THIS A COSMIC WINK?
TO THE DYNAMIC TENSION...
...BETWEEN ALL THE THINGS BEYOND my CONTROL that SHAPE ME...
...AND MY AGENCY...
...TO CHANGE and SHAPE things?
I'M ALWAYS in PROCESS.
ONLY EVER COMPLETED by DEATH.
BUT HEY, EVEN THEN, AM I EVER REALLY DONE?
OR DO I KEEP ON MORPHING and REMAKING?

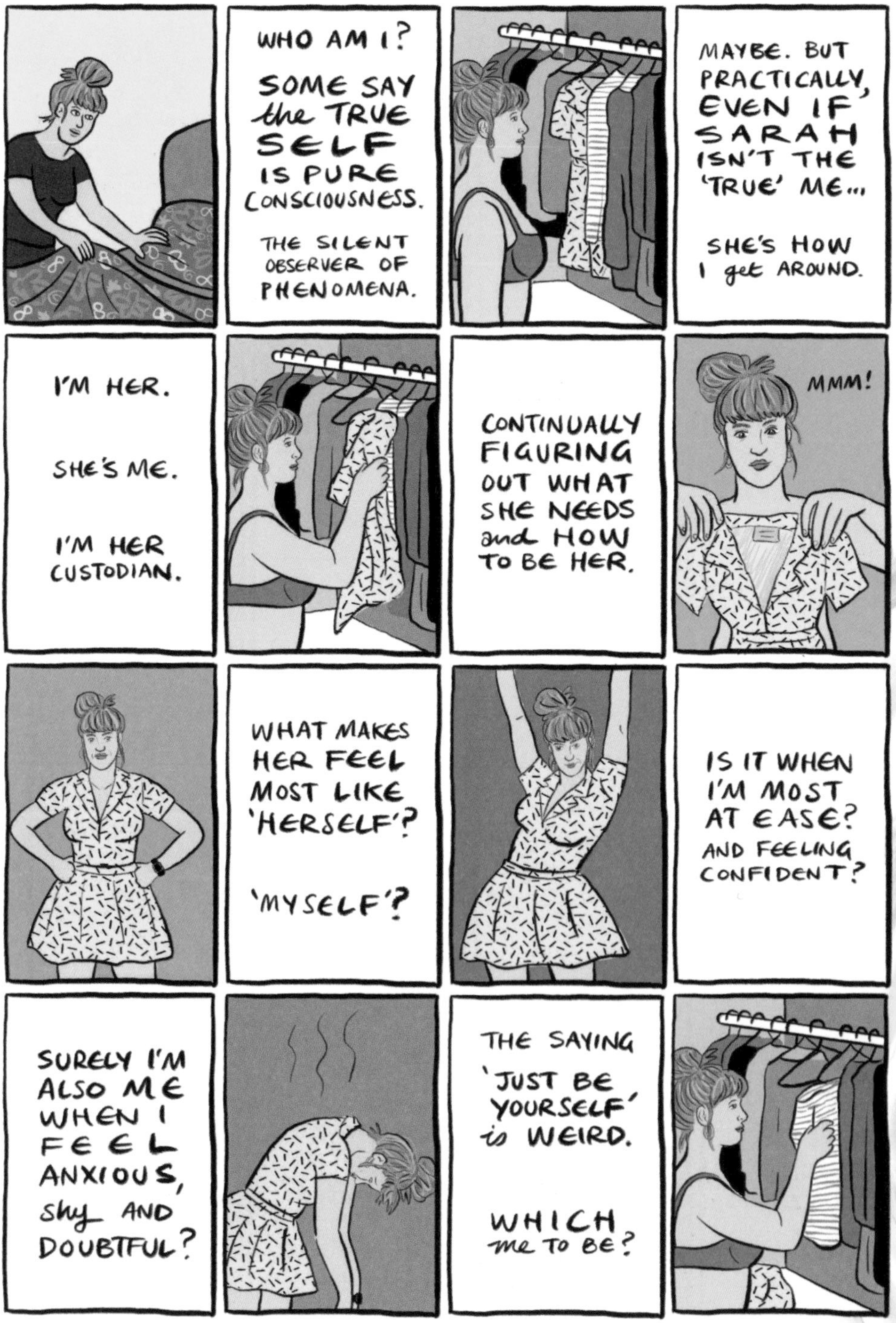
WHO AM I?
SOME SAY the TRUE SELF IS PURE CONSCIOUSNESS.
THE SILENT OBSERVER OF PHENOMENA.
MAYBE. BUT PRACTICALLY, EVEN IF SARAH ISN'T THE 'TRUE' ME...
SHE'S HOW I get AROUND.
I'M HER.
SHE'S ME.
I'M HER CUSTODIAN.
CONTINUALLY FIGURING OUT WHAT SHE NEEDS and HOW TO BE HER.
MMM!
WHAT MAKES HER FEEL MOST LIKE 'HERSELF'?
'MYSELF'?
IS IT WHEN I'M MOST AT EASE?
AND FEELING CONFIDENT?
SURELY I'M ALSO ME WHEN I FEEL ANXIOUS, shy AND DOUBTFUL?
THE SAYING 'JUST BE YOURSELF' is WEIRD.
WHICH me TO BE?

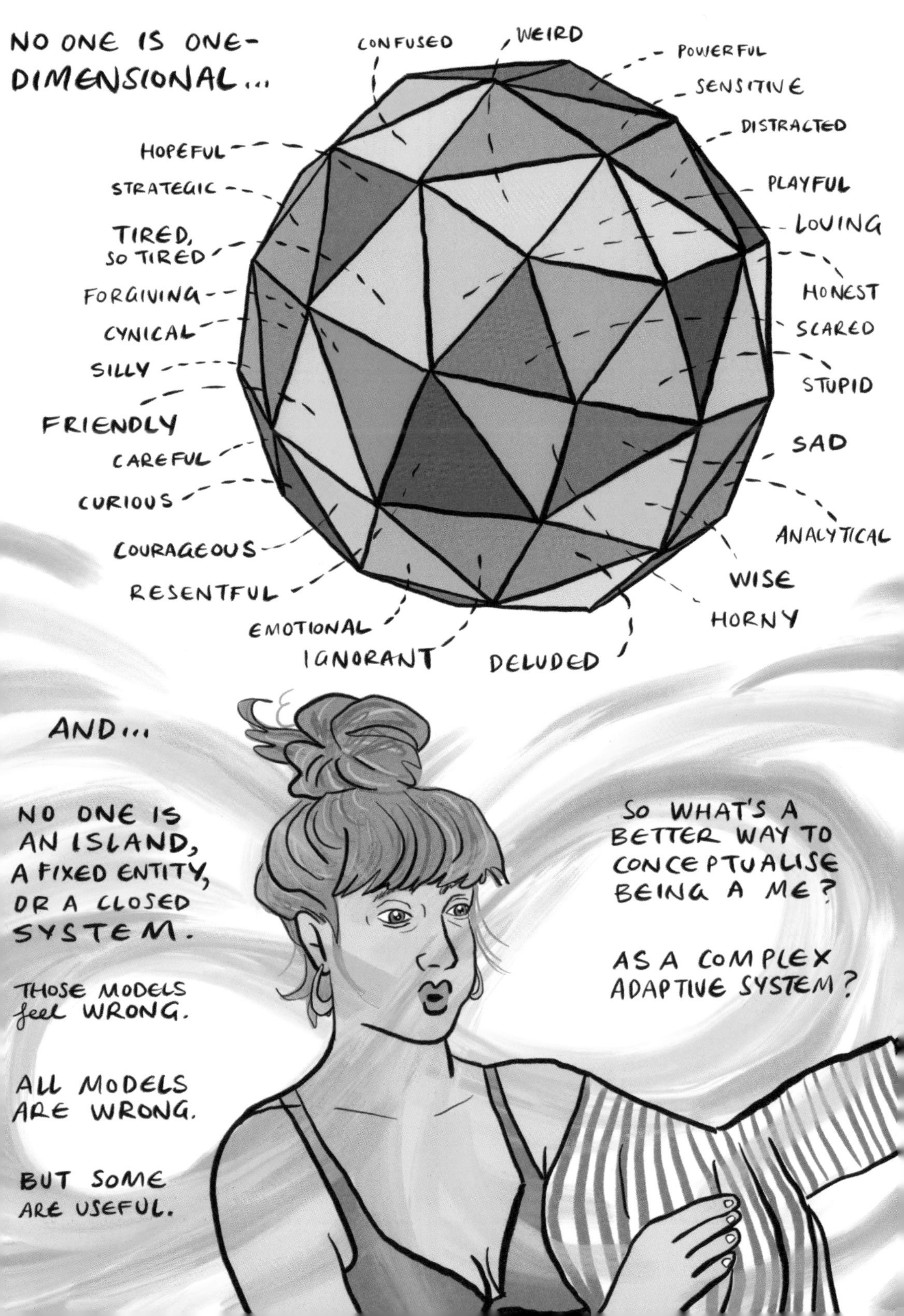

NO ONE IS ONE-DIMENSIONAL...
CONFUSED
WEIRD
POWERFUL
SENSITIVE
DISTRACTED
HOPEFUL
STRATEGIC
PLAYFUL
LOVING
TIRED, SO TIRED
HONEST
FORGIVING
CYNICAL
SCARED
SILLY
STUPID
FRIENDLY
SAD
CAREFUL
CURIOUS
ANALYTICAL
COURAGEOUS
WISE
RESENTFUL
HORNY
EMOTIONAL
IGNORANT
DELUDED
AND...
NO ONE IS AN ISLAND, A FIXED ENTITY, OR A CLOSED SYSTEM.
THOSE MODELS feel WRONG.
ALL MODELS ARE WRONG.
BUT SOME ARE USEFUL.
SO WHAT'S A BETTER WAY TO CONCEPTUALISE BEING A ME?
AS A COMPLEX ADAPTIVE SYSTEM?

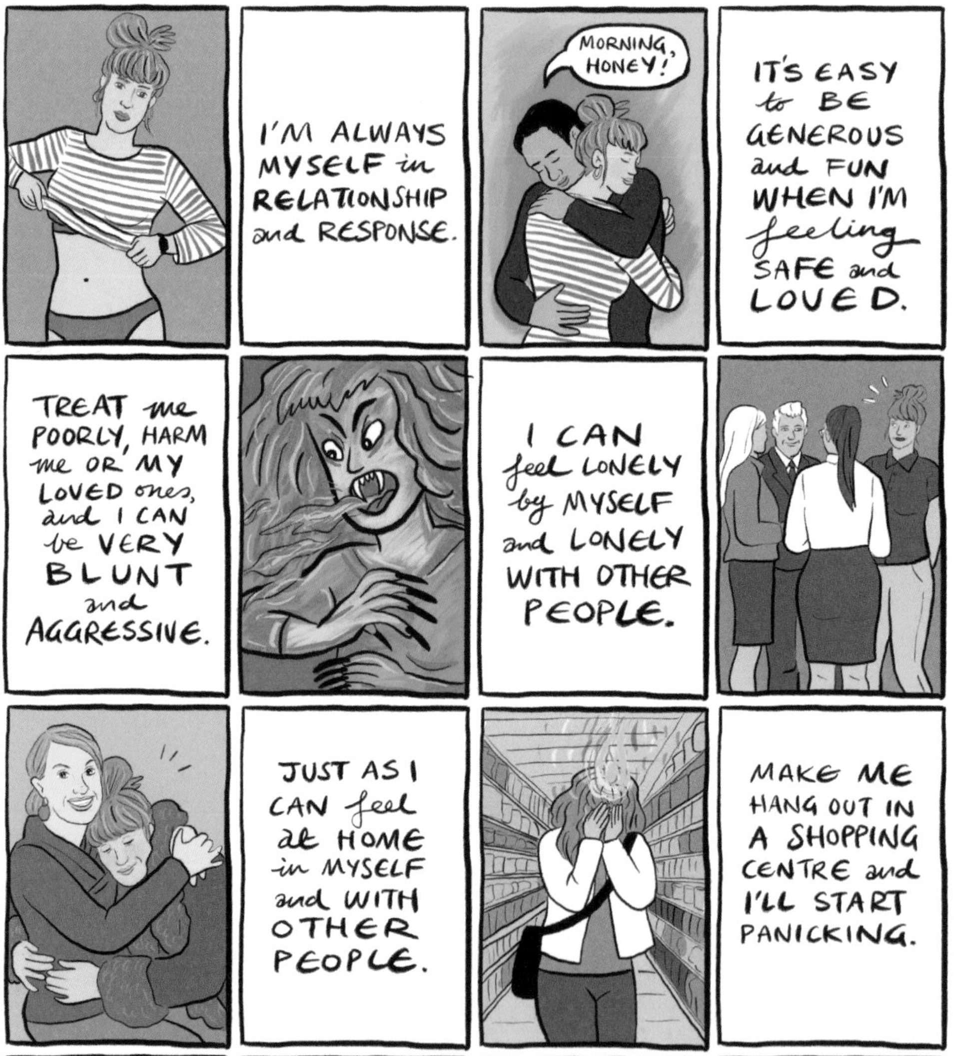
I'M ALWAYS MYSELF in RELATIONSHIP and RESPONSE.
MORNING, HONEY!
IT'S EASY to BE GENEROUS and FUN WHEN I'M feeling SAFE and LOVED.
TREAT me POORLY, HARM me OR MY LOVED ones, and I CAN be VERY BLUNT and AGGRESSIVE.
I CAN feel LONELY by MYSELF and LONELY WITH OTHER PEOPLE.
JUST AS I CAN feel at HOME in MYSELF and WITH OTHER PEOPLE.
MAKE ME HANG OUT IN A SHOPPING CENTRE and I'LL START PANICKING.
PUT me on STAGE SPEAKING and I FEEL NERVOUS BUT FINE.
BEFORE COFFEE I'M ...
OH SHIT! I'VE RUN OUT of COFFEE!

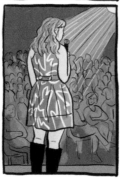

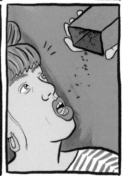

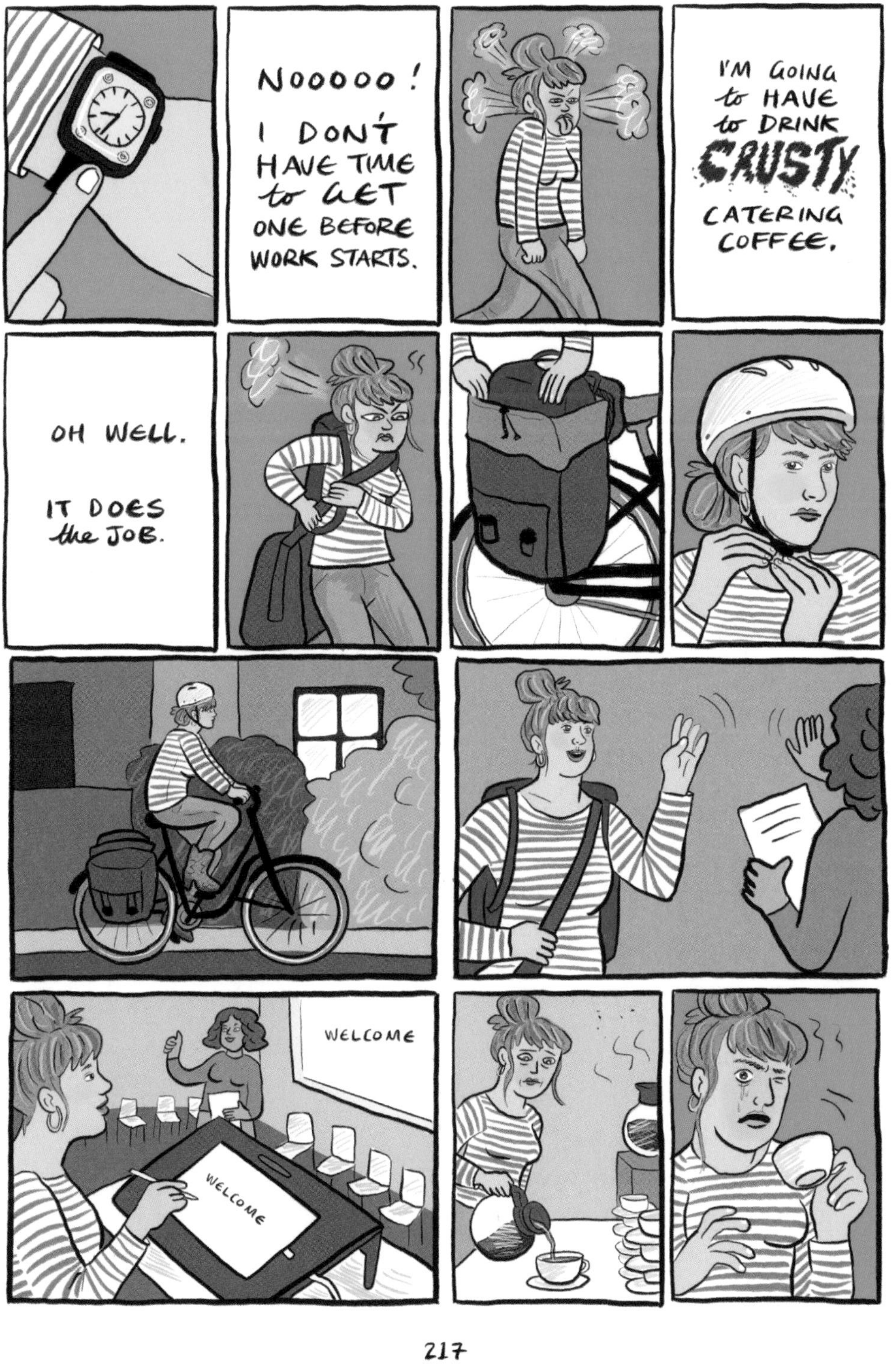
NOOOOO!
I DON'T HAVE TIME to GET ONE BEFORE WORK STARTS.
I'M GOING to HAVE to DRINK CRUSTY CATERING COFFEE.
OH WELL.
IT DOES the JOB.
WELCOME
WELCOME

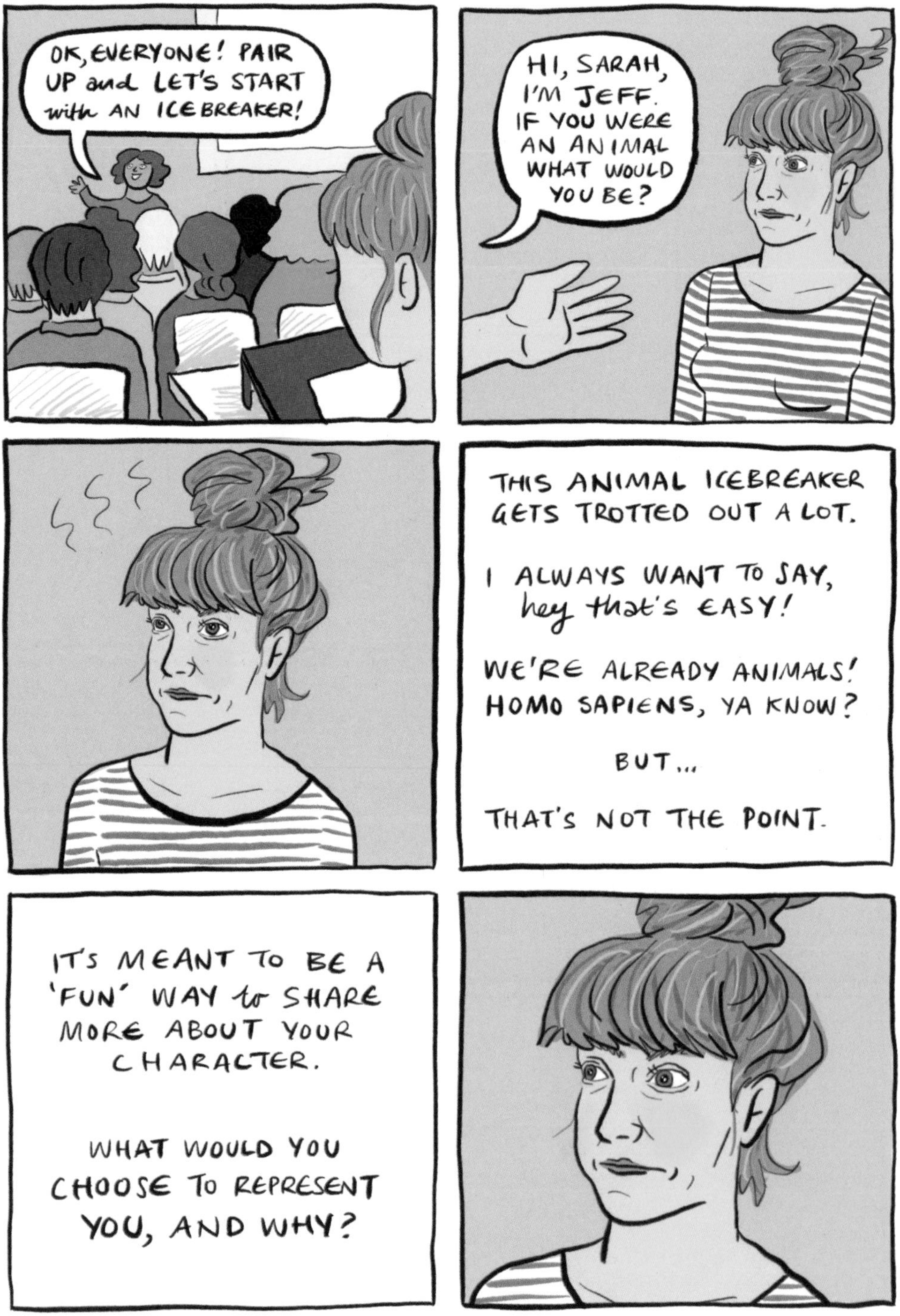
OK, EVERYONE! PAIR UP and LET'S START with AN ICEBREAKER!
HI, SARAH, I'M JEFF. IF YOU WERE AN ANIMAL WHAT WOULD YOU BE?
THIS ANIMAL ICEBREAKER GETS TROTTED OUT A LOT.
I ALWAYS WANT TO SAY, hey that's EASY!
WE'RE ALREADY ANIMALS! HOMO SAPIENS, YA KNOW?
BUT...
THAT'S NOT THE POINT.
IT'S MEANT TO BE A 'FUN' WAY to SHARE MORE ABOUT YOUR CHARACTER.
WHAT WOULD YOU CHOOSE TO REPRESENT YOU, AND WHY?

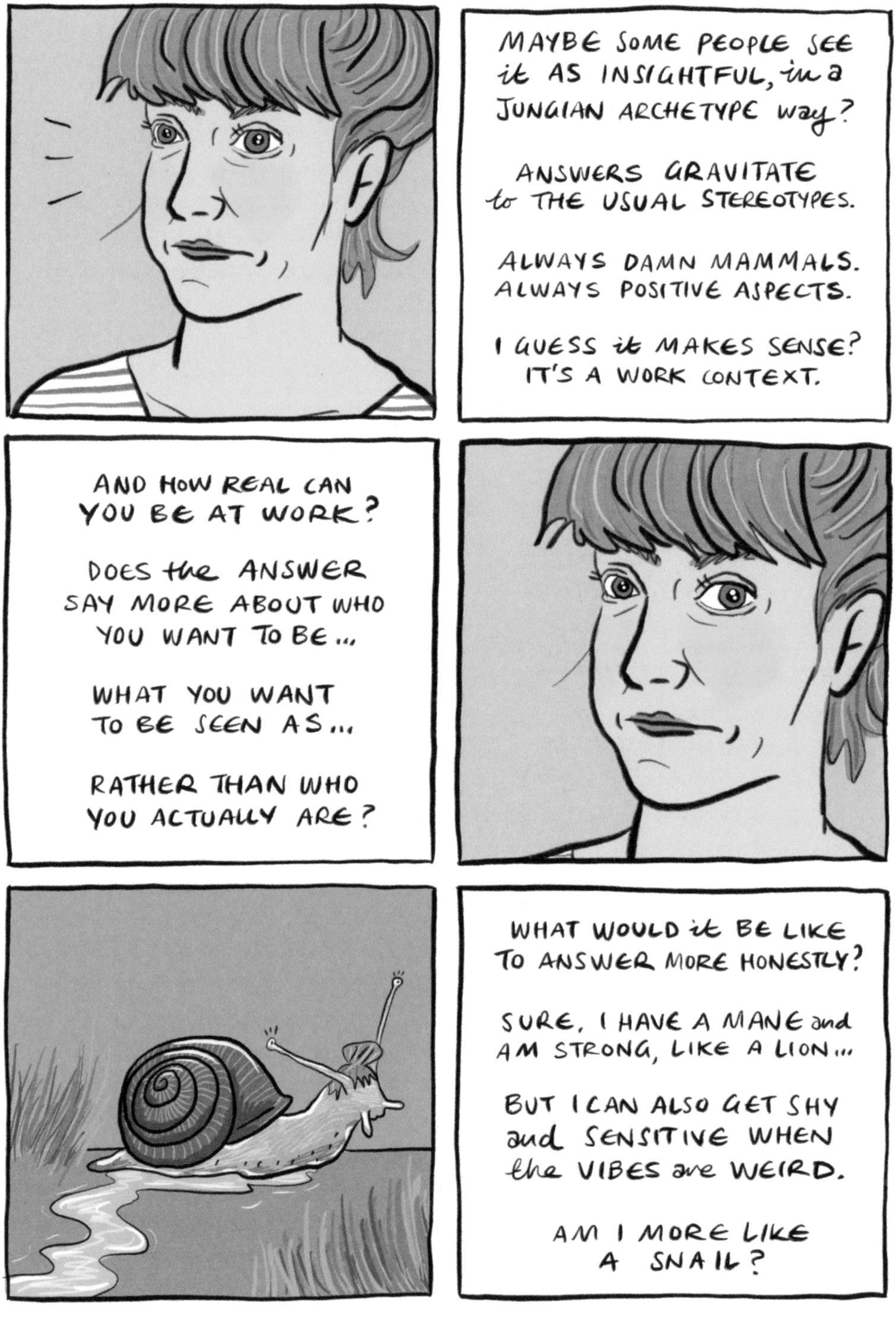
MAYBE SOME PEOPLE SEE it AS INSIGHTFUL, in a JUNGIAN ARCHETYPE way?
ANSWERS GRAVITATE to THE USUAL STEREOTYPES.
ALWAYS DAMN MAMMALS. ALWAYS POSITIVE ASPECTS.
I GUESS it MAKES SENSE? IT'S A WORK CONTEXT.
AND HOW REAL CAN YOU BE AT WORK?
DOES the ANSWER SAY MORE ABOUT WHO YOU WANT TO BE...
WHAT YOU WANT TO BE SEEN AS...
RATHER THAN WHO YOU ACTUALLY ARE?
WHAT WOULD it BE LIKE TO ANSWER MORE HONESTLY?
SURE, I HAVE A MANE and AM STRONG, LIKE A LION...
BUT I CAN ALSO GET SHY and SENSITIVE WHEN the VIBES are WEIRD.
AM I MORE LIKE A SNAIL?

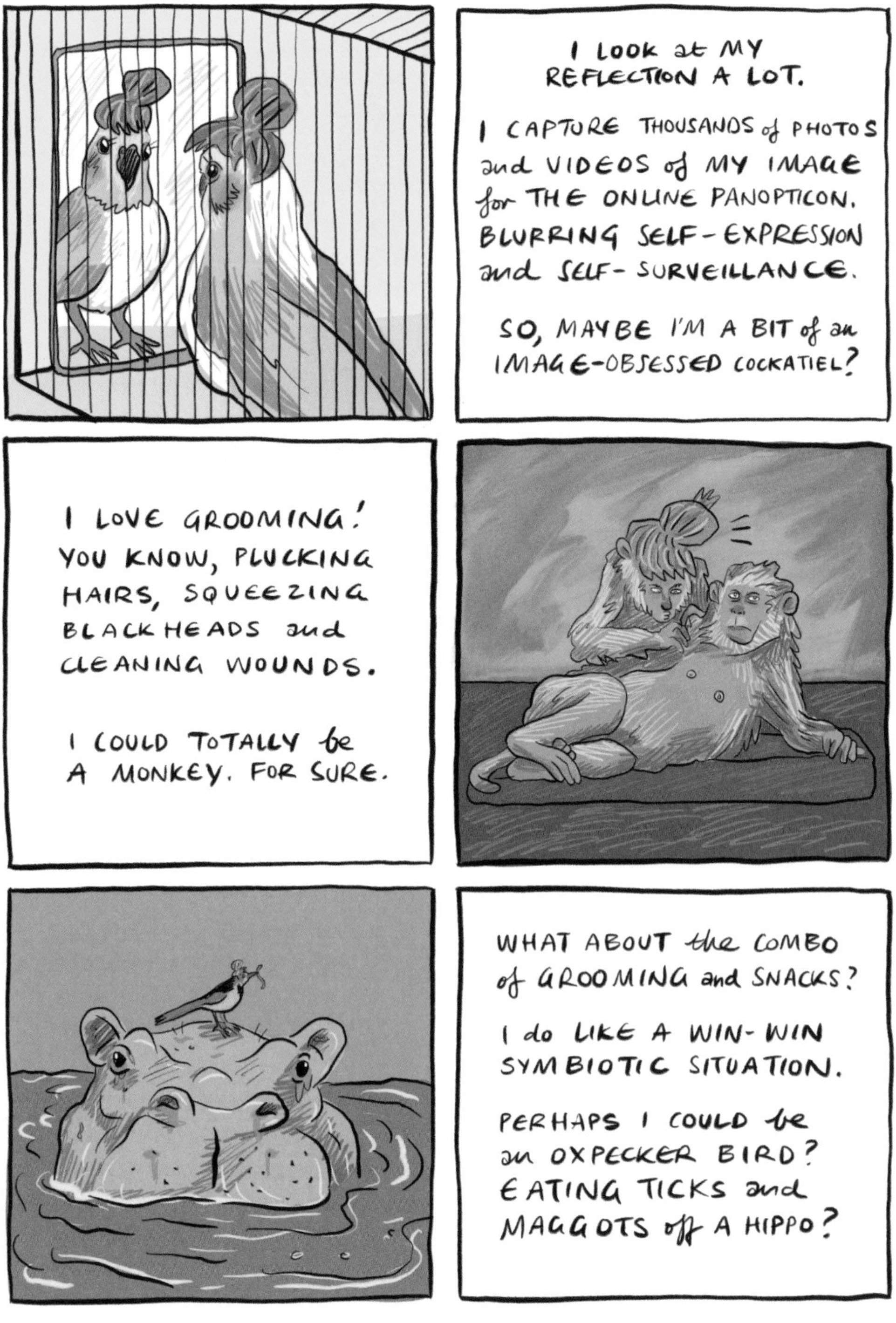
I LOOK at MY REFLECTION A LOT.
I CAPTURE THOUSANDS of PHOTOS and VIDEOS of MY IMAGE for THE ONLINE PANOPTICON. BLURRING SELF-EXPRESSION and SELF-SURVEILLANCE.
SO, MAYBE I'M A BIT of an IMAGE-OBSESSED COCKATIEL?
I LOVE GROOMING! YOU KNOW, PLUCKING HAIRS, SQUEEZING BLACKHEADS and CLEANING WOUNDS.
I COULD TOTALLY be A MONKEY. FOR SURE.
WHAT ABOUT the COMBO of GROOMING and SNACKS?
I do LIKE A WIN-WIN SYMBIOTIC SITUATION.
PERHAPS I COULD be an OXPECKER BIRD? EATING TICKS and MAGGOTS off A HIPPO?

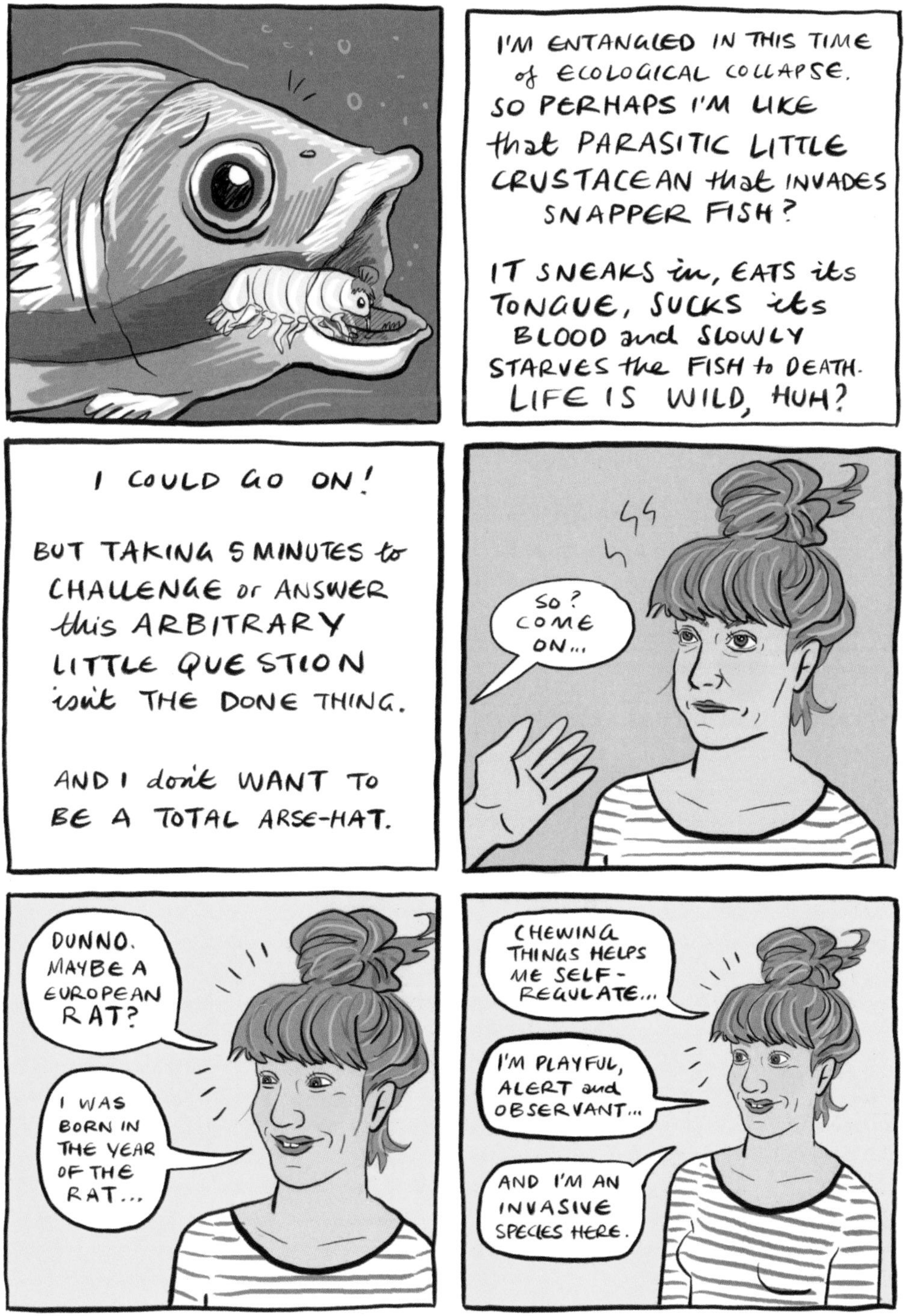
I'M ENTANGLED IN THIS TIME of ECOLOGICAL COLLAPSE. SO PERHAPS I'M LIKE that PARASITIC LITTLE CRUSTACEAN that INVADES SNAPPER FISH?
IT SNEAKS in, EATS its TONGUE, SUCKS its BLOOD and SLOWLY STARVES the FISH to DEATH. LIFE IS WILD, HUH?
I COULD GO ON!
BUT TAKING 5 MINUTES to CHALLENGE or ANSWER this ARBITRARY LITTLE QUESTION isn't THE DONE THING.
AND I don't WANT TO BE A TOTAL ARSE-HAT.
SO? COME ON...
DUNNO. MAYBE A EUROPEAN RAT?
I WAS BORN IN THE YEAR OF THE RAT...
CHEWING THINGS HELPS ME SELF-REGULATE...
I'M PLAYFUL, ALERT and OBSERVANT...
AND I'M AN INVASIVE SPECIES HERE.

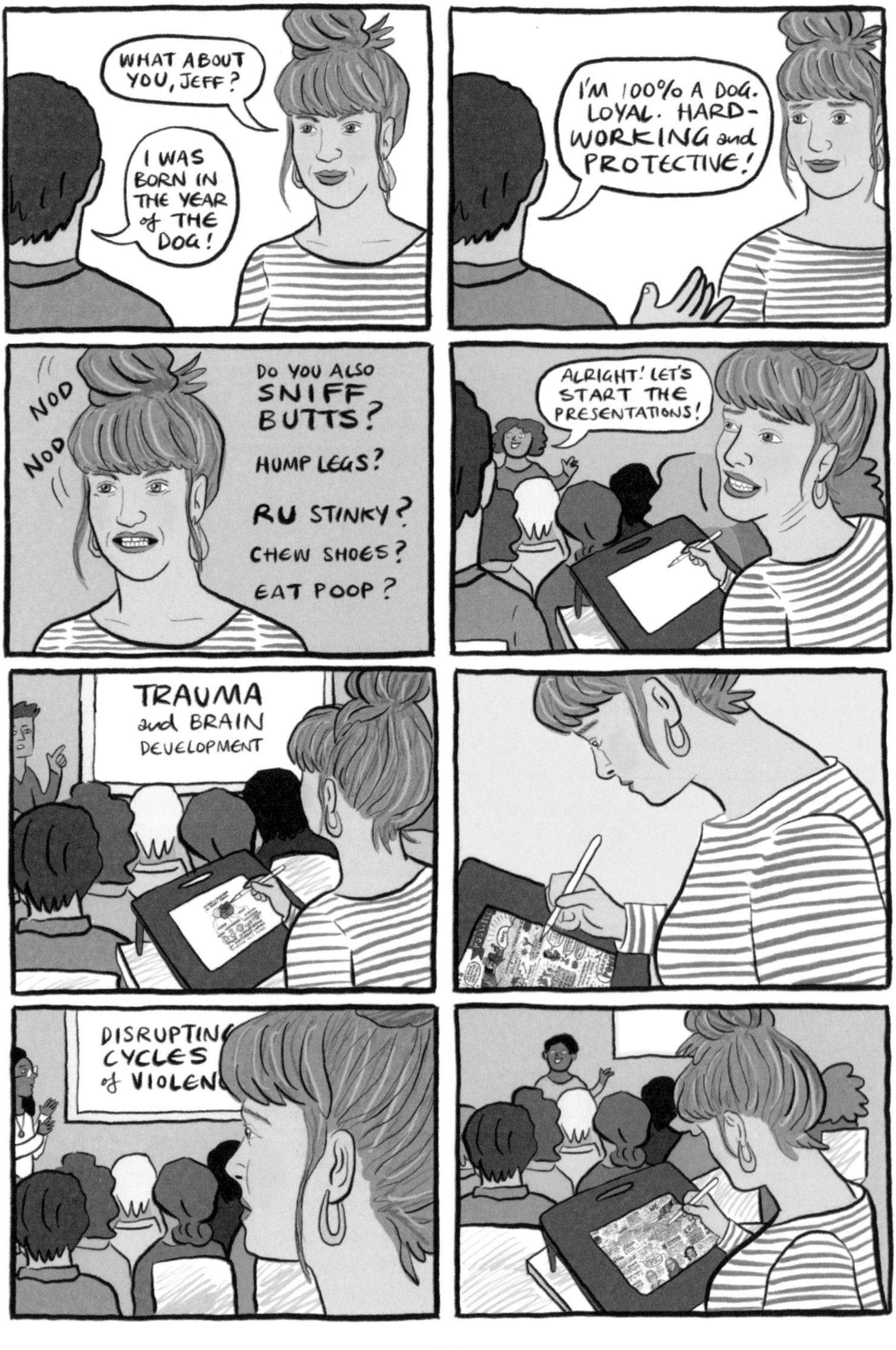
WHAT ABOUT YOU, JEFF?
I WAS BORN IN THE YEAR of THE DOG!
I'M 100% A DOG. LOYAL. HARD-WORKING and PROTECTIVE!
NOD NOD
DO YOU ALSO SNIFF BUTTS?
HUMP LEGS?
RU STINKY?
CHEW SHOES?
EAT POOP?
ALRIGHT! LET'S START THE PRESENTATIONS!
TRAUMA and BRAIN DEVELOPMENT
DISRUPTING CYCLES of VIOLEN

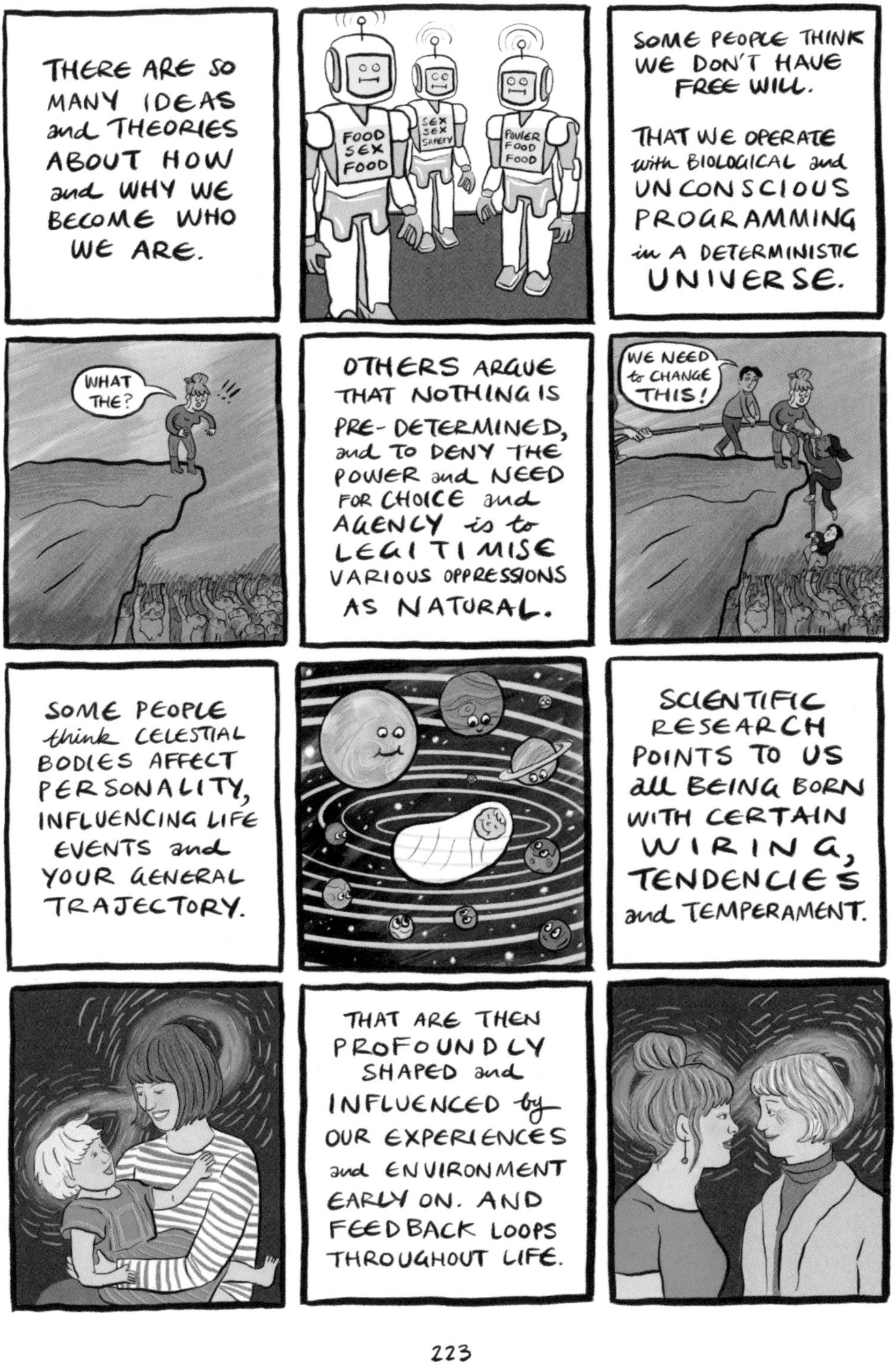
THERE ARE SO MANY IDEAS and THEORIES ABOUT HOW and WHY WE BECOME WHO WE ARE.
FOOD SEX FOOD
SEX SEX SAFETY
POWER FOOD FOOD
SOME PEOPLE THINK WE DON'T HAVE FREE WILL.
THAT WE OPERATE with BIOLOGICAL and UNCONSCIOUS PROGRAMMING in A DETERMINISTIC UNIVERSE.
WHAT THE?
!!!
OTHERS ARGUE THAT NOTHING IS PRE-DETERMINED, and TO DENY THE POWER and NEED FOR CHOICE and AGENCY is to LEGITIMISE VARIOUS OPPRESSIONS AS NATURAL.
WE NEED to CHANGE THIS!
SOME PEOPLE think CELESTIAL BODIES AFFECT PERSONALITY, INFLUENCING LIFE EVENTS and YOUR GENERAL TRAJECTORY.
SCIENTIFIC RESEARCH POINTS TO US all BEING BORN WITH CERTAIN WIRING, TENDENCIES and TEMPERAMENT.
THAT ARE THEN PROFOUNDLY SHAPED and INFLUENCED by OUR EXPERIENCES and ENVIRONMENT EARLY ON. AND FEEDBACK LOOPS THROUGHOUT LIFE.

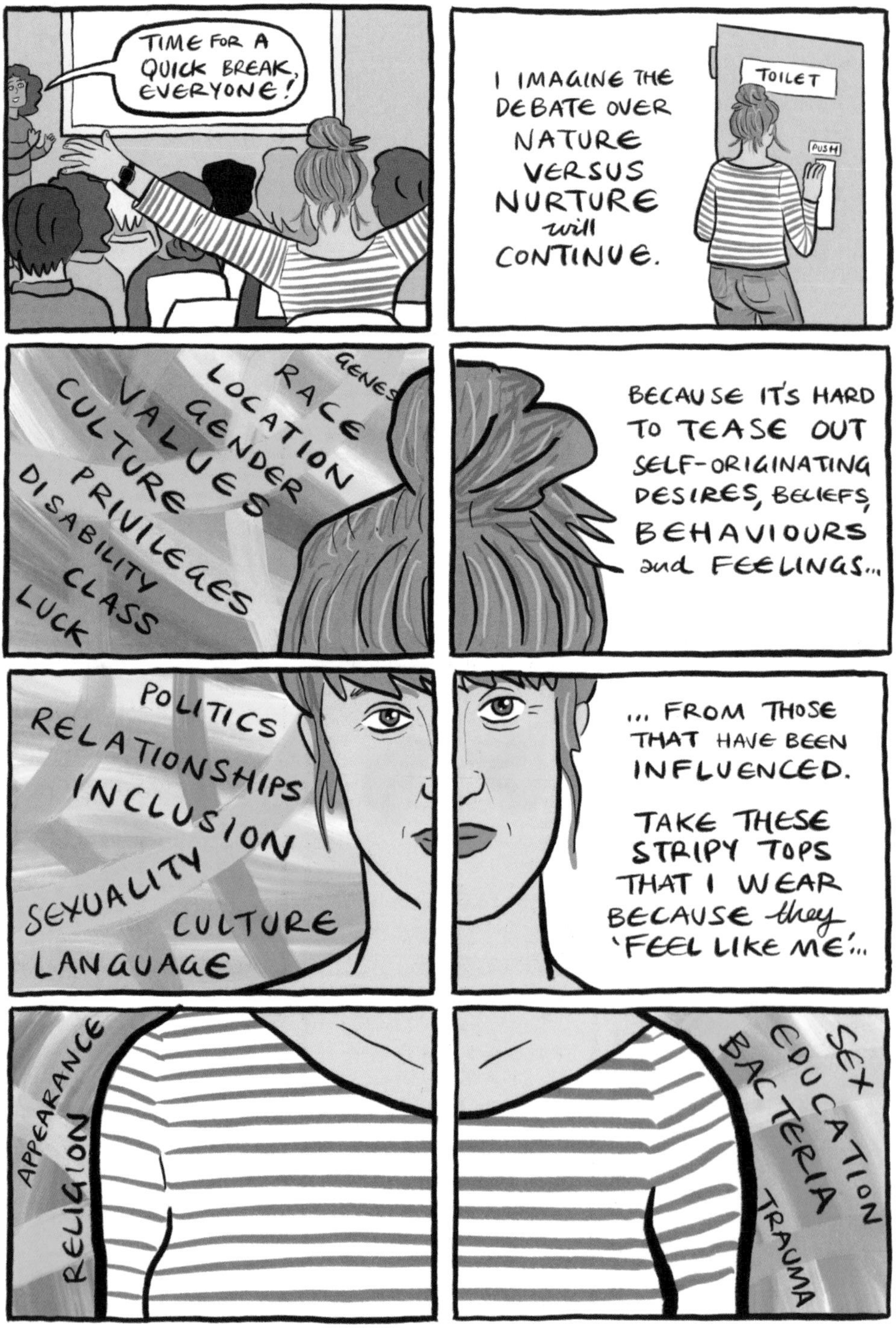
TIME FOR A QUICK BREAK, EVERYONE!
I IMAGINE THE DEBATE OVER NATURE VERSUS NURTURE will CONTINUE.
TOILET
PUSH
GENES
RACE
LOCATION
GENDER
VALUES
CULTURES
PRIVILEGES
DISABILITY
CLASS
LUCK
BECAUSE IT'S HARD TO TEASE OUT SELF-ORIGINATING DESIRES, BELIEFS, BEHAVIOURS and FEELINGS...
POLITICS
RELATIONSHIPS
INCLUSION
SEXUALITY
CULTURE
LANGUAGE
... FROM THOSE THAT HAVE BEEN INFLUENCED.
TAKE THESE STRIPY TOPS THAT I WEAR BECAUSE they 'FEEL LIKE ME'...
APPEARANCE
RELIGION
SEX
EDUCATION
BACTERIA
TRAUMA

o I REALLY LIKE THEM? OR HAVE I BEEN CONDITIONED TO? I WAS
RESSED in STRIPES from CHILDHOOD. FOR MY ARCHITECT FATHER
nd LANDSCAPE ARCHITECT MOTHER, STRIPES ARE SYNONYMOUS
ITH STYLE, ASPIRATIONAL EUROPEAN CULTURE and IDEAS of
REATIVE GENIUS. WHICH is ROMANTIC, but CASTS A LONG SHADOW.

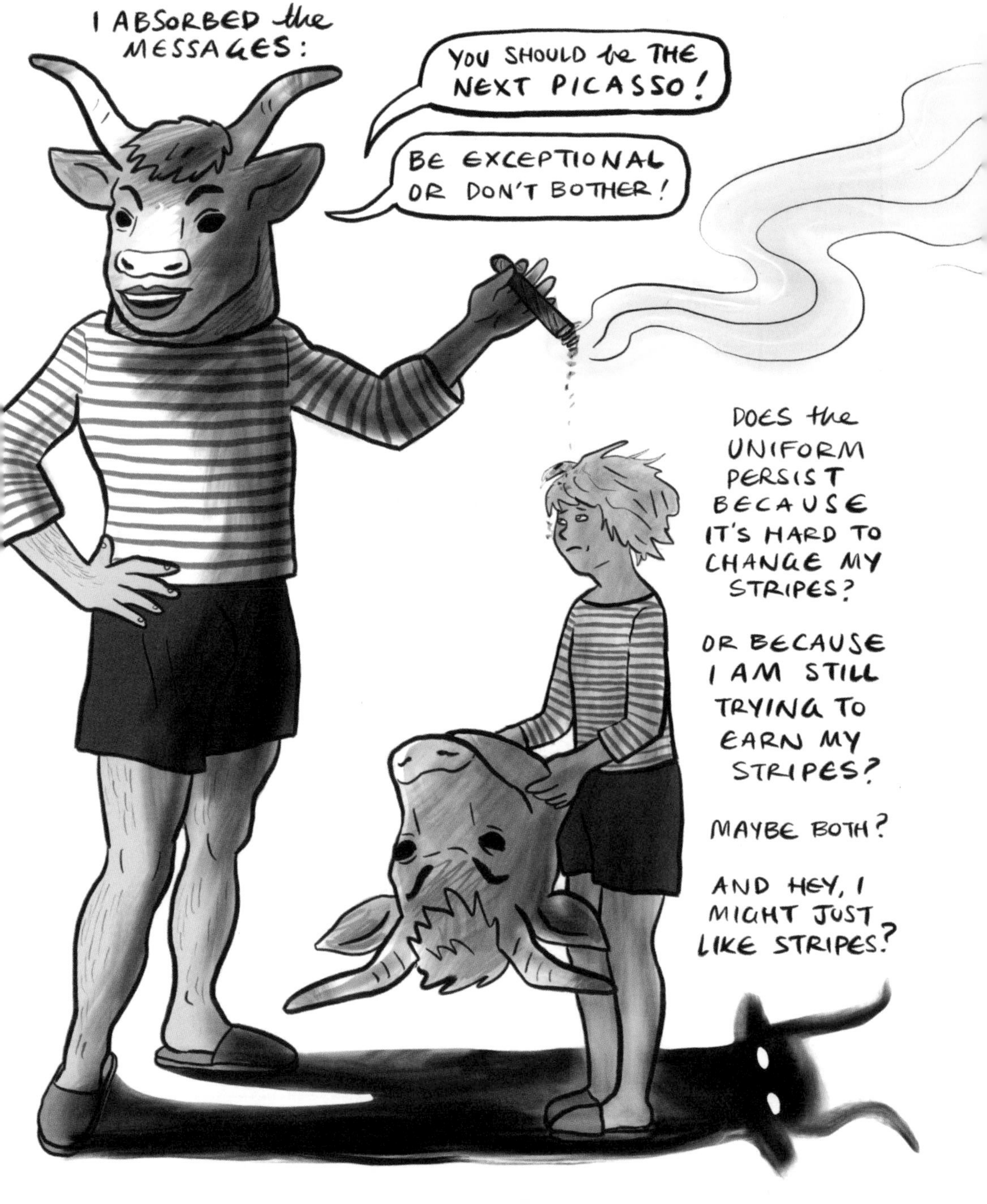
I ABSORBED the MESSAGES:
YOU SHOULD be THE NEXT PICASSO!
BE EXCEPTIONAL OR DON'T BOTHER!
DOES the UNIFORM PERSIST BECAUSE IT'S HARD TO CHANGE MY STRIPES?
OR BECAUSE I AM STILL TRYING TO EARN MY STRIPES?
MAYBE BOTH?
AND HEY, I MIGHT JUST LIKE STRIPES?

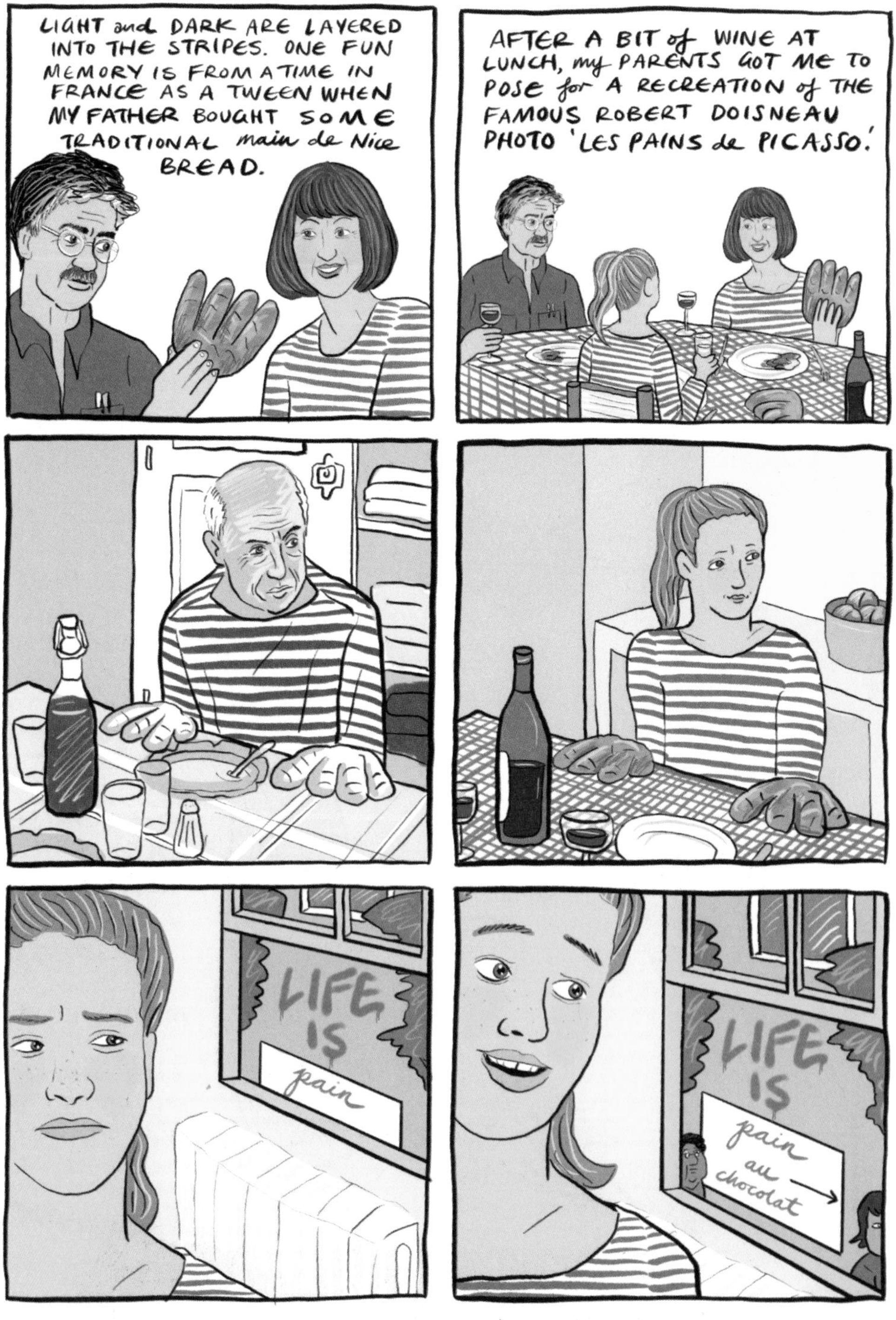

LIGHT and DARK ARE LAYERED INTO THE STRIPES. ONE FUN MEMORY IS FROM A TIME IN FRANCE AS A TWEEN WHEN MY FATHER BOUGHT SOME TRADITIONAL main de Nice BREAD.
AFTER A BIT of WINE AT LUNCH, my PARENTS GOT ME TO POSE for A RECREATION of THE FAMOUS ROBERT DOISNEAU PHOTO 'LES PAINS de PICASSO.'
LIFE IS
pain
LIFE IS
pain au chocolat

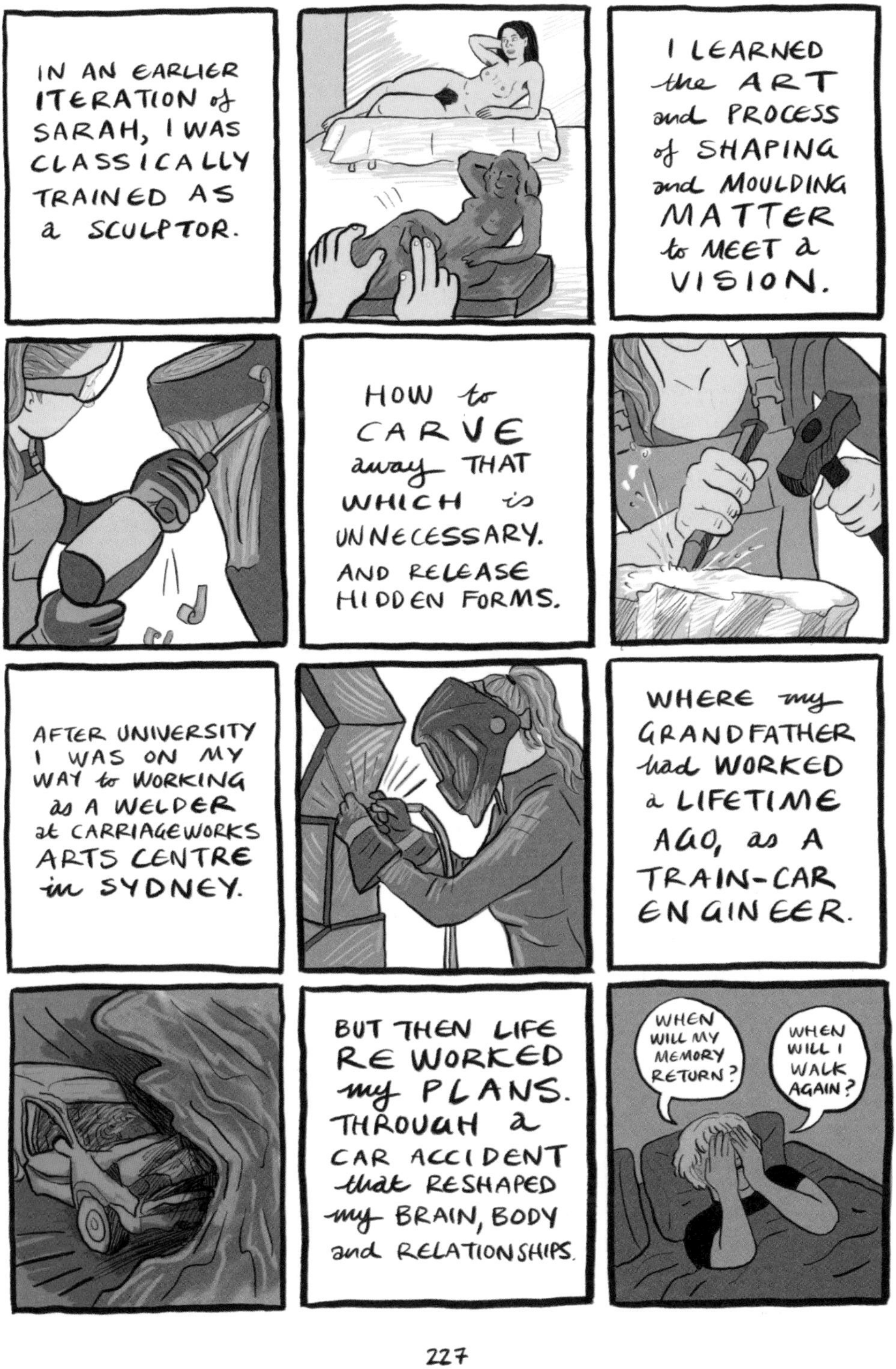
IN AN EARLIER ITERATION of SARAH, I WAS CLASSICALLY TRAINED AS a SCULPTOR.
I LEARNED the ART and PROCESS of SHAPING and MOULDING MATTER to MEET a VISION.
HOW to CARVE away THAT WHICH is UNNECESSARY. AND RELEASE HIDDEN FORMS.
AFTER UNIVERSITY I WAS ON MY WAY to WORKING as A WELDER at CARRIAGEWORKS ARTS CENTRE in SYDNEY.
WHERE my GRANDFATHER had WORKED a LIFETIME AGO, as A TRAIN-CAR ENGINEER.
BUT THEN LIFE RE WORKED my PLANS. THROUGH a CAR ACCIDENT that RESHAPED my BRAIN, BODY and RELATIONSHIPS.
WHEN WILL MY MEMORY RETURN?
WHEN WILL I WALK AGAIN?

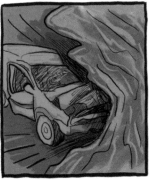

IT WAS A CHALLENGE for ME to FIGURE OUT HOW TO REWRITE, RECONFIGURE, and REBUILD MYSELF.

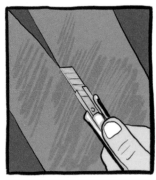

TO CUT AWAY OLD IDEAS of WHO I WAS SUPPOSED to BE. WHILE ALSO REMEMBERING PARTS of ME I HAD FORGOTTEN.

SO MUCH of MY LIFE HAS BEEN THIS ONGOING PROCESS of ADDITION and SUBTRACTION. MOVING AWAY and TOWARDS.

LET YOURSELF be SILENTLY DRAWN by THE STRANGE PULL of WHAT YOU REALLY LOVE. IT will NOT LEAD YOU ASTRAY.

— RUMI, POLYMATH and SUFI MYSTIC

I DON'T KNOW if I BELIEVE in A TRUE ESSENCE of SELF or an INFALLIBLE SELF, but THERE IS SOME KIND of QUIET WHISPER.

SOME SIGNAL in THE NOISE, HELPING me SORT OUT WHAT I ACTUALLY WANT from WHAT I'M SUPPOSED to WANT.

A DEEPER KNOWING, of SOMETHING MYSTICAL?

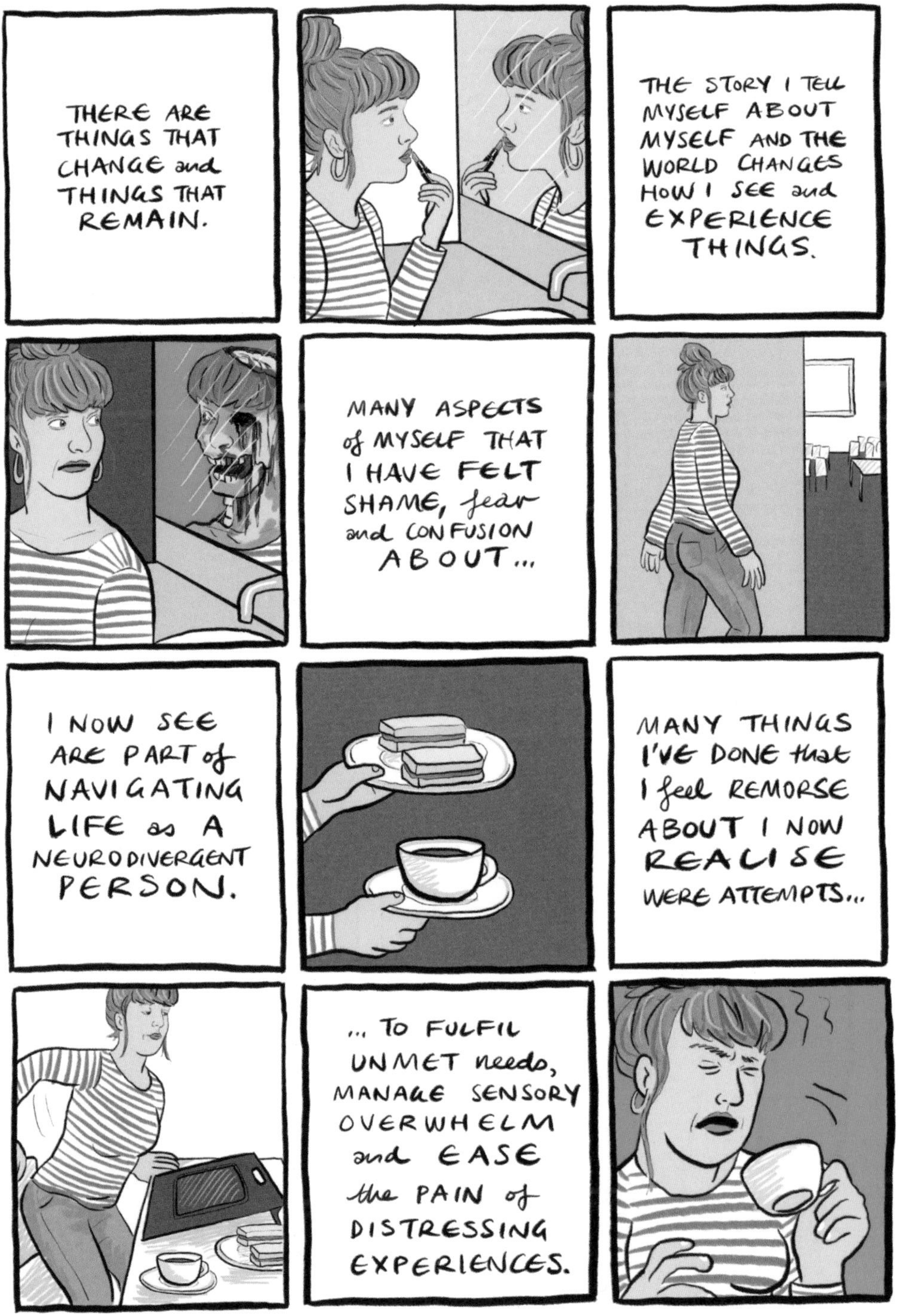
THERE ARE THINGS THAT CHANGE and THINGS THAT REMAIN.
THE STORY I TELL MYSELF ABOUT MYSELF AND THE WORLD CHANGES HOW I SEE and EXPERIENCE THINGS.
MANY ASPECTS of MYSELF THAT I HAVE FELT SHAME, fear and CONFUSION ABOUT...
I NOW SEE ARE PART of NAVIGATING LIFE as A NEURODIVERGENT PERSON.
MANY THINGS I'VE DONE that I feel REMORSE ABOUT I NOW REALISE WERE ATTEMPTS...
... TO FULFIL UNMET needs, MANAGE SENSORY OVERWHELM and EASE the PAIN of DISTRESSING EXPERIENCES.

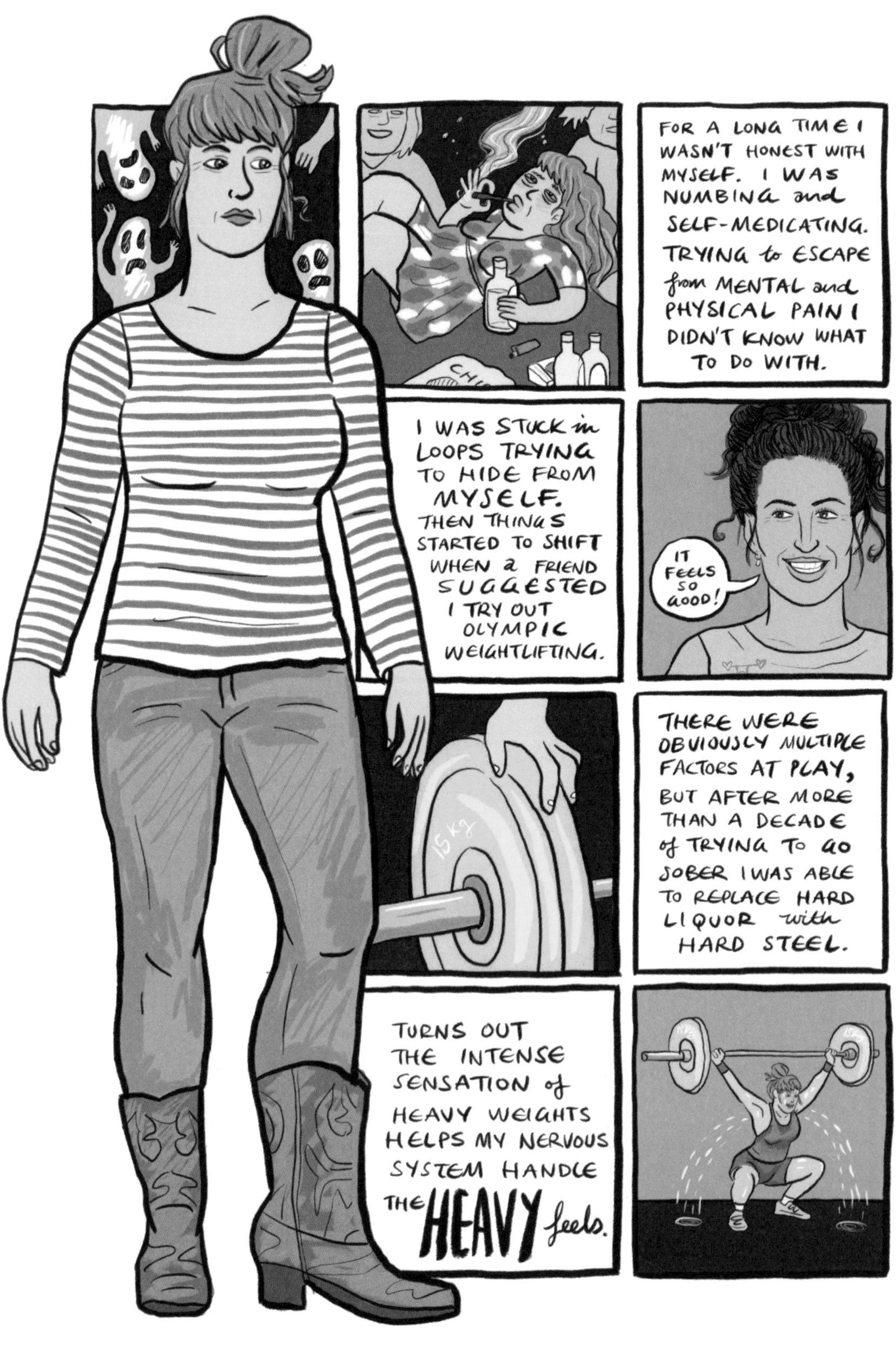

FOR A LONG TIME I WASN'T HONEST WITH MYSELF. I WAS NUMBING and SELF-MEDICATING. TRYING to ESCAPE from MENTAL and PHYSICAL PAIN I DIDN'T KNOW WHAT TO DO WITH.
I WAS STUCK in LOOPS TRYING TO HIDE FROM MYSELF. THEN THINGS STARTED TO SHIFT WHEN a FRIEND SUGGESTED I TRY OUT OLYMPIC WEIGHTLIFTING.
IT FEELS SO GOOD!
15 kg
THERE WERE OBVIOUSLY MULTIPLE FACTORS AT PLAY, BUT AFTER MORE THAN A DECADE of TRYING TO GO SOBER I WAS ABLE TO REPLACE HARD LIQUOR with HARD STEEL.
TURNS OUT THE INTENSE SENSATION of HEAVY WEIGHTS HELPS MY NERVOUS SYSTEM HANDLE THE HEAVY feels.

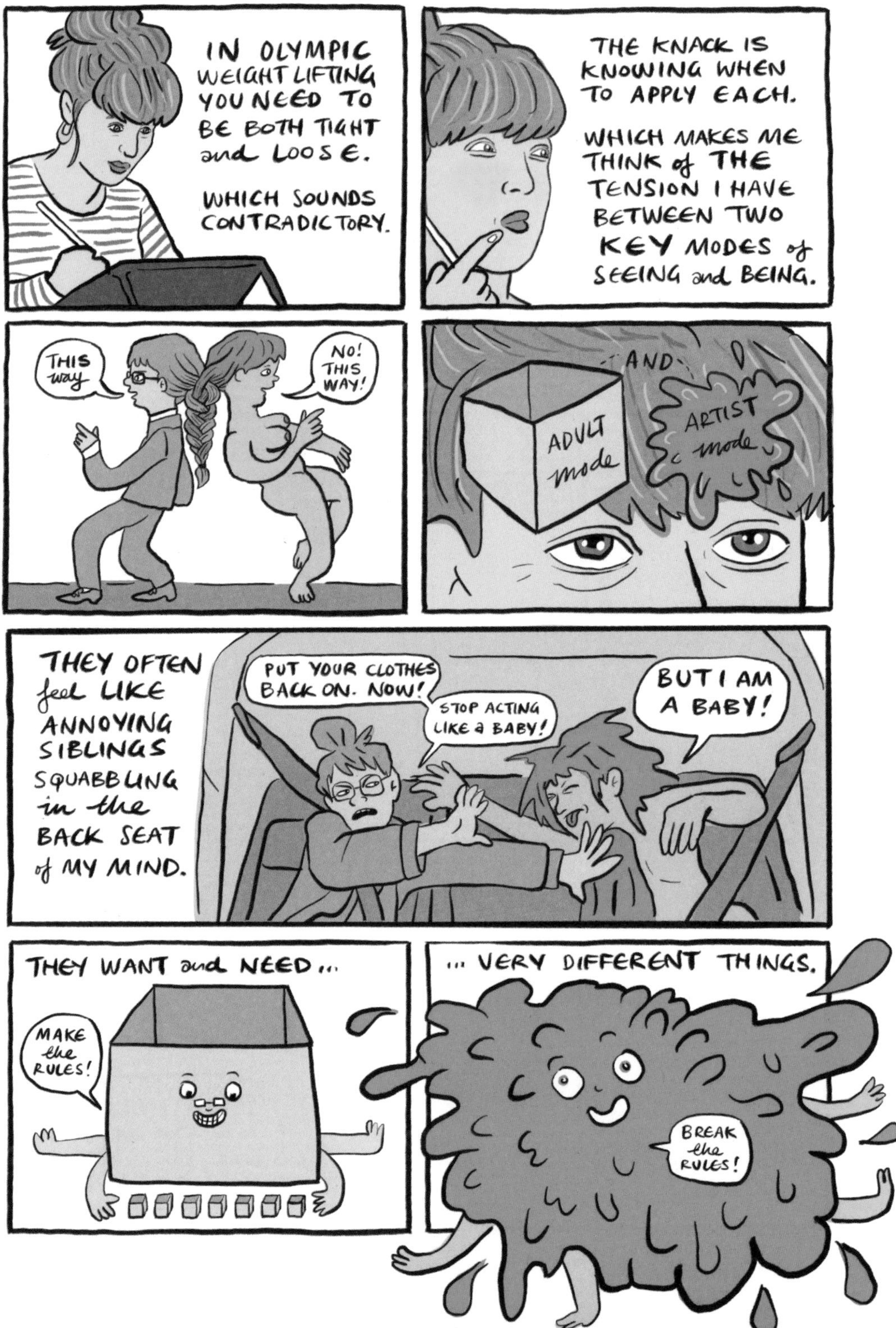
IN OLYMPIC WEIGHT LIFTING YOU NEED TO BE BOTH TIGHT and LOOSE.
WHICH SOUNDS CONTRADICTORY.
THE KNACK IS KNOWING WHEN TO APPLY EACH.
WHICH MAKES ME THINK of THE TENSION I HAVE BETWEEN TWO KEY MODES of SEEING and BEING.
THIS way
NO! THIS WAY!
ADULT mode
AND
ARTIST mode
THEY OFTEN feel LIKE ANNOYING SIBLINGS SQUABBLING in the BACK SEAT of MY MIND.
PUT YOUR CLOTHES BACK ON. NOW!
STOP ACTING LIKE a BABY!
BUT I AM A BABY!
THEY WANT and NEED...
MAKE the RULES!
... VERY DIFFERENT THINGS.
BREAK the RULES!

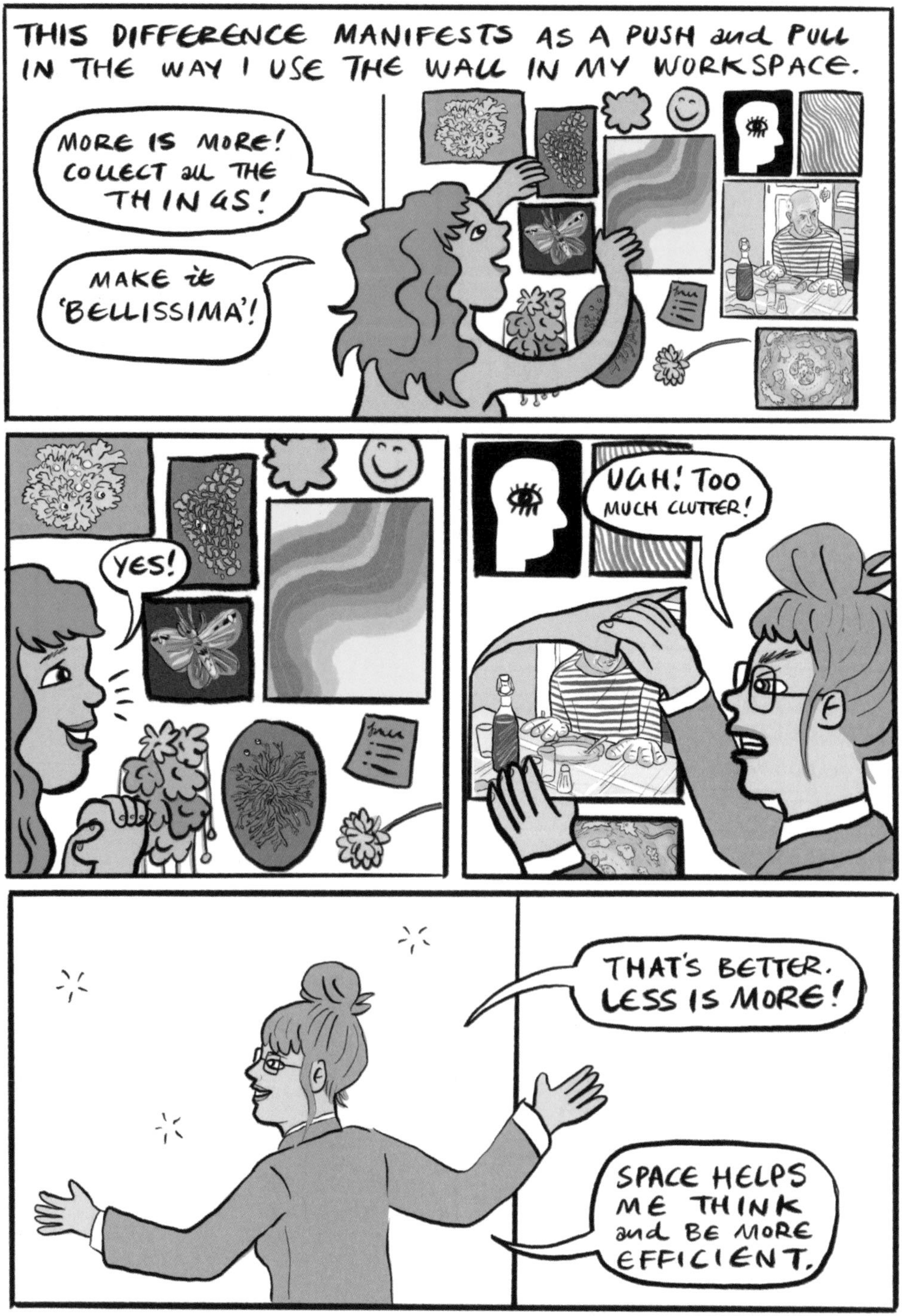
THIS DIFFERENCE MANIFESTS AS A PUSH and PULL IN THE WAY I USE THE WALL IN MY WORKSPACE.
MORE IS MORE! COLLECT all THE THINGS!
MAKE it 'BELLISSIMA'!
YES!
UGH! TOO MUCH CLUTTER!
THAT'S BETTER. LESS IS MORE!
SPACE HELPS ME THINK and BE MORE EFFICIENT.

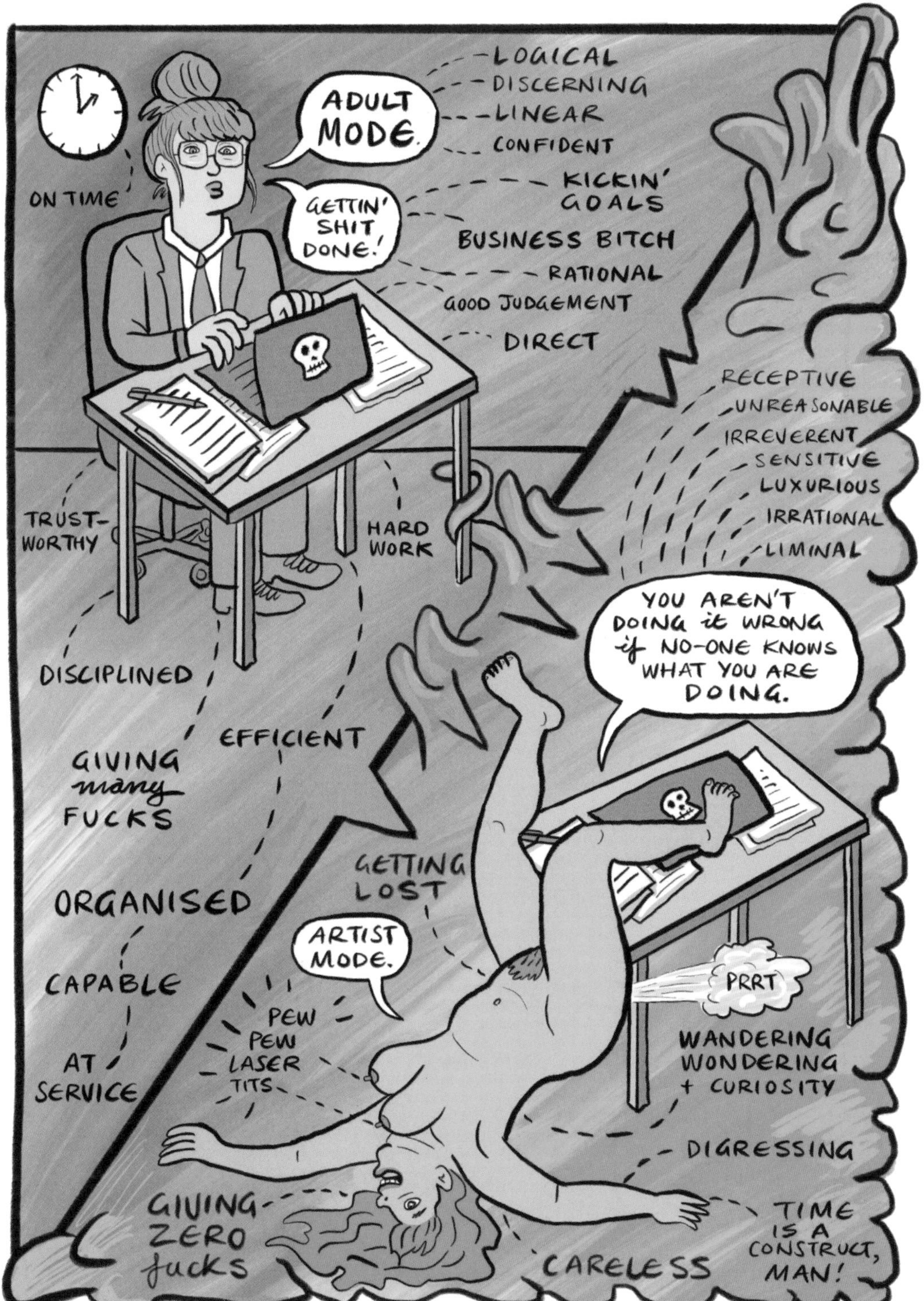
ADULT MODE.
LOGICAL
DISCERNING
LINEAR
CONFIDENT
ON TIME
GETTIN' SHIT DONE!
KICKIN' GOALS
BUSINESS BITCH
RATIONAL
GOOD JUDGEMENT
DIRECT
TRUST-WORTHY
HARD WORK
DISCIPLINED
EFFICIENT
GIVING many FUCKS
ORGANISED
CAPABLE
AT SERVICE
RECEPTIVE
UNREASONABLE
IRREVERENT
SENSITIVE
LUXURIOUS
IRRATIONAL
LIMINAL
YOU AREN'T DOING it WRONG if NO-ONE KNOWS WHAT YOU ARE DOING.
GETTING LOST
ARTIST MODE.
PEW PEW LASER TITS
PRRT
WANDERING WONDERING + CURIOSITY
DIGRESSING
GIVING ZERO fucks
CARELESS
TIME IS A CONSTRUCT, MAN!

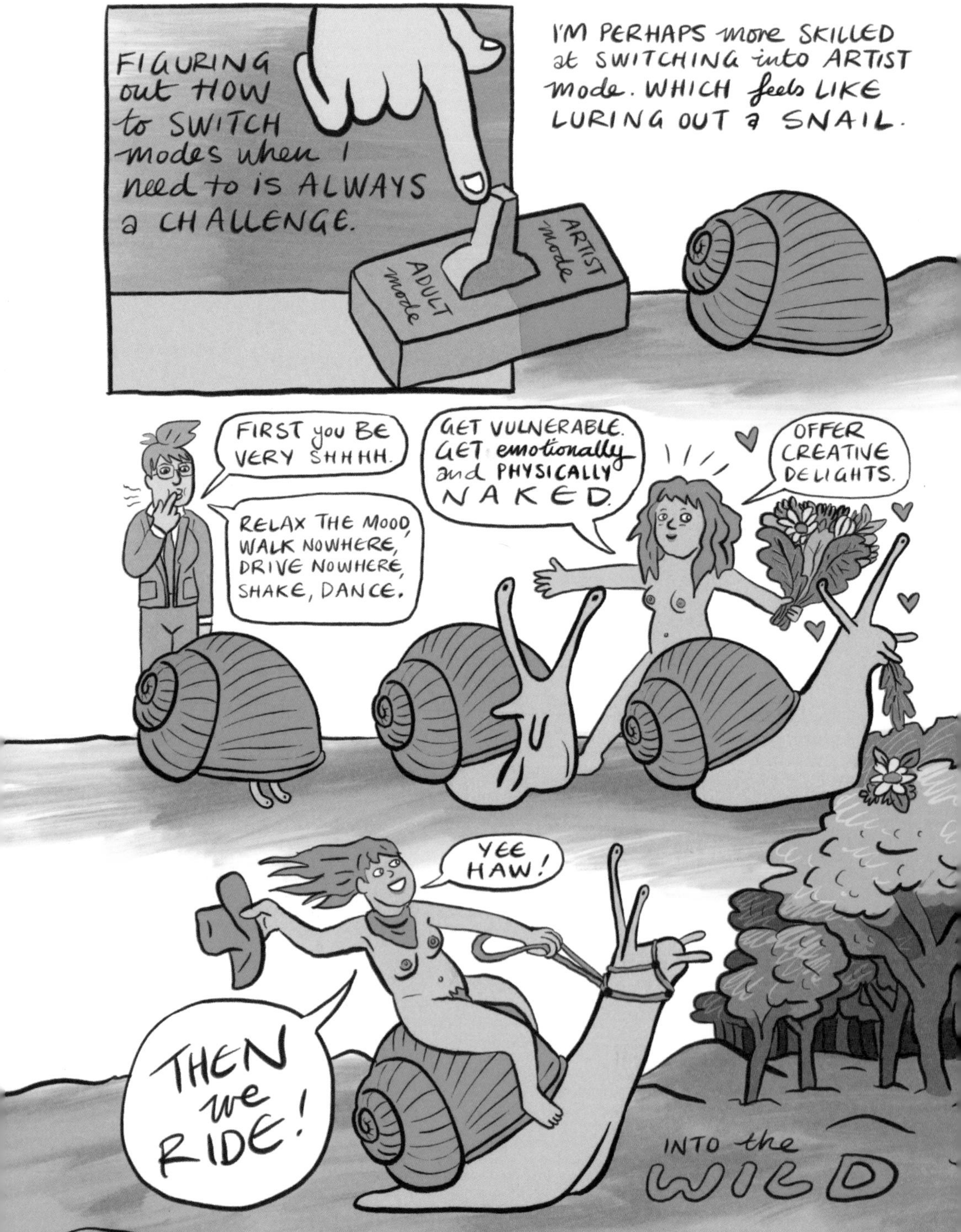
FIGURING out HOW to SWITCH modes when I need to is ALWAYS a CHALLENGE.
ARTIST mode
ADULT mode
I'M PERHAPS more SKILLED at SWITCHING into ARTIST mode. WHICH feels LIKE LURING OUT a SNAIL.
FIRST you BE VERY SHHHH.
RELAX THE MOOD, WALK NOWHERE, DRIVE NOWHERE, SHAKE, DANCE.
GET VULNERABLE. GET emotionally and PHYSICALLY NAKED.
OFFER CREATIVE DELIGHTS.
YEE HAW!
THEN we RIDE!
INTO the WILD

WHEN I'VE BEEN OUT ROAMING FREE in ARTIST mode IT'S A LOT HARDER to SWITCH into ADULT mode.

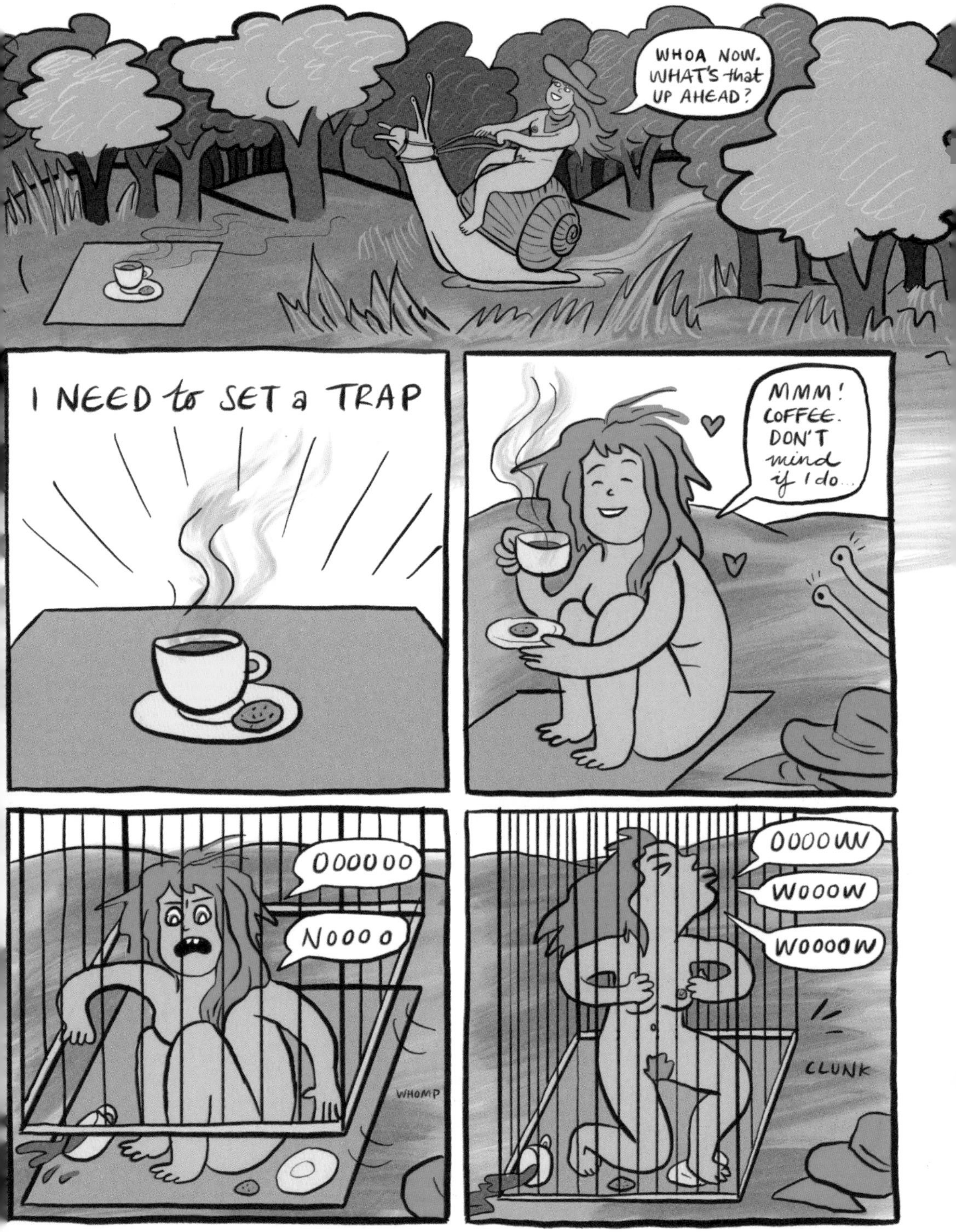
WHOA NOW. WHAT'S that UP AHEAD?
I NEED to SET a TRAP
MMM! COFFEE. DON'T mind if I do...
OOOOOO
NOOOO
WHOMP
OOOOW
WOOOW
WOOOOW
CLUNK

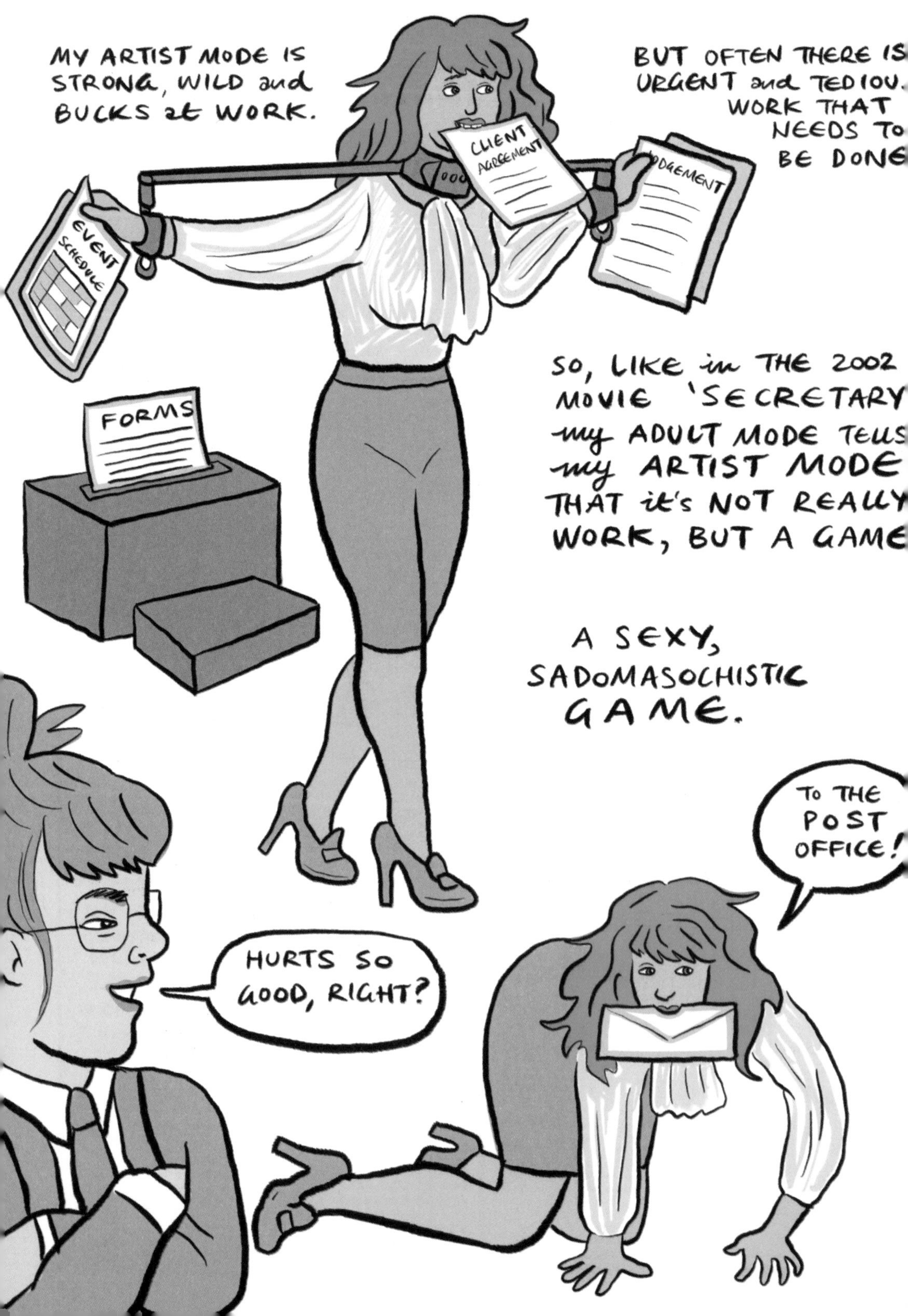
MY ARTIST MODE IS STRONG, WILD and BUCKS at WORK.
BUT OFTEN THERE IS URGENT and TEDIOU. WORK THAT NEEDS TO BE DONE
CLIENT AGREEMENT
EVENT SCHEDULE
FORMS
SO, LIKE in THE 2002 MOVIE 'SECRETARY my ADULT MODE TELLS my ARTIST MODE THAT it's NOT REALLY WORK, BUT A GAME
A SEXY, SADOMASOCHISTIC GAME.
TO THE POST OFFICE!
HURTS SO GOOD, RIGHT?

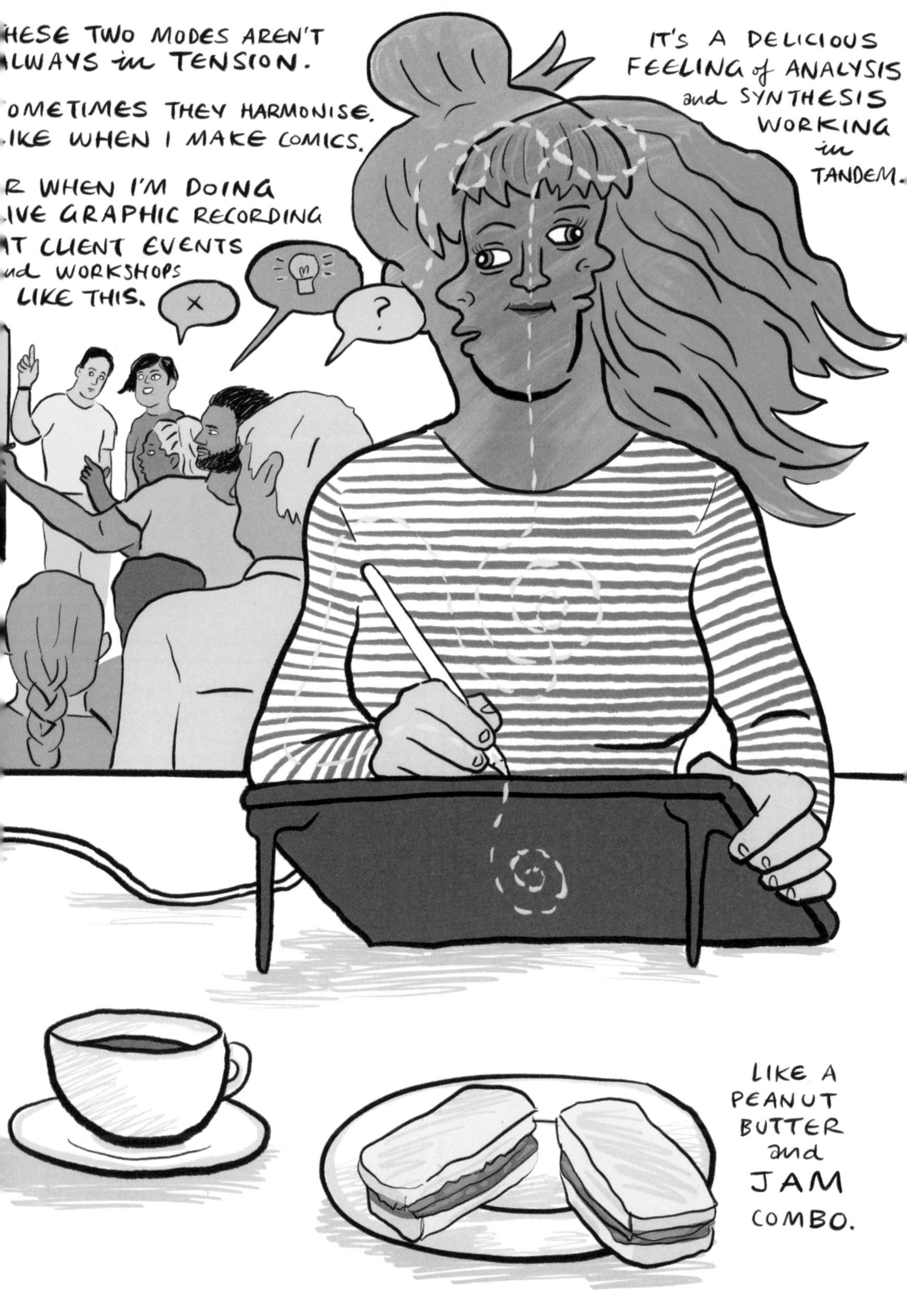
HESE TWO MODES AREN'T
LWAYS in TENSION.
OMETIMES THEY HARMONISE.
IKE WHEN I MAKE COMICS.
R WHEN I'M DOING
IVE GRAPHIC RECORDING
T CLIENT EVENTS
nd WORKSHOPS
LIKE THIS.
X
?
IT'S A DELICIOUS FEELING of ANALYSIS and SYNTHESIS WORKING in TANDEM.
LIKE A PEANUT BUTTER and JAM COMBO.

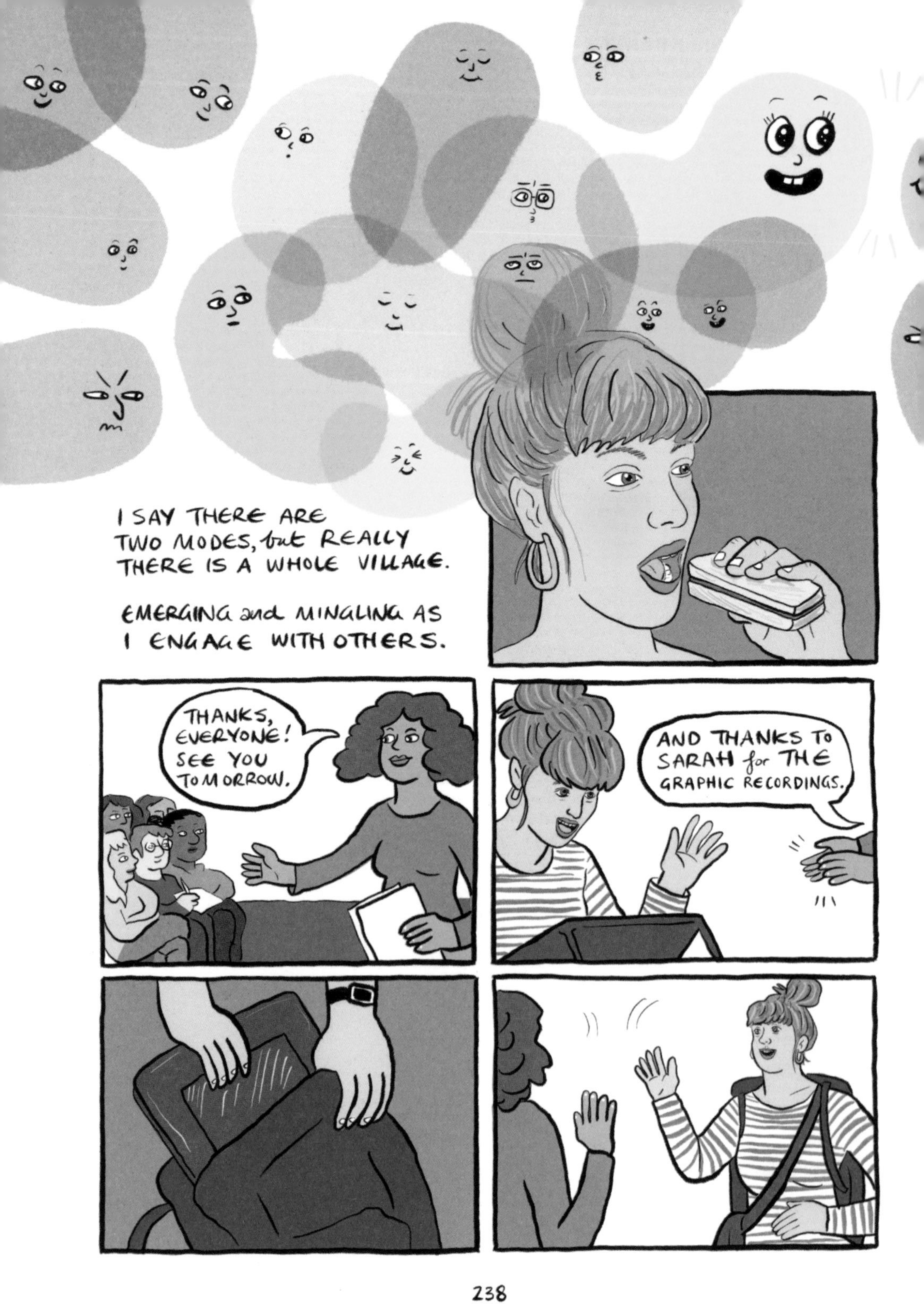
I SAY THERE ARE TWO MODES, but REALLY THERE IS A WHOLE VILLAGE.
EMERGING and MINGLING AS I ENGAGE WITH OTHERS.
THANKS, EVERYONE! SEE YOU TOMORROW.
AND THANKS TO SARAH for THE GRAPHIC RECORDINGS.

CHANGE MY CONTEXT and I CHANGE.

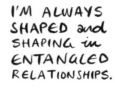
I'M ALWAYS SHAPED and SHAPING in ENTANGLED RELATIONSHIPS.

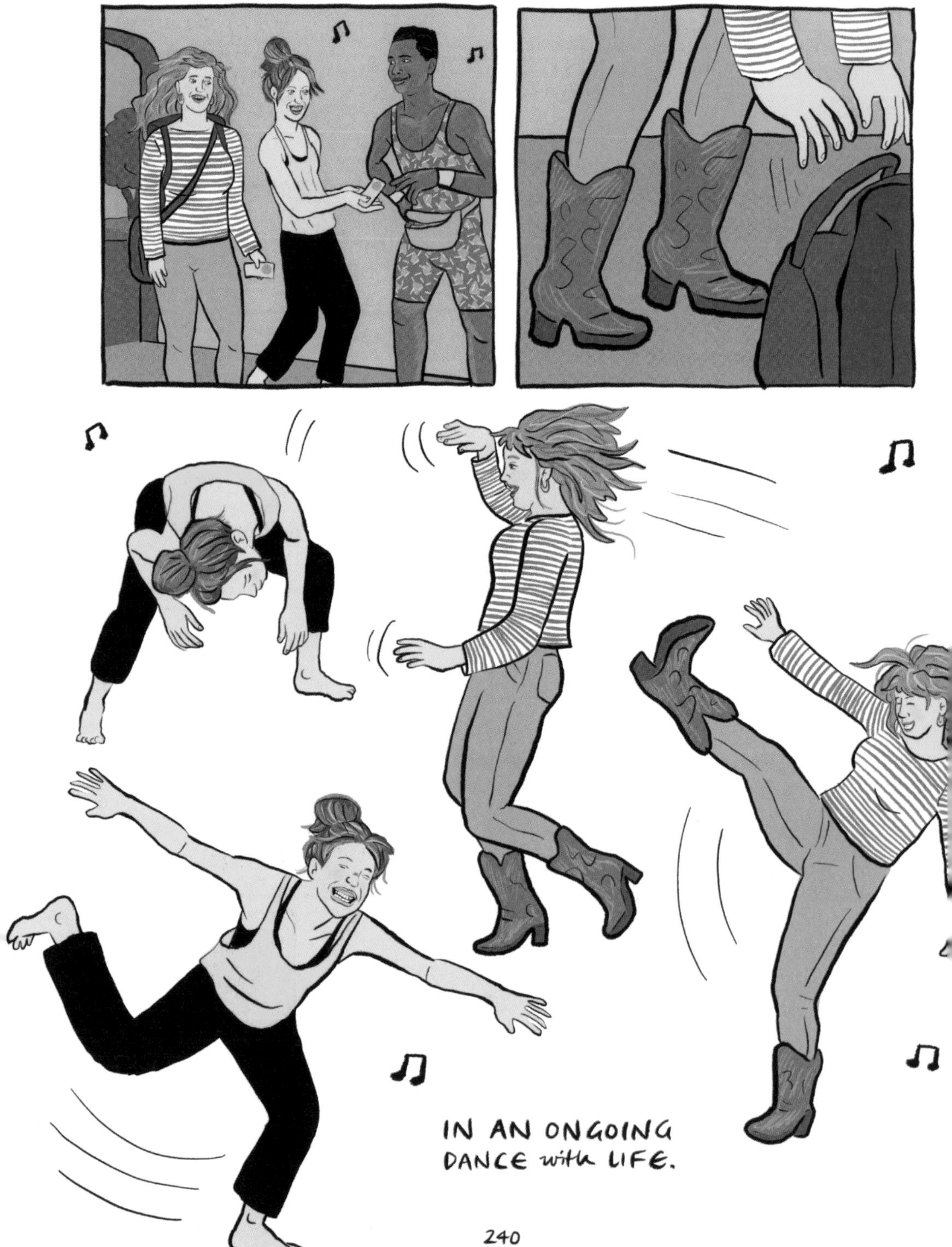
IN AN ONGOING
DANCE with LIFE.

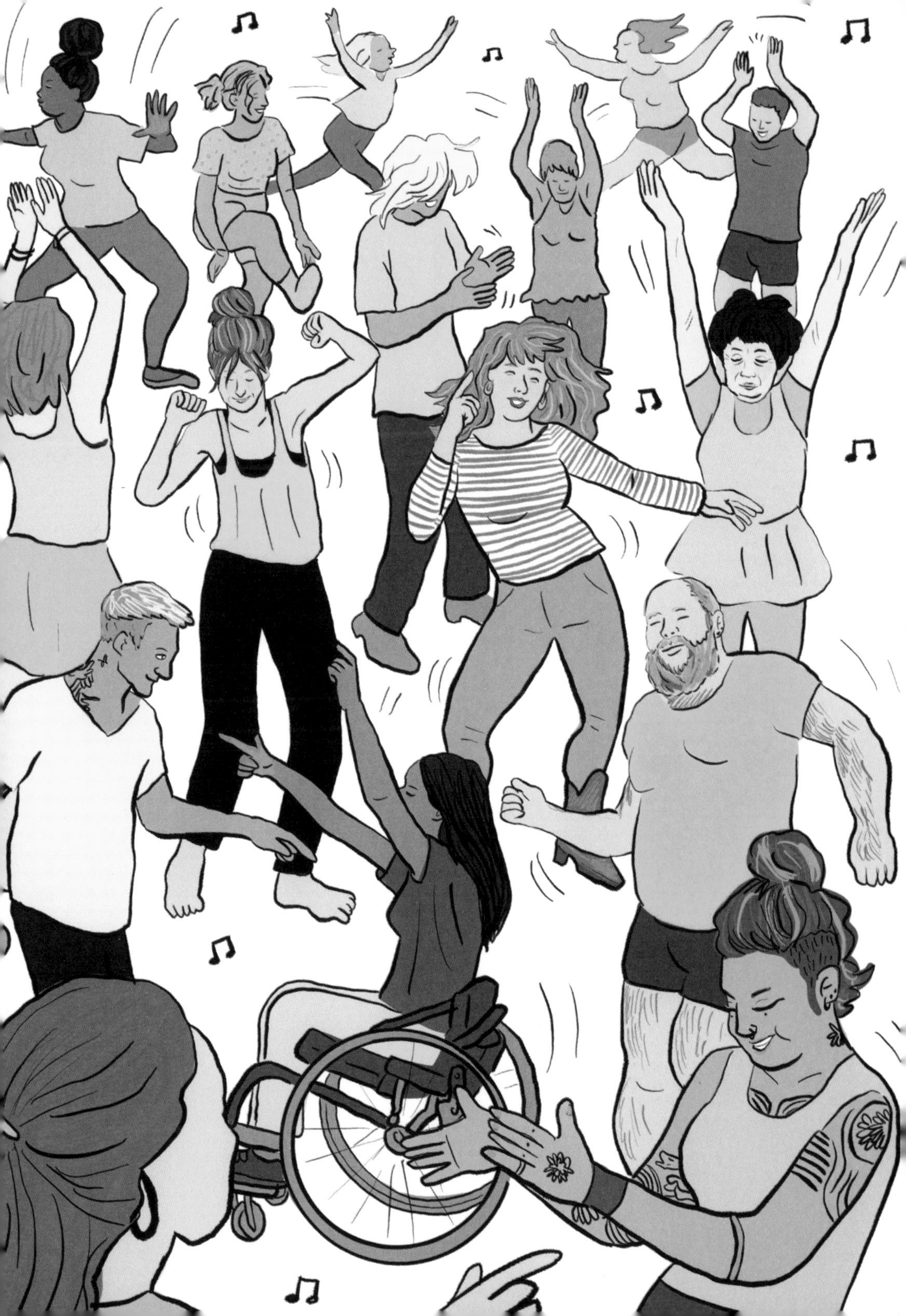

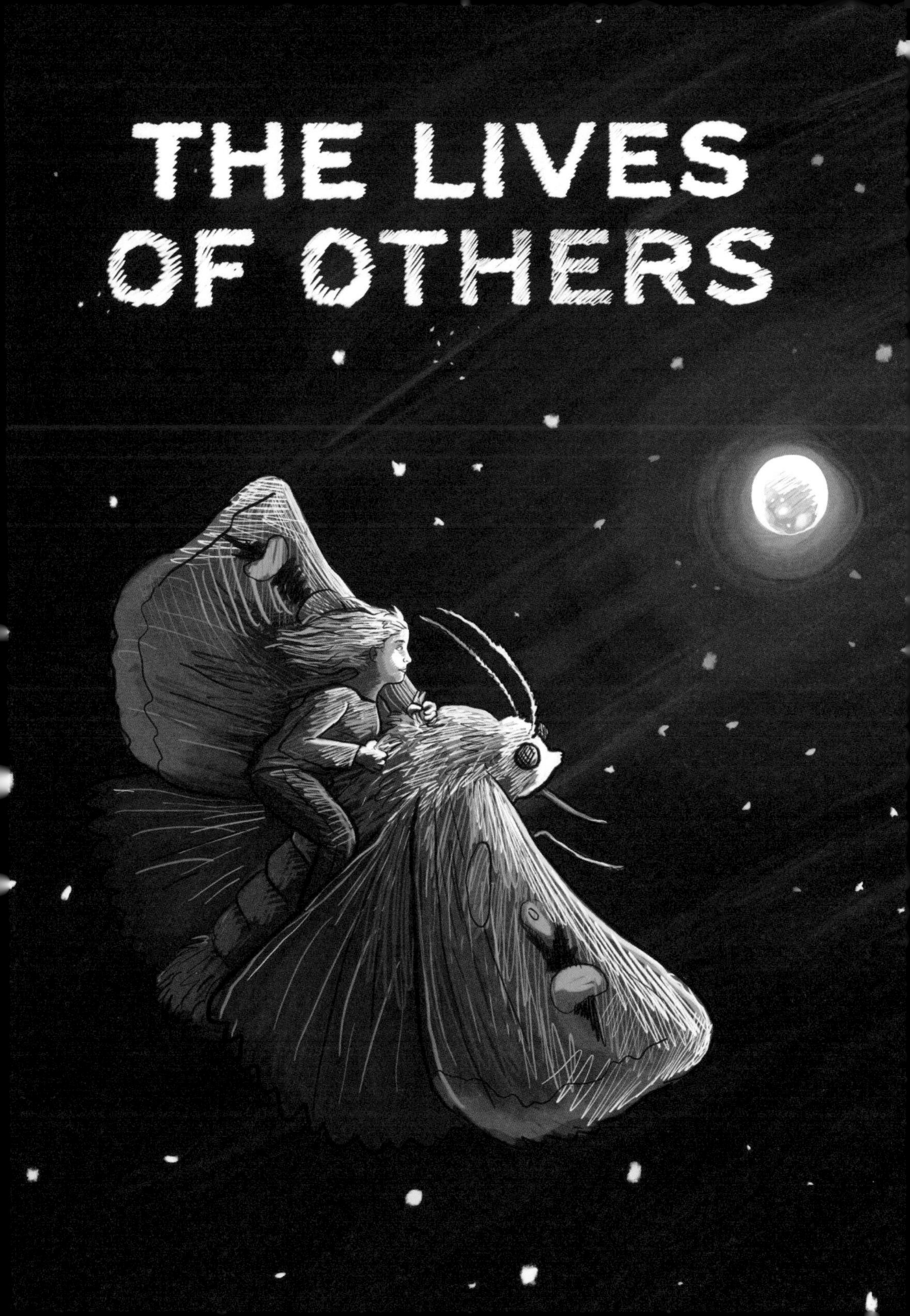
THE LIVES
OF OTHERS

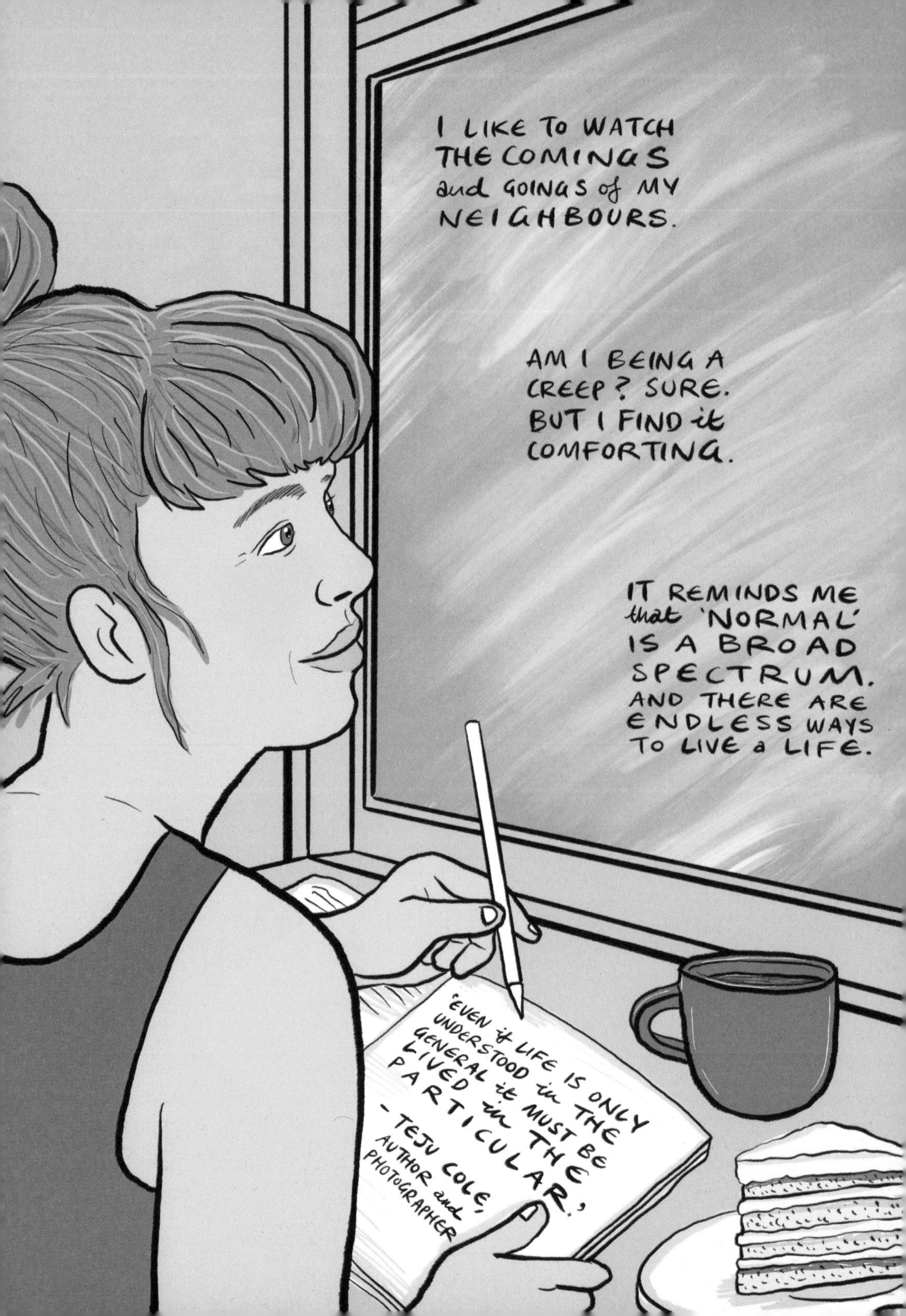
I LIKE TO WATCH THE COMINGS and GOINGS of MY NEIGHBOURS.
AM I BEING A CREEP? SURE. BUT I FIND it COMFORTING.
IT REMINDS ME that 'NORMAL' IS A BROAD SPECTRUM. AND THERE ARE ENDLESS WAYS TO LIVE a LIFE.
'EVEN if LIFE IS ONLY UNDERSTOOD in THE GENERAL it MUST BE LIVED in THE PARTICULAR.'
- TEJU COLE, AUTHOR and PHOTOGRAPHER

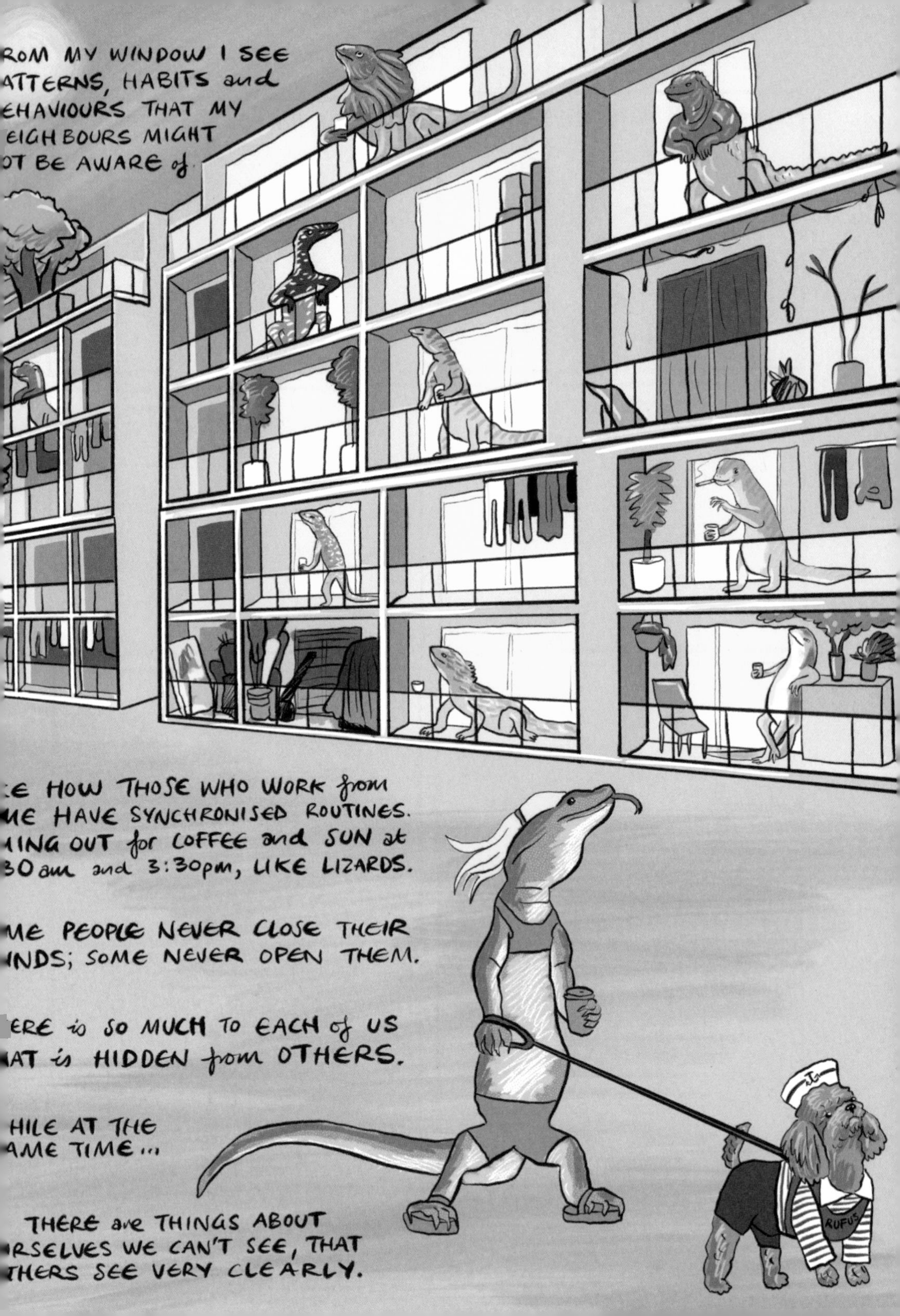

ROM MY WINDOW I SEE ATTERNS, HABITS and EHAVIOURS THAT MY EIGHBOURS MIGHT OT BE AWARE of.
E HOW THOSE WHO WORK from ME HAVE SYNCHRONISED ROUTINES. MING OUT for COFFEE and SUN at 30 am and 3:30pm, LIKE LIZARDS.
ME PEOPLE NEVER CLOSE THEIR INDS; SOME NEVER OPEN THEM.
ERE is SO MUCH TO EACH of US AT is HIDDEN from OTHERS.
HILE AT THE AME TIME...
THERE are THINGS ABOUT RSELVES WE CAN'T SEE, THAT THERS SEE VERY CLEARLY.
RUFUS

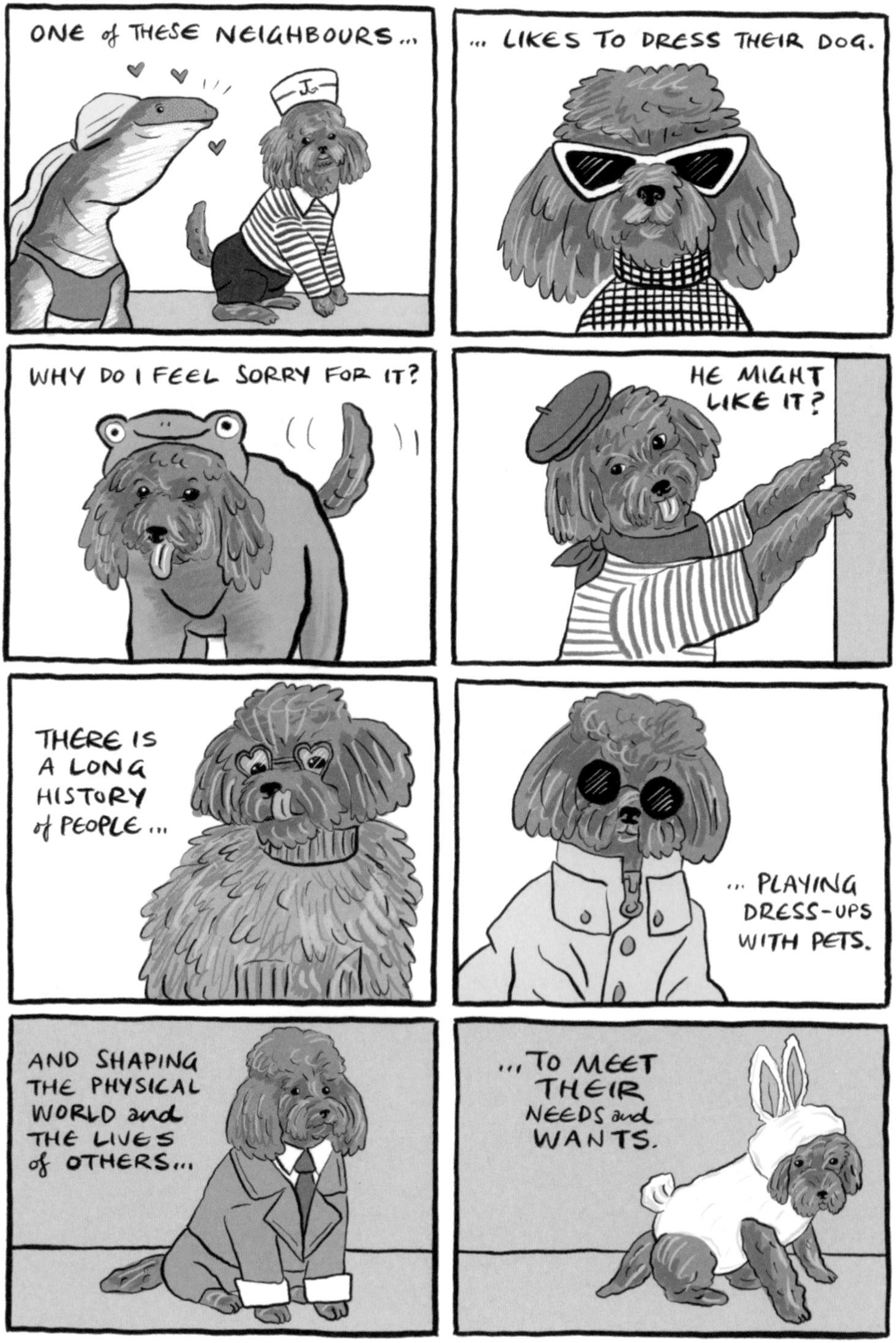
ONE of THESE NEIGHBOURS...
J
... LIKES TO DRESS THEIR DOG.
WHY DO I FEEL SORRY FOR IT?
HE MIGHT LIKE IT?
THERE IS A LONG HISTORY of PEOPLE...
... PLAYING DRESS-UPS WITH PETS.
AND SHAPING THE PHYSICAL WORLD and THE LIVES of OTHERS...
...TO MEET THEIR NEEDS and WANTS.

OST OF THE PLANTS and ANIMALS HUMANS INTERACT WITH
AVE been SELECTIVELY BRED, MODIFIED and DOMESTICATED.
EN 'UNTOUCHED' NATURAL PLACES CAN HAVE A LONG, DEEP
ISTORY of INDIGENOUS CURATION and CUSTODIANSHIP.

T WHAT if HUMANS aren't AS IN CONTROL of THIS AS WE ASSUME?
ULD OTHER LIVES ALSO BE SHAPING US TO THEIR BENEFIT?
ER A LONG TIME THINGS CO-EVOLVE in ENTWINED FEEDBACK LOOPS.

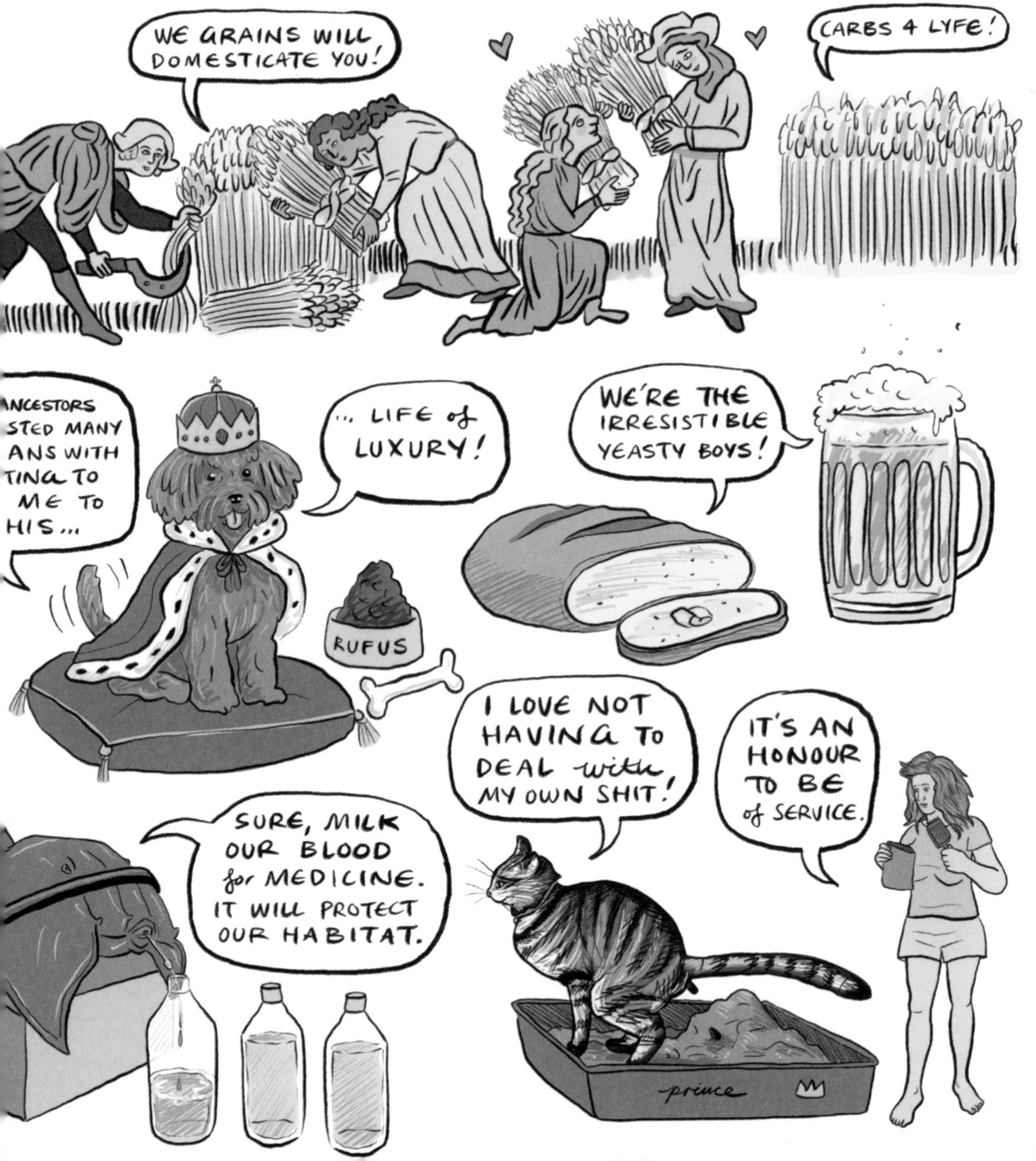

WE GRAINS WILL DOMESTICATE YOU!
CARBS 4 LYFE!
NCESTORS
STED MANY
ANS WITH
TING TO
ME TO
HIS...
... LIFE of LUXURY!
WE'RE THE IRRESISTIBLE YEASTY BOYS!
RUFUS
I LOVE NOT HAVING TO DEAL with MY OWN SHIT!
IT'S AN HONOUR TO BE of SERVICE.
SURE, MILK OUR BLOOD for MEDICINE. IT WILL PROTECT OUR HABITAT.
prince

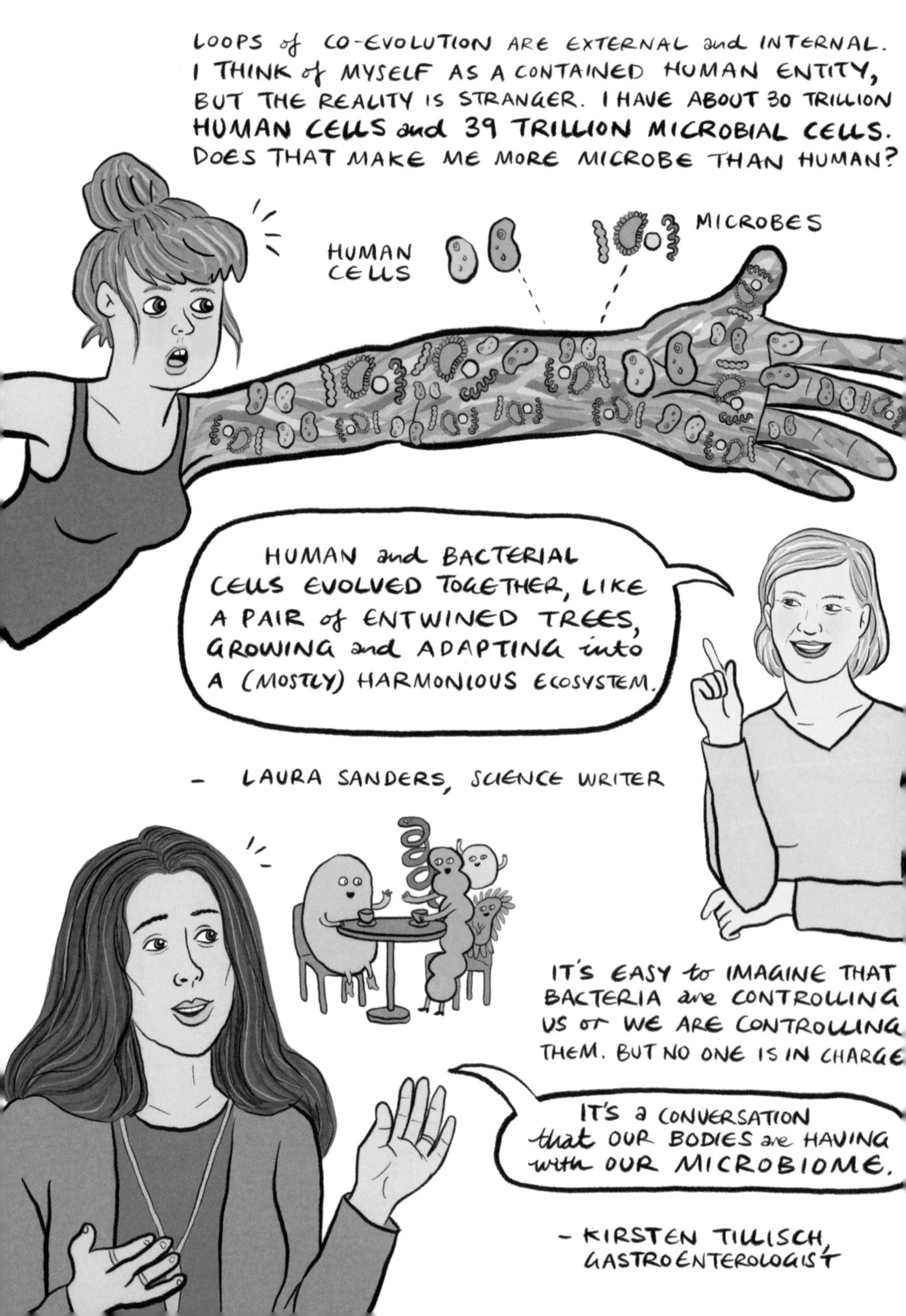
LOOPS of CO-EVOLUTION ARE EXTERNAL and INTERNAL. I THINK of MYSELF AS A CONTAINED HUMAN ENTITY, BUT THE REALITY IS STRANGER. I HAVE ABOUT 30 TRILLION HUMAN CELLS and 39 TRILLION MICROBIAL CELLS. DOES THAT MAKE ME MORE MICROBE THAN HUMAN?
HUMAN CELLS
MICROBES
HUMAN and BACTERIAL CELLS EVOLVED TOGETHER, LIKE A PAIR of ENTWINED TREES, GROWING and ADAPTING into A (MOSTLY) HARMONIOUS ECOSYSTEM.
- LAURA SANDERS, SCIENCE WRITER
IT'S EASY to IMAGINE THAT BACTERIA are CONTROLLING US or WE ARE CONTROLLING THEM. BUT NO ONE IS IN CHARGE
IT'S a CONVERSATION that OUR BODIES are HAVING with OUR MICROBIOME.
- KIRSTEN TILLISCH, GASTROENTEROLOGIST

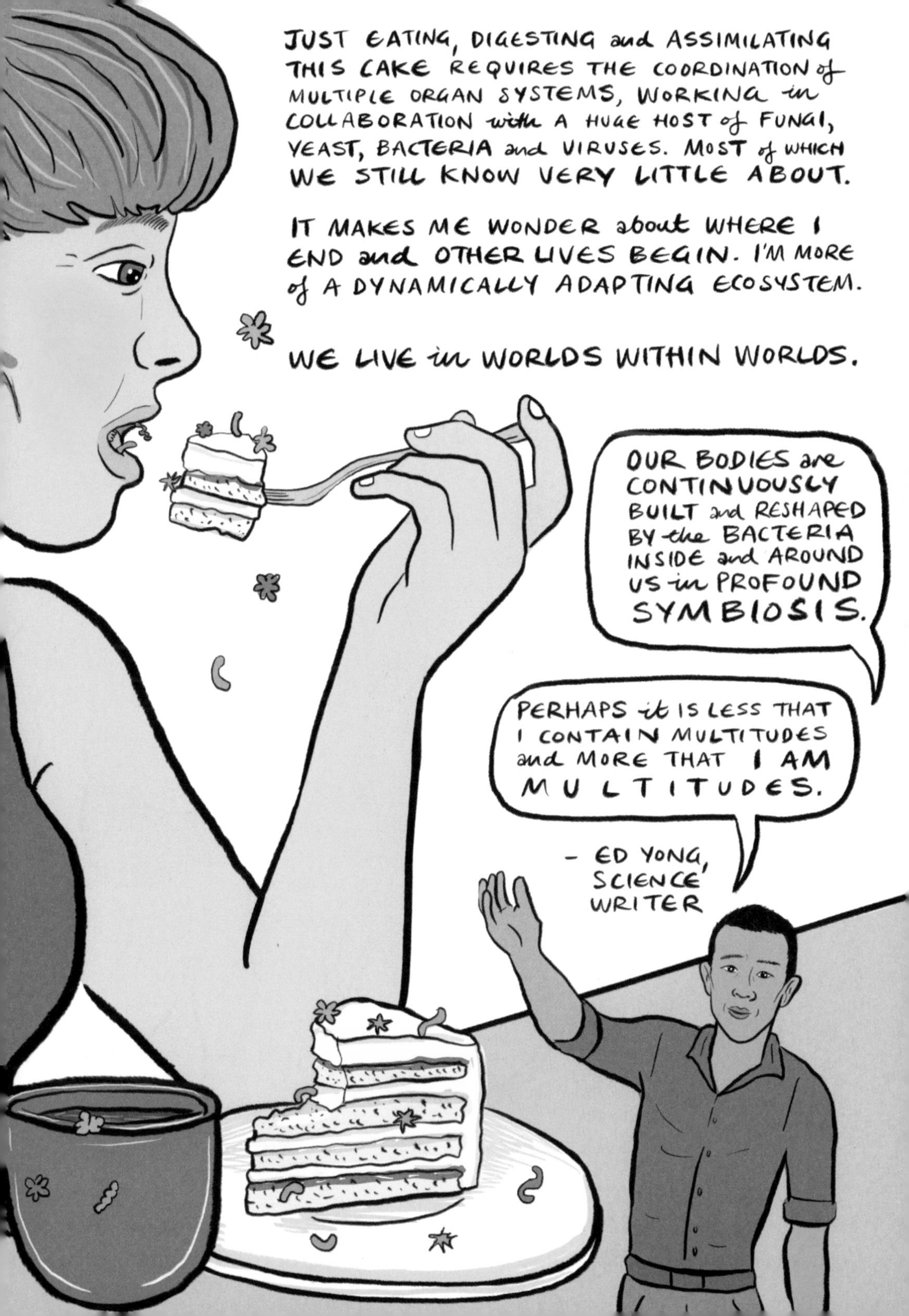
JUST EATING, DIGESTING and ASSIMILATING THIS CAKE REQUIRES THE COORDINATION of MULTIPLE ORGAN SYSTEMS, WORKING in COLLABORATION with A HUGE HOST of FUNGI, YEAST, BACTERIA and VIRUSES. MOST of WHICH WE STILL KNOW VERY LITTLE ABOUT.
IT MAKES ME WONDER about WHERE I END and OTHER LIVES BEGIN. I'M MORE of A DYNAMICALLY ADAPTING ECOSYSTEM.
WE LIVE in WORLDS WITHIN WORLDS.
OUR BODIES are CONTINUOUSLY BUILT and RESHAPED BY the BACTERIA INSIDE and AROUND US in PROFOUND SYMBIOSIS.
PERHAPS it IS LESS THAT I CONTAIN MULTITUDES and MORE THAT I AM MULTITUDES.
- ED YONG, SCIENCE WRITER

ALL THESE LITTLE LIVES in US and on US, ALSO EXTEND OUT of US AS MICROBIAL CLOUDS.

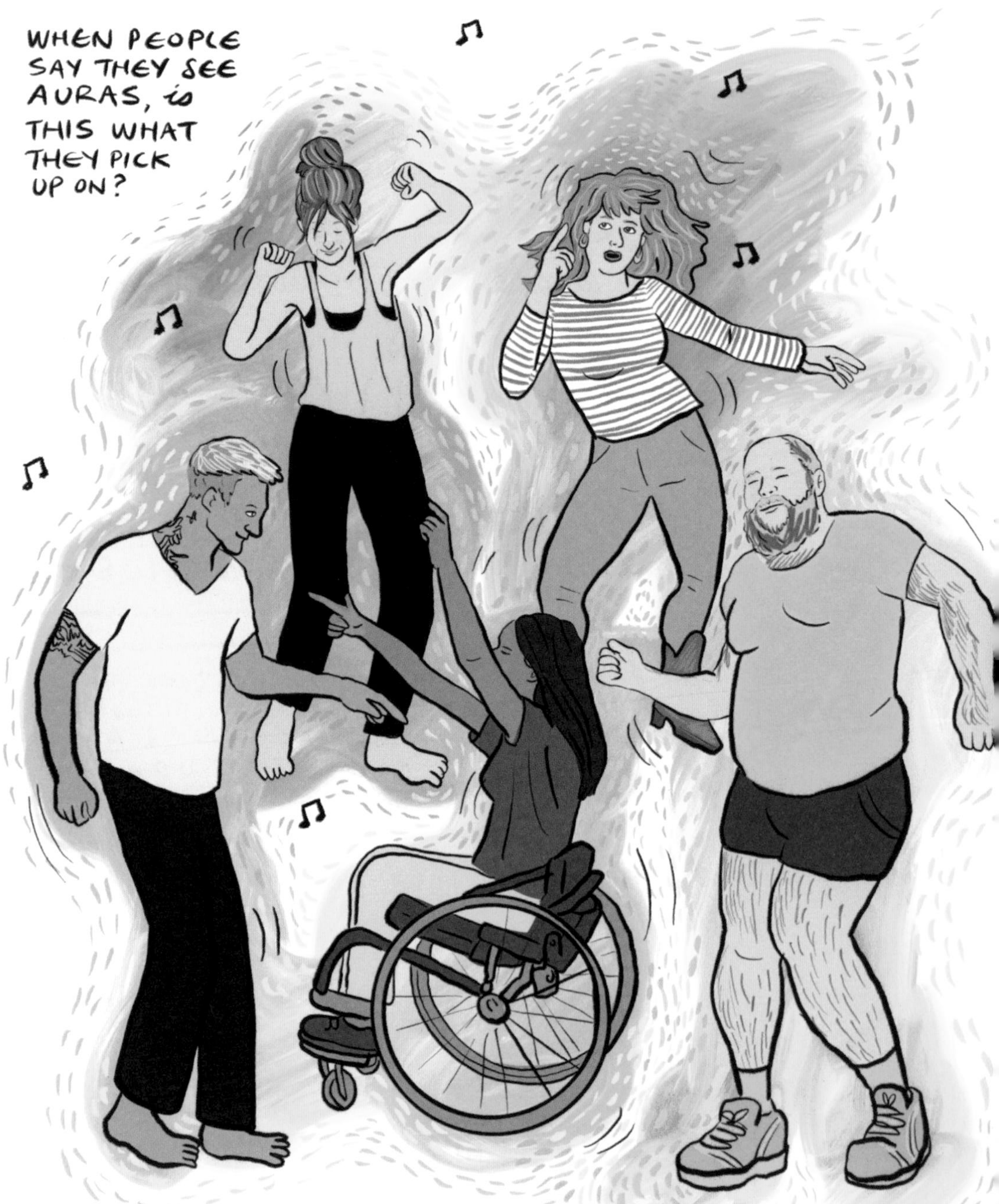
WHEN PEOPLE SAY THEY SEE AURAS, is THIS WHAT THEY PICK UP ON?

BODIES ARE CONTAINED and POROUS. PEOPLE and PLACES LITERALLY RUB off ON US. WE CHANGE EACH OTHER

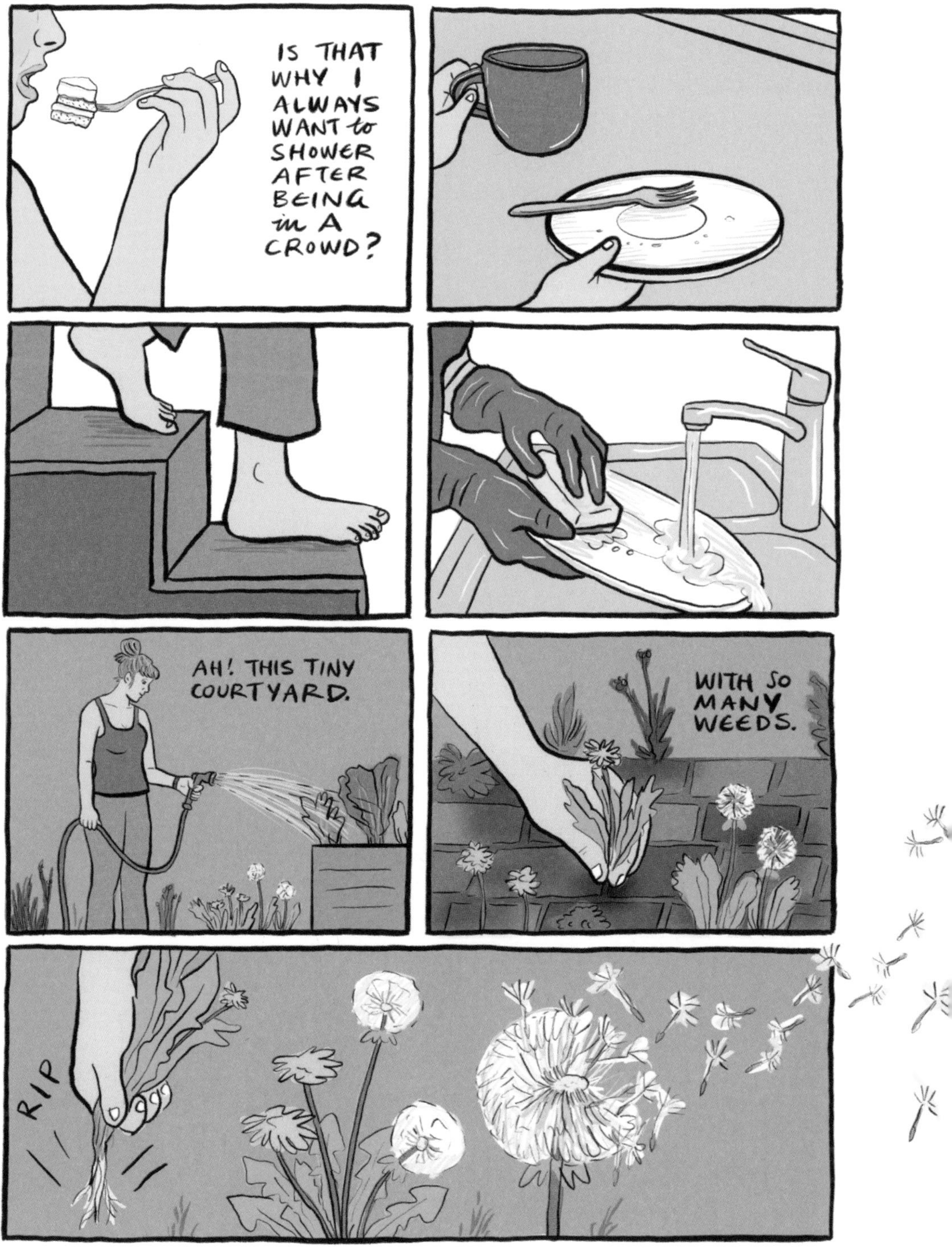
IS THAT WHY I ALWAYS WANT to SHOWER AFTER BEING in A CROWD?
AH! THIS TINY COURTYARD.
WITH SO MANY WEEDS.
RIP

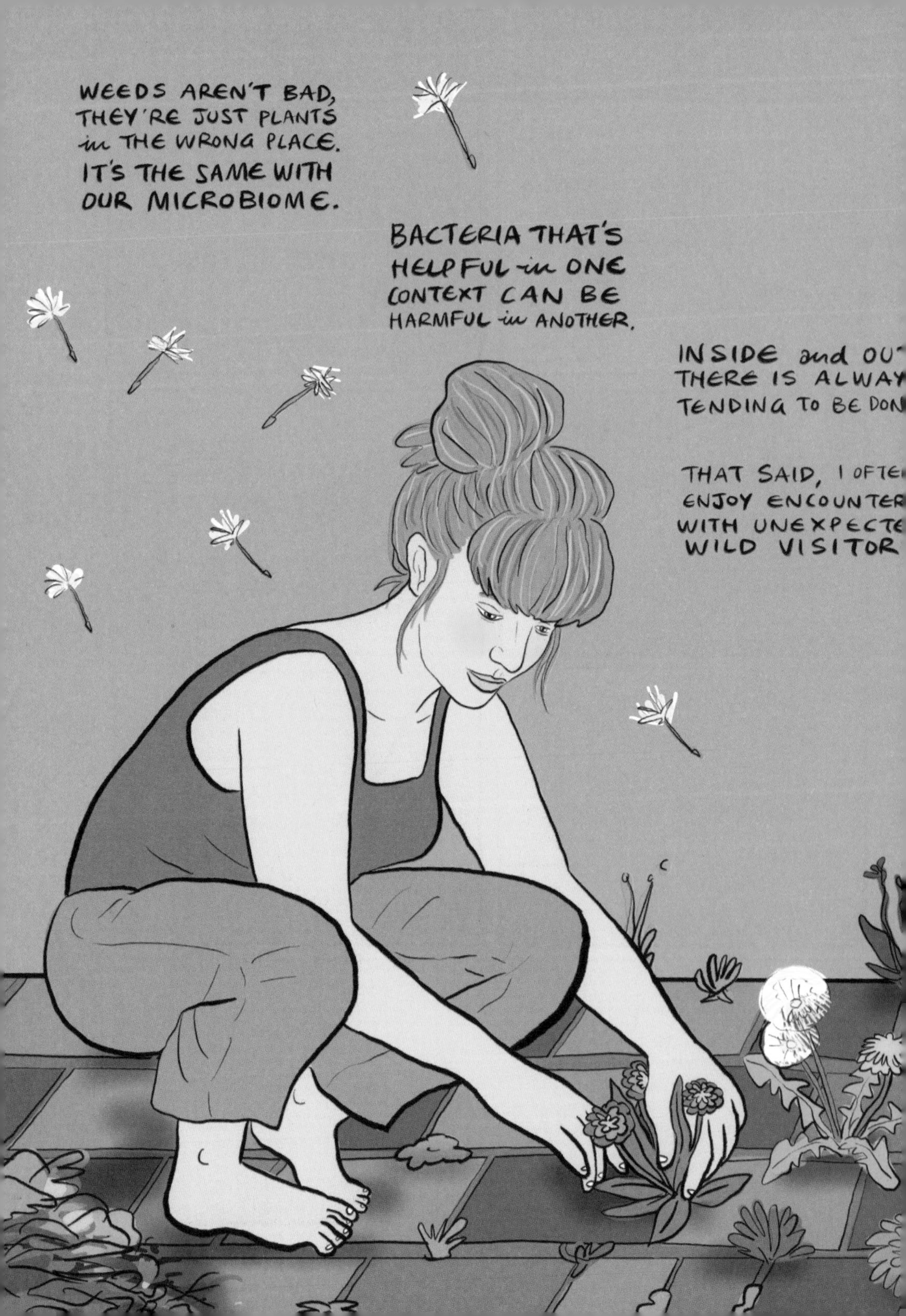
WEEDS AREN'T BAD, THEY'RE JUST PLANTS in THE WRONG PLACE.
IT'S THE SAME WITH OUR MICROBIOME.
BACTERIA THAT'S HELPFUL in ONE CONTEXT CAN BE HARMFUL in ANOTHER.
INSIDE and OU
THERE IS ALWAY
TENDING TO BE DON
THAT SAID, I OFTE
ENJOY ENCOUNTER
WITH UNEXPECTE
WILD VISITOR

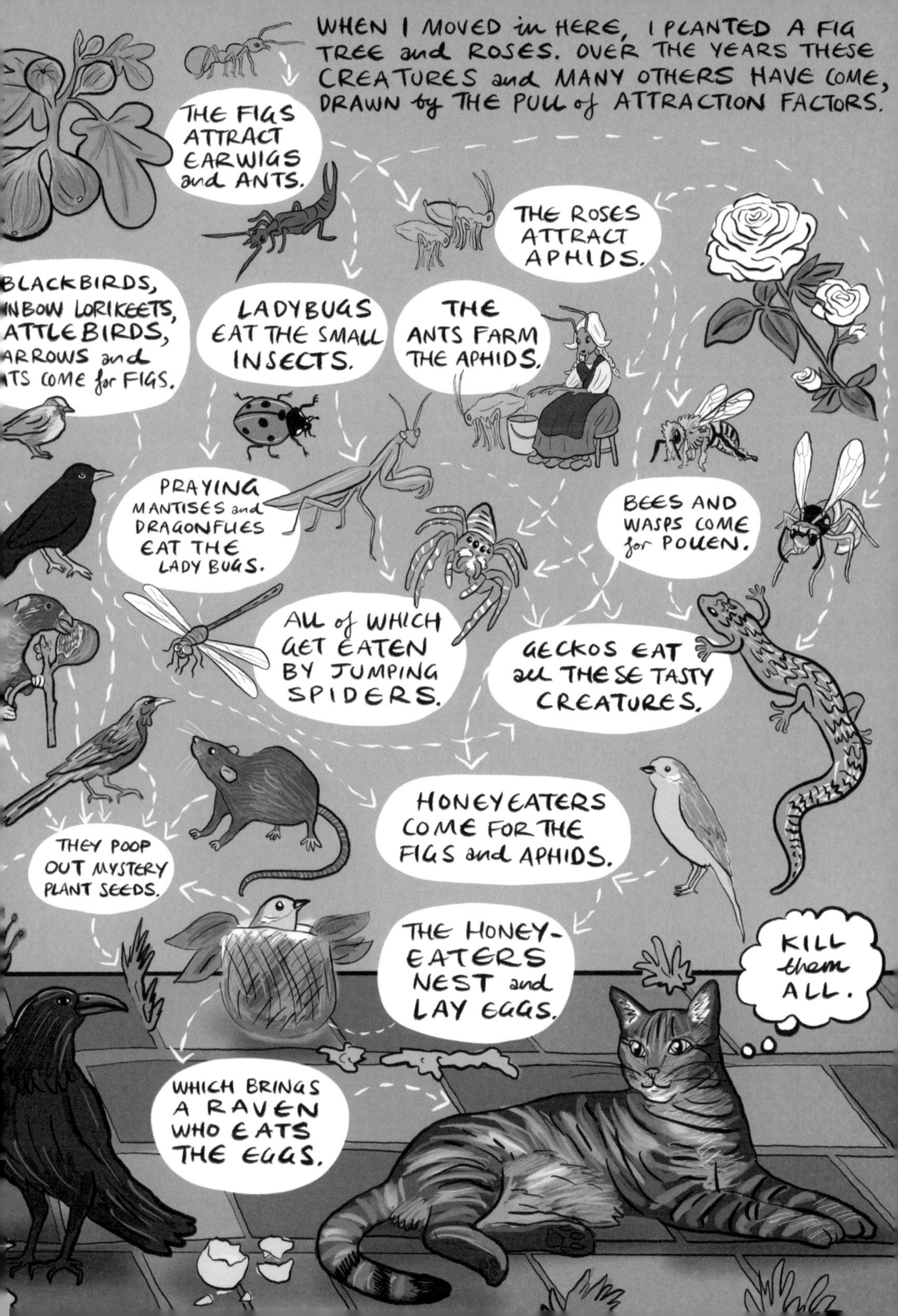
WHEN I MOVED in HERE, I PLANTED A FIG TREE and ROSES. OVER THE YEARS THESE CREATURES and MANY OTHERS HAVE COME, DRAWN by THE PULL of ATTRACTION FACTORS.
THE FIGS ATTRACT EARWIGS and ANTS.
THE ROSES ATTRACT APHIDS.
BLACKBIRDS, INBOW LORIKEETS, ATTLEBIRDS, ARROWS and TS COME for FIGS.
LADYBUGS EAT THE SMALL INSECTS.
THE ANTS FARM THE APHIDS.
PRAYING MANTISES and DRAGONFLIES EAT THE LADY BUGS.
BEES AND WASPS COME for POLLEN.
ALL of WHICH GET EATEN BY JUMPING SPIDERS.
GECKOS EAT all THESE TASTY CREATURES.
HONEYEATERS COME FOR THE FIGS and APHIDS.
THEY POOP OUT MYSTERY PLANT SEEDS.
THE HONEY-EATERS NEST and LAY EGGS.
KILL them ALL.
WHICH BRINGS A RAVEN WHO EATS THE EGGS.

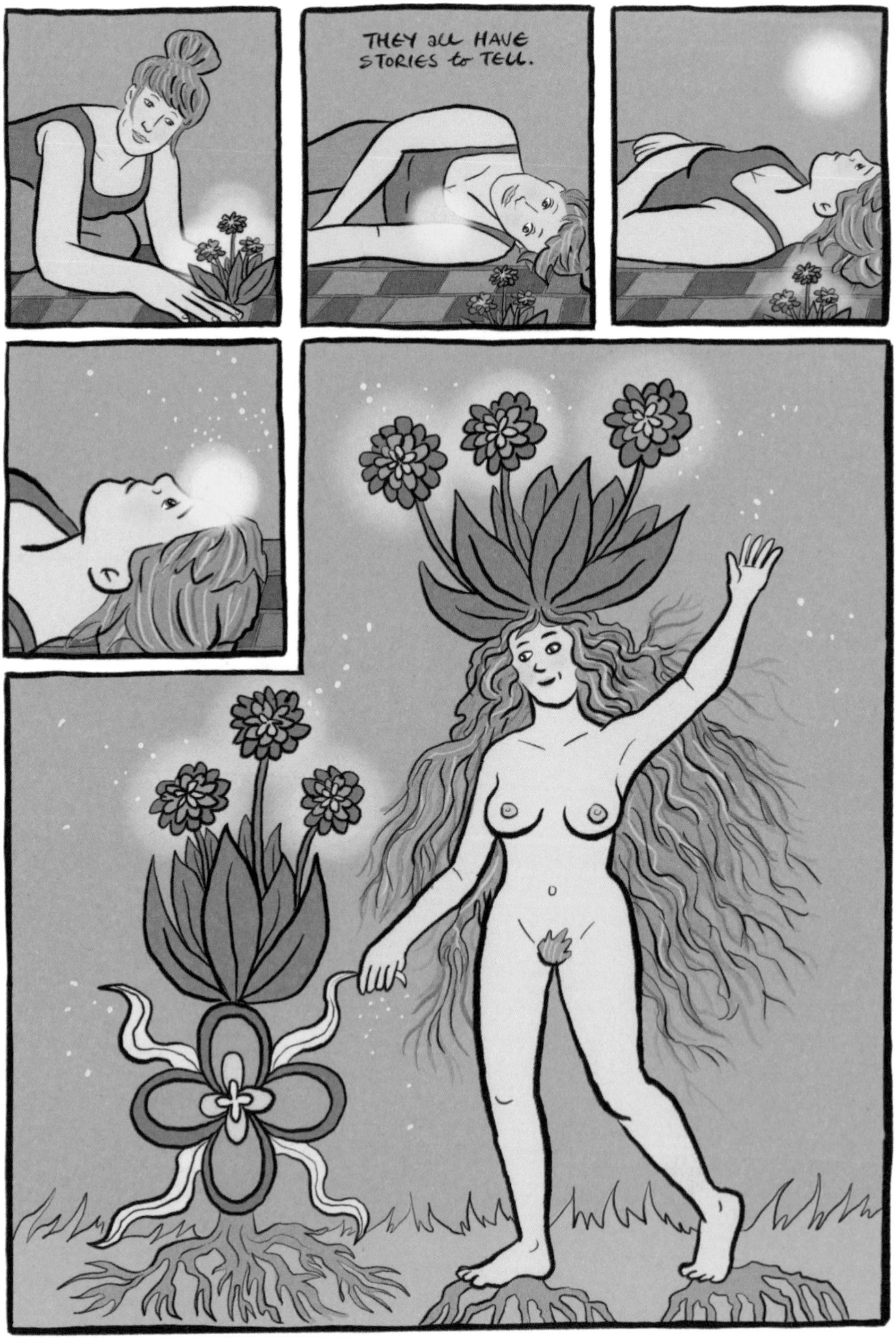
THEY all HAVE STORIES to TELL.

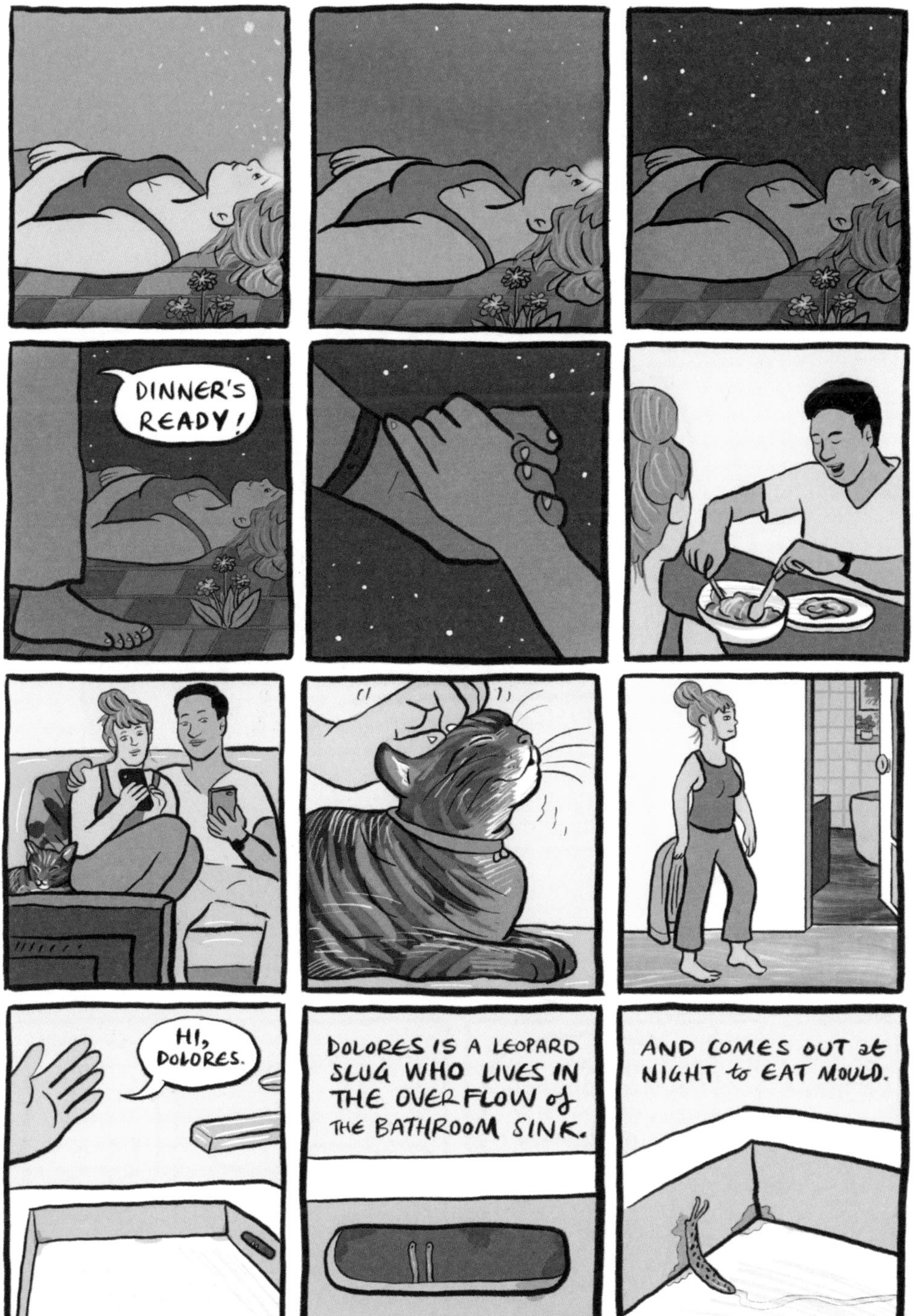
DINNER'S READY!
HI, DOLORES.
DOLORES IS A LEOPARD SLUG WHO LIVES IN THE OVERFLOW of THE BATHROOM SINK.
AND COMES OUT at NIGHT to EAT MOULD.

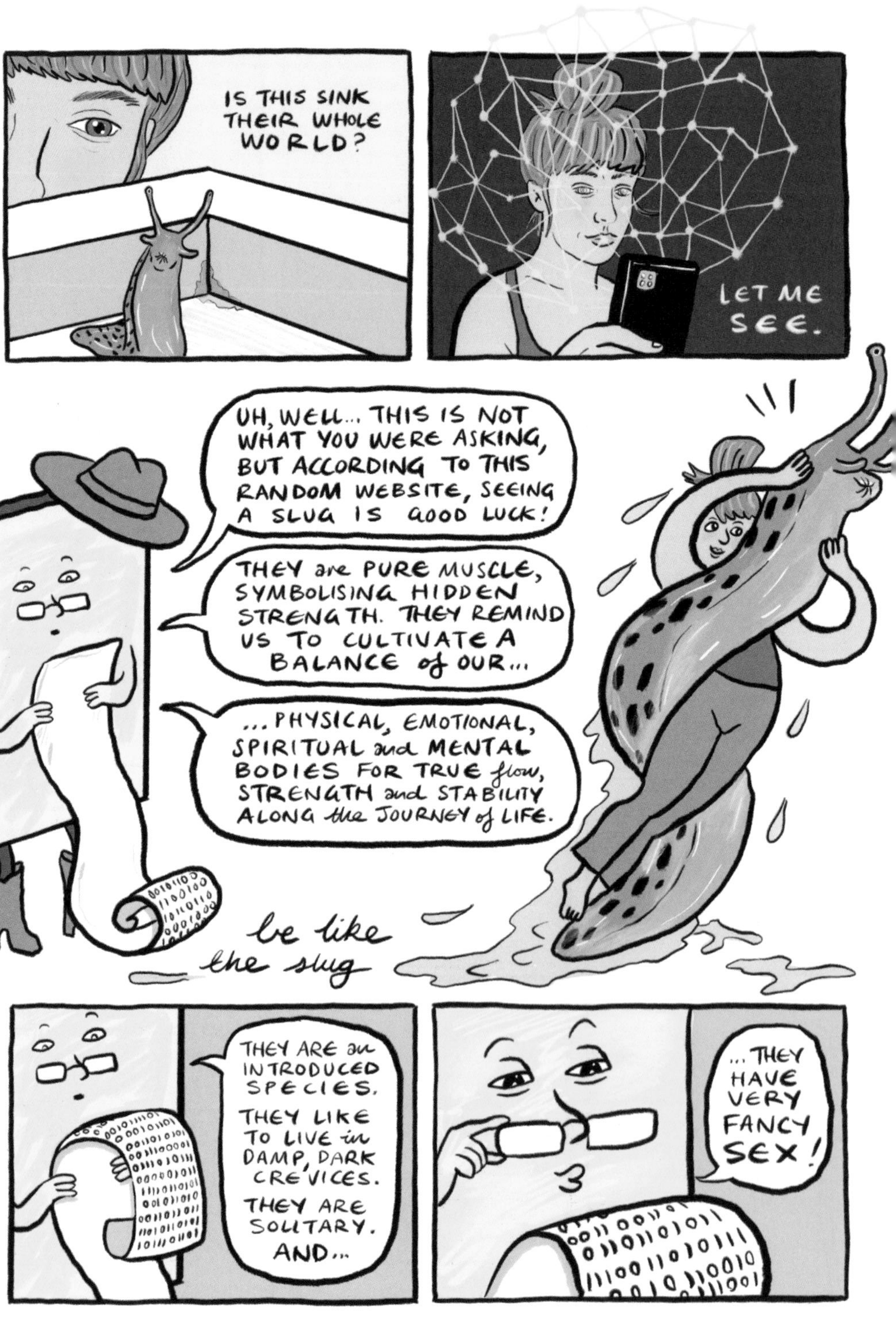
IS THIS SINK THEIR WHOLE WORLD?
LET ME SEE.
UH, WELL... THIS IS NOT WHAT YOU WERE ASKING, BUT ACCORDING TO THIS RANDOM WEBSITE, SEEING A SLUG IS GOOD LUCK!
THEY are PURE MUSCLE, SYMBOLISING HIDDEN STRENGTH. THEY REMIND US TO CULTIVATE A BALANCE of OUR...
...PHYSICAL, EMOTIONAL, SPIRITUAL and MENTAL BODIES FOR TRUE flow, STRENGTH and STABILITY ALONG the JOURNEY of LIFE.
be like the slug
THEY ARE an INTRODUCED SPECIES.
THEY LIKE TO LIVE in DAMP, DARK CREVICES.
THEY ARE SOLITARY.
AND...
...THEY HAVE VERY FANCY SEX!

THEY COURT for HOURS, CIRCLING and LICKING each OTHER.
THEN THEY CLIMB UP HIGH, ENTWINE and SLIDE DOWN A THICK STRING of MUCUS.
FINALLY, BIG FRILLY PENISES ERUPT FROM THEIR HEADS. THEY ENFOLD and TRANSFER SPERM.
LATER, THEY'LL BOTH LAY HUNDREDS of LITTLE EGGS.
WHAT SPECTACULAR DICKHEADS!

SO MANY COMMON THINGS ARE WAY MORE WONDERFUL and STRANGE than I REALISE.

I'VE SHARED BATHROOMS WITH SLUGS BEFORE.

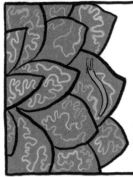

IN MY LAST BATHROOM THERE WAS KINGSTON, WHO ATE PATTERNS ALL OVER MY SUCCULENTS.

YOU'RE A TRUE ARTIST!

AND IN A PREVIOUS HOUSE THERE WAS FRANCIS, WHO LIVED IN THE SHOWER.

LOOK!

MY HOUSEMATE WASN'T A FAN.

UGH! GROSS!

WE NEED TO CLEAN THIS UP!

258

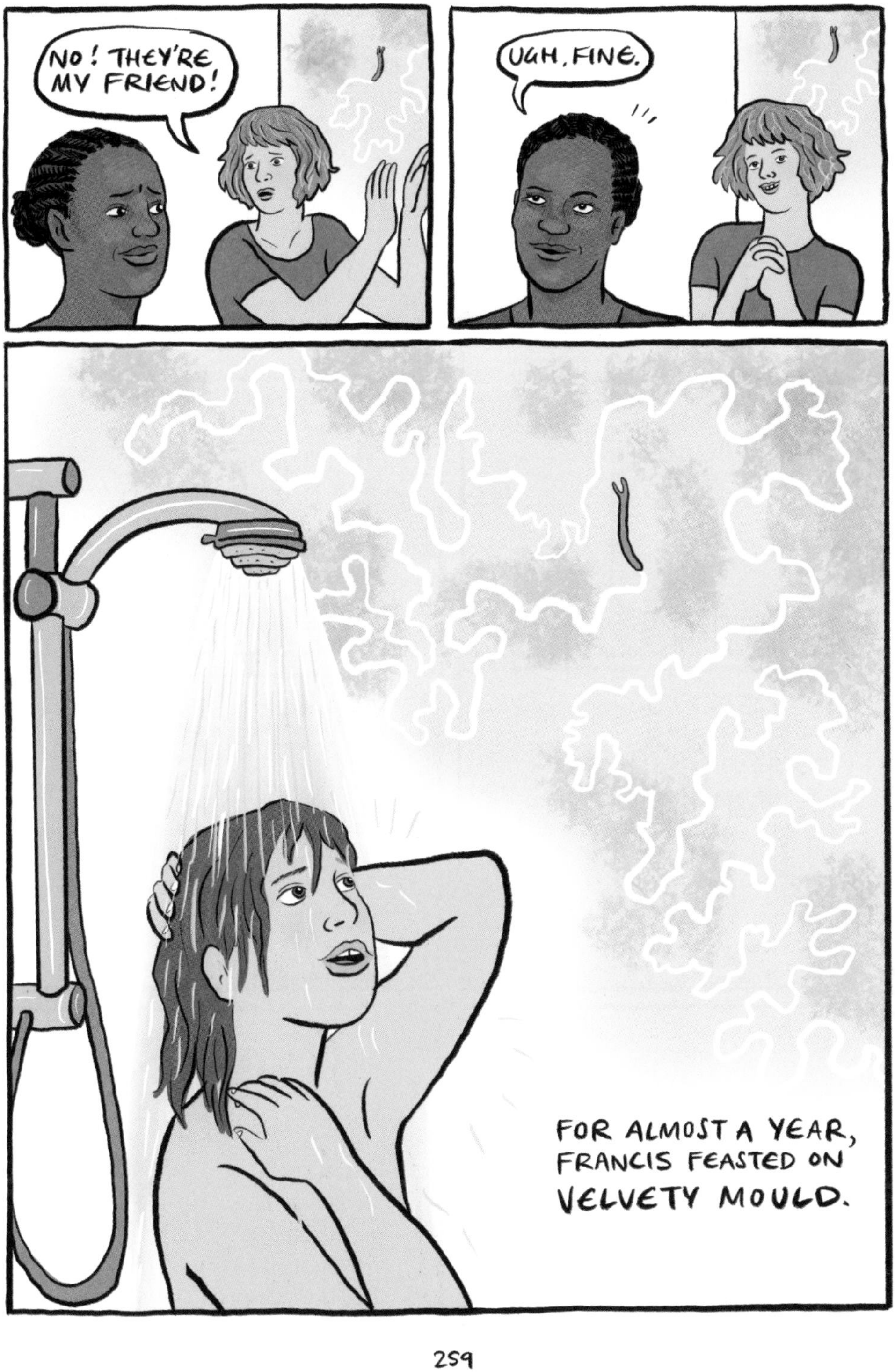
NO! THEY'RE MY FRIEND!
UGH, FINE.
FOR ALMOST A YEAR, FRANCIS FEASTED ON VELVETY MOULD.

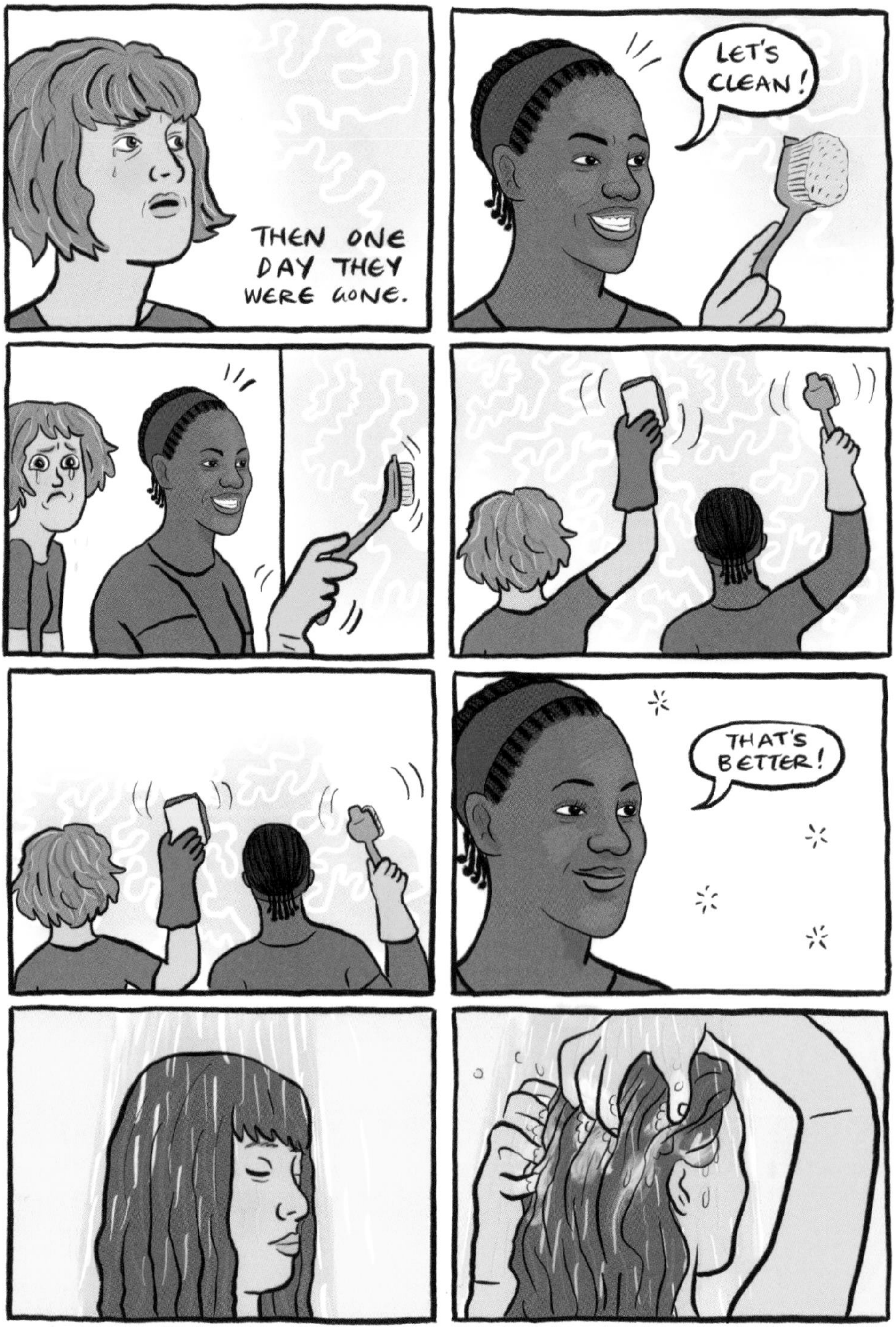
THEN ONE DAY THEY WERE GONE.
LET'S CLEAN!
THAT'S BETTER!

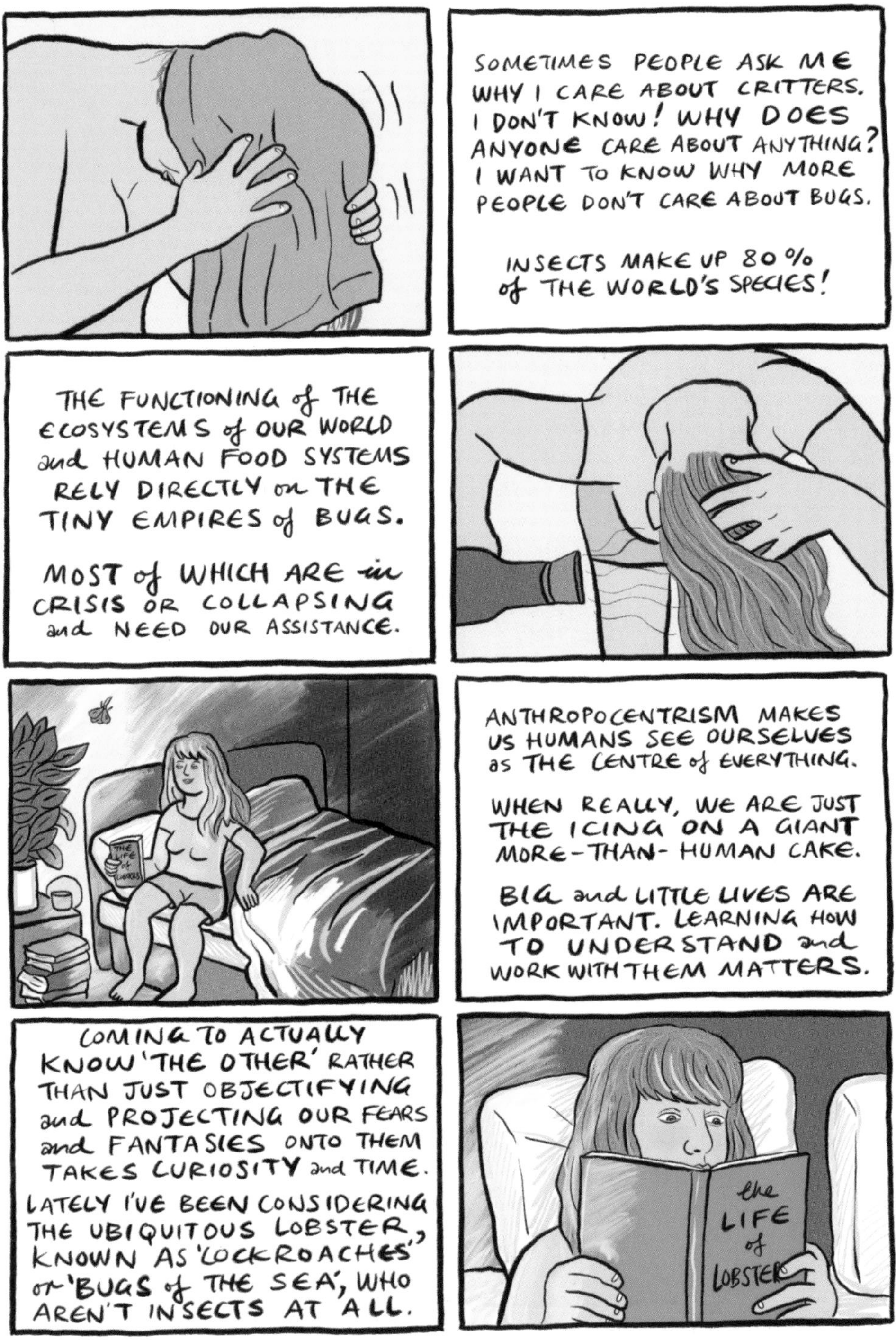
SOMETIMES PEOPLE ASK ME WHY I CARE ABOUT CRITTERS. I DON'T KNOW! WHY DOES ANYONE CARE ABOUT ANYTHING? I WANT TO KNOW WHY MORE PEOPLE DON'T CARE ABOUT BUGS.
INSECTS MAKE UP 80% of THE WORLD'S SPECIES!
THE FUNCTIONING of THE ECOSYSTEMS of OUR WORLD and HUMAN FOOD SYSTEMS RELY DIRECTLY on THE TINY EMPIRES of BUGS.
MOST of WHICH ARE in CRISIS OR COLLAPSING and NEED OUR ASSISTANCE.
ANTHROPOCENTRISM MAKES US HUMANS SEE OURSELVES as THE CENTRE of EVERYTHING.
WHEN REALLY, WE ARE JUST THE ICING ON A GIANT MORE-THAN-HUMAN CAKE.
BIG and LITTLE LIVES ARE IMPORTANT. LEARNING HOW TO UNDERSTAND and WORK WITH THEM MATTERS.
COMING TO ACTUALLY KNOW 'THE OTHER' RATHER THAN JUST OBJECTIFYING and PROJECTING OUR FEARS and FANTASIES ONTO THEM TAKES CURIOSITY and TIME.
LATELY I'VE BEEN CONSIDERING THE UBIQUITOUS LOBSTER, KNOWN AS 'COCKROACHES' or 'BUGS of THE SEA', WHO AREN'T INSECTS AT ALL.
the LIFE of LOBSTER

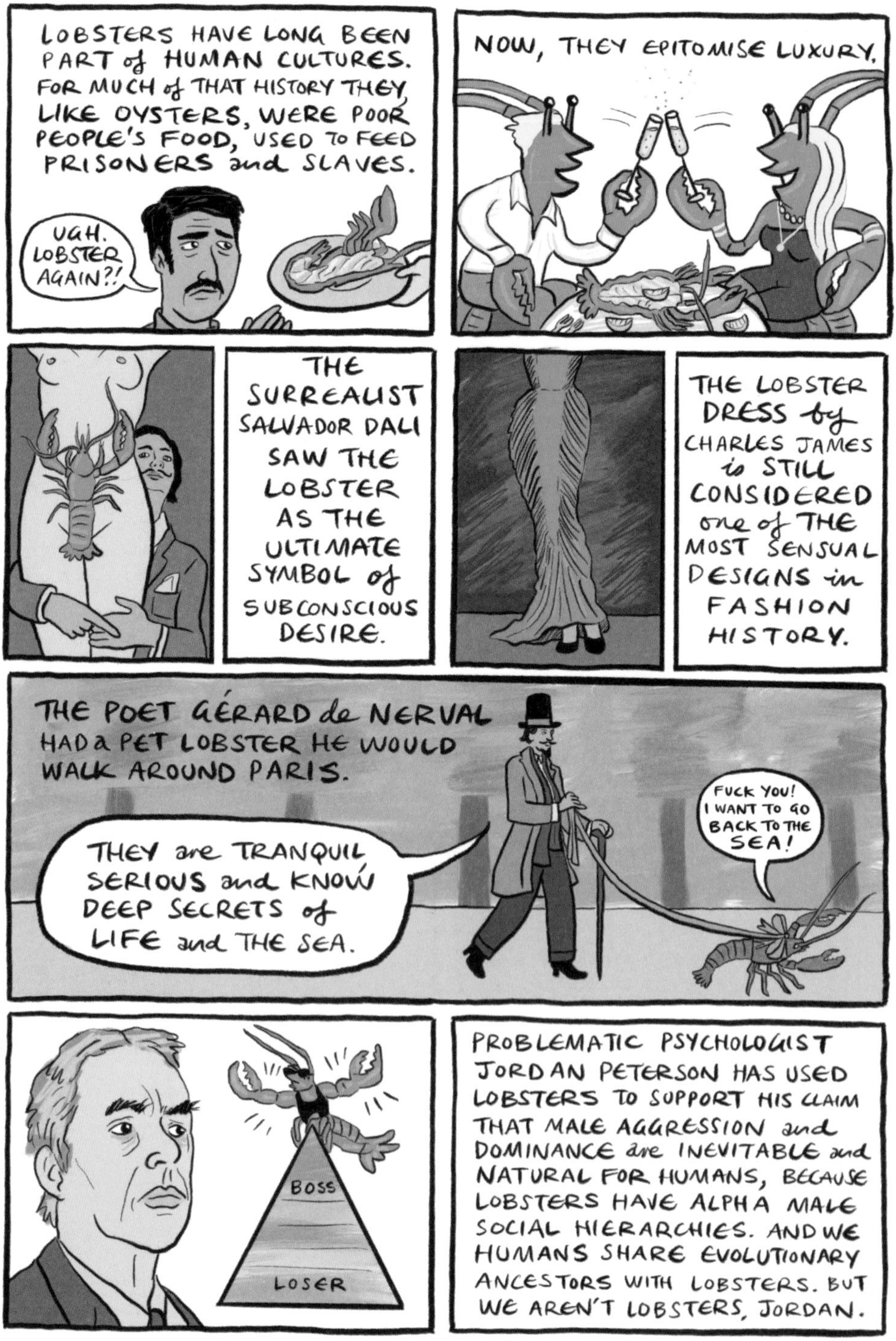
LOBSTERS HAVE LONG BEEN PART of HUMAN CULTURES. FOR MUCH of THAT HISTORY THEY, LIKE OYSTERS, WERE POOR PEOPLE'S FOOD, USED TO FEED PRISONERS and SLAVES.
UGH. LOBSTER AGAIN?!
NOW, THEY EPITOMISE LUXURY.
THE SURREALIST SALVADOR DALI SAW THE LOBSTER AS THE ULTIMATE SYMBOL of SUBCONSCIOUS DESIRE.
THE LOBSTER DRESS by CHARLES JAMES is STILL CONSIDERED one of THE MOST SENSUAL DESIGNS in FASHION HISTORY.
THE POET GÉRARD de NERVAL HAD a PET LOBSTER HE WOULD WALK AROUND PARIS.
THEY are TRANQUIL SERIOUS and KNOW DEEP SECRETS of LIFE and THE SEA.
FUCK YOU! I WANT TO GO BACK TO THE SEA!
BOSS
LOSER
PROBLEMATIC PSYCHOLOGIST JORDAN PETERSON HAS USED LOBSTERS TO SUPPORT HIS CLAIM THAT MALE AGGRESSION and DOMINANCE are INEVITABLE and NATURAL FOR HUMANS, BECAUSE LOBSTERS HAVE ALPHA MALE SOCIAL HIERARCHIES. AND WE HUMANS SHARE EVOLUTIONARY ANCESTORS WITH LOBSTERS. BUT WE AREN'T LOBSTERS, JORDAN.

WE HAVE SO MANY SHARED EVOLUTIONARY ANCESTORS, WITH VARIED WAYS of ORGANISING SOCIETY. JUST AS HUMANS DO!

WE COULD EASILY JUSTIFY ORGANISING AROUND AN ALPHA QUEEN, LIKE ANTS DO, WHERE SHE IS FERTILISED by MANY MALES. AND ONCE THEY'VE DONE THEIR JOB, MALES ARE DRIVEN OUT of THE COLONY TO DIE ALONE.

BRR
BRR
SCRAM!

SOME of WHAT I THOUGHT I KNEW ABOUT LOBSTERS HAS TURNED OUT TO BE MYTH...

... LOBSTERS FALL in LOVE and MATE FOR LIFE. YOU KNOW WHAT? YOU CAN ACTUALLY SEE OLD LOBSTER COUPLES WALKING AROUND THEIR TANK, YOU KNOW, HOLDING CLAWS.

- PHOEBE from THE '90s TV SHOW 'FRIENDS'

THE REALITIES of LOBSTER LIVES ARE MUCH MORE CREATIVE.

TAKE THEIR SEX LIVES FOR EXAMPLE ...

TO PARAPHRASE SCIENCE WRITER MATT SONIAK, they HAVE an ELABORATE SYSTEM of SERIAL MONOGAMY.

FEMALES FIND THE DOMINANT MALE in THE AREA.

THEN FORM A CONGA LINE ...

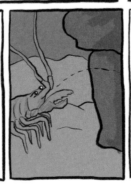

... STAGGERED ACCORDING TO THE TIMING of THEIR MOULTING.

263

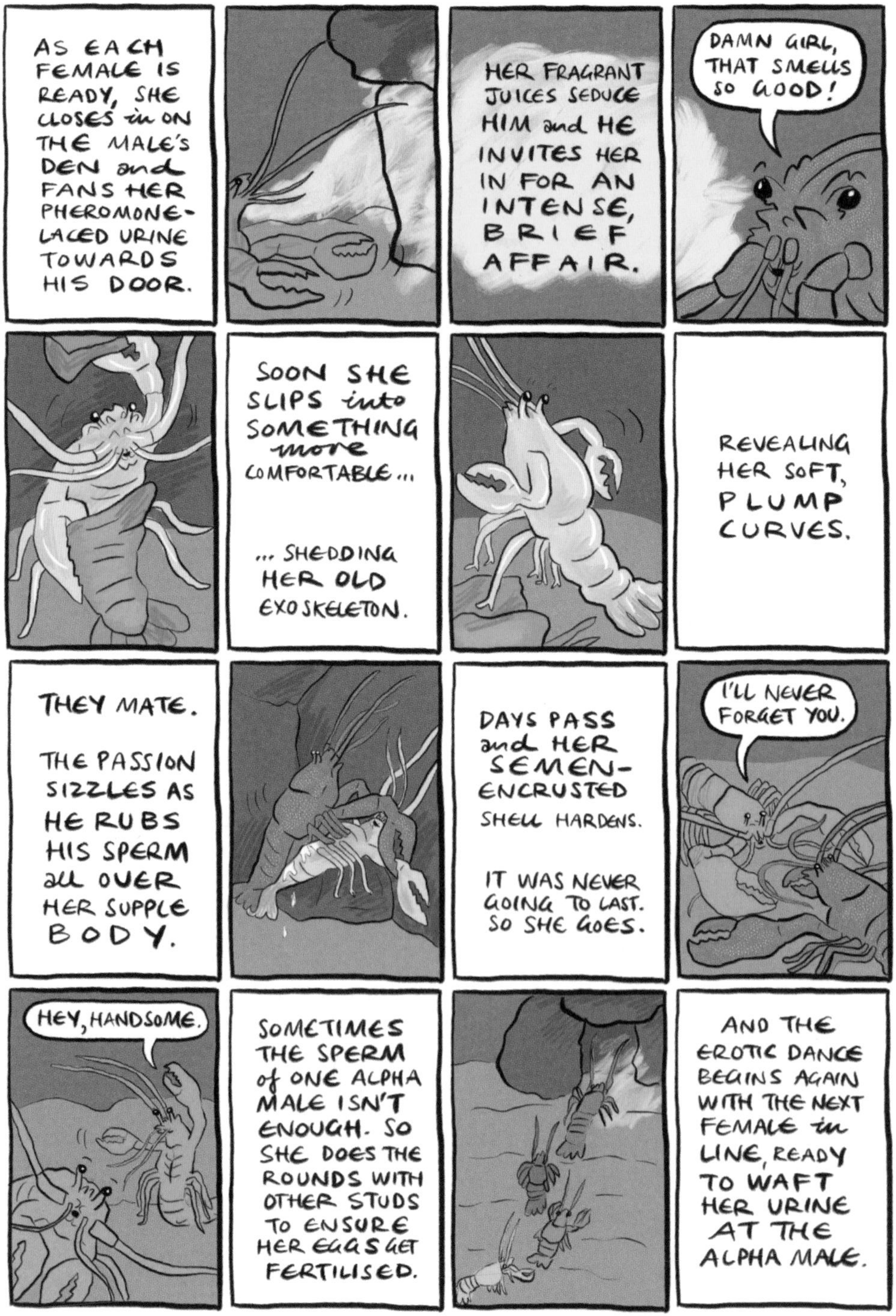
AS EACH FEMALE IS READY, SHE CLOSES in ON THE MALE'S DEN and FANS HER PHEROMONE-LACED URINE TOWARDS HIS DOOR.
HER FRAGRANT JUICES SEDUCE HIM and HE INVITES HER IN FOR AN INTENSE, BRIEF AFFAIR.
DAMN GIRL, THAT SMELLS SO GOOD!
SOON SHE SLIPS into SOMETHING more COMFORTABLE...
...SHEDDING HER OLD EXOSKELETON.
REVEALING HER SOFT, PLUMP CURVES.
THEY MATE.
THE PASSION SIZZLES AS HE RUBS HIS SPERM all OVER HER SUPPLE BODY.
DAYS PASS and HER SEMEN-ENCRUSTED SHELL HARDENS.
IT WAS NEVER GOING TO LAST. SO SHE GOES.
I'LL NEVER FORGET YOU.
HEY, HANDSOME.
SOMETIMES THE SPERM of ONE ALPHA MALE ISN'T ENOUGH. SO SHE DOES THE ROUNDS WITH OTHER STUDS TO ENSURE HER EGGS GET FERTILISED.
AND THE EROTIC DANCE BEGINS AGAIN WITH THE NEXT FEMALE in LINE, READY TO WAFT HER URINE AT THE ALPHA MALE.

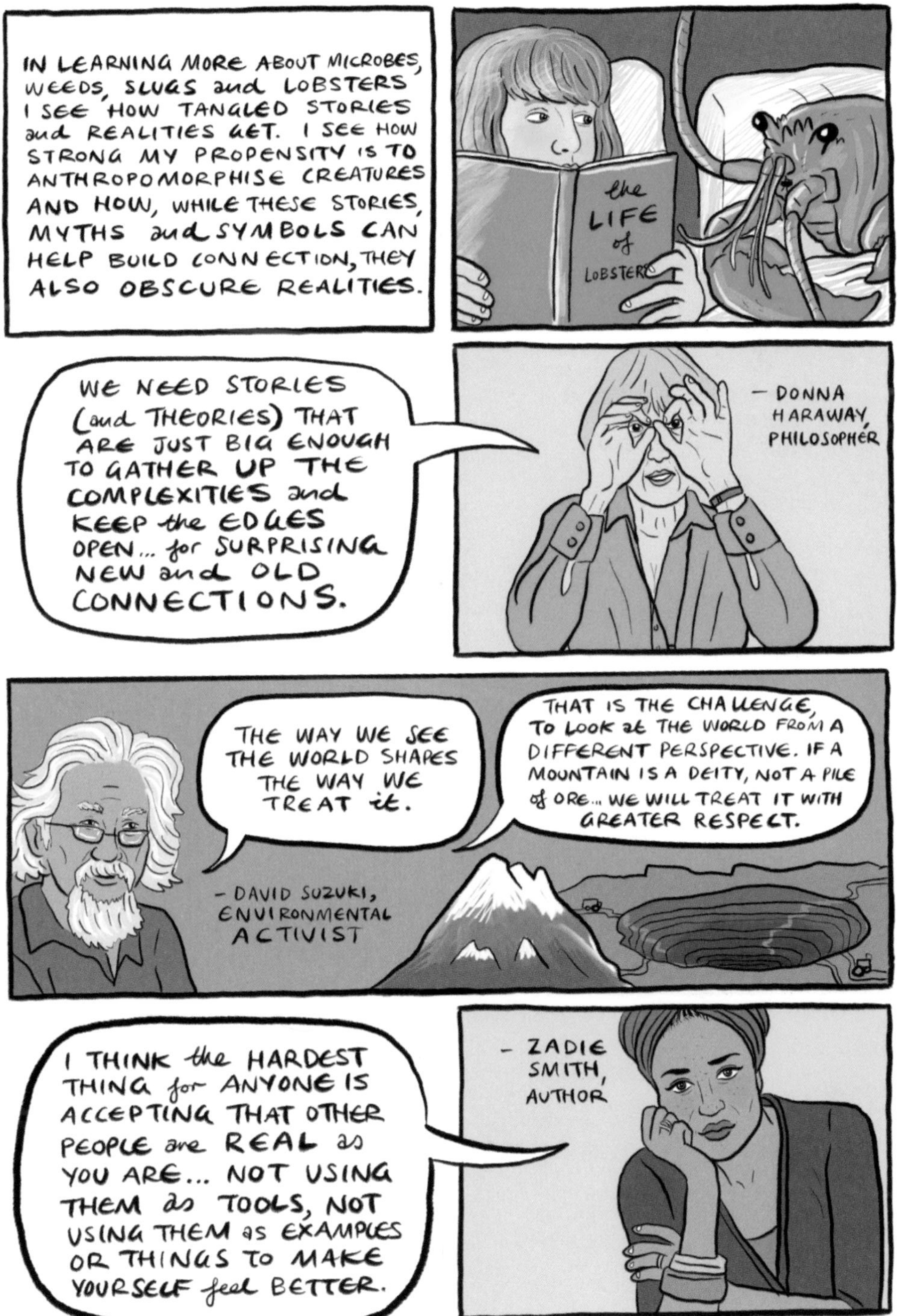
IN LEARNING MORE ABOUT MICROBES, WEEDS, SLUGS and LOBSTERS I SEE HOW TANGLED STORIES and REALITIES GET. I SEE HOW STRONG MY PROPENSITY IS TO ANTHROPOMORPHISE CREATURES AND HOW, WHILE THESE STORIES, MYTHS and SYMBOLS CAN HELP BUILD CONNECTION, THEY ALSO OBSCURE REALITIES.
the LIFE of LOBSTERS
WE NEED STORIES (and THEORIES) THAT ARE JUST BIG ENOUGH TO GATHER UP THE COMPLEXITIES and KEEP the EDGES OPEN... for SURPRISING NEW and OLD CONNECTIONS.
– DONNA HARAWAY, PHILOSOPHER
THE WAY WE SEE THE WORLD SHAPES THE WAY WE TREAT it.
THAT IS THE CHALLENGE, TO LOOK at THE WORLD FROM A DIFFERENT PERSPECTIVE. IF A MOUNTAIN IS A DEITY, NOT A PILE of ORE... WE WILL TREAT IT WITH GREATER RESPECT.
– DAVID SUZUKI, ENVIRONMENTAL ACTIVIST
I THINK the HARDEST THING for ANYONE IS ACCEPTING THAT OTHER PEOPLE are REAL as YOU ARE... NOT USING THEM as TOOLS, NOT USING THEM as EXAMPLES OR THINGS TO MAKE YOURSELF feel BETTER.
– ZADIE SMITH, AUTHOR

CONSIDER THIS BOGONG. I COULD SEE IT AS AN INTRUDER IN MY HOUSE and KILL IT WITH A SHOE.

I COULD BELIEVE IT'S A BAD OMEN AS MANY SUPERSTITIONS DO.

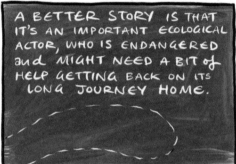

A BETTER STORY IS THAT IT'S AN IMPORTANT ECOLOGICAL ACTOR, WHO IS ENDANGERED and MIGHT NEED A BIT of HELP GETTING BACK ON ITS LONG JOURNEY HOME.

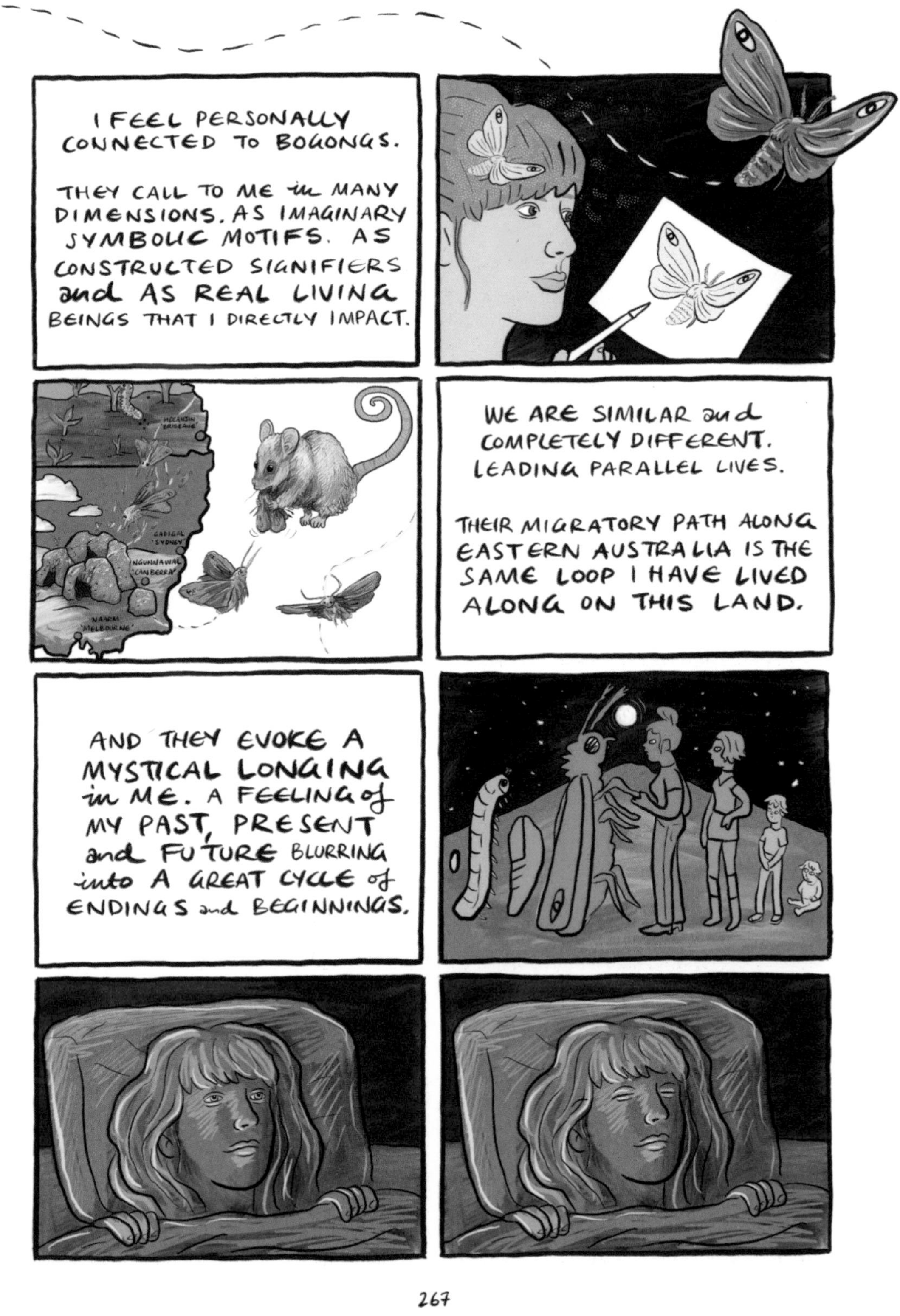
I FEEL PERSONALLY CONNECTED TO BOGONGS.
THEY CALL TO ME in MANY DIMENSIONS. AS IMAGINARY SYMBOLIC MOTIFS. AS CONSTRUCTED SIGNIFIERS and AS REAL LIVING BEINGS THAT I DIRECTLY IMPACT.
MEANJIN 'BRISBANE'
GADIGAL 'SYDNEY'
NGUNNAWAL 'CANBERRA'
NAARM 'MELBOURNE'
WE ARE SIMILAR and COMPLETELY DIFFERENT. LEADING PARALLEL LIVES.
THEIR MIGRATORY PATH ALONG EASTERN AUSTRALIA IS THE SAME LOOP I HAVE LIVED ALONG ON THIS LAND.
AND THEY EVOKE A MYSTICAL LONGING in ME. A FEELING of MY PAST, PRESENT and FUTURE BLURRING into A GREAT CYCLE of ENDINGS and BEGINNINGS.

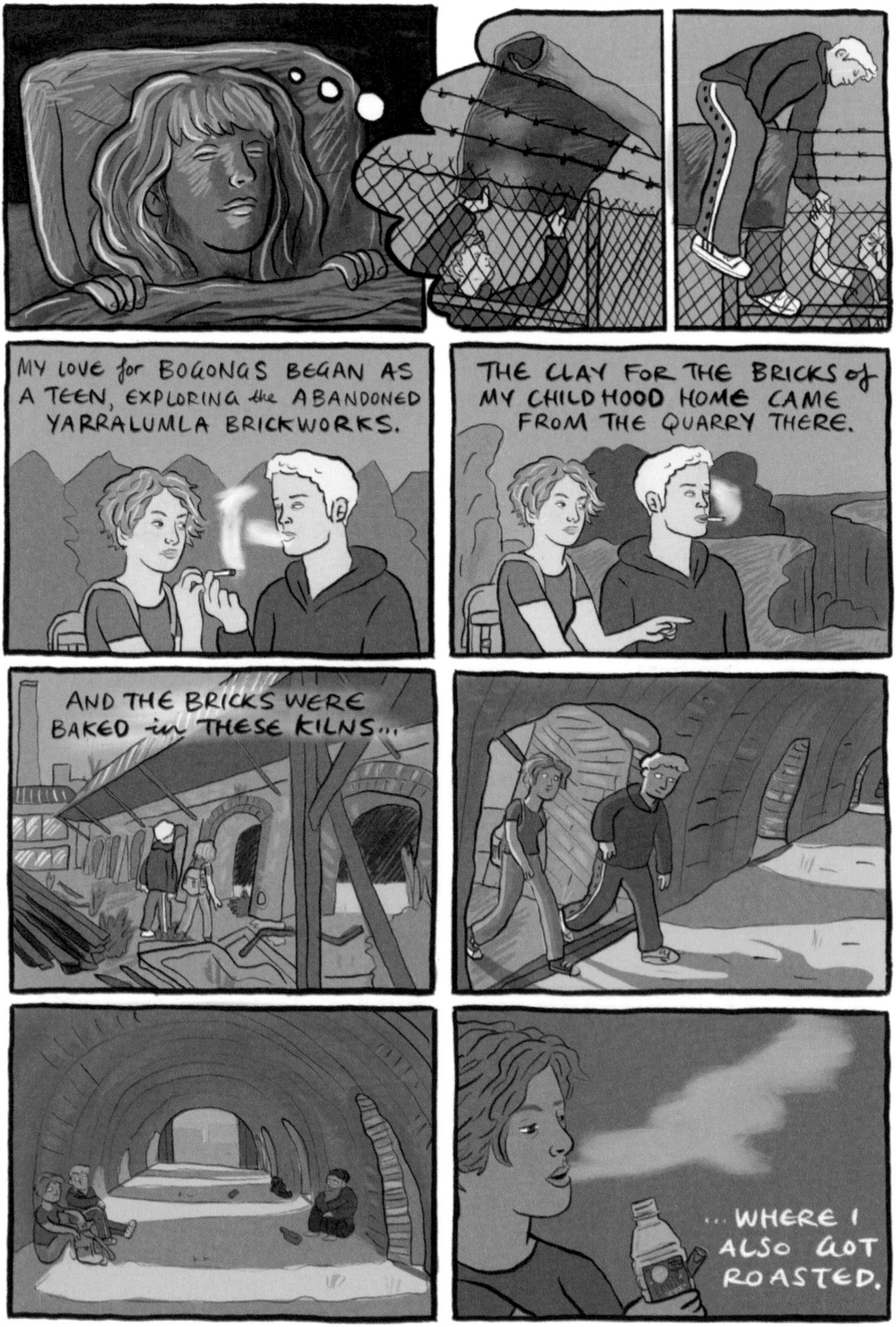
MY LOVE for BOGONGS BEGAN AS A TEEN, EXPLORING the ABANDONED YARRALUMLA BRICKWORKS.
THE CLAY FOR THE BRICKS of MY CHILDHOOD HOME CAME FROM THE QUARRY THERE.
AND THE BRICKS WERE BAKED in THESE KILNS...
...WHERE I ALSO GOT ROASTED.

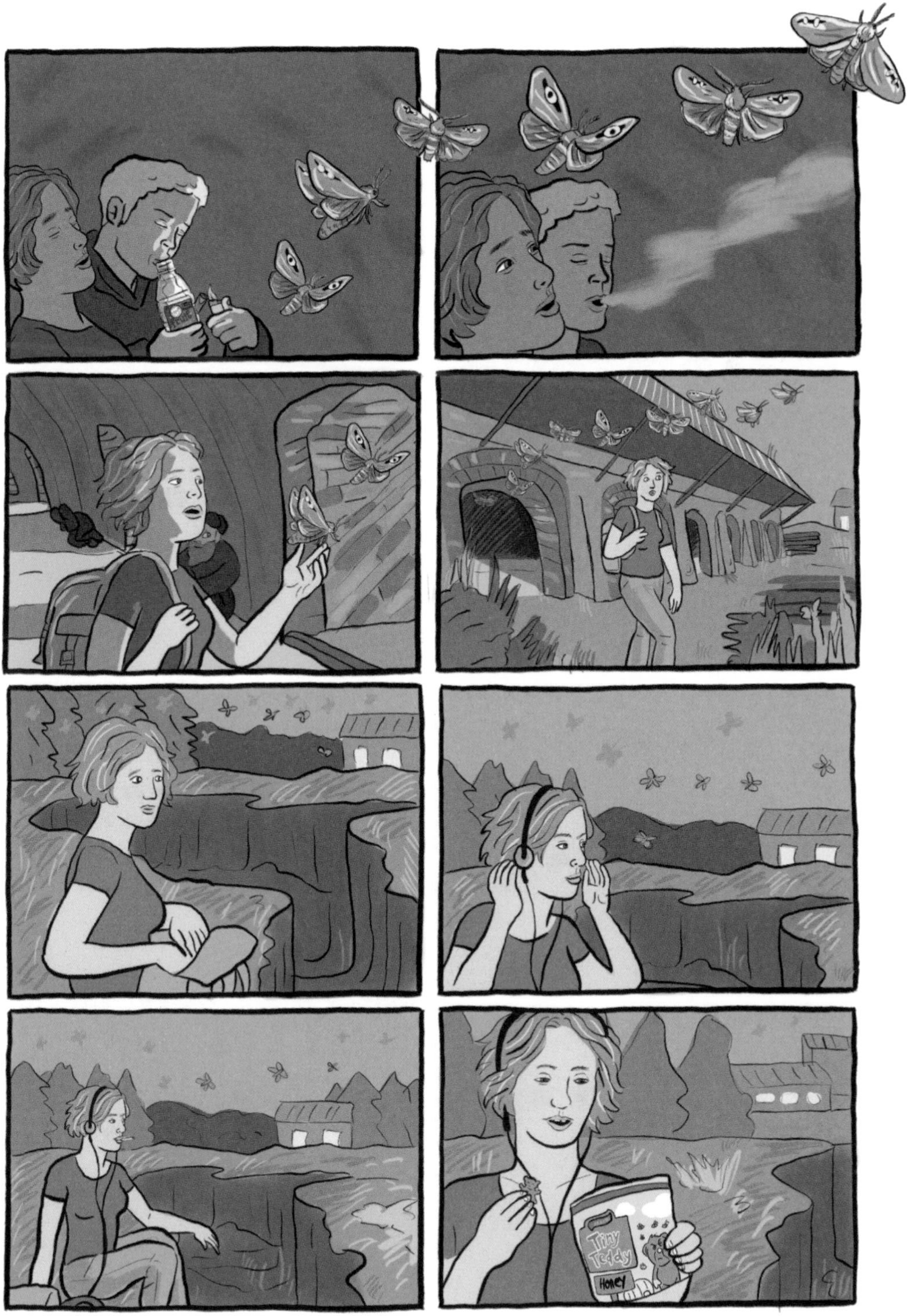
Tiny Teddy
Honey

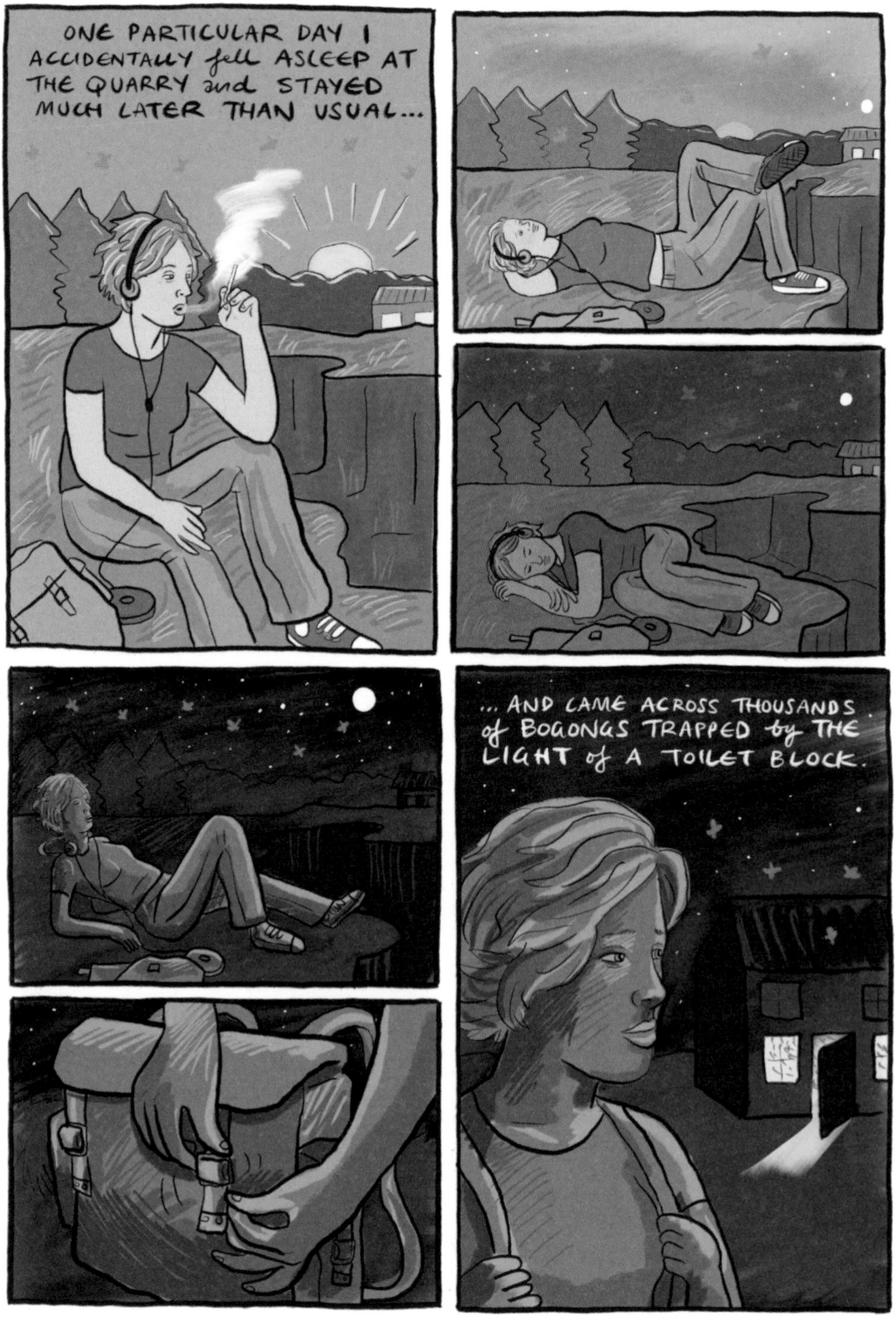
ONE PARTICULAR DAY I ACCIDENTALLY fell ASLEEP AT THE QUARRY and STAYED MUCH LATER THAN USUAL...
... AND CAME ACROSS THOUSANDS of BOGONGS TRAPPED by THE LIGHT of A TOILET BLOCK.

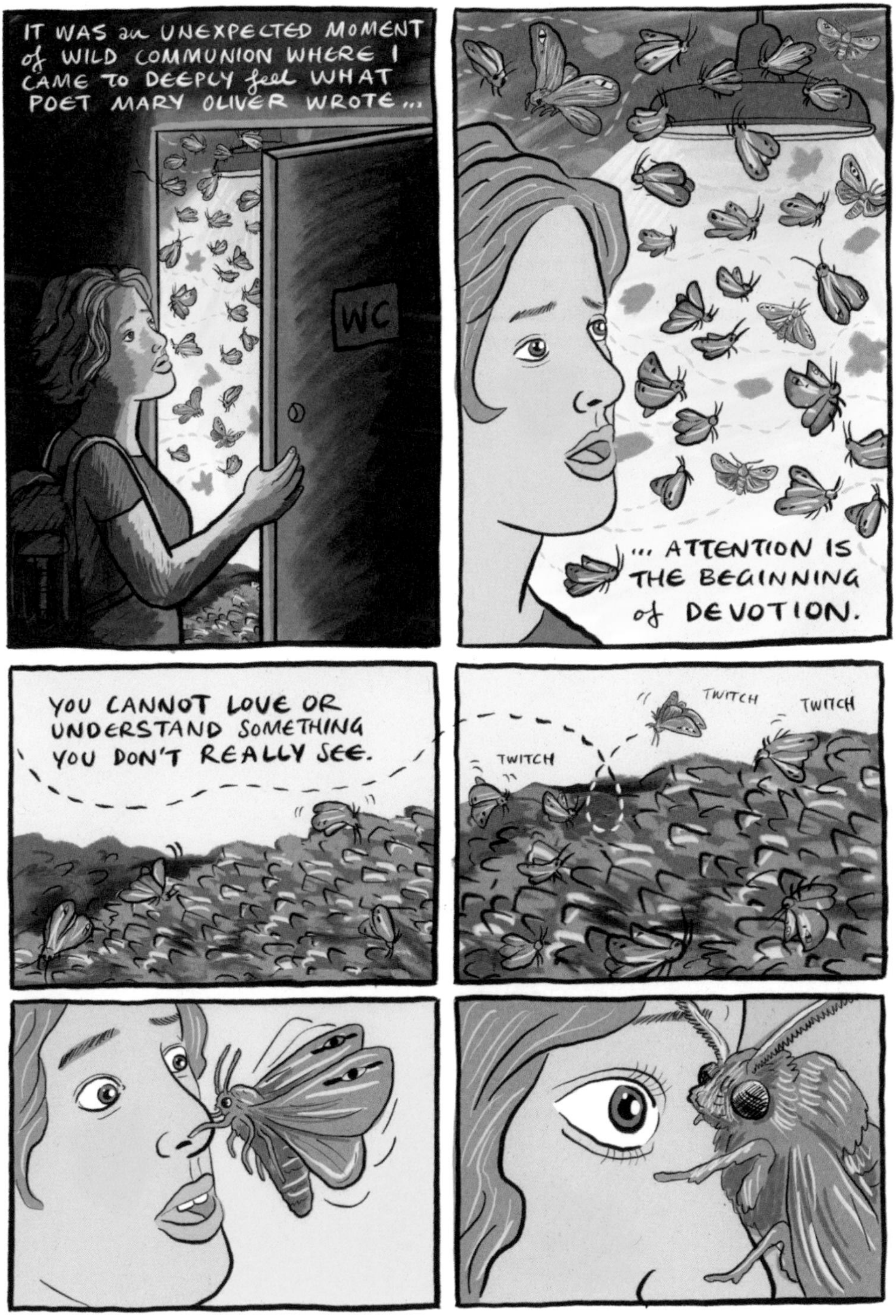

IT WAS an UNEXPECTED MOMENT of WILD COMMUNION WHERE I CAME TO DEEPLY feel WHAT POET MARY OLIVER WROTE...
WC
... ATTENTION IS THE BEGINNING of DEVOTION.
YOU CANNOT LOVE OR UNDERSTAND SOMETHING YOU DON'T REALLY SEE.
TWITCH
TWITCH
TWITCH

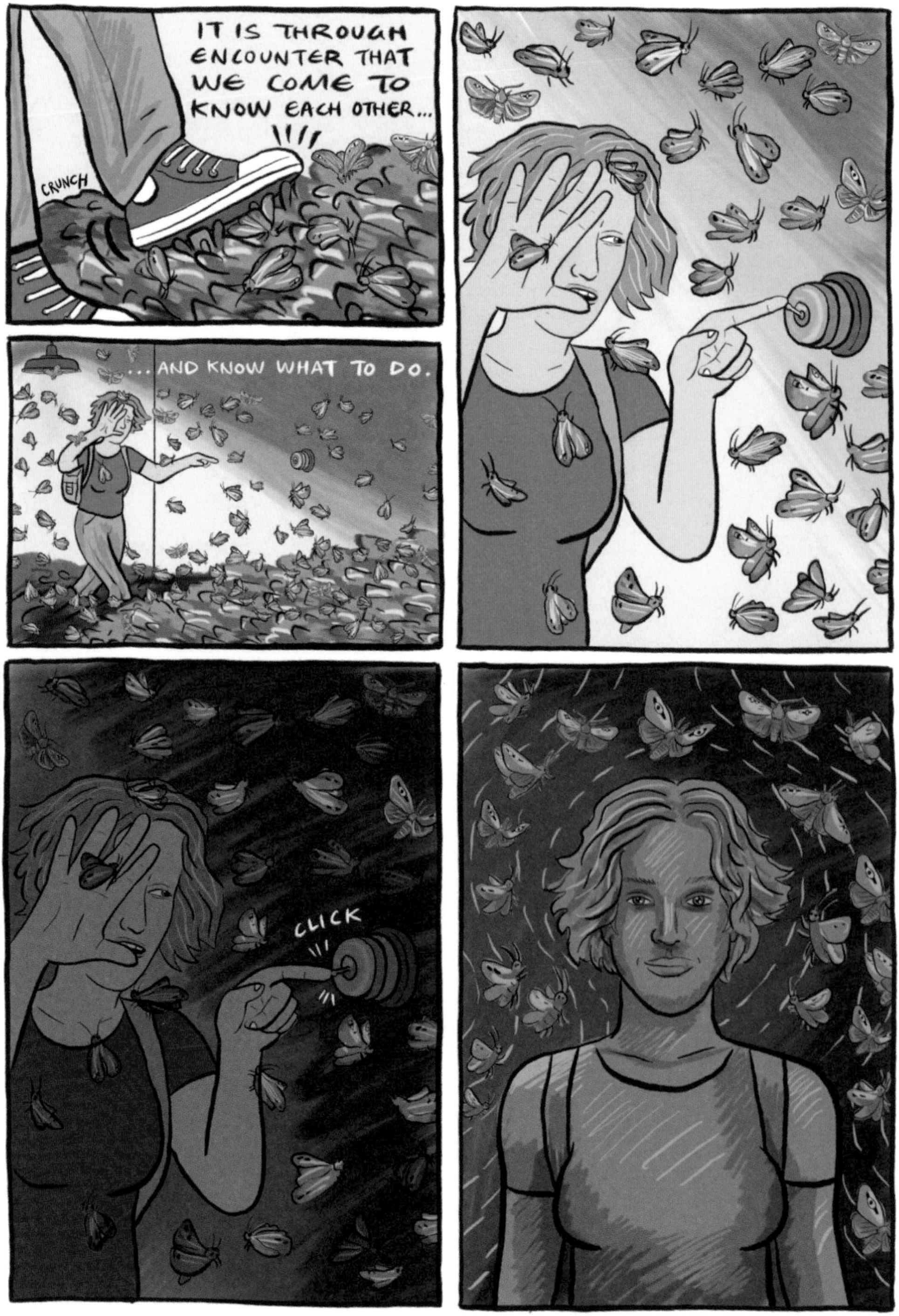
IT IS THROUGH ENCOUNTER THAT WE COME TO KNOW EACH OTHER...
CRUNCH
...AND KNOW WHAT TO DO.
CLICK

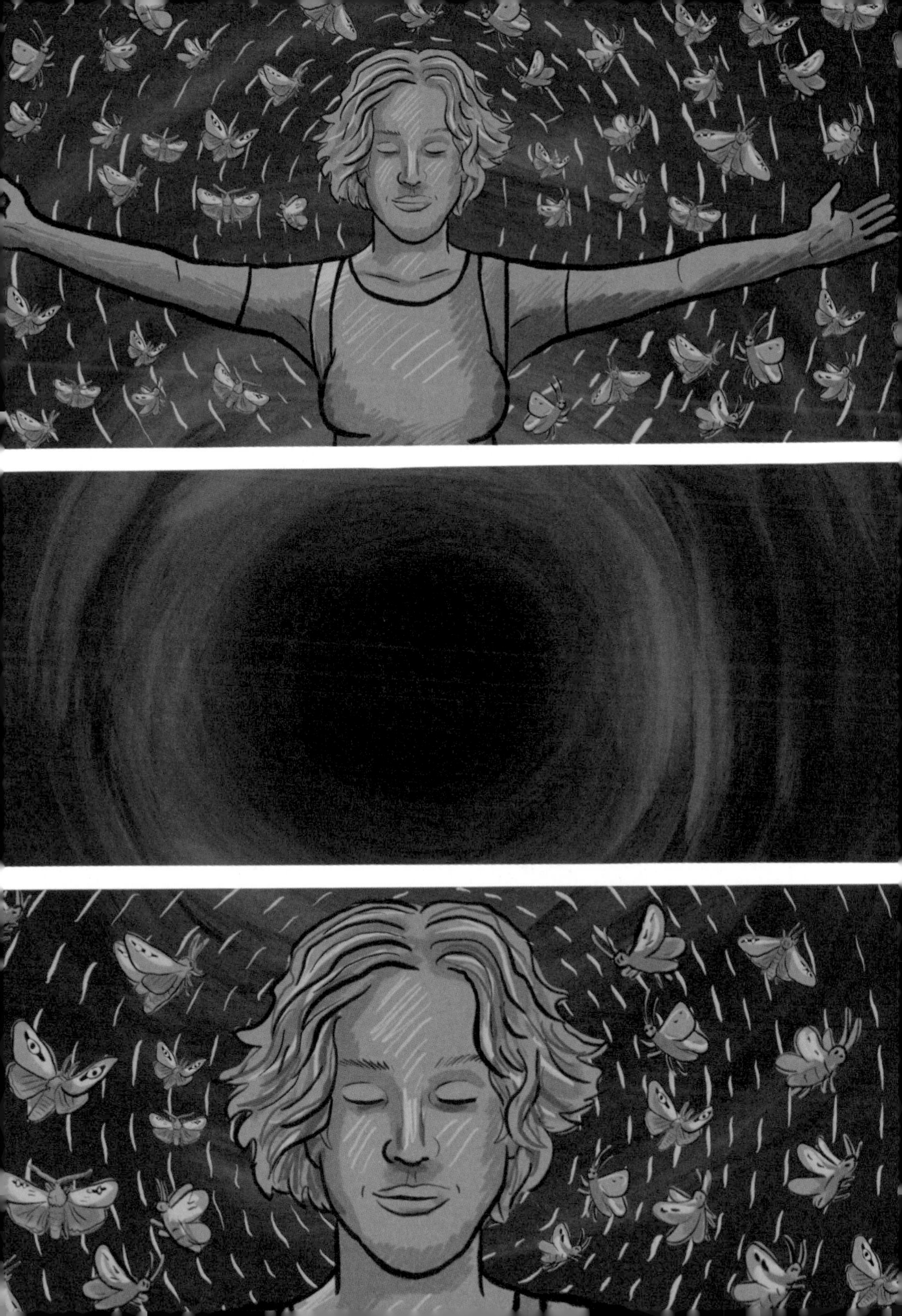

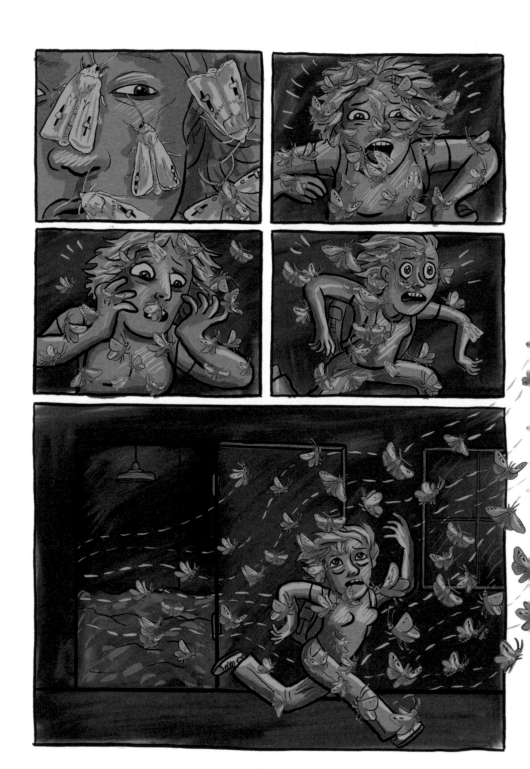

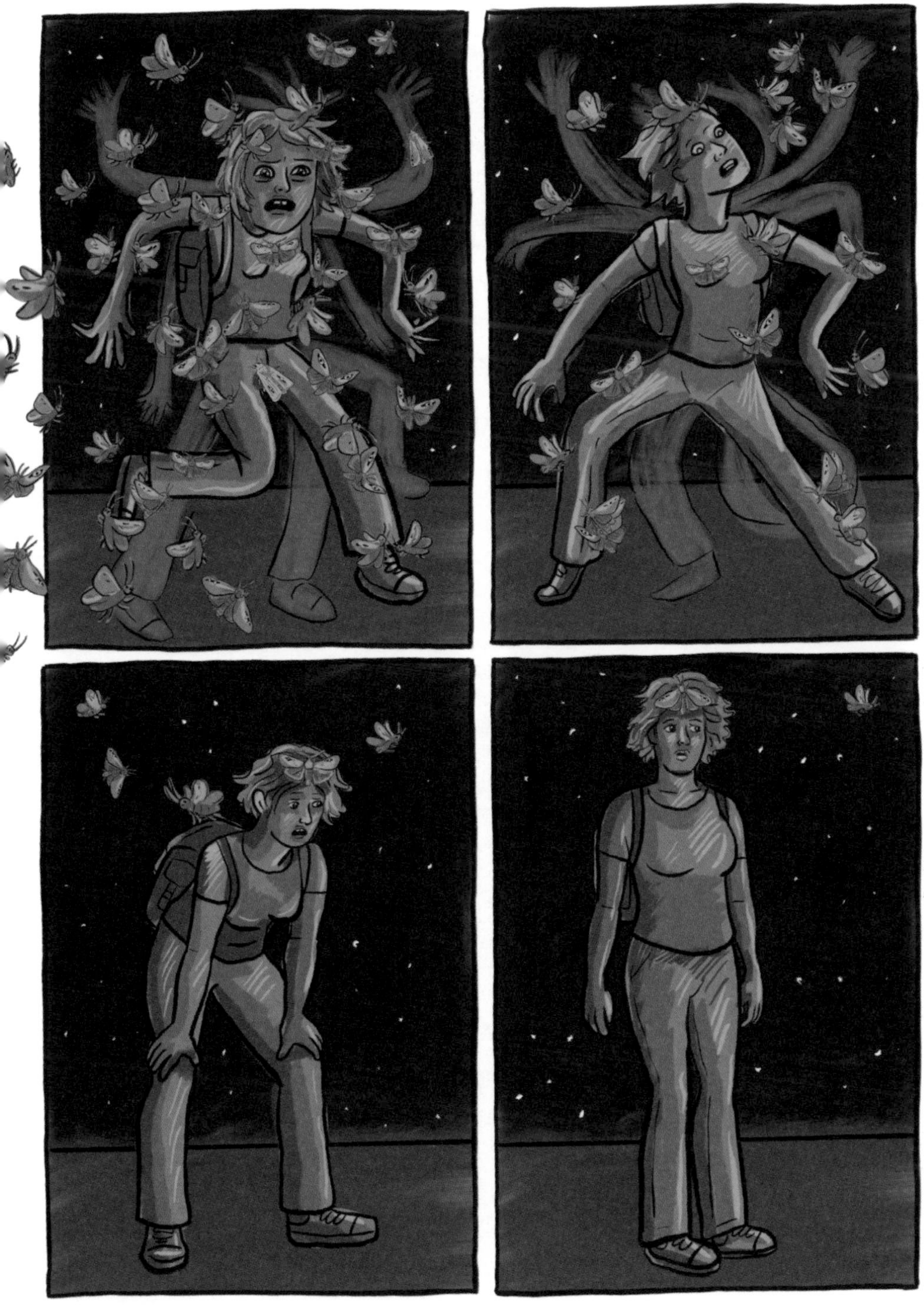

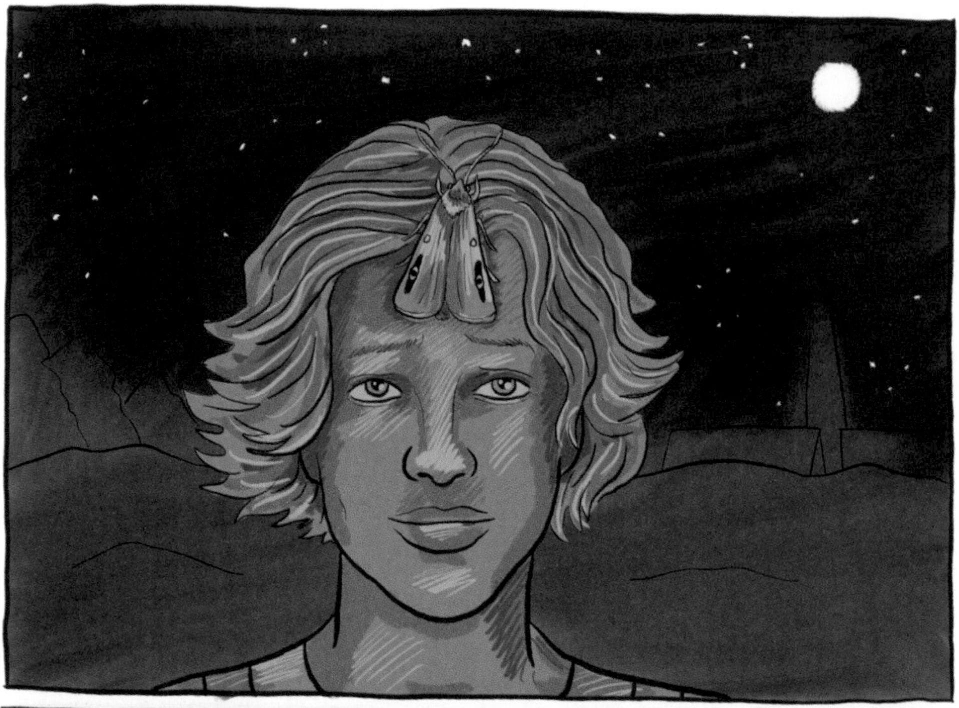

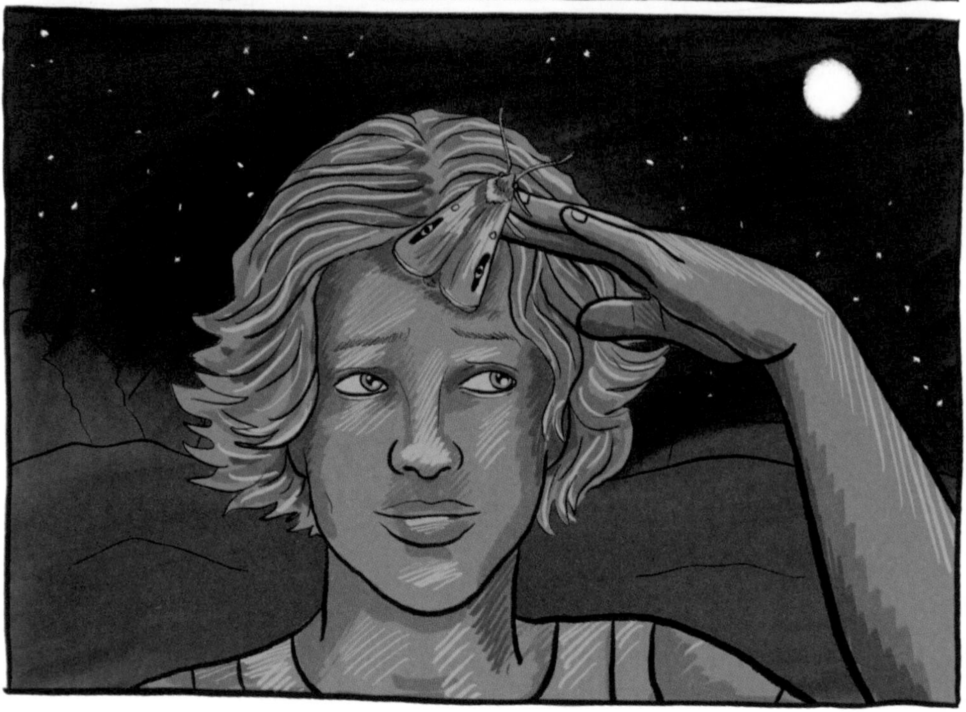

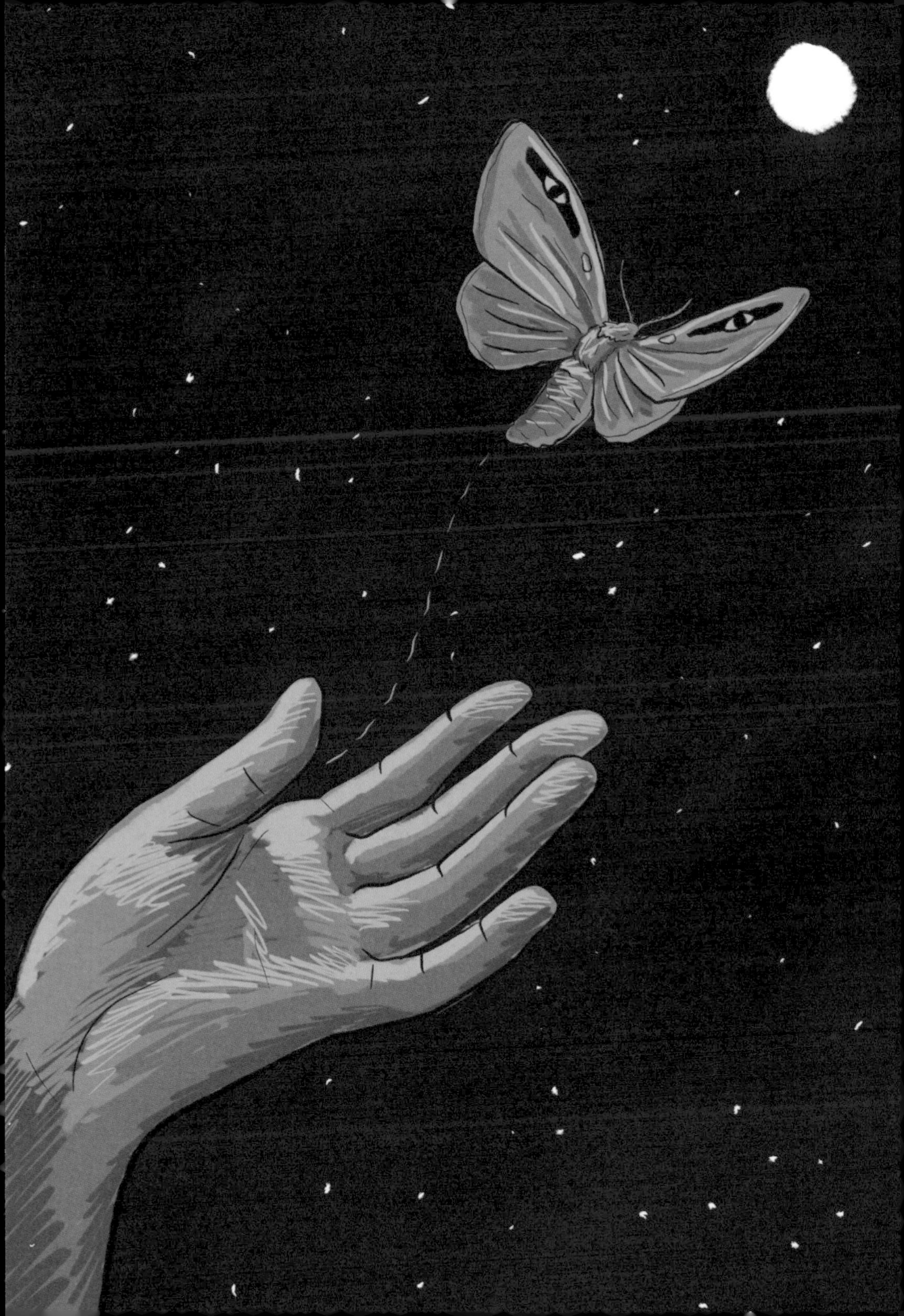

# Thank Yous

THANK YOU to ALL the PEOPLE WHO MADE this BOOK POSSIBLE:

TO ELERI and ERICA for BEING my PRODUCTION and EDITING DREAM TEAM. TO NAKKIAH, KELLY and GEN for BELIEVING IN ME and CHAMPIONING this UNUSUAL WORK. TO MY AGENT, DANIELLE, and JACINTA for SUPPORTING ME and THE BOOK. TO DAN and KENDRA for BRINGING this BOOK TO the USA! TO SAM and JO for THEIR BEHIND-the-SCENES WORK. TO DR LAM, DR FOX, JOSH, FIONN, PAT, GABE, GINA, ZAHRA, RACHEL, SJ, GORKIE, ELOISE, MICHAEL, CHAR and LEAH for THEIR CHATS and THOUGHTS OVER THE YEARS. TO MY BRILLIANT PEERS in the COMIC ART WORKSHOP, for HELPING ME WORKSHOP and THINK THROUGH THIS BOOK at FOUR RESIDENCIES. TO ADI, KIM, WILL, DIANNE, JOHN, BEN, LEO, EMILY, FI, GORKIE, SJ, LEONIE, BETHEL, BRIAR, JESSE, JASON and EMILIE FOR BEING in THE BOOK. AND MOST ESSENTIALLY, to MY PARTNER, JASON, for ALL HIS LOVE, TRUST, PATIENCE, CHATS, READS, EDITS and SUPPORT.

# CREDITS AND ACKNOWLEDGEMENTS

Thank you to all who have kindly given permission for use of their copyright material in this book. Every effort has been made to identify copyright holders and obtain permission for the use of copyright material. The title of this book—*Eventually Everything Connects*—comes from a quote by the famous designer and architect Charles Eames (eamesfoundation.com).

p. iv: John Muir, from *My First Summer in the Sierra* (Boston: Houghton Mifflin, 1911).

p. iv: Excerpt from *No One Is Talking About This* by Patricia Lockwood, copyright © 2021 by Patricia Lockwood. Used by permission of Riverhead, an imprint of Penguin Publishing Group, a division of Penguin Random House LLC. All rights reserved.

**JOIE DE VIVRE**
p. 28: 'A Brief for the Defense' from *Collected Poems* by Jack Gilbert, copyright © 2012 by Jack Gilbert. Used by permission of Alfred A. Knopf, an imprint of the Knopf Doubleday Publishing Group, a division of Penguin Random House LLC. All rights reserved.

p. 29: Excerpt from *Dare to Lead: Brave Work. Tough Conversations. Whole Hearts* by Brené Brown, copyright © 2018 by Brené Brown. Used by permission of Random House, an imprint and division of Penguin Random House LLC. All rights reserved.

**LIKE A MOTH TO A FLAME**
pp. 47–48: Thank you to Uncle Russell Mullett, GunaiKurnai Elder and Registered Aboriginal Party Manager for the GunaiKurnai Land and Waters Aboriginal Corporation for sharing GunaiKurnai cultural knowledge related to bogong history in the Victorian Alps. With thanks also to Professor Bruno David of the Monash Indigenous Studies Centre.

p. 51: Alain Sylvain, reprinted by kind permission, Jillian Rosen and Alain Sylvain.

p. 54: Words and music by Bo Burnham © copyright Fred Chestnut Music. All rights administered in Australia & New Zealand by Kobalt Music Publishing Australia Pty Ltd. Print rights administered in Australia & New Zealand by Hal Leonard Australia Pty Ltd, ABN 13 085 333 713, www.halleonard.com.au. Used by permission.

All rights reserved. Unauthorised reproduction is illegal.

p. 56: Natalie Wynn, from *What's Wrong with Capitalism* (Part 1), ContraPoints, 2017.

**DESIRE LINES**
p. 68: Oscar Wilde, from his play *Lady Windermere's Fan*, 1892.

p. 69: Jack Halberstam, 'Introduction: Low Theory', in *The Queer Art of Failure*, pp. 1–25. Copyright © 2011, Duke University Press. All rights reserved. Republished by permission of the copyright holder, www.dukeupress.edu.

pp. 71–72: Excerpts from *The Joy of Sex: The Ultimate Revised Edition* by Alex Comfort, copyright © 2008 by Octopus Publishing Group Ltd. Used by permission of Crown Books, an imprint of Random House, a division of Penguin Random House LLC. All rights reserved.

p. 89: Words from Agnès Varda's 2008 French documentary film, *Les plages d'Agnès (Beaches of Agnes)*.

p. 90: Lillian Ahenkan (aka FlexMami), from *Flex and Froomes* podcast, CADA network.

p. 93: Excerpt from *Ways of Seeing* by John Berger, copyright © 1972 by Penguin Books Ltd. Used by permission of Viking Books, an imprint of Penguin Publishing Group, a division of Penguin Random House LLC. All rights reserved.

p. 93: Excerpt from *Sex for One: The Joy of Self Loving* by Betty Dodson, copyright © 1974, 1983, 1987, 1996 by Betty Dodson. Used by permission of Harmony Books, an imprint of Random House, a division of Penguin Random House LLC. All rights reserved.

p. 96: Miriam Margolyes from the documentary *Miriam's Dead Good Adventure*, reprinted by kind permission from Leverton Media Ltd.

p. 98: Words by Audre Lorde, 'Uses of The Erotic: The Erotic as Power', a paper delivered at the Fourth Berkshire Conference on the History of Women, Mount Holyoke College, August 25, 1978. Published as a pamphlet by Out & Out Books (available from Crossing Press). Reprinted in *Sister Outsider: Essays and Speeches* by Audre Lorde, Crossing Press, 1984.

## WE WERE HERE

p. 113: Susan Sontag from Peter Hujar's *Portraits in Life and Death*, published by Da Capo Press, 1976.

p. 114: Courtesy Faber Permissions. Excerpt from *Known and Strange Things: Essays* by Teju Cole, copyright © 2016 by Teju Cole. Used by permission of Random House, an imprint and division of Penguin Random House LLC. All rights reserved.

p. 115: Richard Feynman, *The Feynman Lectures on Physics* © 1965, 2006, 2013 by California Institute of Technology, Michael A. Gottlieb, and Rudolf Pfeiffer, published by Basic Books, an imprint of Perseus Books, LLC, a subsidiary of Hachette Book Group, Inc.

p. 118: Joan Didion, *Slouching Towards Bethlehem*, Farrar, Straus and Giroux, 1968.

p. 126: Oliver Sacks, *Gratitude*, Picador, 2015.

p. 127: From *Entangled Life* by Merlin Sheldrake © Merlin Sheldrake, 2020, published by Bodley Head, reprinted by kind permission of David Higham Associates.

p. 130: Courtesy Bill Bryson. Excerpts from *A Short History of Nearly Everything* by Bill Bryson, copyright © 2003, 2008 by Bill Bryson. Used by permission of Delacorte Press, an imprint of Random House Children's Books, a division of Penguin Random House LLC. All rights reserved.

p. 135: Ojibwe saying as appears in the TV show *The Sopranos* ('Mayham', S6E3).

## STATE OF EMERGENCY

p. 156: David Wallace-Wells, reprinted by kind permission.

p. 168: Rebecca Solnit © 2004, *Hope in the Dark*, reprinted by kind permission. Published in the USA by Haymarket Books, updated ed. (15 March 2016), and in the UK by Canongate Canons, main edition (1 Sept. 2016).

p. 171: Copyright © 2016 by Mary Oliver with permission of Bill Reichblum. Reprinted by the permission of The Charlotte Sheedy Literary Agency as agent for the author.

## SEEING THINGS

p. 203: Courtesy Professor Donald D. Hoffman from his 2015 TED talk, 'Do We See Reality as It Really Is?' Reprinted by kind permission.

## WHAT MAKES A ME?

p. 226: Illustration based on Robert Doisneau's 'Les Pains de Picasso', 1952, printed 1981. Yale University Art Gallery, New Haven, CT. Gift of George Hopper Fitch, BA 1932. Accession no.1992.53.65.

## THE LIVES OF OTHERS

p. 244: Courtesy Faber Permissions. Excerpt from *Blind Spot* by Teju Cole, copyright © 2016, 2017 by Teju Cole. Used by permission of Random House, an imprint and division of Penguin Random House LLC. All rights reserved.

p. 248: Laura Sanders © *Science News*, 'Microbes can play games with the mind', March 23, 2016. Used by kind permission.

p. 248: Kirsten Tillisch as quoted in Laura Sanders © *Science News*, 'Microbes can play games with the mind', March 23, 2016. Used by kind permission.

p. 249: Ed Yong, from his talk 'The Microbes Within Us', the Royal Institution, 13 October 2016. Used by kind permission.

p. 254: Plant illustration based on an illumination from the manuscript *Erbario: A 15th-Century Herbal from Northern Italy*, Italy, 14– (pp. 13 and 26).

p. 262: Gérard de Nerval (1805–1855) as reported by Théophile Gautier (1811–1872).

p. 263: Phoebe Buffay (Lisa Kudrow) in season 2 of the 1990s TV show *Friends*.

p. 265: Donna Haraway, 'Anthropocene, Capitalocene, Plantationocene, Chthulucene: Making Kin', in *Environmental Humanities* 6, no. 1: 159–65. Copyright © 2015 Donna Haraway. All rights reserved. Reprinted by kind permission of the author and publisher, www.dukeupress.edu.

p. 265: David Suzuki, reprinted by kind permission.

p. 265: Zadie Smith as quoted in the 8 November 2019 *Toronto Star* article by Deborah Dundas: 'Zadie Smith on fighting the algorithm: "If you are under 30, and you are able to think for yourself right now, God bless you".'

# BIBLIOGRAPHY

**JOIE DE VIVRE**
Brown, Brené. *Dare to Lead*. Random House UK, 2018.

Camus, Albert. *Le mythe de Sisyphe*. Gallimard, 2008.

Chödrön, Pema. *When Things Fall Apart*. Shambhala Publications, 1997.

Gilbert, Jack. *Collected Poems*. Knopf, 2014.

Watts, Alan. *The Wisdom of Insecurity: A Message for an Age of Anxiety*. Vintage Books, 1988.

**LIKE A MOTH TO A FLAME**
Burnham, Bo. *Inside*. Netflix musical special, 2021.

Coper, Ed. *Facts and Other Lies: Welcome to the Disinformation Age*. Allen & Unwin, 2022.

Curtis, Adam. *All Watched Over by Machines of Loving Grace*. BBC television documentary series, 2011.

Montell, Amanda. *Cultish: The Language of Fanaticism*. HarperCollins US, 2021.

Orlowski-Yang, Jeff. *The Social Dilemma*. Netflix documentary, 2020.

Wynn, Natalie. *What's Wrong with Capitalism, Part 1*. ContraPoints, 2017.

**DESIRE LINES**
Bachelard, Gaston. *The Poetics of Space*. 1958. Penguin Classics, 2015.

Berger, John. *Ways of Seeing*. Penguin Modern Classics, 2009.

Halberstam, Jack. *The Queer Art of Failure*. Duke University Press, 2011.

Lorde, Audre. 'The Master's Tools Will Never Dismantle the Master's House'. *Sister Outsider: Essays and Speeches*. 1984. Crossing Press, 2007.

Morin, Jack. *The Erotic Mind*. Harper Perennial, 1996.

Nagoski, Emily. *Come As You Are*. Scribe, 2015.

Perel, Esther. *Mating in Captivity: Unlocking Erotic Intelligence*. Harper, 2006.

———. *The State of Affairs: Rethinking Infidelity*. Harper, 2017.

Russell, Euphemia. *Slow Pleasure: Explore Your Pleasure Spectrum*. Hardie Grant, 2022.

**WE WERE HERE**
Bryson, Bill. *A Short History of Nearly Everything*. Penguin Random House, 2003.

Nelson, Maggie. *The Art of Cruelty*. W. W. Norton & Company, 2012.

Sacks, Oliver. *Gratitude*. Picador, 2015.

Sheldrake, Merlin. *Entangled Life*. Bodley Head, 2020.

Sontag, Susan. *On Photography*. Penguin Modern Classics, 2009.

**STATE OF EMERGENCY**
Brown, Adrienne Maree. *Emergent Strategy: Shaping Change, Changing Worlds*. AK Press, 2017.

Butler, Octavia E. *Parable of the Sower*. Warner Books, 1998.

Chomsky, Noam, and Edward S. Herman. *Manufacturing Consent: The Political Economy of the Mass Media*. Vintage, 1995.

Curtis, Adam. *Can't Get You Out of My Head*. BBC documentary series, 2021.

———. *The Century of the Self*. RDF Television documentary series, BBC, 2002.

———. *HyperNormalisation*. Documentary, 2016.

———. *Living in an Unreal World*. Short film, 2016.

D'Ignazio, Catherine, and Lauren Klein. *Data Feminism*. MIT Press, 2023.

Fiennes, Sophie. *The Pervert's Guide to Ideology*. Documentary, 2012.

Freinacht, Hanzi. *The Listening Society: A Metamodern Guide to Politics*. Kindle edition, 2017.

Giridharadas, Anand. *Winners Take All*. Knopf, 2018.

Haraway, Donna J. *Staying with the Trouble: Making Kin in the Chthulucene*. Duke University Press, 2016.

Johnson, Dr. Ayana Elizabeth, and Alex Blumberg. *How to Save a Planet*. Podcast.

Kimmerer, Robin Wall. *Braiding Sweetgrass*. Penguin, 2020.

Lowenhaupt Tsing, Anna. *The Mushroom at the End of the World*. Princeton University Press, 2021.

Scott, James C. *Seeing Like a State: How Certain Schemes to Improve the Human Condition Have Failed*. Yale University Press, 1999.

Smil, Vaclav. *How the World Really Works*. Penguin, 2022.

Solnit, Rebecca. *Hope in the Dark: Untold Histories, Wild Possibilities*. Haymarket Books, 2016.

Sparrow, Jeff. *Crimes Against Nature: Capitalism and Global Heating*. Scribe, 2021.

Wallman, Sam. *Our Members Be Unlimited*. Scribe, 2022.

Yunkaporta, Tyson. *Sand Talk: How Indigenous Thinking Can Save the World*. Text Publishing, 2019.

Žižek, Slavoj. *Living In The End Times*. Verso Trade, 2011.

**SEEING THINGS**

Barrett, Lisa Feldman. *How Emotions Are Made: The Secret Life of the Brain*. Mariner Books, 2017.

Brown, Derren. *Tricks of The Mind*. Doubleday, 2007.

Chabris, Christopher, and Daniel Simons. *The Invisible Gorilla: And Other Ways Our Intuitions Deceive Us*. Harmony, 2011.

Eagleman, David. *Incognito: The Secret Lives of the Brain*. Vintage, 2012.

Griffiths, David. 'Queer Theory for Lichens'. *Undercurrents* 19 (2015).

Hassan, Steven. *Combating Cult Mind Control*. Park Street Press, 1990.

———. *Freedom of Mind: Helping Loved Ones Leave Controlling People, Cults and Beliefs*. Kindle Editions, 2012.

Hoffman, Donald. *The Case Against Reality: Why Evolution Hid the Truth from Our Eyes*. W. W. Norton & Company, 2019.

Kahneman, Daniel. *Thinking, Fast and Slow*. Penguin, 2012.

Mlodinow, Leonard. *Subliminal: How Your Unconscious Mind Rules Your Behaviour*. Vintage, 2013.

Ronson, Jon. *Them: Adventures with Extremists*. Kindle Editions, 2003.

Vedantam, Shankar. *Hidden Brain*. NPR podcast.

**WHAT MAKES A ME?**

Epstein, David. *Range: Why Generalists Triumph in a Specialized World*. Riverhead Books, 2019.

Martin, Roger L. *The Opposable Mind: How Successful Leaders Win Through Integrative Thinking*. Harvard Business Review Press, 2007.

McGilchrist, Iain. *The Master and His Emissary: The Divided Brain and the Making of the Western World*. Yale University Press, 2012.

Van der Kolk, Bessel. *The Body Keeps the Score: Brain, Mind, and Body in the Healing of Trauma*. Penguin, 2015.

**THE LIVES OF OTHERS**

Cole, Teju. *Blind Spot*. Random House, 2017.

Haraway, Donna. *Manifestly Haraway*. University of Minnesota Press, 2016.

Kimmerer, Robin Wall. *Braiding Sweetgrass*. Penguin, 2020.

Yong, Ed. *I Contain Multitudes: The Microbes Within Us and a Grander View of Life*. Ecco Press, 2016.